Presented to Corps Se
Desmond Rix by the Letchworth
Corps on the occasion of your
retirement.

9th January 1993

Proverbs 3:6

The Life and Work of
CHARLES HADDON SPURGEON

After an engraving by J. Cochran.

Yours very truly

C H Spurgeon

The Life and Work of
CHARLES HADDON SPURGEON

G. HOLDEN PIKE

Volume I

THE BANNER OF TRUTH TRUST

THE BANNER OF TRUTH TRUST
3 Murrayfield Road, Edinburgh EH12 6EL
PO Box 621, Carlisle, Pennsylvania 17013, USA

*

First Published 1894
First Banner of Truth Trust edition 1991

Volume One (Comprising Volumes 1-3 in original edition)
ISBN 0 85151 620 3
Two volume set ISBN 0 85151 622 X

*

Printed and bound at The Bath Press, Avon
in Great Britain

THE

LIFE AND WORK

OF

CHARLES HADDON SPURGEON

BY

G. HOLDEN PIKE,

AUTHOR OF "THE WORLD'S WORKERS—CHARLES HADDON SPURGEON," ETC.

ILLUSTRATED WITH FIFTEEN FULL-PAGE PHOTOGRAVURE PLATES.

VOL. I.

CASSELL & COMPANY, Limited:

LONDON, PARIS & MELBOURNE.

CONTENTS.

LIST OF PHOTOGRAVURE PLATES.

THE LIFE AND WORK

OF

CHARLES HADDON SPURGEON.

CHAPTER I.

THE FATHERLAND OF THE SPURGEONS.

The Spurgeon Family of Dutch Descent—Driven from Holland by Persecution—Philip II. and the Duke of Alva—William the Silent and the Heroic Age—The Siege of Leyden— Interest felt by Mr. Spurgeon in the Country—His Preaching Tour in Holland in 1863 —Dutch Characteristics—Tastes of Mr. Spurgeon—His Sympathy with Netherlanders— Job Spurgeon the Quaker.

THAT the earliest known representatives of Mr. Spurgeon's family were of Dutch extraction is an interesting fact; but none the less on that account the great preacher was an Englishman, who loved his country, and was content in the most unselfish manner to devote his best energies to its welfare. Before his death he had become generally regarded as one who was a servant of the Universal Church and a citizen of the world; but while he commanded the respect of all nationalities, probably it was the English-speaking race alone who could perfectly understand him. Foreigners who had to make their acquaintance with the man through a translation could never fully realise the best qualities of his discourses in their original dress.

Rather more than two centuries and a half before the subject of this work was born, his Protestant ancestors appear to have been driven from their ancient home in the Netherlands by the persecution, on a wholesale scale, which broke out under the hateful rule of Philip II. That fanatical despot had less of political sagacity than his father, Charles V.; and in the end it turned out to be a misfortune rather than an advantage for such a misguided tyrant to be served by able

B

men whose bigotry and general sympathies were in unison with his own ignoble aims. These were the tools who enabled Philip to ruin his empire, as well as to throw away his great opportunities of conferring lasting benefit on the Spanish race and the Spanish dependencies. The Spanish monarch probably had some share in instigating the burning of the Smithfield martyrs under the reign of his wife, our own Queen Mary; but if this too zealous Romanist injured England in this respect, he unintentionally conferred benefit upon our land when he drove away the flower of his own people to seek refuge on our shores. The Spurgeons, with a large number of others who crossed the sea in order to escape death at the hands of Ferdinando Alvarez, Duke of Alva, were the cream of the Protestant population. The Spanish general, who at the head of twenty thousand mercenary troops entered the Low Countries in the year 1567, was a man quite after the heart of Philip II., and he carried out the persecuting policy with alacrity and vigour.

Soon after the death of his English wife and the accession of her Protestant successor, the great Queen Elizabeth, Philip saw that certain symptoms of discontent began to show themselves in his Flemish provinces. Those provinces were rich; they were increasing in wealth. The Reformation had already so far made way among them that numbers of the people, of whom the Spurgeons were but a sample, were sufficiently enlightened to be ready, if need arose, to make sacrifices for their religion. Such subjects did not commend themselves to the phlegmatic mind of Philip II., however. To him the maintenance of Romanism and the Inquisition was of the first importance, and because the inhabitants of the Low Countries were beginning to hold other views on such matters, he treated them in a way which was in strong contrast to his father's benignant policy towards them. At a council held in Spain, the Duke of Feria advised that mild measures should be adopted; the Duke of Alva, on the other hand, declared that severity alone would answer the purpose they had in view, and it was to this Ahithophel that the King yielded. The advice was in accord with his own cruel

nature; and the King's admiration of Alva prompted him to allow
to that able general almost unlimited power. What happened all
readers of history know sufficiently well. In a little over five years
18,000 persons were executed, including the two patriots, Egmont
and Horn, while about 30,000 fugitives made their escape to other
lands, carrying with them their arts and industries.

That was the heroic age in the history of Holland, and William
the Silent, the ancestor of our own William III., or Prince of Orange,
was the hero of the time. One of the most memorable events
was the siege of Leyden by the Duke of Parma in 1573–74, the
story of which has been thus succinctly told in the "Treasury of
Geography":—

"For a period of seven weeks there was no bread within the city; horses, cats, dogs,
with roots of all kinds, were eagerly devoured, but the heroic example of the burgomaster,
Pieter Adrianzoon van der Werff, who offered his own body to such as were clamorous for
surrender, encouraged his fellow-citizens to hold out. Unable to muster an adequate force
for the relief of the place, the Prince of Orange at length formed the desperate resolve of
breaking down the dykes of the adjacent coast and admitting the ocean. It was some
little time before the full effect was produced; at length, impelled by a violent wind, the
sea rushed in, overwhelmed the works of the besiegers, and forced them to a precipitate
flight, leaving above a thousand of their number drowned. A fleet of boats, prepared for
the expected relief of the beleaguered place, immediately advanced from Rotterdam over the
newly-formed expanse of water, and triumphantly reached the walls of the city. The Prince
of Orange, in token of gratitude for the heroism which the defenders of Leyden had shown,
gave them the option of two rewards—relief from certain taxes or the foundation of a
university. The citizens, to their lasting honour, preferred the latter, and thus was formed
an institution which rapidly became among the most eminent in Europe, and which still
preserves a large measure of its fame. The traditions of Holland are heroic, if its plains
be flat and unromantic and its people of phlegmatic temperament and calculating spirit."

Mr. Spurgeon never ceased to feel interest in Holland, and it
yielded him satisfaction to know that his sermons and other works
were extensively circulated in the Dutch language. In the early days
of 1863 the English preacher visited the chief towns of the Netherlands; and it was while making that tour that he was honoured
with an interview by the then reigning Queen. At such a time the
stirring memories of the sixteenth century would come into his mind:
he would think of his own kinsfolk, who escaped with their lives,
and of those who remained behind to lay the foundation of a great
country, and in many instances to pour out their blood in its behalf.

Although he dwells in quite an unromantic country, a chief characteristic of the middle-class Hollander is a love of gardening; and this is a taste which is likely to show itself in successive generations of descendants, even though they may have become associated with the dwellers in another land. That this love of trees, shrubs, and flowers was a characteristic of Mr. Spurgeon was evident to all who were acquainted with his habits. He loved his garden, because it never failed to afford refreshment to his mind when over-wearied with work and care; and choice plants, which friends would sometimes send him from distant lands, were treasured in his glass-houses as carefully as a connoisseur would preserve valuable specimens or works of art. He loved the open air; but from his study he could walk into what might have been called his inner garden, enclosed in glass.

All this is quite in accord with the tastes of the Hollanders at the present day. "Every Dutchman above the necessity of working to-day for the bread of to-morrow has his garden-house in the suburbs of his town, and repairs to it on Saturday evening with his family, to ruralise until Monday over his pipe of tobacco," says Mr. S. Laing, in his "Notes of a Traveller." The same writer adds: "The slip of land is laid out in flower-beds, all the flowers in one bed being generally of one kind and colour; and the brilliancy of these large masses of flowers—the white and green paintwork, and the gilding about the garden-houses—and a row of those glittering fairy summer lodges, shining in the sun, upon the side of the wide canal, and swimming in humid brilliancy in the midst of plots and parterres of splendid flowers; and with the accompaniments of gaily-dressed ladies at the windows, swiftly-passing pleasure-boats, with bright, burnished sides below, and a whole city population afloat, or on foot, enjoying themselves in their holiday clothes—form, in truth, a summer evening scene which one dwells on with much delight."

Such is Holland to-day after generations of progress, and such are the heroic memories associated with the struggle for liberty in the sixteenth century. It is an additional distinction for such a country to have been the original home of the Spurgeon family. Whenever Mr. Spurgeon met a Hollander, especially one who was interested in the extension of religion in the country, the English pastor always at once felt that there was something of kinship which bound them together in sympathy.

The Spurgeon family thus had trouble enough in the era of the Reformation, and they continued to be sufferers in the days of the Puritans a century later. Mention is made of a Job Spurgeon who was imprisoned during the reign of Charles II. This Job Spurgeon is mentioned twice in Besse's "Sufferings" in the following manner:—

"Anno 1677.—Taken for a meeting at Dedham, from Samuel Groom, at whose house it was held, from Job Spurgeon, and others, goods worth £16 15 6."

"Anno 1683.—On the 22nd of the month called July, with three others, Job Spurgeon, of Dedham was committed by warrant to Chelmsford Gaol. They were, after a few weeks, bailed out till sessions, but on their appearance there on the 3rd of October they were required to give sureties for their good behaviour, which, refusing to do, they were recommitted to prison, where three of them lay upon straw about fifteen weeks in the midst of a winter remarkable for extremity of cold; but the fourth, Job Spurgeon, being so weak that he was unable to lie down, sat up in a chair the most part of that time." *

* Quoted by Thomas Sharp in *The Friend*, February 26th, 1892.

CHAPTER II.

BIRTH AND PARENTAGE.

Changes in England—The Condition of the Country in 1834—Hard Times—Ignorance and Degradation of the Common People—The Spurgeon Family at Kelvedon—Historical Memories of
the Place—Removal of the Family to Colchester—Tollesbury, the Scene of Mr. John
Spurgeon's Ministry—Stambourne.

MR. SPURGEON saw many changes brought about in the social
and political world during his not very long life of fifty-
seven years. When, as a very young and newly-married couple, his
parents were living at Kelvedon in 1834, the general outlook was
depressing rather than encouraging. The prolonged and devastating
wars in which the four Georges had indulged had brought on the
inevitable reaction, trade being bad and agriculture depressed. Farmers
found it difficult to make both ends meet; for while prices of produce
had fallen, the rates and other demands they had to meet had largely
increased. In the political and ecclesiastical world there was more
commotion than usual; for, finding that the Reform Bill had not
altogether answered the expectations of those who had set their hopes
extravagantly high, religious equality and the abolition of various
abuses were being loudly demanded. Modern philanthropy, as we
understand it, had not yet commenced. A large proportion of the
common people were in a state of ignorance and degradation. There
were a few charity schools in the towns, and here and there a
village may have had one; but no one believed, as yet, that it
was the duty of the Government to undertake a scheme of national
education. Lord Ashley had commenced to fight the battle of
the working classes and the oppressed; but he made headway slowly
from lack of public sympathy and of friends to second his efforts.

When Mr. John Spurgeon married Miss Jarvis and settled in
Kelvedon, he chose for his home a very typical Essex village. It
is not a large place, the population at present probably not exceeding

two thousand souls. Though not hitherto sought out by tourists, as may come to be the case in the future, it is pleasantly situated, and it has a few historical memories which are of some interest to the topographer. After visiting the small, old-fashioned house in which Charles Haddon Spurgeon was born on June 19th, 1834, the tourist may ramble hither and thither and think of some other things which have happened here in the distant past. Anciently the manor was the heritage of Edward the Confessor; but at present the manor of other days is divided into two, one of which seems to be attached to the See of London, while the other belongs to the master of Felix Hall, from whose Park some beautiful scenery of the vale through which the River Blackwater flows may be looked upon. Centuries ago the northern invaders of England chose these rich lands for settlement; and it is said that the massacre of the Danes at the opening of the eleventh century commenced at Kelvedon. The present Bishop of Rochester, who took part in the late great preacher's funeral, is the patron of the living. The church has a tower, Early English pillars and arches, and a later nave-roof, in all of which ecclesiastical archæologists will find something to interest them.

After the birth of a son and heir, whom they named after his uncle Haddon, Mr. and Mrs. John Spurgeon did not remain long at Kelvedon. In or about April, 1835, they gave up their village home in order to settle at Colchester as a more convenient centre for their business, and where some of their family connections appear to have resided. Hence the statement, which has often been repeated, that the brothers Charles and James Spurgeon went to school together at Kelvedon—one being called Big Chummy and the other Little Chummy—has no foundation in fact. Charles was not a year old when his parents removed to Colchester, and soon after he had completed his first year he went to reside with his paternal grand-parents at Stambourne.

The way in which the name of Haddon came into the family is thus explained. The father of the pastor of Stambourne was a cheese factor, whose working capital was inadequate, but he was always able to procure a loan from his friend Mr. Haddon, a fellow deacon. While he was a model of liberality, Mr. Haddon was eccentric, and none of his odd ways could be disregarded by those who desired to retain his favour. He would lend his friend £500 at once; but although he would accept of no interest, no excuse availed if the money was not returned on the day agreed upon. The great-grandfather of the late pastor of the Metropolitan Tabernacle took care that nothing happened to vex his generous co-deacon; and he showed his regard by naming one of his children Haddon. In due time the mother of the future great preacher called her son Charles Haddon. Mr. Spurgeon was really named after a brother of each of his parents—Charles Parker Jarvis, and Haddon Rudkin Spurgeon. The present pastor of the Metropolitan Tabernacle, the Rev. J. A. Spurgeon, informs me in a private letter: "The family of Haddon are now in America, and keep up correspondence with my dear father. They still consider 'Haddon Hall' to be rightfully theirs, though lost to the family."

While living at Colchester Mr. John Spurgeon had a congregation at Tollesbury, to which he ministered on Sundays. Tollesbury is approached by a creek of the River Blackwater; the parish also has some thousands of acres of water, so that on this account, and also on account of its saline pastures and oyster-dredging, the place has some rather uncommon characteristics. Mr. John Spurgeon's service at Tollesbury continued for some years, or until the children of the family were big enough to accompany their father in his conveyance on Sunday mornings, the distance being nine miles. Meanwhile, the boy Charles remained at Stambourne until he could run about and had become the precocious child. Later on, it was there that he loved to spend his holidays.

CHAPTER III.

JAMES SPURGEON OF STAMBOURNE.

The Last of the Puritans "—Hereditary Rheumatism—Job Spurgeon in Chelmsford Gaol—The Old Pastor of Stambourne—His Characteristics—His Training for the Ministry—Stambourne and its Surroundings—The Hervey Family—Henry Havers, Founder of the Independent Congregation—Settlement of James Spurgeon at Stambourne—The Days of War and of dear Bread—A Village Greatheart—Special Providences—Charles and his Grandfather—Visits to the Squire at Stambourne Hall—Resisting the Devil—A Relic of an older World—The old Pastor's Refusal to visit London—A last Link between the Old Times and the New.

WHEN a man preached, talked, and dressed like old Mr. James Spurgeon, the Independent pastor of Stambourne, it was quite natural that people should think and speak of him as one of the last of the Puritans. As I have heard his chief remaining grandson explain, the veteran preacher, when between eighty and ninety years of age, would significantly rub his knees as he sat by the fire, and give expression to the apprehension that rheumatism would, after all, bring him to a premature end. The rheumatism was hereditary; and though some may trace it back only as far as the time of Job Spurgeon, already mentioned, who for conscience sake was confined in Chelmsford Gaol during some weeks of wintry weather in the reign of Charles II., it is more than probable that the refugees of a century earlier brought the affection with them from the Netherlands.

A correspondent of *The Christian World* has made these references to Mr. Spurgeon and his grandfather:—

"Down in Essex, where I paid a visit one day last autumn, near Kelvedon, I heard that Mr. Spurgeon was regarded as a boy as somewhat shy and reticent, if not, indeed, somewhat morose! As a matter of fact, no doubt he was drinking in everything he heard and saw, to be given forth again, however, with good interest when the time came. He was largely brought up by his grandfather, who was for fifty years Independent minister at Stambourne, and a shrewd, clever old man he appears to have been, whom local tradition regards as the origin—as far as wit and wisdom are concerned, at all events—of that famous personage, John Ploughman."

Old Mr. James Spurgeon was something more than an uncompromising champion of evangelical teaching; he had the old-fashioned habits of the older world in which he had passed his youth and early manhood. Like all veterans of the school to which he belonged, he may probably have had some deeply-rooted prejudices, but he inherited all the strong affections which were characteristic of the Puritan stock from which he had descended. James Spurgeon of Stambourne was of metal not a whit inferior to that of his valiant ancestor, Job Spurgeon. It was of the quality out of which martyrs are made. At whatever time or in whatever form the enemy might appear, James Spurgeon knew not what was meant by showing " the white feather." He was not superstitious; but he no more doubted the existence of a personal devil than his own. The Evil One was not only a real adversary, he was one to be resisted at any cost and at every turn. He might thwart the pastor's best endeavours during the week; he might be found following him up the pulpit stairs with perplexing suggestions on the Sabbath; but no weapons which such a foe could employ could prevail. The congregation were in full sympathy with their pastor; what he preached and practised they carried with them into the world and its everyday life. Nothing was ever said in the pulpit or believed in the pew save what had been thoroughly well tested. It was a rare instance of Puritan fervour burning on through two centuries; and if there had ever been any want of harmony between the Established Church and the Independent Chapel in earlier days, all had given place to peace and friendship in the days of James Spurgeon. The two congregations had much in common; the clergyman and the Nonconformist preacher were fast friends. Depict the village as it was half a century ago, and you have a picture of English country life at its best.

In the opening years of this century Mr. James Spurgeon had been a student at Hoxton Academy, where ministerial candidates were trained for service among Nonconformists. At midsummer, 1804, he was sent to supply the pulpit at the Independent chapel at Clare, a Suffolk town which dates back to Saxon times, and which has an ancient church, and formerly had a strong castle. Mr. James

Spurgeon accepted the pastorate at Clare in the summer of 1806, but four years later he removed to Stambourne, where he remained till his death in 1864.

Stambourne? Of course the reader does not know the locality. It is not even a place one goes past in the train, as there is no railway station. Book to Yeldham on the Great Eastern Railway, and you will have less than three miles to walk; but if you like to alight at Halstead, the post-town of the villages thereabout, you will enjoy a fine cross-country excursion of eight miles. If you do not know the country, be careful in regard to the roads, and ask yourself if you can answer questions such as Mr. Spurgeon might himself have put to you, if in conversation you had aroused his interest by confessing you were a native, or by professing to be tolerably well acquainted with the country. In Mr. Spurgeon's childhood days there was an oak at Great Yeldham which all curious sight-seers went to see, and which, in the days of its prime, before it died of old age, measured thirty feet in circumference four feet from the ground. Toppesfield, two miles farther on in a north-westerly direction, enjoyed some local notoriety on account of the Roman relics which had been unearthed. Wethersfield is also an interesting place, with an ancient church. Finchingfield, on an affluent of the River Pant, was the parish in which the East Essex hounds used to meet when the little boy Charles felt such an interest in their exploits. The manor belonged of old to John de Compes, who received it for the distinguished service of turning the spit at the coronation of Edward III. Steeple, not far away, belongs chiefly to St. Bartholomew's Hospital. Then Hempstead had its Great Oak; and in this parish, too, was Winchlow Hall, belonging to the family of William Harvey, the discoverer of the circulation of the blood.

Such were the surroundings of Stambourne. When you actually arrive in the village, the ancient parish church, with its Norman tower, will be an object of interest; so, also, will the comfortable old mansion called Stambourne Hall. The labourers' cottages, which are gradually becoming tenantless one after the other, will probably

inspire more uncomfortable reflections; but as we are concerned
with the past rather than with the present, no reflection need be made
on that unwelcome symptom of the decay of rural industry.
Another thing to be regretted is the disappearance of the old manse
in which James Spurgeon lived, and the meeting-house, on the same
ground, in which for nearly sixty years he preached the Gospel.

It is pleasant to think of Stambourne as of a typical Essex
village; but apart from that the history of this quiet retreat, lying,
as it were, aside from the thronged highway of modern life and
progress, illustrates some of the best phases of English rural life.
In the seventeenth century there was probably no one in the country
who more ardently loved the Established Church than Henry Havers,
who, as ex-rector of the parish, founded the original Nonconformist
chapel, in which the Common Prayer was read until the reign of
George II. was far advanced. As a man of substance, he founded
the church which has flourished until the present day under nine
successive pastors, and he took care to place the property in the
hands of trustees.

When the late James Spurgeon settled in this retired sphere in
1810 he little thought that he would be the man to give new interest
to a settlement which already could offer some attractions to historical
inquirers. The times were hard as well as threatening; for just
about the date that the pastor's eldest son—the present Rev. John
Spurgeon—was born, wheat rose in price in England to a guinea a
bushel, and in some counties even some shillings higher. Despite
all drawbacks, however, there have been persons living in those days
who were wont to speak of these as the good old times.

Under James Spurgeon, the old fashions of former days held on
until long after the accession of the present Queen; and an extant
diary written fifty years ago we might suppose to have been composed by some Puritan Greatheart of the Commonwealth era. The
writer might occasionally feel the chill of a passing cloud, but his
sun could never be really eclipsed. His faith was far-seeing and
steadfast; his piety was as healthy as a palm-tree refreshed by

perennial springs. James Spurgeon was always himself, and that means that he was unlike any other man who lived in England during the first half of this century. He seems to have been made for country service, and it is not likely that he would ever have succeeded so well amid the more crowded life and excitement of a town.

Many special providences would happen in the life of such a man, and one of the most signal of these was when grandfather and grandson were brought together under the same roof. The two appear to have been made the one for the other. Though the one was close upon sixty years the elder of the other, they seem to have had much in common; at all events, little Charles appears to have taken readily to such things as pleased the venerable pastor. The child was a daily comfort to the veteran Christian, and was, at the same time, learning in the school which, on the whole, was probably the best fitted to educate his heart and mind.

We cannot wonder that a man in Mr. Spurgeon's position should have looked back upon the days of childhood, spent beneath his grandfather's roof, as a sunny period. The truth is, that the conditions of life in the village were favourable all round. In his own way Mr. Spurgeon tells how the rector of the parish and his grandfather were agreed as regarded their doctrinal belief. The squire was a churchman, but he also sometimes attended the Nonconformist chapel; while on Mondays squire, rector, Nonconformist pastor, and the little boy, would all be found at the Hall together—a merry party, enjoying to the full sugared bread-and-butter for their tea. Of these things, and many others, readers should not fail to read for themselves in "Memories of Stambourne," Mr. Spurgeon's last book.

As we have said, few men of his time more strikingly showed the possession of Puritan characteristics than the old pastor of Stambourne. To him the Bible was literally the Word of God, all being verbally inspired. His strong belief in a personal devil has been already referred to; and some of his experiences under this head almost read like something which might have been borrowed from "The Pilgrim's Progress." He had a notion that he was liable to be assaulted by the Evil One at the most unexpected times, and at his weakest point.

More remarkable was the dream he once had when a young man, and in which he thought he saw the devil. He was accustomed to pray alone in a secluded spot formerly called Honeywood Park, between Coggeshall and Halstead; and in this night-vision Satan seemed to declare in his rage that if the young pastor ventured again to walk along the well-beaten path to the oak, he would be torn in pieces. This appears to have been regarded as a genuine threat; and, although the young man would not be turned aside from the path which led straight to the tree beneath which he had been wont to hold communion with God, he reached the spot in a state of nervous excitement, and with the perspiration standing on his face. There was no fiend to be seen; but on the ground lay an enormous golden ring, for which no owner could ever be found. The pastor of Stambourne appears not to have been married at that time; and Mr. Spurgeon's grandmother's wedding-ring was made of the gold so mysteriously discovered. The striking particulars of this incident may be found in "The Spare Half-hour."

The pastor of Stambourne belonged to an older world, and he would appear to have realised the fact. With London, as it was in the first years of the century, he had been somewhat familiar as a student; but, after he had once settled in his secluded Essex pastorate, he never cared to move far away. Whether he actually ever entered a train I cannot say with certainty; for no record with which I am acquainted exists of his ever having undertaken such a journey. The Metropolitan Tabernacle was opened two or three years before his death; but although his constant references to the subject showed that no one was more interested in his grandson's success, the aged pastor of Stambourne could never be persuaded to visit London for the sake of joining in the worship at the Metropolitan Tabernacle. "I am too old," he would say;

and when a man is nearer ninety than eighty there is undoubtedly some force in the plea.

James Spurgeon seemed to live as one of the last representatives of the Old Dissent. In all his tastes, manners, and aspirations, the veteran belonged to a generation which had long since passed away. His faith was old-fashioned in its childlike simplicity; he was never troubled with any of the doubts which are raised by modern criticism. He was a lover of psalmody; but when he sang anything not actually in the Bible it had to be one of Dr. Watts's hymns. All of his habits seemed to tally with his old-fashioned clothes.

The venerable pastor of Stambourne was one of the last connecting links between the old times and the new. During his long life of nearly ninety years, what changes had time brought about in the world! In James Spurgeon's days of childhood Dr. Johnson still ruled as the autocrat of London literary society; the establishment of the Republic of the United States and the French Revolution were events of his youth; and he was in the early years of his pastorate when Napoleon was extinguished by Wellington at Waterloo. As a man and as a pastor, the Stambourne veteran belonged to the older world of the Georges into which he had been born; and it is probable that he had little or no sympathy with the innovations and modern methods of doing things which he lived to see introduced. Had any one of us stepped into the old meeting-house in the middle of this century, it would have been like sitting beneath the shadow of those days of the eighteenth century which elderly people once liked to think and talk about. The occupants of the pews, the preacher in the pulpit, and, after the service was over, the leave-takings at the manse itself, would have seemed to tell of days which can never come again.

CHAPTER IV.

CHILDHOOD.

THE pastor of Stambourne was already growing old before his grandson was sufficiently advanced to take any general interest in the surrounding world—that is to say, when the late pastor of the Metropolitan Tabernacle was a little boy, able to run about the village and its suburbs, the master of the manse was fast nearing his seventieth year. The patriarch and the child seem to have been much together, and each contracted much love and sympathy for the other.* There was a congenial charge to look after, on the one hand; there was, on the other, a teacher worthy of being looked up to and admired. Each was a gainer from association with the other. Though he had borne the burden and heat of the day until old age, the grandsire was still juvenile in heart, and there was a freshness about his piety which made his talk interesting to a developing youthful genius. The Puritan-like quaintness of the old pastor also found a ready response in the child. In the old-fashioned

---

* "It is no wonder that Stambourne had a singular attraction for Mr. Spurgeon. It was there that the foundation of his character was firmly laid. His father and mother had seventeen children, with but scant means for their support. It was no doubt some little relief for the boy to pay long visits to his grandfather's parsonage. There he found himself in an old Puritan world. James Spurgeon was a man of sparkling wit, in whom local tradition afterwards discerned the original of John Ploughman. He was a preacher of rare spiritual force, about whom one hearer said quaintly that a sermon from his lips made 'his wing-feathers grow a foot. He could mount as eagles after being fed with such heavenly food.' A devout working-man paid him a grand tribute: 'He was always so experimental. You felt as if you had been inside of a man.' When Charles became a preacher, there were people who said, 'I heard your grandfather, and I would run my shoes off my feet any day to hear a Spurgeon.'"—JOHN TELFORD, B.A., in *The Methodist Recorder*.

house-place, in the study, or large old parlour, in which the last notes of a sermon would be made, and in the open air, the two would be much together. The child would, of course, take notice of things which did not come within the range of the old pastor's more con-tracted outlook. Thus, not only was he interested in hounds and huntsmen, but being well acquainted with Scripture, he would at times ask questions which no one could answer. Then, like all such questioners, he would not be satisfied until he had found some sort of solution of the problem. At all events, this all showed an interest in religion and religious matters, which the old pastor of Stambourne was careful to stimulate and nurture in the best possible manner.

According to one good authority, Mr. Spurgeon was not only an hereditary Puritan, he at once would have a feeling of kinship with any whose ancestors, in days of persecution, had left home and country for their religion's sake. At Stambourne all that there was of the Puritan in him would naturally become developed.

The late preacher's father, Mr. John Spurgeon, has given some reminiscences of his eldest son's childhood, as follows :—

"It has been said that Charles was brought up by his grandfather and grandmother. The fact is, that my father and mother came to see us when Charles was a baby of fourteen months old. They took him to stay with them, and he remained with them until he was between four and five years of age. Then he came home to stay with us at Colchester, where I was then residing, at the same time carrying on my ministerial work at Tollesbury, some miles distant. Afterwards he often went to spend his holidays with his grandparents, who were very fond of him. . . . Charles was a healthy child and boy, having a good constitution, and he was of an affectionate disposition, and very studious. He was always reading books—never digging in the garden or keeping pigeons, like other boys. It was always books and books. If his mother wanted to take him for a ride she would be sure to find him in my study poring over a book. He was clever, of course, and clever in most directions of study. He learned to draw very well. . . . I have a drawing by him of an ancient pile—from a copy—in another room. It is signed by him, and bears the date 1848, that is, when he had grown rather a big boy, During one of his visits to me before he became ill, Charles said, alluding to his picture, ' Father, I should like you to leave it to me.' I said, ' You can have it now, my boy, if you like.' ' No, no,' he replied; ' it has hung here a long time, and I only want you to leave it to me.' ' It's yours,' I remarked again, ' take it whenever you like.' "

It is not necessary to infer from this and other testimony that Charles Spurgeon was never really a child like other lads. His *bonhomie* in after years, and his open-hearted sympathy with children

c

in general, seem sufficiently to disprove such a notion. It is true that he never contracted any love for such a game as cricket, nor for athletic sports; but one may well believe that when he saw what the Orphanage boys could do on their exercise days he regretted having himself neglected such a method of developing muscle. Then, when he was pastor of the Metropolitan Tabernacle, he would enjoy a game at bowls on his own lawn.

At the same time, the boy had his own well-marked characteristics. He was certainly more thoughtful than the ordinary run of boys of his age, and he would be more impressed by the books he read. Half a century ago, when the precocious child was beginning to read for himself, the literature provided for children was not abundant, the consequence being that some of the old classic favourites, such as "Robinson Crusoe" and "The Pilgrim's Progress," as well as "The Book of Martyrs," by old John Foxe, received greater attention than might otherwise have been bestowed on them. Young Spurgeon was greatly moved and influenced by the reading of such works. Bunyan's characters would become to him like real living beings; many of the better kind would be almost like personal friends, while such a reader would vehemently resolve that he, too, would oppose without mercy such foes of all that was good as Apollyon and Diabolus. Then he would learn to detest the ways of Mr. Worldly-wiseman, Mr. Hate-good, and all those who ill-used the pilgrims in Vanity Fair. At last, perhaps with a little help from his grandfather or his aunt by way of explanation, he would have the truth dawn upon his mind that all in the household were pilgrims; that Vanity Fair was still being held; and that his grandfather was quite as necessary to aunt and the little boy as Greatheart was to Christiana and her children. Defoe's masterpiece, as a book of another kind, would have a different influence, but it was a book which Mr. Spurgeon never ceased to admire; and when he read "Robinson Crusoe" through again some few years before his death, he spoke of it in a way that showed his high appreciation. As regarded old Foxe's great work, it is probable that the pictures at first made deeper impressions upon his susceptible mind than the text. The large folio plates of the burning of the martyrs in Smithfield, and of their sufferings elsewhere, stirred the young heart, and engendered a hatred of the Roman system which was never lost. Hence, when at the age of sixteen he made his first literary essay, he very naturally chose for a subject "Antichrist and her Brood." That performance is still in the possession of Mr. John Spurgeon, and if published now would be read as a curiosity.

Years before this, when the boy was only six years old, he overheard his grandfather deploring the habits of one of his flock, who was accustomed to go to a public-house for a mug of beer and a quiet pipe. Little Charles said, "I will kill him," and shortly afterwards told his grandfather that he had done the deed. "I've killed old Rhodes. He will never grieve my poor grandfather any more." "What do you mean, my child?" asked the minister. "I have not been doing any harm, grandfather," was the reply. "I've been about the Lord's work, that is all." The mystery was presently explained by old Rhodes himself. He told Mr. Spurgeon that the lad had come to the public-house, and said to him, "What doest thou here, Elijah, sitting with the ungodly? You are a member of a church, and you break your pastor's heart! I'm ashamed of you! I would not break my pastor's heart, I am sure." Old Rhodes was angry for a moment, but came to the conclusion that the child was in the right, and now begged pardon.

We have to think of the little boy at this time as being in all things subject to his grandfather. While, however, this veteran was the Eli to whom our little Samuel looked as the final authority on all things, the maiden aunt, the old pastor's daughter, was as good as a second mother to him. The influence of such a woman on such a nature would be great and lasting.*

* "Mr. Spurgeon was the first grandson born in his family, and when of tenderest years was removed from his father's house to that of his grandfather at Stambourne, with whom was residing an unmarried sister of his father, Miss Ann Spurgeon, who lavished on the baby nephew, consigned to her special care, that wealth of love and affection maiden aunts are so often seen to bestow. It was said he was a most amiable child; and even when a mere

All the surroundings of his life at Stambourne appear to have favoured the healthy development of his religious life; and in after days it was with the manse in the old Essex village that the fondest memories of the pastor of the Metropolitan Tabernacle were associated. In many respects the place appears to have been highly favoured. The farmers were tolerably prosperous; the excessive depopulation of the villages had not yet made itself felt; and, better than all, the Nonconformists and the members of the Established Church lived in harmony, and worked in common for the good of their poorer neighbours.

In church, in chapel, and in daily life, many of the old fashions still held on; and the talk of the staid Christians who frequently assembled in old Mr. James Spurgeon's house was of that old-fashioned kind which Puritanism itself might have inspired. These warm-hearted members of the church felt drawn by their sympathies towards the little boy, and the child, on his part, naturally contracted an affection for them. He appears to have occasionally joined in the conversation in a way that surprised his elders; but they did not on that account suspect his uncommon genius. The round-faced child was bright enough for his years; but it needed a shrewder observer than could be found among those Essex farmers and their dependents to detect his uncommon characteristics. To the congregation who attended the old meeting-house he would merely be a forward child, who had caught something of his grandfather's eccentricity, and who in after years would rival the old man in his quaintness and honest outspokenness. As will presently appear, a visitor in due course came to Stambourne who saw greater promise in the little boy than anyone else had seen.

We must not suppose, however, that the old pastor's grandson spent all of the days of childhood at Stambourne. He may have

infant, before his lips had uttered an articulate word, would sit patiently for hours amusing himself with a book of pictures. His love of reading soon manifested itself. Even at six years old, when some children have advanced no farther in spelling than words of one syllable, he could read out with a point and emphasis really marvellous in one so young."—"Traits of Character," by a Contemporary, 1860; II., 80–81.

stayed there until he was over five years of age; he then returned
to his parents' home at Colchester, where he first attended school.
As a schoolboy, it was at Stambourne that he loved best to pass his
holidays—not that he was less happy in the home of his parents
than with his grandfather; for the future great preacher owed more
to his father and mother than he could ever estimate. He would
himself have admitted this fact. No memories he ever had of early
days were out of harmony with the Christian life. While Mr. John
Spurgeon was constantly employed in preaching the Gospel, his wife
devoted herself to the work of caring for the children in a way which
was altogether characteristic of the model Christian matron. She it
was who taught them in the Scriptures; she encouraged them in
what was right, while she prayed for each individually with an
ardour that was in itself a blessing. In a word, the mother of the
future pastor of the Metropolitan Tabernacle was such as a great
man might well be proud of, and her early teaching and solicitude
were ever remembered by him with affectionate gratitude.

CHAPTER V.

VISIT OF RICHARD KNILL TO STAMBOURNE.

Charles and James Spurgeon as Playmates—Characteristics of the Elder—The Toy Ships—*The Thunderer*—Richard Knill at Stambourne—His Work in Foreign Climes—Knill's Mother—An Escape from Drowning—Saturday Evening in the Spurgeons' Best Parlour —Knill's Experience in Madras—His Account of the Great Flood at St. Petersburg—His Prophecy concerning his Young Friend—Permanence of the Friendship.

WHEN Charles and James Spurgeon were boys together they were very much like other children of their age, although in some respect the characteristics of the elder, which at a very early date began to show themselves, were sometimes such as would prove him to be a child above the ordinary standard. Charles seems to have read the Bible for himself with a comprehension beyond his years, and the facts found in Scripture relating to nature and every-day life he made his own, so that the knowledge he possessed of such things in those early days was sufficiently striking to surprise older people who listened to his knowing remarks, and at times possibly corrected their own ignorance.

Charles and James played together; they were greatly attached to each other, but, as there was a difference of three years in their ages, the first must have been almost a man, comparatively speaking, in the eyes of his brother. The younger would, in consequence, take many impressions from the elder, such as would probably have a lasting influence.

Thus, one day the two brothers were seen playing together near some water on which each was sailing his toy ship. They began to talk about the names which should be given to the vessels. Both looked admiringly on the boats, as in their eyes they bore proudly on their way in company, some rare hard service being supposed to be in store for them. Suddenly the features of Charles assumed an expression of determination, and he said with great energy, "I shall call mine *The Thunderer*." He then went on to explain that if one meant to fight and gain the victory, his vessel must carry a name worthy of the cause in hand. " Yes, I shall call mine THE THUNDERER!" Of course the younger brother looked on in admiration, and being· already content to follow one who was born to be a leader, he gave his own little man-of-war a humbler name.

A memorable event, which relieved the monotony of the days of childhood—if, indeed, the daily round ever had aught of monotony in it—was the visit to Stambourne of the late Richard Knill, who appears to have come as the appointed preacher of the anniversary sermon on behalf of the London Missionary Society. As a traveller of varied experience and adventure, as well as a quondam missionary, and at that time as a pastor, Mr. Knill would be cordially welcomed by the Stambourne minister, who was nearly twelve years the senior of his visitor. Mr. Knill had been engaged in Christian service in India and St. Petersburg successively; and during the latter part of his life he had for a time ministered in what had been the pulpit of Rowland Hill, at Wotton-under-Edge, after which he removed to Chester. He was thus in many ways quite an interesting character to come into a country house in days when books and stories of adventure were not so plentiful as they are at present. Then, above all, the great cause of the London Missionary Society, which the visitor came to plead, was more than enough to make him welcome to such entertainment as the manse afforded.

Old James Spurgeon would naturally be charmed with the company of a man who, though younger than himself, had seen so much more of the world. Mr. Knill, having lived in the far East, as well as in distant northern regions, had much new information to give respecting little-known customs and strange peoples, and the progress of the Gospel amongst them.

However much Mr. Knill might take with his host, however,

he appears to have been much more powerfully attracted by the old pastor's grandson, who then must have been passing some of his holidays at Stambourne. He saw something above the commonplace in the bright, speaking eyes of that round-faced child. Then, when the boy was spoken to, there seems to have come a response beyond his years, so that a bond of sympathy presently united the two. At the same time, Mr. Knill may have been drawn towards this engaging child partly because of his yearning love for young people, since his own children had, one by one, been borne to the grave. In the year 1848, which may have been about the date of this visit, Mr. Knill's last surviving son, who had been trained for the Christian ministry, had passed away, leaving in the fond father's heart a void never to be filled.

The visit of the missionary preacher probably extended only from Saturday afternoon to Monday; but as the weather was sufficiently genial, he and the little boy passed some time together in the open air. The two knelt together in the great yew arbour at the bottom of the manse garden, when the elder prayed for his child friend in a way that was believed in after years to have drawn down the blessing of heaven. There was conversation also that related to Christ and His cause, which could not but have deeply impressed the boy's susceptible nature.

But while the veteran missionary and his young friend are together in the manse garden, or while they quietly ramble along the sweet Stambourne lanes, now in their early summer dress, we shall hardly over-shoot the mark in supposing that the inquisitive child had his wholesome curiosity gratified by hearing something about his mature friend's experience and adventures in the world. Was Charles a lad who had to go to school morning by morning? That had once been the lot of Richard Knill; but in those old days of George III. England was nearly always at war, and the times were altogether harder. How interested little Charles would be in hearing of his friend's providential escape from drowning when a boy; and one may well suppose that the anecdote would be told because the circumstance pointed an obvious moral. Down in Devonshire, at the end of the last century, bridges over running streams were not always considered to be absolutely indispensable; and one such river, which had to be crossed morning and evening when going to and returning from school, had nothing better for the convenience of foot passengers than great blocks of stone, to step aside from which would be to risk drowning. On one occasion, while playing on one of these great blocks, Richard Knill fell in; but as it happened, a poor widow, who was carding wool not far away, heard the splash, and hastened to the rescue of what was then the flaxen-haired little boy. Mr. Knill could tell how the old dame—who, of course, was to him a veritable heroine—had saved him by seizing hold of his curls, so that, at times, there was genuine advantage in having long hair. "She could not read, but she saved my life," the old missionary would add.

When the pastor's family and their visitor assembled on the Saturday evening in the best parlour of the Stambourne manse, old James Spurgeon, as an ardent Puritan enthusiast, would naturally be interested in hearing about what was being done in foreign lands. We have no certain record of what passed; but we know full well that the pastor and his grandson, as well as others who may have been there, would listen spell-bound to such accounts of service and adventure as a man like Knill could give. All this, moreover, would increase their interest in the missionary sermons to be preached in the adjoining meeting-house on the morrow.

One seems to hear the pastor of Stambourne, his grandson sitting on a hassock at his feet, ask his brother Knill to tell them something about India, as he had known it in the early days of the century, more than thirty years before. Mr. Knill knew a good deal about life in Madras as he had found it in the year 1816, when it was the fashion for nominally Christian Europeans to lead very unworthy lives. On a certain Sunday, after service, soon after he arrived in the city, the missionary dined with a number of military officers, whose habits reflected the condition of society in general.

"The wine passed round merrily; they pressed me to drink.* I politely declined. The captain said, 'When you are at Rome you must do as Rome does.' I said, 'Captain, if you urge me to drink I will write to your sister about it, and what will she say?' The snare was broken. 'Well,' said he, 'do as you please.' They related soldiers' stories, and I related missionary stories, and by way of application I said: 'Gentlemen, we are going to build a girls' school in Black Town, near our chapel, to correspond with the boys' school, and as this is the first visit I have paid, I should like to make it memorable by your becoming the first contributors. Give me something for a foundation stone.' They cheerfully responded, and sent me home in the captain's palanquin with £15 towards the girls' school. From that time the captain became a regular attendant at chapel, and sometimes ten or twelve officers came with him."

Mr. Knill could talk not only of India, but of Russia; for he was in St. Petersburg at the time of the memorable overflowing of the Neva in November, 1824, and also during the terrible outbreak of cholera in 1830. Had the little boy, who was so interested in all that was taking place in this old Essex village, ever heard of the storm of fire which nearly two thousand years before had overtaken the cities of Herculaneum and Pompeii? If so, his new friend, Mr. Knill, had actually lived in the Russian capital, which, as a great modern city, might possibly one day be overtaken by a flood that would allow none of the hundreds of thousands of inhabitants to escape from death, any more than those in the ancient towns were able to get away from the overwhelming fire.

What the missionary once related concerning the flood in the Russian city is a sample of the anecdotes with which he was able to entertain friends at home in England while sitting as a guest at their firesides :—

"The wind was high, and the waters rose very much, so that guns were fired to warn the inhabitants of those apartments which were nearly on a level with the river. The next morning the guns

* The quotation, of course, is in Mr. Knill's own words.

fired again, as the waters had greatly increased. About ten a.m. some of the streets near the Neva were beginning to be covered; but the people would not believe that the waters could rise much higher, forty-seven years having rolled away since the city was inundated. By half-past ten it was too late to attempt the removal of any property, and all the people were thrown into confusion. Those who could run, ran; and those who could not, cried for deliverance from immediate death. In some instances assistance reached the sufferers, but in many more they were suffocated by the flood. By two p.m. the city presented a scene the most awful that can be conceived. Every place was deserted. There was nothing visible that had life, and the streets were occupied by ships, and boats, and watch-houses, and floating trees, and even coffins from the cemeteries, with property of various kinds. Several entire villages were carried away, with the exception of a cottage here and there to make known where they once stood."

Such was the man who came to the old manse at Stambourne to preach the missionary sermons between forty and fifty years ago, and such were the things he was able to relate from his own varied experience when opportunity offered. We are interested in him because he appears really to have been the first who entered the village with an eye of sufficient discernment to detect the uncommon genius of young Charles Haddon Spurgeon. Mr. Knill had never before heard a child of his little friend's years read the Scriptures at family prayer with such effect; and he had a presentiment, for which he could not account, that the little fellow before him was destined to undertake distinguished service in the Church. All have heard of the striking prophecy that his young friend would grow up to proclaim the Gospel to multitudes; and how he asked that when he preached for the first time in Surrey Chapel he would allow the people to sing Cowper's familiar hymn, " God moves in a mysterious way." All that the devoted ex-missionary had spoken of, and much more besides, at last came to pass; and no one was more delighted with Mr. Spurgeon's early successes than the friend who had met with the future great preacher at his grandfather's manse, had prayed with him, and had admired him as a child of remarkable promise. "I know him!" cried Richard Knill, when news of the vast crowds attending Mr. Spurgeon's services reached Chester; and Mr. Spurgeon still knew and loved Richard Knill. The friendship commenced at Stambourne continued until the old missionary's death in 1857, at the age of seventy. Both the missionary and his younger friend appear to have looked upon their first meeting at Stambourne as quite providential; and although the striking prophecy to the effect that the little boy would one day preach in Rowland Hill's chapel may have helped to bring about its own fulfilment, the episode, as a whole, is sufficiently remarkable to warrant particular notice.

CHAPTER VI.

SCHOOLDAYS AND CONVERSION.

Quality of Spurgeon's Education—Preaching from a Hay-rack—His Mother's Teaching—His first Schoolmasters—A School Incident—Removal with his Brother to Maidstone—A precocious Letter-writer—Incidents connected with his Conversion—Scene in the Colchester Primitive Methodist Chapel—The Sermon—Mr. John Spurgeon's Testimony—Zeal in Christian Work—A Boy's Humour.

WHEN Mr. Spurgeon settled in London in the year 1854 there were those who industriously circulated the report that the young preacher was quite uneducated. This was not the opinion of those who were better acquainted with the facts of the case, however. The truth was, that he was not only as well prepared as circumstances would allow for the distinguished position he was destined to occupy in the world, but was evidently prepared for his future eminent service in the best manner possible. That is the view the late Pastor would himself have taken of the matter, while the tutor to whom he was chiefly indebted—the late Mr. Charles Leeding— would have borne similar testimony. They would both have maintained that the hand of Providence had overruled all things from beginning to end. The parents of the future preacher were not people who undervalued education; they rather exercised becoming self-denial in order to give their children educational advantages. If, therefore, we follow young Spurgeon through the course of his education, and at the same time take full account of the discipline he received in his grandfather's manse, we shall probably also see for ourselves that he was singularly favoured in the days of childhood and youth; that, in point of fact, all things seemed to work together to fit the wonderful boy for the great sphere he was designed to occupy.

What his work in the world would really be appears to have been seen even in the early days of childhood. As a man of observation,

Mr. John Spurgeon saw that his son was destined to become a preacher. " Yes, yes ; he always was to preach," he told a corre- spondent of a daily newspaper who questioned him on this subject ; and the veteran then went on to tell of a characteristic scene he once witnessed in his stable at Colchester. Looking into this building on a certain afternoon, the father observed that his son Charles had climbed into the hay-rack above the horse's manger, and, supposing that to be his pulpit, was addressing an audience below with all the energy he could command. As his chief auditor, the child- preacher's brother James was becomingly accommodated with a seat in the manger, while his sisters occupied a more humble, though probably a more comfortable, position on trusses of hay. There could be no doubt about the bent of such a lad's inclinations, although it might not be possible as yet to discover that he was a unique genius.

Like many other great personages before him, young Charles Spurgeon was no doubt greatly indebted to his mother as a teacher before he went to school at all. When he first left home to get instruction, his first schoolmistress was the wife of a certain Captain Cook, a namesake of the well-known eighteenth-century discoverer, but not related to him, so far as I am aware, although an ancient tobacco- box, which is supposed to have travelled round the world in the pocket of this intrepid discoverer, is still treasured in the family as a memento of the old days at Colchester. The promising lad next went to a school in the same town kept by a Mr. Lewis, under whom he made some progress. Perhaps the young scholar may thus early have been interested in the topography of the ancient Roman town, the old-time associations of which had extended to the Trinobantes among the Britons, to Claudius Cæsar and Boadicea at later dates, and to the Saxons still later. It was at Colchester that Charles first met with his favourite tutor, Mr. Leeding—the friend to whom he was chiefly indebted for painstaking instruction.

It was a good school which young Charles Spurgeon attended at Colchester ; and, as many misrepresentations on this subject have gained currency, I am glad to quote the testimony of Mr. R. D. Cheveley, of Harrogate, given since Mr. Spurgeon's death. The writer was educated at the same academy, and, having grateful memories of the advantages he received, is anxious to correct misleading statements. "Stockwell House, Colchester," he says, "where Charles Haddon Spurgeon was being educated from the age of eleven to fifteen, was a thoroughly good middle-class classical and commercial school. Mr. Henry Lewis, the principal, was a man whose literary attainments were of a superior order, and for years he was assisted by a very scholarly man in the person of Mr. Leeding, whose death occurred only very recently. Mr. Leeding was the classical and mathematical tutor; his teaching was very thorough, and in Charles Spurgeon he possessed a pupil of a very receptive mind, especially with Latin and Euclid. I remember well that in both of these subjects he was very advanced, so that he left Stockwell House a thoroughly well-educated youth; in fact, quite as much so as it was possible for him to attain outside of the Universities. Such statements, therefore, as have appeared in the public press to the effect that Mr. Spurgeon's education, 'such as it was,' was obtained at a school at Colchester, convey the idea that it was education of a most elementary character, and are, in consequence, somewhat incorrect."

"J. B.," of St. Botolph's, Colchester, has also given in the same journal—*The Christian World*—some reminiscences of the old days at Colchester, when he was at school with Spurgeon. Speaking of the rollicking humour, combined with great industry, which was even then characteristic of Spurgeon, this correspondent says:—

"Spurgeon was always top boy of his class—in fact, top boy of the school. Once only I remember he lost his place in class, and lost every place until he reached the very bottom. In vain did his teacher remonstrate with him; he was at the bottom, and couldn't get away. At last it occurred to the teacher, perhaps the *fire* near the bottom of the class might have something to do with it. It was a very cold day, and the top of the class was close to a draughty door. The teacher reversed the class, making the top by the stove. Spurgeon immediately brightened up; not a chance was missed of getting up, and he was soon back in his old place at the top.

"About half-a-dozen boys, who lived at some distance from the school, used to carry their dinners and eat them in the schoolroom. Spurgeon was one of these, and it was his usual custom while eating his own dinner to be turning over the pages of a joke or riddle or anecdote book in search of something to amuse the rest. Anything extra good he would sometimes commence reading before his mouth was quite ready. Many were the laughs we had, and many the half-chokings we had, in trying to feed and read and laugh all at once. The playground was never Spurgeon's forte; play of the intellect was his delight."

The anecdote about the stove I have myself heard Mr. Spurgeon tell at the Pastors' College.

The next move was when, in the year 1848, the brothers Charles and James went together to a college at Maidstone, in which special attention was given to the study of agriculture as a science. The principal was Mr. Walker, a relative. The journey thither from the Eastern Counties was through London; and that was probably the first sight the brothers had of the great metropolis where in the future their united life-work was to be undertaken. Railways were not so universal then as they are at present; and memories of the coach and other things belonging to the journey appear to have lingered in the minds of the travellers.

After leaving Maidstone another move, fraught with still greater consequences, was made, when young Spurgeon became junior tutor in the academy of Mr. Swindell at Newmarket. Some particular account of the progress made in this town will need to be given; but in the meantime some reference must be made to that great crisis in life which we call conversion, which occurred before the situation of tutor was accepted.

In connection with this subject we have to bear well in mind that, all along, the training of this child of genius had been of a distinctly religious character. One reason why he had so readily caught up the modes of thinking and feeling of his Puritan grand-father was because his mind had been prepared for the reception of such impressions by the training of the home. From his earliest childhood the future preacher had lived in a religious atmosphere, and the talk of religious people had been, as it were, his native dialect. In an extant letter, written at the age of fourteen and addressed to an uncle, this precocious child is found using language and scriptural phrases such as might have come from a seasoned Puritan of full experience in the seventeenth century. Mere knowledge of such things, however, does not necessarily affect the heart and life so as to ensure peace of mind.

The great change of conversion appears to have occurred towards the close of the year 1848, or the opening of 1849, when the boy was in his fifteenth year. The family were then living at Colchester. Mr. John Spurgeon was engaged in business, but on Sunday mornings he regularly drove over to Tollesbury, nine miles away, there to minister to a congregation at the Independent Chapel. As the Spurgeon household was a tolerably large family, the custom was observed of the young people accompanying their father to Tollesbury in turn. On a certain Sunday morning in the winter of 1848–49 it had been arranged for Charles to accompany his father to the service, as he had so often done before; but, as the weather happened to turn out cold and stormy, it was thought advisable for the lad not to go. "You cannot go to Tollesbury, therefore you had better go to the Primitive Methodist Chapel in Colchester," his mother said to him, and Charles at once felt disposed to obey. On that particular morning he was not in a happy state of mind; and it was probably quite as agreeable to his feelings to go alone to public worship as it would have been to accompany his father in the chaise through the wind and snow. In point of fact, this son of the Tollesbury Independent minister was in that transition state of doubt and terror—eager for the pardon and peace of soul which he could not yet find—which Bunyan refers to in the opening of his immortal allegory: "Behold, I saw a man, clothed with rags, standing in a certain place, with his face from his own house, a book in his hand, and a great burden upon his back. I looked, and saw him open the book, and read therein; and as he read, he wept and trembled; and not being able longer to contain, he brake out with a lamentable cry, saying, 'What shall I do?'" Tortures of mind, such as Bunyan himself may have endured, and such as he alludes to in another of his works, were at this time oppressing the heart and soul of young Spurgeon.

When the anxious youth walked from his home into the

D

Colchester street on that memorable tempestuous winter morning, he appears hardly to have settled in his own mind whether he would enter the Primitive Methodist Chapel, as his mother had recommended, or whether he would go further afield. He went onward, engrossed with his own thoughts, and little heeding the storm, on account of the weight which well-nigh bore him down. When he presently came up to the Methodist meeting-house he entered, however, thinking he might as well do that as go further, or do anything else.

As Mr. John Spurgeon has explained, "the preacher in the Primitive Methodist Chapel was a local man; a local preacher, who also worked at digging, planting cabbages, and so on." When he entered the pulpit this humble peasant evangelist saw so few persons in the pews that he began to question with himself whether it was worth while to conduct a service at all. The snow and wind would not allow of the people leaving their homes, so that no one was to blame; but, at the same time, what good end would be answered by his wearing himself out by preaching in a practically empty chapel? The good man still hesitated in regard to abandoning the service; however, on taking another survey of his audience his eye may have been attracted by the pale, round-faced, anxious-looking lad sitting by himself, who looked like a subject that needed a good word. At all events, he resolved that the service should go on; and when the time came for the sermon he opened the Bible at Isaiah xlv. 22—"Look unto Me and be ye saved, all the ends of the earth." Presently he became more animated, and again surveying the nearly empty chapel, as though each pew contained an anxious listener ready to receive the life-giving message of the Gospel, he called out with all his energy, "*Look!* Look! LOOK!" The arrow thus shot at a venture went home into at least one heart.

That, indeed, was a supreme moment in the life of young Spurgeon. The word that he most needed to hear had not only been spoken, he had received it with gladness; in an instant he felt that he was not only free, he was a new creature in Christ Jesus. What had really happened corresponds so precisely with what happened to Christian at a certain stage in his pilgrimage, as depicted by our great allegorist, that the passage may well be given. " So I saw in my dream," says Bunyan, " that just as Christian came up with the cross, his burden loosed from off his shoulders, and fell from off his back, and began to tumble, and so continued to do till it came to the mouth of the sepulchre, where it fell in, and I saw it no more. Then was Christian glad and lightsome, and said with a merry heart, ' He hath given me rest by His sorrow, and life by His death.' Then he stood still awhile to look and wonder; for it was very sur‑ prising to him that the sight of the cross should thus ease him of his burden. He looked, therefore, and saw again, even till the springs that were in his head sent the waters down his cheeks. Now, as he stood looking and weeping, behold, three Shining Ones came to him, and saluted him with ' Peace be to thee.' So the first said to him, ' Thy sins be forgiven thee '; the second stripped him of his rags and clothed him with change of raiment; the third also set a mark upon his forehead, and gave him a roll with a seal upon it, which he bid him look on as he ran, and that he should give it in at the Celestial Gate."

This is Bunyan's language in " The Pilgrim's Progress," and Mr. Spurgeon would have acknowledged that the passage exactly de‑ scribed his own condition on the stormy winter's day in 1849, when, for the first time, he realised that he was accepted of God for Christ's sake. The storm had not abated when he again stepped forth into the street; but what cared he for snow or wintry blast now that the burden had rolled from his shoulders, while peace flowed into his heart? He went homeward with a lightened step, for, instead of all things seeming to be against him, all things appeared to be in his favour. Even the elements in their violence seemed to be friendly towards him. Life had now another meaning; the world opened up new prospects. The wonder was that so gloriously simple a matter had not been clearly apprehended before. " Look unto Me and be ye saved, all the ends of the earth!" In that brief sentence the Evangelical Prophet had summed up the Gospel which in the fulness of time was to supersede the dispensation of the law.

Referring to the latter part of that eventful day, Mr. John Spurgeon said to a newspaper representative :—

"We spent the evening as an evening should be spent, reading the Bible, and so on. Then by-and-by I said, 'Come, boys, it's time to go to bed.' 'Father,' remarked Charles, 'I don't want to go to bed yet.' 'Come, come,' said I, whereupon he told me that he wanted to speak with me. We sat up long into the night, and he talked to me of his being saved, which had taken place that day, and right glad was I to hear him talk. 'In the text, "Look, look, look," Charles said to me, holding up his hands, 'I found salvation this morning. In the text, "Accepted in the Beloved," preached at the Baptist Church in the evening, I found peace and pardon.' These, I think, were his words, and so was his conversion to God brought about."

Concerning the preacher at the Primitive Methodist Chapel, Mr. Spurgeon, senior, remarked :—"Some years afterwards, when I was opening a church in Cambridgeshire, a man came up and spoke to me, telling me that he was the local preacher of the Primitive Methodist Church. We had only spoken a few words, when I was whisked away to speak to some other of the many friends, and I never saw him again. About his entering the Baptist Church, Charles used to say that I was a wise father to let my children read the Bible for themselves."

In its attendant circumstances, this conversion was a striking episode in a great man's life ; so that naturally efforts have been made to identify the man who occupied the pulpit on the stormy Sunday when the lad was converted. In after years the convert himself described the preacher as a "lean-fleshed" man, but who he really was does not appear to have been discovered. Some supposed for a time that a Mr. Eaglen was the friend who preached what is now known as the "Look" sermon; but when he was confronted with Mr. Eaglen on one occasion Mr. Spurgeon failed to recognise in him his Primitive Methodist benefactor. Probably it is quite as well that he is hidden among that unknown crowd of honourable workers who have done their duty with great results following, but without having their fame trumpeted through the world.

For such a youth to become converted was for him to become zealous in the various kinds of Christian work that he was competent to undertake. As Mr. John Spurgeon himself has said: "Before he went to Newmarket Charles had been converted, and while at Newmarket he was zealous to do something for religion. He distributed tracts among the people, some of whom, I suppose, were not particularly anxious at that time to have them. Anyhow, Charles adopted a measure to keep him in his house-to-house visitation and distribution. He carried copybooks, and taught the boys of a household to write, while at the same time he distributed the tracts. Indeed, from the very first, Charles was active to do good."

Other characteristics, which became more and more developed as years passed by, are also referred to by the great preacher's father. "Charles," he says, "had always a strong vein of humour, or, if you like, fun, running through him. An illustration of my words strikes me, although it carries me back many, many years. After Charles had begun to preach he used often to drive into Colchester from meetings. I don't mean that he drove himself, because he never would, and on the occasion to which I refer James was driving. It was a four-wheeled machine, and one of my daughters was sitting behind, Charles and James being in front. 'You're asleep, Polly,' said Charles, turning round in his humorous way. 'No, I'm not,' she answered. A little later he turned round again with 'Now you're quite asleep, Polly. If you sleep I'll unhook you, and leave you behind!' Whether she had been dozing in the cold I don't know, but the prospect of being unhooked and left behind—an impossibility—kept her awake."

This reminiscence somewhat anticipates events, however; for at the date at which we have now arrived, Charles Spurgeon was still only a schoolboy, whose education was as yet not nearly completed.

CHAPTER VII.

AT NEWMARKET.

Starting in Life—Newmarket, Past and Present—Mr. Swindell's Academy—Professor J. D. Everett's Reminiscences—Mr. Mattingly's Recollections—Temptation to Infidelity—Adoption of Baptist Views—Baptism at Isleham—Engaging in Christian Work—A Stock Contribution to Albums.

IT was on the morning of August 17th, 1849, that young Spurgeon left his home at Colchester for Newmarket. As this represented something like his first start in life on his own account, Mrs. Spurgeon accompanied her son to his destination, in order to see for herself that all things were arranged satisfactorily and comfortably. Although the youth had only just commenced his sixteenth year, he had accepted the appointment of under tutor in the academy of Mr. Swindell at Newmarket, the return being the privilege of continuing his own education, especially in Greek.

The town of Newmarket was in itself a place which Spurgeon, with such tastes and aspirations as had been particularly characteristic of him since his conversion, would have avoided rather than have selected for a residence; but, as he would be housed with a Christian family, the uncongenial surroundings would not unduly affect him. Newmarket was then what it still remains—the principal centre of racing in Great Britain. There the Jockey Club has its headquarters, and in the neighbourhood are many training establishments. The races are said to have originated in the days of Queen Elizabeth, when some fine Spanish horses, saved from the wreck of the Spanish Armada, were taken into the town. Be this as it may, Newmarket became a favourite place of fashionable resort early in the seventeenth century. James I. there erected for himself a palace which he called a hunting-seat; and this was afterwards rebuilt by his grandson Charles II. Part of the site, and also a portion of the materials of this building, were used for the erection of an

Independent Chapel some years after Spurgeon had left the town. The town was a Roman station, and ancient relics are still occasionally discovered. The race meetings are held seven times every year, and the general surroundings of the place seem to show that sport constitutes its chief business.

At the time that Mr. Spurgeon became an articled pupil in the academy of Mr. Swindell at Newmarket, Professor J. D. Everett, F.S.A., now of Queen's College, Belfast, was also engaged in the same establishment. Mr. Everett was about three years older than the junior tutor, and the two soon became sincere friends. The following reminiscences have been given by the Professor in *The Christian World* :—

"In the summer of 1849, when I was not quite eighteen, I went to Newmarket to assist in a school kept by a Mr. Swindell, who had been an old friend of my father's, and who had my brothers Percy and John as pupils. There were two other assistants, but not long after my arrival they went off, and I was left for a week or so as the sole assistant. I was then relieved of part of my duty by a lad of fifteen, who came as an articled pupil. This was Charles H. Spurgeon, and for the next three months we shared the work between us. We boarded in the house, occupied the same bedroom, took our walks together, discussed our common grievances, and were the best of friends.

"He was rather small and delicate, with pale but plump face, dark brown eyes and hair, and a bright, lively manner, with a never-failing flow of conversation. He was rather deficient in muscle, did not care for cricket or other athletic games, and was timid at meeting cattle on the roads.

"He had been well brought up in a family with strong Puritanical tendencies, and was proficient in the subjects taught in the middle-class schools of those days. He knew a little Greek, enough Latin to gather the general sense of Virgil's 'Æneid' without a dictionary, and was fond of algebra. He had a big book of equation problems (by Bland, I think), and could do all the problems in it, except some two or three, which I was proud to be able to do for him. He was a smart, clever boy at all kinds of book learning; and, judging from the accounts he gave me of his experiences in his father's counting-house, he was also a smart man of business. He was a keen observer of men and manners, and very shrewd in his judgments. He enjoyed a joke, but was earnest, hard-working, and strictly conscientious."

Professor Everett is also able to quote from a shorthand diary which he kept at that time. One of the entries is as follows:—

"*Tuesday*, October 9.—After dinner I took Percy and four other boys to see the races. We saw the Cesarewitch, the most celebrated race at Newmarket; thirty-one horses ran. We also saw four other races. I saw quite enough to gratify my curiosity, and did not wish to stop to see any more races. Mr. Spurgeon did not go, as he thought he should be doing wrong if he went."

We thus see that the young tutor was keeping himself pure and unspotted from the world. He was also making appreciable advances in the Christian life; stimulated as he was in his endeavours to reach to higher things by a devoutly Christian housekeeper in the schoolmaster's household, who, by precept and example, encouraged the young man in every possible way. In his reminiscences already referred to, Professor Everett says something about this honourable woman :—

"As to the early history of his theological views, I can add something to what has been already published. In Mr. Swindell's household there was a faithful old servant—a big, sturdy woman, who was well known to me and all the inmates as 'cook.' She was a woman of strong religious feelings, and a devout Calvinist. Spurgeon, when under deep religious conviction, had conversed with her, and been deeply impressed with her views of Divine truth. He explained this to me, and told me in his own terse fashion that it was 'cook' who had taught him his theology. I hope I am not violating his confidence in mentioning this fact. It is no discredit to the memory of a great man that he was willing to learn from the humblest sources."

Mr. Swindell confirms all that the Professor says about the "cook" or housekeeper at the academy. He also notes that Mr Spurgeon refers to the old servant in his first published book, "The Saint and his Saviour," while on another occasion the great preacher confessed: "I got all the theology I ever needed a good many years ago from an old woman who was cook in the house where I was usher, and I have never had any wish to get a newer sort."

Mr. Robert Mattingly, of Great Cornard Street, Sudbury, has also contributed some interesting information concerning this good woman to the same journal :—

"About twenty-five years ago I became acquainted with the person referred to, Mary King by name. She was then living in cottage lodgings, facing St. Margaret's Church, Ipswich, and was a member of the Bethesda Strict Baptist Church, close by. She was a staunch Calvinist, logical, clear-headed, and had a wonderful knowledge of the Bible. I have often heard from her lips the account of her intercourse with the youthful Spurgeon, of which she was naturally not a little proud, as he had then attained the height of his marvellous popularity. Professor Everett says she was known as 'cook.' She always spoke of herself as 'housekeeper,' and as the intercourse between Mr. Spurgeon and herself seemed to be quite within the order of the household, she probably occupied something more than a menial position. During my acquaintance with her I learned that she had outlived all, or nearly all, of a small income (I do not remember from what source). I wrote to Mr. Spurgeon acquainting him with the facts, and received from him a prompt reply, thanking me for my letter, sending a hearty greeting to his old friend, and with characteristic generosity he enclosed a cheque for £5, with a request that I would minister to her immediate necessities, pay her 5s. a week, and generally use my discretion in dispensing the amount in his behalf. This I did, and reported to Mr. Spurgeon from time to time, always receiving a fresh cheque when the fund in hand became exhausted, and this was continued till her death about three years later."

It was during the Newmarket period that young Spurgeon learned from experience that the Christian life is a serious warfare, the narrow way leading from the strait gate having snares and pitfalls for unwary, youthful feet. He learned for himself all about the dangers of Bypath Meadow, as well as of the terrors of the Slough of Despond. Referring to freethinkers and their unbelief, Mr. Spurgeon confessed many years afterwards in a sermon at Exeter Hall, that he had himself been subject to the temptation to scepticism. In an evil hour, which he shuddered to think about, he let go the anchor of faith, and while starting on a mad voyage, he asked Reason to be his guide. The voyage thus entered upon was tempestuous, but brief, and the lesson learned would never be forgotten. What was spurious in infidelity he had seen for himself; he keenly realised also the horrors from which he had providentially escaped. If any invited him to go that way again he said No; for he had tried those seas for himself, and was personally aware of what was before any voyager who ventured upon them.

Mr. Swindell, the proprietor of the academy at Newmarket, was a Baptist, but I am not aware that it was through coming in contact with this friend that Mr. Spurgeon was led to embrace the sentiments of the Particular Baptist denomination. Mr. and Mrs. John Spurgeon, who, like old Mr. James Spurgeon, were Independents, wished their children to read the Scriptures independently, and then to decide for themselves on such a matter; and, so long as they were conscientious, it was never anything of a cross to the parents that their two sons should think differently from themselves in regard to baptism.

Having become fully persuaded in his own mind that adult baptism by immersion was the only mode sanctioned by Scripture of administering the ordinance, Mr. Spurgeon desired to be baptised and to become a member of a Baptist Church. When he looked around the neighbourhood in which he was living he could discover no pastor of a congregation to whom he cared to apply

nearer than the one at Isleham, eight miles distant. Isleham was
a place of over two thousand inhabitants in the Fen Country; and
at a ferry of the River Lark the Baptists of the district had
been accustomed to have baptisings in the open air periodically since
the latter part of the eighteenth century. Being about half a
mile from the village, the ferry itself is a quiet, sylvan spot, such
as old Isaak Walton would have loved as a retreat where sport and
contemplation could be combined; but when persons were baptised
there a concourse of onlookers was attracted. On his mother's
birthday, May 3rd, 1850, Mr. Spurgeon rose early, and after spending
some time alone he walked the eight miles to Isleham, and was
baptised with some others by the late Pastor W. W. Cantlow, who
was then settled at the place. The school-house, erected in 1888,
was put up in memory of the man who thus immersed Mr. Spurgeon in the neighbouring river, and the memorial-stone of the
building records the interesting event.

Mr. Spurgeon does not appear to have united himself with the
congregation at Isleham, for, being separated from the people
by a distance of eight miles, he could not conveniently have
joined with them in their worship, communion, or Christian
service. From that date, however, the young Christian had but
one aim in life—to promote the glory of God and the good
of his fellow-creatures. Of course, he had as yet no suspicion
that his lot in the world would be more than a commonplace one;
but he was already desirous of doing even commonplace things in
the best manner possible. He keenly realised the responsibility of
being a Christian; and the doctrines he then embraced were such
as remained dear to him until the end. Those doctrines were
identical with what his grandfather and father had preached before
him. As time passed on he may have altered in some respects in
his method of presenting those doctrines, but from the great truths
themselves he never swerved. In after years in London, when, as
was often the case, he was asked to make his contribution to an
album, there was never any difficulty in regard to what should be

written: it was, I believe, the great preacher's invariable custom to give Cowper's well-known verse, which so well expressed the character of his own life-work:—

> "E'er since by faith I saw the stream
> Thy flowing wounds supply,
> Redeeming love has been my theme,
> And shall be till I die."

In his reminiscences Professor J. D. Everett says of Spurgeon at this time:—

"He had a wonderful memory for passages of oratory which he admired, and used to pour forth to me with great gusto, in our long walks, long screeds from open-air addresses, of a very rousing description, which he had heard delivered at Colchester Fair by the Congregational minister, Mr. Davids. His imagination had evidently been greatly impressed by these services, at which, by-the-bye, his father was selected to give out the hymns, on account of the loudness of his voice—a quality which would appear to have run in the family, but which had not at that time shown itself in my young friend. I have also heard him recite long passages from Bunyan's 'Grace Abounding.'

"He was a delightful companion, cheerful and sympathetic, a good listener as well as a good talker. And he was not cast in a common, conventional mould, but had a strong character of his own.

"The school was broken up before the regular time by an outbreak of fever, and I did not return to it; but we exchanged occasional letters for some years afterwards. He remained with Mr. Swindell for a year or so, and then removed to another school, kept by an old friend of his own at Cambridge."

To Cambridge, therefore, we will now follow the young tutor.

CHAPTER VIII.

CAMBRIDGE : THE FIRST SERMON.

Residence at Cambridge—Engages in Christian Work with new Ardour—Mr. Leeding—Robert Hall's Opinion of Cambridge—Troubles in the Church during Mr. Robinson's Pastorate—The Outlook in Mr. Spurgeon's Time—Mr. Spurgeon and the Lay Preachers' Association —Work in the Villages by Local Preachers—Mr. Spurgeon begins his Career as a Cottage Preacher—"Bishop" Vinter's Stratagem—A Walk—Effect on the Congregation—Mr. Spurgeon and the "Gentlemen at Cambridge."

MR. SPURGEON'S residence at Newmarket did not extend to more than about a year, and, as he had a good deal of time which he could call his own, he made some advances in self-improvement, while he was all along assiduous in such Christian work as he had an opportunity of undertaking. In Sunday-school work, in giving addresses to scholars, and in tract distribution, there was no lack of useful service; and whatsoever the hand of this youth found to do he did not fail to do it with all his might.

When the young teacher left Newmarket, in 1850, he went to reside at Cambridge; and although his surroundings had been sufficiently comfortable in the great racing town, things were probably still more to his liking now that he was living beneath the shadow of the University. In the Newmarket academy the articled pupil had found a friend in the head of the household, Mr. Swindell; Mr. Everett had there been to him a companion who was nearly as young as Mr. Spurgeon himself; and the devoted Christian housekeeper had given advice which would influence her youthful friend throughout his whole life. At Cambridge, however, Mr. Spurgeon once more came in contact with Mr. Leeding, the accomplished tutor whom he had first met at Colchester, and who, next to Richard Knill, probably understood his young friend's bent of mind and developing genius better than anybody else. It was no small benefit again to enjoy the tuition of such a man, to whom the pastor of the Metropolitan Tabernacle till the last acknowledged his indebtedness.

Mr. Spurgeon took some interest in topography. He must have seen much to gratify curiosity in such a town as Cambridge; and in this respect he would be a contrast to that ardent lover of nature, Robert Hall, who once remarked, " I always say of my Cambridge friends when I witness their contentedness in such a country, ' Herein is the faith and patience of the saints ! ' *My* faith and patience could not sustain me under it, with the unvarying kindness of my friends in addition." The distinguished pulpit orator of a century ago had even still more pronounced opinions in reference to the drawbacks of the great University town. " 'Tis a dismally flat country, sir, dismally flat," he once remarked. " Ely is twelve miles distant, but the road from Cambridge thither scarcely deviates twelve inches from the same level; and *that's* not very interesting. Before I came to Cambridge," he added, " I had read in the prize poems, and in some other works of fancy, of ' the banks of the Cam,' and of ' the sweetly-flowing stream,' and so on; but when I arrived here I was sadly disappointed. When I first saw the river as I passed over King's College bridge, I could not help exclaiming, ' Why, the stream is standing still to see people drown themselves '; and that, I am sorry to say, is a permanent feeling with me. Shocking place for the spirits, sir; I wish you may not find it so; it must be the very focus of suicides."

These singular notions about Cambridge are quoted because the great and good man who uttered them had formerly been a pastor of the church and congregation of which Mr. Spurgeon now became a member. That congregation, at the period in question, was carrying on its full share of Christian work in and around Cambridge; but there had been a time when the usefulness of the people was threatened by a wave of Socinianism. The distinguished Robert Robinson, author of the well-known hymn, " Come, Thou fount of every blessing," had been the pastor, and it was his unhappiness to let go the anchor of his faith in the Scriptural verities he had once preached with soul-moving power. "Fascinating as a preacher, delightful as a companion, perseveringly skilful in the insinuation of his sentiments, his influence could not but be great," says Dr. Olinthus Gregory. "From the profession of orthodox opinions," adds the same writer, "he had passed by a rather rapid transition, not to Socinianism, but far beyond, to the very borders of infidelity; such, at least, was the substance of his declaration to Dr. Priestley, whom he thanked for preserving him from that awful gulf. Vain speculation was substituted for knowledge, faith, and experience; confession and prayer but seldom made a part of the public worship which he conducted, his effusions before sermon consisting almost altogether of ascriptions of praise; and the congregation became so transformed and deteriorated in consequence that among the more intelligent class, with only two or three exceptions, 'he was esteemed the best Christian who was most skilled in disputation, not he who evinced most of the spirit of Christ.' The majority of the poorer members, however, escaped the contagion, and were ready to co-operate with the late Mr. Foster, who was then the senior deacon, and another of the deacons, who equally deplored the evils which had fallen upon them. Cordially attached to those doctrines which they regarded as fundamental, and therefore as constituting the basis of Church union, they were preparing to call upon the whole body to consider the expediency of requesting Mr. Robinson to resign, when his sudden death at Birmingham, just after he had been preaching in Dr. Priestley's pulpit, rendered such a measure unnecessary."

This dark passage in their history was only a distant memory when Mr. Spurgeon became associated with the church. Mr. Roff, the pastor, had just died, and Mr. Robinson, his successor, was not yet in office. In the middle of this century the people represented a prosperous Christian church; they maintained a number of agencies at work, and they did specially good service by means of the Lay Preachers' Association, which sent its agents into the villages around the University town. When the youthful Spurgeon associated him-self with the congregation in St. Andrew's Street, how little did he think that a student educated in the Pastors' College he was himself to establish would one day be its minister. Such is the case, however; for Mr. T. Graham Tarn, who has been settled with the people for a lengthened period, completed his theological course in the College in the year 1872.

Mr. George Apthorpe, who is still living at Cambridge, was acquainted with Mr. Spurgeon from the time of his first coming to the University town till the last, and he has obligingly sent me some particulars.

In the Sunday-school, Mr. Apthorpe had his class next to Mr. Spurgeon's, and he says, "Many a time I was listening to him while teaching my own boys." There was a select number of friends whose interest in the young man who had just come from Newmarket was very great; and one of the number, named Williamson, then a deacon of St. Andrew's Street church, openly declared of young Mr. Spurgeon, "Whoever lives to see it, he will become one of the greatest men in England." These ardent admirers do not appear to have exceeded eight or nine, however; for as Mr. Apthorpe adds: "The majority of the friends were rather averse to him, thinking what seemed to them his boldness and forwardness was rudeness in one so young." Among those who saw in the new-comer a power that would one day be mightily felt, was Mr. Vinter, who was also a deacon; and as the chief spirit among the members of the Lay Preachers' Association, which had then been established about twenty years, he was naturally ever on the look-out for new talent to press into the service. Mr. Vinter was a robe-maker by trade, and he had some years before been a member of the congregation of the devoted apostle of the Established Church, Charles Simeon, who died in November, 1836. Mr. Vinter was a very genial man, somewhat humorous, and was very highly esteemed. He had two brothers, Charles and Robert, and these also lived earnest Christian lives, the first being described as a tower of strength among the Wesleyans, while the other was equally useful among the Episcopalians. Of course, the attention of the Mr. Vinter of St. Andrew's Street chapel was first attracted towards Mr. Spurgeon in the Sunday-school; for it was obvious that if a youth could speak with such force before an assembly of teachers and children, he could do the work that was required of a lay preacher equally well.

There is also at Cambridge another old friend of the late pastor of the Metropolitan Tabernacle in the person of Mr. Watts. On a certain Sunday, after the Lord's Supper, Mr. Spurgeon followed this latter and showed a desire to become acquainted with him. He asked of Mr. Watts the loan of Scott's Commentary, and this being granted, the two drank tea together, and a friendship of the closest kind was commenced, which lasted until the preacher's death. There is an entry in the Church Book notifying the fact that Mr. Spurgeon had accepted the pastorate of the church at Waterbeach.

While studying under his friend Mr. Leeding, and at the same time teaching younger boys during the week, Mr. Spurgeon thus ardently engaged in Christian work on the Sabbath. For some time his efforts may not have extended beyond the Sunday-school, and tract distribution in the poor districts; but that would not long continue to be the case. He had already become much interested in the successful operations of the Lay Preachers' Association; and, when competent volunteers were always being sought after, it was not likely that a Sunday-school teacher who seemed to be endowed with special genius for giving addresses would escape being pressed into the service.

Since the Revival in the last century, what is called lay preaching has found great favour with Nonconformists; and throughout his life Mr. Spurgeon did all in his power to encourage and extend a practice which has now become common in villages and towns alike throughout the country. The custom is for young men who have gifts for public speaking to undertake cottage services, and these are in sufficient favour with working people and others to ensure their being on the average pretty well attended. The good influence thus exercised is in the aggregate very great; for the general civilising effect can only be adequately estimated when the condition of England is compared with that of other countries. Even the colporteurs who are diffusing Bibles and pure literature throughout the country, are expected to be local preachers as well as booksellers. It is also a fact that some of the most successful ministers of our times have been men who commenced their career as preachers in a peasant's cottage. Young men who had already borne something of the burden and heat of the day in this kind of active service always carried with them a passport to the favour of Mr. Spurgeon. Such candidates alone were eligible for admission to the Pastors' College. That institution was never intended for the training of merely clever young men in whom relatives detected literary gifts, and who thought themselves destined to occupy some commanding position in the world. From the first the College was intended for the encouragement and assistance of men who had already become preachers.

It was as a cottage preacher that Mr. Spurgeon was to commence his great career in the pulpit. When he first became connected with the congregation in St. Andrew's Street, Cambridge, the Lay Preachers' Association represented a numerous as well as an active band of workers—Mr. James Vinter, the directing genius, being familiarly known as "Bishop" Vinter. To the genial nature and Christian zeal of this warm-hearted veteran Mr. Spurgeon in after years bore cordial testimony. He appears to have preached with some acceptance himself; but he was at all times one who encouraged the younger volunteers whom he brought into the service.

On a certain Saturday morning in the year 1850, "Bishop" Vinter called at Mr. Leeding's house to ask young Mr. Spurgeon if he would walk over to Teversham on the following day with a young man who was unaccustomed to preach. To such a proposition there could be no possible objection. Though Mr. Spurgeon himself had given divers Sunday-school addresses, he had never yet attempted to deliver anything so pretentious as a genuine sermon; and had his friend the "Bishop" outspokenly asked him to preach, the young tutor would at once have shrunk from the proposal as an

E

impossibility. It would be a pleasure, however, to accompany another who was to conduct the service.

After tea, in the evening of the next day, Mr. Spurgeon set off along the Newmarket road in company with a young man somewhat older than himself—their destination, Teversham, being a village of less than sixty houses, three miles away, in the Chesterton district. The conversation was of a cheerful character until the younger of the two ventured to give expression to the good-natured wish that his companion would have a profitable time while preaching. The misunderstanding now came to an end. The good brother had no intention of giving a sermon; he had never attempted such a feat; he was not even a member of the Lay Preachers' Association; he had come for the simple object of accompanying the appointed preacher to Teversham! Thus it became plainly apparent that "Bishop" Vinter's young man not much used to preaching was no other than Mr. Spurgeon himself. Mr. Leeding's timidly sensitive assistant was somewhat appalled at the prospect of preaching, even in a cottage, but he bravely faced the inevitable, not heeding the well-meant advice offered by his companion, to the effect that the repetition of an old Sunday-school address would be sufficient for the occasion. That was not Mr. Spurgeon's way of doing things even at this early date, when he stood, as it were, on the threshold of his career, and the fact was of good omen for the future. He resolved at once that, if he must preach, he would do his best; and, although that involved the taking of a new subject, he did not shrink from the ordeal. Though still full of the dread which came of misgiving, he began to collect his thoughts, and presently the two came up to the cottage in which the service was to be held. The congregation were there waiting in expectancy, and no doubt many were surprised when the eager-looking boy took the place at the desk instead of his older companion. After singing, reading, and prayer the preacher, about to give his maiden sermon, announced his text—the familiar words of the great apostle—"Unto you, therefore, which believe, He is precious." How long his first sermon was

Mr. Spurgeon never remembered, but none of the fears which tormented him while on the Newmarket road were realised. A familiar talk on the work of Christ and on the Saviour's worth to His people was really not strange work to the young disciple even at sixteen years of age. His clear voice and plain language would not fail to captivate the people. They were not only edified by what they had heard, their hearts were warmed, although no one in the humble congregation could have suspected that one destined to become the greatest preacher of the century had broken silence in their midst.

At the same time, there were those present who were more or less surprised at the way in which the boy-preacher had acquitted himself. The principal representative of these was an ancient dame, who called out when the sermon was finished, " Bless your dear heart! how old are you ? " Not yet being accustomed to the unconventional ways he may have afterwards favoured, Mr. Spurgeon replied in a rebuking tone, " You must wait until the service is over before making any such inquiries," and he then proceeded to announce the concluding hymn. After the benediction had been pronounced and the people were dispersing, the affectionate dame who had asked the preacher's age still showed no disposition to go away without having her curiosity satisfied. How old was he ? Well, he was under sixty. " Yes, and under sixteen ! " the old lady insisted. She not only wanted to know the lad's age, he was asked to promise to come again, which he was not averse from doing if his superiors at headquarters saw proper to sanction it.

Having broken new ground, the lad may have felt some confidence in his ability to go forward; but he might not be quite so sure about what the gentlemen at Cambridge would say on the point. What, for example, would "Bishop" Vinter say when he heard that the boy of sixteen had been acting as a lay preacher before being formally recognised by the director and the brotherhood ? The youth whose awakening voice was so soon to be heard in London and the great towns of England was as yet a timid amateur, whose humble deference to his superiors was characteristic. The "gentlemen at Cambridge" were still personages of whom the stripling stood in wholesome awe; but to have a lowly opinion of himself, while he entertained becoming notions of the importance of his superiors, was a promising sign. But the days of childhood were over, and although only a boy as regarded his years, Charles Haddon Spurgeon would henceforth have to undertake the work of a man--work, moreover, which only one who stood as a giant among his fellows could accomplish.

CHAPTER IX.

MR. SPURGEON AS A LOCAL PREACHER.

Close of the first half of the Nineteenth Century—The Great Exhibition—Mr. Spurgeon and
Mr. Leeding—Papal Aggression : "Antichrist and her Brood"—The Prospects of the Boy-
Preacher—A great Acquisition to the Lay Preachers' Association—Perseverance in the
Work of Preaching—Reminiscences of surviving Friends at Cambridge—The "Miller of
Houghton" and Mr. Spurgeon—Mr. James A. Spurgeon's Recollections.

THE close of the first half of the nineteenth century was a period
of more than ordinary interest in our national history; and it
was particularly so in the life of the great man whose course we have
followed to the opening of his seventeenth year. Those who are
old enough to look back upon the closing days of the year 1850
will remember that the outlook in general seemed to promise many
things which were destined never to be realised. In Hyde Park
an army of workmen were engaged in erecting the vast, fairy-like
palace of glass for the Great Exhibition, which it was fondly hoped
would introduce or commemorate the opening of the new era of
universal brotherhood. Sanguine persons entertained the most extravagant hopes of the general civilising influence which this
unique industrial and artistic show would exercise over the nations
of the world. Patriots thought that the golden age was at length
beginning. The period of devastating and exhausting wars was
now to be followed by the era of universal peace, so far as civilised
nations were concerned. Social reformers also saw in the Great
Exhibition a promise of better things for the future than had ever
been known. Even Christian missionaries saw in the wonderful
festival to be celebrated in London that which would prepare the
way for the progress of the Gospel. If people of all colours and
of all nations were brought together, the lesson they would learn
would be that all would benefit by all working with heart and
soul for the common good of the world.

Young Mr. Spurgeon and his faithful friend and tutor would be interested in these things, and they would talk about them; they would each give an independent opinion on the outlook, and speculate in reference to the good times coming, which many were predicting with such excess of confidence. As ardent Evangelicals, we may confidently assume that neither of these friends was carried away with over-sanguine feelings in regard to the opening prospect. Art, science, and industries were good things in their way; the welfare of the nation demanded that they should be promoted by every legitimate means; but they could never be expected to bring about a reformation which the Gospel alone could effect. We have some conclusive evidence that at or about the time in question Mr. Spurgeon manifested lively interest in events which were happening, but matters pertaining to religion evidently affected him more than politics or even social reforms. Thus, the year 1850 was the period of what is known in history as the Papal Aggression. When the Pope mapped out this country into bishoprics and appointed his representatives to take possession of them, the public mind became violently agitated, and popular sentiment found expression in Parliament, an Act being passed attaching certain penalties to the assumption of episcopal titles without royal warrant. In addition to what was given in the daily and weekly journals, there was the abundant supply of books and essays usual at such a crisis. Mr. Spurgeon was, of course, an enthusiast on the Protestant side, as well became his notable ancestry. It was in hope of winning the prize offered by a member of the Morley family at Nottingham for an essay on Popery that he penned his still unprinted work on "Antichrist and her Brood." This work is consequently a memento of the Papal Aggression and of the extraordinary excitement it caused in the middle of this century.

But to turn to more personal matters, we can imagine that there would be a little more excitement in the quiet home of Mr. Leeding, the Cambridge schoolmaster, when his youthful pupil-assistant returned to tell how he had been caught by guile, and had been obliged to preach a sermon against his will. Mr. Leeding would probably offer his congratulations. He also saw in his young friend the future popular preacher, as was the case with Richard Knill; for the tutor was shrewd enough to see that Mr. Spurgeon possessed gifts far above the average, while his acquirements were likewise beyond his years. Mr. Leeding was well aware that he had in his house a youth who could with ease have passed an examination at the University, had not all the colleges been closed against him as a Nonconformist. The tutor seems to have been a man who knew when and how to encourage an aspirant. Apart from the ordinary routine of daily work, there was much in Sunday-school teaching, in the writing of essays, etc., and in the giving of addresses in cottages, to develop and draw out latent powers.

Even as a teacher in the Sunday-school, who occasionally spoke to the children collectively, the addresses of Mr. Spurgeon had attracted some notice; but when he had began to preach he found the work grow upon him. "Bishop" Vinter and the other "gentlemen at Cambridge" must soon have perceived that, in securing the services of such a volunteer, they had made an acquisition which would in no small measure redound to the credit of the Lay Preachers' Association.

It might truly have been said that he had been led by a way that he knew not from the days of early childhood till the days of youth, when his powers were developing, and the way in which he would have to go was opening before him and being made plain. The past had been an experience which would inspire gratitude; for step by step he had advanced in a providential manner till the service he loved best promised to become his life-work. Then the enthusiasm he already began to show as a preacher was in itself an augury of success. Now that he had made a beginning, he not only found peculiar pleasure in his work, he was an examplar, as regarded zeal and perseverance in face of any discouragement or difficulty, to all the other members of the Lay Preachers' Association.

Wind and rain, which often enough came in company to dis-
commode foot-passengers across those Cambridgeshire flats, never
sufficed to drive his good humour away or to cool his ardour as an
evangelist. Even the villagers he preached to must have caught
something of the fervour which characterised this youthful Apollos;
for if, on arriving at a village on a stormy evening, the weather
threatened to keep his congregation within doors, he would call at
their houses to remind them that a sermon was about to be given.
Protected with waterproof coverings, and having a stout stick and
a lantern, this representative of the Cambridge Lay Preachers' Association would appear in one village after another;* and long years
after, when the boy-evangelist had developed into the pastor of the
Metropolitan Tabernacle, there were many who fondly remembered
these early days of small things.

Some years ago, in 1875, my friend the late Edward Cressell,
who was then pastor of the Congregational Church at Houghton,
Huntingdonshire, gathered for me some things relative to this period
of Mr. Spurgeon's career, which show how appropriately he was
called the boy-preacher. One gentleman told Mr. Cressell that he
had been present at a service at Somersham, conducted by Mr.
Spurgeon, twenty-six years before, when, as a lad in his seventeenth
year, the preacher wore a jacket and broad, turned-down collar.
The text on that occasion was, " Fear not, thou worm Jacob" (Isaiah
xli. 14). The chapel was one at which an aged minister officiated,
and the contrast between the tones of the venerable pastor and the
voice of the youthful orator is said to have been striking. There
were people about who plainly saw that the itinerant, boy though
he might be, was introducing new methods into the pulpit, and that
he had about him the promise of a powerful, original preacher. One
old man, a Calvinistic Baptist, who was not easily suited by ordinary

---

* "There were thirteen villages comprised in the district which came within the operation
of the Lay Preachers' Association. In one or other of these the boy-preacher was ever to
be found in the exercise of his new functions; the scene of his ministrations being sometimes a cottage or a barn, or, as it occasionally happened, it was in the open air the service
was performed."—"Traits of Character," by a Contemporary, 1860; II. 89.

ministers, having heard Mr. Spurgeon, soon contrived to hear him again and again.

One lady remembered to have heard Mr. Spurgeon in the Congregational Chapel at Houghton when the youthful preacher was the guest of the late Mr. Potto Brown—an occasion of which the great preacher retained very vivid recollections till the end of his days. The discourse he then gave was calculated to make a deep impression; but it was not such as anybody would have expected to hear from a preacher who had the appearance of a boarding-school lad; it was rather such a sermon as a divine of ripe experience might have given. Under the circumstances it was hardly to be wondered at that the "Miller of Houghton," as Mr. Brown was called, should have looked upon his guest as a pretender content to appear in borrowed plumes. The schoolmaster of the village was also greatly impressed with the uncommon power of the preacher. It is to be regretted that many more things of this kind were not gathered while the opportunity offered. Those who re-member these earliest services of Mr. Spurgeon in the villages around Cambridge some forty years ago are now themselves rapidly pass-ing away.

Speaking as President of the Pastors' College Evangelical Associa-tion on May 5, 1892, Mr. James A. Spurgeon gave an interesting account of his brother's early days.

The family home at Colchester, he said, was as godly a household as could be met with in a Christian land, the mother, Mrs. John Spurgeon, being the starting-point of all goodness. In one "Life" the amusing statement was made that Charles Spurgeon was sent to Stambourne at the age of eighteen months because he was "one of seventeen"; but as he was the first-born, that was hardly con-sistent with fact. He returned to his parents' roof when between five and six years old, and after that went only during holiday time. The household at Stambourne was also of the most godly sort, old Mr. James Spurgeon being an earnest preacher of the Gospel, with a magnificent voice. He is still well remembered; and the President

of the Association made the confession that his first notion of a joke
was derived from his grandfather.   One day, when a number of friends
were congregated together, someone said, "Mr. Spurgeon, how much
do you weigh?"   "Well, that depends on where you take me,"
replied the veteran preacher; "in the balances I should be found
wanting, but in the pulpit they say I am heavy enough."   At first
that explanation was hardly apprehended by the child listener, but
presently he was found laughing in company with more elderly people.
Thus, while such an uncompromising Puritan, both as regards his
theological belief and his habits generally, the old pastor could indulge in fun after the manner of his more distinguished grandson
in after days.

Mr. James Spurgeon also remembers his grandmother, the wife of
the Stambourne pastor.   She was remarkable for her good-nature to
children.   On one occasion when he visited Stambourne as a delicate
boy, Master James was to have no pastry, a maternal order which
somewhat disconcerted the good grandmother, who appears not to
have been herself unless children could enjoy themselves.   The old
lady would not let it appear that she directly disobeyed orders from
Colchester; but she whispered to her grandson the information that in
a certain cupboard a plentiful supply of tarts could be found, and
left him to help himself.   He soon discovered that a mistake had
been made, and learned that a mother's restraint was better than a
grandmother's indulgence.

According to Mr. James Spurgeon, his brother got much good
at Stambourne, but he was nevertheless chiefly indebted to the good
influence of the home at Colchester.   It is thought to be a wonderful thing that Mr. John Spurgeon was able to give his sons so
good an education as he did.   They had the best that could be given
them, and the school-books, which are still treasured, are evidences
of the thoroughness with which the work was done.   While the
younger brother kept rabbits and so on, the elder kept to his
books.   He had a mind "as capacious as a barn," and he began to
be a tutor as far back as could be remembered.   He also made

such progress as few could have equalled, and perhaps none surpassed.

Mr. James Spurgeon further remembers when his brother began to preach; for the younger usually drove the elder in the family pony-chaise to the appointed preaching-stations. The Spurgeons' home at Colchester was a rendezvous for preachers, where rest and refreshments were to be had. While delivering some of his earliest discourses, Charles was regarded as a wonderful preacher by his brother; a rare kind of unction attended his sermons, and the impressions made on the country people were as deep as ever was the case afterwards in the town. He was a marvellous example of a preacher leaping at a bound full-grown into the pulpit; and though in after years there might be more depth and spirituality, there was not more genius. There was more of God's Word and its meaning at a later date; but his earliest recollections of his brother were, Mr. James Spurgeon said, the brightest and the best. He remembers his going to Waterbeach, the impression made, and the wonder there was in the Colchester household. He was a God-made and God-sent man—he was sent to the age; and his memory was one of unalloyed joy and happiness.

CHAPTER X.

SETTLEMENT AT WATERBEACH.

Waterbeach Past and Present—Winfold Farm and Denney Abbey—The Doctrines preached—
The Old Chapel—A Time of Preparation for Higher Service—The Young Preacher's
Method of Study—His Ingenuous Nature—An Old Deacon's Recollections—Mr. Spurgeon's
first Sermon in the Chapel—Characteristics of his subsequent Discourses—Reproving
an Old Minister—"The Sauciest Dog that ever barked in a Pulpit."

IN the natural order of things it was impossible that the light of
such a preacher as Mr. Spurgeon could for long remain hidden
under a bushel; or, in other words, that he would be allowed to
work as a mere wandering agent of the Cambridge Lay Preachers'
Association for any lengthened period. As Mr. Spurgeon was
accustomed occasionally to tell his own students, there is always
room for candidates at the top of the tree, however great the
competing crowd may be at the bottom. Not that Waterbeach was
in any sense to be regarded as representing a topmost position; but
it was the very place in which a promising man, with credit to
himself and benefit to others, might make an encouraging start.
The congregation was quite a model one for a thriving Cambridgeshire village; and if the people did not raise much more than the
proverbial forty pounds a year for their pastor's maintenance, it was
probably through their keeping to the old-time fashion rather than
through any want of thought or lack of kindness. In the middle
of the nineteenth century it was a very general thing in English
country places for notions of the most modest description to be
entertained concerning the temporal requirements of a preacher of
the Gospel. The fact was that a pastor's income did not consist
of money alone, the people making him many presents in kind.

Waterbeach itself is an ancient place, and when Mr. Spurgeon
first went there he found the church of the Establishment, dedicated
to St John, to be an interesting building, while there were alms-

houses and a charity-school dating from the seventeenth century.
Though sufficiently flat to call forth expressions of aversion from
Robert Hall, the surroundings are in some respects charming in
genial weather, and have besides some attractions for archæologists.
Mr. Samuel Lewis remarks in his "Topographical Dictionary of
England" :—"About the year 1160 a cell to the monastery of Ely
was established in a small island called Elmeneye, but was shortly
after removed to Denney, both in this parish. In the following
century it was occupied by the Knights Templars, who then possessed
the manor of Waterbeach. In 1293, an abbey for minoresses of
the order of St. Clare was formed . . . .,
which in 1338, the order of the Templars being then abolished,
was transferred to their house at Denney. At the Dissolution there
were twenty-five nuns, and the annual value of the lands was
estimated at £172. The abbey house and the demesnes have been
many years rented as a farm, and the refectory has been converted
into a barn."

These things are worthy of mention because the remains of
mediæval England referred to were objects of rare interest to Mr.
Spurgeon himself in his oft-repeated visits to the scene of his
early labours during the nearly forty years of his ministry in
London. Mr. Spurgeon has often visited Winfold Farm at Waterbeach; and visitors to that charming spot are able to inspect the
remains of Denney Abbey. For many years Winfold Farm had its
"Orphanage Acre," the entire proceeds of which, consisting of flour,
potatoes, etc., were regularly sent to the Stockwell Orphanage as a
gift to the inmates. That fact alone would have been almost
sufficient to attract Mr. Spurgeon to the spot; for persons who were
kind to his great family of orphan children were regarded as being
kind to himself.

It would appear that Mr. Spurgeon first became acquainted with
the village and people of Waterbeach in the course of his travels as
a member of the Cambridge Lay Preachers' Association. He never
had a settled home in the place; and there is reason for believing

that he found so many friends there that during the time of his ministry he had a fresh house of entertainment on the occasion of every visit. The people were a warm-hearted community, who at once showed the most cordial appreciation of the young preacher's services. The doctrines he preached were such as they themselves loved and built their hopes upon; and these doctrines were identical with the teaching which had been given forth from the Baptist pulpit in the village for long generations. In point of fact, Waterbeach was as much a little stronghold of Puritan ideas as Stambourne itself; and that is the reason why the grandson of the aged Essex pastor at once felt himself at home with the congregation. The strong silken cords which bound the boy-preacher and his people together in the bonds of love were never severed. In early days it was as the Garden of Eden; in after years it was a quiet resting-place to which the orator loved to retire for change and refreshment.

In the middle of this century, when Mr. Spurgeon first became associated with the Waterbeach friends, many fashions such as we now associate with a former age had hardly passed away. The railway through Cambridge had not been opened many years; and the many signs of agricultural depression which are now apparent even in the richest tracts of England, did not then sadden the hearts of observant tourists. The evidences of plenty and of quiet progress were seen on every hand. On alighting from the train, the vast dome of the sky—similar to that overhead at sea—would remind the visitor that he was on an extensive plain; but the land was rich and the people were prosperous. To a Londoner, escaping for a brief space from noise and smoke-charged atmosphere, the fine air and rustic charms were irresistible. The chapel itself, a quaint, square building, might almost have been mistaken for a rick of wheat or a haystack, if it had not been for the odd-looking little windows, one above another, which were supposed to let sufficient light into the sanctuary. Other things in the village so far corresponded with this commanding object that probably Waterbeach presented quite a similar outlook to that which greeted the early preachers of the Methodist revival when they gave forth the Gospel in this district a century before.

To come upon such a place and such a community as this, at so interesting a period in his career, must be regarded as a providential circumstance in the experience of Mr. Spurgeon. If the young evangelist had gone straight from the Cambridge Lay Preachers' Association to London, his success would no doubt have been immediate; but the abrupt suddenness of such a transition would have been excessively trying. In after days the achievement of a unique popularity came with sufficient suddenness; but after the experience gained at Waterbeach, and while itinerating among the surrounding towns and villages, the boy-preacher was in some measure prepared for the trial attending the more exhausting labours which awaited him in London. The service rendered at Waterbeach was a time of preparation and of strengthening which could not well have been dispensed with. The preacher already, as it were, saw in miniature the popularity which awaited him in London. The quaint little chapel of which he had become the pastor was nothing like large enough to accommodate the numbers who came to hear the Gospel preached in fulness and freeness; and in proportion as people in other places became acquainted with Mr. Spurgeon's pulpit characteristics, crowds were drawn together when he undertook to preach at anniversaries or on special occasions. The whole period was therefore one of trial, as well as of preparation for a great and unique life-work in the future; for if the metal of which the preacher was made had not given forth the ring of sterling quality at Waterbeach, it could never have borne the severe tests to which it was exposed in London shortly afterwards.

Although Mr. Spurgeon was only about seventeen years of age when he commenced work at Waterbeach, he was thoroughly well equipped. He had not only learned things which were actually of use to him, he had acquired habits of study such as would yield

him good profit. He already knew how to read to advantage, and
a good book once read became his own. His own explanation of
his method, to the effect that he tore things out of books by the
hair of their heads, sufficiently explained his ways to those who
understood him. In point of fact, his knowledge already took an
enlarged range for a preacher of his years. There was nothing
of the mere flash-in-the-pan kind of brilliance about his earliest
sermons. Even among his rustic audience there were those who could
readily enough distinguish between rhetorical fireworks and genuine
sterling eloquence. It was seen by such that a pulpit genius had
arisen; but, if that had been all, the impression made would not
have been the profound one that it was. What chiefly astonished
the members of mature age of the Waterbeach church was the
advanced Christian experience of the youth of seventeen who had
accepted the pastoral charge. If he had been speaking at the dictation of his grandfather, the pastor of Stambourne, this characteristic
could not have been more prominent. His experience was apparently
that of one who had progressed far in the Christian course. This
probably may have occasioned some inconvenience, because some were
led to doubt the preacher's honesty. To keen observers it must have
appeared that the boy in the pulpit could not be giving his own
sermon, but rather the words of some of the Puritan sages of extended
knowledge and experience whom he so often referred to or quoted.
On the other hand, there must have been that about the preacher
which many were able to accept as evidence of his honesty and
earnestness. He had an open face, which did not look like wishing
to deceive anybody; his manners all seemed to testify to his ingenuous
nature. Hence, while the common people heard him gladly, those
who were not of the common people regarded the young preacher
as being somewhat of a phenomenon which needed to be explained.
"Who is this Spurgeon?" was often enough asked in Cambridgeshire
before it came to be one of the stock questions of London quidnuncs.
And as in London in after years, the answer to the question was
generally coloured by the prejudgment, favourable or unfavourable,

H. OAKLEY

AFTER A PHOTOGRAPH BY MR A. HOWARD BENHAM, 4, ALBERT TERRACE, N.W.

MR. SPURGEON'S BIRTHPLACE AT KELVEDON: NOW THE WHEATSHEAF INN.

cf those who gave it. In taking a retrospect of Mr. Spurgeon's early days one writer says :—

"There is something to be said for the paradox that the common people are the real leaders of opinion. They have proved to be so at any rate regarding a great man who has recently left us, and who is now universally spoken about as the greatest of modern preachers. It was not in a sermon by a learned canon in St. Paul's Cathedral, nor in a leading article in *The Times* or *The Standard*, that the boy-preacher was welcomed to the Metropolis, when he came up to it in much fear and trembling from his little chapel at Waterbeach. The new note Spurgeon struck in pulpit oratory sounded harsh and discordant in the ears of cultured people. But it was sweet music to the rude peasantry and humble tradesfolk of Cambridge- shire, and in course of time people in high places came to be of the same opinion. The common people heard him gladly, and the lords and ladies of London, after much scoffing and jeering, were fain to hear him too. Suppose the good folk at Waterbeach had been as diffident about their own judgment in the choice of a preacher as many at the time would think they ought to have been; suppose they had gone to men of light and leading—say bishops of the National Church, or men distinguished in literature, or even experienced ministers of their own body, and asked them to listen to the boy-preacher and pronounce a verdict upon him, what a rating the good folk would have got for their imprudence in dreaming of choosing such a person! They would have heard much about his extreme youth, his inadequate learning, his lack of experience, perhaps of his presumption and the vulgarity of his style and bearing in the pulpit. And if the affairs of Waterbeach had been managed with such ideal perfection that the common herd would have given heed to the counsels of the wise, the career of the great preacher would have been nipped in the bud, and he might have lived and died as unnoted as thousands of others. Happily the Waterbeach people were left to choose for themselves. The seed of genius was allowed to germinate, the promising plant attracted ere long the attention of a slightly higher circle in London, and so step by step this nursling of the people fought his way until the successes of Exeter Hall, the Surrey Gardens Music Hall, and the Metropolitan Tabernacle became the talk of London, and rang over the world."*

More than once I have visited Waterbeach in order, if possible, to obtain information from those who might be able to give personal reminiscences of Mr. Spurgeon's early days. One elderly deacon of the church declared that at the outset the youthful pastor astonished everybody who heard him. The good man spoke of those memorable days with enthusiasm; but that which seemed chiefly to strike him was the fact that the boy-preacher appeared to possess the experience of an elderly or mature Christian. It was as though the preacher had been perfected at once for his work. Others, as we have said, observed the same thing, and to them it was a phenomenon which could not be explained in any ordinary way, because it was of an altogether exceptional character. One who was a friend of Mr. Spurgeon in his early days, gave it as his deliberate opinion that the pastor became fully equipped in youth for his work, and

* *The Daily Chronicle*, April 14, 1892.

that from youth to mature age he never improved like other people. In the nature of things this could not be, but such an opinion shows how the advanced Christian knowledge and experience of the preacher was viewed by friends in the days before he came of age.

Mr. Robert Coe, who was a deacon of the church at Waterbeach in Mr. Spurgeon's time, was quite a typical man of his class; and he maintained a lifelong friendship with the pastor of the Metropolitan Tabernacle. This worthy and his wife, as I found them, were more in love with old-time fashions than with new customs; and they could talk with delight of the great man who had been associated with their little chapel in the past. The good deacon had often been invited to London; but he did not really appear in the great congregation at Newington until he was partly drawn thither by the promise of a new flagon for the communion-table, which should supersede the common wine-bottle previously used. A quarter of a century after Mr. Coe had first seen the young lay preacher from Cambridge, pale with misgiving, enter the Waterbeach pulpit, he visited London for himself, was entertained at Nightingale Lane, and carried back the coveted flagon to his native village.

Mr. Coe's recollections of Mr. Spurgeon's early days in Waterbeach were not only entertaining, they may be regarded as a warning to those who are tempted to form an adverse conclusion respecting a preacher's capacity on account of his youth. When Deacon Coe for the first time met Mr. Spurgeon in the old chapel, he thought that his new friend was too pale and too young to do anything worth speaking of as a preacher; but when he discovered what kind of a voice he possessed, and what he was able to say, he could only sit and listen in admiration and astonishment. Then some of the early sermons had made impressions deep enough to be remembered. The preacher might be carried away with his descriptions of the glorious privileges of believers; but his denunciations of sin, his pictures of the doom of the impenitent, were terrific warnings. He in those days spoke as a decided Calvinist, but accustomed himself to milder phrases when he became a little older.

Many anecdotes respecting his early days are afloat in the neighbourhood of Waterbeach, but there is some difficulty in regard to their authenticity. One may hear that he suffered severely from sickness when he commenced to smoke; and then this is denied, and we are told that his first "churchwarden" never occasioned him the least inconvenience. Such trivialities, however, may well be left in obscurity.

When Mr. Spurgeon first joined the church there were many good and grave people who failed to understand him, and to whom, consequently, he appeared uncouth, forward, or even irreverent. I have heard that a certain person once expressed surprise to the leader of a prayer meeting on account of his having "called upon that rude young man to pray." I have also heard it stated that at the time of his joining the church, Mr. Spurgeon at the conclusion of a meeting went up to one of the leading members and very cordially asked him how he did. The person looked a picture of surprise, and, while quite polite, confessed that he had not the pleasure of knowing his interlocutor. "Not know me! Then you ought to do. I have sat down with you three Sabbaths at the Lord's Table, and you ought to know me!" was the reply. It was now discovered that he was young Mr. Spurgeon. "Then perhaps you will go home with me to tea," was the next remark. "That's just what I'm going to do," was the reply.

Those were also days of adventure, many of which were of sufficient interest to oblige the preacher once to say that there had been almost enough in any one day of his life to make up the materials for a three-volume novel. The particulars of one diverting incident I was the first to give to the world some years ago, having received the facts from Mr. Spurgeon himself as he sat in his study at Clapham while in too weak a condition to work. At such a time, if free from pain, he always seemed to relish entertaining his friends with recollections of those good old times when, in the strength and fresh-ness of youth, he could enjoy life to the full, the heavy burden of the London pastorate not yet having cast its shadow across his path.

In the year 1852 he had already become uncommonly popular for a preacher who was a mere youth, and whose ministerial position was only that of a very small village pastorate, the stipend of which was less than a pound a week. The extraordinary fame of the young pastor occasioned his being invited to preach at anniversaries and on special occasions by friends at a distance, who in some instances may never have seen his face. One of these was an elderly man, whose chapel was not very far away, and who was in himself as faultlessly respectable as he was dry and orthodox. The day of the services would be an important one, because good collections would be expected. When the time at length came round, and Mr. Spurgeon actually appeared on the scenes, he cordially greeted his octogenarian brother; but until he heard his boy-visitor confess that he had come to preach the anniversary sermons, the old man hardly dared to believe his eyes. When polite inquiries respecting his health were made, the veteran abruptly replied, " I am none the better for seeing you ! " Then he paced the room in great concern of mind respecting the success or failure of his anniversary; and in the course of the soliloquy in which he indulged he muttered something about boys who went up and down the country preaching before their mother's milk was well out of their mouths. A great concourse of people had assembled for the anniversary service; but the old pastor was at first half-ashamed to take a place in the chapel where he could be seen by the congregation.

Mr. Spurgeon was not one to be greatly disconcerted by the treatment he had received; but, on the other hand, he would not miss the opportunity of administering a becoming reproof. He already observed the custom, which he kept up to the last, of making explanatory remarks on the passage of Scripture read before the sermon. Now was Mr. Spurgeon's opportunity; and he read what Solomon had said about the honour attending a hoary head, this being accompanied by his own characteristic commentary. "A hoary head is a crown of glory." Was it really always so? The wise man was an authority not to be challenged; but, Solomon or no Solomon, it did not seem to be always so, for there was a tongue in one hoary head which had not been civil to the boy who had come to preach. " If it be found in the way of righteousness." That, of course, altered the case, and Solomon was right, after all; for unless an old man was found in the right path he might as well have red hair as white. The old minister, who had now emerged from his hiding-place, at once saw the reasonableness of this reproof. He had evidently acted wrongly, and it would look handsome to make some honourable amends. As the boy-preacher was descending from the pulpit, therefore, the octogenarian slapped him on the back, at the same time remarking, " You are the sauciest dog that ever barked in a pulpit ! " It may be that he thus gave rise to the itinerant's being called " the saucy young rascal," as he sometimes was about this time.

CHAPTER XI.

PROGRESS AT WATERBEACH.

Increasing Popularity—Stepney College in 1852—A Singular Misadventure—A Voice on Midsummer Common—Resolution not to go to College—Reminiscences—William Jay and John Angell James—Calvinist or Arminian?—The Poor Pastor and his Clothes—The Prayers of Children—Professor Everett's Recollections—Mr. Edward Ingle's Reminiscences of Mr. Spurgeon as a Tutor—"The Old Pope"—A Missionary Meeting in the School—Predictions of future Greatness—A Letter of 1853.

THOUGH not a few may have been tempted to despise his youth, as had been the case with that afterwards sincere friend Deacon Robert Coe, Mr. Spurgeon met with many outsiders who accorded him hearty encouragement while he was at Waterbeach. Among those who visited the village and preached in the meeting-house in those early days was the late Cornelius Elven, a native of Bury St. Edmund's, who devoted fifty years of his life to pastoral labour in that town. Mr. Elven was a giant in stature, and it is said that he was charged the fare of two persons when travelling by coach. When this worthy visited Waterbeach, he appears to have noticed that the boy-preacher's abilities were above the common order, and while encouraging him in his work he ventured to give some common-sense, fatherly advice, which was thankfully accepted and acted upon. Some years afterwards, when Mr. Elven had grown old enough to need a co-pastor, Mr. Spurgeon recommended him one of the best preachers that had been trained in the Pastors' College—Mr. William Cuff, who has since had erected for him the Shoreditch Tabernacle, in which he now ministers. Mr. Elven was also one who watched the progress of Mr. Spurgeon during the early days in London, and preached for his young friend at New Park Street Chapel.

In the meantime, while the pastor of the little old-fashioned chapel at Waterbeach was making rapid progress, and achieving quite an uncommon kind of popularity, the most interested observers of what was happening were naturally Mr. and Mrs. John Spurgeon of Colchester and the aged pastor of Stambourne. Whatever misgivings may have been harboured in relation to the subject in earlier days, it was now plainly seen that Charles had found his life-work. The father, more especially, became particularly anxious that his son should be as well equipped as possible for the service which lay before him. Charles had enjoyed the advantages of a good school education; it was now indispensable that he should add to this a theological training such as could only be obtained at a college established for the purpose. Labour at Waterbeach would have to be suspended for a time; the young pastor must go to college.

At that time the Baptist College at Stepney had existed for between forty and fifty years; but though the surroundings at the time of starting in 1810 may have been of a semi-rural kind, they had now all the characteristics of a murky, East-end London parish. The Principal of the institution was Dr. Joseph Angus, and that veteran tutor still holds the same office at Regent's Park College, to which the Stepney students were removed in 1856. As his son had become a Baptist, Mr. John Spurgeon regarded Stepney College as being the place to supply what was wanted in the way of a more complete theological education.

Mr. John Spurgeon reasoned with his son long and earnestly on the subject, the result being that it was arranged for a meeting to take place between Dr. Angus, the tutor of Stepney, and the young Waterbeach preacher, who might have been called the itinerant evangelist of Cambridgeshire. The place of meeting was to be at the house of a well-known publisher in the University town, and both the Doctor and the proposed student duly kept their appointment; but although both were in the house together, it seemed to be destined that they were not to meet. Mr. Macmillan's servant-maid was apparently not the shrewdest of her sex; at all events, she quite failed to understand that the staid professor and the round-faced lad, who arrived at the house nearly at the same time, had any business with one another. She showed the Doctor into one parlour and closed the door; in his turn, she showed young Mr. Spurgeon into a second parlour and closed the door; and then, probably forgetting all about such a trivial circumstance, she left both of the morning callers to their peaceful cogitations. Having to keep an appointment in London, Dr. Angus had at last to hasten away to the railway station; and when Mr. Spurgeon felt that he could hold out no longer, he rang the bell, to learn when the servant came that the Doctor had gone away.

This was not at first regarded as a circumstance which in anywise indicated that the idea of going to college would have to be abandoned. An application for admission to the College could be made in writing, and, as that plan promised to answer the purpose equally well, Mr. Spurgeon resolved that he would despatch a letter to the committee asking that his desire might be favoured. Man proposes and God disposes, however. Persons of strong Puritanic sympathies, such as the Waterbeach pastor and his grandfather entertained, have always strongly protested against what were to them merely man-made ministers. If a man was really called of God to preach the Gospel, let him go forth in the strength of the Lord, and let all bid him God-speed. If, on the other hand, a man thought he could take his destiny into his own hands, and transform himself into a minister of the Word, let him check presumption by heeding well the inspired warning, "What hast thou to do to declare My statutes, or that thou shouldst take My covenant in thy mouth?"

Probably no one was ever further removed from superstition than Mr. Spurgeon; but such things as we call premonitions or presentiments may have had some meaning for him, just as they have for many others who would shrink from attempting to make everything plain to objectors. There were stranger things in his world than are dreamt of in the world's philosophy.

In the after-part of the day on which he missed seeing the Stepney professor by a seeming accident, Mr. Spurgeon had a strange experience, which would appear to have exercised an influence over the whole of his after-life. His devotion to the cause of the Lay Preachers'

Association was still as ardent as ever, and an engagement had to be kept at a village on that very evening. Lying about a mile to the north-east of Cambridge, Chesterton includes the site of the ancient castle; but it is now the suburb containing the pleasant homes of well-to-do people who are engaged in business in the University town. While crossing Midsummer Common, near to this place, and thinking about various things, certain words of Holy Writ occurred to the mind of the young preacher with such force that it seemed they were actually spoken through the opening clouds, direct from heaven itself—"SEEKEST THOU GREAT THINGS FOR THYSELF? SEEK THEM NOT!"

Whatever may have been the way in which these words were suggested to the mind of the young pastor in a meditative mood, as he crossed Midsummer Common to keep his village preaching engagement, a turning-point in his life had arrived. Where was he? what were his aims? what were the things that his heart was really seeking after? He seemed, as it were, to be brought to a sudden standstill in his life-course, and some serious self-examination had become necessary. The searching questions which a young Christian would ask himself at such a time seem to be sufficiently obvious. Had he given himself unreservedly to his Lord's service, and did the entire unselfishness of his aims testify to his sincerity? If God had called him to the work of preaching the Gospel, and had given him a sphere of labour, was he justified in leaving it for the purpose of spending several years in the seclusion of a London college? Were the claims which the poor but warm-hearted people of Waterbeach had upon him to be altogether ignored? If the Lord appointed His workmen, would He not fully equip them for their service?

Some such questions would suggest themselves to the preacher's mind, and, while seeking an answer to them, his resolution concerning a theological education was taken once and for all. He was plainly called to do the work he was engaged in, and he would not leave it. The idea of seeking any additional benefit from a college training would therefore have to be abandoned. Many had sought great things for themselves in the direction of the College. A large number had undoubtedly derived great benefit from the prescribed studies; but for himself, he must seek them not.

Mr. and Mrs. John Spurgeon did not see things in this light; for, from the standpoint of their wider worldly experience, the opportunity of securing a thorough theological training was a providential opening to be entered without hesitation. The father reasoned long and earnestly with his son on this matter; but it was impossible to shake the young preacher's resolution, which he had arrived at under such singular circumstances. He would not actually be disobedient to so good a parent; if the order, "You are to go," was authoritatively given, he would yield as a duty, but he would never go to college of his own free choice. The pastor of Tollesbury thought that his son was making a mistake; but he judged that, as a father, it was his duty to give way. He may have suspected that, after all, things were not quite what they appeared to be to him, and that everything would be made plain in the course of the good providence of God. In any case, persuasive words fell flat on the ear of the young Waterbeach pastor, while the most forcible arguments were pointless; for all that the father could bring forward in favour of securing a college training was answered by the words which had been so mysteriously suggested on Midsummer Common—"*Seekest thou great things for thyself? Seek them not.*" This, then, is how it happened that Mr. Spurgeon never went to college.

The youthful pastor returned to his little sphere at Waterbeach in a happy and contented state of mind. He harboured no doubt concerning the Divine guidance; and to have the pathway of life made plain before him was really to have a stumbling-block removed out of the way. The outlook of a village pastorate never appeared more encouraging to a pastor. The old, picturesque, thatched chapel still continued to be crowded; conversions were so numerous that Waterbeach itself began to show visible signs of improvement; while the pastor's services were still sought for special and anniversary celebrations. Every step he now took confirmed him in the assurance that he had done right in remaining where he was.

At times Mr. Spurgeon would indulge his friends with anecdotes and reminiscences of those early days, and, as may be seen in the religious papers of that date, one of these occasions occurred during the first week of December, 1880. The fact was then referred to that at Waterbeach baptisms took place in the open air and in the neighbouring river, as had been the case at Isleham, where Mr. Spurgeon was immersed, as already described. This primitive mode of administering the ordinance had some drawbacks, however; and it might become especially trying on a wet day. On one memorable occasion, when that worthy giant, Cornelius Elven, had volunteered his services, it rained heavily; and the Bury St. Edmund's pastor grew more than a little nervous at the prospect of getting wet through, for the weighty reason that he had no change of clothes, and, if it came to borrowing, there were none within a radius of forty miles which would be anything like large enough.

As a young beginner whose preaching had been found to have attractions for large numbers of all ages and of all conditions in life, Mr. Spurgeon himself felt great interest in the ministrations of the leading divines of their day. He took care to hear a sermon from the venerable William Jay, of Bath, when he visited Cambridge, and ever afterwards harboured grateful memories concerning him. Even the text was never forgotten—"Ever let your conversation be as becometh the Gospel of Christ." He also thought it worth while to travel to Birmingham to hear John Angell James, who gave a much appreciated discourse from the words, "Ye are complete in Him." Mr. James was not quite so ardent a Calvinist as his younger friend, and did not suppose that his preaching would always prove so acceptable. He was, however, a man in whom dignity and simplicity were combined.

The preaching adventures of Mr. Spurgeon's early days were many and varied. Thus, at one well-known town in Hertfordshire, he was viewed as an intruder according to the prejudice of different observers.

There were several chapels in the place; but he was too much of a Calvinist for one, and too much of an Arminian for another. However, at last he was admitted to the pulpit of a third. The pastor of the congregation received a stipend about equal to the wages of a farm labourer, so that a visitor to his cottage might well feel some misgivings about accepting his hospitality. "I noticed," Mr. Spurgeon afterwards said, "that my host wore a very shiny alpaca coat; and at the close of the sermon I said to the congregation, 'Now I have preached my best to you. Freely you have received, freely give. The minister of this place looks as if he wants a new suit of clothes: I will give half a sovereign, my friend down below will do the same, and plates will be held at the doors for your contributions.' The effort was successful. After the service, the poor pastor said that his Master had always sent him his living, but that he was beginning to wonder where the next suit of clothes would come from."

Mr. Spurgeon has also told of another experience which he met with in that same town, and on the same day. He offended certain strait-laced Calvinists by telling a company of children that God would hear their prayers even before they were converted. In the estimation of some Christian professors of "high" sentiments, this savoured of the most dangerous Arminianism, and as these gathered together in grave consultation the question triumphantly asked was, whether the prayers of the wicked were not an abomination to the Lord? "What are you battling with this young man about?" asked an elderly dame, whose red cloak served to make her conspicuous. "What do you know about the Scriptures?" she added, with some vehemence. "You say God does not hear the prayers of un- converted people; why, have you never read that He heareth the young ravens when they cry?—and there is no grace in them. If God hears the cry of the ravens, don't you think He will hear the cry of a man made in His own image?" That seemed to settle the point, and it was found more convenient to walk away than to con- tinue the argument.

In such secluded country places as the young pastor from

Waterbeach was called upon to visit from time to time, many eccentric samples of humanity would be discovered—lineal descendants, as it might have been imagined, of the quaint Puritan heroes whose wit left its impression on their age. Think, for example, of a devoted veteran who, after serving the neighbouring farmers as a common shepherd for forty years, took to the more responsible service of tending a flock belonging to the fold of Christ. The force of habit being what it is, such a man would hardly be able to be very greatly different from what he had been during the main part of his life, so that it was quite a natural confession for him to make when he declared that his second flock was far more sheepish than the first.

Professor J. D. Everett has given some interesting facts concerning this period :—" In or about 1852," he says, " I was occupying a post in a high-class school (Mr. Thorowgood's, at Totteridge, near London), and there being a vacancy for another assistant, I wrote, with Mr. Thorowgood's approval, to my old friend Spurgeon, proposing that he should come and fill it. He asked for a few days to decide definitely, and then wrote declining, chiefly on the ground that he was unwilling to renounce the evangelistic work which he combined with the position he then held. He stated then or in a subsequent letter that he had preached more than three hundred times in the previous twelve months, and that the chapel at Waterbeach was not only full, but crowded with outside listeners at the open windows."

These preaching engagements in towns and villages of the surrounding country appear to have yielded the young itinerant great satisfaction ; and they were so far from adding to his burden that they appear rather to have relieved the week-day teaching in Mr. Leeding's school at Cambridge. Those were happy and profitable days, and some of the pupils who were then pursuing their education still survive, and are able to give sunny memories of the time they spent at school under such masters.

Thus, referring to Mr. Spurgeon as he was in the year 1852, my friend Mr. Edward Ingle, now of Willingham, but who was then a pupil in the Cambridge academy, supplies me with some personal reminiscences. In a private letter dated March 23, 1892, Mr. Ingle remarks: "I count myself honoured in the providence of God to have come under his tuition in my schooldays. Newspaper references to his position in Mr. Charles Leeding's school in Cambridgeshire refreshed pleasant memories of study and friendship. As boys, we were, I believe, drawn to love him by a spell similar to what his students of later years have felt."

As he looks back through the vista of forty years, Mr. Ingle can recall to mind that the young tutor—who was himself only of schoolboy age—already showed great force of character, which could not fail to exercise a powerful influence on those lads who came into contact with him. At the same time, Spurgeon had in his character all those attractive traits which come of the freshness of youth and of a sanguine temperament. In the year 1852 he was eighteen years of age, and he resided in the house with Mr. Leeding and his house-keeper, the school and its surroundings being kept quite apart from the house.

On a certain afternoon young Ingle arrived exceptionally early, no doubt hoping to have some play before lessons. Just at that moment Mr. Spurgeon happened to be coming out of the house, and taking hold of his scholar in his kind, familiar way, the young tutor said, "Come along, Ingle, I'll show you what I am writing against the old Pope." The two then entered the school, when from his desk the amateur author brought forth that manuscript entitled "Antichrist and her Brood"[*] which George Smith, the pastor of Poplar, had commended, although, as adjudicator, he had not awarded its writer Mr. Arthur Morley's prize. Mr. Spurgeon

---

[*] I suppose the following refers to this essay, but as it will be seen, it is supposed by Mr. Hodder to have been written some years before the competition actually took place. The prize was not offered by Mr. Samuel Morley, but by his cousin Arthur.

"Both Samuel Morley and Lord Shaftesbury were friends and admirers of Mr. Spurgeon, and both watched his widening sphere of influence with eagerness. Mr. Spurgeon had from his childhood known the merchant philanthropist, and loved him all through his life. When Mr. Spurgeon was a boy of ten, he competed for a prize to be given by Mr. Morley for the best essay 'On Popery.' He was not successful in the competition, but his essay was so good that Mr. Morley awarded him an extra prize of £3—a little fortune in the estimation of the boy."—"Life of Samuel Morley," by Edwin Hodder, p. 235.

"turned over the pages with a relish," says his quondam scholar, and then remarked, with an emphasis worthy of his ancestors who had suffered under the agents of Philip II. in the Netherlands, " How I should like to pull the old Pope from his throne." At that time, as Mr. Ingle can vividly remember, nothing more readily awakened the enthusiasm of his young tutor than a reminder of the unscriptural pretensions and teaching of the Papacy.

To the boys whom he taught, Mr. Spurgeon's mind seemed to be occupied with great subjects, or, at all events, with things which lay beyond the ken of his class. The young tutor was also known to be very warm-hearted; and while there was something in his eye, as well as in the compass of his voice, which already attracted the attention of those who lived or studied with him, Mr. Ingle assures me that, "to a casual observer, his *tout-ensemble* was very extra-ordinary." So long as he was neat and comfortable, the prevailing fashion in dress never troubled young Spurgeon ; whether people were reminded of a former generation or of the present by the cut of his coat or the shape of his stock, was a matter of no concern. The boys thought that their teacher was without doubt an odd-looking young man to have charge of a class of lads ; but, nevertheless, all they saw in him only served to confirm their confidence and com-mand their admiration. He might be singular in some respects, but when he came to be engaged in the serious business of teach-ing, all things save the subject in hand were at once forgotten. Only let this somewhat odd-looking young tutor read a stirring passage from English history, or give a page from Milton's master-piece, or explain in a way that boys could comprehend something relating to astronomy, physical geography, or some other science, and the pupils at once had their attention arrested, the too-frequently dull routine of school-hour lessons became at once invested with a charm which was irresistible. All was the more effective because the teacher never gave himself up to the assumption of airs which would not have been becoming in one of his years. Just as in after-years, when he ranked as the first preacher of his age, Mr.

Spurgeon would say in his jovial manner, "You know, I'm not the reverend gentleman," so at Cambridge he was a youth among boys. Hence Mr. Ingle is able to add, "We used to have plenty of fun; Spurgeon would laugh as heartily as anyone I ever saw."

On one occasion one of the scholars became perplexed over a matter of spelling, although the word consisted of only four letters. "Please, sir, do you spell York, Y O R K or Y E A O R K"? asked the lad, the query at once provoking a round of laughter. Lending strong emphasis to the Y E A, Mr. Spurgeon gave it as his decided opinion that the word should begin as the scholar suggested—as though a new discovery had been made. He then wrote down YEAORK, and, handing the paper to the inquirer to show him how natural it looked, the youngster was obliged to join in the merriment.

On another day there was a lesson in botany, when mention was made of "cruciform plants." Mr. Spurgeon asked, "What is a cruciform plant; what shape is it ?" Then when the boys showed a dull apprehension by not answering, the tutor presently gave the command, "Now then, out you go into the playground or garden, and fetch me in the flower of a cruciform plant." Of course, the young botanists found the adjournment into the open air an agreeable change. One of them was successful in finding on a certain vegetable a flower in the form of a cross. Then followed a reminder of the scientific or Latin name of the plant; but the lesson did not conclude without some passing earnest references to the cross of Christ.

As my friend at Willingham is able to testify, the boys who made up Mr. Spurgeon's class needed no urging to be attentive when the time for going through a Scripture lesson came round. Though the Bible is often regarded as a dry book by boys, the Scripture lessons were given with a freshness which made them of extraordinary interest. "There was no long, sombre face with Spurgeon, no starchiness," remarks his former pupil; "he was very homely and happy in these lessons." While giving them, the young teacher would not only become animated, but seemed to speak about the old-time characters who stood out on the page of inspiration as though they were his own personal acquaintances. One occasion is still memorable—that on which the lesson embraced the passage wherein the prophet Elijah challenges the people to determine by fire whether the Lord of Hosts or Baal was the true God. The great scene on Mount Carmel was depicted before the boys with wonderful vividness. To everyone present it almost seemed that the youth had actually been an eye-witness of the spectacle.

On another occasion, when the class had to read Isaiah lv., which Mr. Spurgeon told them was one of the gems of the Bible, he asked them if they would not commit that passage to memory, and all did so. It was evident to the boys that their tutor read with rarest delight what he would have called the Gospel according to the Evangelical Prophet, although it was hardly to be supposed that the pupils would be able fully to understand their leader's fervour. There was another passage in the Psalms which he seemed to love specially to dwell upon at this time, for in it he saw a wonderful revelation of the Divine character as viewed from the human standpoint: " As far as the east is from the west, so far hath He removed our transgressions from us."*

There were other things than lessons, however, which had to receive attention; for we have to remember that, in addition to the regular work at Waterbeach, the young tutor was also still a member of the Cambridge Lay Preachers' Association. Thus, on a certain dark and damp winter afternoon, just before breaking-up time, the door of the room is opened, and the figure who enters,

---

* This passage appears to have stirred the depths of Mr. Spurgeon's heart whenever he thought of it in after years, *e.g.* :—

" The first time I heard him he preached from the passage ' Who forgiveth all thine iniquities.' The sermon was remarkable for directness, simplicity, and earnestness. When he quoted the passage ' As far as the east is from the west, so far hath He removed our transgressions from us,' he said, ' How glorious is this statement! If it had been as far as the south is from the north, it would have been an immense distance; but no, it is as far as the east is from the west, an immeasurable distance.' From the first sentence to the last he held the attention, and left an impression not easily effaced. I think I never met a man who seemed more in this world and less of it. He feels that his work is among men, and while his associations here are with the earth, yet his conversation, his citizenship, is in heaven."—J. B. GOUGH, "Sunlight and Shadow," p. 296.

G

laughing merrily at what he supposes may be his own somewhat odd appearance, is no other than young Mr. Spurgeon in the costume of an itinerant preacher of the Fens. Completely enveloped in an oilskin suit, the junior tutor had looked in just to show Mr. Leeding and the lads at their desks what he appeared like when fully equipped for the road. "Here I am, going off to fight the battles of the Lord," he remarked; and away he went to keep a preaching engagement in a village not far away.

While he aimed at exercising the best possible moral and religious influence over the boys he had in charge, Mr. Spurgeon was careful at the same time to develop their talents; and he appears to have been particularly anxious to bring out or encourage those who showed any faculty for public speaking. He was at all times ready to make allowances for natural shortcomings, and overflowed with sympathy; but it was not always easy for the scholars to keep pace with such a teacher.

For example, he once remarked, "We will have a little meeting amongst ourselves some evening;" and, because the boys knew well enough that he meant what he said, they somewhat dreaded the novel kind of entertainment in prospect. Though it was such a miniature affair, all the arrangements were to be similar to those of a public gathering in the town. Mr. Spurgeon and several of the lads were to constitute the audience; the subject was to be the foreign missionary cause; a duly qualified boy would be voted into the chair, and the speakers would be expected to say something to the purpose. Mr. Edward Ingle vividly remembers this diverting incident of his schooldays.

In due time the evening came round, and preparations worthy of the occasion had been made in the schoolroom: a platform, with a table and chairs, had been erected; there was a proper seat for the president of the coming meeting, there were forms for the auditors. The chairman who happened to be elected was rather diminutive for his years; but, being a clever little fellow, it was supposed that he might do what was required of him with credit to himself and profit to others. It turned out, however, that both the chairman and those who were to support him showed some symptoms of nervousness just at the time when they should have remained calm and self-possessed. The chairman showed unmistakable weakness about the knees; and when he rose it was not to make a few appropriate remarks on the subject of foreign missions, but earnestly to ask that he might be allowed to resign his office. He had no sooner spoken than circumstances seemed to favour his petition, though in a manner as unwelcome as it was unexpected. In a moment the entire little platform collapsed, the chairman and the table, the appointed speakers and the seats, suddenly showing a striking transformation scene, of which confusion and alarm were the main characteristics. Mr. Spurgeon himself appeared to be terror-stricken, until the welcome discovery was made that no one was much hurt, and that little damage was done.

When Mr. Spurgeon had completed the rescue of his young friends there was a hearty, all-round laugh; and then the serious business of rebuilding the structure in a more enduring way was undertaken. The platform having been rebuilt, a stronger-kneed chairman was elected, and the meeting proceeded in a way which yielded satisfaction to all who took part in it. Instead of the boys being disheartened, as might have been the case, they were encouraged to persevere and to attempt to do better another time. The young tutor well knew the value of an encouraging word, accompanied by a kind pat on the shoulder, at such a time; and it was because the boys became anxious to please one who so greatly appreciated all that they did for him that they were willing to go on to do better.

As Mr. Spurgeon went on his course in this manner, he occasionally came into contact with those who thought that they saw in him that which would develope into something greater. One friend and then another would give opinions as regarded the future which were not always easy to understand at the time, but which were destined to be more than realised. Men of learning, and of experience in the Church and the world, sometimes had to do with him, and they saw that he possessed gifts of no common order. It was customary at times to hear such a remark as, " That Spurgeon will be a wonderful man some day; there's something marvellous about him." Those who lived in the same house with him were sharers of this conviction, and were, if possible, even more convinced that a distinguished future awaited him. This was the case with Mr. Leeding and the housekeeper, both of whom were profoundly impressed with their young friend's character and abilities, as also were many who came to the house. One visitor in particular declared he had an irresistible conviction that the young tutor and itinerant preacher had a great future before him, and that mighty works would be done by him for God. And there was one who at this early date was discerning enough to make the striking prophecy—" That young man will yet shake England like a second Luther ! "

Having been associated in his youth with Mr. Spurgeon, Mr. Edward Ingle naturally watched the progress of his old tutor in London with no common interest; to meet with him, to hear a sermon from him, came to be regarded as one of the greatest of gratifications. On one memorable occasion in 1874 it was my own privilege to accompany Mr. Spurgeon to Willingham, when he preached in the open air to a great crowd on behalf of the building fund of the new chapel, which his brother-in-law, the late Mr. Jackson, had erected. Mr. Ingle, who has supplied the above facts relative to schooldays in Cambridge, vividly remembers this festival, of which some account will appear in the proper place.

During this time, while the young pastor was living at Cambridge, and towards the end of 1853, or about the time that he first came to London, his home was at 9, Union Road, and we find him also at 60, Upper Park Street. Though his ministerial income was then less than a pound a week, his people at Waterbeach made him many presents, while he realised something from teaching the boys who now remember him so fondly. It was not only a time of happiness and of progress, it was also a period of preparation for more arduous service.

A religious newspaper has reproduced the following advertisement, which throws some light on Mr. Spurgeon's movements at this period :—

"No. 60, Upper Park Street, Cambridge.

"Mr. C. H. Spurgeon begs to inform his numerous friends that, after Christmas, he intends taking six or seven young gentlemen as day pupils. He will endeavour to the utmost to impart a good commercial education. The ordinary routine will include arithmetic, algebra, geometry, and mensuration; grammar and composition; ancient and modern history; geography, natural history, astronomy, Scripture, and drawing. Latin and the elements of Greek and French if required. Terms £5 per annum."

While conducting one of the prayer-meetings which were held during the latter half of 1891 to plead for Mr. Spurgeon's recovery, Mr. Stott, who was then assistant pastor at the Metropolitan Tabernacle, read a letter in which the young pastor of Waterbeach referred to his work and prospects in the ingenuous and warm-hearted way which was characteristic of him even in those early years. It was as follows :—

"MY DEAR UNCLE,

"I have two or three reasons for writing to you just at this time. We are going to have a baptising on October 19, and I should be so glad to see my uncle following his Master in the water. I am almost afraid to mention the subject lest anyone should charge me with giving it undue prominence; if they will do so, they must. I can bear it for my Master's sake. . . . Now, with regard to coming for a week to preach at Stambourne and neighbouring villages, I am yours to serve to the utmost. Not on the Sabbath, but all the week. I have a good sphere of labour here, but I want to do more, if possible. It is a great field, and the labourers must work with all their might. I often wish I were in China, Hindostan, or Africa, so that I might preach, preach, preach all day long. It would be sweet to die preaching. But I want more of the Holy Spirit; I do not feel enough—no, not half enough—of His divine energy. . . . I shall not mind preaching two evenings in Stambourne if you cannot get other convenient places; and I should love to have some good thoroughly hot prayer-meetings after the service. . . . I wish to live in unity with every believer, whether Calvinist, Arminian, Churchman, Independent, or Wesleyan; and, though I firmly believe they are tottering, I do not like them well enough to prop them up by my wrangling at them. . . . I am, yours most truly,

"C. SPURGEON.

"9, Union Road, Cambridge,
    "*September* 27, 1853."

CHAPTER XII.

THE "MILLER OF HOUGHTON."

Mr. Spurgeon and the "Miller of Houghton"—Mr. Potto Brown's Characteristics—The Boy-Preacher visits Houghton—"Felicitous Misery"—"The Prophet's Chamber"—A Veteran Arminian and a Young Calvinist—"A Battle Royal"—A Friendly Parting—Mr. R. W. Dixon on Potto Brown's Peculiarities.

A MAN who was a remarkable character in his day now demands some passing reference. The late Mr. Potto Brown, the eccentric "Miller of Houghton," as he is sometimes called, the head of a family which owned large steam flour mills on the Ouse, both at Huntingdon and St. Ives, has to be included among the friends of Mr. Spurgeon's youth while he was pastor at Waterbeach, or during the time of his connection with the Cambridge Lay Preachers' Association. Mr. Potto Brown himself lived at Houghton, a pleasant village which lies about midway between St. Ives and Huntingdon, his house being of the old-fashioned comfortable sort in which a lover of nature and of country life would delight, the gardens being a special feature which had their attractions for all visitors. In addition to the charms of Houghton itself, which in Mr. Brown's time was justly regarded as a model village, the outlying country was of considerable topographical or historical interest. Along that river bank, regarding its characteristics, as well as "Ouse's silent tide," with a poet's eye, Cowper often walked; and in and all around St. Ives memories of Oliver Cromwell seem to be awakened at every step. What young Spurgeon may have thought of such things need not be conjectured; but he would no doubt take notice of them when, as the guest of Potto Brown, he had to occupy the pulpit at Houghton Chapel during one of the most memorable Sabbaths of his early days. This was afterwards referred to by the pastor of the Metropolitan Tabernacle as a time of "felicitous misery"; but the experience may have served to enlarge his views of human life. Although the two were far apart as regarded their theology, there was much in each to win the admiration and esteem of the other.

Born in the year 1797, in the house in which he died in 1871, Mr. Brown was a benefactor to Houghton such as the village may hardly expect to see the like of again. In every direction might be seen the results of his kindness. The best products of his gardens and hot-houses were not considered too choice for the sick poor who needed them. He would have disliked having to enlist the aid of the village constable in dealing with dishonest neighbours, but he would nevertheless find out a way of making such see for themselves the contemptibleness of theft. One who stole Mr. Brown's vegetables would, if traced, probably have a piece of meat sent to him direct from "the house" to make his meal complete; and such a one might feel his punishment as much as many who atone for their misdeeds in prison. In many respects, to an ordinary observer, it might have appeared that the Miller of Houghton was aiming at making himself and his actions a conundrum.

Mr. Brown was associated with the Union Nonconformist Chapel at St. Ives; but he took care that what was to him a chapel-of-ease flourished also at Houghton. When news of the achievements of the boy-preacher of Waterbeach reached the ears of the good-natured but eccentric miller, he seems to have determined that he would hear the youthful prodigy for himself and judge of his merits. The spare room, or "prophet's chamber," in Mr. Brown's house was always available for the pulpit "supplies"; and, for the sake of the entertainment it afforded him, the master liked to have some-body in it.

At the same time, it is a singular circumstance that so far-gone an Arminian as the Miller of Houghton should have invited to his house, as a Sunday "supply," so uncompromising a Calvinist as young Spurgeon. When Mr. Spurgeon reached the village mansion on the Saturday evening, he would be struck with the singular code

of laws by which the household was ruled. At family prayer the
preacher would not be allowed to read a portion of Scripture; that
would be done in turn by one of the servant-maids, and it was
understood to be a great trial to bashful maidens. If, on the
following morning, the "supply" was downstairs before eight o'clock
he would be greeted with approval; for Mr. Brown admired a
preacher who observed what he called his *Sunday time.* "My time
is eight o'clock by my clock in the kitchen, and that always gains
a quarter of an hour in the week, and I let it remain till after
breakfast," the miller would remark, adding, "Then I set it right
that the servants may know the correct time to go to public worship."
At the breakfast-table the preacher would have to take the place
set apart and the food prescribed for him, and he would also have
to eat what was supposed to be best for his personal benefit.
"That is your place," the host would remark; "there are two eggs;
we always provide two eggs for the minister's breakfast on Sunday
morning, because there is a large amount of phosphorus in eggs,
and that acts on the brain, and so we get better sermons." "What
sort of an old fellow *is* this Potto Brown?" once asked an unhappy
student of the miller himself while under the impression that he
was addressing a man-servant. "Oh, a queer old fellow," was the
reply, and a very correct reply it was.

When Mr. Spurgeon found himself the guest of such a host as
this village philanthropist, it was very natural that he should feel
ill at ease, for the two might seem to have little in common.
Probably the Miller of Houghton had as kind a heart as the old pastor
of Stambourne; but in matters which chiefly touched Mr. Spurgeon's
sympathies the two men were a complete contrast. After Mr.
Brown had heard his young "supply" on the Sunday, he spoke of
his preaching in a very disparaging tone. If, as was supposed by
the late Mr. Edward Cressell—who during some years was pastor
at Houghton—Mr. Brown suspected young Spurgeon to be so far an
adventurous impostor that he preached, as his own, the sermons of
mature divines, we can understand the miller's ground of misgiving.

As an enterprising, shrewd business man of Quaker descent, who had seen something of the world, the Houghton miller had never heard a mere boy preach with such force as his present visitor, and he seemed to lay claim to a Christian experience which, in the ordinary course of things, could only belong to a much older person. Then what Mr. Spurgeon would have regarded as a necessary and emphatic enunciation of the doctrines of grace was to Mr. Brown a too out-spoken parade of the doctrines of Calvinism, against which his life and action had been a prolonged protest. A collision between two such champions of opposite teaching was inevitable, one being as determined as the other in speaking out plainly what he believed. No quarter was given on either side; and it is to be regretted that a fuller account of what the younger disputant many years afterwards described as "a battle royal" has not been preserved.

The miller opened the combat by telling the boy-preacher that his discourses might do very well for an apprentice boy; but there was nothing in them beyond that, and then he went on in an animated strain to show how utterly distasteful to an experienced man like himself was the Calvinistic doctrine which had been the groundwork of the sermons. Nettled by being so sharply rebuked, and feeling indignant that the teaching which his Puritanic grand-father and the godly housekeeper at Newmarket had found to be the very marrow of the New Testament should thus be made light of, the youthful evangelist told the Miller of Houghton to his face that his theology was worthless. The discussion continued with great warmth for some time; but as each disputant was able to respect an opponent who believed something for himself, and held his ground against all comers, no scars remained to tell of actual ill-feeling. Indeed, it is not improbable that this very disagreement may have had the effect of heightening Mr. Brown's respect for his guest; for not only would there be demonstration that he could with boldness and honesty defend a faith which he believed to be scriptural, but the dispute would give evidence of the "apprentice boy's" possession of genius and knowledge, which could not possibly have been borrowed for the occasion from a more experienced Christian. From that day Charles Haddon Spurgeon and Potto Brown were very good friends. Seeing that they could not agree, they gave up their wordy combat, and conversed in a friendly way about things which they held in common. When the time for separation came, the two were to all appearances fast friends; they walked together to Huntingdon, and as a parting gift the miller handed to the young preacher a copy of Haldane's " Life."

We properly speak of the good Miller of Houghton as a Christian and a philanthropist *sui generis*. He was no more like any other man than young Mr. Spurgeon himself was; and it would have been as hopeless for any person to attempt to copy the one as the other. He has some attraction for us as an early friend of Mr. Spurgeon, and as such it may be interesting to give what Mr. R. W. Dixon says about him in a memorial *brochure* issued some years ago :—

"The care Mr. Brown took to educate all who came within his influence was very marked; the servants of his household—any friends, especially young friends, who might be staying in the house—he took pains with all. He sought to interest his household in the family worship. He wished to inculcate the feeling that people should not depend upon any priest or one man to lead the devotions, laying stress on the text, 'And hath made us (*all*) kings and priests unto God.' He tried to get all to engage in this service, which he made informal and simple. He would hand a Bible to any one person in the circle, and say, 'Read, please, but don't read a fighting psalm'; or, 'Don't read a *long* piece'; or, 'We are some of us going to market, read something to guide us in buying and selling'; or, 'What good news is there for us to-day?' or, 'We must read our Bibles the same as we read our newspapers.' Sometimes he would interrupt the reading with a remark; as, when that Psalm was read which says David roared in the night, Mr. Brown said, 'What would they say to us if we went on like that?' His younger servants he got to read the Scriptures in turn, the older ones to pray aloud. The younger ones were corrected when they misread; this led them to rehearse their portion before coming in. Sometimes he would make a running commentary on what was read, or show how it applied to every-day life. Thus he redeemed a regular service from what it might have become—a dull routine, and used it as a means of education for those about him. He found it difficult to get women to pray aloud, and would say to them, 'Women should pray aloud, or they may be accused of drunkenness, as Hannah was.' He had great difficulty in inducing his first wife to pray aloud, even in private. She said she could not. He said, 'Could you not repeat words after me?' She thought she could. Then they knelt down, and he said, 'Lord, be merciful'; she repeated, 'Lord, be merciful.' He continued, 'to me a sinner.' He then rose, and said, 'There, you can pray very well.' After a time she took her part in vocal prayer at family worship. Mr. Brown liked to have several short prayers. He did not appeal to anyone in particular, but was troubled if no one followed after he had prayed, when he paused before rising to give them the opportunity." *

A man of this stamp would not only interest Mr. Spurgeon in early life, he would continue to have rare attraction till the last. After the death of the Miller of Houghton an article on his life, work, and characteristics appeared in *The Sword and the Trowel.*

* "Potto Brown: the Village Philanthropist," pp. 180–181. Several facts relating to Mr. Brown were communicated by my late friend, Edward Cressell, who was for some years minister at Houghton, and an admirable preacher.

CHAPTER XIII.

LAST DAYS AT WATERBEACH.

An Invitation from London—New Park Street Chapel—Decaying Prosperity—Mr. Spurgeon's
First Night in London—His Misgivings—First Impressions of the Chapel—Dr. Gill's
Chair—Differences of Opinion—The Evening Sermon and its Effects—Offer and Acceptance
of the Pastorate—Impressions of Outsiders—Entry in the Church Book at Waterbeach.

WE are now approaching the close of the days at Waterbeach, which the great preacher never ceased fondly to remember in London in after days. The manner in which he was
first introduced to a larger sphere of labour in the metropolis
might look like accident; but Mr. Spurgeon himself would have
called it a particular providence. As the reader will be aware,
when the pulpit of an important church and congregation becomes
vacant, any mention of a promising village genius, who might be
able to maintain the prestige of eminent predecessors, is listened
to with interest. Men who have already made a reputation are
commonly too scarce to be available; but it is always just possible
that some rising star may be found who will equally well serve
the anxious deacons' purpose. In the case of Mr. Spurgeon, it
happened that news of his uncommon talents and unexceptionable
teaching was carried to the Baptist Church at New Park Street
Chapel, Southwark, at a time of urgent need in the autumn of the
year 1853, when the pastorate was vacant. The sanctuary, which had
accommodation for twelve hundred persons—not more than a sixth
part of which was occupied—was supposed to be as handsome as
it was spacious. Though the cause was an ancient one, the
chapel itself was comparatively new; it had been erected in the
reign of William IV., in place of one which had been taken down
to clear the approaches to the present London Bridge. As will be
shown in the proper place, quite a succession of notable theologians

had been associated with the people from the seventeenth century downwards; but at the time mentioned the outlook was altogether disheartening. It was becoming more and more difficult to maintain congregational prosperity in crowded industrial centres, from which the best families showed a growing disposition to remove in order to secure the greater quiet and purer air of the suburbs. This was the case with New Park Street Chapel forty years ago; and to any ordinary observer it must have appeared that nothing short of the miraculous could arrest the process of decay.

Mere appearances may be deceptive, however; no actual miracle was needed to turn back the tide to the high-water mark of prosperity; all that was wanted was a man possessing certain gifts and characteristics. Where was such a man to be found? That was a question which the deacons wished to have answered; and at a very opportune moment a friend came forward to give the desired information. The man wanted was down at Water-beach; and one of the friends had become impressed with his talents while noting the way in which he had been somewhat roughly rebuked at a meeting at Cambridge on account of outspoken adherence to what he judged to be the truth. When the late Mr. William Olney heard of this circumstance, he resolved that he would write to the young preacher to see what he might have to say to the proposal that he should make a trial of his gifts before a London congregation. From Mr. Olney's standpoint, all the precedents of the past seemed to favour a successful issue. The church of which he was a member had so repeatedly, with the best results, selected a man for its pastor who was still in his teens, or had scarcely got out of them, that the fact of Mr. Spurgeon being only nineteen years of age was of good omen. It had been much the same with Dr. John Gill, who had been pastor for over fifty years, with Dr. John Rippon, who held the office during sixty-three years, and with Dr. Joseph Angus, who had resigned the post about a dozen years before.

Mr. Spurgeon himself was by no means elated with the proposal that he should visit London. He had had little experience of life in the metropolis; but the vivid portrayals of Ragged London, which had so often had a fascination for him in the columns of *Household Words*, would only tend to make him love all the more the charms of his native East Anglia. The boy-preacher's private address being unknown to the magnates of New Park Street, the letter of application was sent to Waterbeach Chapel, and the mysterious-looking missive was lying on the communion-table when, after the winter-morning drive from Cambridge, Mr. Spurgeon entered the building to conduct the usual service. At first he thought that the letter was not for him; but a deacon was present in the person of Mr. Coe, who knew well enough that the application had reached the person for whom it was intended. There might be another Spurgeon at another place with a larger congregation, but the suggestion that the letter was intended for him was none the less mistaken. The more the preacher looked at the matter all round, the less he appears to have liked the prospect which the proposed visit to London opened before him. The situation was so far peculiar that pride or desire for a higher position must have nothing to do with influencing him in making his decision. It was not long since he had seemed to hear on Midsummer Common the admonition which had entered into his very soul: "Seekest thou great things for thyself? Seek them not." A reply was at first sent to London, saying that a mistake had evidently been made; but at length Mr. Spurgeon agreed to visit the metropolis.

Being in love with the sphere he was occupying, and having no ambition to remove to London, Mr. Spurgeon left home on a memorable Saturday in December, 1853, with a heavy heart. Indeed, the affair was so genuine a trial to him that the passage of Scripture on which his mind continued to dwell was, "He must needs go through Samaria." We have to picture the country youth travelling up the Eastern Counties Railway to the old terminus at Shoreditch, thinking all the way of those he had left behind in Cambridge, and eagerly anticipating the time when he would return to them. In London the signs of approaching Christmas might be apparent on every hand; but all that did not tend to relieve his own lowness of spirits.

Where was the young preacher to find a lodging? Not one of the good deacons who had favoured the notion of asking him to make a trial of the exercise of his gifts before a London congregation had offered him lodging and entertainment. A "supply" could be provided for at a boarding-house in Queen Square, and that was the most convenient arrangement. Though this was a highly respectable place, it was not one calculated to inspire a new-comer with a love of London. Those who commonly frequented the boarding-house were precise religionists of the Evangelical section of the Established Church, and their conversation was not of a kind to exhilarate one who had just come up from the Fens and was destined to strike out for himself a new path in the great centre of the world's commerce and civilisation. The select company of the common-room would at once see that the new-comer not only did not belong to their coterie, but appeared to be in certain respects somewhat of a greenhorn. They all saw at a glance that his clothes had not been made in Bond Street or Regent Street; and while the formidable-looking black satin stock he wore was such as might have come as an heirloom from Stambourne, the red-and-white cotton pocket-handkerchief which occasionally became visible naturally awakened dismay in the hearts of persons whose notions of propriety were of such an approved standard. When these good people learned that the round-faced boy who had suddenly appeared among them was actually engaged to preach on the morrow at one of the great chapels of London, which had its memorable associations, they could not help being amused, although they may have been too polite to show what they felt.

At the same time, the temptation to entertain their young

friend with trustworthy information relative to the men of might
and of miraculous eloquence who then held forth in the various
London pulpits was too great to be resisted. "There were giants
in the earth in those days," and these Anglican Evangelicals
plumed themselves upon being minutely acquainted with their characteristics. Mr. So-and-so who ministered in one quarter was the
oracle of thoughtful people; Mr. Somebody-else in another direction
had an irresistible attraction for men; and then there was another
whose powers were such that City merchants flocked to hear him
a thousand at a time! There may have been others whose powers
of voice and of oratory were too great for human estimation; but
the very thought of having to sleep in the same town with
such men of world-wide fame was more than enough to unnerve
a rustic evangelist who was timidly anticipating having to stand
in the pulpit of Dr. Rippon within the space of a few hours.
After all this it seemed meet that the boarding-house manager
should, for a bedroom, allot Mr. Spurgeon a small place over
the street door, hardly more than large enough to turn round in,
and in which peaceful sleep was impossible on account of noises
from the streets. When, at length, the morning came—a sombre
December morning in London—the Evangelical Churchpeople of
the boarding-house common-room went their several ways to hear
those wonderful magnates of the English pulpit whose genius
and labours imparted such lustre to the metropolis. It was too
much to expect that any one of the number should volunteer
to accompany the odd-looking visitor from the Fens to his singular
destination at the Baptist meeting-house, with which they were
probably only very imperfectly acquainted.

Being a stranger in London, the young preacher's first
business when he left his lodging on the Sunday morning was to
find the way to New Park Street. Turning into the great main
thoroughfare of Holborn, he went on down the hill, the Viaduct
being then hardly thought of, and turning again into Far-
ringdon Street, he went on over old Blackfriars or Southwark

Bridge, to come at last to the chapel which had such a memorable history associated with it. Before entering, there seems to have been another pang of misgiving; but, as the visit to London had not been of his own seeking, he resolved to go boldly forward and do what was expected of him. The meeting-house appeared to be as dull and gloomy within as it was black and uninviting without; but all this was quite in keeping with the state of Mr. Spurgeon's mind. He was still thinking of the words, "He must needs go through Samaria."

At the same time he could not but feel interested in his surroundings when he actually entered the building. There were warm-hearted friends to welcome him, while here and there were memories of a distinguished past. The temptation to sit down in what had been Dr. Gill's chair was irresistible, and there were pictures, etc., to see, as well as things to hear, in which such a visitor would be greatly interested. Some few persons still survive who were present at the old chapel on that memorable Sunday morning; but the one who retained the most vivid recollections of the occasion was my friend the late Mr. William Olney, from whom I received a particular description of what happened.

When Mr. Spurgeon left the vestry to enter the pulpit the outlook was more dispiriting than ever, the mere handful of people dotted about the building representing altogether a much smaller congregation than would have assembled at Waterbeach, or at any of the special services in the parts surrounding that village. Everything associated with the place seemed to indicate that the prosperity of the past had gone down to low-water mark, and this could not but affect the preacher's spirits.

The sermon was founded upon James i. 17, "Every good gift and every perfect gift is from above, and cometh down from the Father of lights, with whom is no variableness, neither shadow of turning." Perhaps some of the veteran Calvinists among the congregation may not have thought it a promising omen when the first text was thus selected from the Epistle of the Apostle of Works.

H

Be that as it may, the original style and method of the youthful preacher struck all discerning persons present. The extraordinary clearness and power of his voice were also noticed. As to the general merits of the preacher, however, there was division of opinion. Some were captivated at once; others, who posed as more discerning, deliberate critics, hesitated to give their approval. This was all very natural. If it needs a great man to introduce original methods, such as will inevitably supersede the old-time ways or fashions, it also needs persons who are something more than commonplace to appreciate the innovation.

But apart from what he had actually done in the way of preaching the Gospel to a London audience, Mr. Spurgeon had given his hearers something to talk about. The two hundred persons present, who on this occasion had an average of six seats each in the Southwark meeting-house, went home not only to dine but to discuss what they had heard and seen. They had passed through a new experience; and while some may have ingenuously confessed that they were charmed, others were persuaded that such preaching would never do. We have to remember that on that first Sunday of his appearance in London, Mr. Spurgeon was a fair sample of what he would surely continue to be in years to come. He gave neither more nor less than one of his ordinary sermons, such as he would have preached to his rustic flock at Waterbeach had he remained at home. Any notion of delivering an elaborately prepared discourse to impress the congregation "with a view" to the pastorate, was far from his thoughts; he was too anxious to get the business over, and to return to dearly-loved Cambridge, to be tempted by such a prospect. At the same time, he was pointed in his remarks and simple in his style; and while his overflowing humour might provoke a titter through the chapel—staid deacons and grave matrons being unable to resist the temptation—the young preacher would actually be seen at times to smile himself. Nothing could be more impressive than the way in which he presented the solemn truths of the Gospel; but, nevertheless, the fact remained that this man was capable of smiling in the pulpit, and did not account it a sin to make others smile as well.

The greater part of those who were present in the morning took care to go in the evening, and the reports they had made about the strange ways of the young man from Cambridge proved to be a sufficient advertisement to draw together a much larger assembly. An eccentric preacher who was only nineteen years of age was sure to prove a powerful attraction to the religious quidnuncs of London of forty years ago. The subject of the evening sermon was taken from the Book of Revelation, " They are without fault before the throne of God." The theme was a congenial one ; the preacher had gained confidence since the morning ; he was in better spirits, so that he was enabled to speak with comfort to himself while he powerfully impressed those who heard him. It was an extraordinary occasion, and those present felt it to be such. At the conclusion of the service it was a somewhat perplexing thing to know what to do with the people. They lingered in and about the chapel in a state of excitement; and the majority were anxious that the young Waterbeach pastor should forthwith be asked to remove to London. The day was thus a success, after all; and the youth whom the company at the Queen Square boarding-house had set down as a mere odd-looking rustic had so far become master of the situation that he had no reason further to fear being put to the test of preaching before a London congregation. The ordeal had not been what he had anticipated; he had succeeded in a signal manner when he thought it more than possible that he might fail; and he had gained new friends where he may not have hoped to find them. The evening repast in the boarding establishment, therefore, was a far pleasanter affair than breakfast in the early morning had been. The boy-preacher was no longer depressed by contrasting his own native littleness with the mighty pulpit orators who were the wonder of London. He might be but an apprentice hand, as Potto Brown had said; but he had a Gospel message to give such as the people were glad to

hear.   All things now seemed to wear a more attractive face; and
though this Cambridge youth was not seeking a London pastorate,
nothing was more certain than that he need not shrink from it if,
later on, he should be disposed to enter upon such a sphere.

The good people at Waterbeach of course felt regret at the
turn which things were taking in connection with their pastor; but
as such a termination of his services in the village was well known
to be inevitable sooner or later, they reconciled themselves to it.
The first letter of invitation arrived at No. 60, Upper Park Street,
Cambridge, where Mr. Spurgeon was then living, in the latter part of
January, 1854, after he had preached again on several occasions in
London. In reply, the young pastor referred to his comfortable
position among a devoted and loving people; and the only reason
that moved him to leave them was the fact that they were
unable to raise sufficient for a minister's maintenance.   This
seemed to indicate that the hand of Providence was opening the
way for work in another direction.   Mr. Spurgeon himself at this
time acted with caution, and he admired the exercise of prudence in
others.   When he had accepted the call to Waterbeach, he would
not bind himself to serve for longer than three months; and when the
deacons asked him to occupy the London pulpit for half a year he
shrank from the unqualified acceptance of their offer.   He reserved the
right to retire should anything like failure attend his ministry;
and, on the other hand, he would not disregard a hint to resign if
the other side felt disposed to give it.   He was quite incapable
then of measuring his own capacity, although after a time, when
he had discovered what he could do, he was remarkable for self-
reliance.   People may have supposed later that he believed in himself;
he really believed in what God was capable of accomplishing through
his means.   In January, 1854, however, he was particularly careful
to keep open a way of retreat into the Fens should the London
experiment not answer his expectations.   He thought that people's
enthusiasm might cool down, and then his popularity would be sure
to wane.   In any case, he would not leave Waterbeach abruptly,

for the people had all been kind and devoted; and they would
heartily welcome him back into their midst if the London arrangement should not become permanent.

Any hope that the people of Southwark would repent of their
choice, or that Mr. Spurgeon himself would see that it was his duty
to retire into the country, was doomed to meet with disappointment.
The preacher's popularity continued to increase in a way that was
quite without parallel. Instead of New Park Street Chapel having
twelve hundred seats for two hundred persons, the doors were soon
besieged by crowds who were content with standing room if seats
were not to be obtained.

At first there was a small minority who were not in favour of
inviting Mr. Spurgeon to accept the pastorate, but eventually these
gave way to the wishes of the majority, so that the call became
practically unanimous. This cordial invitation to the pastorate was
acknowledged by the youth of nineteen, and no difficulty appeared
to stand in the way of his accepting it. He reminded his friends
that he had never sought advancement at their hands; he had had
nervous misgivings about making the experiment of preaching in
London at all, and now the general outlook filled him with astonishment. His one desire was for God to lead him on and open the way.
Since he had seemed to hear that mysterious admonition outside of
Chesterton, he would not dare to harbour any ambition on his own
account; but at the same time he could not but feel some satisfaction at becoming the pastor of a people with so noble a history.
As he thought of his illustrious predecessors—Keach and Stinton,
Gill and Rippon—he asked for the prayers of the saints that such
an inexperienced youth might prove worthy to follow in their train.
He hoped that any unguarded words he might use, or any mistakes
into which he might fall, might be overlooked. While making a
great venture, he did so in faith that the Lord would strengthen
him to undertake the service. This was no vain confidence, but
rather full dependence on the Divine strength.

It is interesting to us to learn what the young preacher

from the Fens appeared like to shrewd observers who were tempted to enter New Park Street Chapel to see and hear for themselves. One who was an excellent judge wrote: " His voice is clear and musical, his language plain, his style flowing but terse, his method lucid and orderly, his matter sound and suitable, his tone and spirit cordial, his remarks always pithy and pungent, sometimes familiar and colloquial, yet never light or coarse, much less profane. Judging from a single sermon, one supposed that he would become a plain, faithful, forcible, and affectionate preacher of the Gospel in the form called Calvinistic; and our judgment was the more favourable because, while there was a solidity beyond his years, we detected little of the wild luxuriance naturally characteristic of very young preachers."

From the first, the Quakers appear to have appreciated Mr. Spurgeon's forcible outspokenness while giving his message; and if Job Spurgeon, who in the seventeenth century was thrown into Chelmsford Gaol, suffered as a Quaker, there was some kinship between the Essex youth and the Friends. Even at this early date there was a notice of the New Park Street pastor in *The Friend* which was characteristic of the quarter whence it came. It ran thus :—

" The interest excited by his ministry, and the conflicting opinions expressed in reference to his qualifications and usefulness, have been altogether without parallel in modern times. It was a remarkable sight to see this round-faced country youth thus placed in a position of such solemn and arduous responsibility, yet addressing himself to the fulfilment of its onerous duties with a gravity, self-possession, and vigour that proved him well fitted to the task he had assumed."

In reference to the transformation scene which had taken place at New Park Street Chapel, it was added:—

" In a few weeks the empty pews were crowded, every sitting in the chapel was let; and ere twelve months had elapsed the eagerness to hear him had become so great that every standing-place within the walls was occupied on each Sabbath, and it soon became evident that increased accommodation must be provided."

In the meantime, while all this was taking place in London, nearly sixty miles distant, the deacons at Waterbeach plainly saw that their young friend would never return to that little pastorate. Then they made this historic entry in their Church Book :—

"Mr. Spurgeon continued to labour amongst us with very great success till the beginning of 1854, when he was called to the more important pastorate of New Park Street, where his popularity and usefulness continue beyond all parallel in modern times, being often called upon to preach on public occasions in all parts of the country."

When Mr. Thompson, the present pastor at Waterbeach, read that passage to his congregation on Sunday, February 7, 1892, he very appropriately added :—

"Our beloved friend has gone from us, leaving no stain behind him. A man greatly beloved by all. He has left a terrible breach. He was a man of great faith, with an unswerving fidelity to the truth, loyal and devoted to his God, docile, childlike before God, fearless before men. He possessed a gentleness of soul known to few men, and when buildings and books shall be no more, Charles Haddon Spurgeon will continue to live, and his works will follow him."

CHAPTER XIV.

THE OLD STYLE AND THE NEW.

The Work in London commenced—The Older Pulpit Models—Characteristics of a "Great" Sermon—Other Ministers of the Time—"The Gold-headed Cane Era"—Professor Everett's Reminiscences—The Situation in London—Mr. W. Ford's Recollections—Lord Shaftesbury's Work.

MR. SPURGEON'S great work in London was commenced before either the preacher himself or his friends were well aware of the fact. Certainly no one as yet understood that a new era in the history of the English pulpit had been opened, and that in time the style of ornate oratory which had been in fashion since the days of Dr. Johnson would give place to a more natural method of public speaking, of which the young preacher from Waterbeach was to become the chief model.

Of course, persons were able to see at once that there was something strikingly novel about the young pastor at New Park Street; but it was not to be expected that they would all at once realise that one of the most far-reaching innovations of modern times was being introduced. There were superfine critics who detected what they called "Saxon" as the leading characteristic of the discourses given at the Southwark meeting-house, and that might be a merit in one who was incapable of soaring higher. The Latinised style of Johnson and Gibbon was still their standard of excellence. To observers of to-day it will appear sufficiently strange that such a standard should have been in favour, while in Addison and Goldsmith, as well as in Matthew Henry and Cowper, models existed which were so infinitely superior. As regarded the common people, who knew little or nothing about either *style* or *Saxon*, Mr. Spurgeon spoke a language they could understand without being obliged to refer to a dictionary, and they heard him gladly.

No doubt it looked something like presumption in so young a man when he thus deliberately set his face against the fashion which had prevailed for generations, and set up a method of his own. Indeed, this appears to have been one of the charges brought against him; and very early in his London career Mr. Spurgeon found it necessary to say something in reply. He did the best thing possible under the circumstances, by acknowledging that the new method of preaching had been introduced; but he explained that he had acted as he had done because he judged the new method to be better than the old.

The reader can best understand the importance of the innovation of which Mr. Spurgeon was one of the pioneers, by reminding himself of the style of preaching exemplified by the leading pulpit orators of those days. There was John Angell James (1785–1859), for instance, whom Mr. Spurgeon himself greatly admired. In a sketch of James's life, Dr. R. W. Dale tells us that " his sermon in May, 1819, for the London Missionary Society, was long remembered and spoken of as one of the most remarkable of the ' great efforts ' which in those times made the annual sermon at Surrey Chapel the chief attraction of the May week. . . . Like all his great sermons preached in his earlier years, it was delivered *memoriter*, and his brother, who sat in the pulpit with the manuscript in his hand, to ' prompt ' the preacher if for a moment he faltered, has told me that hardly an epithet, a conjunction, or a preposition was forgotten."*

A sermon of this kind, with its introduction, divisions, subdivisions, transitions, application, and peroration, was an exceedingly elaborate production, to which people might listen in wondering admiration, but which was not calculated to answer the chief end of preaching; and we can well believe that Dr. Dale is right when he says of the estimable colleague of his younger days, " I think that he was at his best when he did not feel himself under any obligation to make a great effort." Dr. Stoughton, too, speaks of

---

* " Pulpit Memorials," 150–151.

James's rhetoric as being "too ornate and ambitious," although it drew forth encomiums from Lord Holland.

Another pulpit celebrity of those days was Henry Melvill, of whom the late E. Paxton Hood remarks:—" Fine preaching, we say, this of Mr. Melvill's; and the labour bestowed upon it was said to have been immense. During the time that he preached at Camden Chapel in London, the reports in circulation respecting the solicitude manifested by him during the composition of a discourse were many and ludicrous. We heard that he was quite inaccessible for about eight hours of every day in the week, closely locked, it was said, in his study. He, at that time, was said to bestow pains upon his discourses as if, instead of being delivered to two thousand persons, they were to be models for all future ages. We have sometimes doubted this, and are still prepared to believe that they are exaggerators who assure us that at these times he invariably wrote his discourses twice and sometimes thrice; after which they were transcribed by his wife in a clear and legible hand for the pulpit. Suppose the case not to be so bad as this, still is it not dreadful thus to misunderstand the intentions of the Gospel ministry? "*

The introduction of a simpler, more natural style of preaching is not to be traced to Mr. Spurgeon alone, although his was doubtless the chief share in it. We find the Rev. Edward White claiming some share of the work for the late pastor of the Weigh House Chapel:—" He was an epoch-making man, though marking an epoch perhaps as much as making it. Providence seems to have given this eminent person to the Congregational Dissenters just when such an influence was needed to lift them out of the somewhat cramped formulas of the Georgian era. . . . The age of silk and lavender, and of successful suppression of inquiry under devious phrases, was coming to an end. It was inevitable that much of the ancient style of thought, handed down since the age of Charles II., should pass away, and no single person did so much to promote the reform as Mr. Binney." †

* "The Throne of Eloquence," p. 466.   † "Pulpit Memorials," pp. 327–328.

In the course of an address to his old students, given just twenty years after he first came to London, I overheard Mr. Spurgeon characterise the old times as the " Gold-headed Cane Era." He would also occasionally refer to those antique ornaments of the London pulpit who, in the first place, took care to be gentlemen, whatever they might be, or might not be, besides. When such portrayals were carefully examined, they were found not to be so charged with exaggeration as some may have been disposed to think.

Mr. R. J. Curtis, of the Ragged School Union, communicates the following concerning Mr. Spurgeon and the " Gold-headed Cane Era":—

" An early impression of his was that of want of contact between the people and the pulpit. The ministers, with a sort of kingly or priestly dignity, awed the people into a sort of slavish timidity of anything approaching familiarity with such dignified personages. He determined to smite this, and he did it with a blow of a giant, and this smaller dignity soon gasped itself away. A friend of mine, a great admirer of Mr. Spurgeon, relates the following :—' Mr. Spurgeon had been preaching during the week, I think, at Bexley. After the service a great many persons remained to see him, and, if practicable, to shake hands with him. When apprised of the same he said, ' I will come and shake hands with them like one o'clock ' ! "

What Mr. Spurgeon was at the opening of his London career, and what kind of world seemed to be opening before him, we have well depicted in the reminiscences of Professor J. D. Everett, from which I have already quoted. Mr. Everett visited his old Newmarket comrade soon after his settlement at New Park Street.

" I spent half a day with him," he says, " and he poured forth to me, without reserve, the full tale of his successes, telling me of the distinguished men who continually came to hear him, and of the encomiums pronounced on his delivery by elocutionists like Sheridan Knowles.

" He showed me the small manuscript books in which he wrote his morning sermons, in a plain round-hand (his evening sermons being less carefully prepared), and read me one of the sermons as thus written. It did not consist of notes and jottings, but was complete in itself, and occupied about a quarter of an hour in the reading. I estimated that it must have been amplified about threefold in actual delivery. He told me that he could always say exactly what he intended, and in exactly the time which he intended.

" His fame was not then known to the general public, and it was only from himself that I learned it. There was something ludicrous in the idea of a man talking so big about his own performances, but it was the simple truth, and he told it with the simplicity of a child. His great power was to him a simple matter of fact, of which he had no more reason to be proud than a bird of its power to fly, or a fish of its power to swim.

" One of his most marked characteristics was the consummate ease with which he did his work, and he was fully conscious of this strong point. He certainly was a thorough believer in himself from the time that he first went to London. He knew what he meant to do, and he did it in his own way, without troubling himself about adverse criticism. He did not break his heart at being scorned or misrepresented.

"This characteristic of being always at his ease was at the root of what was called his irreverence. I remember suggesting to him, in this connection, that a man ought to feel and show some sense of awe in the presence of his Maker; and his reply was to the effect that awe was foreign to his nature—that he felt perfectly at home with his Heavenly Father."

At this time the outlook in London was sufficiently gloomy to discourage and even alarm anyone whose nerves were not of the strongest. In certain parts of the town something like a panic actually prevailed, while the sights and sounds must have reminded some observers of the time of plague in the seventeenth century. Thus in and around Golden Square on Saturday morning, the 9th of September, the scene is thus described:—"There was scarcely a street free from hearses and mourning-coaches. A number of the tradespeople left their shops and fled, the closed shutters bearing the announcement that business had been suspended for a few days. Messrs. Huggins, the brewers, have issued an announcement that the poor inhabitants may obtain any quantity of hot water for cleaning their dwellings, or other purposes, at any hour of the day or night." *

The official report at this time was as follows:—"In the seven days extending from the 3rd to the 9th of September, the deaths of 3,413 persons were recorded, and 2,050 of the number were caused by cholera; which had, in partial eruptions all over London, destroyed in nine weeks, 5, 26, 133, 399, 644, 729, 817, 1,287, 2,050, or in the aggregate 6,120 lives. The outbreak began later than the corresponding outbreak of 1849, which by the same date had, in sixteen weeks, been fatal to 10,143 persons. Will the epidemic pursue its ravages? Will it observe its own times, disregard the seasons, and exact its full tale of victims? Such were the questions that were asked, with no little anxiety, by those who watched over the public health during the last week." It is then added that "no exertion should be spared to save the thousands whose lives are still threatened; and the dread lesson, before

* *The British Banner*, September 13, 1854.

regarded so little, should never be forgotten—that men can no longer drink polluted water, breathe impure air, neglect sanitary measures year after year, with impunity."

Like others whose lot was cast in the thickly inhabited part of the town, Mr. Spurgeon was much affected by this terrible visitation; but the young pastor had an encouraging experience which is thus referred to by Mr. W. Ford, of Westminster:—

"In the year 1854, the first year of Mr. Spurgeon in London, the cholera raged in the locality of his church, and the neighbourhood where he resided. The parochial authorities were very thoughtful for the poor, and caused bills to be placed at the corners of the streets, headed 'Cholera,' in large type, informing the public where advice and medicines would be supplied gratis. At that time I lived in the Great Dover Road, and Mr. Spurgeon lived a little further towards Greenwich, in Virginia Terrace. Seeing the bills above named at every turning, I was forcibly impressed that they were very much calculated to terrify the people. With the concurrence of a friend I procured one, and wrote in the centre these words:—'Because thou hast made the Lord, which is my refuge, even the Most High, thy habitation, there shall no evil befall thee, neither shall any plague come nigh thy dwelling.' This bill I placed in my shop window, hundreds read it, and I am not aware of one jeer or improper remark—so subdued and solemnised were people by the awful visitation. Among the readers of the bill was Mr. Spurgeon, and he graphically describes the incident in his work entitled 'The Treasury of David.'" *

In his notes on Psalm xci., Mr. Spurgeon refers to this incident, and tells how he was refreshed and strengthened by reading the inspired words which the Christian tradesman exhibited in his window.

We do not find any mention of the name of Mr. Spurgeon at the Baptist Union meetings in 1854, and this may perhaps be accounted for by the general distrust with which he was regarded by the more elderly ministers. The following general resolution passed by the members of the Union, shows that the prospect before the churches was not so very cheering at that time:—

"That the Union learn with unfeigned regret that the rate of increase in the churches, as shown by the Association Returns of 1853, is smaller than in preceding years, and smaller than it has been in any year since 1834, the limit of the Union records, it being only at an average of 1⅓ per church per annum; that while the impression made by this numerical statement might be somewhat modified by a regard to the temporary causes —such as emigration, for example—which have operated to the diminution of the churches (and the statement cannot alone be taken as a satisfactory basis on which to form an estimate of the spiritual state of the churches) in the judgment of the Union it presents at once an occasion for humiliation and a loud call to united activity and prayer: the former in every department of the work of the Lord, the latter for the gracious outpouring of His Holy Spirit."

* "The Best Refuge in Times of Trouble," by W. Ford.

While the future seemed gloomy, we find complaint in regard to the inadequate supply of able preachers. "At no period since the Reformation from Popery was there so much need for a constantly increasing supply of competent ministers, both for home and foreign service," one authority declared. "The outcry is very great of the deficiency, both in Great Britain and in America. It is stated that the reasons are to be found partly in the extremely straitened circumstances in which large numbers of ministers, both in and out of the Established Church, are placed, and the temptations which commerce, in its varied walks, holds forth to men of ability." *

In its social aspect, London itself was probably in a transition state. The town was beginning outwardly to improve in appearance; but those earnest Christian people who headed the Ragged School crusade needed all the heroism which they could command, and all the perseverance of which human nature was capable, to ensure success in their self-imposed tasks. The late Lord Shaftesbury and his colleague Judge Payne devoted a large part of their time to the encouragement of such service. The office of the Ragged School teacher had not ceased to be a service of peril. The slums were in the condition in which they had been for generations, and large areas which have since been cleared to have large and imposing buildings erected on their sites were then an eyesore as well as a common danger. Lord Shaftesbury explored the most notorious districts, and what he saw inspired him with sentiments akin to despair. It was just about the time of Mr. Spurgeon's coming to London that this great philanthropist passed his Bill for the control of common lodging-houses, which till this time had been the *inferni* of poverty wherein tens of thousands of miserable beings languished or rotted "in lairs fitter to be the habitation of hogs than of human beings." Crime and pauperism were extending their domain; and in view of the great increase of offences among children and young persons, the authorities had to face the alternative of more schools or more prisons. In the

* *The British Banner*, 1854.

course of a year, "according to a return, there were 3,098 children under fourteen years of age found in London, living either as mendicants or thieves. Of these, 1,782 were living in lodging-houses, and 1,316 'at large,' as the return says. There were 148 of them parentless, 336 of whom the parents appeared to be in a condition of life to educate and maintain them, and 844 whose parents sent them to beg and lived, at least, partly on their earnings. Captain W. Hay, the Commissioner of Police, states that there are 20,641 children under fifteen living in idleness, without education, and apparently neglected by their parents, and of these 941 have been charged with other offences than as mendicants and thieves." Altogether, there must have been at least 100,000 children growing up in London without education. Temperance was in its infancy, and an enormous number of persons were arrested every year on account of drunkenness.

For a youth of nineteen to leave the congenial sphere of Water-beach to enter upon work in an already overgrown metropolis, with characteristics such as have been depicted, was a trial in more senses than can well be comprehended. At the very outset, when cholera was working havoc among the members of his church, young Spurgeon was brought face to face with death in its worst form; but he never shrank from duty, though at times he was tempted to think that his first year in London would be his last.

CHAPTER XV.

MR. SPURGEON'S PREDECESSORS.

A Church with a Notable History—The Days of Strafford and "Thorough"—The Brownists and Early Puritans—Accomplished Scholars in straitened Circumstances—William Rider, the first Pastor—Henry Jessey—Benjamin Keach—Old-time "Justice"—Benjamin Stinton—Divisions after his Death—John Gill—An eminent Scholar—Life in the City of London—Gill's "Commentary"—A social Age—Clubs and Coffee-houses—The Singing at Carter Lane Chapel—Dr. Rippon—A long Pastorate—New London Bridge and New Park Street Chapel—Dr. Joseph Angus—James Smith—William Walters—Long Pastorates.

THE church and congregation which had succeeded in securing the services of the young itinerant preacher of the Fens could boast of a notable history, extending back as far as the stirring days of the Commonwealth. Even before the ascendency of Cromwell, in the early days of the Long Parliament, the Baptists of Southwark began to show sympathy on the side of the people and against the king in the dispute that was to be settled by war. Strafford, with his scheme of "Thorough," and his friend "William the Fox," as many already called the Archbishop of Canterbury, were not any more in favour "over the water" than they were in the City. We hear of Brownists being imprisoned in the Clink because they would not use prayers "made by bishops"; and it was by such interference with the right of private judgment, as well as by the imposition of illegal taxes, that the crisis of civil war was hastened. The Brownists became somewhat numerous in Southwark during the reign of James I.; and, though they were more sweeping in their desires for reform than the Puritans of after days, these sectaries were really the forerunners of the Puritans. What is especially striking in the character of these early Nonconformists is their devotion to duty and their indifference to worldly comfort or distinction so long as conscience was satisfied. Those were the days when even accomplished scholars who refused to be timeservers had to be content with coarse fare and a poor lodging. We find Ainsworth, a first-class Hebraist, working as a bookseller's porter. Roger Williams lived on a few pence a day, and John Canne, the Baptist itinerant preacher, who was the first to collate marginal references for the English Bible, appears to have worked as a printer.

In the dangerous times of Charles I., the Baptists of Southern London met in private houses in order to elude the informers, and their first recognised pastor appears to have been William Rider, of whom little is known beyond the facts that he was tolerably well-to-do in the world, and published a book to advocate the practice of laying of hands on such as were baptised. Although the rule of the country had passed from the king to the Parliament, a teacher who held Baptist views and did not hesitate to proclaim them had no easy time of it. Rider was one of those who became sufferers for conscience' sake. Then it happened that Henry Jessey, who held the living of St. George the Martyr, Southwark, was converted to the views of Rider, the consequence being that many others followed. Popular excitement on the question of baptism by immersion found vent in public disputes.

When or where the first pastor died is not known; but he was succeeded by the more celebrated Benjamin Keach in the year 1668, when London was recovering from the ravages of plague and fire. Born in 1640, Keach was a native of Buckinghamshire, and like young Spurgeon, about two hundred years later, he at the age of fifteen gave up the Pædobaptist views in which he had been educated to accept the faith and practice of the Baptists. Keach, as a youth, also preached up and down his native county, just as his successor afterwards did in the Fens; the difference being that in the seventeenth century a preacher might have his labours interrupted by the military and be haled off to gaol. Persecution, however, could never repress such a man's ardour. On one occasion he was arraigned for publishing a primer for children. The language used by the judge in passing sentence is remarkable for the insight it affords into the character of the times. "Benjamin Keach," remarked the representative of English justice as it was understood in the seven-

I

teenth century, "you are here convicted for writing, printing, and publishing a seditious and schismatical book, for which the Court's judgment is this, and the Court doth award: That you shall go to gaol for a fortnight without bail or mainprize, and the next Saturday to stand upon the pillory at Aylesbury, in the open market, from eleven o'clock till one, with a paper upon your head with this inscription: '*For writing, printing, and publishing a schismatical book entitled, "The Child's Instructor; or, a New and Easy Primer."*' And the next Thursday to stand in the same manner and for the same time in the market at Winslow; and there your book shall be openly burnt before your face by the common hangman in disgrace of you and your doctrine. And you shall forfeit to the King's Majesty the sum of twenty pounds, and shall remain in gaol until you find sureties for your good behaviour, and for your appearance at the next assizes, there to renounce your doctrines and make such public submission as shall be enjoined you. Take him away, keeper."

Even an experience of this kind could not discourage such a man; he persisted in preaching and teaching as opportunities offered, and the country people had more admiration for the evangelist than for his persecutors. Truth could not be repressed by burning in market-places piles of the books which contained it. I believe that the meeting-house at Winslow in which this worthy preached is still standing.

In his twenty-eighth year, Keach left Buckinghamshire to succeed William Rider in the pastorate at Southwark; but on arriving at his destination he was penniless, robbers on the road having taken his money. He was cordially welcomed by the Baptists, and his loss made good. The chapel in which he preached was, for those days, an attractive-looking building. On entering the iron gates a visitor passed on through a pretty avenue of lime-trees. There Keach laboured amid many difficulties until the atmosphere of the religious world was cleared by the Revolution. The meetings were often disturbed by representatives of the law, and when liberty of conscience was ensured by the accession of William III., other troubles disturbed the peace of the congregation. The pastor was in favour of introducing the practice of singing hymns during public worship; but others were so violently opposed to what they believed to be a mere anti-Christian innovation that they seceded, and founded a rival congregation. Others were for observing Saturday as the true Sabbath; and it was this latter agitation which led to the publication of Keach's book on "The Jewish Sabbath abrogated." Keach was much loved by his people, and till the last maintained a spotless character. The labours in which he engaged were so abundant that he was quite worn out at the time of his death, in the summer of 1704. He had a son named Elias, who planted two Baptist churches in Pennsylvania and afterwards preached at Wapping. With the death of Benjamin Keach the Puritan age of the church may be said to have closed. How sincerely he was mourned is shown by a broadside poem issued at the time in accordance with a practice then common :—

> "Is he no more? has heaven withdrawn his light,
> And left us to lament in sable shades of night
> Our loss?
> Death boasts his triumph, for the rumour's spread
> Through Salem's plains, KEACH, dear KEACH, is dead."

In all, Keach left over forty published works; and while one of these, "The Rector Rectified," shows his taste for controversy, the best remembered is his "Key to open Scripture Metaphors." His remains were laid to rest in a graveyard owned by the Baptists in the Park, Southwark. Hence the future name of New Park Street, in which was situated the chapel wherein Mr. Spurgeon opened his London ministry a century and a half later.

Keach had a son-in-law, named Benjamin Stinton, who now became pastor of the church. The responsible office was accepted very reluctantly, however, for Stinton was at this time thirty years old, and he had received no proper training for ministerial work. He did the best he could under the circumstances: he studied hard under a competent tutor, and was soon able to discharge, in more than a creditable manner, the duties required of him. The old Baptist historian, Thomas Crosby, speaks of him as "a very painful and laborious minister of the Gospel," adding that, "though he had not the advantage of an academical education, yet by his own industry, under the assistance of the famous Mr. Ainsworth (author of the Latin Dictionary), after he had taken upon him the ministerial office, he acquired a good degree of knowledge in the languages and other useful parts of literature, which added lustre to those natural endowments which were very conspicuous in him."

Mr. Stinton was zealous as a pastor, and, although we do not know very much about him, he was a commanding figure in the Southwark of the days of Queen Anne and of the earlier part of the reign of George I. The pastor was before his times; and it was not until the Protestant Succession had triumphed by the Crown passing to the House of Brunswick that a charity-school for Dissenters could be established. He also collected materials for a work on the denominational annals, and these appear to have been largely used by Crosby in the compilation of his History. Neal, the historian of the Puritans, also had the papers in his possession for several years, but without making any particular use of them. Another distinguished piece of service on the part of Benjamin Stinton was the part he took in founding the Baptist Fund in the year 1717. This fund remains until our own day; and Mr. Spurgeon, being one of the trustees, always manifested becoming interest in its welfare on account of the eminent service rendered by the distribution of a large sum annually amongst aged or necessitous ministers.

The death of Benjamin Stinton occasioned a division in the congregation, through one section wishing to have William Arnold for his successor, while the choice of others fell upon John Gill, of Kettering, who was then a youth very nearly corresponding in age to Mr. Spurgeon when he left Waterbeach. The chapel was then in Goat Street; but some time afterwards a more convenient building was erected in Unicorn Yard. This was at length forsaken, in 1757, for the chapel in Carter Lane, Tooley Street, and this was the place of meeting until its removal necessitated the building of New Park Street Chapel. Should any-one be interested in discovering the site of this eighteenth century chapel, it may be seen at the south end of London Bridge, at the entrance to the railway-station yard.

John Gill, who now succeeded to the pastorate which he retained for more than fifty years, was a native of Kettering, and was born in 1697. In childhood and youth he was famed for his genius and acquirements; and a proverb which became current among the market people indicated his general character—"As surely as John Gill is in the bookseller's shop." Immediately after his birth, a stranger who happened to be passing is said to have voluntarily made the prophecy that the child would become a great scholar. He began to preach in 1716, and soon attracted some attention. It is possible, however, that he may have been too hard a Calvinist for some of the critical hearers of Southwark, who raised a loud outcry against his election, and would not rest until they had submitted their case to the ministerial *coterie* which then assembled at the Hanover Coffee-house. The only thing to do was for each section of disputants to retain its man, and live in peace with those who thought differently from themselves. The fact was, that those who objected to the young preacher were as little aware of his power as those who at first thought little of Mr. Spurgeon were aware of his wonderful gifts. Although John Gill was not a Spurgeon, he soon established his claim to rank as the foremost man of his denomination. Apart from his idiosyncrasies, he was one of the best scholars of his time, and, judged by the quantity he wrote, its most industrious author. When it was customary to live in the City, he found a congenial home in Gracechurch Street. In tastes and habits he was a man of the eighteenth century.

As a Hebrew scholar Dr. Gill had few equals among his contemporaries. The Baptist Fund, which still annually supplies a

number of young pastors with grants of books, assisted him to
purchase a valuable collection of Hebrew works; and being
competent to read the Talmud and the Targums in the original,
Gill turned this advantage to excellent account. He read
systematically with a view to the exposition of Scripture, and after
more than twenty years of labour commenced the publication of
that voluminous commentary which originally extended through nine
folio volumes. This achievement won for its author the distinction
of Doctor in Divinity, the diploma coming from Marischal College,
Aberdeen. The work also attracted the admiring notice of the
pious Hervey, to whom the annotations on Solomon's Song, more
especially, were "a paradisiacal garden." Of the honour which
came to him from the Scottish University, Dr. Gill spoke in a
characteristic way when he remarked, "I neither thought it, nor
bought it, nor sought it."

While as a commentator he had accomplishments which were
peculiar to himself, Dr. Gill was also an ardent controversialist.
Such was his unceasing industry that a proverb which now became
current in London was to the effect, "As surely as Dr. Gill is
in his study." On a certain day he was not in his sanctum,
however; but his temporary absence seemed to be providential when
a heavy stack of chimneys crashed through the roof and shattered
the writing-table. The doctor appears not to have possessed even
the elementary social qualities; he had lived as a recluse in his
study until he seemed to have little or no talent for conversation.
To Samuel Johnson, who was then passing his time in London, and
who made talking about the chief business of life, this would have
looked like a serious drawback to life itself. The London of the
middle of the last century, when traders and merchants who had
their businesses in the City lived there, seems to have attractions
of its own as we look back upon it. What a centre of social
enjoyment such a town must have been when a large circle of
friends all lived within the bounds of so comparatively small an
area! Thus while Dr. Gill lived in Gracechurch Street, his son-in-

law and publisher, George Keith, was at the "Bible and Crown" hard by. Other friends, who were also booksellers, were found in Mr. Ward of the "King's Head," in Little Britain, and Mr. Whiteridge, of Castle Alley, near the Royal Exchange. The age seems to have been a more social one than our own, and that may have been because people had more leisure. Everybody of any importance had perforce to belong to some club or *coterie;* and, despite his shyness in conversation, the presence of Dr. Gill was necessary to make complete the circle of the club whose members met at the Gloucestershire Coffee-house. Then there was the weekly dinner which Mr. Thomas Watson, of Cripplegate, gave regularly on Tuesdays to Nonconformist ministers of every denomination. The members of the church also had a grand dinner at Christmas, when the wants of the poor were the appropriate topic of conversation.

In his later days Dr. Gill lived at Camberwell; but though his strength was well maintained, and he could till the last read the smallest print without glasses, he survived long enough to see the congregation to which he ministered decline. The people, who valued his ministry as greatly as ever, would have engaged an assistant; but he persistently objected to such an arrangement. "Christ gave pastors, but not co-pastors," he said; and that was an intimation that nothing more was to be said on so distasteful a subject.

In the middle of the eighteenth century psalmody in Nonconformist chapels appears to have been in a very primitive condition; and while £4 a year was considered a good salary for a pew-opener, a mere precentor had to be content with an annual stipend of forty shillings. It is hardly to be wondered at that, in such a case, persons with musical ears were able to detect flaws in the singing. One worthy woman, in particular, was moved to ask that some improvements might be introduced, and to effect her purpose she boldly waited on the commentator himself. When he had listened to her well-founded complaints respecting the precentor's shortcomings,

Dr. Gill asked, "What tunes would you like, good woman?" "Why, sir, I should very much like David's tunes," responded the old lady. "Well, if you will get David's tunes for us, we will try to sing them," replied the doctor.

As a pastor and preacher, the good doctor met with experiences such as might have happened to Mr. Spurgeon himself a century later. There was a man who, after sermon, would meet the pastor at the foot of the pulpit stairs with the question, "Is this preaching?" or, "Is this the great Dr. Gill?" The doctor was not one to be very much irritated by such annoyances; but on one occasion he said rather brusquely, "Go up and do better!" Those were also the days when even Baptist ministers wore the white bands, which imparted to them a very ecclesiastical appearance. A lady at one time became so profoundly impressed with the length of the doctor's bibs, that soon afterwards she called at his residence, armed with a pair of scissors, and asked to be allowed to shorten them. Consent was readily given; but when the bands were reduced to the approved length the doctor remarked, "Now, my good sister, you must do me a good turn also." Consent being given, the pastor went on, "You have something about you which is a great deal too long," and having borrowed the scissors to use as he pleased, he added, with grim emphasis, "Come, then, good sister, put out your tongue!"

Dr. Gill died in October, 1771, and was buried in Bunhill Fields. Many funeral sermons on his life and work were published. Toplady, who was well acquainted with him, regarded him as the greatest divine of his age, and not merely the leading man of the Baptist body.

When a successor had to be elected to the great commentator, the choice of the majority of the people fell on John Rippon, then a student at Bristol College, and twenty years old. A body of members seceded, but, as the pastor moved that they should have a sum of £300 voted to them to aid them in building a chapel, an excellent spirit prevailed. In time the seceders may have discovered their mistake; for the church they had left prospered.

Dr. Rippon had neither the gifts nor the acquirements of his predecessor, but his character commanded respect, and he was a man of great industry. The church and congregation grew in numbers and in wealth; and the high position the pastor was supposed to occupy caused his opinion to carry great weight in all denominational councils. In a degenerate age discipline appears to have been well maintained; and such diversions as theatre-going, card-playing, dancing, etc., were rigorously proscribed. The members were expected to avoid even such a place as Vauxhall Gardens— then a very fashionable recreation-ground. Nor might enthusiasts presume to teach religion without receiving proper license. One excellent characteristic of the well-to-do people was their liberality to the poor; for not only were these liberally dealt with in general, but Dr. Rippon, in the year 1803, founded the almshouses which on being rebuilt were afterwards endowed by Mr. Spurgeon with a sum of £5,000. The old chapel had to be enlarged in 1792, and the fact that at that time a collection on a special occasion would amount to £40 or £50 shows the comfortable circumstances of the congregation.

Though not possessing talents of the first order, Dr. Rippon showed some literary ambition. His compilation of hymns was for long exceedingly popular, and the copyright was equivalent to a large estate. Among his unpublished works is a full history of Bunhill Fields burial-grounds, the MS. of which is still preserved.*

The pastorate of Dr. Rippon was one of the longest on record; it extended through the sixty-three years ending with 1836. He was over eighty when the first stone of New Park Street Chapel was laid in the spring of 1832, and he was present at the opening some months later, although he is supposed to have outlived his usefulness. The compulsory turning-out of the people from the old sanctuary at Carter Lane to seek a home in a damp, low-lying locality like New Park Street, was a genuine disaster. The site

* I believe that this work may be seen at the Heralds' College, Doctors' Commons, and that it extends through twelve folio volumes.

was a most out-of-the-way place for a chapel, and the disadvantages
attending it were so many that Mr. Spurgeon might well find the
congregation seemingly on the verge of extinction when, twenty
years later, he first visited the uninviting locality. When the builders
of the present London Bridge necessarily swept away many buildings, there was naturally a keen competition for other sites, and
New Park Street was probably chosen by the builders of the new
chapel because the land was cheap and was near the old river.

Dr. Rippon was succeeded in the pastorate by the present Dr.
Joseph Angus, of Regent's Park College, who at that time was a
youth only twenty-one years of age—the time-honoured custom of
the church in choosing a very young pastor, when one had to be
selected, being still maintained. He was a native of Newcastle, and
after attending the Grammar School in that town he studied successively at Stepney College and the University of Edinburgh. It was
while at New Park Street that Mr. Angus produced his prize essay
on "Church Establishments." This was in reply to the views of
Dr. Chalmers on the same subject, set forth by the Edinburgh Professor in lectures delivered in London. Dr. Angus resigned his
charge in 1840 to accept the secretaryship of the Baptist Missionary
Society.

From 1841 to 1850 the pastorate was held by Mr. James Smith,
who had been stationed at Cheltenham, and who again returned to
that town. He was a good preacher and the author of a large
number of printed works. The air of London did not suit him;
but though he at last acted on medical advice and sought a purer
air, he died in 1861, at the comparatively early age of fifty-nine.
He was succeeded by Mr. William Walters, of Preston, who afterwards removed to Birmingham, and who had only recently resigned
when Mr. Spurgeon was invited to occupy the vacant pulpit.

It will be seen from this outline that the church and congregation
of which Mr. Spurgeon was invited to accept the pastorate was
just about two hundred years old when the young preacher left
Waterbeach. He was proud of his predecessors, and in his early

days, more particularly, he would refer at times to Dr. Gill with great satisfaction. It will be observed that the election of a new pastor, when the need arose, nearly always occasioned a division; but the seceders soon saw that the fears which prompted their action were groundless. It was also a singular thing that the pastors should successively have been so often chosen at or about the age of twenty, to be retained till death. Probably no other congregation in the country could show a record in which only two pastors were elected during the space of one hundred and seventeen years. Thus Dr. Gill occupied the pastorate in 1719, and his successor, Dr. Rippon, held on until 1836. The next longest pastorate was that of Mr. Spurgeon himself, which extended to almost thirty-eight years.

When Dr. Gill arrived in London the Dissenters were troubled by disputes concerning the Trinity. As the eighteenth century advanced many congregations drifted from their old moorings of orthodox belief; but these Baptists of Southwark went on unaffected by the passing storms.

CHAPTER XVI.

FIRST MONTHS IN LONDON.

Beginning of the Work in London—The First Printed Sermon—Spurgeon's Relations with his Brother Ministers—Paxton Hood's Opinion—Mr. Spurgeon's Style—Popularising the Gospel—Resolve to enlarge New Park Street Chapel—An American Divine's Estimate—Mr. Spurgeon and the Pastor of Helensburgh.

MR. SPURGEON'S great work in London was now fairly begun. After a few weeks it was seen that the six months' probation agreed upon would be needless, and hence an invitation to the pastorate was given and accepted. Some time necessarily had to elapse before the great outlying world became aware of the presence of a pulpit phenomenon in a back street of Southwark; the news spread, nevertheless, for thus early the young preacher's sermons began to be sent abroad in large numbers by means of the printing-press. The earliest printed sermon I have discovered is No. 2,234 of *The Penny Pulpit*, entitled " Harvest Time," and preached at New Park Street on August 20, 1854. It seems that the numbers, as they appeared at irregular intervals, at once commanded a large circle of readers, and this was the reason that, in the first week of 1855, the regular weekly issue was commenced. Not only did hearers in the pews perceive a novelty in the preacher's manner, there was a novelty about the style as the sermon appeared in print which captivated the reader. From the first, Mr. Spurgeon well understood that the heart had to be touched if any good was to be done.

As illustrative of his style at this time take this passage from one of the earliest published sermons, " A View of God's Glory " :—

"I can say no more concerning God's goodness. But this is not all that Moses saw. If you look to the words which follow my text, you will see that God said, 'I will make all My goodness pass before thee.' But there was something more. No one attribute of God sets God out to perfection; there must always be another. He said, ' I will be gracious to whom I will be gracious, and will show mercy on whom I will show mercy.' There is another attribute of God. There is His sovereignty. God's goodness without His sovereignty does not completely set forth His nature. I think of the man who, when he was dying, called me to see him. He said, 'I am going to heaven.' 'Well,' I replied, 'what makes you think you are going there?—for you never thought of it before.' Said he, 'God is good.' 'Yes,' I answered, 'but God is just.' 'No,' said he, 'God is merciful and good.' Now that poor creature was dying and being lost for ever, for he had not a right conception of God. He had only one idea of God—that God is good; but that is not enough. If you only see one attribute, you have only half a God. God is good, and He is a sovereign and doeth what He pleases; and though good to all in the sense of benevolence, He is not obliged to be good to any. 'I will be gracious to whom I will be gracious, and show mercy to whom I will show mercy.' Do not you be alarmed, my friends, because I am going to preach about sovereignty. I know some people, when they hear about sovereignty, say, 'Oh, we are going to have some terrible high doctrine!' Well, if it is in the Bible, that is enough for you. Is not that all you want to know? If God says, 'I will be gracious to whom I will be gracious, and will show mercy to whom I will show mercy,' it is not for you to say it is high doctrine. Who told you it is high doctrine? It is good doctrine. What right have you to call one doctrine high and one low? Would you like me to have a Bible with 'H' against high and 'L' against low, so that I could leave the high doctrine out and please you? My Bible has no mark of that kind; it says, 'I will be gracious to whom I will be gracious.' There is Divine sovereignty. I believe some are afraid to say anything about this great doctrine, lest they should offend some of their people; but, my friends, it is true, and you *shall* hear it. God is a sovereign. He was a sovereign ere He made this world. He lived alone, and this was in His mind, 'Shall I make anything, or shall I not? I have a right to make creatures or not to make any.' He resolved that He would fashion a world. When He made it, He had a right to form the world in what size and shape He pleased; and He had a right, if He chose, to leave the globe untenanted by a single creature. When He had resolved to make man, He had a right to make him whatever kind of creature He liked. If He wished to make him a worm or a serpent, He had a right to do it. When He made him He had a right to put any command on him that He pleased; and God had a right to say to Adam, 'Thou shall not touch that forbidden tree.' And when Adam offended, God had a right to punish *him* and all the race for ever in the bottomless pit. God is so far sovereign that He has a right, if He likes, to save anyone in this chapel, or to crush all who are here. He has a right to take us all to heaven, if He pleases, or to destroy us. He has a right to do just as He pleases with us. We are as much in His hands as prisoners in the hands of her Majesty when they are condemned for a capital offence against the law of the land; yea, as much as clay in the hands of the potter. This is what He asserted when He said, 'I will be gracious to whom I will be gracious, and I will show mercy on whom I will show mercy.' This stirs up your carnal pride, does it not? Men want to be somebody. They do not like to lie down before God and have it preached to them that God can do just as He wills with them. Ah! you may hate it, but it is what the Scripture tells us. Surely it is self-evident that God may do as He will with His own. We all like to do as we will with our own property. God has said that if you go to His throne He will hear you; but He has a right not to do it if He likes. He has a right to do just as He pleases. If He chose to let you go on in the error of your ways, that is His right; and if He says, as He does, 'Come unto Me all ye that are weary and are heavy laden, and I will give you rest,' it is His right to do so. That is the high and awful doctrine of Divine sovereignty."*

Mr. Spurgeon was so thoroughly well acquainted with human nature that he knew just what humanity wanted; and he preached the Gospel with a freedom and a fulness which had not been out-rivalled since the eighteenth century revival preachers. At the same

* Quoted in *The Earthen Vessel*, x. 279-280, from *The Penny Pulpit*, 1854.

time, he was most remarkably situated, quite apart from his popularity. In the year 1854 no Baptist weekly newspaper existed in the British Isles, and the idea of attempting to found such an organ was regarded as being somewhat Utopian. There were several Nonconformist journals, however, each conducted with great ability; but so far as my own investigation has gone, the editors did not consider that the youthful innovator was worthy of much recognition. Mr. Spurgeon's friend of after years, the late Dr. John Campbell, was then reigning at Bolt Court as chief of *The British Banner*; but from New Year's Day to December 31 of that memorable year the name of Spurgeon has not been discovered in the paper. The various denominational gatherings were, of course, held in due course —those of the Baptists, as well as of the Independents, being pretty fully reported; but the shadow of the pastor of New Park Street Chapel cannot be traced. He was shunned by many of his brethren who ought to have accorded him the heartiest of welcomes; and then it very naturally followed that he shunned them in return.* The treatment which Mr. Spurgeon received from his brethren in the ministry at this time struck the late Mr. Paxton Hood as being remarkable. "Shall we say 'brethren in the ministry'?" said Mr. Hood, who had the sense to see where the shoe pinched. He had strong doubts whether they really were brethren of Mr. Spurgeon in the Scriptural sense; for he was obliged to add: "We understand they have pretty generally agreed to regard him as a black sheep. His character is good—unexceptionable; his doctrines have no dangerous heresy in them; still he is tabooed. . . . No; usually the ministers have not admired his advent; the tens of thousands of persons who flock to hear the youth preach his strong,

---

* On October 17, 1855, six ministers, out of thirty-three churches which then represented the London Association, met at the Baptist Mission-house. "Alas, 'how hath the fine gold become dim,'" says *The Baptist Messenger*. "Who can wonder at the low state of the churches when the princes among the people are thus negligent and supine?" It is then added: "The Rev. A. C. Thoas, of Islington, is appointed to preach the annual sermon, and the Rev. C. H. Spurgeon to be chairman; the Revs. Messrs. Katterns and Harcourt are to deliver the addresses at the annual public meeting of the Association, to be held at New Park Street Chapel."—*The Baptist Messenger*, iii. 122.

nervous Gospel do not at all conciliate them—perhaps rather exasperate them." *

In point of fact, the prejudice against this youthful innovator was far stronger than people at this distance of time can realise. It was illustrated in a painful, and yet somewhat comical, way at a country anniversary about this time. One of the most eminent of the London ministers was engaged to preach in the evening; but on hearing that Mr. Spurgeon was to take the morning service the great man at once declined to risk having his reputation tarnished by association with him. Jealousy of another's success is always a symptom of a mean mind, and it seems to be especially mean when entertained towards one who successfully preaches the Gospel. If the elder ministers were jealous of Mr. Spurgeon, however, there was plenty to stimulate their envy. Others had from time to time come to London to be successful in their chosen work; but no such popularity as was now manifesting itself had been known during the centuries which had elapsed since the primitive age. We find it spoken of as "a kind of madness, and a mania, most extraordinary in itself, but the more so because it is certainly difficult to discover on what the excitement is based." Probably the people themselves could have given a more satisfactory explanation than the professional critics.

There was nothing which Mr. Paxton Hood liked better than hearing first one and then another of the great preachers of his day, whether in London or in the provinces. About this time he was naturally attracted by Spurgeon, and being unable to afford any time on a Sunday, he made his way to New Park Street Chapel on a Thursday evening. The time for commencing was seven o'clock, but the doors were opened at half-past six, and to make sure of a place, the expectant hearer took care to be one of the crowd which assembled before the doors were opened. Though this was only a week-night service, the people thronged the building, so that at a quarter to seven the

* "Lamps of the Temple," p. 544.

pews were not merely crowded, but those unable to obtain seats were standing in the aisles. Mr. Hood also tells us that, "of course, on the Sabbath the crowd is far greater—the crush at the doors sometimes fearful." Thus popular at home, the preacher seemed to be, if possible, still more popular in other parts of London or in the provinces. If he preached in any one of the largest sanctuaries that existed, such, for example, as Finsbury Chapel, the admission had to be by ticket; but this was at a somewhat later period. In provincial towns the desire to hear Spurgeon was even more striking. Such was the popular curiosity that people would leave their work, or they would attend at any unseasonable hours, in order to see and hear for themselves the pulpit phenomenon from South-wark. When he first visited Bristol, it was commonly reported that people listened with wonder; and that if a building in the western city capable of accommodating ten thousand persons could have been secured, every seat would have been occupied. People began to endeavour to account for his popularity. He was thought to owe something to his enemies as well as his friends. Hence, we find it said, "He is flattered by a hurricane of acrimonious remark and abuse, and perhaps owes his popularity in no small degree to this sweeping condemnation." One of his characteristics was that he could hold his own, and sometimes he paid back his detractors in their own coin with interest. Mr. Hood's sketch of the Park Street pastor in his early days is drawn with a good deal of discrimination :—

"One thing is certain, Spurgeon's back is broad, and his skin is thick; he can, we fancy, bear a good deal, and bear a good deal without wincing. . . . He is the topic and theme of remark now in every part of England, and severe as some of his castigators are, he returns their castigations frequently with a careless, downright, hearty goodwill. Beyond a doubt the lad is impudent, very impudent; were he not, he could not, at such an age, be where he is, or what he is. We were greatly amazed, as we stood at his chapel doors waiting to enter, to see him, as he came and passed along to the vestry, repeatedly lift his hat and bow again and again to his waiting auditors: there was so much audacious, good-natured simplicity, both in the act itself and in the face of the actor, that we could not help smiling right heartily. It was evident he was not indisposed to appropriate to himself a considerable amount of personal homage. His face is not coarse, but there is no refinement in it; it is a square face; his forehead is square; we were wishing, albeit we are not phrenologists, that it had evidenced a little more benevolence of character. But

THE OLD MANSE AND MEETING HOUSE, STAMBOURNE.

THE OLD CHAPEL AT WATERBEACH.

there is a good-nature in the face—something which looks, even on so youthful a countenance, like *bonhomie;* certainly it does not look earnest, nor does earnestness, in the *highest* sense, belong to his individuality. That he is in earnest we do not for a moment doubt; but at present we may doubt whether his earnestness has within it deep capabilities. He may preach after the manner of Peter, but he cannot doubt and suffer like Thomas, nor flame like Paul, nor love like John."*

Those old days of nearly forty years ago, when Mr. Spurgeon had just opened his career in London, have been represented as the age of young men; but then men of extraordinary capacity commonly begin their life-work early. It has been shown how this happened in the case of Mr. Spurgeon's predecessors in the pastorate; and at the date in question, people recalled to mind how such admirable preachers as John Angell James, Thomas Spencer, of Liverpool, and William Jay, had all accepted pastorates at an age when others are commonly at college. Thus readiness to work at an exceptionally early age showed the possession of exceptional talents; and some thought that in Mr. Spurgeon's case his impudence alone was a talent. In illustration of this Mr. Hood has a piquant anecdote :—

"Mr. Spurgeon is characterised rather by celerity than intensity—nimbleness rather than insight. He adroitly seizes all things, and adapts and arranges them to suit his purpose. What he is able to receive, he digests well. He gave a most impudent answer the other day to a London minister who came to hear him preach on a week-day morning in one of the large chapels of London. It is probable that there was a good deal of impudence in the brother to whom he spoke; for ministers can be impudent, and some of them, when they like, insolent. 'I can't make it out,' said the minister, 'when you study, brother Spurgeon. When do you make your sermons?' 'Oh,' Spurgeon is reported to have replied, 'I am always studying; I am sucking in something from everything; if you were to ask me home to dine with you, I should suck a sermon out of you.'"†

There were those who talked about the young preacher's models; but it was evident to more shrewd observers that he was too much of a cosmopolitan to slavishly follow any mere human standards, although, without doubt, that fine standard of good English, the Authorised Version of the Bible, had greatly influenced his style. To suppose that either Jay or Robert Hall was his chief master was absurd. Paxton Hood professed to have made the discovery that Spurgeon was "not at all qualified to shine in the brilliant

* "Lamps of the Temple," pp. 545–546.
† *Ibid.*, p. 547.

J

intellectual firmament" in which Mr. Hall had had his place; but would anyone now deny that the young pastor of New Park Street was by far the greater genius? To say that he had some of the best traits of Hervey, Berridge, and Rowland Hill might be true; but what was chiefly true was that this man knew how to speak to the common people in plain but forcible language. It was well said, "The popularity of Mr. Spurgeon is to be traced greatly to his homeliness of manner. The people love to see that when it is real and not assumed; and how little we have of it!" The time had come when the Gospel needed to be popularised; and in Mr. Spurgeon the man was found to do it. He cared nothing for the mere flowers of rhetoric in which the representatives of the old school he was superseding so greatly delighted; but illustrations gathered fresh from nature, or appropriated by him during his contact with the world, had a rare charm for him, and they had a still greater charm for the crowds he addressed. The people had found what they wanted, and Mr Spurgeon's unique popularity was the best proof of how they rejoiced in what they had found.

When observers of this remarkable success—so unexampled in all respects—asked of one another whether it would last, whether such a man would wear during many years, the unwavering faith and easy naturalness of the young preacher should have checked any misgiving. As the year 1854 went on, even the war abroad and the alarming ravages of pestilence in London could not hinder ever-increasing attention being given to the ministrations of the pastor of New Park Street Chapel. The newspapers at last began to notice him, while still more conclusive evidence of his popularity was seen in artistic caricatures. The majority of those who ventured on making prophecies lived long enough to find themselves mistaken; but Mr. Paxton Hood very sagaciously gauged the situation :—

"Our preacher's fulness and readiness is to our minds a guarantee that he will wear, and not wear out. His present amazing popularity will, of course, subside, but he will still be amazingly followed, and what he is now, we prophesy, will on the whole remain. For polished diction we shall not look to him; for the long and stately argument we shall not look to him; for the original and profound thought we shall not look to him; for the clear and lucid criticism we shall not look to him; but for bold, convincing statements of Evangelical truth, for a faithful grappling with convictions, for happy and pertinent illustrations, for graphic description, and for searching common-sense, we shall look, and we believe we shall seldom look in vain. In a word, he preaches not to metaphysicians or logicians; neither to poets nor to *savants*; to masters of erudition or masters of rhetoric; he preaches to men. Fastidiousness holds up its hands horrified. The Intelligence of the Age is quite shocked. If Oxford should hear of him, and condescend to listen, it will musingly compliment Dissent by saying it's just what it thought of the horrid thing. The young B.A. of the London University will regard him as a dreadful apparition, and will hasten into his study to compose an elaborate essay for the rising watering-place of Small-tooth-comb, ' On the Foolishness of Preaching.' The religious beau, who would wish to pass muster among Christians if he may be allowed his cigar, his glass, and his seat midway between the chapel pew and the chair of the scorner, will look into Park Street, but pronounce the discourse decidedly very vulgar. *The Christian Wasp*, the organ of the large and influential body of Arminian Rationalists, will purchase one of the preacher's sermons in *The Penny Pulpit*, and construct an elaborate review to prove that looking at God as we look at the sun, through a logical telescope, is the best test of religious life and truth; and that as man is free to be good whenever he likes, Spurgeon is shockingly wrong because he intimates that man is as free to fly to God as a stone to the sun. Meantime, our preacher will pursue his way, we trust, entangling himself with none of their criticisms, but saying the word in all plainness which God shall give him to utter." *

Whatever people might say about their pastor, however, and whether critics were severe or generous, the difficulty of the good deacons at New Park Street was no longer associated with empty pews, but with the crowds which, at night especially, when the gas was alight, made the heat of the chapel terribly oppressive. The pastor, who was such a lover of fresh, pure air, might seek temporary relief by putting his stick through a pane of glass; but, if possible, something else would have to be done. The site of the chapel made it possible for an enlargement to be carried out; and before the young preacher had been many months in his new pastorate, funds for carrying out this enterprise were being collected. It may have occurred to some discerning people even thus early that the mere enlargement of an old chapel would never meet the requirements of the case; and that a chapel larger than any that had ever before been·erected would have to be provided.

The phenomenon was the more unaccountable because there were people, passing for shrewd observers, who did not discover in the preacher what they would have regarded as necessary qualifications

* " Lamps of the Temple," pp. 584–585.

for popularity. One American writer who attempted to depict Mr. Spurgeon as he was at this time says:—"He was unpractised in either the art of oratory or of preaching, his public efforts having consisted of addresses before Sunday-schools, and a very brief but successful pastorate over an obscure Baptist Church at Waterbeach. In personal appearance he was not prepossessing; in style he was plain, practical, simple; in manner, rude, bold, egotistical, approaching to the bigoted; in theology, a deep-dyed Calvinist; in Church relations, an uncompromising Baptist. We could scarcely imagine a more unpromising list of qualifications, or rather disqualifications, for public favour."

One of the first to recognise and acknowledge the great abilities of Mr. Spurgeon is said to have been the late Mr. John Anderson, who was pastor of the Free Church at Helensburgh; and it was out of compliment to that friend that Mr. Spurgeon's house in Nightingale Lane, Clapham, was called after the name of the Scottish town. Mr. Anderson's opinion was that all would have to yield Mr. Spurgeon the honour of being the chief preacher of the day. A warm friendship soon afterwards sprang up between the two pastors, as will be shown; the Scotch divine loved to meet his friend in London; and Mr. Spurgeon would occasionally be found in after years conducting a service on the lawn in front of the Free Church Manse at Helensburgh. Scotland appears to have been holiday-ground which was always appreciated; and though they were not hasty in making their decision, the Scottish people at last became among the most devoted of his admirers. In after years, however, what were called holidays in the North were little other than preaching tours.

CHAPTER XVII.

MR. SPURGEON'S FIRST PRINTED SERMON.

National Difficulties—Spurgeon's unwavering Faith—Detractors' false Stories—A Service at
New Park Street Chapel—A Harvest Discourse.

ALTHOUGH the summer of the year 1854 appears to have been a trying time in many respects, with unwavering faith in God the pastor of New Park Street Chapel went on his way, apparently unaffected by the public trials which arose from pestilence and war, an oppressively high income-tax, dear bread, and an increase of pauperism. If he had a special mission to accomplish, he would be specially protected while carrying it out. To preach like Spurgeon did at this time, and in the intervals of preaching to devote hours to the visitation of the plague-stricken members of the church, who had a first claim on his regard, had the appearance of genuine heroism. Here, at all events, was a God-called minister of the Gospel.

In the meantime, in London itself by day, in the suburbs of an evening after business hours, and in villages and towns of the more distant provinces, what a talk there was concerning this young man's work, and of the daring, original way in which he did it. The present writer was then living in Somersetshire; and he remembers on a certain day the late Mr. Sutton, of Watchet—a veteran who had served with honour in the mission field of India—coming to his father and commencing a conversation about Spurgeon; and, having read the printed sermons, Mr. Sutton added, "But he can never keep on like this!" Mr. Paxton Hood calls attention to the fact that at this time the discourses were very unequal. This was inevitable; for no preacher, public speaker, or writer can at all times maintain one level uniform standard of excellence.

Nothing was more striking than the way in which early detractors had to change their tone. Thus the late Dr. Binney was one who

at first regarded his younger neighbour with dislike, and there is
reason for thinking that he was the "eminent London minister," mentioned by Mr. Hood, who refused to become associated at a country
anniversary with the young man from New Park Street. It was not
long, however, before Dr. Binney, while addressing some students,
had to confess: "I myself have enjoyed some amount of popularity;
I have always been able to draw together a congregation; but in
the person of Mr. Spurgeon we see a young man, be he who he
may, and come whence he will, who at twenty-four hours' notice
can command a congregation of twenty thousand people. Now, I
have never been able to do that, and I never knew of anyone else
who could do it."

The stories which soon began to be circulated about Mr. Spurgeon
were, of course, numerous; the majority were more or less amusing;
but the drawback was that so many of these personal tit-bits
were untrue. Many years ago, a friend of the late pastor showed
how these idle tales were circulated and often garnished by those
who told them. "I was for a time at a well-known health resort
on the south coast. At the *table d'hôte* I sat next to a young
married lady, who was, alas! consumptive, and of that temperament
which is so common in such cases, *très spirituelle*, and very learned
and accomplished. You may be sure she never lacked auditors for
her lively conversation. At dessert one day she was 'telling stories,'
in the juvenile and literal sense of the phrase, about yourself. I
let her go on for some time until I thought the fun was getting a
little too fast, and then I said: 'I hope, Mrs. ——, you do not
believe the stories you are detailing, because I assure you I heard
nearly all of them in my childhood before Mr. Spurgeon was born,
and that most of them were attributed to Rowland Hill—doubtless
with equal lack of authenticity.' She looked me calmly in the face,
with a very comical expression, and replied: 'Oh, Mr. ——, we
never ask whether such stories are true; it is quite sufficient if we
find them amusing.' 'Well,' I said, 'so long as that is understood
all round, by all means keep on.'" This was one of the penalties

of popularity to which Mr. Spurgeon submitted with as much grace
as could have been expected under the circumstances.

Having thus taken notice of so many things connected with the
preacher, or with his contemporaries and the times, I will now
suppose that the reader is about to accompany me to New Park
Street Chapel, where we shall hear the young preacher for ourselves.
It is Sunday, August 20, and, despite the summer weather which
is tempting people abroad to hear the popular preacher, our minds
do not escape the depressing influences of the times. Parliament
having just been prorogued, the London season is coming to an end.
The scourge, no doubt, chiefly affects what are called the lower orders;
but in one instance, at least, when Lord Jocelyn actually died in
Lord Palmerston's drawing-room, it has rudely stalked into the
world of fashion itself. The armies in the Crimea are also finding
it a more destructive foe than the Russians, for thousands of the
French and hundreds of the English have died of it. To escape
forthwith into the country, instead of seeking out the damp, low-
lying back street in Southwark where Mr. Spurgeon will preach,
might seem to be the wiser thing to do; but we will, for this
once, at least, go with the crowd.

The preacher strikes you as being somewhat pale and even
younger-looking than you had anticipated, but there is nothing
about him which will add to the depression consequent upon the
sombre nature of the times. On the contrary, many a troubled soul
will on this morning find the New Park Street sanctuary just such a
quiet resting-place as they desire. In any case, that appears to be the
young pastor's wish; he will endeavour to raise the people to something higher, rather than depress them by talking about dark topics.
You notice that the hymns are of the old-fashioned kind, and are
selected from Dr. Rippon's book; the reading of Scripture is
animated, and you are struck with the freshness of the exposition
with which it is accompanied. The prayer is remarkable for its
fervour and naturalness, reminding you of a truthful child speaking
to his father.

Then you are in a state of expectancy for the sermon; and you are pleased to find that the preacher has been studying a seasonable subject, but of the brighter kind. In the country around Colchester and Stambourne the farmers and their labourers have been gathering in the wheat, barley, and oats; and the sweet Essex fields have been such a contrast to the London cholera-stricken streets that the youth in the pulpit has been refreshing his mind by dwelling upon their charms. Turn with him to 1 Samuel xii. 17, and you have the text: "Is it not wheat harvest to-day?" Now listen well, and you will not go away wondering what it is that makes Mr. Spurgeon so popular:—*

"I shall not notice the connection, but I shall simply take these words as a motto; and my sermon will be founded upon a harvest-field. I shall rather use the harvest for my text than any passage that I find here. 'Is it not wheat harvest to-day?' I suppose the dwellers in cities think less of times and seasons than dwellers in the country. Men who were born, trained up, nourished, and nurtured among corn-fields, harvests, sowings, and reapings, are more likely to notice such things than you who are always engaged in mercantile pursuits, and think less of these things than rustics do. But I suppose if it is almost necessary that you should less regard the 'harvest' than others, it ought not to be carried to too great an extent. Let us not be forgetful of 'times and seasons.' There is much to be learnt from them, and I would refresh your memories this morning by a harvest-field. What a wondrous temple this world is; for in truth it is a temple of God's building, wherein men ought to worship Him. What a wondrous temple it is to a mind spiritually enlightened, which can bring to bear upon it the resources of intellect and the illuminations of God's Holy Spirit! There is not a single flower in it that does not teach us a lesson, there is not a single wave, or blast of thunder, that has not some lesson to teach to us, the sons of men. This world is a great temple, and as, if you walk in an Egyptian temple, you know that every mark and every figure in the temple has a meaning, so when you walk this world you must believe that everything about you has a meaning. It is no fanciful idea that there are 'sermons in stones,' for there really are sermons in stones; and this world is intended to teach us by everything that we see. Happy is the man who only has the mind and has the spirit to get these lessons from nature. Flowers, what are they? They are but the thoughts of God solidified—God's beautiful thoughts put into shape. Storms, what are they? They are God's terrible thoughts written out that we may read them. Thunders, what are they? They are God's powerful emotions just opened out that man may hear them. The world is just the materialising of God's thoughts; for the world is a thought in God's eye. He made it first from a thought that came from His own mighty mind, and everything in the majestic temple that He has made has a meaning."

The preacher then shows that nature is a temple which had its four evangelists, these, of course, being the four seasons. These

---

* This sermon, entitled "Harvest Time," and previously mentioned (*The Penny Pulpit*, No. 2,234), is the first discourse by Mr. Spurgeon that was ever printed. I have heard of a large price being given for a copy.

follow one another, Spring leading the way; and what have these to say to man on the earth?

"We look, and we behold that by the magic touch of Spring, insects which seemed to be dead begin to awaken, and seeds that were buried in the dust begin to lift up their radiant forms. What says Spring? It utters its voice, it says to man, 'Though thou sleepest, thou shalt rise again; there is a world in which, in a more glorious state, thou shalt exist; thou art but a seed now, and thou shalt be buried in the dust, and in a little while thou shalt arise.' Spring utters that part of its evangel. Then comes Summer. Summer says to man, 'Behold the goodness of a merciful Creator; He makes His sun to shine on the evil and on the good, He sprinkleth the earth with flowers, He scattereth it with those gems of creation, He maketh it blossom like Eden, and bring forth like the garden of the Lord.' Summer utters that; then comes Autumn. We shall hear its message this morning. It passes, and, fourth, comes Winter, crowned with a coronal of ice, and it tells us that there are times of trouble for man; it points to the fruits that we have stored up in autumn, and it says to us, 'Man, take heed that thou store up something for thyself, something against the day of wrath; lay up for thyself the fruits of autumn, that thou mayest be able to feed on them in winter. And when the old year expires its death knell tells us that man must die; and when the year has finished its evangelistic mission, there comes another to preach the same lesson again."

The preacher will not enlarge on each of this captivating train; time will only allow of his devoting attention to the golden-tressed Autumn, which had come forth to ask the question, "Is it not wheat harvest to-day?" It was a time to consider the harvest and to learn something from it. There were joyful harvests to be spoken of, and that of the field was one of them:—

"We cannot forget the harvest of the field. It is not meet that these things should be forgotten; we ought not to let the fields be covered with corn, and to have their treasures stored away in the barns, and all the while to remain forgetful of God's mercy. Ingratitude, that worst of ills, is one of those vipers which makes its nest in the heart of man, and the adder never can be slain until Divine grace comes there and sprinkles the blood of the cross upon man's heart. All vipers die when the blood of Christ is upon them. Let us just lead you for a moment to a harvest-field. You shall see there a most luxurious harvest, the heavy ears bending down almost to touch the ground, as much as to say, 'From the ground I came, I owe myself to the ground, to that I bow my head, just as the good Christian does when he is full of years. He holds his head down the more fruit he has upon him.' You see the stalks with their heads hanging down because they are ripe. And it is goodly and precious to see these things. Now just suppose the contrary. If this year the ears had been blighted and withered, if they had been like the second ears that Pharaoh saw, very lean and very scanty, what would have become of us? In peace we might have speculated on large supplies from Russia to make up the deficiency; now, in times of war, when nothing can come, what would become of us? We may conjecture, we may imagine, but I do not know that we are able to come to the truth; we can only say, 'Blessed be God, we have not yet to reckon on what would have been; but God seeing one door closed has opened another.' Seeing that we might not get supplies from those rich fields in the south of Russia, He has opened another door in our own land. 'Thou art My own favoured island,' says He, 'I have loved thee, England, with a special love; thou art My favoured one, and the enemy shall not crush thee; and lest thou should starve, because provisions are cut off, I will give thee thy barns full at home, and thy fields shall be covered, that thou mayest laugh thine enemy to scorn, and say to him, "Thou thoughtest thou couldest starve us and make us afraid; but He who feeds the ravens has fed His people, and has not deserted His favoured land."' There is not one person here who is uninterested in this matter. Some say the poor ought to be thankful that there is abundance of bread. So ought the rich. There is nothing which happens to one member of society which does not affect all. The ranks lean upon one another; if there is scarcity in the lower ranks, it falls upon the next, and the next, and even the Queen upon her throne feels in some degree the scarcity when God is pleased to send it. It affects all men. Let none say, 'Whatever the price of corn may be, I can live'; but rather bless God who has given you more than enough. Your prayer ought to be, 'Give us this day our daily bread'; and remember whatever wealth you have you must attribute your daily mercies as much to God as if you lived from hand to mouth; and sometimes that is a blessed way of living—when God gives His children the hand-basket portion instead of sending it in a mass. Bless God that He has sent an abundant harvest! Oh, fearful one, lift up thy head, and thou discontented one be abased, and let thy discontent be no more known. The Jews always had a feast of the Tabernacles when the harvest time came. In the country they always have a *harvest home*, and why should not we? I want you all to have one this day. Rejoice! rejoice! rejoice! for the harvest is come. 'Is it not wheat harvest to-day?' Poor, desponding soul, let all your doubts and fears be gone. 'Thy bread shall be given thee, and thy water shall be sure.' That is one joyful harvest."

These passages undoubtedly show the young preacher at his best at this period in his history. He next goes on to describe that joyful harvest which it is within the power of every Christian to gather in:—

"In one sense he is a seed sown by God which is to grow, and ripen, and germinate till the great harvest time. In another sense, every Christian is a sower sent into the world to sow good seed, and to sow good seed only. I do not say that Christian men never sow any other seed than good seed. Sometimes, in unguarded moments, they take garlic into their hands instead of wheat; and we may sow tares instead of corn. Christians sometimes make mistakes, and God sometimes suffers His people to fall so that they sow sins; but the Christian never reaps his sins; Christ reaps them for him. He often has to have a decoction made of the bitter leaves of sin, but he never reaps the fruit of it. Christ has borne the punishment. Yet bear in mind, my brethren, if you and I sin against God, God will take our sin, and He will get an essence from it that will be bitter to our taste: though He does not make us eat the fruits, yet still He will make us grieve and sorrow over our crimes. But the Christian, as I have said, should be employed in sowing good seed, and as such he shall have a glorious harvest. In some sense or other the Christian must be sowing good seed. If God calls him to the ministry, he is a seed-sower; if God calls him to the Sabbath-school, he is a seed-sower; whatever his office, he is a sower of seed. Here I stand, Sabbath after Sabbath, and on week-days, too, and sow seed broadcast all over this immense field; I cannot tell where my seed goes. Some are like barren ground, and they object to the seed that I sow. Let them—I have no objection that any man should do so. I am only responsible to God, whose servant I am. There are others, and my seed falls upon them and brings forth a little fruit; but by-and-by, when the sun is up, because of persecution, they wither away and they die. But I hope there are many here who are like the good ground that God has prepared, and when I scatter the seed abroad it falls on good ground and brings forth fruit to an abundant harvest. Ah! the minister has a joyful harvest, even in this world, when he sees souls converted. I have had a harvest time when I have led the sheep down to the washing of baptism, when I have seen God's people coming out from the mass of the world, and telling what the Lord has done for their souls—when God's children are edified and built up it is worth living for, and worth dying ten thousand deaths for to be the means of saving one soul. What a joyous harvest it is when God gives us converted ones by tens and hundreds, and adds to His Church abundantly such as shall be saved! Now, I am like a farmer just at this season of the year. I have got a good deal of wheat down, and I want to get it into the barn, for fear the rain comes and spoils it. I believe I have got a great many here—good, pious, Christian persons—but they will persist in standing out in the field. I want to get them into the barns. They are good people, but they do not like to make a profession and join the church. I want to get them into my Master's granary, and to see Christians added to the church. I see some holding down their heads and saying, 'He means me.' So I do. You ought before this to have joined Christ's Church! and unless you are fit to be gathered into Christ's little garner here on earth, you have no right to anticipate being gathered into that great garner which is in heaven.

"Every Christian has his harvest. The Sabbath-school teacher has his harvest. He goes and he toils and ploughs very stony ground often, but he shall have his harvest. Oh, poor labouring Sabbath-school teacher, hast thou seen no fruit yet? Dost thou say, 'Who hath believed our report, and to whom is the arm of the Lord revealed?' Cheer up, my brother, thou dost labour in a good cause, there must be some to do thy work. Hast thou seen no children converted? Well, fear not, you cannot expect to see the seed spring up very early, but remember—

> "'Though seed lie buried long in dust,
> It shan't deceive your hope;
> The precious grain can ne'er be lost,
> For God insures the crop.'

Go on sowing still, and thou shalt have a harvest when thou shalt see children converted. I have known some Sabbath-school teachers who could count a dozen, or twenty, or thirty children who have one after another come to join the church and know the Lord Jesus Christ. But if you should not live to see it on earth, remember you are only accountable for your labour and not for your success. Sow still, toil on! 'Cast thy bread upon the waters, and thou shalt find it again after many days,' for God will not allow His word to be wasted; 'It shall not return unto Him void, it shall accomplish that which He pleases.' But there is a poor mother who has been often sad. She has got a son or a daughter, and she has been always praying that God might convert their souls. Mother, thy son is an ungainly boy still; he grieves thy heart; still the hot tears scald thy cheeks on account of him. And thou, father, thou hast reproved him often; he is a wayward son, and he is still running the downward road. Cease not to pray! Oh, my brethren and sisters who are parents, you shall have a harvest. There was a boy once—a very sinful child—who hearkened not to the counsel of his parents; but his mother prayed for him, and now he stands to preach to this congregation every Sabbath. And when his mother thinks of her first-born preaching the gospel, she reaps a glorious harvest that makes her a glad woman. Now, fathers and mothers, such may be your case. However bad your children are at present, still press toward the throne of grace and you shall have a harvest. What thinkest thou, mother? Wouldest thou not rejoice to see thy son a minister of the Gospel? thy daughter teaching and assisting in the cause of God? God will not suffer thee to pray and thy prayers be unheeded. Young man, thy mother has been wrestling for thee a long time, and she has not won thy soul yet. What thinkest thou? thou defraudest thy mother of her harvest! If she had a little patch of ground hard by her cottage, where she had sown some wheat, wouldest thou go and burn it? If she had a choice flower in her garden, wouldest thou go and trample it under foot? Thou art going in the ways of the reprobate, thou art defrauding thy mother and father of their harvest. Perhaps there are some parents who are weeping over their sons and daughters who are hardened and unconverted. God turn their hearts! for bitter is the doom of that man who goes to hell over the road that is washed by his mother's tears, stumbles over his father's reproofs, and tramples on those things which God has put in his way—his mother's prayers and his father's sighs. God help that man who dares to do such a thing as that! And it is wondrous grace if He does help him.

"You shall have a harvest, whatever you are doing. I trust you are all doing something. If I cannot mention what your peculiar engagement is, I trust you are all serving God in some way; and you shall assuredly have a harvest wherever you are scattering your seed. But suppose the worst—if you should never live to see the harvest in this world, you shall have a harvest when you get to heaven. If you live and die a disappointed man, you shall not be disappointed in the next world. I think how surprised some of God's people will be when they get to heaven. They will see their Master, and He will give them a crown. 'Lord, what is that crown for?' 'That crown is because thou didst give a cup of cold water to one of My disciples.' 'What! a crown for a cup of cold water?' 'Yes,' says the Master, 'that is how I pay My servants. First I give them grace to give that cup of water, and then having given them grace, I will give them a crown.' 'Wonders of grace to God belong.' He that soweth liberally shall reap liberally, and he that soweth grudgingly shall reap sparingly. Ah, if there could be grief in heaven, I think it would be the grief of some Christians who had sown so very little. After all, how very little the most of us ever sow? I sow but very little compared with what I might. How little any of you sow. Just add up how much you give to God in the year. I am afraid it would not come to a farthing per cent. Remember, you reap according to what you sow. Oh, my friends, what surprise some of you will feel when God pays you for sowing one single grain. The soil of heaven is rich in the extreme. If a farmer had such ground as there is in heaven, he would say, 'I must sow a great many acres of land,' and so let us strive; for the more we sow the more we shall reap in heaven. Yet remember it is all of grace, and not of debt."

Having noticed these happy harvests—that of the field and that of the Christian—the preacher had another of a joyful kind to dwell upon—that of the Lord Jesus Christ Himself:—

"Christ had His sowing times. What bitter sowing times were they! Christ was one who went out bearing precious seed. Oh, I picture Christ sowing the world. He sowed it with tears; He sowed it with drops of blood; He sowed it with sighs; He sowed it with agony of heart; and at last He sowed Himself in the ground, to be the seed of a glorious crop. What a sowing-time His was! He sowed in tears, in poverty, in sympathy, in grief, in agony, in woes, in suffering, and in death. He shall have a harvest, too. Blessings on His name, Jehovah swears it; the everlasting predestination of the Almighty has settled that Christ shall have a harvest. He has sown, and He shall reap; He has scattered, and He shall win His prize. 'He shall see His seed, He shall prolong His days, and the pleasure of the Lord shall prosper in His hand.' My friends, Christ has begun to reap His harvest. Yea, every soul that is converted is part of His reward; everyone that comes to the Lord is a part of it. Every soul that is brought out of the miry clay and set on the King's highway is a part of Christ's crop. But He is going to reap more yet. There is another harvest coming in the latter day, when He shall reap armsful at a time, and gather the sheaves into His garner. Now, men, come to Christ in ones and twos and threes; but then they shall come in flocks, so that the Church shall say, 'Who are these that come in as doves to their windows?'

"There shall be a greater harvest-time when time shall be no more. Turn to the fourteenth chapter of Revelation, and the thirteenth verse—'And I heard a voice from heaven saying unto me, Write, Blessed are the dead which die in the Lord from henceforth: Yea, saith the Spirit, that they may rest from their labours; and their works do follow them.' They do not go before them and win them heaven. 'And I looked, and behold a white cloud, and upon the cloud One sat like unto the Son of man, having on His head a golden crown, and in His hand a sharp sickle. And another angel came out of the temple, crying with a loud voice to Him that sat on the cloud, Thrust in Thy sickle and reap: for the time is come for Thee to reap; for the harvest of the earth is ripe. And He that sat on the cloud thrust in His sickle on the earth; and the earth was reaped.' That was Christ's harvest. Observe but one particular. When Christ comes to reap His field, He comes with a crown on. Oh! see that Crowned Reaper on His throne! There are nations gathered together—

> "'They come, they come, the ransom'd tribes,
>   Where'er they rest or roam;
> They heard His voice in distant lands,
>   And hastened to their home.'

There they stand, one great army before God. Then comes the Crowned Reaper from His throne; He takes His sharp sickle, and see Him reap sheaf after sheaf, and He carries them up to the heavenly garner. Let us ask the question of ourselves, whether we shall be among the reaped ones—the wheat of the Lord. Notice, again, that there was first a harvest, and then a vintage. The harvest is the righteous; the vintage is the wicked. When the wicked are gathered, an angel gathers them; but Christ will not trust an angel to reap the righteous. 'He that sat on the throne thrust in His sickle.' Oh, my soul, when thou comest to die, Christ will Himself come after thee; when thou art to be cut down, He that sits upon the throne will cut thee down with a very sharp sickle, in order that He may do it as easily as possible. He will be the reaper Himself; no reaper will be allowed to gather Christ's saints in, but Christ the King of saints. Oh, will it not be a joyful harvest when all the chosen race, every one of them, shall be gathered in? There is a little shrivelled grain of wheat there that has been growing somewhere on the headland, and that will be there. There are a great many who have been hanging down their heads, heavy with grain, and they will be there, too. They will be all gathered in.

> " 'His honour is engaged to save
>   The meanest of His sheep;
> All that His heavenly Father gave
>   His hands securely keep.'

"But now we are obliged to turn to the three sad harvests. Alas! alas! the world was once like an Eolian harp; every wind that blew upon it gave forth melody; now the strings are all unstrung, and they are full of discord, so that when we have the strains of joy we must have the deep loss of grief to come after it."

Then follow references to what the preacher calls three sad harvests—the harvest of death, the harvest that will have to be reaped by the wicked, and the harvest of the wrath of God. It is probable that some things are put in a way different from what would have been the case twenty or thirty years later; but the mode of expression is eminently characteristic of Mr. Spurgeon's youth, and of the first year of his ministry in London:—

"The first sad harvest is the harvest of death. We are all living, and what for? For the grave. I have sometimes sat me down and had a reverie like this: I have thought— Man, what is he? He grows, he grows, till he comes to his prime, and when he is forty-five, if God spare him, perhaps he has then gained the prime of life. What does he do then? He continues where he is a little while, and then he goes down the hill; and if he keeps on living, what is it for? To die. But there are many chances to one, as the world has it, that he will not live to be seventy. He dies very early. Do not we all live to die? But none shall die till they are ripe. Death never reaps his corn green; he never cuts his corn till it is ripe. The wicked die, but they are always ripe for hell when they die; the righteous die, but they are always ripe for heaven when they die. That poor thief there, who had not believed in Jesus perhaps an hour before he died, he was as ripe as a seventy years' saint. The saint is always ready for glory whenever death, the reaper, comes, and the wicked are always ripe for hell whenever God pleases to send for them. Oh, that great reaper! he sweeps through the earth, and mows his hundreds and thousands down. It is all still; death makes no noise about his movements, and he treads with velvet footfall over the earth—that ceaseless mower, none can resist him. He is irresistible, and he mows, and mows, and cuts them down. Sometimes he stops and whets his scythe; he dips his scythe in blood, and then he mows us down with war; then he takes his whetstone of cholera, and mows down more than ever. Still he cries, 'More! more! more!' Ceaseless that work keeps on! Wondrous mower! Wondrous reaper! Oh, when thou comest to reap me I cannot resist thee, for I must fall like others; when thou comest I shall have nothing to say to thee. Like a blade of corn I must stand motionless, and thou must cut me down! But, oh! may I be prepared for thy scythe! May the Lord stand by me, and comfort me and cheer me; and may I find that death is an angel of life—that death is the portal of heaven; that it is the outward porch of the great temple of eternity; that it is the vestibule of glory!

"There is a second sad harvest, and that is the harvest that the wicked man has to reap. Thus saith the voice of inspiration, 'Whatsoever a man soweth, that shall he also reap.' Now, there is a harvest that every wicked man has to reap in this world. No man ever sins against his *body* without reaping a harvest for it. The young man says, 'I have sinned with impunity.' Stay, thou young man; go thou to that hospital and see the beings writhing in their disease. See that staggering, bloated wretch, and I tell thee stay thy hand, lest thou become like him. Wisdom bids thee stop, for thy steps lead down to hell. If thou 'enterest into the house of the strange woman' thou shall reap a harvest. There is a harvest that every man reaps if he sins against his *fellows*. The man who sins against his fellow-creatures shall reap a harvest. Some men walk through the world like knights with spurs on their heels, and think they may tread on whom they please; but they shall find their mistake. He who sins against others sins against himself; that is nature. It is a law in nature that a man cannot hurt his fellows without hurting himself. Now you, who cause grief to other minds, do not think the grief will end there; you will have to reap a harvest even here. Again, a man cannot sin against his *estate* without reaping the effects of it. The miserly wretch who hoards up his gold, he sins against his gold. It becomes cankered, and from those golden sovereigns he will have to reap a harvest; yes, that miserly wretch, sitting up at night and straining his weary eyes to count his gold, that man reaps his harvest. And so does the young spendthrift. He will reap his harvest when all his treasure is exhausted. It is said of the prodigal that 'no man gave unto him'—none of those that he used to entertain—and so the prodigal shall find it. No man shall give anything unto him. Ah! but the worst harvest will be that of those who sin against the *Church of Christ*. I would not that a man should sin against his body; I would not that a man should sin against his estate; I would not that a man should sin against his fellows; but, most of all, I would not have him touch Christ's Church. He that touches one of God's people touches the apple of His eye. When I have read of some people finding fault with the servants of the Lord, I have thought within myself, 'I would not do so. It is the greatest insult to a man to speak ill of his children.' You speak ill of God's children, and you will be rewarded for it in everlasting punishment. There is not a single one of God's family that God does not love, and if you touch one of them He will have vengeance on you. Nothing puts a man on his mettle like touching his children; and if you touch God's Church you will have the direst revenge of all. The hottest flames of hell are for those who touch God's children. Go on, sinner, laugh at religion if thou pleasest; but know that it is the blackest of sin in all the catalogue of crime. God will forgive anything sooner than that; and though that is not unpardonable, yet if unrepented of, it will meet the greatest punishment. God cannot bear that His elect should be touched, and if you do so it is the greatest crime you can commit.

"Now we must conclude the third sad harvest; and that is the harvest of Almighty wrath, when the wicked at last are gathered in. In the fourteenth chapter of the Revelation you will see that God commanded the angel to gather the grapes, and they were all put in the wine-press together, and after that the angel came and trod them down until the blood ran out, so that it was up to the horses' bridles for the space of one hundred and twenty miles. Wonderful figure to express the wrath of God! Suppose, then, some great wine-press in which our bodies are put like grapes; and suppose some mighty giant comes and treads us all under foot until the blood runs out; that is the idea—that the wicked shall be cast together, and an angel shall crush them under foot until the blood runs out up to the horses' bridles. May God grant of His sovereign mercy that you and I may never reap such a harvest as that; that God may never reap us in that fearful harvest; but rather that we may be written amongst the saints of the Lord!"

In finishing up his subject, the preacher gave a word to those genuine Christians who would be sure to reap such a harvest as they desired if they fainted not :—

"Sow on, brother; sow on, sister; and in due time thou shalt reap an abundant harvest. Let me tell you one thing before you go away, if the seed thou hast sown a long while has never come up. I was told once, 'When you sow seeds in your garden, put them in a little water over-night; they will grow all the better for it.' So, my brother, if thou hast been sowing thy seeds, put them in tears, and it will make thy seed germinate the better. 'They that sow in tears shall reap in joy.' Steep your seed in tears, and then put it into the ground, and you shall reap in joy. No bird can devour that seed; no bird can hold it in its mouth, no worm can eat it, for worms never eat seeds that are sown in tears. Go thy way, and when thou weepest most, then it is that thou sowest best. When most cast down, thou art doing best. If thou comest to the prayer-meeting, and hast not a word to say, keep on praying, do not give it up; for thou often prayest best when thou thinkest thou prayest worst. Go on, and in due season, by God's mighty grace, you shall reap if you faint not."

CHAPTER XVIII.

MR. SPURGEON AND THE STRICT BAPTISTS.

Interest of Friends at Cambridge—Mr. George Apthorpe—Mr. T. W. Medhurst's Recollections—
Mr. Spurgeon's First Platform Speech in London—Further Accounts of the Cholera—
Death of Mr. Josiah Denham—Mr. Spurgeon's Address at the Grave-side—The Strict
Calvinistic Baptists—James Wells—Charles Waters Banks—Questions as to the Character
of Mr. Spurgeon's Teaching—Extracts from Early Sermons—"A very Questionable
Personage"—The New Park Street Pastor portrayed.

THE friends at Cambridge continued to feel the keenest interest
in the progress of the young preacher who had gone out from
their midst. When he took charge of the congregation at Waterbeach
the fact had been duly recorded in the church records; and when
he set out for London he was followed by the prayers and good
wishes of many friends. The day before he finally left Cambridge
he told Mr. George Apthorpe of his plans for the future, and added
that he did not intend to study harder in London than he had
done in the country. By that he simply meant that there would
be no mere showing off in the metropolis; and that the needs of
Londoners being identical with those of country people, he would
continue to do as he had done—to preach the Gospel to the best of
his ability, still looking for Divine help in the service. As one of
the earliest friends of the great preacher, Mr. Apthorpe has many
sunny memories of him, and he treasures many letters which he
received from time to time. It is a singular fact that when the
publication of the New Park Street discourses began in London, the
booksellers of the University town did not deign to traffic in them.
For a long time such readers as desired to possess the numbers
had to make their purchases at the grocery establishment of Mr.
Apthorpe, who naturally felt more than ordinary satisfaction in thus
acting as the Cambridge publisher of his former companion in the
St. Andrew's Street Sunday-school. In course of time the booksellers

included Spurgeon's sermons in their ordinary stock; and when it was no longer unfashionable to read such productions many purchasers were found for them.

There are still a few persons remaining who have vivid recollections of what took place in 1854. Among these is Mr. T. W. Medhurst, now settled in the pastorate at Cardiff, who believes that he was privileged to hear Mr. Spurgeon's first platform speech in London. On a certain day in the early part of the year in question, and even before Mr. Spurgeon was actually chosen pastor of New Park Street, an anniversary meeting of the Sunday-school at Maze Pond Chapel was held, Mr. Spurgeon being among the speakers. Then Mr. Medhurst saw and heard his future friend for the first time. Sufficient impression was made for the questions to go round, " Who is he ? " " Where does he hail from ? " And the answer came from those who did not know very much about the matter, " He is a young man from Waterbeach, who is supplying at New Park Street not far away." *

* Here are other reminiscences of those early days, contributed by an anonymous correspondent to *The Freeman* :—

"Before he was really elected to the pastorate of the church in New Park Street, I heard him make what was probably his first platform speech in London, at Maze Pond, the occasion being the annual meeting of the Sunday-school. The grandfather of Mr. Archibald G. Brown was in the chair; so you see the relationship of the two churches, originally one, had promise of continuity. No doubt Mr. William Olney introduced him to us, and knew he would help the cause. What a stripling he then was! What an impression he made! It was then that he related the difficulty he felt when a child as to how the apple got through the narrow neck of the bottle, and then the application, 'Oh then you must put it in while it is a little one.' And again at about the same period he preached a sermon in the same chapel one Sunday afternoon for one of the societies, when my mother pronounced judgment on him and said, 'He will be a second Whitefield!' The minister of Maze Pond, the Rev. John Aldis, at once foresaw for him a very distinguished career, and was the first amongst the London ministers who took him by the hand, and Mr. Spurgeon never forgot it. For he was not so generally well received by his brethren. As to what was said, that is better forgotten, for nearly all of them came round to him at last. But at a devotional meeting, where Mr. Spurgeon had been invited to be present, a London pastor prayed for our 'young friend who had so much to *learn*, and so much to *unlearn*.' The narrator of this told me, however, that it did not at all affect him, nor did he betray the least feeling of annoyance. The importance of a united diaconate was never made more palpable than in Mr. Spurgeon's settlement at New Park Street. They were mostly men of middle age, and with much experience of the exigencies of church life. Had it been otherwise, how different might have been the pastor's career! 'Tis true there was one opponent who would not give in to the last, and his attitude necessitated the services being continued in the old place even after the Tabernacle was built, and it was not till his death that the building could be disposed of."

K

Some references have already been made to the alarming prospect in the summer of 1854, occasioned by war and pestilence. Writing on this same subject early in the autumn, Mr. Spurgeon's early London friend, the late Charles Waters Banks, draws a dark picture of the surroundings of a South London pastor, although there was the cheering fact of an abundant harvest:—"The scenes around us have been of the most solemn character. We could not walk the streets but we saw the doctors driving hither and thither—hearses, mourning coaches, and funeral processions, at almost every turn; and the unhappy tidings constantly coming of one and another suddenly removed from this world of sorrow and of sin. These are indeed heart-aching days for the fallen sons of men; our faces have turned pale; our spirits have trembled."*

Mr. Banks himself suffered from an attack of cholera; and when here and there a friend died the national trouble seemed to come home to the individual heart. Among those who died suddenly was one of the first of the steadfast friends who stood by Mr. Spurgeon on his first coming to London—Mr. Josiah Denham,† of Unicorn Yard Chapel, who had greatly profited by his ministrations at New Park Street. Mr. Denham was, in life, a great benefactor of the poor, although little was known of what he did among them. He died on September 1, and the funeral took place on the 5th at Nunhead Cemetery. Several ministers took part in the funeral services, but the most interesting feature was the eloquent address at the grave-side by Mr. Spurgeon. This has long since been forgotten, and will now be read with new interest. It was as follows:—

"Sleep on, my brother, sleep on; for so He giveth His beloved sleep! Though thy bed be dark and cold, thou shalt not be alone; for thy dust is guarded by angels. Though thou art covered by the earth, thou shalt hear the trump of the archangel; thou shalt throw aside thy cerements, and in an incorruptible body thou shalt awake from thy long sleep. Oh, my friends, let us die with him; for to the believer death is the consummation of life; it is the close of the conflict; the sheathing of the sword. Sleep on, my brother, sleep on! The battle is fought, and thy work is done!

* *The Earthen Vessel*, x. 221.
† I am not certain that he died of cholera.

"But dost thou sleep? Doth thy spirit slumber? Nay! nay! Thy body sleeps, but thou art far away from that cold clay. Methinks I hear thy voice beyond the clear sky. Methought I heard thee! Yea, thou art there, my brother—thou art there! Thy voice comes down to me like sweet music. I hear thee say, 'I have washed my robe, and made it white in the blood of the Lamb.'

"Oh, can I weep for thee? Dare I wish thee to return? No, thou glorified one! I shall come to thee, but I cannot wish thee back again. Yet I must weep for thee; as of old the weeping Jeremiah penned the lamentations over a slain Josiah, so would I mourn over thee, my brother! A Josiah indeed! Could benevolence have kept thee alive, thou hadst not died. Could religion have warded off the death-shaft, thou wouldst not lie there. But these avail not to avert the hour of death. With all thy loveliness and kindness thou wast a mortal, and mortals must die. Oh, tenderly beloved of thy wife, she could not save thee from the tomb! Nor can the mingled tears of sons, and brethren, and friends, restore thy form to life. But the word of the Omnipotent shall do it. The voice of Jesus shall arouse thy sleeping body. As a sinner thou hast died; but, accepted in the Beloved, thou shalt live.

"Oh, thou hast no righteousness of thy own; but thou hast an infinitely better one. He who loved thee with an everlasting love has clothed thee in a spotless robe of righteousness, and through His merits thou art received within the pearly gates. Farewell, my brother, till the resurrection morning!

"Now, my fellow-mourners, there is much to mitigate your woe; much to cause you joy; the dark cloud has a silver lining: 'Ye sorrow not as those without hope.' Follow the track which he pursued—the footsteps of Jesus—and may you, an unbroken circle, meet around the throne."

When Mr. Spurgeon settled in London there was one other preacher on the south side of the Thames who had an extensive following, and whose chapel, better known as the Surrey Tabernacle, was thronged at every service. I refer to the late James Wells, a pulpit genius of great powers, who, notwithstanding some prejudices, and an impetuosity which led him to make some mistakes, is still remembered as a chief apostle of the nineteenth century by members of his denomination. He was a Strict Calvinistic Baptist,* he was regarded as being more extreme in his views than the pastor of

* The question arose, Was it right for Calvinistic ministers to preach for others of a different faith? "Mr. Spurgeon did so at Cannon Street on Tuesday, the 2nd October; and I am told that Mr. James Wells has done the same; but it appears by their conduct either Wesleyanism is not so bad as represented, or they are to be blamed for so doing. You know John says, 'He that biddeth them God-speed is partaker of their evil deeds.'"— "RHODA," in *The Earthen Vessel*, November, 1855.

To this "VERITAS" replied a month later:—"In regard to Mr. Spurgeon, I am not sufficiently acquainted with his line of doctrine to make any particular comment upon his amalgamation with this or the other sect. But in reference to Mr. Wells, whose views of truth I love and cherish, I must confess it as my honest opinion, that I cannot see why his preaching the Gospel of God's free grace to Wesleyans should prompt us to believe any better things of them than has been represented. Neither do I see it mitigates his principles, or renders him in fault as an ambassador of the living God. He is by no Scripture authority commanded to contract his labours, or limit them among any one class."

New Park Street; but at the outset of Mr. Spurgeon's London career, it seems to have been a question with many whether he would not eventually cast in his lot with this body. How he fraternised with them is seen by his friendship with Mr. Charles Waters Banks, by his visits to Unicorn Yard Chapel, by his taking part in the funeral of Mr. Denham, and by the assistance soon afterwards given to *The Christian Cabinet* weekly paper, which had a Strict Baptist for its editor. Thus it happened that Mr. Spurgeon's early critics viewed him from two separate standpoints, one being that of the extreme Calvinists, to some of whom the young preacher was a mere legalist adventurer; the other, that of those who were in the *via media* of Baxter, if they were not Arminians outright, and to these Mr. Spurgeon's talk about the predestination of sovereign grace was distasteful. Mention has been made of the way in which other London ministers held aloof from the New Park Street pastor —the chief exceptions being Dr. Alexander Fletcher, and Paxton Hood; it may now prove interesting for the reader to learn how he was regarded by the more pronounced Calvinists.

The fact of Mr. Spurgeon's amazing success was candidly admitted. "But then very solemn questions arise," said the monthly organ of the Strict party. These "solemn questions" turned out to be of a very searching kind, as, for example, "What is he doing? Whose servant is he? What proof does he give that, instrumentally, his is a heart-searching, a Christ-exalting, a truth-unfolding, a sinner-converting, a Church-feeding, a soul-saving ministry?" In starting such questions, and in endeavouring to give what he wished to be accepted as an impartial answer to them, the editor of the magazine referred to had to write with excessive caution, well knowing that his constituency was divided in opinion in regard to Mr. Spurgeon's claims to be recognised as a duly qualified preacher of the Gospel. The editor himself was favourably disposed towards Mr. Spurgeon; but knowing that his individual testimony would go but a very little way with his hard-headed subscribers if unsupported by the opinions of others, he was glad to be able to show that believers as sound in the faith as himself saw some good—at all events a promise of good—in the youth from Waterbeach. One genial comrade wrote to him in this reassuring strain :—

"I went last night to hear Mr. Spurgeon at Park Street, and after much squeezing got into a seat. It appeared to me that a very great number, after ineffectual attempts to gain ingress, went away again without being able to hear him. He preached from these words : 'He shall see of the travail of His soul and be satisfied.' And, much to my satisfaction, he delivered a short, pithy, and, to me, powerful epitome of the grand and fundamental doctrines of the Bible ; powerfully proving, under the head concerning Christ's satisfaction, that if but one of His elect body, the Church, could possibly be missing at last, He could not be satisfied.

"God has wonderfully gifted this stripling ; he has a powerful voice ; an easy and abundant flow of matter. In fact, from the impression I was under, upon the whole, I could not help concluding that this young man is destined of the Lord to be a very useful and laborious servant of Christ. He speaks as one having authority, and not as the Scribes and Pharisees of our day. There are some of my friends who regard his youth as an obstacle to their well receiving him ; but, surely, God is able to work by means of a David or a Timothy as effectually as by more aged and experienced instruments ; and a very few years' time will remove this objection. To all appearance, however, a course of very great usefulness is laid out for this youthful champion ; and if he does somewhat closely —but not too closely—insist upon fruits corresponding with a profession of the Gospel, we must not call this legality, when we know him to be sound in the main ; indeed, I think this is what the acknowledged ministers of truth, in our time, have long neglected to enforce."*

Having explained in what a Divine call to the Christian ministry consists, the editor thought he saw in Spurgeon evidences of having received such a call. In youth he had been preserved from straying into paths of vicious worldliness, and in that respect showed a favourable contrast to many others who had become acceptable preachers of the Word. Mr. Spurgeon was believed to be "as great a lover of free grace and of real Calvinism as any man ;" but he was discouraged by those who were too bigoted to accept the truth unless it were expressed in a certain style of phraseology. The Moderates, on the other hand, bit their tongues with rage at what they called his higher doctrines.

The most effective way of testing the preacher was to appeal to his teaching, however. Extracts were given from the eloquent discourse on the harvest, while a number of sentences were selected from a powerful sermon on "The Testimony of Christ and the

* *The Earthen Vessel*, x. 277.

Christian's Inwrought Evidence of the Truth of that Testimony." As these passages will show how Mr. Spurgeon's utterances at this time commended him to the more charitable of the Strict section, and also how surprising his knowledge of theology was for his years, they may be given in this place:—

"When Christ spake, He always spake directly from Himself. All the rest spake that which they had received from God. They had to tarry till the winged cherub brought the live coal, they had to gird on the ephod and the curious girdle with its Urim and Thummin; they must stand listening till the voice saith, 'Son of man, I have a message for thee.' They were but instruments blown by the breath of God, and giving sounds only at His pleasure; but Christ was a fountain of living water—He opened His mouth and the truth gushed forth, and it all came directly from Himself. In this, as a faithful witness, He was superior to every other."

It was then shown that the testimony of Christ was uniform, and that could not be said of any other teacher.

"Look at Noah, he was a very good testifier to the truth, except once, when he was intoxicated; he was a sorry testifier to the truth then. David was a testifier to the truth; but he sinned against God and put Uriah to death. The same might be said of Isaac; and if you go through the whole list of holy men you will find some fault in them, and we shall be obliged to say they were very good testifiers certainly, but their testimony is not uniform. There is a plague-spot which sin has left upon them all; there was something to show that man is nothing but an earthen vessel after all. But Christ's testimony was uniform. There never was a time when He contradicted Himself; there never was an instance in which it could be said, 'What you have said you now contradict.'"

When the Strict Calvinistic critic comes to examine what Mr. Spurgeon had to say about the testimony of Christ in the believer's own experience, he has to confess to being "a little disappointed," for the subject was "hardly touched." It might be that he was keeping the subject back for some special occasion; but in any case, he was urged to be faithful—"Oh, thou valiant little pastor of Park Street! for Christ's sake, and for the sake of poor, tried, and tempted souls, we pray thee hold not back from us a full and faithful declaration of God's gracious dealings with thine own soul!" At the same time, it was not to be supposed that the young preacher never referred to himself: he had done so in a taking way, and probably a promise of better things to come was discerned, *e. g.* :—

"Oh, beloved, that is the best confirmation of Gospel truths which every Christian carries about with him. I love Butler's 'Analogy'; it is a very powerful book. I love Paley's 'Evidences.' But I never need them myself for my own use. I do not want any proof that the Bible is true. Why? Because it is confirmed in me. There is a witness which dwells in me which makes me bid defiance to all infidelity, so that I can say—

> " ' Should all the forms that men devise
>   Assault my soul with treacherous art,
> I'll call them vanity and lies,
>   And bind the Gospel to my heart.'

I do not care to read books opposed to the Bible; I never want to wade through mire for the sake of washing myself afterwards. When I am asked to read an heretical book, I think of good John Newton. Dr. Taylor, of Norwich, said to him, 'Have you read my "Key to the Romans"?' 'I have turned it over,' said Newton. 'You have turned it over!' said the Doctor. 'And is this the treatment a book must meet with which has cost me so many years' hard study? You ought to have read it carefully, and weighed deliberately what comes forward on so serious a subject!' 'Hold!' said Newton, 'you have cut me out employment for a life as long as Methuselah's. My life is too short to be spent in contradictions of my religion. If the first page tells me the man is undermining truths, it is enough for me. If I find the first mouthful of a joint tainted, I do not want to eat it through to be convinced I ought to send it away.' Having the truth confirmed in us, we can laugh all arguments to scorn; we are plated in a sheet of mail when we have the witness within us of God's truth. All the men in this world cannot make us alter one single iota of what God has written within us. Ah, brethren and sisters, we want to have the truth confirmed in us. Let me tell you a few things that will do this. First, *the very fact of our conversion* tends to confirm us in the truth. 'Oh,' says the Christian, 'do not tell me there is no power in religion, for I have felt it. I was thoughtless like others; I laughed religion to scorn and those who attended to it; my language was, "Let us eat, drink, and enjoy the sunshine of life"; but now, through Christ Jesus, I find the Bible a honeycomb, which hardly needs to be pressed to let the drops of honey run out; it is so sweet and precious to my taste that I wish I could sit down and feast on my Bible for ever.' What has made this alteration? That is how the Christian reasons. He says, 'There must be a power in grace, otherwise I never should be so changed as I am; there must be truth in the Christian religion, otherwise this change never would have come over me.'

"Some men have ridiculed religion and its followers; and yet Divine grace has been so mighty that these very men have become converted and felt the new birth. Such men cannot be argued out of true religion. You may stand and talk to them from dewy morn to setting eve, but you can never get them to believe that there is not truth in God's Word. They have the truth confirmed in them.

"Then, again, another thing confirms the Christian in the truth, and that is when *God answers his prayers*. I think that this is one of the strongest confirmations of truth when we find God hears us. Now I speak to you on this point of things which I have tasted and handled. The wicked man will not believe this; he will say, 'Ah, go and tell those who know no better.' I say I have proved the power of prayer a hundred times, because I have gone to God and asked Him for mercies, and have had them. 'Ah,' say some, 'it is only just in the common course of Providence.' *Common course of Providence!* It is a blessed course of Providence! If you had been in my position you would not have said that; 1 have seen it just as if God had rent the heavens, and put His hand out and said, 'There, my child, is the mercy.' It has come so plainly out of the way that I could not call it a common course of Providence. Sometimes I have been depressed and downcast, and even out of heart, at coming to stand before the multitude; and I have said, 'What shall I do? I could fly anywhere rather than come here any more!' I have asked God to bless me, and send me words to say; and then I have felt filled to the brim, so that I could come before this congregation or any other. Is that a common course of Providence? It is a special Providence—a special answer to prayer. And there may be some here who can turn to the pages of their diary and see there God's hand plainly interposing. We can say to the Infidel, 'Begone! The truth is confirmed in us; and so confirmed that nothing can drive us out of it.'

"You have the truth confirmed in you, my dear friends, when you have found great *support in times of affliction and tribulation.* Some of you have passed through trouble, for one can never expect a congregation which is free from it. Some of you have been tried and have been brought very low. And cannot you say with David, 'I was brought low, and the Lord helped me'? Can you not think how well you bore that last trouble? When you lost that child, you thought that you could not bear it so well as you did; but you said, 'The Lord gave, and the Lord hath taken away; blessed be the name of the Lord.' Many of you have loved ones under the sod—your mother, father, husband, or wife. You thought your heart would break when you lost your parents; but is not the promise true, 'If thy father or mother forsake thee, the Lord will take thee up'? He told thee, woman, that He would be a father to thy children; and hast thou not found it so? Canst thou not say, 'Not one good thing has failed of all the Lord hath promised'? That is the best confirmation of the truth of God. Sometimes persons come to me in the vestry and they want me to confirm the truth outside of them. I cannot do that; I want them to have the truth confirmed in them. They say, 'How do you know the Bible is true?' 'Oh,' I say, 'I never have to ask such a question as that now, because it is confirmed in me. The Bishop has confirmed me—I mean the Bishop of souls, for I never was confirmed by any other—and so confirmed in me the truth that no one can confirm me out of it." *

This, and much besides, was regarded by certain observers as being all very good as far as it went; but it was not sufficient to satisfy them. Probably without quite realising the plain fact, they too much despised the New Park Street pastor's youth. Elderly and experienced Christians found that they could not readily submit to be taught in the deep things of God by a divine who was only twenty years old. There were also some who thought that at times Mr. Spurgeon said things which "fell with an ill grace" from the lips of one so young. The answer was, that a preacher free from imperfections would be altogether contrary to the common rule; and it was not doubted that if this youth was spared he would develop into a servant of God of great usefulness and far-reaching influence.

There was, however, a more select *coterie* of extreme Calvinists to whom any recognition of Gospel teaching outside of their own denomination savoured of apostasy from the truth. One critic of this school asked even of Dr. Cumming, "Who, taught of God, ever once thought his ministry to be that of life and freedom in

---

* Quoted in *The Earthen Vessel*, x. 281–283, from *The Penny Pulpit*, 1854.

the Gospel and new covenant sense of the word?"* The same writer naturally regarded Mr. Spurgeon as "another very *questionable* personage"; and as this person's views were representative of one section of opponents, who turned from the young preacher as from a false prophet during the first months of his ministry in London, some passing notice may be taken of them.

When the organ of the High Calvinists came out as an apologist for Mr. Spurgeon, there was "unbounded astonishment in one part of the camp." The article was thought to be an oversight committed through excess of good nature, although the belief was also current that "canting professors" had had something to do with the business. If the magazine was about "to change masters, let it do so at once, and the living in Jerusalem will have done with it." Here is a pen-and-ink sketch of Mr. Spurgeon in 1854, drawn from life by the "Job" to whom we have already referred :—

"It is, then, in the first place, clear that he has been from his childhood a very industrious and ardent reader of books—especially those of a theological kind; and that he has united with his theological researches books of classic and of scientific caste; and has thus possessed himself of every kind of information, which by the law of association he can deal out at pleasure; and these acquirements by reading are united in Mr. Spurgeon with good speaking gifts. The laws of oratory have been well studied, and he suits his action to his words. This mode of public speaking was, in the theatres of ancient Greece, carried to such an extent that one person had to speak the words and another had to perform the gestures, and suit, with every variety of face and form, the movement to the subject in hand. Mr. Spurgeon has caught the idea, only with this difference, that he performs both parts himself.

"Mr. Spurgeon is too well acquainted with Elisha Coles not to see in the Bible the sovereignty of God; and too well acquainted with the writings of Toplady and Tucker not to see in the Bible the doctrine of predestination and an overruling Providence; and too well versed in the subtleties of the late Dr. Chalmers not to philosophise upon rolling planets and methodically moving particles of earth and water, each particle having its ordained sphere. But in addition to these he appears to be a well-disposed person : kind, benevolent, courteous, full of good-will to his fellow-creatures, endearing in his manners, social—a kind of person whom it would seem almost a cruelty to dislike. The same may be with equal truth said both of Dr. Pusey and of Cardinal Wiseman."†

Having thus depicted the more pleasing traits in the New Park Street pastor's character, the critic is too conscientious to shrink from completing the portraiture. How characteristic of such a writer is the following passage :—

* "Job," in *The Earthen Vessel*, xi. 13.
† *Ibid.*

"But then it becomes us to beware, not only of the rough garment of a mock and 'arrogant humility,' but also of Amalekite-measured and delicate steps, and also of the soft raiment of refined and studied courtesy (Matt. xi. 8), and fascinating smile, with '*Surely the bitterness of death is past*' (1 Sam. xv. 32). But Samuel had too much honesty about him to be thus deceived. We must, then, beware of words that are softer than butter and smoother than oil (Psalm lv. 21). Not one of the Reformers appears to have been of this *amiable* caste; but these creature-refinements pass with thousands for religion, and tens of thousands are deluded thereby. It was by great, very great, *politeness* that the serpent beguiled Eve; and, unhappily, her posterity love to have it so; so true it is that Satan is not only a prince of darkness, but transformed also as an *angel of light*, and shall deceive, if it were possible, even the very elect."

But according to common belief, Mr. Spurgeon was a converted man, one who had undergone a change of heart. "Heaven grant that it may be so, for the young man's sake and for that of others also!" adds the writer already quoted; "but I have—*most solemnly have*—my doubts as to the Divine reality of his conversion. I do not say—it is not for me to say—that he is not a regenerated man; but this I do know, there are conversions which are not of God." By this it was meant that it was possible to have some knowledge of Christian faith and of practice, and yet not to be regenerated in a Scriptural sense. What were the paths marked out by the prophets and the apostles? "I believe Mr. Spurgeon well capable of talking about those paths; but I cannot see that he is walking therein," we find it remarked. Hence, such a ministry was put down as being "most awfully deceptive," although it might be "morally and socially beneficial to some people." What Mr. Spurgeon was at that time it was believed he would still continue to be. "His orbit may seem to be eccentric, but he will go intellectually shining on, throwing out his cometary attractions, crossing the orbits of all the others, seeming friendly with all yet belonging to none." The attraction of the preacher for the multitude consisted in a fine voice, and a capacity to use in the pulpit the materials which he so industriously collected in his study. In that respect he was a rebuke to such as were idle, and who, while pluming themselves on being sound in the faith, were tempted to think that hard work could be dispensed with.

At the time this discussion among the High Calvinists as to

whether the pastor of New Park Street Chapel was worthy of their recognition as a preacher of the Gospel, created much excitement among the members of the Strict Baptist denomination. The chief assailant, some of whose strictures have been here quoted, appears to have been himself a minister in an influential position ; but Mr. Spurgeon took no notice of the attack. In after years, he had many friends among the body which *The Earthen Vessel* represented ; but I am not aware that his relationship to the denomination itself was ever of that exceptionally cordial kind which, when he first came to London, some thought would turn out to be the case.

CHAPTER XIX.

WORK AND PROGRESS IN 1855.

Opening of the year 1855—Commencement of *The New Park Street Pulpit*—Sermon for the London Association—Enlargement of the Chapel—Services at Exeter Hall—Caricatures— A Pen-and-Ink Sketch—False Anecdotes—Mr. Spurgeon at Tottenham—Reopening of New Park Street Chapel—Large Sale of the Sermons—Birthday Celebration—*The Christian Cabinet*—The Mission of the Cheap Press—Visit to Scotland—In the Highlands—In Danger on the Clyde—A Friend's Reminiscences of New Park Street.

ALTHOUGH the year 1854 had closed in gloom, people were looking hopefully into the future when the New Year opened. Things could not be expected to be worse than they had been, and the probability was that there would be an improvement. As regarded Mr. Spurgeon, he was now able to consider himself thoroughly established in London. So far was his popularity from waning, that it had continued to grow, and promised to become greater than ever during the year which was then opening. The appetite of sermon-readers throughout the country had been sufficiently whetted by the samples of the young pastor's discourses which had already been printed; and, accordingly, it was now determined to publish regularly, as a weekly periodical, *The New Park Street Pulpit*. The desire to undertake such an enterprise did not originate with Mr. Spurgeon himself; but Mr. Joseph Passmore, who was then a young man engaged in the printing and publishing business, saw the golden opportunity which offered itself, and resolved to take advantage of it. Mr. Passmore was associated with the New Park Street Church and congregation, and his family was related to that of the late Dr. Rippon. The young printer and the young preacher passed some time together on Mr. Spurgeon's memorable first Sunday in London, and thus a lifelong friendship was commenced. If the weekly publication of the sermons was likely to become a successful undertaking, there would be no objection

in Mr. Spurgeon's mind to a trial being made. Mr. Passmore and
Mr. Alabaster, his partner, were both trustworthy men whose
characters naturally inspired him with confidence.

On the opening Sunday of the year Mr. Spurgeon preached at
New Park Street on the Immutability of God, the sermon being
founded on Malachi iii. 6—"I am the Lord, I change not;
therefore ye sons of Jacob are not consumed." The discourse is
throughout quite in the preacher's early style, and, notwithstanding
that the doctrines of his later days were identical with those
he taught at the outset of his career, the phraseology is here
and there not altogether such as Mr. Spurgeon would afterwards
have used. Probably Milton's imagery—in the passages he had
loved to recite to his pupils at Cambridge—had still great fascination for him. The High Calvinists must have found much in
the sermon that was reassuring from their peculiar standpoint.
In proof of the doctrine of election, John Newton's story relating
to a worthy woman, who had something to say on the subject,
was retold. "Ah, sir," said this dame of Old London to the
rector of St. Mary Woolnoth, "the Lord must have loved me
before I was born, or else He would not have seen anything in me
to love afterwards." The discourse at the evening service, which
preceded the administration of the Lord's Supper, was founded on
1 Cor. xi. 24—"This do in remembrance of Me."

During that same week, on Wednesday afternoon, January 10,
Mr. Spurgeon preached at New Park Street on behalf of the
London Baptist Association, and among the congregation some well-
known London ministers might have been observed. In one pew,
some time before the service commenced, was Thomas Binney,
of the Weigh-House Chapel, and a few minutes later John De
Kewer Williams, of Tottenham, took a place beside the City pastor.
The sermon was founded on 2 Cor. x. 4—"For the weapons of
our warfare are not carnal." Mr. Williams, who still retains a vivid
recollection of the occasion, especially remembers what he calls "the
intensely graphic way in which the young preacher described how

the strongholds of Satan should be taken by storm and destroyed."
It was remarked in the course of the sermon that "the Baptists are
the elect of the elect," which made it clear that, young as he was,
the preacher was thoroughly persuaded in his own mind. Here is
an extract from this discourse relating to the opposite doctrines of
Antinomianism and Arminianism :—

"I dread Arminianism (and my church and my people equally do), and every Christian
ought to dread Antinomianism. I tremble sometimes when I think how much of its spirit
there is amongst us. I think that Antinomianism differs from Arminianism in this—
Arminianism is an enemy of truth altogether, and is entirely a system of error, but
Antinomianism is the abuse of truth. It is the taking the stones of the sanctuary to
build a house for Belial. It is building upon the truth of Jesus the wood, hay, and
stubble of carnal man's imaginings. Arminianism is false from top to bottom, but this
Antinomianism is true at the foundation, and on this basis are built up inferences so
abominable, so horrifying, that well might St. Paul say, at the mention of one of them,
'God forbid!' 'What! shall I continue in sin, that grace may abound?' What! shall
I despise God's holy law because I cannot perfectly fulfil it? What! shall I make an
excuse for myself because of the corruption of my heart? What! shall I say I am never
to strive after nearness to perfection because I feel I cannot, in the present state, get
quite up to it? What! shall I sit myself down in sloth, and sing 'Jehovah Jireh,' and
imagine that because God will bring about His awful decrees and work out His gracious
purposes I am to sit down and wait for them, without using the means God has
appointed for the obtaining of the purposed and promised blessings? Let it be far from
us; yea, let us abhor it. It is a 'deep ditch, and he that is abhorred of the Lord shall
fall into it.' God deliver us from it! Oh that Antinomianism!—which administers opiates
to the ungodly; which brings men together in the house of God, and tells them that if
they are lost it is not their fault; lulls them off to sleep, lets them go to hell blindfold,
with the conviction that if they are to be damned they shall be damned. Horrible beyond
expression! You and I, each of us, must be united in a holy league, as much against
Antinomianism as Arminianism. We shall have our hands full if we attempt to do
anything against either of these things, but God help us and we yet shall overcome and
wave the palm branch of victory." *

This striking sermon, the tea-meeting which followed, and the
crowded public meeting of the evening, marked a new era in the
history of what was then called the London Association of Baptist
Churches. The denominational organ thus contrasted the old times
with the new :—

"Whatever reason may be assigned for the fact, it is certain that an Association
meeting in London is very different from one in the country. Perhaps the ministers and
members of the several churches meet so often that an annual gathering is no novelty;
perhaps the walk through London streets, or the jolt in an omnibus or cab, has fewer
attractions than the Whitsuntide jaunt by railroad or pleasant country lane; or perhaps
the thing has escaped due attention amid the throng of metropolitan claims—but certain it
is, that the London Particular Baptist Association, holding as it does, from a sense of

* The Baptist Messenger, ii. 25.

duty, a meeting every year, has only given generally the impression of being a somewhat dull affair. Indeed, it is not enlivening either to preacher or hearer to find one's self in New Park Street Chapel with a congregation of seventy people on a January week-day afternoon! This year, we are bound to say, all was different. The popularity of the Rev. C. H. Spurgeon, the recently-settled pastor at New Park Street, attracted a crowded audience on the afternoon of the 10th instant. The metropolitan churches of the denomination appeared for the most part well represented, the only noticeable exception being the absence of several leading ministers, owing, as was explained, to the Quarterly Mission Committee being holden, by some mischance which will probably not occur again, upon the same day. The preacher treated with much earnestness on the 'strongholds' of the Evil One that we are called to subdue, and on 'the weapons of our warfare,' which are 'mighty through God' to the task. The vigour and originality of the sermon, we cannot forbear remarking, sufficiently accounted to us for the popularity of the youthful preacher, and indicated powers which, with due culture, may by the Divine blessing greatly and usefully serve the Church in days to come." *

At that time older preachers saw something to admire, and in a sense to envy, in what they called Mr. Spurgeon's assurance. Thus, as Mr. Williams remarks, "Although he must have seen Mr. Binney among the congregation, he was apparently not in the slightest degree disconcerted." The fact was, as the present writer can himself testify, the youthful pastor was in some measure troubled at his own unparalleled popularity, and dreaded the crowd far more than he did any individuals, however celebrated they might be.

By this time the managers at New Park Street had decided that something must be done with the old chapel in order to provide some additional accommodation for the ever-increasing crowds. The site admitted of some enlargement of the building being carried out; and funds having been collected for this enterprise, the congregation removed to Exeter Hall—then a comparatively new building only two or three years older than the preacher who was to conduct the services in its great room.

It was quite a new departure for a congregation to hire such a building as this for ordinary services; and on the first day of meeting—Sunday, February 11—large numbers were attracted by curiosity. Hitherto, Exeter Hall had seemed to belong to the Sacred Harmonic Society on the one hand, and to the conveners of May meetings on the other; for a preacher to arise who could

* *The Freeman*, January 24, 1855.

crowd its benches and even its aisles to the last standing-place, was altogether a novel experience. What was the meaning of the Strand being partially blocked soon after ten on Sunday mornings by a well-dressed crowd of people carrying Bibles and Rippon's Selection of Hymns? The inconvenience was caused by a young man from New Park Street, whom people seemed determined to hear at any hazard. The question went round from one to the other, "Who is he?" and the answer was, "He is a stripling from Waterbeach." One thing after another leaked out about this young Spurgeon. It was soon told abroad that he was the son of an Independent minister, that he had turned Baptist, and that he was an uncompromising Calvinist.

The Press, in the main, appears to have been fair and generous. Thus, one of the ablest and most respectable of the London evening papers gave this notice :—

"The circumstances under which this gentleman has recently come before the public are curious, and demand a passing notice. Some months since he became minister of New Park Street Chapel, and it was soon found that the building, capacious as it was, was far too small to accommodate the crowds of persons who flocked to hear the young and eloquent Divine. In this state of affairs, there was no alternative but to enlarge the chapel; and while this process was going on, Exeter Hall was engaged for him. For some weeks past he has been preaching there every Sunday morning and evening; but he has filled the great hall just as easily as he filled New Park Street Chapel. A traveller along the Strand, about six o'clock on a Sunday evening, would wonder what could be the meaning of a crowd which literally stopped the progress of public vehicles, and sent unhappy pedestrians round the by-streets, in utter hopelessness of getting along the wide thoroughfare. Since the days of Whitefield—whose honoured name seems to be in danger of being thrown into the shade by this new candidate for pulpit honours—so thorough a religious furore has never existed. Mr. Spurgeon is likely to become a great preacher; at present his fervid and impassioned eloquence sometimes leads him astray, and mars the beauty of his singularly happy style." *

About the same time, *The Glasgow News* had something to say concerning a popular minister in London and "the green-eyed monster," as follows :—

"To the horror of some pious rival, New Park Street Chapel has become rapidly crowded, so that the congregation has had to resort to Exeter Hall till their chapel is enlarged. Even Exeter Hall is found too small to accommodate the crowds which go to see and hear the youthful and now renowned Rev. C. H. Spurgeon. Someone, who, we suspect, could give a beggarly account of empty benches, has written to some of the

* *The Globe*, Thursday, March 22, 1855.

newspapers, holding up this successful rival to scorn because he does not preach and pray to his satisfaction—that is, we presume, in the usual jog-trot, sleepy fashion. Young Spurgeon must, therefore, be held up to contempt in the columns of such papers as choose to lend themselves to these purposes. We have seen gentlemen who have worshipped in his crowded congregation, and who state that the services are conducted with strict propriety, and that there is nothing in the service to offend even 'ears polite.' They assure us that his discourses are replete with substantial matters, and that they are couched in language vigorous and appropriate. He pays no attention to the dogmas of schools, and chooses to express his views in language of his own, which is free from the stereotyped phraseology of the pulpit; but there is no expression used unworthy of the subject, and none which judges of theology would repudiate. A number of letters have appeared in his vindication, and to these the names of highly respectable parties are attached. It were well for rivals to mind their own business, as a young man of such energy as Mr. Spurgeon is not to be put down by envious rivals. Like other young preachers, he has his peculiarities; but these are often the indications of a genius which ripens into a brilliant maturity."

The name and doings of the youthful pastor thus soon became a theme of common talk outside of what is conventionally known as the religious world. The caricaturists set themselves to work. In one production, which was sufficiently popular in its day, the New Park Street pastor was depicted as Mr. Brimstone; and in order that no mistake might be made, another contemporary celebrity, Mr. Treacle, had his portrait given in the same drawing. Another picture was "Catch-'em-alive-O," Mr. Spurgeon's preaching being thus compared with the stick-fast fly-papers then in use. Meanwhile, busy tongues, pens, and pencils contributed to increase a popularity which was already unexampled.

A pen-and-ink sketch of the preacher at this time says :—

"A young man, in the twenty-first year of his age, has just appeared under this name, among our metropolitan preachers, and is creating a great sensation in the religious world. He had only been a few weeks settled as minister of Park Street Chapel, Southwark, before that commodious place was filled to overflowing, while hundreds at each service went away who were unable to effect an entrance. The result was that it was agreed to enlarge the chapel, and that the youthful minister should preach in the large room of Exeter Hall for eight Sundays, until the reopening of his own place of worship. It will easily be believed how great must be the popularity of this almost boyish preacher, when we mention that yesterday, both morning and evening, the large hall, capable of containing from 4,000 to 5,000 persons, was filled in every part. Mr. Spurgeon belongs to the Baptist denomination, in which his father is a minister in the neighbourhood of Cambridge. He is short in stature, and somewhat thickly built, which, with an exceedingly broad, massive face, gives him the appearance of one of twenty-six or twenty-seven years of age, instead of twenty-one. His doctrines are of the Calvinist school. He is a young man, we are told, of extensive information, especially on theological subjects, and of a highly cultivated mind. There can be no doubt that he possesses superior talents, while, in some of his happier flights, he rises to a high order of pulpit oratory. It is in pathos

L

that he excels, though he does not himself seem to be aware of the fact. But for some drawbacks in the young Divine, we should anticipate great usefulness from him, because he not only possesses qualities peculiarly adapted to attract and rivet the attention of the masses, but he makes faithful and powerful appeals to the consciences of the unconverted. In the spirit of sincere friendship we would impress upon him the indispensable necessity of relinquishing those theatrical attitudes into which he is in the habit of throwing himself. In Exeter Hall yesterday, instead of confining himself to the little spot converted into a sort of pulpit for him, he walked about on the platform just as if he had been treading the boards of Drury Lane Theatre, while performing some exciting tragedy. We hope, however, that in these respects he will improve. It is with that view we give him our friendly counsels. He is quite an original preacher, and therefore will always draw large congregations, and, consequently, may be eminently made the means of doing great good to classes of persons who might never otherwise be brought within the sound of a faithfully preached Gospel. He has evidently made George Whitefield his model; and, like that unparalleled preacher, that prince of pulpit orators, is very fond of striking apostrophes. Like him, too, he has a powerful voice, which would, at times, be more pleasing, and not less impressive, were it not raised to so high a pitch." *

It was admitted by Mr. Spurgeon's friends at this time that a man who had taken such a position as he had done was open to criticism. A magazine which consistently defended him remarked:—

"The pulpit and the forum alike invite attention, and challenge criticism; and so long as this test is legitimately and truthfully applied, no public character, if right-hearted, will shrink from its decisions. But if the criticism be made the vehicle of calumny, and if the censors of the Press, instead of employing their pens in commending excellencies, or in censuring and correcting faults, however severely, if fairly done, seek by detraction and falsehood to damage the reputation and lessen the usefulness of those whose efforts they decry, then do they degrade an otherwise honourable occupation into that of a dirty and despicable slanderer. Several of Mr. Spurgeon's critics, we regret to say, have thus disgraced themselves." †

The London correspondent of *The Ipswich Express* wrote a description of one of the services at New Park Street at this time, and besides making out that all the discourses were "redolent of bad taste, vulgar, and theatrical," gave a poor account of the preacher generally. Then came certain apocryphal anecdotes, one especially about a great number of worked slippers being received from young ladies. The editor of the Ipswich paper appears to have freely admitted letters in defence of the pastor, and correspondents indignantly denied what was false, while they gave evidence of truthfulness and zeal which was unanswerable. The story of the slippers was a well-worn fable which any shrewd journalist should

* Quoted in *The Baptist Messenger,* ii. 54–55.
† *The Baptist Messenger,* ii. 72.

have avoided. After all, fact was stranger than fiction in the case of Mr. Spurgeon; for as one friend, who had very generally attended the services, said:—

"The foot of the young pastor never trod the floor of schools or the halls of colleges; he boasts no birth, and has no pride of ancestry; but still, spite of this, his people increase, his church enlarges, his hearers become more numerous, and his ministrations are made more extensively useful; and now that he is placed upon a lofty eminence which he has 'won by the consistency of his character, the power of his preaching, the pure piety of his ministerial life, and the earnestness of his pastoral labours, the shafts of calumny and envy are showered on him thick and fast. So let it be; 'Thrice armed is he who hath his quarrel just,' and I trust Mr. Spurgeon will live to outlive it all." *

While standing forth as a defender of Mr. Spurgeon, a certain provincial minister urged other friends to be more sober in their estimate of the preacher:—

"He neither possesses nor lays claim to such gigantic powers of mind as some have enthusiastically asserted. His greatness is his usefulness. . . . The extravagant encomiums bestowed upon him by some of his injudicious friends are as little approved by Mr. Spurgeon as the envenomed shafts of calumny hurled at him by unchristian assailants are effective for the purpose intended. Of the animus by which the latter are influenced, as well as of the success they are likely to realise, the fables of Old Father Æsop may serve strikingly to illustrate. The fox may contemn the grapes because they happen to be beyond his altitude, and the empoisoned fangs of the asp will only be damaged by the object on which it wreaks its envious rage." †

The writer of this letter recommended Mr. Spurgeon's opponents to leave off detraction, and to try instead to imitate their gifted brother in his "laborious and incessant efforts both as a pastor and an evangelist."

Sincere friends were sometimes candidly critical in these early days, however; and by way of illustration take this utterance:—

"We have it not in our hearts to criticise that which, on the whole, is so very excellent, and which, too, was meant only to benefit the souls of our fellow-immortals; else it would be very easy to discover and to direct attention to faults both as to style and taste. That they should exist to any extent is a great pity, as it is very evident if these defects were regarded by Mr. Spurgeon as matters of very great importance, he has only to exercise his own better judgment to render his discourses worthy the popularity he has so suddenly and, we think, also most justly acquired.

"We understand he has entered into an engagement with a publishing house of high respectability to prepare for publication a volume of sermons, for the copyright of which, rumour states, he is to receive a very extraordinary sum. Let Mr. Spurgeon follow his own intuitions, under the direction of the Holy Spirit, and he will speedily falsify the uncharitable predictions of envious and prejudiced critics; and thus, from a sacred afflatus,

* W. Lemon Oliver, in *The Baptist Messenger*, ii. 73.
† "A Country Pastor," in *The Baptist Messenger*, ii. 74.

and the promptings of his own genius, he will not fail to take his place in the foremost rank of pulpit orators. May God long preserve him to the Church, and enable him to continue such utterances as those which are given forth in the Exeter Hall sermons." *

Some of the things said of Mr. Spurgeon in those days are not a little astonishing when read in the light of his subsequent career. To many the young preacher's popularity was quite an ephemeral thing, and only a very short time would be needed to finish up what was sensational in his adventurous course. To such people it was very much like a display of fireworks; the rocket might go up like a stream of fire, but the stick must inevitably come down in smoke and darkness. The preacher would find his level— the dull level of mediocrity—when his too ardent followers ceased like sheep to follow one another. At one service in a provincial town, a church official hoped that such a discourse as that by Mr. Spurgeon, who had just preached in the chapel, would not be accepted as a sample of the average preaching of the denominational ministers. For a time, even Mr. Binney looked upon Spurgeon as a young man who went up and down the country preaching in an incoherent manner. To others, he was an adventurer who talked more nonsense than truth, a man whose acquaintance with theology was no greater than his knowledge of English grammar. Then, what piquant anecdotes were told about him!—anecdotes that had done duty for more than one generation of eccentric ministers. Thus, it was said that to give expression to his satisfaction at the death of an obnoxious deacon, the pastor preached a funeral sermon for the worthy gentleman founded on the words, " And the beggar died." He was also reported to have slid down the pulpit balustrade to illustrate the ease of backsliding, and then to have sought to clamber up to emphasise the difficulty of recovery. What chiefly gave offence, however, was the new method of preaching which the Essex youth had introduced. Instead of humbly learning from his betters, Spurgeon, with his simple Saxon, was even presuming to teach them how the thing ought

* *The Baptist Messenger*, iii. 36.

to be done. To many it appeared as though native impudence could not further go.

The fact was, that a time of transition had come, and it was impossible to check the progress of events. The ill-success of the Russian war, and the intense sufferings of the allied armies in the Crimea, were teaching the people a lesson which they might be slow to learn, but which would be wholesome in the end. The abolition of the compulsory stamp on newspapers was also giving an impetus to the general diffusion of knowledge, especially as the paper duty would be sure to follow. More interest was also being shown in popular education. These things made it evident that such a pulpit phenomenon as the young pastor of New Park Street had appeared at an opportune time; but whether that was so or not, no adverse criticism, specious warning as regarded what was proper or improper, or even violent detraction, could stop the crowd from following one to whom they had taken a fancy. Much more was being effected than appeared on the surface to ordinary observers. Mr. Spurgeon had not only caught the popular ear to give the people the Gospel, he was sweeping away many things which had become sufficiently obsolete to be a hindrance rather than a help to ardent evangelists; and others would soon reap the good fruits of his wisdom and courage. If the late Rowland Hill looked on his large round chapel with satisfaction because Satan could not find a corner to hide in, was it not equally commendable in Spurgeon to be the first man who thought it a shame that the devil should have all the largest places in London and elsewhere? The Rev. Mark Guy Pearse has remarked on this subject:—

"If to-day we gather in St. James's Hall without prejudice or loss of sanctity, let us thankfully remember the bold hand that first opened the door of such places for such purposes. And if to-day preaching is no more 'as dying man to dying men,' but rather as living man to living men, who have got to get their living, and need all the grace of God to do it honestly and well, it is largely due to the courage and sanctified common sense of this blessed man."

That was something to do; but Mr. Spurgeon could never have enjoyed the popularity he did from the first if it had not been for his character. Commanding as his talents were, his character became his chief passport to public favour. Hence the eminent Wesleyan preacher was able to add:—

"I cannot refrain from adding my testimony to the memory of this servant of God—a man greatly beloved. There is none living to whom I owe so much as to him. I have never taken up one of his sermons without finding my soul quickly aglow with love and praise. If, when I am dull and cast down, I begin to read something of his, it is to me what the harp of David was to the troubled soul of old. Many a time I have come to my work kindled with hope and ringing with praise, because God had spoken to me by the printed word of His servant. I loved and honoured him. To me he was another Luther— the same sturdy faith, the same fearless defiance, the same ready humour, the same love of all things bright and pure, the same simplicity and self-forgetfulness."

Mr. De Kewer Williams, who now ministers at Hackney, but who in 1855 was stationed at Tottenham, is able to tell some interesting things about the days when Mr. Spurgeon was commencing his ministry in London. During the summer of 1855 the young pastor preached for Mr. Williams in the then new Tottenham and Edmonton Chapel from the words, "To know the love of Christ, which passeth knowledge." The congregation was a very full one, and among those who came were one or two Plymouth Brethren, who after the service remarked, "That young man will require great grace." "Just so; we all require it, if we did but know it," replied Mr. Williams. Not very long afterwards, the young pastor visited the Baptists of Tottenham, and during the sermon referred to various preachers and their ways in his own characteristic manner. He did more, however; for without knowing it he "took off" the excellent minister of the church in a way which must have not a little astonished the audience. The text on that occasion was, "Never man spake like this man"; and the advice given to preachers themselves was of a kind not likely to be forgotten by any who heard it. "What is the use of preaching the Gospel if people do not come to hear it?" was asked. It was then added, "I would preach in a red coat, or in any way, rather than have an empty chapel." Some time afterwards a sermon was preached at Deptford from the words, "We have seen the Lord"; and the people were asked if they had ever told Thomas such a thing as that. "There is a stuck-uppishness among us English people that prevents one man speaking to another on this all-important subject," said Mr. Spurgeon. "When I first joined a church I thought that Christian people must be brothers. I attended the Communion twice, but no one spoke to me; and I found out that numbers of fellow-Christians were brethren, but not brothers exactly." It was on this occasion that Mr. Williams met Mr. Spurgeon in the vestry with some others, and a certain Congregational minister, on joining the company, asked the latter if he would give a sermon at a chapel at Islington. The gentleman who asked this favour was incautious enough to add, "If you could come on Sunday it would be of most service to us, and I could take your place." We are told that "Mr. Spurgeon looked surprised" on hearing this novel proposition, but he at once gave a turn to the conversation and got out of the difficulty without giving any offence. He said, "You know, Mr. ——, if the devil were announced to give a discourse, and did not appear, but the archangel Gabriel, happening to be there, discoursed instead of him, the audience would not like it, because they did not come to hear him, you know." *

On Thursday, the last day of May, New Park Street Chapel was reopened after what was called "extensive enlargement." Mr. Sherman, the ex-pastor of Surrey Chapel, preached in the morning, and Mr. Spurgeon himself in the evening, when large numbers had to be turned away from the doors unable to obtain admission.

On the first Sunday in June, 1855, therefore, pastor and people were again found assembling in Southwark; but, although New Park Street Chapel would accommodate about three hundred more hearers, the difficulty of dealing with the crowd was practically as great as before. To preach at Exeter Hall twice a week for about four months must have had the effect of making the preacher better known among the *élite* of society, however; and ramblers from the West-end would now be found crossing the Thames in

* "My Friend Spurgeon," by J. De Kewer Williams, in *The Baptist*, March 11, 1892.

still greater numbers to hear the youthful prodigy in Southwark. Pastor and congregation must now have been more than ever impressed with the fact that a new chapel would have to be provided.

The sermons, which were by this time published regularly, stimulated the expression of opinion for and against the preacher which had begun in the previous summer. Despite the fact that he was a High Calvinist himself, Mr. Spurgeon's most violent detractors still appear to have been found among the more extreme members of that denomination. Hence we find a leader of that sect, who was more favourably disposed to the young preacher, warning his followers that they might possibly be found fighting against God in opposing him. "Therefore, brethren, be careful," he said. "Let us remember, also, that infidel *Reasoners*, Jesuits, Mormonites, and hosts of open enemies, are working hard to deceive men, to lead them on to the gates of death, and to cast contempt upon the glorious Gospel." *

While people were disputing about the merits of Mr. Spurgeon, some writers protested against new preachers of Arminian sentiments being admitted into pulpits in which Calvinistic doctrines were preached. One of Mr. Wells's followers who went to New Park Street received somewhat of a severe shock when he found that Mr. Sherman, of Surrey Chapel, was actually held in favour by Mr. Spurgeon. "Still, I would by no means condemn the stripling," he charitably remarks. "He is young, soldier-like, full of zeal for his adorable Lord, and apparently desirous to spread abroad His mighty acts." The pastor of New Park Street was not the only one who indulged in such pulpit "matrimonial connections," however; and it was insisted by those who were disposed to deal fairly all round that people who dwelt in glass houses should not throw stones. "I have thought, for some time past, that many of those men who are so very forward in pointing out what they call errors in Mr. Spurgeon, are far more faulty than

* *The Earthen Vessel,* **xi.** 204.

he is," says the writer just quoted; "and that it is (do pardon me for so saying) nothing but envy which makes them so spiteful as they are against the young man—his pulpit talents being so great. I should not wonder, if those gentlemen were narrowly watched in their preaching, that we should at times, at least, be shocked at their *unsound sentiments.*"* Still, although some might be found to be well disposed towards him, a large proportion of the High Calvinistic section ardently joined in the cry concerning Mr. Spurgeon, "It is a second-hand ministry, deeply tainted with an Arminian spirit."

That the judgment of the public was different was proved by the increasing desire to hear the preacher, and by the large sale which his Exeter Hall discourses commanded when collected into a volume. Soon after the return to the enlarged chapel at New Park Street, or on the 19th of June, Mr. Spurgeon completed his twenty-first year, and this was celebrated by a special service, the sermon entitled "Pictures of Life" being published at twopence, accompanied with the first portrait of the young pastor that was ever engraved. The sale was large, but it is only with difficulty that a copy can now be obtained.

The birthday discourse is founded on James iv. 14—"What is your life?" The opening refers to the swiftness of existence on earth. To the youth entering upon the world, life might seem to be long, but to the aged who were finishing their course, it was ever short. It was a span when compared with the ages of the universe, or a drop when compared to the ocean. Then follows this characteristic passage :—

"Life is swift. If you would picture life you must turn to the Bible, and this evening we will walk through the Bible-gallery of old paintings. You will find its swiftness spoken of in the book of Job, where we are furnished with three illustrations. In the ninth chapter and at the twenty-fifth verse we find, 'Now my days are swifter than *a post*.' We are most of us acquainted with the swiftness of post-conveyance. I have sometimes, on emergency, taken post-horses where there has been no railway, and have been amused and pleased with the rapidity of my journey. But since, in this ancient book, there can be no allusion to modern posts, we must turn to the manners and customs of the

* "B," in *The Earthen Vessel*, xi. 204.

East, and in so doing we find that the ancient monarchs astonished their subjects by the amazing rapidity with which they received intelligence. By well-ordered arrangements, swift horses and constant relays, they were able to attain a speed which, although trifling in these days, was in those slower ages a marvel of marvels; so that to an Eastern, one of the greatest ideas of swiftness was that of a post. Well doth Job say our life is like a post. We ride one year until it is worn out, but there comes another just as swift, and we are borne by it, and it is gone, and another year serves us for a steed; post-house after post-house we pass, as birthdays successively arrive; we loiter not, but vaulting at a leap from one year to another, still we hurry onward, onward, onward still. My life is like a post; and not like the slow waggon that drags along the road with tiresome wheels, but, like a post, it attains the greatest speed."

Other illustrations of the swiftness of life were given, after which something was said about its uncertainty. What was life other than a vapour? In speaking of its changes, the preacher compared it to a pilgrimage, as the patriarch Jacob had done in his day.

"That hoary-headed patriarch, when he was asked by Pharaoh what was his age, replied, 'The days of the years of my *pilgrimage* are an hundred and thirty years. Few and evil have the days of the years of my life been, and have not attained unto the days of the years of the life of my fathers in the days of their pilgrimage!' He calls life a pilgrimage. A pilgrim sets out in the morning, and he has to journey many a day before he gets to the shrine which he seeks. What varied scenes the traveller will behold on his way. Sometimes he will be on the mountains, anon he will descend into the valleys; here he will be where the brooks shine like silver, where the birds warble, where the air is balmy, and the trees are green, and luscious fruits hang down to gratify his taste; anon he will find himself in the arid desert, where no life is found, and no sound is heard, except the screech of the wild eagle in the air, where he finds no rest for the sole of his foot—the burning sky above him, and the hot sand beneath him—no roof-tree and no house to rest himself; at another time he finds himself in a sweet oasis, resting himself by the wells of water, and plucking fruit from palm-trees. One moment he walks between the rocks in some narrow gorge, where all is darkness; at another time he ascends the hill Mizar; now he descends into the valley of Baca; anon he climbs the hill of Bashan, 'a high hill is the hill Bashan'; and yet again going into a den of leopards, he suffers trial and affliction. Such is life—ever changing. Who can tell what may come next? To-day it is fair, the next day there may be the thundering storm; to-day I may want for nothing, to-morrow I may be like Jacob, with nothing but a stone for my pillow, and the heavens for my curtains. But what a happy thought it is; though we know not where the road winds, we know where it ends. It is the straightest way to heaven to go round about. Israel's forty years' wanderings were, after all, the nearest path to Canaan. We may have to go through trial and affliction; the pilgrimage may be a tiresome one, but it is safe; we cannot trace the river upon which we are sailing, but we know it ends in floods of bliss at last. We cannot track the roads, but we know that they all meet in the great metropolis of heaven, in the centre of God's universe. God help us to pursue the true pilgrimage of a pious life!"

As regards the changes of life, the words of David are quoted— "We spend our years as a tale that is told"; and then occurs a passage which gives some of the preacher's own experience :—

"Now David understood about tales that were told; I daresay he had been annoyed by them sometimes. There are in the East professed story-tellers, who amuse their hearers by inventing tales such as those in that foolish book, the 'Arabian Nights.' When I was foolish enough to read that book, I remember sometimes you were with fairies, sometimes with genii, sometimes in palaces, anon you went down into caverns. All sorts of things are conglomerated into what they call a tale. Now, says David, 'we spend our years as a tale that is told.' You know there is nothing so wonderful as the history of the odds and ends of human life. Sometimes it is a merry rhyme, sometimes a prosy subject; sometimes you ascend to the sublime, soon you descend to the ridiculous. No man can write the whole of his biography; I suppose if the history of a man's thoughts and words could be written, scarce the world itself would contain the words that should be written, so wonderful is the tale that is told. Our lives are all singular, and must to ourselves seem strange, of which much might be said. Our life is 'as a tale that is told.'"

The discourse closed with some allusions to the end of life, the words of Samuel being quoted—"Water that is spilt upon the ground, and cannot be gathered up again":—

"Man is like a great icicle, which the sun of time is constantly thawing, and which is soon to be water spilt upon the ground that cannot be gathered up. Who can recall the departed spirit, or inflate the lungs with a new breath of life? Who can put vitality into the heart, and restore the soul from Hades? None. It cannot be gathered up. The place shall know it no more for ever. But here a sweet thought charms us. This water cannot be lost, but it shall descend into the soil to filter through the Rock of Ages, at last to spring up a pure fountain in heaven, cleansed, purified, and made clear as crystal. How terrible if, on the other hand, it should percolate the black earth of sin, and hang in horrid drops in the dark caverns of destruction!"

It was also during this year that Mr. Spurgeon once more took up the pen, which he may not have felt encouraged to use as an author since his little essay on "Antichrist and her Brood" had failed to win Mr. Arthur Morley's prize. This time he came out as a journalist, *The Christian Cabinet*, to which he lent his aid weekly for nearly a whole year, being the first penny paper of the kind ever published in England. "Although on the one hand the Press was so mighty an agent for diffusing light," we find it remarked, "it has also proved too often a means of spreading darkness and error, and it was to check in some measure the growth of this evil that Mr. Banks bent all his powers in starting *The Christian Cabinet* and other religious papers, which he fondly hoped would counteract the influence of more doubtful literature." *

* "Life of Charles Waters Banks," p. 135. On one occasion, in writing to Mr. W. H. Collingridge, editor of *The City Press*, Mr. Banks gave this entertaining account of himself :—

"I venture to affirm that you will nowhere find a more curious specimen of a pioneer,

The late Charles Waters Banks became pastor of the ancient congregation at Unicorn Yard, Tooley Street, in the same year that Mr. Spurgeon settled in London. Mr. Banks was a very able man; he looked upon the mission of the Press with genuine enthusiasm; and although he belonged to the High Calvinists, he entertained the most profound respect for Mr. Spurgeon. The young pastor never went over to the denomination of his more elderly friend, but as regarded aggressive Christian work, both were heartily agreed. Mr. Banks was an advocate of open-air preaching and of general mission work; but to certain professors of the more extreme type, all such enterprise savoured of legalism. One such was somewhat shocked when in New Park Street Chapel he heard some allusions to what it was proposed to do for the surrounding neighbourhood in the way of Christian work. That of course stamped the pastor as a man whose tendencies were towards legalism. Nevertheless, through good report and evil report, the work went bravely forward. In the summer of Mr. Spurgeon's second year in London, he and his people undertook Home Mission service in earnest, the chief centre being the Southwark Mission

---

printer, publisher, sub-editor, under the late William Mudford, Esq. (whose son is now editor of *The Standard*), pulpit-preacher all over England and Wales, etc., than is, and has been, your little old-fashioned, hard-working servant for sixty-five years, whose singular name is Charles Waters Banks. Do you recollect him? Fourteen years in Cranbrook Church a choral singer; printer and publisher of the first Unitarian magazine, called *The Inquirer*; editor, printer, and publisher of the first-known provincial magazine, called *The Weald of Kent Mirror*. In Canterbury, I printed for the late Rev. Dr. Molesworth the first Church of England penny publication, called *The Penny Sunday Reader*, of which hundreds of thousands were issued. Under William Mudford, Esq., a grand Conservative writer, I was the sub-editor of *The Kentish Times, The Kentish Observer, The Canterbury Journal*, and *The Canterbury Magazine*. Mr. Mudford would come and hear me preach, and told me he approved of all I said and did, except my pronunciation of 'Amen'; I should pronounce it 'Ah-men.' In London, nearly forty years ago, I started and edited the first Christian penny weekly paper ever known, *The Christian Cabinet*. Have been originator, sole editor, proprietor of *The Earthen Vessel* for more than forty years. It goes now by thousands all over the English-speaking world. Thirty-three years editor and proprietor of *Cheering Words*, which little child creeps into many a cottage, and ladies tell me into some mansions too, to cheer the heart when overwhelmed with grief. If all my works and wars were written, they'd show I have been sorely smitten; yet still a lad both brisk and glad in any work God calls me to. Have been an editor for sixty-five years, and a preacher over fifty-three, and still at both, and God's almoner to scores of His poor."
—"Life of Charles Waters Banks," pp. 41-42.

Hall, opened in connection with the chapel. An effort like this naturally looked like something savouring of legalism to persons who held extreme views; but Mr. Banks sympathised with such enterprises quite as heartily as Mr. Spurgeon did himself.

In July, 1855, Mr. Spurgeon took a journey to the North, and visited Scotland for the first time. He appears to have called at various great towns on the road. On a Sunday morning at Bradford he preached in the Music Hall to a congregation which included a thousand more persons than could have been got into Exeter Hall; but quite as many went away unable to gain admission as were admitted. In the evening the excitement rose still higher; the streets around the music-hall were thronged, while the great building itself was so closely packed that the preacher was scarcely able to move about sufficiently while giving his sermon. A similar experience was passed through at Stockton-on-Tees. At Edinburgh there were great crowds at Queen Street Hall, although the heavy rain would probably have damped the ardour of many if the attraction had been any other preacher. At Glasgow there were, if possible, still greater crowds; and in that commercial metropolis of Scotland the newspapers devoted much space to reports of the sermons and to articles on the preacher. *The Glasgow Examiner* acquitted itself creditably while endeavouring to give an impartial estimate of Mr. Spurgeon's methods and genius. People might put him down as an empiric because he had courage enough to leave the old-time routine to beat out a path for himself; but such daring had been characteristic of the greatest reformers ever known, from the Apostle Paul down to the sixteenth-century veterans Luther and Knox. It was not necessarily a mark of originality or of exceptional talent to leave the beaten track; but it might be advisable to do so :—

"Routine in religious services is extremely liable to beget a listless, lukewarm compliance with prescribed forms, while the spirit or *animus* gradually subsides. The preacher speaks his usual time; the people sit patiently enough perhaps; a few may even listen; the usual number of verses are sung and the business of the day is over; there is generally no more about it. No one can deny that this is neither more nor less than a simple statement of the real state of matters in the majority of our churches at the present day. Should the preacher sharpen his intellect with a sprinkling of snuff, let fall his handkerchief on the Psalm-book, or give one thump louder than usual with the fist ecclesiastic, that will be noted, remembered, and commented on, while there is all but total oblivion of the subject and the nature of the discussion. To break up this deadening process, to shake the dry bones and make them live, ought to be the great aim of the preacher of the present day; but it is not everyone who can do it. Affectation of manner or style won't do it; talent, we may say genius, of a peculiar nature is required; and we have no hesitation in saying that Mr. Spurgeon possesses the requisites in an unusual degree."

Nevertheless, it seemed to be quite a legitimate thing for sensible persons to regard with some misgiving certain of the "uncanonical expressions of this young preacher"; and even if they found themselves calling him a quack or an empiric they were to be excused; for had not common report spoken of this youth's unsystematic training and native boldness? Still, there was something in him, the success of his ministry was a fact "that could not be stifled with a sneer." Why was he so successful?

"It could not be any novelty in the theme itself, as there were thousands of preachers and millions of books and tracts dilating on it before Mr. Spurgeon made his appearance; it could not be any new doctrine, for this was the same as John Calvin, and preached by all the evangelical denominations around him; neither could it be his youth, as there are in the churches of Britain scores of preachers as young as he is; neither could it be the few *outré* sentences that were scattered through the discourses, for there are many in London who say stranger and odder things than any that he has yet uttered."

Reference is then made to the character of the average congregations which Mr. Spurgeon drew together; and these are set down as "fair examples of the respectable church-going community, perfectly capable of judging rationally on all subjects that engross public attention." Looking back on those days, and remembering what kind of a figure Mr. Spurgeon made in the world at that remarkable period in his history, I do not regard such an estimate of his influence as being in any wise a correct one. The striking thing about the young preacher in the early years of his unique career was the fact that his influence extended far beyond "the respectable church-going community." "The profound, the ignorant, and the illiterate, the light-hearted and frivolous young people of the metropolis," were not only the exceptions among the many who heard the Gospel from his lips, the classes who seem to be outside of the church altogether were attracted in large numbers. The youth from Waterbeach became a phenomenon to such as well as to more sober-minded people. His name became a household word in the by-streets of working-class neighbourhoods; and people who were strangers at public worship went to " hear Spurgeon " just as they would have gone after any other novelty. In this respect Glasgow did not differ from London; for the immense audiences which are reported to have been spell-bound at the services were really made up of all classes and ages, as was the case in England, and proper account should have been taken of such a speaking fact. It is acknowledged that his later sermons were better than those which had gone before. What, then, was the secret of such uncommon success? *The Glasgow Examiner* gave these reasons:—

" In the first place, there is about him that hearty, open, English frankness which has no hesitation in giving full and free utterance to its opinions, loves, and dislikes. There is the ready, acute perception which never fails to bring out fresh and striking illustrations from any text on which the attention is directed. Again, there is an extensive acquaintance with literature, which, by the aid of a retentive memory, can at a moment's notice furnish the speaker with choice and appropriate material. And lastly, there is a power of voice, and volubility of utterance, which enable him to get on with great care, and at the same time to give powerful effect to his sentiments. We may have heard many preachers who could reason more correctly and profoundly, who displayed more classical elegance and polish, but we have not heard one who can more powerfully arrest the attention, and carry the sympathies of an audience along with him."

The critic dealt with the discourses as he found them, and it was thought that if readers who looked through the reports did the same, they would see little in them to which they would take exception. Still, he was too original in his method to please every-body :—

"Those who think that preaching the Gospel is the harping on one or two cardinal points, or the repetition of some favourite dogma in language strictly ecclesiastical, must be offended with the freedom, independence, and variety of the preacher's style and thoughts. Instead of limiting himself to commonplace illustrations, he opens his eyes on nature, on science, on society, and gathers from them all that he reckons suitable to illumine his sub-ject. Instead of confining himself to the language of the schools, and of divines and theologians, he ransacks all the stores of literature, and reckons not a sentence disqualified to take a place in his discourse because it was coined or used by a Shakespeare, a Scott, a Johnson, or even a Burns. Language hitherto reckoned fit only for plays, novels, and songs is seized by this preacher, and oftentimes most ingeniously and aptly brought into his dis-cussions. We do not inquire whether in every case the sentiments and language are appropriate, but refer to the fact that such is his independence that he, with equal freedom, selects from sacred writers; and such is his miraculous power of assimilation, that what would come from others as a motley, incoherent mass, becomes in his hand unique, complete, and beautiful."

The arrangement of his discourses was thought to be good, although he used no notes; and although he made much of doctrines, such teaching—that of an ordinary Calvinist—was thought to be essential. Mr. Spurgeon's prayers had been described as "irreverent, presumptuous, and blasphemous"; but nothing of the kind had been noticed by his Glasgow critic. "On the contrary, they were correct, appropriate, and beautiful. He certainly has not followed the usual pulpit style, but has opened his eyes on the state of society in all its forms and phases, and adapted his confessions, and petitions, and thanksgivings. He confesses the peculiar sins of the times, as well as the inherent and changeless depravity of man's nature; the sins of the parlour, of the counting-house, and public assembly; the sins of individuals, families, and nations. He offers petitions for various classes and characters—for the profligate and careless, for the old, the young, and for little children; petitions for churches, for nations, for the world, all in a somewhat novel manner. While he gives thanks for special blessings, and employs language which none but the genuine believer can appropriate, and which even he must sometimes acknowledge with hesitancy, he forgets not the common benefits which all share, and the common blessings with which all are crowned."

Hence the keen observers of Glasgow, with whom the young preacher now came in contact for the first time, were not able to detect any of the "undue familiarities" or the "daring impieties" with which some others had charged him. They thus learned what many others learned in time, that the Spurgeon of the newspapers and the Spurgeon of real life were not always identical. Instead of all the objectionable things which had been so industriously reported concerning the preacher, the truth now turned out to be that he was characterised by "an earnestness, an unction, a fluency, and an urgency, which are but too seldom imitated."

The reading of the Scriptures with the exposition was thought to be quite as good as the preaching, the attention given to tone and emphasis being especially observable. There were those who preferred to have the Bible read without running comments; but even to such there would be nothing objectionable in Mr. Spurgeon's methods. His preaching is then described :—

"Some preachers owe much to their *personnel* in the pulpit. Before they open their mouths, there is something about them which causes a sort of awe and respect to creep over the audience. The appearance of this preacher may be said to be interesting rather than commanding. He is quite a youth, and his countenance boyish. He is under, rather than over, the middle size, and has few or none of the physical advantages of the orator in his appearance. But what he lacks in appearance he has in reality. Soon as he commences to speak, tones of richest melody are heard. A voice full, sweet, and musical falls on every ear, and awakens agreeable emotions in every soul in which there is a sympathy for sounds. That most excellent of voices is under perfect control, and can whisper or thunder at the wish of its possessor. And there is poetry in every feature and every movement, as well as music in the voice. The countenance speaks—the entire form sympathises. The action is in complete unison with the sentiments, and the eye listens scarcely less than the ear to the sweetly flowing oratory. But among the thirty thousand English preachers, and the three thousand Scotch ones, there are many sweet voices as well as this, and many who have studied the art of speaking with the greatest assiduity, and yet they fail to attract an audience. Mr. Spurgeon is more than a 'voice crying'; he has rare powers of observation, recollection, assimilation, and creation. His field of observation is wide and varied. He seems to have opened his eyes to *nature* in all its varieties, to *science* in all its discoveries, and to *literature* in all its departments. Everything which the eye of man can look upon, or the ear hear, seems to have made an indelible impression on his mental powers. The impression is not only distinctly made, but ineradicably maintained. Every mountain, every valley, every book, every sentence, which has once come in his way, becomes for ever fixed in his recollection. And not only fixed, but becomes the material on which marvellous powers of assimilation vigorously operate. Out of the forms of beauty which his eyes see, other still lovelier forms are created. The loveliest natural landscape is adorned with additional beauty by the aid of a refined and chastened fancy. The thoughts that have come floating down the long bygone ages are placed in the crucible of his mind, and, purged of the objectionable, come out bearing his own image and superscription. There is evidently in him great power of *assimilative* genius, and occasional indications of even a higher order of genius—even that which creates fresh and new forms of beauty which bear the distinct mark of his own mind."

Glasgow was the preacher's headquarters during this visit to the North, and the largest congregations ever gathered in the Scottish commercial metropolis are said to have been drawn together at this time. On Sunday, July 15, morning service took place in Dr. Patterson's church, Hope Street, and that of the evening in Dr. Wardlaw's chapel in West George Street. Mr. Spurgeon was greatly charmed with the scenery of Scotland as he proceeded on his way. He went northward to Perth, Dunkeld, and Aberfeldy; and while

M

viewing the rocks at the last-named place he is said to have clapped his hands for joy at such a manifestation of the power of God. He did not succeed in awakening any of the Highland enthusiasm, however. At Aberfeldy the bellman went round to summon a congregation in characteristic fashion. " Your auld playmate and auld acquaintance, Shony Carstairs, wants to see you all at the Independent Chapel at seven o'clock, to hear my dear friend, the Rev. C. H. Spurgeon, preach. Mind, he has come five hundred miles to tell you something for your good, and the Rev. C. H. Spurgeon and myself expect you all to come and give us a hearty shake hands." There was plenty of snuff-taking during the sermon, and immediately the benediction was pronounced there was a rush for the door, when the popular preacher and his friend, Shony Carstairs, had the building to themselves.

What seems also to have struck observers at this time was the fact that the young preacher had not been unduly lifted up by his success. With such vast crowds at his feet, anxious to listen to what he had to say, there was some danger of others being led to the footstool of God in penitence without the preacher himself partaking of the same spirit. Perhaps it was well for him at that early date that he had violent detractors as well as enthusiastic admirers. The two extremes of opinion were continually finding expression in the public journals. It was therefore remarked, " He has been denounced as mean in stature, inexpressive in countenance, and contemptible in intellect. On the same day his *personnel* has been extolled as attractive, his intellectual power tremendous, and his oratory overwhelming. He has heard voices innumerable denouncing him, and voices innumerable admiring him. Many a pen has been dipped in gall by jealous rivals, and many a pen in honey by generous critics."

The result seems to have been that the preacher did not think of himself too highly or too lowly. He was conscious of his own power; but while he knew that he was not so mean a mediocrity as numbers insisted, he seems to have had no temptation to exalt himself. Thus early he was without doubt a wonderful example of the power of the grace of God to keep a man from sinking down into a state of pride. There are those who think that in after-life Mr. Spurgeon's frequent illnesses were a kind of necessary thorn in the flesh to keep him humble; but in the halcyon days of youth, when his health was perfect, there seems to have been no danger of his falling into that condition of pride which would have destroyed his usefulness. Even thus early, if he did not do so in all cases, he frequently refused fees for preaching.

Before he returned home from this tour, Mr. Spurgeon was at one time in danger of drowning on the Clyde. "I crossed the Clyde in a ferry," he remarked himself; "the man who had the management of the boat had taken 'a wee drap of the cratur,' and was not able to manage it at all, and had put twenty-six persons into a boat that ought to have contained far less.* I have been informed by one or two ladies that report was current that I was thrown into the water and fished up by the hair of my head. Now, that was not so. We were simply in danger, but by a little management and expostulation, which was resented by oaths and curses, we came safe to land." A trip was made to Lake Windermere in the course of this excursion. In every town visited immense crowds were attracted, the climax being reached at Glasgow, when on one occasion twenty thousand persons were said to have been unable to gain admission to one service.

In his early days Mr. Spurgeon would occasionally see a contrast to this awakening of the congregation of a whole city. He did not always have an overflowing audience; but that did not happen on account of want of popularity, it rather came about because he was too popular. Thus, when he visited Enfield, the then little chapel at Chaseside was nearly empty because people

---

* "One gains a glimpse of his decision of character from an incident in his northern trip. Finding that the ferryman on the Clyde had allowed six-and-twenty persons to get into a boat fit for no more than twelve, and that the man was drunk, Mr. Spurgeon took the oars from him, and, in spite of his oaths, insisted that so many lives should not be at the mercy of his unsteady hands."—*The Patriot*, September 21, 1855.

stayed away in order to avoid the crush which was supposed to be inevitable. There was also one elderly dame living near who stayed away on principle, because she could not conscientiously encourage the young man's vanity.*

A correspondent of *The Freeman*, who remembers Mr. Spurgeon as he was at New Park Street during the first months of work in London, says the congregation was then "mainly a juvenile audience," as the preacher had not yet been "quite ' received ' by the church at large." The impression produced is vividly remembered. "The pulpit was then the old-fashioned one, entered by a staircase from the vestry, the door being closed behind, as was the fashion at an early period," it is remarked; and it is added that "his action was much too lively to be confined to the limits of the pulpit, and he occasionally sat upon the side of it as one would do on the bulwark of a ship." His success appears to have silenced those students who maintained that sermons needed to be read. On one occasion, in preaching from Eccl. ix. 4, "For a living dog is better than a dead lion," he remarked, "Now, if I had said this I should be accused of coarseness and vulgarity." The lessons or conclusions he drew from his subject are said to have been always serious and practical. "The Emperor of Russia was then lying dead, and I remarked to him what use he might have made by the comparison," says this early friend. "'Why didn't you tell me?' he replied with energy; of course my only answer was that I was not previously let into the secret of the discourse." Another early sermon, which is said to have produced a deep impression, was founded on Lev. xix. 19, "Neither shall a garment mingled of linen and woollen come upon thee." Many of these discourses which were thus memorable, and

---

* One other instance of this kind occurred. About thirty years ago, Mr. William Winters wrote to Charles Waters Banks : " A short time after the Surrey Gardens catastrophe Mr. Spurgeon came to preach in the Strict Baptist Chapel, College—then Water—Lane, Cheshunt, and, singular enough, he had only a very few persons to hear him, everybody thinking the chapel would be crowded to excess. Consequently he had to preach to an exceedingly small audience; and as soon as he got into the pulpit he began to feel himself cramped up, and with his usual bluntness called it ' A tub of a thing.' Some time after I heard you preach there, for the first time in my life, and there was an excellent congregation "—" Life of Charles Waters Banks," p. 154.

are even still remembered, were never printed. On a certain week-day afternoon he preached for a Baptist society from 1 Cor. xiv. 8, "For if the trumpet give an uncertain sound, who shall prepare himself to the battle?" He then said some trenchant things against Arminianism; and it was on this occasion that the late Dr. Binney made the remark which was long remembered, "He is the most impudent young rascal I ever heard in my life." There were staid persons who gave the preacher some very proper advice. "Take care, you are a very young man." Mr. Spurgeon's reply was, "Who were the great sinners, the old or the young, as given in Holy Writ? There were Noah, Lot, David, etc.; therefore, I say, 'Take care, old man.'"

One rule observed at this time, that is, not to attempt to answer adverse critics, was adhered to throughout life; and this, no doubt, preserved Spurgeon from much irritation. Perhaps, how-ever, some little trouble might have been taken in contradicting erroneous statements or anecdotes, but even these were allowed to go on their way unchallenged. Many things which had thus no foundation in truth may have been accepted as fact. Thus, for years it was circulated in Mr. Spurgeon's "Life," issued by his own publishers, that there had been only four pastors at Stambourne in two hundred years; and the four was not corrected into eight until "Memories of Stambourne" appeared.

In the course of some interesting reminiscences of Mr. Spurgeon in *The Christian Union* of New York, Dr. Wayland Hoyt makes some references to the great preacher's early days, which may be given in this place :—

"With Mr. Spurgeon religion was never in the least anything put on. It was always a steady and pervasive influence and colour, flushing everything. I never met a man who was so absolutely free from cant. I never met a man whose tongue so thoroughly refused to run over the routine and usual religious phrases. In everything he said and in everything he did there was the completest naturalness. I was walking with him in the woods one day just outside of London, and, as we strolled under the shadow of the summer foliage, we came upon a log lying athwart the path. 'Come,' said he, as naturally as one would say it were he hungry and bread were put before him, 'come, let us pray.' And, kneeling beside the log, he lifted his soul to the Lord in the most loving, outpouring, and yet reverent prayer. Then, rising from his knees as naturally, he went strolling on, talking about this and that. The prayer was no parenthesis interjected. It was something that belonged as much to the habit of his mind as breathing did to the habit of his body. . . . Mr. Spurgeon was a man of the most singular ability of self-marshalling and self-control. In this respect he always reminded me of Mr. Beecher. He seemed to be absolutely sure of himself for any moment, for any occasion. . . . His pulpit preparations were always just before each service. He once said to me that if he were appointed to preach on some great occasion six months beforehand, he should not think at all of preparation for the duty until just as the time struck—he would occupy himself about other things. This surprising power of quick self-control and marshalling of powers gave him a perpetual consciousness of ease. He had never the fear that he would not be equal to the time. He knew that when the moment came he would be ready; so, instead of being strained and anxious, his mind was in a beautiful openness for whatever might flow in upon it. And yet, especially in his earlier years, after his preparation had been made, and just as he was about to confront the throngs he knew were gathering to listen to him, he used to have the most fearful nervous anxiety, almost convulsions. He told me once that for years and years in his early ministry he never preached but that he had had beforehand the most straining time of vomiting. His stomach was able to retain absolutely nothing. In later years he vanquished this nervous tendency. Nothing was more delightful about Mr. Spurgeon than his evident childlike faith. That God should do great things for him through him, seemed to him to be as much expected as that a mother should meet the necessities of her child. He had been telling me once about the amount of money he must disburse in order to sustain his various enterprises. We stopped talking for a little, and I sat looking at him. He was as unconcerned as is a little child holding its mother's hand. There were no lines upon his brow, there was no shadow of anxiety upon his face, only the large, good-natured English smile. I was thinking of the orphans he must feed, the old Christian women he must care for, the professors' salaries in his Pastors' College he must pay, the students he must supply with teaching, many of them with bread and clothing, since they were too poor to buy these for themselves. I said to him in a kind of wonder, 'How can you be so easy-minded? Do not these responsibilities come upon you sometimes with a kind of crushing weight?' He looked at me with a sort of holy amazement, and answered, 'No; the Lord is a good banker. I trust Him. He has never failed me. Why should I be anxious?'"

In his young days, as in his maturer years, Mr. Spurgeon won favour by having about him no airs of the "great man"; and the attention he would show to the poor of "the household of faith" was all along characteristic. When out preaching, I have heard of his choosing to go and drink tea with very poor people whom he happened to know, rather than be entertained at the mansion where he was expected. When he visited Ponders End as a very young man, he passed much of the time between the services with a bed-ridden aged Christian in South Street, with whom he sat and conversed while his congregation was being regaled at a tea-meeting. Such things more than answered the adverse criticisms to which he was subjected.

CHAPTER XX.

MR. SPURGEON'S CALVINISM.

A Service at Unicorn Yard Chapel—A Centre of High Calvinism—Extracts from the Sermon—
Extension of Mission Work at New Park Street—Opening of a Ragged School.

SOON after his return from Scotland in the year 1855, Mr.
Spurgeon preached a memorable sermon at the old chapel in
Unicorn Yard, Tooley Street, on behalf of the Ministers' Relief Society.
This charitable agency had been formed not very long before by
Mr. Charles Waters Banks, who was then pastor of a church which
met in a chapel in Crosby Row. Mr. Banks soon afterwards
removed to what he called his Old Vicarage in Unicorn Yard. He
had a great love for this place, and we find him speaking of the
old sanctuary in a truly affectionate manner.* Mr. Banks succeeded
in interesting his friend Spurgeon in the work of what he had
called the Gospel Ministers' Relief Society. As pastor of the
church in New Park Street, Mr. Spurgeon was already a member of
the Particular Baptist Fund, which his predecessor Benjamin Stinton
had founded in 1717, and he would be expected to make a collection
annually for that institution. He nevertheless appears to have had
a strong liking for the supplementary agency which his friend and
neighbour had founded. Accordingly, on Wednesday evening,
August 29, the young pastor might have been seen walking along

* "That old, and truly ancient, that long-honoured house of prayer—which for a
century and a half, or more, had been the birthplace and a Bethel to many thousands—
was fast falling into decay. It was nearly deserted, and report said, and men of practical
judgment said, it was not safe to meet in. The Lord, in His kind and gracious
providence, called me to gather the gold and silver of His willing saints, and entirely to
renovate and re-establish this long-honoured Gospel sanctuary. On the day previous to
the reopening, I besought our gracious God to give me a word from Himself with which
to enter upon my new scene of labours, and these words were impressed on my mind:
Son, go work to-day in My vineyard. Never shall I forget the sight when I stood up
in the pulpit—the crowds of anxious eyes, and the flood of happy feelings, in the midst
of which I delivered the message the Master had given."—"Life of Charles Waters
Banks," p. 61.

Tooley Street towards Unicorn Yard.　He was probably in better spirits than he would have been a year before, for the work to which he had set his hand seemed to be going bravely forward; and while the national outlook was less disheartening, Mr. Spurgeon himself was more firmly established as the most prominent preacher of the age.　The war with Russia still went wearily on; but some occasional success had elated the French, and the Queen and Prince Albert had just returned from their eight days' visit to the French Emperor at Paris, where some brilliant pageants had been witnessed.

The sermon preached on the occasion referred to was entitled, "Christ's Prayer for His People," * and the text was John xvii. 20 —"Neither pray I for these alone, but for them also which shall believe on Me through their word."　The sermon itself is very characteristic of Mr. Spurgeon's early style, and as such the passages which follow will be acceptable to all who are interested in the preacher's early progress in London.　It will be noticed that the distinguishing doctrines of Calvinism are strongly insisted upon. To those who were not fully in sympathy with them, these sentiments, so boldly expressed, would, no doubt, be sufficiently distasteful; but to the High Calvinists, who regarded James Wells and Charles Waters Banks as representative apostles of sound doctrine, the question must have suggested itself whether Mr. Spurgeon was not really being drawn into closer sympathy with the stricter denomination.　In the introduction the preacher dwelt on Christ's peculiar love for His people :—

"In the very opening of this subject one feels inexpressibly delighted to see the wondrous love of our Saviour towards His people.　He here promises that He will intercede for everyone of them before His Father's throne.　He declares that He not only prays for 'these'—that is, the elect who are called out from the ruins of the fall—but that this intercession also arises for those who are yet uncalled, unconverted, and unregenerated.　Mark the depth of His affection—He spends all His time continually in interceding for His people.　I marvel at the condescension of Jesus Christ—that His people's name is ever on His lips.　When we consider that, notwithstanding all His exceeding grace and affection towards them, they transgress and rebel, it appears wonderful that He should mention their names, or that He should regard their persons.　But when we remember that day by day in that land where there is no night, He who stands before His Father's throne bears perpetually on His breast their names deep-cut in the precious

* *The Penny Pulpit*, No. 2454.

jewels and stones of the breastplate, and always with outspread hands pleads for them, we cannot but admire His love for them, and feel a deep veneration for that grace which makes Him declare—'For Zion's sake will I not hold My peace, and for Jerusalem's sake I will not rest, until the righteousness thereof go forth as brightness, and the salvation thereof as a lamp that burneth.'

"You must note here also the peculiar knowledge which our Saviour, Jesus Christ, has of all His people, as well as His particular love for them; for He says He prays for those who are yet uncalled. Now, none of us who have faith in God, none of those called and led to believe in Jesus, are unknown to Him. He knows His redeemed as well in one condition as another. He knows which of two drunkards shall turn and become one of His family. There are none so sunk into the depths of sin and wickedness that, if they are His by the covenant of His grace, do not even now share His intercession. He knows His beloved when there is no mark to know them by. He discerns His sheep when to other people they seem like wolves and goats. He recognises His family when they are black as the tents of Kedar, and He knows they shall be fair as the curtains of Solomon. He knows His children when they do not know themselves; when they fancy they are lost beyond rescue, or when they foolishly conceive that they can save themselves. Yea, and when all hope fails them, when it seems that the Lord does not know them, and the Gospel does not know them—when no Christian knows them, and the minister can give them no comfort, Christ knows them even then, for still it is written, 'I pray for them'— I pray not for the world, I pray also for those whom Thou hast given Me out of the world; who have not believed yet; but who shall believe through the word of those who are already called.

"Another thought before we pass to the subject; for we like to suggest a few of these thoughts just to start with, as they are in the text. The other thought is this—mark how Jesus loves all His people with the same affection. He could not pray for those few who in His lifetime had believed, without suddenly (to speak after the manner of men) recollecting that these were but a handful; and, therefore, He stirs Himself up, and says, 'My Father, neither pray I for these alone, but for them also who shall believe'; as much as to say, These are not My especial favourites because they are converted so early; I do not love these better than others—I pray for those also who shall be called. I pray as much for one of My people as for another. It is well said by one of the Apostles, 'There is no difference'; and verily, beloved, there *is* no difference in the affection of God towards His children. There is an elect out of the elect, I will acknowledge, as to gifts and standing, and as to the labour which they may accomplish in this world; but there is no election out of the elect as to a deeper extent of love. They are all loved alike; they are all written in the same book of eternal love and life. They were all purchased with the selfsame precious blood of the Saviour. One was not purchased with His foot, another with His hand, but all with His very heart's blood. They are all justified with the same righteousness, all sanctified by the same Spirit, and they shall all enter into the same heaven. I am not sure that there will be any difference in degrees of glory; one star may differ from another star in its peculiar colour and form, but not in brightness or in lustre; they shall all shine alike as stars for ever and ever. They are all saved by the same grace; loved by the same love; heirs of the same inheritance; and Jesus Christ puts them altogether when He says—'Neither pray I for these alone, but for them also which shall believe on Me through their word'!"

The first point insisted on is, that God loved His people before they believed. Christ would never pray for those He did not love; and thus such prayers were different from those of the hypocrite. There were too many hypocritical prayers, and they were not worth picking up in the street; they were even wicked. That God loved His people before they were in a state of grace was shown to be a Scripture doctrine, although many talked against it. If men came to God, it was owing entirely to grace.   All this brought out the Calvinistic belief of the preacher, so that when, in the second place, he explained the use of a Gospel ministry, he had to take some notice of the objections which would be urged against his teaching :—

"Now, then, the second thing—the use of a Gospel ministry? Now, many captious and cavilling persons will object—'You may say that God loves His people, and, therefore, they will be saved; then what is the good of your preaching?' *Then what is the good of preaching!* When I say that God loves a multitude that no man can number, a countless host of the race of men, do you ask me what is the good of preaching? *What is the good of preaching!* To fetch these diamonds of the Lord out of the dunghill; to go down to the depths, as the diver does, to fetch up God's pearls from the place where they are lying. What is the good of preaching? To cut down the good corn and gather it into the garner. What is the good of preaching? To fetch out God's elect from the ruins of the fall, and make them stand on the rock Christ Jesus, and see their standing sure. Ah, ye who ask what is the benefit of preaching, because God has ordained some to salvation, we ask you whether it would not be a most foolish thing to say, because there is to be a harvest, what is the good of sowing? There is to be a harvest, what is the use of reaping? The very reason why we do sow and reap is, because we feel assured there is to be a harvest. And if, indeed, I believed that there was not a number who must be saved, I could not come into this pulpit again. Only once make me think that no one is certain to be saved, and I do not care to preach. But now I know that a countless number must be saved, I am confident that He shall 'see His seed; He shall prolong His days': I know that if there is much to dispirit me in the ministry, and I see but little effects, yet He 'shall keep all that the Father has given to Him'; and this makes me preach. I am not among those who say—'Who hath believed our report, and to whom hath the arm of the Lord been revealed?' at present; but if I could say that, nevertheless, I know they will be saved, and that would comfort and cheer me, and make me go on again. I come into this chapel to-night with the assurance that God has some child of His in this place not yet called; and I feel confident that He will call someone by the use of the ministry, and why not by me? I know there are not a few souls whom God has given me through my ministry, and not hundreds, but thousands. I have seen some hundreds of those who profess to have been brought to God through my preaching in Park Street and elsewhere. And with that confidence I must go on. I know that Jesus must have a 'seed,' His people must increase, and it is the very purpose of the ministry to seek them out and bring them into God's fold. Our Saviour tells us the use of the ministry is, that they may 'believe on Me through *their* word!' There is one peculiarity about this. It says, 'They shall believe on Me through *their* word. Have you never heard people call out about running after men? They say, 'You are all running after such a *man!*' What, then, would you have them run after a woman? You say, 'The people go after one particular man!' Who else shall they go after? Some persons may say, 'Ah, I went to so-and-so, and the people there love their minister too much—oh, it is worshipping a man.' Ah, that is very dreadful, no doubt. But then it is not so. There is very little love towards our fellow-creatures anywhere, and so far as ministers being in danger of being ruined by love, it very seldom falls to their lot. Very generally they get quite as many kicks as anything else; and if they do get too much love in any particular place, they get too much of the reverse somewhere else. If we get a little sweet, somebody else is sure to put in much that is bitter. Is it not singular that the Holy Ghost should say—'that they may believe on Me through *their* word'? Now, do God's people believe through the word of the ministry? We know it is written, 'We do not receive it as the word of man, but as, in truth, the word of God.' Our faith does not stand in the word of man, but in the word of God. We do not rest on any man, yet it is through *their* word—that is, through the word of the Apostles, through the word of every faithful minister. I take it, the Gospel is the minister's own word when he speaks from experience and manifestation. What is in the Bible is God's word; what God speaks to me by experience becomes my word as well as God's. And it is then *their* word, when ministers come into the pulpit with the word in their hearts. I think a minister is not only called to preach what he finds in the Bible—the mere naked doctrine—but what he has experienced in his own heart—what he has tasted, and felt, and handled. If he does this, he will be greatly in danger of being charged as an egotist. He will use too many 'I's' very likely. Well, he cannot preach John Smith's experience, or anybody else's experience; he can only preach his own, and then he will have to say 'I.' But if he does not preach experimentally what he has felt himself, it will not be 'that they may believe on Me through *their* word.' When we speak that which we know, and testify that we have seen and felt; if we say we know the Saviour will pardon sinners because He has pardoned us, then it is not only God's word, but our word. If I say to a child of God—'Go, and cast thy burden on the Lord, and thou wilt find relief,' and I say 'I have done so,' then it is not only God's word, but my word. When he has proved the Saviour's word by experience, then it becomes the minister's word, as also when he has it manifested to him by the Holy Spirit. Some people say that these manifestations are all nonsense. I have heard many object to applied texts. Such men do not understand much about the real law of piety, or else they would see texts manifested to them at one time which they had never seen before. I know many of my ministering brethren who now testify that they have sometimes taken a text and tried to break it. They have smitten it with a sledge-hammer, but they could not get an atom off it; and they have had to throw it aside. But another time, my friends, when that same text comes before us, though it seemed hard as granite when we took it up in our hands before, it now crumbles and breaks in pieces. Why? Because God's Holy Spirit shines upon it now, and He did not do so before. And we might have continued hitting it till we broke the head of our hammer, and not a scrap would come off it; but the manifestation afterwards reveals the text; and most texts are to be learnt so. It is not by sitting down in deep thought often that you get at the meaning. It is by leaving it until in some hallowed hour of high spiritual intercourse we get into the very secret chamber where the meaning of the text lies. In some solemn moment we dive down into the very depths where the meaning of the text is hidden. God teaches us the meaning, and then it becomes *our* word. It is ours by application; and we believe, my brethren, that sinners will be converted to God only by preaching the Gospel we find in our hearts, 'known and read of all men!' That they also may believe on Me through their word!

"Let us then come into our pulpits with this determination (I speak to my brethren in the ministry), that by the help of God we will bring our own experience to bear upon it. We will sometimes talk of ourselves, and not be ashamed of it, for whatever the Lord our God saith unto us, not only in His word, but by experience, and by His Spirit, that we speak to the people."

Notwithstanding all, however, God could do without ministers if He chose. When it was insisted that ministers were necessary, it was speaking of them as concerning men, and after the manner of men. The preacher continued:—

"With God ministers are not necessary. He could do without them. I thought to-day as I walked along, 'God could do without me.' I thought of many men who were preaching, and I thought, 'God could do without them; strike them all away, and God could do without them.' I thought of some members of my church, dear to me, who seem to be pillars of it, and I thought, 'What could I do without them?' And then the thought came across my mind, 'God could do without *them*.' The people of God would still be saved just as well without them if God so pleased. God is enough in Himself, without the addition of any one of His preachers. When He made angels it was not because He wanted them. He could have accomplished His will without the wing of a flaming seraph, and without the voice of a glorious cherub. When He made the stars it was not because He needed them. He was light Himself without the light of sun, stars, or moon. When He made man it was not because He wanted man, it was because He would make him, and for no other reason. There was no necessity for it. He would be the same eternal God were all His creatures dead; and if He were to blot out those lines of wisdom and grace written in the universe, He would be just as glorious and great as ever. And especially in the Gospel ministry God can do without His servants. But this being a dispensation of means, He is not a God acting without means. God *does* not do without them, though He could if He would. God elected His people without ministers; He did not want any ministers to help Him in that. He redeemed His people without ministers. What great divine could have helped Christ to redeem His people? Yea more, He can, if He please, call His people without ministers; for we know how some have become the subject of grace by the reading of the Word without the assistance of the ministry, and some in the Sabbath school have received the words of eternal life. This should make our pride subside at once. I know it is a great honour, and should comfort us much, to know that God is making use of us; but He could, if He pleased, well enough accomplish His ends and purposes without you and without me. If to-morrow we were laid low in our coffins, and if our people should go out weeping because their pastor was dead, God has other men whom He could raise up; or, if He did not choose to raise other men up, He could perfect His ends without us. And, possibly, there is a time coming when Gospel ministers shall not be wanted; when men shall need no man to say to his brother, 'Know the Lord, for all shall know Him, from the least even to the greatest.' There may be happy days coming, 'when the knowledge of the Lord shall cover the earth as the waters cover the sea'; and when there shall be no need of the messengers upon the mountains to 'make glad the city of our God'; when the sunshine of the Lord shall supplant our poor farthing rushlight, and when Jesus shall 'come in His glory, and all His holy angels with Him'; and we shall have too much to do to stand and admire Him, without standing up to men to preach concerning Him who is present in their midst."

The orator went on to show that God would never do without ministers; that so long as there were a people to be gathered in, according to the elective grace of God, there would be those abroad who would gather them in. He then proceeded to say some trenchant things about the true and the false "successors of the apostles" :—

"Christ says in the text, 'Neither pray I for these alone, but for them also which shall believe on Me through their word.' Someone may object and say, 'Yes, but their word signifies the word of the apostles.' Then another person might say, 'Are you the successors of the apostles?' There has been a vast deal of fudge in these days about 'the successors of the apostles.' We have people who pretend to be the successors of the apostles. There are the Roman Catholics; they are the successors of the apostles. But, I think, if Peter and Paul were to come and see their successors, they would think there was a mighty difference between themselves and them. By way of parable, suppose the Virgin Mary, Peter, and Paul should come one Sunday and go to a cathedral; well, when they entered, the Virgin heard them singing something to her honour, and praise, and glory; she jogged Peter, and said, 'What are these people after? they are worshipping me. My Son said to me, "Woman, what have I to do with thee?" He never worshipped me,' she said; 'let us turn out of this.' They stopped a little longer, and they heard one of them say that the apostle Peter was the head of the Church, and his successor, the Pope, was therefore the head. Peter jogged the Virgin Mary and said, 'What a lie that is; I was never head of the Church at all. Did I not fall into sin? I head of the Church! A pretty head I was.' Soon afterwards Paul heard them preaching justification by works. 'Come out,' said he, 'there is no Gospel here; I preached justification by faith without works, and they are preaching justification by works'; and so, upon that, they all three of them went out. By-and-by they came to a place where they heard them singing, 'Glory, honour, praise, and power be unto the Lamb that sitteth on the throne'; and they heard them speak of those who were 'kept by the power of God through faith unto salvation.' 'Ah,' said Peter, 'this is the place, and here I will stay.' Those are the successors of the apostles who are like the apostles. Are those the successors of the apostles who take our money from us by force to pay for their religion? Are those the successors of the apostles who go to brother so-and-so's house and take away his table, and his spoon, and his candlestick to pay rates for a religion he does not believe in? I should like to read about a church-rate in Corinth, or about the apostle Paul distraining upon some man in Jerusalem. Such men successors of the apostles! They may be in godliness—for holy men are sometimes very much mistaken—but they are not like the apostles. I say again, those who are like the apostles are their successors; not men who are ashamed to speak to anybody else, because they think they are above them; not those who cannot speak plain words. Oh! have we not some ministers to understand whom you need take a dictionary always to chapel with you? Do you call them the successors of the apostles? Your judgment answers 'No.' A downright honest man, who speaks what can be understood, who declares God's Gospel in unmeasured terms, as God would have him speak it, he is a successor of the apostles; and it is through *their* word (the apostles' word, and the successors of the apostles) that men are to be saved. Successors of the apostles! I am as much a successor of the apostles as the Bishop of Bath, the Bishop of London, or the bishop of anywhere else, and perhaps more so. We are all bishops who are called of God, ordained by the Most High. We trace our ordination to the hands of the Almighty, who has put His hands on our head. There will always be successors. The ministry shall never cease till the latest period of time. Never has there been a spiritual night so dark when there have been no stars to illumine it; never a sky so beclouded that the sun could not shine through it. There have always been some lights; and until the latest hour there shall always be some who are girded with the strength of the Omnipotent, and made strong in the mighty God Jehovah; who shall testify their words, which is, after all, God's word, that thereby men shall be saved.

"Now, my dear brothers and sisters, having directed your attention to the fact that we are quite sure God will always have a ministry and always use it; and since a ministry under God is necessary, though He could do without them, what should we do for them? I will tell you what some people say—*starve them.* Some people have a notion that a minister cannot preach experimental godliness, if he has anything more than £1 a week; and supposing he should have enough to keep himself just the same as his people, he will get ruined —of course he will! He is subject to infirmities like other people, and, therefore, he will naturally get proud. Money in the pocket of a man who sits in a pew is all very just and right; but if it was in the hands of his minister, it would make him worldly; and, therefore, some people try to starve him. I do not say it is so here, or with my people, but it is so in many country villages. Unfortunately, there are many farmers who could afford to give much to the cause of God, who, while their servant Betty sits in the gallery, and pays her shilling a quarter for her pew, the master only pays a shilling a quarter, too. The poor girl, renting a pew at a few shillings a year, gives as much to the cause of God as the rich man who has his thousands. He says, 'I pay my pew rent'; but how much is that pew rent? And there are many ministers among the Baptists who do not get much above £30 a year. They manage to make both ends meet, but how they do it I do not know. They have to keep a shop. And then, on Sunday, many will go away and say, 'It was a very poor sermon; there was not much in it; our minister could not have studied it.' How could he, while he had to stand behind the counter? But Christ's ministers give themselves to the work, because they feel they must preach; and they would rather preach on dry bread than be silent. Now, we have formed this Society, just to help them. I can assure you, if any one of our dear friends stood in the position I have occupied for a single year, when you came to cast up your income, if you felt any benevolence, you would have a very little left; indeed, you would have nothing left if you listened to the claims made upon you. Talk about Baptist ministers being overpaid! I am sure they are worse paid than bricklayers' labourers.

"When the Emperor of Russia sent an ambassador here, he used to have a fine house, and everything else. I do not ask for such grandeur for God's ambassadors; but I ask a decent maintenance; and when they have it not, I think we should do something to help them.

"Now, one other thought. If God sends ministers into the world to preach His Gospel, how ill does it become us to hurt them—'He that toucheth you, toucheth the apple of Mine eye.' I have always felt very careful about touching a child of God. You know there is nothing puts a man so much on his mettle as to touch his children. I have seen a father calm and placid, and very gentle—someone has touched his children, the father flashed into his face at once. Do what you like; touch my property, or my house, and I may be vexed; but touch my child, and then my fury comes up at once. He cannot stand that. Oh, my friends, a heavy responsibility rests on the heads of some, even of God's people, if you view it in that light. Touch God's people; touch God's chosen; touch God's favourites; touch God's darlings! Oh, let us take heed! We had better suffer one to pass who professes to be a child of God and is not, than that we should treat harshly or unkindly any of those who really are His. And, I think, if there is any difference in the case of gospel ministers, this has a special force. We should, above all, seek not to injure their character by spreading evil reports about them. They will have enough of that from the wicked world. But we had need be tender of them, and plant a hedge around them to protect them in every way. They are the standard-bearers of Christendom; and if the standard-bearer falls, what a disgrace it brings on everything! We ought to stand by them; pray for them, plead with God for them that He will hold up their hands; for there is very little sympathy and very little kindness in this world."

These extracts will sufficiently show in what light Mr. Spurgeon regarded preaching and preachers. To help this cause ever afforded him keenest pleasure; and many a time has his heart been gladdened by a liberal collection at the Metropolitan Tabernacle for the Particular Baptist Fund.

Reference has already been made to the home mission work undertaken at New Park Street. The day school and missions were in Guildford Street, where larger and convenient premises for the purpose were obtained. In August an excursion of four hundred persons to Rosherville came off, by which a sum of £44 was realised; and on the 9th of November there was a public tea-meeting, at which Mr. Spurgeon presided. Dr. A. Fletcher and others gave addresses; but next to the young pastor himself, the late Judge Payne seems to have been a chief attraction. Just at that time there was a vacancy in the representation of Southwark, and very naturally "the philanthropic barrister," as we find him called, made capital out of that fact. "It had caused much talk, and the question was, who should succeed to the honourable position of M.P.? He thought their chairman (Mr. Spurgeon) was an M.P. already; for he was a Man of Principle, Made on Purpose, to Move the People; a Magnificent Preacher, Marvellously Patient, and Mightily Persevering." Mr. Payne went on to speak of four classes of preachers —"the freezing, the teasing, the pleasing, and the squeezing." Then what about causes and effects? In the pastor he detected juvenility, capability, versatility, and true humility; the effects of which, as seen on that Lord Mayor's day, were "A stirring call, an opening hall,* a social greeting, and a glorious meeting."

The fact that Mr. Spurgeon thus early engaged in aggressive mission work shows him to have been in hearty sympathy with the ragged-school crusade, of which at that time Lord Shaftesbury was the distinguished leader. Though more squalid than it is now, London had then more novelties to arrest the attention of explorers, and the low-lying quarters on the south side of the Thames had many relics of olden times which have since, in numbers of instances, been improved away. Mint Street, one of the old sanctuaries in which criminals had been wont to retreat, was still one of the notorious plague-spots of London. There the first case of cholera in the terrible outbreak of 1832 had occurred. The Mint was still what one writer had called it—"the land of

* The meeting celebrated the opening of the hall. The accommodation was for six hundred children. When one hundred and fifty children had been brought in, it was discovered that a hundred out of the number had never been to school before. See *The Baptist Messenger*, iii. 141; and also *The Freeman*, November 21. 1855.

death, through which the pestilence stalked, like a destroying angel, in the deep shadows of the night, and the open noon of day." Despite its squalidness at the time of Mr. Spurgeon's coming to London, however, the district was one of singular interest. The houses remained just as they had been built two or more centuries before. "There is a smell of past ages about these ancient courts," remarked one writer of the period. "The timber of these old houses looks bleached and dead, and the very brickwork seems to have been never new. In them you find wide, hollow-sounding, decayed staircases, that lead into great ruinous rooms, where echoes are only awakened by the shrieking and running of large black-eyed rats, which eat through the solid floors, through the wainscot, and live and die without being startled by a human voice." The people who inhabited the lower apartments of some of these antique dwellings seemed to be peculiar to their district; and if you had seen them standing at the entrances of their courts to enjoy a view of the outer world of the main thoroughfare, you would not have included them among "the working classes," or with any class at all apart from themselves. Such was the home mission field which in those days may be said to have been attached to the New Park Street Chapel, though others also worked in it. One of the most curious places of its kind in London was the famous Farm House of the Mint, which, as a common lodging-house, had two hundred beds in its forty rooms. In the great kitchen preachers from Surrey Chapel held services.

In the case of Mr. Spurgeon and his people, work similar to that inaugurated at the Guildford Street Hall grew on their hands, until the Metropolitan Tabernacle was surrounded by many such stations. Although times have altered, some of these are still really of the old ragged-school type—such, for example, as the station at Lansdowne Place, in the vicinity of the notorious Kent Street, in the rear of St. George's Church.

OLD SURREY GARDENS MUSIC HALL

FROM A PHOTOGRAPH BY HERBERT HARTWELL, CLAPHAM ROAD, S.W.

SURREY GARDENS MEMORIAL HALL

THE

LIFE AND WORK

OF

CHARLES HADDON SPURGEON

BY

G. HOLDEN PIKE,

AUTHOR OF "THE WORLD'S WORKERS—CHARLES HADDON SPURGEON," ETC.

ILLUSTRATED WITH FIFTEEN FULL-PAGE PHOTOGRAVURE PLATES.

VOL. II.

CASSELL & COMPANY, Limited:

LONDON, PARIS & MELBOURNE.

CONTENTS.

PHOTOGRAVURE PLATES.

CHAPTER XXI.

MR. SPURGEON AND *THE PATRIOT.*

An Extended Review of the Preacher's Life and Work—Characteristics—High Qualities and Shortcomings—A Watch-Night Service at New Park Street Chapel.

THE oldest of the London Nonconformist newspapers, *The Patriot,* appears to have been the first to give any extended notice of Mr. Spurgeon as a preacher, and, on the whole, the opinions expressed of the young pastor were generous and encouraging. The review of his life and work which appeared in the fall of 1855, soon after the visit to Scotland, would fill four columns of *The Times.*

Some biographical facts having been given, special reference was made to the temptation to infidelity noticed by the preacher himself at Exeter Hall. A very generous estimate is then given of his preaching :—

"We found him neither extravagant nor extraordinary. His voice is clear and musical; his language was plain; his style flowing, yet terse; his method lucid and orderly; his matter sound and suitable; his tone and spirit cordial; his remarks always pithy and pungent, sometimes familiar and colloquial, yet never light or coarse, much less profane. Judging from this single sermon, we supposed that he would become a plain, faithful, forcible, and affectionate preacher of the Gospel in the form called Calvinistic; and our judgment was the more favourable because, while there was a solidity beyond his years, we detected little of the wild luxuriance naturally characteristic of very young preachers."

The weekly numbers of *The New Park Street Pulpit* were now being very widely diffused; and *The Patriot* reviewer admitted that after a perusal of some of these his opinion of the preacher had become "somewhat modified." In a number of printed discourses, the characteristics of the preacher showed him to be even a more extraordinary man than had at first been supposed; but, at the same time, he was not quite so far removed "from extravagance" as had been thought. This was not mentioned "with a view to criticism," however; for "there would be little use in pointing out

N

the faults and errors of a public speaker so absolutely independent of opinion." According to his own confession, Mr. Spurgeon was not over-scrupulous about the means he used for doing good. He had told the people of Scotland that they did not understand him —"Why, bless your hearts, I would preach standing on my head, if I thought I could convert your souls, rather than preach on my feet. I am not very particular about how I preach." Then "that ranting fellow," as some called him, had said, "My motto is *Cedo Nulli*—I yield to none. I have not courted any man's love; I asked no man to attend my ministry; I preach what I like, when I like, and as I like." He refused to be bound by any rules of art, so that while he was evidently free from conceit, the critic had to take such a preacher as he found him, and to value him for what he was. This was fair; but the critic may possibly have made a mistake in too readily accepting Mr. Spurgeon's own too humble estimate of himself—an estimate which in some measure may have accounted for the opinion getting abroad that he had burst upon the world without education or proper equipment for his lifework. "Recollect who I am, and what I am," he had said: "a child having little education, little learning, ability, or talent." Without the Spirit of God he declared himself to be unable to speak. "I have not those gifts which qualify men to speak; I need an afflatus from on high; otherwise, I stand like other men, and have nought to say." He would not have spoken like this at a later date, and when it was spoken, it was probably misunderstood. Despite his own lowly opinion of himself, *The Patriot* detected his originality :—

"From whatever cause it springs, whether from force of native character, or from a vigour superinduced upon that basis by the grace of God, there is that in Mr. Spurgeon's reported sermons which marks him a superior man. Models of different styles of preaching are so numerous, that originality must be of rare occurrence; but he appears to be an original genius. To the pith of Jay and the plainness of Rowland Hill, he adds much of the familiarity, not to say the coarseness, of the Huntingtonian order of ultra-Calvinistic preachers. 'It has been my privilege,' he says, 'to give more prominence in the religious world to those old doctrines of the Gospel.' But the traits referred to present themselves in shapes and with accompaniments which forbid the notion of imitation, and favour the opinion of a peculiar bent. Neither in the style and structure, nor in handling, is there appearance ot art, study, or elaboration.   Yet each discourse has a beginning, a middle, and an end; and the subject is duly introduced and stated, divided and discussed, enforced and applied.   But all is done without effort, with the ease and freedom of common conversation, and with the artlessness, but also with the force, of spontaneous expression. 'This,' he says, 'I am sure of: I tell you all I know, and speak right on. I am no orator, but just tell you what springs up from my heart.' 'Speak, my heart!' he exclaims in another place, 'for heart-thoughts are the best thoughts.' "

In his early days, Mr. Spurgeon was persistently accused of being an egotist; but in the eyes of *The Patriot* this reproach is toned down to "characteristic references to his own history, feelings, and habits."   This is a true representation of the case; and any careful reader of the early sermons and other utterances might collect sufficient to give a tolerably full portraiture of the man as he then lived and worked.   Thus we find him, as *The Patriot* went on to show, speaking of the delight he found in reading old books, and his almost total disregard of new ones—a disregard which was certainly given up in later years.   Then we find him confessing that he was almost wholly indebted to the Bible for the discipline of his mental faculties.   Christ was his Sun; and in his quaint way he advised his hearers to allow other acquirements only to revolve as satellites around that centre.   Mount Calvary was the place for a young man to build either his studio or observatory.   It was thus early, moreover, that he made the confession that formerly he had his knowledge in "glorious confusion," but now everything was in its place ready for use when called for or wanted.   His great facility for borrowing illustrations from nature, books, and all things around him, is also taken notice of; and that of course, in its way, showed the bent of a peculiar genius.   Attention is drawn to the less attractive characteristics of the preacher's style, and this is how *The Patriot* refers to them :—

"Sometimes, no doubt, he lapses into a rude colloquialism bordering upon coarseness. 'If,' he observes, 'I were to preach nothing but what would please the whole lot of you, what on earth should I do?' The questionable colloquialism in the second clause occurs more than once or twice ; and, what is worse still, such appeals as 'Good God!' and 'By Heaven !' At the same time that he insists upon preaching that only which he believes true and fit, he declares himself to have no fear that 'an honest British audience will turn away from the man who does not stick, and stutter, and stammer in speaking the truth.' In citing the following as a specimen of his sayings, justice requires the acknowledgment that appropriations so little felicitous are extremely rare:—'I should like to take you this morning, as Samson did the foxes, tie the fire-brands of prayer to you, and send you in among the shocks of corn till you burn the whole up.'"

By way of contrast to this, many things are quoted which show "a high degree of eloquence"; and it is admitted that the sermons abound with aphorisms and pointed sayings, many of them quaint, and all of them having the genuine mark of genius upon them. Some passages are given at length, and all are more or less powerful. The review comes to a close by enumerating certain shortcomings. Mr. Spurgeon was not thought to be sufficiently tolerant towards those who differed from him, and his habit of judging others was held to be both "unlovely and presumptuous." The reviewer proceeds:—

"If asked who is fortunate enough to escape his sarcasm and invective, we should really be at a loss to answer. All, in turn, come under the lash of the precocious tyro. He alone is a consistent Calvinist; all besides are either rank Arminians, licentious Antinomians, or unfaithful professors of the doctrines of grace. College training does but wean young men's sympathies from the people; and 'really ploughmen would make a great deal better preachers.' The doctrine of election is, 'in our age, scorned and hated.' 'The time-serving religion of the present day' is 'only exhibited in evangelical drawing-rooms.' 'How many pious preachers are there on the Sabbath-day who are very impious preachers during the rest of the week!' He 'never hears' his brother ministers 'assert the positive satisfaction and substitution of our Lord Jesus Christ.' These fishers of men 'have been spending all their life fishing with most elegant silk lines and gold and silver hooks, but the fish will not bite for all that; whereas we of the rougher sort,' adds the self-complacent censor, 'have put the hook into the jaws of hundreds.' Still 'rougher,' if possible, is Mr. Spurgeon's treatment of theologians not of his own especial school. 'Arminian perversions, in particular, are to sink back to their birthplace in the pit.' Their notion of the possibility of a final fall from grace is 'the wickedest falsehood on earth.' Mr. Spurgeon was quite at liberty to uphold the comfortable and Scriptural doctrine of the final perseverance of the true believer with all his might; but this was possible without indulging, as he has indulged, in vituperation of opponents more gross than any words we have quoted. Nor, to any right-minded man, Arminian or Calvinist, will it be a compensation that he has dealt with the Antinomians just as bitterly. To the erring professor who conceives himself to be a child of God because he is in trouble, he replies, 'I know a great many rascals in the same condition.' He is too charitable, however, when he ascribes Antinomian licentiousness to a perversion of the Gospel; for it is attributable more correctly to the substitution of 'another Gospel.' But these are subjects on which we cannot enlarge, or we might point out several mistakes into which Mr. Spurgeon's doctrinal zeal has betrayed him. We therefore take our leave of him with this admonition—to cultivate more assiduously the modest spirit of which, after all, he is far from destitute; to remember 'his own youth and inexperience; to reflect upon the inconsistency of complaining that he is himself subject to hostile animadversion, when he deals wholesale in sweeping censure of ministerial brethren older and more experienced than himself; and, in fine, to bear in mind his own very just remark, that 'John Knox did much, but he might, perhaps, have done more if he had had a little love'—that love which 'thinketh no evil.' "*

As one of the first and one of the ablest notices of Mr. Spurgeon's life and work which appeared in the Nonconformist Press, the lengthened article in *The Patriot*, from which the above extracts are taken, attracted much notice at the time. On the whole, this seems to have been written without prejudice, and the writer showed an honest desire to recognise the more extraordinary qualities of the young preacher which accounted for his popularity, although what were regarded as weaknesses were at the same time candidly mentioned. Every great man has some flaws of character, or he would not be human; but probably some of the things complained of in Mr. Spurgeon would not have been so apparent if at the outset he had been less exposed to detraction and misrepresentation.

On the last night of the year 1855, New Park Street Chapel was densely crowded at the watch-night service. Mr. Spurgeon expounded the first twelve verses of Psalm xc.; he also preached a sermon from Lamentations ii. ·19—"Arise, cry out in the night," etc. At two minutes to twelve the preacher stopped in his discourse and asked all to engage in silent prayer. It was altogether a striking scene, and one which some who were present still remember. The occasion appears to have been taken advantage of for preaching the Gospel, and many penitents are said to have been present at this midnight service. The watch-night service was not then so popular an institution as it is now; but, as Mr. Spurgeon explained, he was ready to preach the Gospel at any hour.

The crowded assembly might have been called a prayer-meeting, for others beside the pastor prayed; and very fervent were the petitions for a prosperous time during the year 1856. How little did pastor or people know what was before them! The great and comprehensive work in hand would assuredly extend in all directions; but times of fiery trial were also near, when the work and the workers would be tested in no ordinary way.

* *The Patriot*, Friday, September 21, 1855.

CHAPTER XXII.

MARRIAGE.——INTEREST IN SUNDAY-SCHOOL WORK.

Mr. Spurgeon marries Miss Thompson—Scene in New Park Street Chapel—A Sunday-School Teachers' Entertainment—First Volume of the Weekly Sermons—Estimate of *The Freeman*—"Why so Popular?"—A Doctor's *Brochure*.

THE first sermon which Mr. Spurgeon preached in New Park Street Chapel in 1856 was founded on the text which had been instrumental in his own conversion at Colchester some years before—" Look unto Me, and be ye saved, all the ends of the earth"—Isaiah xlv. 22. Particular reference was made by the preacher to his experience on that ever-memorable Sunday which has already been described.

In the old days of Highbury College, which was a favourite seat of education when Mr. Spurgeon was a little boy at Stambourne, Mr. Thomas Wilson, the treasurer, was accustomed to advise the students not to think of getting " engaged" as students, because no woman worth having would think of accepting a man before it was seen what kind of a position he would be likely to occupy in the world. Though he married young, Mr. Spurgeon practically acted on this advice; for when he came to London he appears to have had no experience whatever in the art of love-making. At that time there happened to be living in Falcon Square one Mr. Robert Thompson; and it was a member of the Olney family who first called the young pastor's attention to the worth of Susannah, the only daughter, who became Mrs. C. H. Spurgeon on Tuesday, January 8, 1856.

When the American Dr. Wayland was in this country, and visited Westwood some years ago, he heard facts relative to this matter which are of general interest. He had some things told him which had reference to the first time that Mr. Spurgeon ever preached in London. According to Dr. Wayland, "on that Sunday morning there were perhaps eighty persons present. The deacons had made a great effort to get people out, so as to swell the audience. One of the deacons went to a young lady and said, 'Do come on Sunday; there will be a young man from the country, and we do want to make as much of a show as we can.' The young lady went and saw the young man from the country, and heard him preach. She told me this herself; she has seen him a good many times since; and, in fact, a couple of years later, she took him for good and all; and what a blessing she has been to him and to the world only eternity can tell."

The marriage service was conducted by Dr. Alexander Fletcher, of Finsbury Chapel, and the entire scene was as singular as anything of the kind ever witnessed. "Shortly after eight o'clock, although the morning was dark, damp, and cold, as many as five hundred ladies, in light and gay attire, besieged the doors of the chapel, accompanied by many gentlemen, members of the congregation and personal friends. From that hour the crowd increased so rapidly that the thoroughfare was blocked up against vehicles and pedestrians, and a body of the M division of police had to be sent for to prevent accidents. When the chapel doors were opened, there was a terrific rush, and in less than half an hour the doors were closed upon many eager visitors, who, like the earlier and more fortunate comers, were favoured with tickets of admission." * According to one report, some two thousand people braved the raw January atmosphere in hope of getting inside the chapel and failed. Dr. Fletcher is said to have been especially fervent in prayer on behalf of the young couple, after which the congregation sang with great heartiness the hymn, "Salvation, O the joyful sound!" The young couple went off followed by the good wishes of all who were assembled in the chapel; but their honeymoon tour was really little more than a flying visit to the Continent. Twelve days later, on Sunday, January 20, the pastor was again preaching in New

* *The British Banner*, January 10, 1856.

Park Street Chapel. Was it through the preacher's being in a more than usually happy state of mind that he gave a sermon on the Beatific Vision?

On Sunday morning, February 10, 1856, Mr. Spurgeon preached at New Park Street on behalf of the Particular Baptist Fund, which had then existed in London for one hundred and thirty-nine years. The object of the Fund is the relief of aged, infirm, or necessitous ministers; but a sum of £400 is annually voted for the education of students, while numerous grants of books are made every year to a number of young pastors who are just commencing their course. Mr. Spurgeon made a strong appeal for contributions; but his faith that nothing would really be lacking was reflected in the text on which his sermon was founded—" The young lions do lack, and suffer hunger : but they that seek the Lord shall not want any good thing "—Psalm xxxiv. 10.

On the following evening Mr. and Mrs. Spurgeon were the guests of the teachers of the New Park Street Sunday-school, who now rejoiced in a new schoolroom. The object was to do honour to the pastor and his bride; for as a former teacher himself, Mr. Spurgeon had all along, since his first coming to London, manifested the warmest interest in the work of the Sunday-school. Great enthusiasm prevailed; and, anxious to appear at their best on such an occasion, the teachers had spared neither pains nor expense to make the entertainment a success. The provision was all of the best, while the choicest flowers and plants which the greenhouse could supply adorned the tables. After tea, Mr. Cutler, the superintendent, presented the pastor with a proof impression of an engraving of the picture, " Liberty of Conscience," representing the Assembly of Divines at Westminster in the seventeenth century. Several speeches having been made, one by Mr. Spurgeon himself, the company adjourned to the chapel, where the weekly prayer-meeting was held. Nearly all the congregation afterwards passed through the schoolroom to view the picture and to express their admiration.

The pastor's zeal for the Sunday-school cause was not confined to his own congregation. One sermon published about this time, and entitled "Come, ye children," was preached on behalf of the Western Kent Sunday-school Union; and another, entitled "A Visit to Calvary," was given at Hanover Square Rooms on behalf of a ragged-school in the locality. According to a contemporary reviewer, the latter "is highly characteristic of this popular preacher, whose earnestness and power in preaching Mr. Howard Hinton, a few days since, commended as a study to an assembly of Baptist preachers educated at the several collegiate institutions belonging to our denomination." *

Passages from this discourse would sufficiently show that the young pastor still had his heart in Sunday-school work, and that he spoke with all the force of one who understood from actual experience what he was talking about.

The first volume of the sermons, issued weekly, had appeared; and the preface shows the varied feelings with which the experiment had been regarded by persons in different quarters. The preacher had been unduly praised and unmercifully abused; but he professes to be invulnerable to detraction on account of the service the discourses had rendered in bringing about conversions. When he looked abroad in the dark world, and saw what was being achieved by means of the wide diffusion of the sermons, the preacher was not only comforted, he had the kind of answer to adverse critics he most desired. Mr. Spurgeon happened to go and see a suffering bed-ridden woman, who had lain for ten years without any ability to rise, and when she confessed to having been brought from darkness to light, and declared that for nine years the sermons week by week had been as marrow and fatness to her soul, the young pastor thought that the printers had abundant cause for encouragement, as well as the preacher himself.

At the time the first volume of sermons preached at Exeter Hall and New Park Street appeared, the Baptist newspaper, *The*

* *The Baptist Messenger*, iv. 153.

Freeman, had been in existence about a year, and the paper had been conducted in a way which reflected some literary credit on the denomination, though many thought that in theology the editors were rather broad. In reviewing the volume the writer felt that he laboured under certain difficulties which could not be ignored; for while venturing to give a candid opinion, there was some risk of seeming to favour those who were reported to be decrying the preacher, or otherwise dealing out to him unjust treatment. Nevertheless, at all hazards, an honest verdict would be given "in the spirit of Christian charity."

It was admitted that since such great orators as Robert Hall, Thomas Chalmers, and Edward Irving had gone home, no modern preacher had made such a sensation as Mr. Spurgeon; but no one was to suppose that the pastor at New Park Street was one of the same class. "Whatever Mr. Spurgeon's merits may be—and he has some rare ones—they are of a very different order from those which distinguished the mighty preachers of the last generation. They were all men of gigantic reasoning powers, of refined taste, of profound scholarship, and of vast theological learning. Of all these qualities Mr. Spurgeon has little enough; nor, to do him justice, does he pretend to any of them, except, perhaps, in some unlucky moments to the last. But it will probably be admitted by all competent judges, that neither Irving nor Hall, nor even Chalmers, was so well fitted to carry the Gospel to the poor as is this modern orator of the pulpit. Their writings will last for many generations, and will be as fresh to the latest as they are to-day; Mr. Spurgeon's sermons will, perhaps, soon be forgotten for ever."

Still, it was allowed that the preacher showed the possession of undoubted genius; for a strong imagination, an easy colloquial manner, and ardent enthusiasm, were all so well combined that no one could hear him "without acquiring for him a sentiment of respect." Of course, something had to be said concerning those "thoughtful" people who are always so sensitive and so discerning :—

"If offended by his extravagances, as the thoughtful certainly will be, the offence is so immediately atoned for by some genuine outburst of feeling, that you remember that his extravagances are but the errors of a youth, and that the material on which these excrescences appear is that out of which apostles and martyrs have, in every age, been fashioned. You pardon his follies, for they are nothing else, for the sake of his unquestionable sincerity and impassioned·zeal. You wish that it had been possible that a mind so gifted might have received more culture before it was called into its present dangerous position; but finding it as it is, you accept it with gratitude, and pray God, the All-wise, to be its guide and protector."

The Freeman not only rejoiced in the young preacher's success, it was hoped that this would be "prolonged and increased"; but his faults, as they appeared to this critic, were freely pointed out. Mere blemishes of style, or offences against good taste, such as "fluent eloquence rushing into rant," or "imaginative flights that sometimes soar so high that they only reach sublimity and fall on 't'other side,'" were passed by. The faults had in view "were rather moral than intellectual, and need the more to be corrected, because they else will grow more palpable and grievous with the lapse of time." They would be sources of weakness, and if indulged persistently, would "prove disastrous to the last degree."

It is instructive, after the lapse of nearly forty years, to have the preacher's shortcomings pointed out by a friendly adviser, who when most severe proposed to speak in charity. What were these faults—real or imaginary?

"Perhaps, indeed, we should be right in summing them up all in one—the vice of vanity; for they all seem to spring from this fruitful root. This may originate his daring method of expounding Holy Writ, his intense egotism, and his habit of decrying his fellow-Christians and fellow-ministers. And these, we fear, are the illegitimate attractions which help to swell his popularity; though we sincerely believe that Mr. Spurgeon would be the first himself to rebuke the followers who loved him for such faults. It is amusing, but it is also painful, to hear a young man of twenty-one speaking of his experience as if he had lived threescore years and ten. Surely some sort of glamour must invest him when he says, 'I have always found through life,' or his audience would burst into a titter; but it is far worse to find him denouncing Arminians (whose creed he evidently does not understand) in almost every sermon. . . . It is sad to see so young a man so deeply imbued with the *odium theologium*. . . . If, already, he can not only preach but print mere vulgar abuse of men who, in the sight of God, may be as sincere as he, and as holy, to what lengths of ribaldry may he not descend when he finds that this knack of 'cordially hating' brings around him a crowd of fulsome flatterers?"

Such was the opinion of a very candid friend who thought it his duty to utter cautions or warnings as well as to give commendation. There were undoubtedly in Volume I. of the Sermons some things, or modes of expression, which Mr. Spurgeon himself might have altered had he ever carried out the design he once formed of revising his early discourses. The doctrines are identical with those of later years, however; and there were hardly so many breakers ahead as the candid critic of *The Freeman* supposed.

Meanwhile, many still professed to be puzzled on account of Spurgeon's unique popularity. Just about this time a certain Doctor in Divinity published a *brochure* on the subject of the hour, and apparently settled matters to his own satisfaction, while offering what he considered to be some very necessary advice. The doctor was not so candidly severe as is the critic in *The Freeman*. "Lend me a chair, my honoured brother," remarks this worthy, "that, sitting at your side, I may discharge the duty and enjoy the privilege of presenting my warm congratulations on the ministerial eminence to which divine Providence has so speedily raised you; accompanied with such paternal counsels as a knowledge of that position—as full of peril as it is of honour—may suggest."*

Having introduced himself in this cordial manner, the worthy doctor comes at once to the subject of his young friend's popularity :—

"Your ministry has attained the dignity of a moral phenomenon; you stand on an eminence which, since the days of Whitefield, no minister—with a single exception, if, indeed, there be one—of any church in this realm has attained. You have access to a larger audience than the magic of any other name can gather; you have raised a church from dignity to eminence—perhaps I might add (rumour is my authority) from spiritual indigence to affluence. You entered on a sphere where, to use the mildest word, languor 'held unbroken Sabbath'; and in less than three short years you have, instrumentally, gathered a large, united, zealous, energetic church, second in numbers, in burning zeal, and in active effort, to no other church in the metropolis. 'The little one has become a thousand, and the small one a great' congregation."

So much for work at home; but the pastor of New Park Street had become as great a favourite as an evangelist in the provinces as the greatest of the Revival preachers of the eighteenth century. The doctor proceeds :—

* "Why so Popular? An hour with the Rev. C. H. Spurgeon." By a Doctor of Divinity. London. 1856.

" Blessed with a vigorous mind, and with great physical energy—*mens sana in corpore sano*—you have consecrated all to your Master's service, and hence you have become an untiring evangelist. East, west, north, south—in England, Wales, and Scotland, your preaching is appreciated by the people, and has been blessed of God. No place has been large enough to receive the crowds who flocked to hear 'the young Whitefield'; and on many occasions you have preached the glorious Gospel, the sward of the green earth being the floor on which, and the vault of the blue heaven the canopy under which, you announced, to uncounted thousands, 'all the words of this life.' Your name has thus become familiar 'as a household word' in most of the churches and many of the families of our land; and the young pastor of Southwark has taken his place among the celebrities of our land, and among the ecclesiastical portion of them he is 'higher than the highest.' "

Having made these concessions, which were obvious truths to all observers, the doctor goes on to offer his congratulations on far higher ground; he takes account of the actual results of Mr. Spurgeon's preaching :—

"Usefulness is the law of the moral universe. This, in relation to the Christian ministry, means the moral renovation, the saving conversion, of human souls. Nothing short of this can satisfy the desires of any 'godly minister of Christ's Gospel'; and, therefore, all such will estimate the amount of their success by the number of well-sustained instances of conversion, which are the fruit, under God's blessing, of their ministerial labours. Subjected to this test, the ministry of him to whom my congratulations are now presented is placed above all the ministries with which I have any acquaintance, or of which I possess any authentic information. He states—so I am informed—that more than one thousand souls have been hopefully converted to God during the past year by the instrumentality of his ministry; and that, as the result of his metropolitan and provincial labours during the period of his short but successful pastorate, several thousands who had erred from the truth, or never known it, had been raised or restored to holiness and God. 'This is the Lord's doing, and it is marvellous in our eyes.' I know something of the state of religion in the British churches, and I do not hesitate to avow my belief that among the thousands—and happily their name is legion—who now Sabbatically proclaim the fundamental verities of the Christian revelation, there is not one who can truthfully say, as you can, that during three short years thousands, as the fruit of his ministry, have been added to the fellowship of his own church and of other churches."

To the mind of the writer these facts were sufficiently singular, and they appear to have been more so the more deeply they were studied. The preacher was only just turned twenty-one; he had no high social standing and no exceptional educational advantages; he had no college distinctions; his only Gamaliel had been his own father; and yet in the metropolis of England, or of the world, the youthful preacher could draw a larger audience than the Archbishop of Canterbury could ever hope to do. That seemed to be a fact for which no moral casuist could satisfactorily account. As, however, every effect must have a cause, it might be possible to throw some light on the subject. The doctor asks his young brother, "How shall we account for your acceptance and success as a minister of Christ?" and then proceeds :—

"In your ministerial career you are subjected to not only the hostile attacks of the malevolent and prejudiced, but to the unintentional mistakes of the virtuous and wise. Keeping all your detractors before the mental eye, let me examine their statements so far as I know them. I ask one, 'Why is he so popular?' He answers, 'You have a large amount of dramatic genius, a melodious voice, and great eloquence as an orator.' But we more than hesitate to accept this explanation. No dramatic genius, no popular eloquence, no melodious harmony has ever done this in the past history of human nature. Macaulay, Garrick, Jenny Lind, Rachel, Gough, have not done it. The theatre must change its 'star' monthly, the singer must emigrate to other climes, and the orator must make 'angel visits few and far between,' to secure the audiences which the charm of your name will surely and speedily convene. And the phenomenon is more remarkable because your gathering is around the pulpit, where no art wins and no pleasure stimulates. I bear you witness, that judging by your published sermons, I know no minister who more emphatically denounces—and few, if any, who so emphatically denounce—the vitiated tastes, the degraded sensualities, and the immoral practices of our country and age. If we connected popularity with a desire to pander to a vitiated public taste, you are almost—if not altogether—the last minister in England whom I would expect to secure popular applause. You not only condemn sin, you do it emphatically, and *con amore*. 'But,' says another, 'he is so original —not in manner alone, but even in matter—that his originality is popular.' I know something, my friend, of the theology of those sainted men—now with God—with whose writings you are equally, probably better acquainted than I am; and I do not hesitate to say that your theological opinions harmonise substantially with those of Gill and Toplady, of Hervey and Romaine; and that in the tone and texture of that theology I find nothing to account, to my satisfaction, for their or for your popularity."

But perhaps Mr. Spurgeon himself might have an answer to give, if plainly asked to account for his popularity and usefulness. The doctor felt sure that he would reply, "I am nothing; God is all; and to His sovereignty I ascribe all my popularity and all my success." That was very becoming, and so on; but at the same time it was not a sufficient explanation. Though God acted in His sovereign right, He never acted without reason. It might not be always discernible, but there always was a reason. How, then, was the thing to be accounted for?

"If I cannot discover the secret of your popularity in *what* you preach, can I find it in any peculiarity in your mode of preaching? Here is, in my judgment, the explanation of the secret. *You have strong faith, and as the result, intense earnestness. In this lies,* as in the hair of Samson, *the secret of your power.*"

The doctor then exhorted the young preacher to remain steadfast in the faith, and to go on preaching the Old Gospel as he had begun.

In that case, "What a glorious prospect of honour, happiness, and usefulness presents itself to your view!" it was added. "A star in the churches; a star of no mean magnitude, of no ordinary brilliancy, you may be honoured to diffuse, very luminously, the derived glories you possess; and having run your appointed course, ultimately set—but far distant be the day!—as sets the morning star—

> "'Which falls not down behind the darkened west,
> Nor hides obscured amid the tempests of the sky,
> But melts away into the light of heaven.'"

Utterances of this kind have a curious interest to readers in these days; and they bear emphatic testimony to the extraordinary popularity of the young pastor in those early times, when he had been labouring in London hardly more than two years. At this time he was making friends faster than had previously been the case; and this would be the natural result of such genial and ably-written apologies for Mr. Spurgeon as now from time to time appeared. He was seen to be wearing well, and that was a sure sign of sterling metal. It was becoming also more apparent that there was no self-seeking in his preaching; for notwithstanding his many engagements from home, the preacher himself, at the end of his third year in London, found himself many pounds out of pocket on account of travelling expenses and other necessary expenditure.

CHAPTER XXIII.

"THE RIVULET" CONTROVERSY.

"THE Rivulet" controversy, which belongs to this period, was so far associated with Mr. Spurgeon that he was one of the combatants, so that no biography of our great preacher would be complete without a chapter devoted to this "passage-at-arms" in the theological field, which once shook the religious world in a way which now excites one's wonder as one looks back upon it. It is not necessary to enter into such a matter at length; it will suffice to state succinctly the main facts as illustrating the part which Mr. Spurgeon himself took in the dispute.

In November, 1855, appeared a small volume entitled "Hymns for Heart and Voice, The Rivulet." The author, Thomas Toke Lynch, was pastor of a chapel in Grafton Street, the congregation being a small one. Born in 1818, he was still hardly more than a young man; he had become known as a contributor to the monthly magazine, *The Christian Spectator;* but the poetical pieces which created such a *furore* had been composed during a time of domestic affliction in 1854, and some succeeding months. It is said that the author found much solace in the work of composition.

The volume did not attract any extraordinary notice until the review by Mr. James Grant appeared in *The Morning Advertiser*. In that article the writer admitted, as he no doubt considered with generous frankness, that Mr. Lynch was amiable, intellectual, cultivated, and was even largely imbued with the poetic spirit; but at the same time the work was calculated to inspire sadness in the minds of those who knew in what true religion consisted. Mr. James Grant then continued :—

"It is with regret and pain we are compelled to say that, though the volume in many places displays much fine feeling, there is not, from beginning to end, one particle of vital religion or evangelical piety in it. At least, if there be, we have not been able to discover it. Occasionally—but even that is comparatively seldom—the name of the Saviour is introduced; but there is not one solitary recognition of His divinity, of His atoning sacrifice, or of His mediatorial office. Neither is the inherent depravity of man, nor the agency of the Spirit in the work of conversion and sanctification, even indirectly recognised from the first to the last page of the volume. Nearly the whole might have been written by a Deist; and a very large portion of the Hymns might be sung by a congregation of Free-thinkers. . . . The hymns of Watts, of Doddridge, of Hart, of Cowper, of Newton, of Montgomery, and others, have, in innumerable instances, proved the source of unspeakable consolation to believers in seasons of sorrow, and on the bed of death; but what a cruel mockery it would be to put into the hands of believers, in such circumstances, such a book as this, or to repeat to them any of its verses! The author, if such were his pleasure, had a perfect right to pen and publish the contents of this volume; but, then, instead of palming them off as 'Christian Poems,' which he expressly does in his preface, he should have given them their proper character of mere tributes to the beauties and beneficence of Nature; or, if he liked the expression better, as endeavours to 'look through Nature up to Nature's God.'"*

Referring to this review, the biographers of Dr. Campbell remark : "Such is the marrow of that criticism which gave rise to 'The Rivulet' controversy."† They speak of the dispute in a dispassionate common-sense manner, like Christian men whose literary training sufficed to preserve them from violence in expression either on one side or the other. In this respect Drs. Ferguson and Morton Brown set a more worthy example to writers who, after the noise and smoke of battle have passed away, seem desirous of reviving some of the worst phases of "The Rivulet" controversy itself.‡

---

* *The Morning Advertiser*, February 7, 1856.

† "A faithful review we admit it to be, and one which evidently came from the pen of a man who has deep and heartfelt convictions as to the importance of all that bears the Christian name, or has the distinctive features of the Christian system fairly exhibited thereon. This is no fault, and cannot be alleged to be so, since it is only asking for what is honest and obvious. The review gives full prominence to the respectability, the amiability, the learning, and the genius of Mr. Lynch; it eschews the personal in the matter, though it does not shrink from regarding the responsibility of the official. This is fair ground, in connection with any published book, by any public man; and we wonder, in looking back through the vista of years, that this should ever have been doubted, and that the critique should have called forth, because of its supposed personality, the opposition which it did."—"Life and Labours of John Campbell, D.D." By Robert Ferguson, LL.D., and A. Morton Brown, LL.D. Page 367.

‡ Thus, in speaking of Thomas Toke Lynch in "Pulpit Memorials," page 438, the writer says:—"The one semblance of excuse to be made for his unscrupulous assailants is that

o

It is conceivable that Dr. Campbell, of *The British Banner*, and James Grant, of *The Morning Advertiser*, may have made mistakes, but that they were *bad*—ignorant and unscrupulous—no one less than a far-gone fanatic on the other side could ever suppose.

The first to reply to Mr. Grant's notice of "The Rivulet" was *The Eclectic Review*, which in former years had been associated with the honoured names of Robert Hall and John Foster. Just at this time *The Eclectic* had a new editor, which probably occasioned the opinions put forth to be looked upon with the greater misgiving. In due course *The Morning Advertiser* reviewed the notice in *The Eclectic*, and then, in answer to this, the latter published a protest signed by more than a dozen of the leading Nonconformist ministers. "This was a new feature in the case—a new feature, indeed, in relation to reviewing," remark the biographers of Dr. Campbell. "Here was a rush into the field of a whole band of helpers to overpower the opinion and to condemn the condemnation of one man." Of course, Mr. Grant, as the chief of a great daily newspaper, was not to be easily suppressed. He republished the Protest, and made remarks upon it, and, after quoting some of the hymns, asked certain of the Protesters whether they would give out such pieces to be sung by their congregations. As the body of Protesters included such men as Henry Allon, Newman Hall, and Thomas Binney, the commotion increased.*

---

they were as utterly incapable of understanding him as a hound is incapable of understanding the sweet and luminous mystery of moonlight at which he bays. The only wonder is that they were not instantly whipped into silence, and forbidden to meddle with things too high for them. It would, perhaps, have been well for Mr. Lynch, personally, had he simply strove on, paying no heed to the din below. But 'study and suffering' had made him sensitive; and his righteous soul was vexed with the unlawful deeds of these ignorant and unscrupulous men, not for his own sake alone, but because of their open and insolent opposition to all freedom and largeness of thought."

* "Wherefore do these rev. gentlemen appear in the field at all? It had been far better for themselves, and for *The Eclectic Review*, had they heeded the counsel of the wise man, 'Leave off contention before it be meddled with,' and had left the criticism and remonstrances of Mr. Grant to their own merits, than for them to have interfered at all in the affair. We do most deeply deplore the position these fifteen reverend gentlemen have voluntarily and heedlessly taken in this business, inasmuch as we greatly fear it betokens on their part an evident leaning towards a transcendental theology—the blighting influences of which have proved most fatal to many once flourishing churches."—*The Baptist Messenger*, iv. 116.

Dr. Campbell was the last of the Nonconformist editors to enter into the fray; but when he did speak the excitement greatly increased. There was no indecision or hesitation: "The Rivulet," taken as a whole, was "the most unspiritual publication of the kind in the English language." The doctor published "Seven Letters," and addressing these to the "Principals and Professors of the Independent and Baptist Colleges of England," he insisted that there was less of distinctive evangelical truth in Mr. Lynch's pieces than in the hymns used by the Unitarians.

Mr. Spurgeon had something to say on the controversy, and though he may have made passing references to the subject in speaking or preaching, his chief utterances concerning the matter were given through *The Christian Cabinet*, for which, as already explained, the pastor of New Park Street Chapel wrote pretty regularly through friendship for his friend Mr. Charles Waters Banks. Unhappily for itself, *The Cabinet* appears to have reviewed "The Rivulet" favourably before Mr. Spurgeon undertook to examine the matter for himself, with very different results. Hence we find Mr. Lynch remarking, "*The Cabinet* is getting now a little more self-consistent. Its conduct towards me has been ridiculous; but wishing it, under its new management, more wisdom, I can heartily wish it, as *wiser*, a good success." Mr. Lynch himself thus refers to the part which Mr. Spurgeon took in this dispute :—

"Amongst the oddities of this controversy, the conduct of *The Christian Cabinet* deserves a word or two. Did the reader ever hear of *The Christian Cabinet?* Truly it is a cabinet not without curiosities. It is a little penny journal, just big enough to make a paper boat of to swim for a moment's sport, and then perish. The wind is very inconstant, but not so variable as this paper, which, indeed, changes its mind, like the wind its direction, without any very discoverable reason. On December 28, 1855, just after the appearance of 'The Rivulet,' its opinion was that the volume abounded with passages adapted 'to brighten and exhilarate the mind—to recover it when it is losing the proper tone of feeling, to exalt it with happy, holy thoughts—to clothe the waste and desolate places of the soul with fruitfulness and verdure, and prepare it for doing brave battle amidst the trials and discouragements of daily life.' *The Cabinet* quoted three hymns in illustration of these sentiments, and concluded, as well it might, by cordially wishing the volume a wide circulation.' But on March 21 *The Cabinet* discovered that it had never seen the volume, and on May 16 called it 'a little penny rattle of rhymery by one Mr. Lynch.' This was somewhat of a descent both for it and me. However, when things get to the worst, they begin to mend. So on May 23 out came 'Mine opinion,' that is to say, Mr. Spurgeon's opinion, which was communicated to the world through this important organ. Mr. Spurgeon acknowledged that he could 'scarce see into the depths where lurked the essence of the matter.' 'Perhaps the hymns,' said he, 'are not the fair things that they seem.' He saw enough in the 'glistering eyes' of the mermaids to suspect they might have a fishy body and a snaky tail. But he confessed that he did not see the said tail. In fact, it lay too deep for him to see, or for anybody else. This review of Mr. Spurgeon's enjoys the credit with me of being the only thing on his side—that is, *against* me—that was impertinent, without being malevolent. It evinced far more ability and appreciation than Grant or Campbell had done, and indicated a man whose eyes, if they do not get blinded with the fumes of that strong, but unwholesome, incense, Popularity, may glow with a heavenlier brightness than it seems to me they have yet done. Mr. Spurgeon concluded by remarking that 'the old faith must be triumphant,' in which I entirely agree with him, doubting only whether he is yet old enough in experience of the world's sorrows and strifes to know what the old faith really is. He says, 'We shall soon have to handle truth not with kid gloves, but with gauntlets—the gauntlets of holy courage and integrity.' Ay, that we shall, and some of us now do. And, perhaps, the man who has a soul that 'fights to music,'

'Calm 'mid the bewildering cry,
Confident of victory,'

is the likeliest to have a hand with a grip for battle, and a grasp for friendship alike strong and warm. Mr. Spurgeon spoke on May 23; and now in October *The Cabinet* scarce knows what to think. A week or two ago it compared me to Apollos, and recommended Priscilla and Aquila to invite me to tea, and 'teach me the way of the Lord more perfectly.' And in the last number that I have seen, it expresses a hope that I 'shall turn out well.' I am sure I hope I shall, and that soon, and the controversy too, for time loiters not." *

As the controversy widened, "The Rivulet," which had started the disputants, was no doubt in the main lost sight of, and the battle centred around the standards of orthodoxy and negative theology. Thus, the controversy, on the whole, had the effect of clearing the air, the general result being, as one authority tells us, "an untold amount of good to the Church of God." Neither the severe criticism nor the abuse was confined to one side; but it is pleasant to find that many of the combatants who were at open war afterwards became good friends. In a general way the bulk of these would probably have united in confessing that good had come to the churches all round. In common with Dr. Campbell and Mr. Grant, Mr. Spurgeon desired nothing different from this; they sought neither fame nor aggrandisement by what they did. Hence, when they found that truth had been the gainer by what they had done, these leaders must have felt themselves compensated for all

* "Memoir of Thomas T. Lynch," edited by William White, pp. 174–178. Mr. Lynch died May 9, 1871, and his biography appeared in 1874.

their pains. "I am able to testify that the agitation has proved a mighty impetus to the ministry," said one; "the cardinal elements of the Gospel have had more prominence than for many years." In some instances it appeared that the ministry itself had been revived. "Never did I feel so concerned clearly and unmistakably to set forth the atoning sacrifice of Christ in all its fulness as now," wrote one preacher; while another added, "Emerging from painful discussions, we shall enter on new and united plans of Christian usefulness." The gain was on the side of truth.

CHAPTER XXIV.

JAMES GRANT AND OTHER FRIENDS.

The Morning Advertiser defends Mr. Spurgeon—James Grant's early Life—A general Criticism—Jubilee Services at Stambourne—Exeter Hall and New Park Street Chapel—An unfulfilled Prophecy.

THE late Mr. James Grant was one of Mr. Spurgeon's earliest friends in London; and as editor of *The Morning Advertiser*, which at that time ranked next to *The Times* among the daily papers of the metropolis, he was able to exercise a powerful and widespread influence. Mr. Grant's journal was probably the first newspaper which cordially recognised the abilities of the young pastor, or which undertook to offer him advice under the name of impartial criticism. As the veteran editor's name may several times occur in the course of the life-story which still remains to be told, a few facts about him will enable the reader the better to understand why he so closely identified himself with the cause which Mr. Spurgeon had at heart.

James Grant was a native of Elgin in Scotland, and he was quite thirty years the senior of the pastor at New Park Street, for whom he at once contracted a strong liking because they were agreed in theology. Mr. Grant commenced to write for London papers as early as 1820, and seven years later he and a relative successfully founded *The Elgin Courier*. In 1833 he removed to London, and became connected with *The Morning Chronicle* at or about the same time that Charles Dickens was on the staff. In the following year, or in the year of Mr. Spurgeon's birth, Mr. Grant accepted an appointment at the office of *The Morning Advertiser*, and there he remained until he retired more than a third of a century later. In 1850 the paper was permanently enlarged to a double sheet, and Mr. Grant became editor. In this sphere the young Scotsman became an indefatigable worker, and the result was that the journal vastly improved its position, so that the chief more than held his own, notwithstanding the efforts which were made by a noisy section of the Licensed Victuallers' Society, to whom the paper belonged, to displace him.

Mr. Grant's family belonged to the Scotch Secession Church; but like his younger friend, the preacher at New Park Street Chapel, he embraced the views of the Baptists in early life. He attended the chapel at John Street, Bedford Row, where James Harington Evans and the Hon. Baptist Noel successively ministered. At one time Mr. Grant was editor and proprietor of *The Metropolitan Magazine,* the publication price of which, sixty years ago, was the old-fashioned one of three shillings and sixpence a month. In addition to all, he contrived to write a number of books, which alone seem to be almost sufficient for a life's work. A critic like Thomas T. Lynch would make some stinging remarks, when retaliating for the part taken by *The Morning Advertiser* in "The Rivulet" controversy, comparisons being drawn between Grant's religious professions and certain characteristics of the Licensed Victuallers' paper which he conducted. Others looked at the matter in a somewhat different light. Thus, one authority declared that much might be said about the advantages which had resulted from such an editor's connection with *The Morning Advertiser.* "The presence of such a man at the head of such a journal is an affair of unspeakable moment, in consequence of the immense influence which he exercises for good by the insertion of religious matter, in which respect *The Advertiser* is a wonder unto many, as it often furnishes reports of important religious services which the religious journals themselves overlook." *

Such was James Grant, journalist and Christian teacher, who at the time of Mr. Spurgeon's coming to London was in the prime of his days and at the height of his success in life, after some years of anxiety in regard to the progress of the journal he edited. When

---

* *The Baptist Messenger,* iv. 149.

the sudden transformation scene at New Park Street occurred, the news did not travel with leaden feet to the well-known office in Fleet Street; the lynx-eyed newspaper had intelligence of what was going on, and the editor-in-chief himself walked to New Park Street to learn for himself what the attraction was which drew together a greater crowd than could get into the lately nearly empty chapel. *The Morning Advertiser* gave its opinion of the preacher—of course, favourable on the whole; and then some months later, when the first volume of sermons appeared, there was a return to the subject, thus:—

"About twelve months ago, when Mr. Spurgeon was preaching in Exeter Hall to the most densely crowded audiences that ever assembled within the walls of that spacious place, we called especial attention to his qualities as a preacher and as a theologian. We pointed out freely, but in the spirit of sincere friendship, what we conceived to be his faults, and expressed not only a hope but a belief that, as he was so young a man—not having then reached his majority—he would, with the lapse of time, which generally matures the judgment as well as mellows the mind, get rid, in a great measure, if not wholly, of what we then specified as defects. It gives us great gratification to say that, having heard him recently in his own chapel in New Park Street, Southwark, we discern a decided improvement, both as regards his matter and manner. Not that there is any change in Mr. Spurgeon's doctrinal views, or in his mode of illustrating, enforcing, and applying them, but that there is less of the pugnacious quality about him when grappling with the views of those from whom he differs. He does not speak so often with asperity of other preachers of the Gospel, whom he conceived—and we must say, in the main, rightly —to be unfaithful to their high calling. There is, too, a marked and gratifying improvement in Mr. Spurgeon as regards the manner of his pulpit appearances. He was always profoundly earnest in his appeals to the conscience of the unconverted, and spoke with an emphasis which showed how deeply he felt when dwelling on the joys and sorrows, the hopes and fears, of believers. And yet, strange to say, there was at times associated with this a seeming irreverence which we know frequently caused much pain to some of his greatest friends and admirers. In this respect also, we are happy to say, we can discern a decided amendment. Still, truth compels us to add that there is room for yet greater improvement, both in his matter and manner. We see something of a spirit which we cannot commend in the preface to this volume. There is a lack, too, of good taste in many parts of the volume itself. More charity of feeling and gentleness of expression are yet wanting, and may be attained without any deficiency in the faithfulness with which he advocates and enforces the distinguishing doctrines of the Gospel. It were well, too, that he should be especially careful to avoid the very semblance of irreverence when engaged in the most solemn and responsible work which a human being was ever delegated to perform —namely, the proclamation of mercy from heaven to fallen man, regarded in conjunction with the awful consequences to those who reject the message. We would, with great earnestness, urge on Mr. Spurgeon the propriety of studiously avoiding the use of expressions calculated to excite a smile, or to make hearers think lightly of the purpose for which they are met together. There is no inconsiderable number of such expressions in the volume before us, which, to the eyes of all who have right views of the sacred mission of the pulpit, must be exceedingly painful to witness.

"We point out these defects in the preaching of Mr. Spurgeon with all the greater freedom, because he is, in various respects, an uncommon man. Never, since the days of George Whitefield, has any minister of religion acquired so great a reputation as this Baptist preacher in so short a time. Here is a mere youth—a perfect stripling, only twenty-one years of age—incomparably the most popular preacher of the day. There is no man within Her Majesty's dominions who could draw such immense audiences, and none who, in his happier efforts, can so completely enthral the attention and delight the minds of his hearers. Some of his appeals to the conscience, some of his remonstrances with the careless, constitute specimens of a very high order of oratorical power. When pronouncing the doom of those who live and die in a state of impenitence, he makes the vast congregation quail and quake in their seats. He places their awful destiny in such vivid colours before their eyes that they almost imagine they are already in the regions of darkness and despair. In his preface he tells us that such has been the impressions produced by some of his sermons, that he has ascertained upwards of twenty cases of conversion as the result of one discourse; to say nothing of those instances of a saving change wrought on his hearers which will be unknown until the world to come has made its important and unexpected revelations.

"When this able and eloquent preacher first made his appearance in the horizon of the religious world, and dazzled the masses in the metropolis by his brilliancy, we were afraid that he might either get intoxicated by the large draughts of popularity which he had daily to drink, or that he would not be able, owing to the want of variety, to sustain the reputation he had so suddenly acquired. Neither result has happened. Whatever may be his defects, either as a man or as a preacher of the Gospel, it is due to him to state that he has not been spoiled by public applause. Constitutionally, he has no small amount of self-esteem; but so far from its growing with its daily extending fame, he appears to be more humble and more subdued than when he first burst on our astonished gaze.

"With regard, again, to our further fear that his excellence as a preacher would not be sustained, the event has, we rejoice to say, no less agreeably proved the groundlessness of our apprehensions; here is no falling off whatever. On the contrary, he is, in some respects, improving with the lapse of time. We fancy we can see his striking originality to greater advantage than at first. There is no sameness in his sermons. The variety of his matter —not, of course, as regards his doctrines, but as relates to his expositions, illustrations, and applications of Divine truth—is as great as ever." *

This was intended to be generous, and at the same time impartial, and the preacher recognised in Mr. Grant a friend who would stand by him in an emergency. Mr. Spurgeon was now supposed to be established in the world; his following was greater than ever. But while the pastor at New Park Street was living down detraction and gathering to himself new friends, the time was fast coming when allies on the Press who would stand by him would be of the utmost service.

About this time appeared "The Baptist Confession of Faith; with Scripture Proofs, adopted by the Ministers and Messengers of the General Assembly which met in London in 1689; with a Preface by the Rev. C. H. Spurgeon." The young pastor regarded this "Confession" as a most admirable summary of what the Fathers

* *The Morning Advertiser,* February 18, 1856.

of the denomination had believed, and he thought that while it was calculated to confirm faith in those who came after, it was really a body of divinity in small compass which would be of great service in controversy, especially to young people and the less-informed classes generally. To the end of his days Mr. Spurgeon set a high value on this little work.

"A Graduate of the London University" also published "Who and What is the Rev. C. H. Spurgeon? A Voice from one of the Colleges." This *brochure* consists of a dialogue between two students, the object being to show what such observers thought of the preacher of whom all London seemed to be talking. Written with some power, this was regarded as a generous tribute to Mr. Spurgeon's worth and far-reaching influence.

On Tuesday, May 27, of this year, Mr. Spurgeon visited the scenes of his childhood at Stambourne, where he preached in celebration of the jubilee of his grandfather. The text was Isaiah xlvi. 4—"Even to your old age I am he; and even to hoar hairs will I carry you. I have made, and I will bear; even I will carry, and will deliver you." In a contemporary newspaper account this interesting festival is thus described:—

"On Sunday week a large concourse assembled, by public invitation, at the Hill Farm, Stambourne, to celebrate the Jubilee of the Rev. James Spurgeon, who has just attained the forty-sixth year of his ministry in this village, as pastor of the Independent Chapel. Considerable preparations had been made, and there were probably from fifteen hundred to two thousand persons present at the services. The public duties were conducted by members of Mr. Spurgeon's family; the Rev. C. H. Spurgeon, of London, being the preacher, assisted by his younger brother (a student) and his father in leading the devotions of the meeting. Many of the surrounding ministers of churches, with their congregations, came from great distances to testify their respect for the venerable pastor of Stambourne meeting. The devotional exercises and the sermons, on the whole, were suitable to the occasion. The collections were liberal. In the course of his sermon the preacher animadverted very severely on the Rev. Thomas Binney's book, "On Making the best of both Worlds," which he denounced as a specimen of the 'new heretical theology.' At the close a minister rose up and protested against Mr. Spurgeon's remarks on Mr. Binney. A general state of confusion ensued in the congregation. Some clapped, some shouted 'Hear, hear,' others cried, 'Turn him out.' The reverend gentleman, however, persisted in defending Mr. Binney, and explained that the design of Mr. Binney's book was to prove and illustrate the Scriptural doctrine that 'Godliness is profitable unto all things, having promise of the life that now is, and of that which is to come.' He said, 'I charge Mr. Spurgeon with having uttered a public falsehood.' In reply, Mr. Spurgeon denounced the speaker for wishing to gain public notoriety by means of his popularity; and in his subsequent prayer at the close of this painful scene, he petitioned that the Lord would forgive him for the sin he had committed, and make him sensible of the wrong he had done in not having first gone privately and reproved him, according to the Scriptural rule." *

Meanwhile, the continued interest which the young pastor took in Sunday-school work became manifest from time to time. Mr. Cutler, the superintendent of the Sunday-school, and Mr. Kimber, the secretary, resigned their offices, and on a summer evening, after the week-night service, we find Mr. Spurgeon presenting them " with tokens of affection and grateful remembrances of their past services," in the names of the teachers. A suitable address was given, after which the one was presented with a timepiece, while the other received a gift of books. †

The enlarged chapel at New Park Street did not suffice for the requirements of the congregation, and thus the experiment was made of using the chapel in the morning, and of hiring Exeter Hall for the vast crowd which regularly gathered to hear Mr. Spurgeon in the evening of each Sunday. The second series of services in the great hall was commenced on June 8, the sermon being founded on Heb. vii. 25—" Wherefore He is able also to save them to the uttermost that come unto God by Him, seeing He ever liveth to make intercession for them." The new arrangement did not answer according to expectation, not that the crowds, which partially blocked the thoroughfare of the Strand, showed any falling off, but the proprietors of Exeter Hall itself were not willing that the building should be used exclusively by a representative of one denomination. It was now that the preacher had his views misrepresented as being " profane," " blasphemous," and even " diabolical," and he directed people to the " Confession of Faith " if they wished to see what his sentiments really were. Meanwhile, a visitor thus describes a service in the Hall and the scene outside.

* Quoted in "Spurgeon, the People's Preacher," pp. 57–58. The contemporary chronicler is mistaken in making it appear that Mr. Spurgeon conducted services at Stambourne on a Sunday. The visit to his grandfather and the scenes of his childhood really took place on a Tuesday, and the sermon preached was the same in substance as that given to the congregation at New Park Street on the Sunday preceding. See *The New Park Street Pulpit*, Nos. 81–82.

† *The Baptist Messenger*, iv. 95.

This really relates to a later series of services, but it is so characteristic of one and all of these memorable occasions, that I give it in this place:—

"A few Sundays since I went, with some friends, to hear him at Exeter Hall. As it was an *impromptu* visit, we were unprovided with tickets, so had to wait in the Strand from the time of our arrival at the Hall, ten o'clock, to that fixed for the opening of the doors, half-past ten. During this period it amused us to notice that not one omnibus passed by, whether from the East or from the West, which did not stop to deposit one or more persons at Exeter Hall. One omnibus *debarked* its whole freight of passengers there. The hall was crowded to suffocation. Indeed, I know nothing to compare with the way in which the people were wedged together but the packing of figs in a drum. Yet, despite the heat and exceeding discomfort many must have felt from their position—for a vast number had to stand all the time—I was rejoiced to observe the decorum and devotional aspect of all. The auditory was composed mainly of men—young men—one-tenth part only were women, I should say; and to hear, as one stood in the crowd, the loving, honouring way in which all were speaking of him, the good they said he was effecting, was really a blessed gratification." *

To many observers there was nothing lasting in all this; Spurgeon was only one of those passing phenomena which, like shooting stars, brilliant for the moment, would soon be lost sight of and forgotten. How often was a similar prophecy made during these days! "Will his popularity last?" was asked by one and another, and one then popular journal somewhat later in the year gave this reply to the question:—

"Will his popularity last? We more than doubt it. It stands on no firm basis. Thousands who now go to hear him only go through curiosity. Men are very much like sheep; one goes through a hedge, then another, and another, at last . . . the whole flock rushes madly forward. This has been a good deal the case with Mr. Spurgeon's congregation, but the current will soon turn and leave him; and as to those who have gone from a slightly different, if not better, motive, it is hardly likely he will retain them long. There is one excuse for Mr. Spurgeon, he is very young—only twenty-two. When he shall be a few years older . . . he will wish that much of his earlier career and strange utterances may be forgotten." †

* "Traits of Character," ii. 100–101.
† *Illustrated Times*, October 11, 1856.

CHAPTER XXV.

THE PASTOR OF HELENSBURGH.

The Rev. John Anderson one of the first to predict the Preacher's lasting Popularity—
Visits New Park Street Chapel—Graphic Description of the Service—Mr. Spurgeon
visits Helensburgh.

SOON after Mr. Spurgeon came to London, a certain Scottish minister, already mentioned, was attracted to New Park Street Chapel, a man who was destined to become a friend and supporter of the most sterling kind of the young Baptist preacher. On one occasion a North British newspaper, published at Greenock, referred to " Mr. Spurgeon's first visit to this district, made at the very onset of his ministerial life as the guest of the late Rev. Mr. Anderson, of Helensburgh. That excellent man and able divine was the first person of any note in the North to take the New Park Street preacher by the hand; and Mr. Spurgeon evinced his gratitude by calling his first residence in London by the name of Helensburgh." This does not appear to be quite correct, however; for as the reader is aware, when Mr. Spurgeon first visited Scotland in July, 1855, his headquarters were at Glasgow; Helensburgh, where his future friend resided as pastor of the Free Church congregation, being twenty-four miles away in a north-westerly direction. The town lies at the mouth of the Gareloch, and is a branch of the Firth of Clyde, being opposite to Greenock, which is about four miles away. Named after Lady Helen Colquhoun, a former proprietor of the land, it is pleasantly situated; while the gardens surrounding the houses impart to it a charm which is wanting in some other places. As a convenient centre for visiting the sites and scenes around Glasgow, Helensburgh is much frequented during the holiday season. It is also such a growing place that the population is probably double what it was in days when Mr. Spurgeon used to

be an occasional visitor during his early ministry in London. I am
not aware that he actually visited Helensburgh during the time of
his first tour in Scotland in 1855, but he may then have first
become acquainted with the genial Free Church minister.

Mr. Anderson was thirty years the senior of the London pastor,
and he had been settled at Helensburgh as far back as the year 1827,
when the now popular holiday resort was a mere village of seven
hundred souls. " The charge, indeed, was a small one ; but in feeling it
his duty to accept it, he was no doubt attracted also by the character
of the locality, which, for the scenes of loveliness and splendour that
surround it, both seaward and landward, is the finest of the many
favourite spots on the noble Firth of Clyde." *

Mr. Anderson was so successful in his sphere that a new church
was erected in 1853 at a cost of £4,500, and soon afterwards a new
manse also was provided. The pastor was no mean scholar, and
while he was himself an accomplished writer, his love for the Old
Gospel was quite as ardent as that of Mr. Spurgeon. " Nothing
pleased Mr. Anderson better than to meet with specimens of fresh,
simple, and impressive preaching ; such, for instance, as he recognised
in Mr. Spurgeon's sermons." Soon after the boy-preacher left
Waterbeach Mr. Anderson became acquainted with him, and to
his credit, he at once formed a high estimate of his young friend's
worth and capacity for usefulness. " Mr. Anderson had the discernment to perceive, while others looked on with doubt and suspicion,
the rare and sterling qualities which now stamp that remarkable
man, in the judgment of all, as one of the prodigies of the age." †

Being thus struck with Mr. Spurgeon's superlative gifts, Mr.
Anderson sought a closer acquaintance. During a visit to London
in the early part of the year 1856 he attended at New Park Street,
and it is a great pleasure to be able to give the genial Scotsman's
graphic description of the service. " He was satisfied that his
splendid voice and effective gesture, his burning zeal and sound

* " Memoir of John Anderson," by John Oatt, p. 6.
† *Ibid.*, p. 32.

doctrine, his affluence of striking illustration, and the Saxon energy of his diction, were all combining to render Mr. Spurgeon the first preacher of the day. And this he had no hesitation in publicly declaring, in face, too, of all the ridicule that was being poured upon the young Baptist minister, on account of the offences against good taste and pulpit decorum that were then laid to his charge. Soon afterwards, Mr. Spurgeon, on Mr. Anderson's invitation, visited Helensburgh, where he repeatedly preached to admiring crowds, and thus was formed an endearing and enduring friendship."* As the narrative proceeds, something may be said concerning these services in the proper place; but in the meantime the reader will be glad to have Mr. Anderson's own realistic account of what he saw and heard at New Park Street Chapel on Sunday, March 30, 1856. Before starting for London he had said to his friends, "I have heard of the fame of this young preacher, and I am going to hear him." On his return he related his experience † :—

"When Mr. Spurgeon was in Glasgow last summer, the fame of his eloquence had reached me in my seclusion here, by the shores of the sounding sea, the noise of whose waves delight me more than the 'din of cities' or the tumult of the people. I had heard him 'spoken against' by some, but spoken of by others as a preacher of remarkable and, since the days of Whitefield himself, of unprecedented popularity. But being one of those who judge for themselves in the matter of preaching, and whose opinions as to what constitutes good preaching are somewhat peculiar, I did not attach much—I may almost say any—importance whatever to what I heard of Mr. Spurgeon and his popularity in Glasgow. One of his printed sermons, however, having fallen in my way, I had no sooner read a few paragraphs of it than I said, 'Here, at last, is a preacher to my mind; one whom not only I, but whom Paul himself I am persuaded, were he on earth, would hear, approve, and own.' I forget what was the subject of the discourse; but I remember well saying to myself, 'I would rather have been the author of that sermon than of all the sermons, or volumes of sermons, published in my day.' I had lately before this been reading Guthrie and Caird, but here was something entirely different, and to my mind, in all that constitutes a genuine and good Gospel sermon, infinitely superior.

"For some time after this I heard little, and thought little, about Mr. Spurgeon. Having been, however, in London on the last Sabbath of March, and having been unexpectedly released from an engagement to preach, I thought I could not do better than go and hear for myself the preacher of whom I had heard so much in my own country. Along with two young friends, see me, then, early on the beautiful morning of that beautiful Sabbath day, when as yet there were few people on the streets, and all the 'mighty heart' of that great city was 'lying still,' on my way from Islington to New Park Street Chapel,

---

* "Memoir of John Anderson," pp. 31–32.

† Mr. Anderson's graphic sketch is taken from *The Baptist Messenger*, iv. 130–132. I am indebted to Miss Kate Stewart, of Sea-Bank House, Helensburgh, for many particulars.

Southwark, a distance of nearly four miles. We arrived at the chapel about eleven, but found that the service had commenced a quarter before eleven. The church was filled, and there were crowds of people at the gate uncertain what to do. Seeing one of the doorkeepers near the great entrance, I went up to him and said 'that I was from Scotland, and that having come so far I really *must* get in.' He asked me from what 'part of Scotland I came.' I said, 'Glasgow.' He asked no more, but said, 'Come, follow me; I really must get you in,' or words to that effect. He led the way into a wing of the building, fitted up and evidently used as a school; and here, where there were many assembled, we found seats; and though, from the crowd which choked the doors and passages, we did not see the preacher very well, we—and this was what we wanted—heard him distinctly. When we entered he was expounding, as is his custom, a portion of the Scriptures. The passage expounded was Exodus, fourteenth chapter, which contains an account of the Israelites at the Red Sea—a passage of Scripture peculiarly interesting to me, having stood on its shore and sailed on ʃthe very spot where the waters were so wondrously divided. The remarks of the preacher on each of the verses were very much in the style of Henry, and were rich and racy. His text was from the 106th Psalm, and the subject of the discourse was the same with that of the chapter he had just expounded— 'The Israelites at the Red Sea.'

"Regarding them as typical of the people of God under the Gospel, he said there were two things which he intended to consider. First, their difficulties; secondly, their resources· Their difficulties, he said, were occasioned by three things—first, the Red Sea before them; second, the Egyptians behind them; and third, the weakness of their faith. These difficulties were in the way, he said, of believers: first, the Red Sea of trials—trials peculiar to them as Christians, and caused by their coming out of Egypt, or their renouncing the world; second, the Egyptians are behind them—sin, Satan, and the world, seeking to recover them to their yoke, and, failing this, to harass and distress them. But the greatest difficulty in the way of both was unbelief. Had they trusted in Him that was *for* them, they would have made little of all them that were *against* them.

"Second, their resources. These were three—first, the providence of God. He had brought them to the Red Sea; and He who had brought them *to* it, was able and wise enough to bring them *through* it. Second, His covenant, in virtue of which He was under engagement to do so, and was bound in honour to do so. Third, the intercession of Moses. He prayed for them when they knew it not. So Christ prays for His people, and Him the Father heareth always; and in answer to His prayers, delivers, and will continue to deliver, them out of all their troubles, etc.

"Such was the method of one of the richest and ripest sermons, as regards Christian experience, all the more wonderful as being the sermon of so young a man, I ever heard. It was a sermon far in advance of the experience of many of his hearers; and the preacher evidently felt this. But, notwithstanding this, such was the simplicity of his style, the richness and quaintness of his illustrations, his intense earnestness, and the absolute and admirable naturalness of his delivery, it told upon his audience generally, and told powerfully. Many, most of them, were of the 'common people,' and when I looked upon their plebeian faces, their hands brown with labour, and, in many cases, their faded attire, I could not help remembering Him of whom it is said, 'And the common people heard Him gladly.' Yes, Mr. Spurgeon is the minister of the 'common people'; he considers himself, I am told, to be such, and well he may. Happy London people, if they but knew their happiness, to have such a minister! But to return to the sermon, and its effects on the faces! How intensely fixed were they on the preacher—how eager to hear every word he uttered—how fearful lest they should fail to catch the least! Tears were now to be seen trickling down them; and then, again, pale and careworn though many of them were, they might be seen beaming with light and joy, and brightening into smiles. One man I noticed in particular. He was evidently of humble rank, but had a noble and intelligent countenance; his face was a perfect study; every time the preacher said a striking thing, he looked expressively to me and I to him. At the close of the service I could have given him a hearty, brotherly shake of the hand, but I lost him in the crowd, and did not see him again.

"Thus much for the morning. A word or two now about the evening sermon. We were told that, if we wanted to get in, to come early, as the crowd would be greater than in the morning. With two friends, I returned about six; the service was to commence at half-past six. To our dismay, when we arrived, we found crowds already at the door waiting for admission. Those only who had tickets were now permitted to enter; as we had none, we almost despaired of getting in. One of my friends, however, knowing how I had got in in the morning, went up to a police officer, and told him I was a clergyman from Scotland, and was anxious to be admitted. The police officer, hearing this, said, very politely, he would allow us to enter the church, but would not promise us seats. This was all we wanted. One of us (a lady) was kindly favoured with a seat; my other friend and myself thought ourselves happy, like Eutychus of old, in being permitted to sit 'in a window,' with a dense crowd in the passage at our feet. I asked a man near me if he came regularly; he said he did. 'Why, then,' I asked, 'do you not take a seat?' 'Seat!' he replied; 'such a thing is not to be had for love or money. I got a ticket for leave to stand.' The church, I was told, is seated for 1,500; but what with the schoolroom and the passages, which were choke-full, there could not have been fewer in it than 3,000. The service commenced with a hymn, which was sung by the congregation standing. Never did I hear such singing; it was like the 'voice of many waters,' or the roll of thunder. No need was there of an organ in that congregation; the most powerful organ would not have been heard in the loud swell of so many living human voices. Then came the prayer. Phrenologically speaking, I should say veneration is not largely developed in Mr. Spurgeon; yet that prayer was one of the most remarkable and impressive I ever heard. He prayed first for confirmed believers, then for declining ones, then for sundry other conditions. Then there was a pause; after which he prayed for the unconverted. 'Some,' he said, 'were present who were in this state, who, in all likelihood, would never be in that or any other church again—who were that night to hear their last sermon—who, ere next Lord's day, would not be in this world; and where would they be? There was but one place where they would be—in hell!' He then said, or rather cried out, 'O God, God! must they perish? wilt Thou not save them, and make that sermon the means of their conversion?' The effect was overwhelming; many wept, and I am not ashamed to say I was one of them. The text was in Psalm cxxvi. 1, 2—'When the Lord turned again the captivity of Zion, we were like them that dream. Then was our mouth filled with laughter, and our tongue with singing.' The subject raised from the text was the 'joy of the young convert.' This sermon, in some respects, was not equal to the one in the morning; but in other respects, and in particular in its suitableness to a large and promiscuous audience, was superior.

"Some of the sketches, and that in particular of a slave newly emancipated, drunk with joy that he was free, was equal to anything ever drawn by a Dickens, or any of our great masters of fiction. Equally fine was that of the sick man restored to health, and going forth for the first time after his recovery to take his walk in the streets of London. But it would be impossible to mention all the fine touches of nature in that sermon, which made the whole of that vast congregation for the moment 'kin.' His denunciations of the Sabbath-breaker and others were as terrible as his delineations of the penitent were tender and melting. Mr. Spurgeon is equally great in the tender and the terrible. Nor is he without humour. Here many will refuse him their sympathy, and think him censurable. I scarcely think he is. Others will think, and do think, differently. His taste, according to others, is bad. It is, I admit, often so. But, then, think of the immaturity of his years. I was told he was conceited. I saw no proofs of it; and if I had, was I on that account to think less of his sermons? I do not say I will not eat good bread, because the maker of it is conceited. His conceit may be a bad thing for himself—his bread is very good for me. I am far from thinking Mr. Spurgeon perfect. In this respect he is not like Whitefield, who from the first was as perfect an orator as he was at the last. In respect

P

of his power over an audience, and a London one in particular, I should say he is not inferior to Whitefield himself. Mr. Spurgeon is a Calvinist, which few of the dissenting ministers in London now are. He preaches salvation, not of man's *free will*, but of the Lord's *good will*, which few in London, it is to be feared, now do. On all these accounts, we hail the appearance of Mr. Spurgeon with no ordinary delight, and anticipate for him a career of no ordinary usefulness. 'Happy are they which stand continually before him, and hear his words of wisdom.' As for myself, I shall long remember with delight the day on which I stood among them, and recommend such of my countrymen as may have a Lord's day to spend in London, to spend it as I did at New Park Street Chapel in hearing Mr. Spurgeon."

In the course of this life-story of Mr. Spurgeon, some other things will need to be said about the close friendship which existed between the young preacher of Southwark and the pastor of Helensburgh. In a sense, John Anderson, like Charles Haddon Spurgeon, seemed to be born to preach the Gospel. If the one in childhood was found preaching from a hay-rack, the other, at a corresponding age, showed similar inclinations. "His own desire was to be a minister of the Gospel, and the indications of his early ambition were not to be mistaken," remarks his biographer. "When a mere boy, he was in the habit of preaching. His pulpit was a tree that grew in the vicinity of the school he attended, and his audience a company of schoolmates." He was no mean poet; his reading was wide and varied; and while travelling in warmer climes in search of health, he showed himself to be a keen observer as well as an accomplished writer. Visitors to Helensburgh became familiar with the sight of "the erect and manly form" of the pastor, while "the lustre of the dark eye" told in his favour. In 1841 the first symptoms of the bronchial affection from which he afterwards suffered showed themselves, so that he was more or less of an invalid during the twelve years of his acquaintance with Mr. Spurgeon. The two had much in common; and "Helensburgh House," Nightingale Lane, Clapham, was a name which told of a friend far away in the beautiful North—"my own John Anderson."

There is a working man now in Helensburgh who remembers standing on the pier when Mr. and Mrs. Spurgeon took their departure after their first visit to the manse. Mrs. Spurgeon walked down leaning on Mr. Anderson's arm, while a worthy porter, who was himself a Baptist, carried the bag belonging to the pastor of New Park Street Chapel with no little pride. According to the honest man's own confession, it had afforded him no small satisfaction to do such a service for one whom he characterised as "the greatest preacher of the day."

The following was written in a book which the pastor of Helensburgh received from his younger friend in the early days of their acquaintance :—

"To my dear friend John Anderson,

"Whose boundless generosity compels me to add an injunction to all men, women, and children on the face of the earth, that none of them dare to accept this volume of him when he shall offer it, seeing that this is a small token of the undying love of

"C. H. SPURGEON.

"February 21, 1859."

CHAPTER XXVI.

THE FOUNDING OF THE PASTORS' COLLEGE.

The Work commenced—Mr. T. W. Medhurst—His History—Becomes the first Student—Early
Difficulties—George Rogers the first Tutor—Spurgeon's favourite Institution—A Work of
Self-denial—An American Testimony.

WHEN Mr. Spurgeon had been in London about two years, the
work of what afterwards became known as the Pastors' College
was commenced; but neither the young pastor, nor those associated
with him in encouraging a few young men who desired to preach
the Gospel, had any idea of the extent to which this service
would develop. They seemed to be providentially directed to the
work, and in every stage afterwards they believed that God was
opening the way. "C. H. Spurgeon's first student," as he is still
called, is Mr. T. W. Medhurst, pastor of Hope Chapel, Cardiff;
and to tell something of his early life-story will be the readiest way
of showing how the college was really commenced.

Mr. Medhurst, who was born in the same year as Mr. Spurgeon,
was associated with the Strict Calvinists; and while, as a young
man, he carefully avoided all low and vicious tendencies, he really
understood little or nothing of that heart religion of which to many
the young preacher of Southwark had become the prophet. The
theatre had a fascination for him which he could not resist; he
devoted many of his week-nights to the drama, and on the Sabbath
he regularly attended the preaching of James Wells at the Surrey
Tabernacle. The discourses of that pulpit orator exercised a wonderful
influence over young Medhurst, who, feeling secure in the citadel
of Antinomian doctrine into which he had retreated, felt perfectly
safe while endeavouring to serve two masters.

It has already been mentioned that Mr. Medhurst stepped into
Maze Pond Chapel early in 1854, and heard what he believes to
have been Spurgeon's first platform speech in London. The speaker

seemed to show the possession of some extraordinary qualities, and having thus met him at a Sunday-school anniversary, Mr. Medhurst was tempted to hear him at New Park Street Chapel. At first, however, he actually trembled at the thought of leaving a teacher so sound in the faith as James Wells to hear a mere Arminian like Spurgeon. It was leaving the assembly of the saints to hear an adventurer, who was giving the people a stone in place of the true bread; and though he summoned sufficient courage to enter the chapel, he felt that it would be a righteous judgment if the walls fell and crushed so notorious an offender out of exist-ence. The sermon happened to be one of a rousing kind, founded on Hosea vi. 3—"Then shall we know, if we follow on to know the Lord." It turned out that Mr. Spurgeon was no Arminian after all; and the discourse made so deep an impression that the young tradesman gave up the theatre, and saw himself "a sinner, lost, ruined, undone." The state of his mind may be judged of from the letter he sent to Mr. Spurgeon, as follows :—

"Will you be kind enough candidly to inform me whether I have any room for hope that I belong to the elect family of God, whether Jesus Christ His Son has died for me, while my affections are in the world? I try to pray, but cannot. I make resolutions only to break them. I from time to time listen to you when you speak of the glory set apart for the saints, when you describe their joys and their feelings, but I feel myself as having nothing to do with them. Oh! sir, that Sunday morning when you spoke of the hypocrite I felt that you described me. I go to chapel to hear the Word preached, I return home and make resolutions; I go to work, then out into the world, and forget all until the time for preaching comes again. I read the Bible, but do not feel interested; it seems no more to me than a book I have before read, dry and insipid. Christ has said that of all who come to Him He will not send any away. How am I to come? I feel that I cannot come. I would if I could, but I cannot. At times I think that I will give it all up, that I will not go to chapel any more; yet when the time comes I cannot stay away, but feel compelled to go again once more. Do, dear sir, tell me how am I to find Jesus? How am I to know that He died for me, and that I belong to His family? Dear sir, tell me, am I a hypocrite?"

After a time, but not before he had passed through an experience similar to what Mr. Spurgeon and John Bunyan himself had endured, young Medhurst found peace of mind, and was ever afterwards considered by the New Park Street pastor as a son in the faith. He was baptised in September, 1854. On a recent occasion Mr.

Medhurst gave an interesting account of how the college really came
to be commenced :—

"Immediately after being baptised, though I had not then any idea of entering the
ministry, I commenced preaching in the open air at Bankside, Southwark, and also on
Tower Hill and at Billingsgate Market. Two persons who were drawn into the church
at New Park Street by my preaching soon after I started led Mr. Spurgeon to suggest
that I should prepare myself for pastoral work. I was just then out of my time. I consented to the proposal, and immediately arrangements were made by Mr. Spurgeon with
the Rev. C. H. Hosken, of Bexley Heath, where I went to reside, once a week spending
several hours with Mr. Spurgeon (who was then lodging at 75, Dover Road, Southwark),
and studying theology with him. After having been preparing for the ministry six months,
I received an invitation to preach at Kingston-on-Thames, and this led to my receiving
a unanimous invitation to the pastorate of the Baptist church there. Acting on Mr.
Spurgeon's advice, that invitation was accepted temporarily until two years of study had
expired. It happened in this way :—Mr. Spurgeon himself made arrangements with the
church that in addition to the amount they were giving me for my services they were to
give him the amount he was expending in the payment of my tuition at Bexley Heath ;
and at the expiration of the first quarter he handed me a cheque, saying, 'That is yours;
the deacons would not have given that extra if I had not put it in the way I have done.'
On my refusing to accept the cheque he at once said that as he had given the money to
the Lord for two years he must take a second student. In that way the Pastors' College
was commenced. After being with the Rev. C. H. Hosken (who is still living at Norwich),
I studied with the Rev. George Rogers, at Albany Road, Camberwell." *

The above will clearly show how the idea of the college took
shape in Mr. Spurgeon's mind. The young pastor's preaching, like
a trumpet-call of one of the old prophets, was bringing in young men
from the world, and they were, in many instances, anxious to engage
in Christian service. The success of Mr. Medhurst was an encouragement to take others, so that before long the work of education had
developed into quite a costly institution. One of the chief difficulties
at the outset was that of getting the necessary funds; for the
students taken in were generally of a class too poor to do anything
in the way of paying for their own support, while there would have
been little or no hope of their being accepted by any other college.
Mr. Spurgeon's ideas of educating students were thus not of the
conventional kind. While he did not undervalue scholarship, mere
educational acquirements alone were never any recommendation ; his
aim from the first was to assist and encourage men who were already
preachers. Both Mr. William Olney and Mr. Winsor, as deacons
of the church, were in hearty sympathy with the new enterprise,

* *The South Wales Daily Press.*

and contributed liberally to its support. The next difficulty was that of finding a suitable tutor, a man who, to ripe scholarship, united soundness in the faith. In regard to funds, the establishment of the weekly offering at the Sabbath services ensured a regular income; while the very kind of Principal needed was found in George Rogers, then pastor of Albany Chapel, Camberwell.

Although an uncompromising Pædobaptist, Mr. Rogers was otherwise a man quite after Mr. Spurgeon's own heart. He was born in 1799, and lived to be the oldest Congregational minister in England. Like Mr. Spurgeon, he was an Essex man, and his birthplace, Ardleigh Hall, was not far from the spot where in Puritan times a famous preacher known as Roaring Rogers carried on his ministry. George Rogers was one of a family of thirteen, all of whom strongly adhered to nonconformity. George even refused on principle the offer of a free education at Cambridge University. As it was, he completed his studies at Rotherham College, and on coming to London as a very young man, he served for a time as assistant at the Weigh House Chapel, London, under Dr. Binney's predecessor, John Clayton. He afterwards settled for a time at Upminster, and he was young when he returned to London to take charge of the congregation at Albany Chapel.

In London Mr. Rogers settled down to hard work, and desiring, above all things, the sphere of a theological professor, he actually prepared himself for such an office. To discover such a man just at the time he was needed was quite " a find " for Mr. Spurgeon. The pastor of Albany Chapel was then fifty-seven years of age, and being so well qualified for what was required of him, he entered on his new duties with the greatest satisfaction. His acceptance of the orthodox doctrines was as hearty as that of Spurgeon himself, while he was Catholic-minded, witty, and judicious. In the early days of the college the students were lodged in the house of Mr. Rogers, and from the first the tutor showed that he was willing to make sacrifices for the enterprise. When on one occasion the funds were low, Mr. Spurgeon suggested that he should sell his own carriage and horses to aid the cause. The tutor would not listen to such a proposition, and declared that he would even prefer to make sacrifices himself. Mr. Rogers became in time so ardently in love with the work that he was wont to say the college could do better without him than he could do without the college. His students contracted the greatest love for him, and few, indeed, ever departed from the evangelical doctrines which were even dearer to the Principal than life itself.

There can be no doubt that the college was Mr. Spurgeon's favourite institution, and in one place he speaks of it himself as " his first-born and best beloved." The ·importance the young pastor attached to such educational effort was shown by the self-denial he was prepared to exercise in order that the work might be vigorously maintained. When we think of a young man who had recently married, and who was still under twenty-three years of age, devoting a main part of his income to such service, his wife in the meantime practising the most rigorous economy in the house-hold in order to enable him to do it, we shall not doubt his enthusiasm. Mr. Spurgeon thought he saw a great opportunity, and he was determined to seize it. Like the young pastor's method of preaching, the idea of this college was in itself sufficiently original to be an innovation, and as such it was regarded both by friends and objectors. The constituency catered for was unlike that for which any other college provided. In all other similar institutions married men were not eligible for admission; but Mr. Spurgeon would not be hampered by any hard-and-fast rules. Even a young married man, who could be made more useful by a couple of years' theological and literary study, would be taken in. Another might actually be settled in the ministry; but if by leaving his people for a time he could be helped to become a more effective preacher, he also would be welcomed. In short, the design was to help men who were already preachers to become better servants of God and of the Church—workmen who needed not to be ashamed. So long as he detected genuine talent for the work, Mr. Spurgeon did not greatly concern himself in regard to a young man's educational shortcomings. They could be in some measure repaired; but zeal in Christian service was not to be acquired apart from a change of heart effected by the agency of God's Holy Spirit alone. The pastor always looked with extreme suspicion on a man who proposed himself on account of the possession of exceptional literary talent, whether genuine or imaginary. From time to time a few somewhat ludicrous examples of self-satisfied genius came before him, but with keenest eye and unerring judgment Mr. Spurgeon never failed to take the measure of such men; and none knew better than he how to administer an effective *quietus* to such aspiring egotists.

From the first, the founder of the college never favoured the idea of lodging a considerable number of young men under one roof. It is true that for a time the household of Mr. Rogers included the whole of the students, but that was not a permanent arrangement. When the number increased they were lodged in twos and threes in houses surrounding the Tabernacle; and when the college building itself was erected about eighteen years ago no accommodation for lodging students on the premises was provided.

Mr. Spurgeon's experience in this service confirmed him in the belief that he was doing the right thing, and that his methods were such as would be most fruitful in good results. He was always a man who adopted Christ's way of judging a tree by its fruits; and in this instance he saw fruit which yielded satisfaction while it inspired gratitude. Objectors arose who insisted that he was training men for whom ministerial spheres would never be found; or that the prescribed curriculum was quite inadequate to equip preachers for active service whose early advantages had been so inconsiderable. The most conclusive answer to this objection was found when the young men made spheres for themselves in the Colonies, or in the foreign mission field; or when, as often happened, they secured some of the best positions at home. This has actually occurred in more cases than can be mentioned.

Since the college was Mr. Spurgeon's favourite service, we shall find, as we proceed, that he devoted to it his best energies. Year by year, beginning with 1865, we shall find him at the annual conference, on each occasion giving one of those instructive and stimulating addresses which seemed at the time to call forth at once all his powers and all his enthusiasm. Friday afternoons were devoted to the students; and the lectures then given can never be forgotten by those who heard them. It was a work of self-denial all along so far as the founder was concerned; but he never grudged either the toil or the money that it cost him.

Since Mr. Spurgeon's death, one of his American friends has remarked concerning this work :—

"The curriculum of the Pastors' College has been criticised as too meagre, and as not affording the student an education sufficiently comprehensive for the times; but it ought always to be remembered that the plan of study adopted by this institution was never designed to be a substitute for university training, and its President never under-estimated the value of higher and ampler advantages. Nor should it be forgotten that until within a recent period it has not been an easy thing for Nonconformists to obtain the privileges of Oxford or of Cambridge. Indeed, I have the honour of being myself acquainted with one among the first of dissenting scholars permitted to graduate at Cambridge, and he is not yet an exceedingly venerable gentleman. We must consequently make allowances both for the peculiarities of Mr. Spurgeon's surroundings and for the pressure of necessity for what may seem to be superficial in the Pastors' College. It was devised and inaugurated as an institution for practical equipment, and as such it has unquestionably justified its existence. While the students may not have been taught the art of interweaving much of polite literature in their discourses, and while they may not have been able to acquire the rare lucidity of their President's style, nevertheless they have received valuable and accurate information. They have likewise obtained a complete knowledge of Holy S ripture; and have listened to sagacious suggestions regarding pastoral duties, and cautions against overdoing, against fanaticism, and against perpetually running after this or that tribe of religious gipsies who insist on encamping in the environments of God's holy city." *

Such a testimony from the New World the late President of the Pastors' College would have greatly valued.

* "The Puritan Preacher in the Nineteenth Century." By George C. Lorimer. Boston: 1892. This is a monograph by one who was intimately acquainted with Mr. Spurgeon.

CHAPTER XXVII.

A GREAT DISASTER.

Beginning to collect for a Great Chapel—The Surrey Gardens Music Hall—Engaged for Spurgeon's Services—Scene in the Building and Grounds—A Panic—Accounts by various Spectators —The Killed and Wounded—Effect on the Preacher.

AT the best Exeter Hall was not a very conveniently situated place for a congregation which had its home on the south side of the river; and, apart from that, the proprietors of the hall were not willing to have the place too regularly occupied by a congregation representing one denomination. To other objections, Mr. Spurgeon himself might have added that of the building not being large enough. The great room was densely crowded on every occasion of a service being held in it, and had it been twice the size it would still have been too small.

On Michaelmas-day, 1856, a meeting was held in New Park Street Chapel to initiate the scheme for the erection of what we find already spoken of as "the largest chapel in the world." Drs. Leask and Fletcher, Counsellor Payne and George Moore, were among the notables present in addition to Mr. Spurgeon himself, and very liberal contributions were promised. This "mammoth undertaking" now began to excite increasing interest, and this first meeting was densely crowded.*

Hence, looking at things all round, a crisis appeared to have come on, and a crisis of a kind which neither Mr. Spurgeon nor his friends well knew how to deal with. London seemed to be so aroused by the simple preaching of the Gospel, that the largest buildings in the town were too small to accommodate the throngs who wished to hear. Exeter Hall itself was one of the most spacious rooms that could be obtained; but if that was not available for any lengthened period, what was to be done in the meantime?

* *The Baptist Messenger*, v. 120.

Persons of an ardent, go-ahead temperament might advocate the immediate erection of a building worthy of the occasion, but that would need a large sum of money, and, even if the needful funds were available, the mere building of such a chapel would require some considerable time. Was it not possible to make some temporary arrangement which would enable the popular young preacher still to give his message to the multitude?

It so happened that just about that time a building capable of receiving an audience of some ten or twelve thousand persons was erected. This was the Music Hall in the Royal Surrey Gardens, and of which the musical conductor, M. Jullien, was the presiding genius. There was, indeed, a strange kind of connection between Exeter Hall and the popular recreation ground at Walworth, but of this many were probably not aware. When the wild beasts were taken away from old Exeter Change, and gave place to the present Exeter Hall, they for a time found a home at the King's Mews, Charing Cross, whence they afterwards found their way to what had been the gardens of the Manor House at Walworth. There they were housed in a great round conservatory, the whole being under the management of the proprietor, Edward Cross. Fireworks and panoramic pictures were afterwards added to the attractions, and at last, in 1856, when the Gardens belonged to a limited liability company, a great hall was erected for the popular concerts of M. Jullien.

The idea occurred to several friends that this Music Hall might be utilised for Spurgeon's services, but when this was suggested to others they at once opposed as impious the thought of preaching the Gospel in a place which was a mere temple of worldly amusement. If Mr. Spurgeon and certain of his friends did not see things in such a light, it was because they were innovators who were before their time. As Christians they were aggressive in a sense which many of those whose co-operation they desired were altogether unable to understand. The idea of giving the Gospel to people in halls, theatres, or similar places, was new, and was far from being universally accepted. Mr. Spurgeon was quite free from such prejudices; he would take his message anywhere, feeling that it was everywhere alike wanted. It is true that in after years the Music Hall was forsaken because it was to be used as a place of amusement on Sunday nights, but that was because the congregation should not seem to support a management which wantonly profaned the Sabbath.

Before it was finally decided to hire the great Music Hall, Mr. Spurgeon and his friend William Olney went to look over the building, and both being impressed with the immense size of the structure, they could not help thinking that it was a somewhat hazardous thing to open such a place to the crowd for religious services on the Sabbath. Nothing of the kind had ever before been attempted, for the largest audiences ever addressed by Wesley and Whitefield had been in the open air, because no buildings were large enough to contain them. In this instance the pastor and his friend found a building of which the seating capacity does not appear ever really to have been measured, though if it be said that over twelve thousand persons could be accommodated, the statement is probably quite within the truth.* As the two looked over the vast area, and then glanced upward at the three great galleries, they might well have some misgivings as to the propriety of trying an experiment of which no one could prophesy what the outcome might be.

At the same time, both the preacher and his faithful friend were reassured by the thought that it would be a glorious thing to preach the Everlasting Gospel to twelve thousand or more at one time; and, putting their trust in God, they resolved to go forward. Those who rejoiced at the prospect of what was about to be done, and those who regarded the great enterprise with misgiving, prayed together for its success. Sunday evening, October 19, was the time fixed for the first service.

When the news went through London that Spurgeon was to hold Sunday services in the hall in which M. Jullien, with his

* "On the first occasion of Mme. Alboni's appearance during the present season not less than 13,000 persons were comfortably accommodated within its walls."—*The British Banner*, October 21, 1856.

great band and opera " stars," had entertained the multitude of pleasure-seekers, expectation ran high, and probably the desire to be present at the service on the part of the common people was such as had never been equalled. People, from children upwards, of every social grade seemed to be desirous to attend. Even in the afternoon of that memorable autumn day, and almost before the shades of evening had begun to fall, the streets leading to the Gardens began to be thronged with people. When Mr. Spurgeon himself arrived, the sight of the people for the time unnerved him; and certainly it was enough to make even a strong man feel sick and faint to find himself the hero of such an occasion. For a considerable distance away the streets appeared to be alive with streams of people, while the entrance-road in the Gardens was blocked with a dense crowd which was unable to enter the hall. When the building itself was filled there were still over ten thousand persons in the grounds; and at last the outer gates were closed to keep in check the encroaching multitude in the streets beyond.

The doors of the building were opened at six o'clock, and such was the pressure at the doors that in a few minutes the three galleries, the orchestra, and the area were all densely crowded. " Notwithstanding the immense size of the place," says one account, " there was not sufficient room for a dozen more to enter, and when the seats became filled there were some two or three thousand persons who were content to stand in the passages, and there were considerably more on the greensward outside, looking through the windows." In its way the scene was unique; no such congregation had ever before been gathered in any building to hear the Gospel simply preached. Dr. John Campbell, the editor of *The British Banner*, sat near the pulpit, and he thus wrote of the occasion :—

"The spectacle, of its kind, was one of the most imposing, magnificent, and awful ever presented to the human eye. No adequate idea of it can be conveyed by description; to be understood it must have been seen; and they who beheld it received an impression which no time will ever obliterate. The sight of ten or twelve thousand people, more or fewer, assembled to listen to the Word of the Living God, in such a place, at such a time, and addressed by a man with a voice of such power and compass that the remotest might hear with ease and pleasure, was sufficient to excite intense joy in the hearts of all good men who witnessed it, nor is it extravagant to say that it was enough to wake the attention of the angelic world." *

A friend who is still living, and who, with his wife, was present on the occasion, says :—

"We reached the place in good time; the building was rapidly filling. We occupied the first gallery, and sat immediately opposite the pulpit; we were not able to sit together. At length, the three galleries were not only full but overcrowded, and so was the floor of the building. The thought came to me and my wife also that the walls of the building were subject to such a degree of pressure as to render their collapse a probability. We both, without concert, determined, as soon as the service should be quietly proceeding, to leave the building." †

If any such thoughts had possession of other minds, the getting up of a panic by thieves for their own purposes was a com‑ paratively easy thing. All began in a promising manner. The preacher, who had recovered from the faintness and sickness which had come upon him, appeared to be quite himself. He opened with a few appropriate words; reading of Scripture and a hymn followed. "There was no dry disquisition, no curious criticism," adds Dr. Camp‑ bell, "but an address directed to the hearts of the hearers, showing from the first that the speaker came strongly intent upon most important business, and that nothing was to be regarded short of its accomplishment. The general prayer next followed; and here, too, the same pertinent and peculiar air was manifested. The one great thing which animated the preacher was most obviously the salvation of men."

It was just after the commencement of the general prayer that the conspirators, who had so skilfully prepared their mine, saw that their opportunity had come. It seemed as though well-instructed agents were stationed in various parts of the hall, each section carry‑ ing out its own allotted part of the programme. At all events, just after Mr. Spurgeon had commenced his prayer there was suddenly heard from one quarter a cry of "Fire!" In another part a different cry was taken up—"The galleries are giving way!" Then from another part was heard another cry in tones of assumed terror— "The place is falling!" The scene which at once followed was

* *The British Banner*, October 23, 1856.
† Communicated by Mr. R. J. Curtis, of the Ragged-School Union.

such as will never be adequately described. Mr. R. J. Curtis, already mentioned, says that "immediately there was a hurried and disordered rush from all parts of the building, especially from the upper galleries. I very soon left, and on reaching the landing and moving towards the stairs—not to go down, but to look—someone, fearing that I was rushing into danger, pulled me back. While standing there, the people in terror rushed on like a resistless wave, the forward portion of which rolled over the banisters, and was precipitated to the bottom of the stairs." The manner in which some jumped from dangerous heights, in order to escape imaginary danger, was unaccountable. I know of one gentleman who sat in one of the galleries, and who, seeing that there was no cause for alarm, did his utmost to reassure a lady who happened to be sitting next to him. His endeavours were fruitless, however; for the woman, beside herself with terror, sprang from her seat, and jumped into the area, to break both of her legs, leaving a shawl in the hand of the friend who would have held her back.

The frenzy of this woman was typical of the uncontrollable fright of others, which in a number of instances resulted in death and broken limbs. The rush from the galleries to the staircases was such that the banisters gave way, and what was hoped would prove ways of escape at once became fearful pitfalls of death.

Describing the height of the commotion a few minutes after the conspirators had fired their mine, a contemporary account says:—

"The cries and shrieks at this period were truly terrific, to which was added the already pent-up excitement of those who had not been able to make their exit. They pressed on, treading furiously over the dead and dying, tearing frantically at each other. Hundreds had their clothes torn from their backs in their endeavours to escape; masses of men and women were driven down and trodden over heedless of their cries and lamentations; men appeared not to care for women, and women appeared equally callous of their own sex, one object only appearing to fill the mind of all—that of self-preservation. Some climbed over the galleries and dropped upon the heads of those below. All this time the pressure from those behind became greater and greater; many who would not otherwise have been injured were crushed by the surrounding multitude. Women, and even strong men, fainted, dropped upon the floor, and were trodden over by those following them.

"Notwithstanding the number that had fallen from the gallery, the crowd still pressed on to the staircases, and had it not been for the providential circumstance that there was an iron pillar supporting the end of the gallery, the loss of life must have been most awful.

While this scene of devastation and terror was proceeding at the north-west end of the building, similar horrors were being enacted at all other outlets.

" As soon as the shrieks of the unfortunate creatures who were suffering in the inside were heard by those who had obtained ingress into the gardens, but could not obtain admission into the hall, they made a desperate rush for the outer gates; but by a strange arrangement they could find no means of getting outside the gates, they having been firmly closed to prevent the great crowd, which had been outside all the evening, from entering the gardens. Men, women, and children climbed, were drawn and thrown over the iron railings, many of them being seriously injured in consequence. As soon as it was known by those outside that a terrible accident had occurred, the wildest rumours prevailed. Some asserted that the entire building had fallen in, burying all beneath; others that the galleries had given way, carrying their occupants upon those below. Then the most fearful excitement prevailed outside. Fathers, whose wives and daughters were in the building; mothers, whose children were there; and in fact every person who knew of a relative of any kind that had gained admission, raised their wildest lamentations for those who they believed were lost to them for ever.

" By this time the greater portion of the audience had escaped from the hall, and of course with all precipitancy made for the street. Those who had been fortunate enough to escape without injury assisted in bringing out their more unfortunate friends and companions, which at once realised the fact of the sad calamity to those outside, who, as quickly as possible, made their way toward the building for the purpose of seeking their relatives and friends. All those who had the power to do so had left the hall, and only the dead, dying, and wounded were to be seen." *

My friend Mr. R. J. Curtis communicates a description of the scene inside the building and nearer the pulpit as it appeared to him :—" After a short time I returned to my seat and remained till nearly the close of the service. During the uproar occasioned by the causeless cry of ' Fire ! ' Mr. Spurgeon retained perfect self-possession, and to allay the panic vociferated, ' Take care of your pockets ! ' His text on the occasion—no doubt impromptu—was the words, ' The curse of the Lord is in the house of the wicked ' (Proverbs iii. 33). The sermon was to the point, and as effectively delivered as on the most auspicious occasion. He was not aware of the cruel consequences of the false alarm till after the service. On leaving the place we saw at the bottom of the stairs a large pool of blood partially covered by a carpet."

This is identical with the view taken by the leading journal so far as the preaching is concerned :—" The preacher kept his place, preaching, praying, and giving out psalms; the surviving congregation returned to their seats, the boxes for the new chapel were rattled about, and the service concluded almost as if nothing had happened." †

* *The British Banner,* October 21, 1856.   † *The Times,* October 20, 1856.

Q

The truth is, nevertheless, that Mr. Spurgeon did not even attempt to give a sermon until calls of "Preach! preach!" from different quarters of the hall prompted him to do so; and it has to be remembered that the preacher and those around him in the vicinity of the pulpit knew nothing of what was really happening in distant parts of the building.

A pretty full account of what Mr. Spurgeon actually said was given in the denominational newspaper. The preacher desired that the people should retire while a hymn was being sung; but the vast majority of the congregation, who knew nothing of the extent of the calamity at the doors, still cried, "Go on! Preach!"

"My friends, what shall I preach about?" said Mr. Spurgeon. "You bid me preach to-night. I am ready to do all I can, but in the midst of all this confusion what shall be my subject? May God's Holy Spirit give me a subject on this solemn occasion. My friends, there is a terrible day coming, when the terror and alarm of this evening shall be as nothing. That will be a time when the thunder and lightning and blackest darkness shall have their fullest power; when the earth shall reel to and fro beneath us; and when the arches of the solid heavens shall totter to their centre. The day is coming when the clouds shall reveal their wonders and portents, and Christ shall sit upon those clouds in glory, and shall call you to judgment. Many men have gone away to-night in the midst of this terrible confusion, and so shall it be on that great day. I can, however, believe that the results of that day will show that there will be a great many—not a less proportion than those who have left—who will stand the ordeal of that great day. The alarm which has just arisen has been produced in some measure by that instinct which teaches us to seek self-preservation. But in the more numerous of the cases it is not so much the dread of death which has influenced them as the dread of something afterwards— that undiscovered country from whose bourne no traveller returns. 'Tis conscience that makes cowards of us. Many were afraid to stop there, because they thought it was to stop and be damned. They were aware—and many of you are aware, that if you were hurried before your Maker to-night you would be brought there unshriven, unpardoned, and con- demned. But what are your terrors now to what they will be on that terrible day of reckoning of the Almighty, when the heaven shall shrink above you and hell open her mouth beneath you? But know you not, my friends, that grace, sovereign grace, can yet save you? Have you never yet heard the welcome news that Jesus came into the world to save sinners? You are the chief among sinners. Believe that Christ died for you and you may be saved from the torments of hell that await you. Do you not know that you are lost and ruined—that none but Jesus can do the sinner good? You are sick and diseased. Jesus can do you good, and will. I thought this night of preaching from the text, 'The curse of the Lord is in the house of the wicked, but He blesseth the habitation of the just.' I feel that I cannot preach as I wish. You will have another alarm yet, and I would rather that some of you would seek to retire gradually, in order that no harm may be done. My text will be found in the 3rd chapter of Proverbs, at the 33rd verse." *

Something like silence was obtained, but soon the agitation again broke out. "You ask me to preach, but how can I after this terrible

* *The Freeman*, October 22, 1856.

scene ? " asked Mr. Spurgeon. " My brain is in a whirl, and I scarcely know where I am, so great are my apprehensions that many persons must have been injured by rushing out." The hymn, "His sovereign power without our aid," was then sung, and the congregation was urged to retire quietly.

As regards the effect of the panic on the preacher himself, several accounts were given. According to one he was carried senseless from the pulpit ; but the truth seems to be that the service was brought to a close when the worst was known. In the words of one chronicler, " Mr. Spurgeon commenced his sermon by observing that he could not, of course, after such an occurrence, preach to them as he would wish, but he would preach to them for the usual time if they thought fit to remain."* Another remarked, " Mr. Spurgeon's mind during the terrible scene manifested a composure truly astonishing. He seemed in no respect unnerved, but manifested a meek yet resolute determination to proceed ; but the thieves, who must have comprised hundreds, continued their noises with such pertinacity as to render it utterly hopeless. Mr. Spurgeon then intimated that the meeting would dissolve, and exhorted the immense multitude to withdraw slowly." †

Seven persons were killed, while a larger number were injured. In regard to the originators of the panic, an inspector of police who was present expressed the opinion that the mischief had not been occasioned by thieves. It was rather thought that certain enemies of Mr. Spurgeon had merely resolved to cause him some annoyance. ‡

* *The British Banner*, October 21, 1856.

† *The Morning Advertiser*, October 20, 1856.

‡ The disaster was not unparalleled, for this account of a similar instance of causeless panic was given at the time :—

"On Sabbath, the 18th October, 1801, an appalling accident befell the people assembled in the Low Church of Kilmarnock, Ayrshire. On the afternoon of that day the edifice was crowded to excess before the arrival of the minister. About the time when the bell had ceased ringing, the end of a seat cracked ; two persons on it immediately exclaimed that the house was falling. The alarm communicated like lightning, and everyone believed what he heard and saw what imagination readily presented. On this a rush was made to get out lest they should be buried in the ruins ; and, as the stairs from the gallery lead down into the area of the church, the crush was tremendous. . . . The spectacle presented in and around the church on that day was truly heartrending — thirty individuals being crushed to death ! "

CHAPTER XXVIII.

CRITICISMS OF THE LONDON PRESS.

THE cases of death were some of them touching instances of young persons going out from their homes in a state of health and expectancy, and in a few hours being carried back stiffened corpses, with features blackened by suffocation. The great building contained neither flue nor fireplace of any kind, and hence did not seem to be a place likely to become a prey to fire. On the morning after the accident the hall was found to be strewn with all kinds of garments which had belonged to men, women, or children, the quantity being so great that the police-station at Lock's Fields could hardly find sufficient storage room for them. Both inside the hall and among the crowd outside a number of thieves committed many robberies, but not one of these offenders appears to have been apprehended. During the night the wildest rumours were current throughout London, and the excitement was certainly not allayed when the newspapers appeared on the following morning with reports of the catastrophe, accompanied by leading articles which more or less misrepresented the facts of the case. It was now that the young pastor realised the advantage of having two such friends to stand by him as James Grant of *The Morning Advertiser*, and Dr. John Campbell of *The British Banner*.

A correspondent of *The Morning Advertiser* said :—

" A variety of absurd and inaccurate statements have been made as to the causes which led Mr. Spurgeon to leave Exeter Hall, and, consequently, necessitated the use of some larger building than his own chapel, and thus eventually led him to the Surrey Music Hall, where this catastrophe occurred. Exeter Hall was taken while the New Park Street Chapel was being enlarged; but when that edifice was duly finished the Exeter Hall committee refused to allow Mr. Spurgeon the use of that building any longer. The fact is, that it would have been contrary to their rules, inasmuch as, to prevent any infringement of their non-sectarian character, they have provided that no minister or sect shall be allowed to take possession of the Hall any longer than they may be necessitated to do so by their own buildings being under repair. When, therefore, Mr. Spurgeon's chapel in New Park Street was re-opened on its completion, the committee of Exeter Hall could no longer, consistently with their rules, permit him the use of it, or the building would have become identified with his name, and thus its unsectarian character, which has been so jealously guarded, would have been lost. These are the facts of the case, and they will be a sufficient answer to the divers wild imaginings of those who sought to account for a result, while they were ignorant of the circumstances which led to it."

On the Monday evening there was a meeting at New Park Street Chapel, when Mr. Moore, one of the deacons, said :—

" With reference to the origin of the alarm, there is no doubt that it originated from wicked designing men. Oh, that dreadful scene! You are anxious to hear about our poor pastor— he is very bad. Very bad I say, not from any injuries or bruises he has received, but from the extreme tension on his nerves, and his great anxiety. So bad is he that we were fearful for his mind this morning. Under these circumstances, only one thing could be done—that is, to send him into the country away from the scene. As we knew that a great number of persons would call at his house during the day, we sent him early this morning, so that none of his engagements can be entered into this week. From information I have just received I am enabled to tell you that to-night he is a little better, but still very prostrate. Mr. Olney (another deacon) is still in bed. Let us be more merciful to our enemies of last night than they were to us. That wicked wretch—that man whom we are justified in calling a miscreant— who first gave the dreadful signal by which so much life was lost—let us even pray for him. Who knows but that he may one day stand in this room and own his great crime, and seek for repentance ? " *

In referring to the accident *The Freeman* maintained that Mr. Spurgeon and his friends were right in hiring the hall, and dismissed as puerile "the charges of ambition or vanity against the preacher or his deacons for following what seemed to be the leadings of Providence and the dictates of Christian zeal."

The Times made some strange mistakes in reference to the disaster. It was said that 20,000 persons went to a new hall to hear a preacher who was "only twenty-five;" and for whom "they are building a place somewhere to hold 15,000." The writer inferred that due care had not been taken, and that under the circumstances

---

* *The British Banner*, October 21, 1856. News of another death having occurred cast additional gloom over this gathering. A collection was made for the sufferers, and the fact came out that a sum of £8 had been voluntarily placed in the boxes at the Music Hall on the preceding evening. Mr. Moore, the deacon, who made the statement given, had been the first to propose that popular services should be held in the great Music Hall, and he had urged on the enterprise notwithstanding that Mr. Spurgeon himself shrank from the thought of preaching in a place of such vast dimensions.

the accident was just of the kind that might have been expected.* Some advice was then given to Mr. Spurgeon, the impression being that he was ambitious of addressing greater multitudes than had ever been spoken to before by any popular orator :—

"The human voice is limited. Stentor himself could not be heard by the whole human race. On certain occasions 20,000 people are assembled in St. Paul's, but they do not hear, or expect to hear; on the contrary, as soon as the preacher appears in the pulpit they take out sandwiches, buns, brandy-flasks, and newspapers. No church in the metropolis holds 3,000, though some have a name for more. There is something, then, very ambitious, to say the least, in the attempt to have five times as many hearers as anybody has had before. Let Mr. Spurgeon be at least content with as many as the Surrey Music Hall was intended to hold sitting in comfort and with sufficient means of exit. . . . Would Mr. Spurgeon be so good as to attend to the subject at once? Next Sunday, instead of 20,000, the Surrey Gardens will be blockaded from four o'clock by at least 50,000. They will expect to hear, not only Mr. Spurgeon, but also a sermon from him on the sudden fate of the victims last Sunday. The prospect is rather a serious one, and if this gentleman and his friends have the means of providing against a crush, or the effects of a panic, they will be held responsible for omitting to do so." †

It may be interesting to quote some additional opinions on this terrible incident which appeared in the London papers. *The Daily News* had an article, and Dr. Campbell characterised its representations as "cruel in the extreme":—

"But the crowd had been assembled to collect a subscription towards the erection of such a mammoth chapel, and Mr. Spurgeon and his friends were unwilling that the opportunity should be lost. Therefore this untimeous reminder; therefore Mr. Spurgeon's exclamation to the panic-stricken fugitives, that they were more afraid of temporal than

---

* "Such incidents are not uncommon, though it is not quite true to say that they cannot be helped, and every fresh instance suggests fresh cautions. A good many years ago, when St. Luke's, Chelsea, was newly built, and thought a paragon of Gothic architecture, there were floating rumours as to the stability of its stone vaulting. It was a new experiment; the old secret was lost; the pasteboard walls and light flying buttresses were mistrusted. So one evening, after a charity sermon, while the hymn was singing and the plate was going round, the officials aloft thought the congregation had gone out and let down the chandeliers; the people in the free seats made way for the falling galleries in haste; the benches were overturned; there was a cry, 'The roof! the roof!' In an instant all was confusion, noise, and dust, and one could only see that the whole congregation was flying over the pews to the doors like leaves in the autumn wind. Happily, the panic was more on the ground than in the galleries, and by the time the congregation had packed the passages so closely that they could not get out, they came to their reason and returned to their places —not, however, before the clergyman, who had been reading the prayers, after a vain attempt to open the door of the reading-desk, vaulted clean over it. St. Luke's has acquired a character for stability by this time, and so it is to be hoped the Surrey Music Hall will in the end. But let not the warning pass wholly away. All the wonder is that, the alarm once given, the results were not worse on Sunday night."—*The Times*, October 21, 1856.

† *The Times*, October 21, 1856.

eternal death; therefore the indecent rattling of money-boxes in their ears. We might go further, and remark on the callous manner in which Mr. Spurgeon and his friends left the meeting, without one attempt to aid or soothe the sufferers; but we are willing to make allowance for the bewilderment which such a spectacle was calculated to produce." *

For many years previous to Mr. Spurgeon's death, *The Daily Telegraph* showed a truly generous appreciation of him and his work. On the morning after the Surrey Gardens calamity, however, this journal probably exceeded all the other London newspapers in the harshness of its censure, *e.g.* :—

"Mr. Spurgeon is a preacher who hurls damnation at the heads of his sinful hearers. Some men there are who, taking their precepts from the Holy Writ, would beckon erring souls to a rightful path with fair words and gentle admonition; Mr. Spurgeon would take them by the nose and bully them into religion. Let us set up a barrier to the encroachments and blasphemies of men like Spurgeon, saying to them, 'Thus far shalt thou come and no further;' let us devise some powerful means which shall tell to the thousands who now stand in need of enlightenment, This man, in his own opinion, is a righteous Christian, but in ours nothing more than a ranting charlatan. We are neither strait-laced nor Sabbatarian in our sentiments, but we would keep apart, widely apart, the theatre and the church; above all, we would place in the hand of every right-thinking man a whip to scourge from society the authors of such vile blasphemies as on Sunday night, above the cries of the dead and the dying, and louder than the wails of misery from the maimed and suffering, resounded from the mouth of Spurgeon in the music hall of the Surrey Gardens. And lastly, when the mangled corpses had been carried away from the unhallowed and disgraceful scene—when husbands were seeking their wives, and children their mothers, in extreme agony and despair—the chink of the money, as it fell into the collection-boxes, grated harshly, miserably, on the ears of those who, we sincerely hope, have by this time conceived for Mr. Spurgeon and his rantings the profoundest contempt."

After the majority of the morning papers had spoken in a strain which seemed to suit the temper of their readers, one of the

* In reply to *The Daily News*, which he quoted, Dr. Campbell wrote:—"The foregoing is full of misrepresentation or misapprehensions. The crowd was *not* assembled for the purpose alleged. Nothing could be more pertinent to the occasion than the awful reference made by Mr. Spurgeon to another day, and the necessity of preparing for it. The '*indecent rattling* of the money-boxes' is a pure fabrication; but to speak of the 'callous manner in which Mr. Spurgeon and his friends left the meeting, without attempting to aid or soothe the sufferers,' is to perpetrate a heinous wrong on a most meritorious and, at this moment, a much afflicted man. Mr. Spurgeon could hardly be induced to withdraw from the pulpit even after the benediction had been pronounced, so intense was his anguish, and so acute his disappointment at not being permitted to testify the Gospel of the Grace of GOD. He was literally led down by his friends, and by them all but carried into the room appropriated as a vestry, which he reached almost in a state of insensibility, and fell prostrate on the floor. A considerable time elapsed before he was able to be raised or converse. He now, but not till now, obtained a hint, but nothing more, of the probability that some people were seriously injured; and that hint suggested to his humane and sensitive spirit the agonising fear that someone might possibly be killed."—*The British Banner*, October 23, 1856.

most influential of the evening journals was more generous in its testimony :—

"We have inquired of respectable persons who were present, and they inform us, up to the moment, during the prayer, when the bell was heard to tinkle, and the cry of 'Fire!' was raised, no worship they ever attended was conducted with more solemnity and decorum; that the singing of a hymn by so many thousands of persons, in so vast a building, was peculiarly impressive; and that but for the intentional disturbance, the effect of the whole must have been all that could be desired. We hardly think anyone can be held responsible for not conjecturing that any even of the lowest roughs and rowdies could be found wicked enough to hazard the lives of so many persons, however willing they might have been to annoy one whom they, of course, judged a fanatical preacher." *

The Evening Star, then a widely circulated penny journal, also joined in the discussion with some vigour, showing that other questions than the mere structure of buildings, or the protection of excited panic-stricken multitudes from harm, were raised by the accident at the Surrey Gardens. That mishap had brought the vocation of the preacher and the secret of his power within the range of newspaper discussion. The *Star* then proceeded to deal with things as they were. It often happened that a curate, who preached better than his rector, gave offence rather than satisfaction to his employer. The so-called popular preacher was rarely found to belong to the common people. To go into any ordinary church or chapel was to see a middle-class congregation :—

"But where are the artisan classes — that keen-eyed, strong-minded race, who crowd the floor at political meetings or cheap concerts, fill the minor theatres, and struggle into the shilling gallery of the Lyceum or Princess's? So very scanty is their attendance upon the most noted preachers, that it is their adhesion to Mr. Spurgeon which has made that gentleman a prodigy and a phenomenon. The first that we heard of him, two or three years since, was that the Bankside labourers went to hear him on Sunday and week nights. The summer before last we found the artisans of Bethnal Green, a much more fastidious race, flocking round him in a field at Hackney. And in the list of the killed and wounded at the Music Hall are journeymen painters, tanners, and milliners' girls. It is worth while to ask the reason why.

"A simple hearing is sufficient to answer the question, supposing that the hearer can also see. There never yet was a popular orator who did not talk more and better with his arms than with his tongue. Mr. Spurgeon knows this instinctively. When he has read his text he does not fasten his eyes on a manuscript and his hands to a cushion. As soon as he begins to speak he begins to act; and that, not as if declaiming on the stage, but as if conversing with you in the street. He seems to shake hands with all round, and put everyone at his ease. There is no laboured exordium, making you wonder by what ingenious winding he will get back to the subject; but a trite saying, an apt

* *The Sun*, October 22, 1856.

quotation, a simple allegory, or two or three familiar sentences, making all who hear feel interested and at home. Then there is no philosophical pomp of exposition, but just two or three catch-words, rather to guide than to confine attention. Presently comes, by way of illustration, a gleam of humour; perhaps a stroke of downright vulgarity—it may be, a wretched pun. The people are amused, but they are not left at liberty to laugh. The preacher's comedy does but light up his solemn earnestness. He is painting some scene of death-bed remorse or of timely repentance; some Magdalene's forgiveness or some Prodigal's return. His colours are taken from the earth and sky of common human experience and aspiration. He dips his pencil, so to speak, in the veins of the nearest spectator and makes his work a part of every man's nature. His images are drawn from the homes of the common people, the daily toil for daily bread, the nightly rest of tired labour, the mother's love for a wayward boy, the father's tenderness to a sick daughter. His anecdotes are not far-fetched, and have a natural pathos. He tells how some despairing unfortunate, hastening with her last penny to the suicide bridge, was stopped by the sound of psalmody, and turned into *this* chapel; or how some widow's son, running away from his mother's home, was brought back by the recollection of a prayer, and sits now in *that* pew. He does not narrate occurrences, but describes them with a rough, graphic force and faithfulness. He does not reason out his doctrines, but announces, explains, and applies them. He ventures a political allusion, and it goes right to the democratic heart. In the open air someone may interrupt or interrogate, and the response is a new effect. In short, this man preaches Christianity, his Christianity, at any rate, as Ernest Jones preaches Chartism, and as Gough preaches temperance. Is it any wonder that he meets with like success? or is he to be either blamed or scorned? Let it first be remembered that Latimer was not less homely when he preached before the king, nor South less humorous when he cowed Rochester; nor Whitefield less declamatory when he moved Hume and Franklin; nor Rowland Hill less vulgar though brother to a baronet. To us it appears that dulness is the worst fault possible to a man whose first business it is to interest; that the dignity of the pulpit is best consulted by making it attractive, and that the clergy of all denominations might get some frequent hints for the composition of their sermons from the young Baptist preacher who never went to college."

This was more generous and reassuring, and before many days had passed certain of the writers who had suffered their feelings to bias their judgment may possibly have discovered that they had made a mistake. *The Sun, The Morning Advertiser, The Evening Star,* plainly showed that Mr. Spurgeon was in no way responsible for the loss of life which had occurred; and hence it only needed the veteran divine and journalist, Dr. Campbell, to give his judgment to make the case for the defence of the young preacher complete. The Nonconformist organ spoke with no uncertain sound in regard to Mr. Spurgeon and his friends :—

"We repeat and contend that, instead of being held up to contempt and execration, they deserve to be lauded for their marvellous courage, patience, and perseverance. Supposing them to have pursued a course directly contrary, such as the bulk of the Press, it appears, would have suggested; supposing them to have fled on the outburst of the storm, such flight would have increased the panic tenfold, and where there is now one death to deplore, there might probably have been a score or even twice that number. By the plan they adopted they did more than can be easily estimated to allay fear, inspire courage, and abate the tempest, and thus to prevent further loss of life. There would otherwise, in all likelihood, have been a rush at all the doors, each contributing more or less—and all fearfully—to the mortality of the occasion! If, notwithstanding the unparalleled exertions of Mr. Spurgeon and his deacons, it was impossible so to quell the commotion as to admit of the resumption of peaceful worship, it may readily be inferred how easily the waves might have been lashed up into an all-devouring fury.

"Let Mr. Spurgeon and his friends, then, think on these things and be comforted; while they did nothing whatever to destroy, they did much to preserve the lives of their fellow-men. The death which ensued was a thing with which they were wholly unconnected; the life which was preserved, the result of an extraordinary exercise of all but superhuman manhood." *

While the newspapers were thus commenting on what had occurred, and freely offering their opinions on the preacher himself and his pulpit methods, Spurgeon himself hardly heard even the faint echoes of the tumult in the quiet rural retreat to which his friends had taken him. For a time it seemed as though the powers of evil had broken loose and would overwhelm the strong man who had been recognised at so early an age as a champion of the truth. Dark and heavy was the cloud which hung over him; but suddenly it seemed to lift and pass away. He was in the garden of a friend's house, when, like a gleam of warm reviving sunshine, the truth suggested itself that Christ was still stronger than the devil, so that He who had a name which was above every name would, in the end, be conqueror. Mr. Spurgeon there and then gave thanks in prayer, and was himself again. He returned to his own house, where his wife, with her twin sons—then just about six weeks old— was the light of his home.

* *The British Banner*, October 28, 1856.

CHAPTER XXIX.

DR. CAMPBELL'S ESTIMATE.

Reappearance of the Pastor at New Park Street—First Service in the Music Hall after the Accident—False Rumours—Death of Richard Knill—Spurgeon at Birmingham.

ALTHOUGH for the time it seemed as though the young pastor's mind would be unhinged by the terrible ordeal he had passed through, he was only absent from his pulpit for one Sunday—the last in October, when Dr. Alexander Fletcher preached at New Park Street Chapel. Mr. Spurgeon's voice was again heard in his own pulpit on November 2, when the chapel was so densely crowded that two thousand persons are said to have been present. We find it remarked that "the greatest decorum was observed in every part of the spacious edifice, and throughout the whole of the service." It was announced that the fund on behalf of the injured sufferers, who numbered twenty-eight, amounted to £70. The sermon was founded on Philippians ii. 9, "Wherefore God also hath highly exalted Him, and given Him a name which is above every name." In commencing, the preacher said :—

"Now, my dear friends, I almost regret this morning that I occupy this pulpit. I regret it because I feel utterly unable to preach to you to your profit. I have thought during the period of relaxation I have had since that terrible catastrophe which has befallen us, that I had thoroughly recovered; but on coming back to this spot again I feel some- what of the same feelings which prostrated me before. You will therefore excuse me this morning if I make no allusion, or scarcely any at all, to recent circumstances; for were I to enter into the subject, and to bring to your remembrance that solemn scene, I should speedily be forced to be silent. It might not have been the malice of men so much as some have thought. It was probably the intention of the parties to disturb the congregation, but not to commit the terrible crime which resulted in the death of several individuals. God forgive those who did it! They have my forgiveness from the bottom of my soul. I may say, however, dear brethren, that we shall not be daunted at what has taken place; and I shall preach again in that place yet! God shall give us souls there, and Satan's empire shall tremble more yet; for I believe that God is with us, and who is he that can be against us? The text is one which has comforted me and enabled me to come here to-day in order to try and comfort you. I shall not attempt to preach from the text, I shall only make a few remarks; for I have been utterly unable to study, and I trust your loving hearts will excuse me."*

At the service preceding the communion in the evening, the chapel was, if possible, even more crowded than in the morning.

On Tuesday afternoon, November 11, Mr. Spurgeon preached a sermon at the Tabernacle, Tottenham Court Road, his appearance in that pulpit being a part of the programme of the centenary commemoration of the chapel. The discourse was founded on Hab. iii. 2, "O Lord, revive Thy work;" and it may be read entire in *The Baptist Messenger* for February, 1856.

When the Surrey Gardens Music Hall was engaged in the first instance it was for four Sundays; but in consequence of the catastrophe the meeting of October 19 was not taken into the reckoning. "The directors of the Surrey Gardens Company acted most generously in regard to the unfortunate evening on which Mr Spurgeon made his *début* in the Music Hall. They gave that night for nothing, the New Park Street congregation paying half the damage; and, consequently, yesterday was the first of the four Sundays for which the hall is engaged."† The meeting on this occasion was a grateful contrast to the former one; for as one account says, "perfect order and sacred silence" reigned throughout.

The members of the New Park Street congregation were admitted by ticket before the general public; but the latter did not muster in anything like the numbers of the first meeting, as the total assembly was not supposed to exceed eight thousand. A strong body of police was in attendance; great precautions were taken to prevent any recurrence of panic; and in case of any false alarm being given, people were advised to keep their seats, and, if possible, to detain the offenders. The newspapers of the time call attention to "the enormous pulpit," which at that time was quite of a novel pattern, being in reality a platform with a low desk, which allowed the preacher sufficient space to move about.

* *The British Banner*, November 4, 1856.
† *The Morning Advertiser*, Monday, November 24, 1856.

This first service, after the terrible affair of four weeks previously, was no doubt a severe trial to the young preacher; and it was evident that memories of October 19 were still afflicting him. In the course of the general prayer Mr. Spurgeon said:—

"Wherever people are assembled to worship God, that place is sacred, whether beneath the magnificent canopy of the blue sky, or in a building such as that in which we are assembled; every place is sacred when devoted to such a purpose, for God is everywhere. May God be in our midst at this time! Let nothing frighten His sheep. Grant that they may feed in quietness. Grant that the preacher may preach with that earnestness which becomes a man who must soon stand before his Maker's bar—a dying man to dying men. May this be a time of great display of the grace of God. Let sinners be saved. Let the people be saved, and glory be gotten to the name of the Most High God by this service. Thou who hast given us great troubles wilt quicken us again and bring us from the depths of our woe. Thou who hast smitten us and wounded us to the quick, lift up the light of Thy countenance upon us, and multiply Thy blessings amongst us. Grant that music, sweeter than is often heard here, may arise, even the music of the penitential sigh, and the aspiration of the breaking heart, mourning over its own wickedness."

The quaint way in which the preacher announced the portion of Scripture to be read, attracted much notice. "Let us read that ancient story of the God who became flesh and dwelt among us, and was crucified for our sins; the story of the crucifixion as it is contained in the 15th chapter of Mark's Gospel." It was thought that the comment was coloured by the recent strictures of the Press on the preacher himself in connection with the disaster of a month before.

"Our Lord knew the dignity of silence. He is a wise man who can hold his tongue. 'In the multitude of words there wanteth not sin.' Our Saviour bore insults, endured scorn, obloquy, and calumny, but 'opened not His mouth.' Let us learn to do the same; for often it is the best way to contend with our enemies to keep our swords in their scabbards. It is the best way to win battles to refuse to enter the lists with our enemies. If men speak evil of us, it is the height of folly to wage battle with them. True knights fight only with true knights. So let true men think it folly to fight with liars. If they lie against us, we are too great to repulse them." Further on it was added that the cross they had to bear was only a wooden one, though it may be painted in colours of iron; and in any case crown-wearers would have first to be cross-bearers.

Among the exaggerated rumours which had gone abroad since the attempt to preach in the Music Hall, was one relating to the vast dimensions of the new chapel it was proposed to erect. On this theme Mr. Spurgeon made a statement which corrected some misapprehensions :—

"There have been a great many rumours abroad respecting the new chapel, the building of which has been contemplated by a number of my friends. It has been asserted that we want to build a Tabernacle capable of holding 15,000 people. With respect to that I will only say that some truthful person has thought fit to put a '1' before the '5,' for we have never entertained even a thought of building such a place. It has, however, been thought that a place of worship capable of accommodating about 5,000 persons was necessary. For my own part I have no wish for such a place, only I cannot bear to see, Sabbath after Sabbath, as many people go away as enter the chapel where we have been accustomed to assemble for worship. It is the will of people to come in large multitudes to listen to my feeble proclamation of the truths of the Gospel. I have not asked them to come, it is their own free will; and if it is a sin in me that they should do so, it is at least an uncommon sin, which many others would like to commit if they could. It has been said, 'Let those who wish to hear me pay for their seats.' That would defeat the object I have in view. I want to preach to those who cannot afford to pay for seats in a chapel, and it is my wish to admit as many of the general public as possible. There will be no collecting-boxes passed round to-day; but as there are necessarily expenses attending the celebration of Divine worship in this hall, the contributions of such as are disposed will be received at the doors on leaving. Do not think we are begging. If you think so, we would not have your money as a gift. It is open for all to do just as they like. Many of my friends, I know, are most anxious on the subject of a larger place of worship than we have at present, and would give double what they have done if they could afford it. It is proposed to hold a service here on the three following Sunday mornings. It is much to the inconvenience of my congregation to attend here. We have a comfortable place of worship elsewhere. There we are very happy together; there I have a congregation, and as many members as any mortal man can desire. It is only with a view of winning souls to God that we have come to this larger place, and should we be accused of other objects the judgment-day will lay bare what our motives have truly been." *

There can be no doubt that the disaster at the Music Hall had the effect of increasing Mr. Spurgeon's fame, great as it had been before ; and very strong evidence of this is seen in the number of newspaper and other articles which appeared even after the excitement of the accident had passed away. One of the chief among veteran journalists who defended Mr. Spurgeon on all occasions, and towards the end of the year 1856 published several articles in a separate form, was the Dr. Campbell, from whom we have quoted, and who was then editor of one or two monthly magazines as well as of *The British Banner*, which paper he relinquished at the end of

* The quotations from Mr. Spurgeon's utterances at this service are from *The British Banner*, November 25, 1856.

1856, however, to start on his own account *The British Standard.* Born in 1795, the doctor was nearly forty years older than his friend of New Park Street, so that there was some propriety in his standing forth as a defender on the one hand and offering advice on the other. At first he had regarded Spurgeon as an upstart. Throughout a large section of the religious world Dr. Campbell's opinions were received with the deference due to one of such ability and character. Some weeks after the Surrey Gardens calamity the doctor gave an elaborate review of Spurgeon as a preacher. The subject, he remarked, had drawn forth much from observers or critics who had too slight a knowledge of the subject to warrant their being heard. In any case, the pastor of New Park Street had a manner which was his own, and those who disliked it were not obliged to sit as hearers at his feet :—

"Mr. Spurgeon is, in all respects, an original—a preacher of heaven's own formation; and hence all is nature and all is life, while that life and that nature are among the millions a power. Is he abrupt, blunt, direct? It is nature. Is he idiomatic, colloquial, playful, dramatic? It is nature. But it is needless to dwell on these subordinate points. 'Every man in his own order,' whether he there stand as an individual or one of a multitude. Nature is power, artifice impotence. Without nature no man can please much and please long. Nature responds only to nature; it turns a deaf ear to all that is contrary. Art may captivate the fancy; nature alone can subdue the heart."

Deserved or undeserved, the popularity of Mr. Spurgeon was a fact which no one could deny; no other man had such a hold of the people. It was not for such a man to cut his locks to suit his critics. The doctrines he preached were identical with those preached by the fathers of a former generation. How was such popularity to be accounted for?

"He owes nothing to the pomp and circumstance of priesthood. There the youthful preacher stands in all the simplicity of his unsophisticated character. He owes nothing to relation or rank, or the accidents of life, which have sometimes contributed to great temporary popularity. What, then, is the source of this unprecedented attraction? It lies partly, but not merely, in the externals of his eloquence; it is primarily in the *soul of the man*—a soul large, liberal, and loving; a soul stamped by the characteristics of a little child, while putting forth the powers of one of David's 'mighties.' He is one of a favoured class, few in number but great in importance. He belongs to the noble fellowship of the Berridges, the Grimshaws, the Whitefields, the Hills, and the Wilkses. Mr. Spurgeon has much in common with all these men, and sustains to the public of his time substantially the same relation as they did. In the name of justice, then, let Mr. Spurgeon have the benefit of their history. If despised, ridiculed, and calumniated by their contemporaries, men unworthy to live in the same age with them, they have had ample justice done them by succeeding generations, who have acknowledged their greatness, revered their virtues, and have acknowledged slowly, yet frankly, the signal, the unparalleled services they were honoured to render in their day and generation.

"Let it be remembered that none of the worthies above named had, at the same age, and during the first two years of their ministry, aught to show in the way of evangelical trophies to be compared with even the ascertained results of Mr. Spurgeon's ministry. Nay, it would be no violation of truth if it be affirmed that all of them united could not have presented, in the shape of ascertained conversions, so much fruit."

Quite apart from his preaching, it was a fact that the chapel at New Park Street was often quite crowded at a prayer-meeting; and the production of such a meeting and its sustentation was a striking evidence of the power of his ministry. The multiplication of such preachers would be the greatest blessing the country could receive. Then follow some comparisons between Spurgeon and such old-time preachers as Bunyan and Whitefield :—

"Since the days of Whitefield no man has excited so much attention in this metropolis as Mr. Spurgeon; and the result, as in a former age, has been great diversity of sentiment. In the daily press, *The Morning Advertiser* was the first to give a just, or, perhaps, a generous account of this extraordinary young man. While with much discrimination it set forth his surpassing excellence in his own line, it was not silent upon his defects, but tendered such counsel as the case required in a spirit calculated to render it palatable. Another daily paper has recently favoured the public with an estimate of Mr. Spurgeon's capabilities, and a portraiture of his performances, displaying more capacity than charity, and a gift fitting rather for the criticism of the theatre than of the house of prayer. Such things, however, would seem, as in the case of Whitefield, only to help him onward. When Foote, of unhappy memory, wrote *The Minor*, bringing Whitefield on the stage in the character of Dr. Squintum—for the great orator was marked by that visual peculiarity—he did much further to excite public attention and confirm Whitefield's hold of the better section of society. Mr. Spurgeon has been the subject of discussion even in the American Press, where he has been most shamefully caricatured. He has made several appearances in Scotland, where he has been well received, and where a portion of its comparatively pure and upright Press has done him justice.

"All such opposition and misrepresentation only tend to further the popularity it is sought to check. It operates like air on the furnace, which would languish and die but for the action of the atmosphere. Mr. Spurgeon's popularity is a mystery, both in the Church and in the world. The enlightened but unreflecting onlookers in both are at an utter loss to account for it. They only seem attracted to his peculiarities, which, viewed through the medium of taste, are defects to be regretted, and, by others, to be shunned rather than imitated. The secret of his power with the masses consists, however, not in these, but in something hid from the mere vulgar eye. In his mighty effusions there is a substratum of Christian truth which he pours forth in an unbroken stream; or, rather, it may often be likened to a cataract bearing down everything before it, and subduing the largest assemblies. Mr. Spurgeon is no negative theologian. Whitefield, in this, as in other respects, had much in common with Spurgeon. The former had vastly more acting, so called, than the latter, and quite as much dry humour, by which congregations are ofttimes excited to laugh; but there was this peculiarity which distinguished him from Spurgeon, that they were as frequently melted into tears.

"Essences must not be confounded with accidents. The peculiarities which often distinguish great men have no necessary connection with the truth which they hold and propagate in common. A firm friend of Whitefield has left it on record that, whether he looked grave or gay, it was nature acting in him. His laugh was hearty, his weeping 'loud and passionate,' and, while his manner was natural, his language was simple— John Bunyan's English. It was, indeed, his boast that he used 'market language;' and, as to the looseness of his harangues, his defence was, 'You complain of my rambling; you ramble more than I do, and I must ramble after you.' Spurgeon, too, we repeat, is in everything a child of nature; he is everywhere at home. His air, his accent, whether he rebuke or woo the soul, all is natural; and his illustrations are generally such as, without wounding the taste of the multitudes, come home to their breasts. He is in sympathy with his audience and with mankind. A master of dialogue, he is not less master of powerful declamation—the two great things for which Whitefield himself was remarkable. What he spoke he felt. Everything found its way to the heart of the assembly. Whitefield's defects, such as they were, were mainly confined to his earlier career; and if it be remembered that he commenced at the age of twenty-one, much allowance is to be made for him. Why not then for Mr. Spurgeon, who had filled the land with his fame long before he had attained to his majority? We say, then, let Mr. Spurgeon have justice. He is working a great work, and let no man hinder him! No other living preacher can command the ear of the millions as he commands it; and we submit it is only fair to bid him God-speed. Time and circumstances will do much to perfect that which needs emendation." *

On the second day of January, 1857, Mr. Spurgeon's old friend, Richard Knill, died at Chester at the age of about seventy years. He had laboured in Chester since the opening of 1848, and under his pastorate the church had increased fourfold. He was in all respects a remarkable man, whose influence was very far-reaching; and his service through the Press was no less extraordinary than his preaching. Thus we find it stated that "No man ever had so many of his tracts circulated as Mr. Knill. Between six and seven millions of them have been printed in England; translated into ten different languages, they have been scattered over the whole world. In America more than seven millions have been printed, so that between the two countries more than fourteen millions have been put into circulation." † He laboured on till the last with apostolic fervour.

The heavy and continued strain of preaching at the Surrey

* Dr. Campbell was considered to be "an excellent judge of pulpit eloquence;" and in orthodox circles his opinions carried great weight. The doctor's editorial articles, which appeared in *The British Banner*, were republished in a pamphlet under the title of "The Modern Whitefield." Another *brochure*, "Mr. Spurgeon Defended," referred more especially to the Surrey Gardens catastrophe.

† *The British Standard*, January 9, 1857.

R

Gardens, besides conducting special services during the week in different parts of the country, began to tell on the pastor's strength. While proceeding with his sermon in the Music Hall on Sunday morning, February 15, when, by the way, he had a bishop among his hearers, Mr. Spurgeon's voice failed, and he was compelled to conclude "somewhat abruptly," as the contemporary account tells us. The congregation appeared to be much concerned on account of the preacher's apparent suffering. In the ordinary course that sermon would have been No. 117 of the regular weekly issue, but it did not appear, and a discourse given at New Park Street some months before had to take its place.

The visit to Birmingham early in the year 1857 was a notable occasion. The curiosity to hear the orator appears to have been very great, as he had never spoken in the town before. The first sermon, in the afternoon, was on the Name of Jesus; and that which followed in the evening was on the text, "To know the love of Christ, which passeth knowledge." On the following day two services were held in Mount Zion Chapel, one discourse being on self-examination, while the other was on seven texts, "I have sinned," or the same that had been given in the Music Hall on January 18. Thus to visit a great town and conduct four exhausting services was a fair example of the way in which Mr. Spurgeon worked at this time. He laboured on in the most self-denying manner, all the while living in accord with the injunction which he had seemed to hear on Midsummer Common, "Seekest thou great things for thyself? Seek them not."

CHAPTER XXX.

THE SERVICES AT THE ROYAL SURREY GARDENS.

Unique Popularity—*The National Review*—A Sunday at the Music Hall described—A Hoax— The Daily Press—Remarkable Letter in *The Times*—Adverse Opinions—Collecting for the Tabernacle.

THE Sunday morning services at the Royal Surrey Gardens had now become one of the chief attractions or wonders of London. As we learn from *The Nonconformist*, Lord Palmerston was prevented by illness alone from being present on one of the Sundays of January :—

"Mr. Spurgeon's popularity does not seem to be at all on the wane. Lord Mayors and Lord Chief Justices jostling journeymen carpenters in the same religious assembly ; peers and peasants listening to the Word of Life from the same lips, and joining in the same chorus of praise, to the tune of the glorious Old Hundredth which rises from eight or ten thousand voices, present a novel and instructive spectacle, however the phenomenon may be explained. What may have been the Premier's motives for taking a ticket for the Surrey Gardens Music Hall last Sunday, of which, however, his old enemy the gout prevented him from availing himself, it is not for us to conjecture. It may be hoped that it was something beyond mere curiosity. At all events, the Cabinet is committed, and it is not easy to see how it could now consistently advise the Crown to withhold from the Dissenting divine the sanction of its presence, at least, in a quiet and unostentatious way. Old George the Third, when at Windsor, used now and then to slip in *incog.* amongst the congregation of that excellent Nonconformist minister, the father of the present Dr. Redford, and in due time, we daresay, amongst the thousands of female head-dresses at the Music Hall, a modest little bonnet will find its way, beneath which will be the evidence of the Royal countenance afforded, in spite it may be of mitred protests, to the uncanonical ministrations which have taken such a hold of the lieges."

The number of notices of Mr. Spurgeon in newspapers, magazines, and reviews now abundantly testified to his increasing and unique popularity. Even *The National Review* for January had something to say on the all-engrossing topic, and while showing no sympathy with the preacher's Calvinism, the reviewer believed that the doctrines preached largely accounted for the success achieved :—

"Mr. Spurgeon's style appears to us quaint and grotesque, with a strong dash of genuine humour. He is obviously to the last degree vivacious and susceptible. There is nothing vulgar, for example, in the following, though it is as grotesque as a gargoyle : 'Oh, may God awaken us all, and stir us up to pray : for when we pray we shall be victorious. I should like to take you this morning, as Samson did the foxes, tie the firebrands of prayer to you, and send you in among the shocks of corn till you burn the whole up.' The following has a sort of rough energy and force of conviction which is not unlike many of the stories told of Luther and his conflicts with the devil: 'A poor tried countryman said the other day, I have been troubled with that old devil lately, and I could not get rid of him for a long while; until at last, after he had been adding up all my sins, and bringing them all before my remembrance, I said to him, "You rascal you, did I not transfer all my business to Jesus Christ long ago, bad debts and all? What business have you to bring them here? I laid them all on Christ; go and tell my Master about them. Don't come troubling me." Well, I thought that was not so bad. It was pretty rough, but it was gloriously true.' A man who had always considered his sins as so many debts in the strict sense of the word, and whose mind is habitually occupied with small business transactions, shows a very forcib'e and genuine conviction by this kind of language. In fact, if his language is to be genuine and striking at all, it must be taken from the subjects which are familiar to him. To say 'You rascal, don't trouble me; you must speak to my Master,' is a phrase which has, at any rate, a positive, definite meaning. A man who should say on a similar occasion 'I dwelt on the all-sufficient sacrifice,' or 'I rejoiced in the blessed blood which cleanseth from all sin,' would speak, in our opinion, far less sincerely and far less reverently. The one man believes in a real master, a real legal obligation, a real devil in the likeness of a harsh creditor, and a discharge such as he could plead in the county court; and the other, in a great proportion of cases, only expresses an indefinite feeling in conventional language. The common feelings which form the lasting bonds of human society are generally definite in proportion to their strength. Conjugal and family love, friendship, a sense of duty, a sense of honour, may be described in the very simplest language, and the fact that it is usually considered reverent to speak of God, Christ, heaven, hell, the devil, and the feelings which they excite, in an obscure and indefinite manner has always appeared to us one of the strongest proofs of the prevalence amongst us of an unacknowledged scepticism. To speak of such matters very seldom and very plainly, would seem to be the course pointed out, both by reverence and common sense; but if we must choose between the two, we do not know whether it is not less bad to handle spiritual truths as you would handle a bullock, than to handle them as you would handle a mist. No Italian friar was ever more perfectly at home in the legends of the saints than Mr. Spurgeon is in what he calls the three R's—Ruin, Redemption, and Regeneration."

The writer in *The National Review* was evidently desirous of dealing fairly with the subject, but he was one of those who caricatured the Calvinistic doctrines through misunderstanding them. It seemed strange, moreover, that while seeking to account for amazing success, nothing was said about the wonderful voice and powerful imagination which were such striking characteristics of the preacher.

Thus the services at the Music Hall created extraordinary and ever-widening interest. Among the many sketches, the *brochure* of "An Eye-Witness," issued in the spring of 1857, attracted some attention. This writer found that the ticket system was enforced to prevent the entrance of thieves and disreputable characters. His estimate of the building was that it would seat 9,000 and allow of standing-room for 5,000 more. He remarks that " even so early as ten o'clock all the seats on the floor and first gallery were occupied, and one only succeeded in procuring seats on the second gallery, and that on the fifth row from the front." At half-past ten, when the doors were opened to the public without tickets, there was "not one seat in the huge hall unoccupied." Meanwhile, the spectacle from the centre gallery was an extraordinary scene—"We heard a strange noise, it sounded like the rushing of mighty waters; and, on looking down, we saw that it was caused by the rushing in of immense crowds of excited and hurried people. In ten minutes' time every inch of standing-room was occupied." Dr. Livingstone sat on the platform, and the Princess Royal, as well as the Duchess of Sutherland, was said to be present. The hymn, "All hail the power of Jesus' name," was sung with overpowering effect. On coming to the close, Mr. Spurgeon remarked, "Dear friends, whilst you are singing this last verse, elevate your hearts to heaven, and let your innermost prayer be that you may join the angelic throng in hymning your dear Redeemer's name. Fancy that you hear the ten thousand times ten thousand that are, at this moment, swelling the anthem above, and feel as if you were mingling your voices with theirs in chanting His praise."

The prayer is described as being of "the most spiritual character... as if Mr. Spurgeon was standing on Pisgah's top, gazing in ecstasies on the promised land." The petitions for persons of all sorts and conditions showed how thoroughly in earnest the preacher was. The way in which he sought strength for himself was also characteristic. "O Lord! help, help thy servant to preach the Gospel to this vast multitude. Fill his soul with heavenly fire. Thou art mighty, but thy servant is weak; make him, O Lord, the honoured instrument in thy hands of converting many here. Thou, in times past, madest the sound of a ram's horn level to the dust the hard, strong, and fortified walls of Jericho; make, I beseech thee, thy servant like a ram's horn on this mighty occasion, so that the hard and strong hearts in thy presence may melt and tumble down at the sound of thy Gospel as proclaimed by him, and that heaven may ring with the hallelujahs of victory." When the people opened their Bibles to find the text, "Let the whole earth be filled with His glory; Amen, and Amen" (Ps. lxxii. 19), the rustling resembled the "pattering of a heavy hailstorm on the leaves of trees." During the sermon, everybody could hear perfectly in all parts of the building, even when the voice was allowed to sink low. The preacher, then under twenty-three years of age, is described as being pallid, without whiskers, his hair being long, and parted nearly in the middle. The desire to hear him became stronger, so that the ordinary tickets of admission had been raised to five shillings a month. "An Eye-Witness" is of opinion that the "cavilling and raising frivolous objections to his preaching, simply proves that *unrenewed* human nature is just what it was eighteen hundred years ago." He adds that Spurgeon "is stirring up all classes, and proving most conclusively that if the Gospel be plainly proclaimed, there will be no lack of hearers."*

In the early part of May, 1857, someone found pleasure in imposing a silly kind of hoax on Mr. Spurgeon's former friends in the Fen country. The town-crier of Soham, and also the town-crier of Ely, received a parcel of printed bills from the "Society for the Diffusion of the Gospel, 28, Park Street, London," announcing that Mr. Spurgeon would preach on the Horsefen at three o'clock on Sunday, May 10. It was a clumsy invention, for at this time the preacher rarely indeed ventured to leave his own people on Sunday.†

Among those attracted to the Music Hall was a correspondent of *The Sun*, who wrote :—

"If what we heard last Sunday be a specimen of Mr. Spurgeon's usual preaching, there was certainly nothing at all more extravagant than would be heard from most of the Evangelical clergymen and Dissenting preachers in the country. There were no outrageous descriptions of divine anger and future punishment, or any wire-drawn refinements on the theology of repentance. His statements on the latter point were characterised by remarkable common sense; they were forcibly expressed and illustrated, as were his arguments for the necessity of repentance. Indeed, there was little in which preachers of all creeds would not have concurred. His voice is a noble one, filling the whole place with the greatest ease; at the

---

* "A Sabbath Morning with the Rev. C. H. Spurgeon. At the Surrey Music Hall, London, April 26, 1857. By an Eye-Witness." This pamphlet was printed at Cheltenham.

† *The Baptist Messenger*, v. 167.

further end of the building we did not miss a syllable. His manner was perfectly unrestrained, but not irreverent. His command of language is very considerable, but does not lead him, for an extempore speaker, into verbosity. His style is unfettered, homely, forcible, and abounds in pointed remarks. There was a total absence of anything humorous or ludicrous, if it has been his habit to indulge in such things. The secret of his popularity, taking last Sunday as a specimen, appeared to us to be something very different. It was impossible not to feel that the preacher was absorbed, not in himself, but in his audience. The formal separation of the pulpit did not separate him from his hearers. He conversed with them—he was one of them. He did not lecture them *ex cathedrá*, or indulge in disquisitions on topics out of their line of thought, but spoke with them as he would have done on a solemn subject in their own houses. Most of our pulpits 'die of dignity,' but, while there was nothing unbecoming on Sunday, the preacher placed himself on a level with all. Of course, a vivid fancy, and considerable powers of expression, aided by a first-rate voice, will account for much; but we think what we have pointed out was the chief reason why, among so many thousands of hearers, we could not, and we looked carefully, detect a single sleeper.

"Our more dignified preachers might study with advantage the phenomenon of this youth's popularity. We can only say that, for our part, his manner disarmed criticism, and we could think only of his probable usefulness to the thousands present, who, we are confident, by their appearance, are not listeners to our customary pulpit prosaics. Lord Chief Justice Campbell, with his son, was present on the platform, and seemed to take the same view with ourselves; he remarked several times to one of the managers after the service in our hearing, and also to Sir Richard Mayne (Commissioner of Police), who was likewise present, 'He is doing great good, sir, great good! London could find room for twenty such preachers; they are just what the populace needs.'"

The London daily Press, which had treated Mr. Spurgeon so badly in the matter of the Music Hall catastrophe, now began to make some amends. It was soon seen that in regard to the character of the preacher himself, a mistake had been made; and among the first to make reparation for the wrong done in passing a too harsh and hasty judgment was *The Times*. In those days that great journal commanded a truly national influence, so that its publication of the famous letter by "Habitans in Sicco," accompanied by a leading article, marked that turn of the tide in the young preacher's favour which was sure to come sooner or later. Extracts from this letter have frequently been given, but few persons of this generation will ever have seen it entire, although it is necessary for such a production to be read as a whole for its true significance to be understood. It was one of the most amusing things of the kind which ever appeared in the leading journal:—

"Sir,—One Sunday morning about a month ago my wife said, 'Let us send the children to St. Margaret's to hear the Archbishop of ———— preach on behalf of the Society for Aged Ecclesiastical Cripples, which is to celebrate to-day its three hundredth anniversary.'

So the children went, though the parents, for reasons immaterial to mention, could not go with them. 'Well, children, how did you like the Archbishop of ——, and what did he say about "the Aged Ecclesiastical Cripples"?' Here the children—for it was during their dinner—attacked their food with great voracity, but never a word could we get out of their mouths about the spiritual feast of which they had just partaken. No! not even the text could they bring out. The more they were pressed the more they blushed, and hung their heads over their plates, until at last, in a rage, I accused them of having fallen asleep during the service. This charge threw my first-born on his defence, and he sobbed out the truth, for by this time their eyes were full of tears. 'Why, papa! we can't say what the Archbishop of —— said, because we could not hear a word he said. He is very old and has got no teeth; and do you know I don't think he has got any tongue either, for though we saw his lips moving, we could not hear a single word.' On this I said no more, but I thought a good deal of 'the Aged Ecclesiastical Cripples' and their venerable advocate, and being something of a philologist, I indulged in dreamy speculations on the possibility of an alphabet composed entirely of labials; and if my wife had not roused me by some mere matter-of-fact question, I almost think I should have given my reflections to the world in the shape of a small pamphlet entitled 'The Language of Labials; or, How to preach Sermons without the Aid of either Tongue or Teeth: published for the benefit of the Society of Aged Ecclesiastical Cripples, and dedicated, of course by permission, to the Archbishop of ——.'

"Now listen to another story. A friend of mine, a Scotch Presbyterian, comes up to town and says, 'I want to hear Spurgeon; let us go.' Now, I am supposed to be a High Churchman, so I answered, 'What, go and hear a Calvinist—a Baptist—a man who ought to be ashamed of himself for being so near the Church and yet not within its pale?' 'Never mind, come and hear him.' Well, we went yesterday morning to the Music Hall in the Surrey Gardens. At first I felt a strange sensation of wrong-doing. It was something like going to a morning theatrical performance on Sunday; nor did a terrific gust of wind which sent the 'Arctic Regions,' erected out of laths and pasteboard in a style regardless of expense, flying across the water of the lake, tend to cheer a mind depressed by the novelty of the scene. Fancy a congregation, consisting of 10,000 souls, streaming into the hall, mounting the galleries, mumming, buzzing, and swarming—a mighty hive of bees, eager to secure at first the best places, and at last any place at all. After waiting more than half an hour—for, if you wish to have a seat, you must be there at least that space of time in advance—Mr. Spurgeon ascended the tribune. To the hum and rush and trampling of men succeeded a low, concentrated thrill and murmur of devotion, which seemed to run at once like an electric current through the breath of everyone present, and by this magnetic chain the preacher held us fast bound for about two hours. It is not my purpose to give a summary of his discourse. It is enough to say of his voice that its power and volume are sufficient to reach everyone in that vast assembly; of his language that it is neither high-flown nor homely; of his style, that it is at times familiar, at times declamatory, but always happy and often eloquent; of his doctrine, that neither the Calvinist nor the Baptist appear in the forefront of the battle which is waged by Mr. Spurgeon with relentless animosity, and with Gospel weapons, against irreligion, cant, hypocrisy, pride, and those secret bosom sins which so easily beset a man in daily life; and, to sum up all in a word, it is enough to say of the man himself that he impresses you with a perfect conviction of his sincerity.

"But I have not written so much about my children's want of spiritual food when they listened to the mumbling of the Archbishop of ——, and my own banquet at the Surrey Gardens, without a desire to draw a practical conclusion from these two stories, and to point them by a moral. Here is a man not more Calvinistic than many an incumbent of the Established Church, who 'mumbles and mumbles,' as old Latimer says, over his liturgy and text. Here is a man who says the complete immersion, or something of the kind, of adults is necessary to baptism. These are his faults of doctrine, but if I were the examining chaplain of the Archbishop of ———, I would say, 'May it please your Grace, here is a man able to preach eloquently, able to fill the largest church in England with his voice; and, what is more to the purpose, with people. And may it please your Grace, here are two churches in this metropolis, St. Paul's and Westminster Abbey. What does your Grace think of inviting Mr. Spurgeon, this heretical Calvinist and Baptist, who is able to draw 10,000 souls after him, just to try his voice, some Sunday morning, in the nave of either of these churches? At any rate, I will answer for one thing, that if he preaches in Westminster Abbey, we shall not have a repetition of the disgraceful practice now common in that church, of having the sermon *before* the anthem, in order that those who would quit the church when the arid sermon begins, may be forced to stay it out for the sake of the music which follows it.

"But I am not, I am sorry to say, examining chaplain of the Archbishop of ———, so I can only send you this letter from the devotional desert in which I reside, and sign myself,

"*Broad Phylactery, Westminster.*   "HABITANS IN SICCO."

In the course of a leading article, *The Times* itself found something to say on the subject of the above letter:—

"It is not surprising that the sudden phenomenon of a monster preacher excites some astonishment, and if our correspondent, 'Habitans in Sicco,' regrets that the Church has not the benefit of similar services, it is quite natural to ask why should such demonstrations be confined to Dissent? Why cannot the Church have a monster preacher drawing its crowds?

"Physically speaking, there can be no reason why the Church should not have, at any rate, once or twice in a generation, a natural orator in its clerical ranks endowed with a voice as loud as Mr. Spurgeon's, and, if she has, there can be no cogent reason why she should not use him. A loud voice is a decided gift, an endowment; it may be thrown away, in the prodigality of nature, upon a man who has no purpose to turn it to, no thought to utter from that splendid organ; upon a man, in fact, who is a mere pompous stentor in a pulpit; but give it to one who has a thought and a purpose, and see the effect. How is it, then, that the Church never has a monster preacher?

"The reason is, that a loud voice requires its proper material to exert itself upon. The voice is notoriously the most sympathetic thing in nature. It cannot be loud and soft indiscriminately. Some things are made to be shouted and others to be whispered. Nobody shouts out an axiom in mathematics; nobody balances probabilities in thunder— *Nemo consilium cum clamore dat.* There must be a strong sentiment, some bold truth, to make a man shout. In religion there must be something rather extravagant in the shape of doctrine. The doctrine of conversion or of irresistible grace can be shouted, but if a man tried ever so hard to shout in delivering a moderate and sensible doctrine on freewill he would find himself talking quietly in spite of himself. A loud voice, then, must have 'loud' doctrine to develop it. But the Church of England has rather a distaste for 'loud' doctrine; her general standard is opposed to it; her basis is a balanced one, mixing opposite truths, and qualifying what she teaches with judicious protests and disclaimers. She preaches Catholicity with a protest against Rome, and Protestantism with a protest against Geneva.

"This is very sensible and very true, but it is not favourable to popular preaching. Of the two parties into which she is divided one thinks it wrong to shout as being against the principle of reverence. This school specially contrasts itself in this respect with the 'rude world,' which is supposed to be always shouting and doing everything that is noisy and vulgar, and with heretics who are audacious and immodest; and it plumes itself on its refinement and good taste in the delivery of religious truth, which it thinks ought to be done in a sort of veiled and fragmentary way, so as to reach the sensitive ears of the good and pass over those of the profane. All this is very excellent and refined, but it is against popular preaching. So much for one party. The other party might speak loud if it liked; it has no theory against it, and its doctrines admit of it, but it does not like the trouble. And besides, this party, though it professedly holds strong doctrine, practically tempers it considerably, and bends to the moderate standard of the Church.

"Thus, what with the fear of criticism, the deference to a recognised standard, idleness, reverence, and a great many other things; what with some thinking it heretical to shout, and others thinking it impolite to be popular, there is no monster preaching in the English Church. It does certainly admit of a question whether in our general policy we are not over-cautious, and gain greater theoretical correctness at the cost of much practical efficiency. It admits of a question whether a little extravagance and a little onesidedness might not be tolerated for the sake of a good, substantial, natural, telling appeal to the human heart. We should have no objection, for our part, to an Evangelical clergyman, with a strong voice, doing what Mr. Spurgeon does. The doctrines of the two are in reality much the same, and that being the case, why should fear of criticism prevent the Evangelical school from making themselves as effective as they can? But such is the influence of a conventional standard, which, like conscience, 'makes cowards of us all.'" *

At this time meetings were held now and again in aid of the building fund of the proposed new Tabernacle. What was called the first of a series of such meetings had been convened in the Tabernacle, High Street, Hoxton, on March 10, when Mr. Spurgeon gave a discourse from the words of Psalm cii. 16, "When the Lord shall build up Zion, He shall appear in His Glory." He also gave an account of his first coming to London, with some reference to the blessing which had attended his ministrations. On Monday, March 23, another meeting came off at New Park Street, and the speech of the chairman, Mr. W. Joynson, of St. Mary Cray, had an excellent effect on account of "its fervour, spirituality, and practical common sense." From a contemporary account we learn that "he repeatedly challenged the meeting to contribute sums equal to those he himself offered conditionally to give; and during the evening his own donations in this form amounted to nearly one hundred and seventy pounds, in addition to a previous donation of twenty-five pounds. Mr. Spurgeon made a fervid and eloquent appeal to his own congregation, such a one as they will never forget." † The following is an extract from the "Appeal to the Christian Public" issued at this time :—

* *The Times*, April 13, 1857. In a contemporary statement "Habitans in Sicco" was declared to be none other than the Jupiter of the Press himself.
† *The Baptist Messenger*, v. 95.

"The great and almost unprecedented success which, under the Divine blessing, has accompanied the labours of the Rev. C. H. Spurgeon during his ministry at New Park Street has rendered it imperatively necessary that a new chapel of large dimensions be erected forthwith. . . .

"Shortly after the accession of the Rev. C. H. Spurgeon to the pastorate, in May, 1854, the numbers attending the chapel rapidly increased, until it was deemed absolutely necessary to enlarge the chapel. This object was effected in May, 1855, at a cost of £1,800. No sooner was the chapel reopened than every sitting was engaged, and hundreds of applications were refused for want of room. The church also increased at such a rapid rate that the chapel was found to be inadequate for the reception of the members at the Lord's table, the members being upwards of 860 persons, more than 550 of whom have been added during the period of two years and nine months."

Meanwhile the services at the Music Hall so increased in public favour that large numbers had to be turned away from the doors on every occasion, after the last standing-place was occupied. On Sunday, May 17, more than a thousand persons were thus disappointed. Many lords and ladies, whose titles are mentioned, were present, Lady Franklin, the widow of the ill-fated Arctic explorer, being of the number. Others were present whose experience was of more interest to the ordinary members of the congregation. There was, for example, a man there who had been an active advocate of Secularist opinions at Norwich ; but having been converted from the error of his ways at one of Mr. Spurgeon's services, he had not only embraced the Christian faith, but had publicly burned all his infidel publications. Another man had not attended a religious service for thirty years.*

Referring to the service of Sunday, August 9, *The Morning Advertiser* says that the congregation was held "in a state of breathless attention." The subject of the sermon was, "Thou shalt love thy neighbour as thyself." Mr. James Grant appears to have been present, for it was remarked in his paper, "We never heard a subject handled in a more masterly manner." The discourse was a practical one; and it is added that, "in choosing occasionally such themes for his ministrations, Mr. Spurgeon only follows the example of his Master, whose preaching was remarkable for its preceptive character." The chief defect of the ordinary preaching was that it was either too exclusively doctrinal or too practical.

* *The British Standard*, May 22, 1857.

The preacher at the Music Hall happily blended the two; and the suggestion is made that the discourse should be widely circulated. It is added that " there was not one single passage in the sermon to which anyone, be his denominational or theological opinions what they may, could take exception; and yet it was faithful, bold, and searching beyond any pulpit address of the kind to which it ever was our lot to listen. Were the world at large to embody habitually in their lives and conversation the great ethical duties which Mr. Spurgeon enforced with such intense earnestness and transcendent power, we should at once witness the advent of a great social and moral millenium." *

While opinions similar to the above were harboured by an increasing number of friends, however, there were still many who professed to see nothing attractive in Mr. Spurgeon apart from a fine voice. His preaching, they held, was vulgar, while his gifts were not above mediocrity. It is even probable that in 1857 no small proportion of the young preacher's brother ministers would have partially agreed with such an estimate as the following:—

"On the pulpit, or rather the platform, Mr. Spurgeon imitates Gough, and walks up and down, and enlivens his sermons with dramatic representations. He is 'hail fellow well met' with his hearers. He has jokes and homely sayings and puns and proverbs for them. Nothing is too sacred for his self-complacent grasp; he is as free and unrestrained in God's presence as in man's. Eternity has unveiled its mysteries to him. In the agonies of the lost, in the joys of the redeemed, there is nothing for him to learn. His 'sweet Saviour,' as he irreverently exclaims, has told him all. Of course at times there is a rude eloquence on his lips, or, rather, a fluent declamation, which the mob around takes for such. The orator always soars with his audience. With excited thousands awaiting his lightest word, he cannot be passionless and unmoved. Words and thoughts are borne to him from them. There is excitement in the hour; there is excitement in the theme; there is excitement in the living mass; and, it may be as the preacher speaks of a physical hell and displays a physical heaven, some sensual nature is aroused, and a change may be effected in a man's career. Little causes may produce great events; one chance word may be the beginning of a new and a better life; but the thoughtful hearer will learn nothing, will be induced to feel nothing, will find that as regards Christian edification he had much better have stayed at home. At the best Mr. Spurgeon will seem to him a preacher of extraordinary volubility. Most probably he will return from one of Mr. Spurgeon's services disgusted with the noisy crowding, reminding him of the Adelphi rather than the house of God; disgusted with the commonplace prayer; disgusted with the questionable style of oratory; disgusted with the narrowness of the preacher's creed, and its pitiful misrepresentations of the glorious gospel of the blessed God; disgusted with the

* Quoted in *The British Standard*, August 14, 1857.

stupidity that can take for a divine afflatus brazen impudence and leathern lungs. Most probably he will come back confessing that Mr. Spurgeon is the youngest and the loudest and the most notorious preacher in London—little more; the idol of people who dare not go to theatres, and yet pant for theatrical excitement.*

Mr. Spurgeon's older friends at the Metropolitan Tabernacle are able to call up in memory many things relating to the preaching excursions into the country which were then constantly being undertaken. An intimate friend of the late pastor, and one who was for many years associated with him in Christian work, Mr. George Goldston of Hastings, has supplied the following pleasant countryside reminiscence, which at heart tends to prove that, despite what superfine critics in the Press might say, Spurgeon was pre-eminently the favourite preacher of the common people † :—

" In the early days of his ministry Mr. Spurgeon was peculiarly happy when surrounded by large gatherings of country people, to listen to the Gospel, as he preached to them in the green fields or country meadows. But of late years he had been compelled to avoid the risk of exposure to the open air; consequently, but few of his addresses so delivered are to be obtained from the printers of his sermons.

" Some of the old members of the church under his charge, however, can call to remembrance the wonderful scenes they witnessed on such occasions. What throngs of country folk, and from what distances they came, the variety of carts, vans, waggons, gigs, and carriages of almost every description !

" It was on such an occasion, in the summer of 1857, that several thousands of people met in a meadow of Mr. Jas. Rawlings, at a little village called Melbourne, a few miles from Cambridge. This lonely village, probably, was never so disturbed before; for more than a week previously busy hands were making preparation. Triumphal arches of evergreen, intermixed with bright flowers, surmounted with mottoes

* " The London Pulpit," second edition, pp. 157–159.

† I may be allowed here to explain, that this account, and also some similar things from other friends, were sent by their writers to Mr. Gawin Kirkham, whose intention it was to depict Mr. Spurgeon as an open-air preacher for this work. Mr. Kirkham died on May 8, 1892, deeply regretted by a wide circle of friends; and the papers sent to him were placed in my hands by the secretary of the Open Air Mission.

or words of welcome, greeted us from the village green and other open spaces. The shops displayed such bunting as their keepers possessed, while many of the cottages of the poor gave lively signs of the interest felt concerning the visit of the youthful preacher.

"At last the day arrived, and the weather being all that could be desired, the people came in from Cambridge, Royston, Baldock, Hitchin, and many other places round, until the meadow (a very large one) in which the service was to be held was nearly half filled with vehicles of various sorts and sizes, from the humble donkey cart to several superb carriages, drawn by valuable horses. When the preacher saw these carriages as he stood in a waggon from which to address the patient multitude, many of them having been waiting for hours, he said: 'I think our friends would do well to have the horses taken out of the carriages. We cannot edify the horses, but the carriages will be a great comfort to the occupants.' This being done, and it being now three o'clock, the time announced for the service to commence, Mr. Spurgeon, in full and clear voice, prayed; every heart seemed touched, a solemnity came upon the people, and attention to what would follow was evidently secured. Then came a cheerful hymn, sung so heartily that every face amongst that great gathering of people was lighted up with joy.

"And now followed the address, so sweetly simple, so full of tender earnestness—the Gospel put in language that all could understand; the appeals so direct that many felt the words were intended for themselves individually.

"The meadow having been cleared, preparation was made to have tea in the open air; and another address was given in the evening. It was estimated that eleven hundred persons took tea in the meadow that afternoon, a very small proportion being able to sit down.

"In the evening the congregation consisted for the most part of the working people living within a few miles of the place, the carriage folk who had come from a distance having returned. Yet the numbers seemed not less than in the afternoon. And there was the same eagerness to hear: such is the attractive power of the Gospel over the human mind. The service, which lasted until dusk, was most impressive; and many hearts in Melbourne were made glad that day. A selected few accompanied the beloved preacher to the house of a friend where he was entertained; being one of the company, it is with vivid recollection that I think of the family gathering for prayer that night, when a blessing was sought for every helper in the day's work, as well as every hearer."

In preaching away from home, Mr. Spurgeon now usually made it a condition that a collection should be taken for the building fund of his new Tabernacle. At first it was thought that a sum of £12,000 would suffice for such a chapel as was needed; but when, in the autumn of 1857, £5,000 had been collected, a total of £20,000 was being asked for; and not until half that amount had been secured would building operations be commenced.

The Metropolitan Tabernacle eventually cost nearly £32,000, a sum which would have inspired feelings akin to despair if it had been known from the first that such an amount would be needed.

CHAPTER XXXI.

A SERMON IN THE CRYSTAL PALACE.

Spurgeon's Popularity still an Enigma to many—*The British Quarterly Review*—A Thanksgiving Meeting—Day of Prayer on Account of the Indian Mutiny—Spurgeon Preaches at the Crystal Palace—Reports concerning the Preacher—Spurgeon at Lowestoft,

THE reaction of public feeling in Mr. Spurgeon's favour seemed to become more and more marked as the year 1857 advanced. The eager crowd at the Music Hall Sunday after Sunday so far increased in volume that, on every occasion of the doors being opened, a multitude which would in itself have constituted a large congregation had to turn away disappointed, unable to gain admission. The unique spectacle was a phenomenon which the town and its quidnuncs still professed to be unable to understand. Some, however, were knowing enough to find an explanation—it was the easiest thing in the world to command an audience in London, and if any doubted that simple truth it could be put to the test by their standing still for a time in Cheapside. Still, such reasoning as this went but a very little way; for anyone with common sense was well aware that for a preacher to attract and then keep a crowded congregation was really one of the most difficult of achievements. Competent judges who were not in full sympathy with Mr. Spurgeon's teaching, but who, nevertheless, wished to write impartially, saw this and made generous allowance in the preacher's favour. Some went further, and in what was being done recognised the hand of God. Thus, in the course of an article on the two annual volumes of sermons already published, a leading Quarterly remarked :—

"We believe ourselves that, to explain the fact presented in the Sunday meetings at the Surrey Gardens, we must go beyond the personal as found in the preacher, beyond the scheme of truth which he propounds, and beyond the nature to which he propounds it—that we must rest in nothing short of the Divine hand itself. The All-wise has often worked by instruments, and in ways, which would seem to have been chosen for the purpose of making a mock of the world's wisdom. He did so when he founded Christianity—he may do much like it again." *

Certain characteristics which had contributed to Mr. Spurgeon's success have some reference made to them, such, for example, as his elocution, his dramatic power, his unflagging earnestness, and his faith in the Gospel to supply all the needs of man. The subject is then summed up:—

"But here comes a man—no Whitefield in voice, in presence, in dignity, or genius, who nevertheless, as with one stroke of his hand, sweeps away all this sickly sentimentalism, this craven misbelief. It is all to him as so much of the merest gossamer web that could have crossed his path. He not only gives forth the old doctrine of St. Paul, in all the strength of Paul's language, but with exaggerations of his own, such as Paul would have been forward to disavow. This man knows nothing of doubt as to whence the Gospel is, what it is, or wherefore it has its place among us. On all such subjects his mind is that of a made-up man. In place of suspecting that the old accredited doctrines of the Gospel have pretty well done their work, he expects good from nothing else, and all that he clusters about them is for the sake of them. The philosophical precision, the literary refinements, the nice discriminations between what we may know of a doctrine and what we may not, leaving us in the end, perhaps, scarcely anything to know about it—all this, which, according to some, is so much needed by the age, is Mr. Spurgeon's utter scorn. He is the direct, dogmatic enunciator of the old Pauline truth, without the slightest attempt to soften its outline, its substance, or its results—and what has followed? Truly Providence would seem once more to have made foolish the wisdom of this world. While the gentlemen who know so well how people ought to preach are left to exemplify their profound lessons before empty benches and in obscure corners, the young man at the Surrey Gardens can point to his 9,000 auditors before him and ask—Who, with such a sight before him, dares despair of making the Gospel, the good Old Gospel, a power in the great heart of humanity?"

The business of collecting funds for the erection of the new Tabernacle still went on. Any person walking along the Southwark High Street on Monday, September 7, would have noticed bills announcing a meeting for that evening at New Park Street for the purpose "of returning thanks to the Most High for the success that has attended the labours of the Rev. C. H. Spurgeon in his endeavours to obtain the means for erecting a large Tabernacle where the masses may assemble to hear the Word of Life."

On this occasion Mr. Spurgeon himself made a statement of some length which enabled all who were interested in the movement clearly to understand the situation. Reference was made to the services which had been held in Exeter Hall—services which had

* *The British Quarterly Review*, July, 1857.

S

been derided and scouted at the time as undesirable innovations, but which had been fruitful in conversions, and otherwise so successful that the bishops of the Established Church were then doing the same kind of thing on their own account. Having then shown that the enlargement of New Park Street Chapel had been of little use, for the services were as crowded as they were before, he continued:—

"In order to assist in raising a fund for that purpose, a second series of services was commenced in Exeter Hall, which were being conducted with as great success as the first, when they were told, for some reason mysterious to him, that they could have the hall no longer. He did not wish to impute motives to anyone in respect of that matter, but he could never yet understand the reason why the hall was refused them, and why they were obliged to discontinue their services in it. That being the case, however, what were they to do? It was no use going back to their old chapel, as it could not contain the half of the numbers who came to attend the services, and the Surrey Music Hall having been found to be eligible, it was resolved to secure it, and try the holding of the services there as an experiment. He would not pain their feelings by alluding to the untoward circumstances attending their first meeting there. It was a painful prelude to most magnificent results, and Satan never met with a greater failure than he did in that attempt at coercion. Had it not been for the lamentable accident which took place on that occasion, so many thousands would never have been brought within the sound of the Gospel. That accident was the means of causing their meeting there to be known among the highest of the land; and although he considered this of little consequence, many of these had since attended their service, and heard the Gospel in its simplicity. Their meetings there had been eminently successful; but, in order fully to carry out their object, they must have a place of worship of their own, where they could have service when they pleased, and which would afford sufficient accommodation to those who might attend. At the present moment he could with certainty state that, had they such an edifice, 5,000 seats, at the least, would find occupants, and he did so from seeing far more than that number, Sunday after Sunday, regularly hearing him in the Surrey Music Hall. They were, in fact, regular attenders, occupying always the same seat, and might be safely calculated on as hearers in a new place of worship had they one erected, and he had no doubt that could they effect their object, they would have the best and strongest church in London. To carry out that object then, a committee had been appointed, who had been unremitting in their labours to procure money for the erection of the building, and a site on which to erect it. Some three months ago he had the honour of breakfasting with Sir S. M. Peto, who promised him a hundred pounds donation when the foundation-stone of such a building was laid, and another hundred pounds when it was finished, besides a promise of further assistance. He also told him that he would cause his agent to look out for a site suitable for the erection of such a structure, in respect of which he was to communicate with the committee, but as he understood Sir M. Peto had been in Portugal mostly ever since, no conclusion had been come to in that respect."

At this time some £4,000 appeared to be in hand, more being promised; and nearly £600 of the total had been collected by the pastor himself in the way of collections after his services. During the preceding week he had secured £179 by such means, but then he had had to travel long distances, and to preach twice each day. The object of the meeting was to inspire the people with the enthusiasm in the enterprise which animated the pastor.*

The chief preaching occasion of the year was the great service at the Crystal Palace on Wednesday, October 7, which was set apart as a day of humiliation and prayer on account of the Indian Mutiny. Younger persons of the present generation will not be able to realise the intensity of feeling which the atrocities of that outbreak aroused; and even so good a friend as Dr. Campbell thought that Mr. Spurgeon spoke in too vindictive a strain. It was not always easy to be calm when reading details of the horrors which characterised the action of the rebels.

The day was too wet and cold for the convenience of those who wished to turn the occasion into a holiday; but a sermon in the transept of the palace of glass at Sydenham had attraction for thousands. The trains commenced running at half-past seven in the morning; and by noon an immense congregation had assembled. The pulpit erected at the north-east corner of the transept was the one which had already done such good service at the Surrey Gardens.† In the course of a brief prayer, the

* An account of what took place on this occasion is given in *The British Standard* for September 11, 1857.

† Writing in *The World*, "Atlas" gives a reminiscence of this memorable day:—"A personal experience of Mr. Spurgeon was at the Crystal Palace, where he preached to 25,000 people. Seated near to the pulpit, I observed Mrs. Spurgeon take her place just before her husband appeared, and that she was visibly affected by the mighty concourse of souls, all with upturned faces and fixed gaze upon one man, and all about to be thrilled to the core by that man's impassioned appeals to them to be saved alive. While Mrs. Spurgeon was concealing her emotion as best she might, I saw the pastor beckon far off with his forefinger to one of the deacons, a stout, grey-haired man of rubicund complexion, and with a defect in one eye. He was in the very glossy black which was the orthodox Dissenting uniform in those far-off days, and walked with a limp which made his progress up the pulpit, or rather platform, stairs tantalisingly slow. Some brief, but evidently important, instruction was at last whispered by Mr. Spurgeon in the lame man's ear, and 25,000 people were at once agog with curiosity to know what this could possibly be at such a time, when the whole vast place was quivering with anticipation and suppressed emotional excitement. I happened to be seated so near Mrs. Spurgeon that when the worthy deacon 'made for her' in his crab-like ponderous way, it was unavoidable that I, at least, out of the vast and silent crowd of expectants, should hear what had delayed the pastor and what the urgent matter was he had at such a critical moment to communicate. In a hoarse whisper I heard this:—'Mr. Spurgeon says, please will you change your seat

preacher commended to God those who had suffered through the
mutiny—the widows and the fatherless. As regarded the soldiers
he prayed God " to bid them remember that they are not warriors
merely, but executioners, and bid them go with steady tramp to
battle, believing that God wills that they shall utterly destroy the
enemy that has defied Britain and defiled themselves among men."
The people sang a second time, the volume of sound producing a
grand effect in the vast building; and then came the sermon, which
was founded on Micah. vi. 9, "Hear ye the rod, and who hath
appointed it."

In the course of a sermon which lasted thirty-five minutes, the
preacher said he looked upon the events in India as a national
punishment inflicted upon this country by means of the Sepoys,
who had voluntarily joined their standard, and had taken the oath
of fidelity to her Majesty and her officers, and who had no cause to
find fault, because they had been always petted and dandled on the
knee of favouritism. If the people of India revolted, they might
think they had patriots in their midst who sought to relieve their
country from a tyrannical nation; but it was only men who were
actuated by lust and ambition that had risen against them. They
had now rebels to be executed, and he looked upon every gallows
as a fearful evil, and regarded every gibbet as a dreadful visitation
upon the land. Whenever the arm of the ruler was outstretched
for the punishment of death, it must always be looked upon by the
country as a serious affliction; but these men must be punished;
both heaven and earth demanded it. He did not believe this was
a war at all in the proper sense of the term. Their troops were
not fighting with the troops of an enemy, but were going forth
against revolted subjects, who, by their crimes and murders and other
unmentionable sins, had incurred the punishment of death. It was
a horrible and dreadful thing to think of taking away the lives of
their fellow-subjects, and they had that day to bemoan, amongst

so that he will not be able to see you; it ['it' was doubtless Mrs. Spurgeon's emotion]
makes him nervous;' and the lady moved immediately to another seat not visible from the
preacher's place."

MR. SPURGEON PREACHING AT THE CRYSTAL PALACE.

other evils, that the sword must be taken from the sheath to cut
off their fellow-subjects by thousands. He saw God's hand in this
war, and he hoped He had only ordained this evil in order that
great good might follow from it. The sins of the Government of
India had been black and deep; and those who had heard the
shrieks of the tormented natives and the cries of dethroned
princes might well prophesy that it would not be long before God
would unsheath His sword to revenge the oppressed. Had it been
the Indian nation that had revolted, he should have prayed to
God that they might be brought under British rule again, for the
sake of civilisation; but they should not preach a crusade against
them lest they should be smiting patriots who were endeavouring to succour an oppressed country. He considered that the
Indian Government should never have tolerated the religion of the
Hindoos; but they had aided and abetted the folly for which God
now visited them with His punishment. It was said that one part
of the cause of the evil was the sin of the English people themselves, and there were certainly sins in the community that should
never have been allowed. The horrible nuisance of Holywell
Street had been long allowed to exist, although it was now pretty
well done for; but what did they see in Regent Street and the
Haymarket? If there was a crime for which God should punish
England, it was the crime of allowing infamy to work out its
designs in such places before their eyes. They knew likewise that
lords and ladies sat in playhouses and listened to plays that were
far from decent; and those sins of the community had in part
brought the rod upon them. He also attributed the evil to the
acts of those who only thought of their fellows as stepping-stones
to gain. But he could not enumerate all the evils that had led to
it. The Christian Church, in his opinion, had been remiss in its
duty; but he hoped that its revival had begun, because last year
had seen more preaching than any year since the days of the
Apostles. They prayed that day; but when victory came to them,
they would praise God by buying fireworks, by firing off rockets,

and by illuminations, as they had done at the close of the late war.

The preacher made a strong appeal on behalf of the sufferers in the mutiny. "Lives there a man who will refuse his help for those of his countrymen who have suffered? No, there does not live such a man; at least, none such in Britain. Was there such a miserable miscreant without a heart, who would, when God had given him enough, shut up his bowels of compassion? No! he would not slander them with the suspicion. He could not think there was such a monster present. When the plates were handed round let them give their pence if they could not give pounds; but let all give in accordance with their means."* The collection for the Indian Relief Fund amounted to £675 16s. 11½d., including £200 from the Crystal Palace Company out of the day's proceeds. Mr. Spurgeon's services were understood to be gratuitous. The "Hallelujah Chorus" and the benediction closed the service. The number of persons who entered the building was 23,654.

This service was acknowledged to be the most notable thing which took place in connection with the fast day; but that class which can never be satisfied with anything, found plenty of reason to find fault. It was a dexterous dodge on the part of the Crystal Palace Company on the one hand; on the other hand it was not a becoming thing to make a religious service a chief attraction in a place devoted to amusement. Dr. Campbell stood forth as Mr. Spurgeon's defender. No reasonable objection could be raised; the place was a proper one to preach in on such an occasion. The collection was not far short of all the other collections in London put together; while "the assembly was the largest ever addressed by a preacher of the Gospel in Europe or the world."

Having thus spoken on behalf of his friend, and expressed his satisfaction at the tone of the several pulpit utterances generally, Dr. Campbell went on to disclaim sympathy with the spirit of the prayer offered at the Crystal Palace, a part of which has been quoted. It

* *The British Standard,* October 9, 1857.

was thought that the young preacher "somewhat forgot himself," which was much to be regretted. "For Mr. Spurgeon, however, large allowances ought to be made," it was added. "Had his profession been that of arms, he would probably have made a second Havelock, if not a Napoleon I. He has a soul within him equal to great enterprises. But the idea of military butchery is most incongruous with the exercise of devotion." *

On Sunday, November 22, Mr. Spurgeon preached from Rev. iii. 19, "As many as I love, I rebuke and chasten : be zealous therefore, and repent." He stated that through the death of a child he was somewhat disqualified from preaching, and had almost felt that he would be unable to be present. The discourse was spoken of as "not so vigorous as usual ; " but the congregation was in hearty sympathy with the pastor, and the hall was densely crowded in every part.

The London correspondent of *The Glasgow Examiner* happened to be present at this service, and some kindly references to the preacher and his work appeared in the paper of that same week. Scottish readers were told that Mr. Spurgeon had preached from the text in the Epistle to the Hebrews, "Whom the Lord loveth He chasteneth ; " and having thus quoted the wrong text, the Scottish journalist proceeded to make a somewhat singular comment upon it. "Mr. Spurgeon now lives in a splendid mansion," he remarked, " keeps a handsome one-horse carriage, and a large retinue of servants —four female and two male servants. His income is said to be a long way over a thousand pounds. His works will now considerably augment his stated income." Of course, good Dr. Campbell wished that people should beware of accepting such statements. They entrenched " a little on privacy." In this case the report was supposed to be " too good to be true ; " but if it was correct, no man, it was averred, better deserved what had fallen to this young pastor's lot.†

Tuesday, December 1, was a memorable day at Lowestoft, for

* *The British Standard*, October 9, 1857.   † *Ibid.*, December 4, 1857.

Mr. Spurgeon preached twice in the town on behalf of the Baptist Chapel, and the collections amounted to almost £100. The services were held in the Continental Goods Depôt of the North of Europe Steam Navigation Company, and three thousand persons were present on each occasion. Being carried at low fares, people came from the surrounding country in large numbers. The late Sir S. Morton Peto, the vicar of Lowestoft, and many of the clergy and Dissenting ministers, were also present, as were also representatives of the principal families resident in the district.

CHAPTER XXXII.

"A CONTRADICTORY GOSPEL."

The Strict Baptists again—James Wells refuses to Preach with Spurgeon—Various Opinions—
"The Saint and his Saviour"—Sample Extracts—A Prophecy.

DURING the year 1857 the doctrines preached by Mr. Spurgeon were again subjected to the criticisms of the Strict Baptists, who were also extreme Calvinists. The leader of the attack was no other than James Wells himself, who, as the ablest man of his denomination, was the recognised champion of his party. The veneration this eloquent preacher inspired was extraordinary; the influence he exercised was that of an apostle. "James Wells is sent of God to bring His people out of bondage," remarked one of his disciples; "this is his peculiar work; and where is there a man that can knock down a 'duty-faith' fabric and wheel away the rubbish like him?" *

In the spring of 1857 Mr. Wells had engaged to preach for a brother minister at Brighton, but when he learned that Mr. Spurgeon was invited to preach in the same building, the Strict Baptist teacher declined. He disavowed harbouring any unkind feelings towards Mr. Spurgeon, some things in whose ministry were right enough, although on the whole his teaching was "divided against itself." Hence, it would be more comfortable to keep "at an honest distance," as that was better than hypocritically professing to receive his message, and then to do as many had done, go and backbite the preacher. The man who could speak thus had no manner of sympathy with "the reproachful things said in the public papers of Mr. Spurgeon's ministry;" for he believed such things arose "from ignorance, envy, and prejudice." After all, the New Park Street pastor was honest

---

* S. B. Seely, in *The Earthen Vessel*, xiii. 221.

and outspoken in uttering what he believed to be the truth. Mr. Wells then showed in brief in what sense he understood Mr. Spurgeon's preaching to be faulty when tested by the touchstone of Scripture. "Mr. Spurgeon informs us that he cannot reconcile Matt. xi. 20, 21, 23, 24, with verses 25, 26, or with verses 28, 29, 30; so that by exalting mere Ninevite repentance (first five verses) into that repentance which God alone can bestow, he hereby makes the Holy Ghost a self-contradictory witness. He thus preaches a *suicidal* Gospel, a Gospel divided against itself. This is that piece of delusion which softens the great truths of the Gospel down to the taste of the carnal mind; and from such a Gospel I do most solemnly and conscientiously differ; and however this may tend to my unpopularity, a good conscience before God is with me a greater treasure than all the world can give."

Mr. Wilkins, the pastor at Brighton, to whom this was addressed, protested that he had no more sympathy with anything short of "a full, free, and effectual Gospel" than Mr. Wells himself. He might not agree with all that was taught at New Park Street, but there was too much of sovereign grace in the young pastor's teaching to allow of its being altogether rejected. "Seeing the many thousands in this metropolis regardless of God, the Bible, or the Sabbath, as I saw them yesterday in Whitechapel and elsewhere, I could say, 'Would to God a thousand Spurgeons were raised up to attract the multitude to hear the Word of Life.'"

Mr. Wells, however, was deaf to all entreaty to visit Brighton; he could have no fellowship with one who believed in duty-faith, or who held that men perished because they refused to believe in Christ. "Though I receive not the mark of error in my forehead so as openly to avow that error, yet if I give the right hand of fellowship to it, I do hereby receive the mark of error, though not in my forehead, yet I receive it in my hand." To talk about "a thousand Spurgeons" to preach to the crowds of East London was of no avail. Popularity counts for very little; it was "the hugeness of Popery, Church of Englandism, Wesleyanism, Mahometanism," which had awed so many into submission. Beyond that, "the nearer the counterfeit is in weight and appearance to the real coin the greater the danger, and the more complete the deception."

The publication of the letters which were written by Mr. Wells and Mr. Wilkins produced many others which showed in what light Mr. Spurgeon was viewed by the straitest section of the Strict Baptists. One representative writer said:—"It may suit the giddy million to make sport with the bewitching philosophy of dramatic display, and to riot in the amusing freaks of art's airy-footed lore; but are the 'children of light' to be caught in the snare of popular talents and to be cheated by mere pulpit eloquence? Are dreams and delusions to captivate Zion? . . . I have not a particle of prejudice against the young and amiable aspirant after pulpit fame; but I have read his sermons, heard his preaching, and closely observed the profession and conduct of his followers; and upon the face of these things I see not the *lively features of a healthy child.*"

A number of letters having appeared, Mr. Wells returned to the subject; and after an examination of several sermons, the statements of which were compared with Scripture, the conclusion arrived at was, "Mr. Spurgeon belongs to the duty-faith class of preachers. . . . He preaches a self-contradictory Gospel." Mr. Wells then adds:—"Poison is generally given in something *good;* or else who that wished not to be poisoned could be so deceived as to take it? Duty-faith is a doctrine which secretly and in a most deadly manner poisons the mind against the very truths in connection with which it is preached. Some of the old duty-faith churches have become the greatest enemies to the truth which the truth has ever known; and yet because Mr. Spurgeon unconsciously throws this poison into the food, or that he does not believe it to be poison, I am to be hated because I will not join in partnership with such unscriptural trading. Be it so; I am content with my lot; and hope to my latest breath to prove the sincerity of my decision."

It would be a mistake to suppose, however, that the whole of the Strict Baptist denomination agreed with Mr. Wells. Many had their prejudices strengthened by what he said; but others honestly believed him to be altogether mistaken. Mr. C. W. Banks, as preacher and editor, had cordially welcomed Spurgeon to London in 1854, and he was still the young pastor's friend. "We have bidden him God-speed in all that was godlike, and of a true Gospel character," wrote Mr. Banks. "In these things we have had an advantage, perhaps, over Mr. Wells, who has, we believe, never either seen or heard Mr. Spurgeon." *

It was towards the end of the year 1857 that Mr. Spurgeon's first book, apart from the published sermons, appeared. The work consisted of twelve chapters, and was entitled, "The Saint and his Saviour: the Progress of the Soul in the Knowledge of Jesus." The copyright, which was far more valuable than the author suspected, was sold for £50, and notwithstanding the extensive sale of the work, that modest honorarium was never supplemented. I could never quite understand how such a bargain came to be made at a time when the writer was already phenomenally popular.† Being in the study at Helensburgh House, some years ago, I ventured to ask for some explanation, and the answer was, "At that time I thought £50 to be a good deal of money." More than twenty years after its production, Mr. Spurgeon had the opportunity of buying back the copyright for £80; but he refused the offer, with the remark that he preferred writing a new book to giving that amount for an old one. ‡

---

* The letters and articles relating to this subject will be found in *The Earthen Vessel* for May, June, July, and August, 1857.

† In point of fact this first book, as we may properly call it, had a somewhat singular history. "It is natural to ask, if composition be such a task to Mr. Spurgeon, and seeing that his pulpit labours are so incessant and overwhelming, how came he to add to his burdens the toils of producing the present volume? There was surely no obligation so to do. This is plausible. Such, however, is not the fact; the truth is, we believe—and it is due to Mr. Spurgeon to state it—that he entered into an arrangement with the respectable house whose name the volume bears, to produce it soon after his arrival in London, and consequently, when he had no anticipation of the unparalleled favour with which he has since been honoured. In those days he had leisure enough, and, but for subsequent events, he would probably long ere this have finished his task, and he might even have become a popular writer."—*The British Standard*, February 12, 1858.

‡ Looking at the matter from the standpoint of self-interest, even this offer should not have been refused. The copyright was then purchased by Messrs. Hodder and Stoughton.

Although, as he tells us, Mr. Spurgeon prepared his work "chiefly for the Lord's family," there are passages in it addressed specially to unconverted readers. Taken altogether, the book is of great interest; for not only have the pages the freshness of youth upon them, but one may see who were the authors who had attraction for the preacher at the age of twenty-three. He gives attention to Byron and Thomson, Tennyson and Herbert, among poets; Seneca also has some share of attention; while among divines, Gill and Charnock, Udall and Chandler, are referred to. Like some of the early sermons, the book might have been the production of a man of long and wide Christian experience; and hence we find one reviewer saying that the book excites surprise when the author's age is remembered. There are also many passages in it which extreme Calvinists would have said were the offspring of duty-faith. The success of the book was immediate, and a steady sale appears to have continued until the present time. A passage or two may be given as examples of Mr. Spurgeon's early written style. This passage on the duty of not neglecting to look after penitent sinners shows his wide sympathy :—

"We find an excuse for inaction in the fancied hopelessness of sinners; while fastidious delicacy, by the fear of pollution, seeks to mask at once our indolence and pride. If we had right views of *ourselves*, we should judge none too base to be reclaimed, and should count it no dishonour to bear upon the shoulders of our sympathy the most wandering of the flock. We have amongst us too much of the spirit of 'Stand by, for I am holier than thou.' Those whom Jesus would have grasped by the hand, we will scarcely touch with a pair of tongs; such is the pride of many professors that they need but the name to be recognised at once as the true successors of the ancient Pharisees. If we were more like Christ, we should be more ready to hope for the hopeless, to value the worthless, and to love the depraved. The following anecdote, which the writer received from the lips of an esteemed minister of the Church of England, may perhaps, as a fact, plead more forcibly than words. A clergyman of a parish in Ireland, in the course of his visitations, had called upon everyone of his flock with but one exception. This was a woman of most abandoned character, and he feared that by entering her house he might give occasion of offence to gainsayers, and bring dishonour upon his profession. One Sabbath he observed her among the frequenters of his church, and for weeks after he noticed her attention to the Word of Life. He thought, too, that amid the sound of the responses he could detect one sweet and earnest voice, solemnly confessing sin, and imploring mercy. The bowels of his pity yearned over this fallen daughter of Eve; he longed to ask her if her heart were indeed broken on account of sin; and he intensely desired to speak with her concerning the abounding grace which, he hoped, had plucked her from the burning. Still, the same delicacy of feeling forbade him to enter the house; time after time he passed her door with longing look, anxious for her salvation, but jealous of his own honour. This lasted for a length of time, but at last it ended. One day, she called him to her, and with overflowing tears which well betrayed her bursting heart, she said, ' *Oh, sir! if your Master had been in this village half as long as you have, He would have called to see me long ago! for surely I am the chief of sinners, and therefore have . most need of His mercy.*' We may conceive the melting of the pastor's heart, when he saw his conduct thus gently condemned by a comparison with his loving Master. From that time forth he resolved to neglect none, but to gather even the 'outcasts of Israel.' " *

He refers in one place to the friend at Newmarket from whom he learned much of his theology:—"The writer confesses his eternal obligations to an old cook, who was despised as an Antinomian, but who in her kitchen taught him many of the deep things of God, and removed many a doubt from his youthful mind." †
The following refers to losses by death:—

"We remember to have heard a preacher at a funeral most beautifully setting forth this truth in parable. He spoke thus:—'A certain nobleman had a spacious garden, which he left to the care of a faithful servant, whose delight it was to train the creepers along the trellis, to water the seeds in the time of drought, to support the stalks of the tender plants, and to do every work which could render the garden a Paradise of flowers. One morning he rose with joy, expecting to tend his beloved flowers, and hoping to find his favourites increased in beauty. To his surprise, he found one of his choicest beauties rent from its stem, and, looking around him, he missed from every bed the pride of his garden, the most precious of his blooming flowers. Full of grief and anger he hurried to his fellow-servants, and demanded who had thus robbed him of his treasures. They had not done it, and he did not charge them with it; but he found no solace for his grief till one of them remarked:—"My lord was walking in the garden this morning, and I saw him pluck the flowers and carry them away." Then truly he found he had no cause for his trouble. He felt it was well that his master had been pleased to take his own, and he went away smiling at his loss, because his lord had taken them. So,' said the preacher, turning to the mourners, 'you have lost one whom you regarded with much tender affection. The bonds of endearment have not availed for her retention upon earth. I know your wounded feelings when, instead of the lovely form which was the embodiment of all that is excellent and amiable, you behold nothing but ashes and corruption. But remember, my beloved, THE LORD hath done it; HE hath removed the tender mother, the affectionate wife, the inestimable friend. I say again, remember your own Lord hath done it; therefore do not murmur, or yield yourselves to an excess of grief.' There was much force as well as beauty in the simple allegory: it were well if all the Lord's family had grace to practise its heavenly lesson, in all times of bereavement and affliction." ‡

One notable passage is really autobiographical; for it refers to that distressing time, just after the Surrey Gardens catastrophe, when the preacher was unable to continue his daily work, and when to his friends it seemed that reason herself would be dethroned. I have heard Mr. Spurgeon refer to that time, and whenever he spoke of

---

* "The Saint and His Saviour," pp. 34–36.
† *Ibid.*, p. 131.   ‡ *Ibid.*, pp. 282–283.

what he then passed through, he would vividly picture his experience. Here are the passages relating to this period as given in his first book :—

"On a night which time will never erase from my memory, large numbers of my congregation were scattered, many of them wounded and some killed, by the malicious act of wicked men. Strong amid danger, I battled the storm, nor did my spirit yield to the overwhelming pressure while my courage could reassure the wavering or confirm the bold. But when, like a whirlwind, the destruction had overpast, when the whole of its devastation was visible to my eye, who can conceive the anguish of my spirit? I refused to be comforted; tears were my meat by day, and dreams my terror by night. I felt as I had never felt before. 'My thoughts were all a case of knives,' cutting my heart in pieces, until a kind of stupor of grief ministered a mournful medicine to me. I could have truly said, 'I am not mad, but surely I have had enough to madden me, if I should indulge in meditation on it.' I sought and found a solitude which seemed congenial to me. I could tell my grief to the flowers, and the dews could weep with me. Here my mind lay, like a wreck upon the sand, incapable of its usual motion. My Bible, once my daily food, was but a hand to lift the sluices of my woe. Prayer yielded no balm to me; in fact, my soul was like an infant's soul, and I could not rise to the dignity of supplication. . . . Then came the 'slander of many'—barefaced fabrications, libellous slanders, and barbarous accusations. These alone might have scooped out the last drop of consolation from my cup of happiness, but the worst had come to the worst, and the utmost malice of the enemy could do no more. Lower they cannot sink who are already in the nethermost depths. Misery itself is the guardian of the miserable. All things combined to keep me for a season in the darkness where neither sun nor moon appeared. I had hoped for a gradual return to peaceful consciousness, and patiently did I wait for the dawning light. But it came not as I had desired, for He who doeth for us exceeding abundantly above what we can ask or think, sent me a happier answer to my requests. I had striven to think of the immeasurable love of Jehovah, as displayed in the sacrifice of Calvary; I had endeavoured to muse upon the glorious character of the exalted Jesus; but I found it impossible to collect my thoughts in the quiver of meditation, or, indeed, to place them anywhere but with their points in my wounded spirit, or else at my feet, trodden down in an almost childish thoughtlessness. On a sudden, like a flash of lightning from the sky, my soul returned unto me. The burning lava of my brain cooled in an instant. The throbbings of my brow were still; the cool wind of comfort cooled my cheek, which had been scorched in the furnace. I was free, the iron fetter was broken in pieces, my prison door was open, I leaped for joy of heart. On wings of a dove my spirit mounted to the stars—yea, beyond them. Whither did it wing its flight? and where did it sing its song of gratitude? It was at the feet of Jesus, whose name had charmed its fears, and placed an end to its mourning. The name—the precious name of Jesus—was like Ithuriel's spear, bringing back my soul to its own right and happy state. I was a man again, and what is more, a believer. The garden in which I stood became an Eden to me, and the spot was then most solemnly consecrated in my most grateful memory. Happy hour, thrice blessed Lord, who thus in an instant delivered me from the rock of my despair, and slew the vulture of my grief! Before I told to others the glad news of my recovery, my heart was melodious with song, and my tongue endeavoured tardily to express the music. Then did I give to my Well-Beloved a song touching my Well-Beloved; and oh! with what rapture did my soul flash forth His praises! but all—all were to the honour of Him, the first and the last, the Brother born for adversity, the Deliverer of the captive, the Breaker of my fetters, the Restorer of my soul. Then did I cast my burden upon the Lord; I left my ashes and did array myself in the garments of praise, while He did anoint me with fresh oil. I could have riven the very firmament to get at Him, to cast myself at His feet, and lay there bathed in the tears of joy and love. Never since the day of my conversion had I known so much of His infinite excellence, never had my spirit leaped with such unutterable delight. Scorn, tumult, and woe seemed less than nothing for His sake. I girded up my loins to run before His chariot, and shout forth His glory, for my soul was absorbed in the one idea of His glorious exaltation and divine compassion." *

This shows that the young pastor's mind was near upon being unhinged by the experience he passed through during this season. He was never quite the same after the catastrophe that he had been previously. Until the age of twenty-two he had hardly known the meaning of illness; but after the year 1856, his ailments were many and frequently severe.

When it appeared at this time, the book struck certain critics as being a curious production. "It is not a didactic treatise," remarked one reviewer, "it is, in fact, not a treatise at all, but a leviathan sermon, addressed to a mixed congregation, comprising a variety of classes, between whom there is an intimate relation. . . . The thunder and lightning, the rant and rapture, by which he rules supreme over a mixed audience of any magnitude, have no place here. All is calm and gentle and tender. To attain the success which, in this respect, marks the effort, has doubtless been no easy matter; the work may be designated Mr. Spurgeon's penance volume. His talents, tastes, and habits all look in an opposite direction, and go some way to unfit him for literary effort in solitude." †

While confessing that the work had been composed amid other incessant toils, and that writing was to him the work of a slave, the author still expressed the hope that he might serve his Master with the pen as well as the voice, but he was told by the critic just quoted "to moderate his expectations in this quarter;" and then it was shown how small was the number of eminent men who had succeeded with both tongue and pen. It was not likely that the eloquent pastor of New Park Street would be any exception as a mere orator to a number of illustrious men who were named. "Their indisposition to use the pen increased with time; and so will his," we find it remarked; "and to such a length did their self-created

* *Ibid.*, pp. 371–375.
† *The British Standard*, February 12, 1858.

incapacity grow on them that they became almost incapable of correspondence; and so will he. We believe he is well-nigh so now." Probably, a prophecy more wide of the mark was never made. The truth is that the love of authorship grew on Mr. Spurgeon as he advanced in life; and the number of his books and magazine articles, apart from sermons, would represent quite a respectable life-work had he been nothing more than a *littérateur.* He also wrote a larger number of private letters than any great man I ever heard of, or than one might have thought possible in the case of a public servant who constantly had a thousand other calls on his time and energy.

T

CHAPTER XXXIII.

A GREAT MISSIONARY SERMON.

THE year 1858 was remarkable for many things. It had a great comet, the like of which modern sky-gazers had never seen; there was a nearly total eclipse of the sun; there was a great Revival in the United States, and some awakening at home, especially in connection with the continued services of Mr. Spurgeon at the Surrey Gardens. The strain of this work now began to tell on the young preacher, however; and before the close of the year we shall find him overtaken by his first serious illness.

At the opening of the year the bank had a sum of £5,000 in hand on account of the new Tabernacle, £2,000 being promised in addition. In regard to the services, conversions were reported to be very numerous, additions being made to the Church every month. At this time Mr. Spurgeon himself baptised the persons accepted for Church membership, a practice he was compelled to relinquish in after years. On one memorable week-night evening at New Park Street Chapel, after the pastor had immersed eighteen, a young person was also immersed by a Pædobaptist minister, who was present as representing an Independent congregation at Kennington. While thus practising adult baptism by immersion, however, the Independent, from the baptistery, stoutly defended the practice of infant baptism as being in accordance with the teaching of Scripture.*

The popularity of the preacher was now quite unparalleled so

* *The Baptist Messenger*, viii. 50.

far as the English-speaking race was concerned; the crowds continued to be phenomenal whenever and wherever he was announced
to preach; and Spurgeon had become an attractive subject for newspapers both at home and in the United States, where his published
sermons commanded an immense sale. Dr. Campbell pronounced
this popularity not only to be " a great fact," but "the most
remarkable thing of the sort on the face of the earth."

We can well suppose that it was not altogether pleasing to
certain of his compeers to see Mr. Spurgeon monopolise the Music
Hall as though no other preacher was competent to preach in such
a building. Just after the Christmas holidays, therefore, street
placards announced that Mr. James Wells would give a discourse
in the place on Sunday evening, January 10, 1858. While speaking
on St. Paul's address to Felix in the morning of that day, Mr.
Spurgeon's voice gave some signs of failing.

When Mr. Wells ascended the pulpit there were over 10,000
persons present to hear him. He mentioned thirteen charges which
the Holy Spirit brought against the human race, and which had
been met by Christ. Some of his followers, who were even more
strict in their notions than James Wells himself, were very angry
at such an experiment being made. Mr. Charles Waters Banks, as
editor-in-chief of the body, quite approved of the Surrey Tabernacle
being closed for once, especially as the great assembly at the Surrey
Gardens contributed £50 to the funds of the Christian Blind Relief
Society. The congregation was as large as Mr. Spurgeon's in the
morning, and though held in a dark winter evening, passed off
without the slightest hitch.

Early in February Dr. Campbell again favoured the world with a
review to date of Mr. Spurgeon's work and writings. The young
preacher had marked out a path for himself, his one unselfish aim
being to do good. He did not, as some had done, get up a number
of sermons with care, preach them all over the land, and then
publish them; he preached as well as printed for usefulness. The
discourses were divinity for the million; while as an orator the

Music Hall preacher had outdone Erskine himself, who spoke three volumes of published speeches in three weeks. "Nothing like this has been heard of since the world began," it is added. "The man who preaches ten times weekly has no leisure for the manufacture of glittering paragraphs and polished periods." Of the discourses already published it was remarked: "There are no other volumes in the English tongue from which the preacher may obtain so much insight into the most efficient methods of addressing mixed multitudes." A reference was also made to the United States :—

"The Americans of the present hour may be received as standing somewhere between the living generation of Englishmen and the generation to be born; and it is not improbable that the judgment they form will be substantially the judgment of posterity. They are far removed from the scene of strife, where there has been, in relation to this subject, such a display of ignorance and folly, and misapprehension, misrepresentation, and falsehood. Mr. Spurgeon has, beyond question, been the best abused and the most exalted man of this generation; but there is reason to believe he has been very little influenced by the one or the other."

The catholicity of the sermons is also warmly commended :—

"Thorough Baptist though Mr. Spurgeon is, and ever ready to avow it where circumstances, in his view, require it, he is not one of those who preach the Gospel knee-deep in water. The New Park Street pulpit is perfectly dry. Only in one instance the Baptist appears, and even then but for a moment, and neither his aspect nor his utterance is at all offensive. Many and terrible, however, are the thrusts dealt out to bitter bigotry of every description."

The English of the sermons is pronounced perfect; "so fine and so idiomatic that it would scarcely lose by comparison with the writings of John Bunyan himself." Another peculiarity is then pointed out—the sermons were "an extraordinary mixture of prose and verse. They comprise a larger amount of poetic fragments than any other in any language published. We doubt if the memory of any other living man be the depository of so much sacred poetry. Were all the collections extant to be burnt to-morrow, Mr. Spurgeon, we think, would have no difficulty in producing from memory one or more every way sufficient for all the purposes of worship. . . . But it will be perilous for any man, in this respect, to imitate Mr. Spurgeon without the possession of his peculiar powers. However telling these poetic pellets may be, well selected Scriptures in the lips of Mr. Spurgeon would be infinitely better; and Mr.

Spurgeon, even, without diminishing his exaction from the poets, would greatly improve his preaching by drawing more extensively on the prophets and apostles." *

On April 7, in what was really wintry weather, Mr. Spurgeon visited Halifax, where a disaster occurred which might have surpassed in evil consequences the panic at the Music Hall, had it happened a little earlier in the day. " We are not prepared to say that the accident arose from any defect in the temporary building erected for the occasion in the Peace Hall," says a contemporary account; " but as the occupants of the gallery were dispersing, a number of boards or planks gave way with a loud noise, and a host of people were thrown heavily upon one another. Frightful screams were heard from the women, and a report was circulated that the gallery had given way." † A high wind and a heavy fall of snow appear to have been the cause of the accident. A man and a woman were carried away, each with a broken leg, and some inconvenience was caused by thieves. That no lives were lost was always attributed by Mr. Spurgeon to providential interposition.

The increasing popularity of the pastor of New Park Street Chapel led to his services being more often sought for special occasions. Whatever may have been thought of him before he was fully " received " by the London ministers, it no longer answered to ignore a man as an adventurer who could achieve what was far beyond the power of any other living preacher. It occurred to the committee of the Baptist Missionary Society to ask Mr. Spurgeon to preach the annual sermon on behalf of their cause, and this he consented to do, the result being that the occasion surpassed anything that had ever been known in the history of the denomination. It was arranged for the service to be held in the Music Hall at the Surrey Gardens on Wednesday morning, April 28, and before the time for commencing the vast building was densely crowded with an expectant audience, who put £150 into the plates at the collection. Dr. Campbell, who would appear to have been present,

---

* *The British Standard,* February 12, 1858.   † *Ibid.,* April 16, 1858.

describes the meeting as " a magnificent affair." He also remarks that " the great preacher was, as usual, completely at home, full of heart, vivacity, and business." What a contrast the scene was to the anniversaries at Surrey Chapel in years before, when one or another leading minister gave a " great " sermon. " Mr. Spurgeon cannot devote weeks, if not months, to the preparation of such a sermon, and then take a fortnight's rest to recruit his strength before the great day. All his days are great, and they come in such rapid succession as to exclude the possibility of finish and elaboration, even if he aspired to it. But with him there is no aiming at greatness ; exhibition has no place in his thoughts. . . . In the proper sense he preaches, and preaches not to the ministers but to the people, and he has his reward." *

The sermon was founded on Psalm xlvi. 8, 9, " Come, behold the works of the Lord, what desolations He hath made in the earth. He breaketh the bow, and cutteth the spear in sunder ; He burneth the chariot in the fire." In opening his subject the preacher described what had already happened in the world, giving some account of the origin and progress of the society for which he pleaded. He then went on to speak of what would ultimately be achieved. As regarded the desolations which had happened from time to time in the world's history, all had in the course of God's good providence worked for good :—

"War and tumult were but the rough physic which God used to purge the world. As it was in the beginning, so should it be until the end ; the blood of their sisters would be avenged, not by the sword, but by the Gospel. In India the arm of God would be felt, the name of God would be acknowledged. Let them not, therefore, now tremble, for all things would work together for good. The preacher then called the attention of the audience to the desolations of false worship, passing in review the idolatry of Babylon and Assyria, observing that, to a large extent, their worship had been broken down, and they had become memorials of past ages. He then called their attention to the idols of Rome, remarking that they had long ago been cast to the moles and the bats. The attention of the audience was then called to the desolation God had made in false philosophy, noticing in order the various descriptions of infidelity, in the course of which he said he believed that he one day should see the last infidel buried, and at the funeral there would be some other person to start up a new system. This text, he said, had special reference to the desolations of war. If they went through the world, everywhere they would see what war had done and the desolations it had made. The people of India

* *The British Standard,* April 30, 1858.

should be subdued, not by the sword, but by the Gospel. The shot of the Gospel should be fired against them. The time he believed was coming when the statue of Nelson on the top of the monument would be upset, and that of Whitefield would be placed up instead; when the statue of Napier would be thrown down and John Wesley erected there. There was a day coming when every statue representing this world's greatness in London would be sold for old iron or old brass. They gave all honour to those men now, but these were the days of their ignorance; when the Gospel superseded them they would be enlightened, and they would then be forgotten. They were to look at the text as a prophecy that it was to be fulfilled. They were to look at the figure of the text. Some day he thought they would be awakened, and one would say to another, 'Come, behold the works of the Lord; what desolation He has made in the earth.' They would see their soldiers march rank and file and lay down their arms. Someone, he was sure, would see it; and happy he who was permitted to do so. The preacher closed with an earnest desire that all those churches who were not connected with the Baptist Missionary Society—and he knew there were many—would speedily become so. He thought there was not enough interest taken in missions. Many, he believed, never thought anything about them till the annual sermon was preached, when they, on that day, put the very smallest piece of coin—a threepenny-piece—in the plate. They liked the mission; but they were like the girl that never told her love; and when there was anything to be done they pinched and screwed the mouth of their purse to the smallest possible point. Mr. Spurgeon then referred to the want of missionaries for foreign lands, remarking on the various things they required. It was the want, he said, of true religion at home that prevented them from looking for any great success abroad. They wanted the brethren to be more earnest in prayer, more earnest in labour. He did agree with those who said the former days were better than these. They wanted an outpouring of the Divine Spirit at home. They were to begin to preach the Gospel at home and then go abroad; and then the Gospel would spread, like a sea of glory, from shore to shore." *

What was called "An Ecclesiastical Duty Day" came off on Friday, June 11, when Mr. Spurgeon preached in the saloon of the Grand Stand on Epsom racecourse on behalf of a chapel at Epsom. "The appearance of such a man in such a place is a new thing in the earth—another remarkable sign of the times," remarked Dr. Campbell. "We shall not be surprised next year to find Mr. Spurgeon a chief performer on the Derby Day! He is clearly born for deeds of daring, and nothing seems beyond his devout ambition, or above his singular powers." The day was long remembered as a remarkable one; about 1,500 persons attended at the afternoon and at the evening service, and a sum of £60 was collected for the chapel fund.

On Sunday, June 13, Henry M. Field, one of the editors of *The New York Evangelist*, visited the service at the Surrey Gardens, and of course sent home his impressions. Spurgeon was described

* *The British Standard*, April 30, 1858.

as "one of the lions of London—a rather young lion to be sure; but one who, since his appearance in the field, has roared so loudly as to make all the nation hear; and every stranger who wishes to 'do' the sights of Babylon, must, for once at least, see and hear him." The description of the preacher's appearance was by no means true to life; but justice was done to his matchless voice, which rang through the hall "like a clarion." The singing was especially grand on account of the multitude of voices. Before the sermon commenced a little scene occurred which must have awakened the sympathy of the whole assembly:—"Mr. Spurgeon announced that a telegraphic despatch had just been received, calling for a person who was supposed to be present, and who was summoned away by a severe domestic calamity. The man whose name had been called came forward much agitated to the pulpit, to receive the message."

The sermon was on the Wicked Man's Life, Funeral, and Epitaph, the text being Ecclesiastes viii. 10. The American visitor had gone to the service with some misgiving, but he came away perfectly reassured:—

"I had seen Mr. Spurgeon criticised and ridiculed in the English journals as a clerical mountebank, and I did not know but he might appear as a theatrical performer in the pulpit. But the critic who can deride Mr. Spurgeon as a charlatan must be insensible to any demonstrations of oratorical power. . . . The same evening we heard him again in his own chapel in New Park Street, and after the service we saw him in the vestry and had a very pleasant interview. I had a natural apprehension that he must be breaking down from excessive labour. But he assured me that he was in robust health. He said that his constant speaking was the best exercise for him, and that he should die if he did not preach ten or twelve times a week. I asked him when he found time to study, to which he replied that he could give but little preparation to his sermons, often entering the pulpit with not more than fifteen minutes' previous thought of his subject.

"But he has lately contrived to have some degree of leisure. He has taken a house out by Clapham Common, at several miles' distance from his church, to avoid interruptions. His deacons do all his visiting, and hence, in the intervals of his public duties, he is able to snatch a few hours for study and books. I suspect, too, that he has read largely in former years. He appears to be very familiar with the old divines, especially with Bunyan, whom he calls the greatest of Englishmen. . . . I think he would have been injured rather than benefited if he had been educated at one of the universities, and spent the years in studying Latin and Greek which he has turned to much better account in studying Bunyan and the people of England."

On July 2 we find Mr. Spurgeon again preaching in the pretty Cambridgeshire village of Melbourne, on behalf of the Baptist

Chapel, of which a young man, Mr. E. Bailey, educated in the College, and at that time not twenty years old, was the pastor. Tents were erected, and 600 persons sat down to tea, though the weather was unsettled. The services appear to have been held in the open air. About 3,000 assembled in the afternoon, and over double that number in the evening, when the text was, "Come, buy wine and milk, without money and without price." A year before, services had been held in Melbourne, and the collections for the great Tabernacle in London exceeded in amount any collection that had been made, with the single exception of that given at Sheffield. The success of young men like Mr. Bailey encouraged the founder of the Pastors' College to persevere in his enterprise.*

On Tuesday, July 6, Mr. Spurgeon was at St. James's Hall, where he preached the centenary sermon of the Orphan Working School, Haverstock Hill. At this time a report was circulated that the Music Hall at the Surrey Gardens was about to be opened for amusements on Sunday evenings, in which case, it was intimated, Mr. Spurgeon would refuse to use the hall in the morning. At the same time it would be necessary to find some other spacious place in which those who flocked in such multitudes to hear the Gospel could be accommodated; for the young pastor publicly announced at the Surrey Gardens that he would not attempt to preach at New Park Street more than once on the Sunday, and he even spoke of going to America if no suitable building were found for him at home. This called forth a letter from the manager of the Surrey Gardens Company, intimating that the directors had no intention of opening the great hall on Sundays for any other purpose than that of divine worship.†

During this summer an interesting visit to Ireland came off; and from particulars given by observers, Mr. Spurgeon's preaching was hardly more successful with the Irish of certain classes than it had been with the equally critical Highlanders. Dr. James Morgan, who

---

* *The Earthen Vessel,* xiv. 194.
† *The British Standard,* July 2, 1858.

was the pastor of Fisherwick Place Church, Belfast, attended several
of the services, and he remarks :—

"*August* 28.—We have had a visit from Mr. Spurgeon, of London. He preached four
times, and I heard him thrice, and must say I was not disappointed, although the mass of
the people were so. His sermons were sound and able, and interspersed with good and
appropriate anecdotes. There was sometimes more humour or drollery in them than suited
the solemnity of the pulpit. Still, one charm of his services lay in these. Had they not
been used, I question if his popularity would have been so great, or, indeed, have
existed at all. His elocution is very good, and his voice most admirable. When he
preached, as he did once, in the Botanic Gardens, he was well heard by 7,000 persons—the number said to have been present. I trust good results may be gathered from
his ministry. He was well received, and deserved to be so, for his plain, honest, and good
preaching and deportment. I much question, however, if his influence was so good as that
of Mr. Guinness, who preceded him by a few months. There was a great contrast between
them. Mr. Spurgeon was gay, lively, and humorous ; but Mr. Guinness was solemn and
earnest and very reserved. Mr. Spurgeon is by far the abler man. Yet were there a
poll to-morrow in Belfast for the two, it would be in favour of Mr. Guinness. Deep
seriousness and earnestness go far—very far. I have no doubt they were very prominent
in our blessed Lord. I have traced happy and gracious results to the ministry of Mr.
Guinness." *

On the last Sunday of September, Mr. Spurgeon was able to
acquaint his congregation with the fact that at length a site, near
the "Elephant and Castle," had been secured for the new Tabernacle,
for which the owners, the Fishmongers' Company, would receive a
sum of £5,000, so that it was desirable for all to continue their
efforts in collecting for the building fund. While all were thus
working for the erection of a house in which the multitude could
hear the Gospel in London, it must have been a great joy to the
young preacher to know that a chapel suitable to the needs of the
villagers was being erected at Teversham, where, only about seven
years before, he had preached his first sermon. Another cause of
satisfaction at this time was the success of Mr. James Spurgeon, who
was attracting very large congregations in the North of England, and
who, some thought, would become as popular as his brother.

As regarded the chapel at Teversham, a desire was expressed to
undertake the enterprise in the year 1855, but the design was not
completed until 1858. It was proposed that the little sanctuary
should be named Spurgeon Chapel; but when that was mentioned
to Mr. Spurgeon he did not at all fall in with the idea. In reply

* "Recollections of My Life and Times," by James Morgan, D.D., pp. 314-315.

to an invitation to preach at the opening in September—the suggestion of the name being also mentioned in the letter—the following reply was received by the secretary:—

"Clapham, August 7, 1858.

"My Dear Brother—

"There is a little mistake somewhere about opening the chapel at Teversham. I told Mr. Vinter that I would preach there to clear off any debt that might remain, but I never thought of *opening* it. September is long since *over* with me as to any promises or engagements. I am prepared, however, to give a service, say in the summer of next year, on that account; as to the name, that was but a freak of my fancy. It is true there are one or two chapels here and there which I have mainly built, and these bear the builder's name, but this was done by French leave and without any desire on my part.

"I feel a veneration for the *old house* in which I first preached, and I confess I am silly enough to believe that the fact will not be forgotten, but I have no desire to have that commemorated which will not be forgotten. Treat that as one of my jokes, and, above all things, *do not do it*; especially as some stronger brethren would not like it.— I am, ever yours truly,

"C. H. Spurgeon."*

As already intimated, it was in the fall of this year that Mr. Spurgeon was overtaken with the first serious illness since his coming to London. He preached at the Surrey Gardens on Sunday, October 10, but did not occupy the pulpit there again until November 7. Meanwhile, very alarming reports were current concerning the gravity of the crisis. It was evident that the preacher had been drawing too heavily on his strength, and that the breakdown was the result of overwork. "We confess to the most entire and intense sympathy in this matter," wrote Dr. Campbell. "The accounts we heard were of so grave a nature that we could not rest satisfied without making special inquiry, which, we regret to say, resulted in the confirmation of nearly all that we had heard; but we rejoice to add, it was also found that the worst was apparently past, and that there is now good ground for hope for a perfect, although it may be a slow, recovery. The marvel is not that Mr. Spurgeon, unparalleled in the present century, should at length have been reminded that with all his mental and moral might and physical capability, he is still mortal."† A few days later the sufferer was reported to be rapidly gaining strength; and on the first Sunday in

* Original in possession of Mr. George Apthorpe, of Cambridge.
† *The British Standard*, October 29, 1858.

November the familiar voice was once more heard ringing through the Surrey Gardens Hall.

By this time the site for the new chapel had cost altogether £5,400, and a large board erected on the spot invited subscriptions. On Monday evening, December 13, a tea-meeting to report progress, at which 900 persons sat down, was held at New Park Street Chapel. A sum of nearly £10,000 had been collected. The congratulations on Mr. Spurgeon's recovery were many, and all rejoiced that, after very tedious negotiations, a freehold site had been secured. It is curious to find thus early the question being asked, "What would become of the great Tabernacle if the pastor should die?" One who was present answered, "That the same God who had sent Mr. Spurgeon would send his successor." Mr. Spurgeon himself said:—

"I do not feel in speaking order to-night, because I feel to have something in my heart so big that I am not able to get it out, and I do not think I can add anything to what has already been said. I cannot, however, resist the temptation of saying a few words on a topic which you may think far remote from the object of the meeting. The times in which we live are most wonderful; and I wish that this church should be in the future what it has been in the past—the advance-guard of the times. I cannot help observing that during the last four or five years a wonderful change has come over the Christian mind. The Church of England has been awakened. How has this been accomplished' and what means have been used? Great services have been held. I cannot help remembering that God honoured us to let us stand in the front of this great movement. From our example the blessed fire has run along the ground and kindled a blaze, which shall not soon be extinguished. When I first heard that clergymen were to preach in Exeter Hall, my soul leaped within me, and I was ready to exclaim, 'Lord, now lettest thou thy servant depart in peace.' When I heard that Westminster Abbey was opened for the preaching of the Gospel, and then St. Paul's Cathedral, I was overwhelmed with gratitude, and prayed that only the truth as it is in Jesus might be preached in these places; that the ministers might travail in birth for souls; that Christ might be found in them the hope of glory. I never felt such a union to the Church of England as I now do. The fact is, that when a youth in the country, I was accustomed to associate with the name of clergyman that of fox-hunting and such-like; I abhorred them, for I thought they were all like that. Now I see them anxious to win souls to Christ, and I love them. I can't help loving them; and as long as they go on to feel the value of souls I shall continue to pray for them. Now, seeing that the Lord has thus honoured us, we must lead on; our movements are observed and we must not take one step backwards. We must progress with our movements. I don't like to hear anything said in our disparagement; we must still lead the van. What if God should spread the late revival, and let the New Park Street Church still go on as the advanced guard? Now, as to the Tabernacle. I am quite certain that it will be built, and that I shall preach in it; and I have no doubt that the money will be forthcoming—that is no burden to me. Some of you have done a very great deal, but you ought to have done a very great deal more. There are others who, if measured by 'oughts,' ought not to have done so much, while others have spared themselves and kept their unholy mammon. Yet we have not done so badly after all; for after purchasing the site we have a balance in hand of £3,600. I hope that you will all agree that the spot is a most eligible one; though some recommended Kensington, others Holloway, and others Clapham." *

The year 1858 thus came to a close happily. The future was bright with promise. Eventually one friend in the west gave £5,000 to the building fund, while another lent a large sum free of interest, so that there should be no difficulty in paying the accounts.

* *The Baptist Messenger*, viii. 165. The account of this meeting does not appear in all copies of the magazine.

CHAPTER XXXIV.

" DE PROPAGANDA FIDE."

ON Tuesday evening, January 4, 1859, I had the happiness of being one of the crowd that had assembled at Exeter Hall to hear Mr. Spurgeon's lecture to the Young Men's Christian Association entitled "De Propaganda Fide." The winter course of lectures had opened on November 17, the 300th anniversary of the accession of Queen Elizabeth, and taken as a whole the series appeared to be of somewhat exceptional interest. The appearance of the name of the young preacher of the Surrey Gardens Music Hall among the other literary or reverend magnates whose services had been secured awakened very general curiosity. This was partly accounted for by the fact that Mr. Spurgeon would appear in a new character, for since his coming to London he had not ventured to appear before the public as a lecturer. Then the title of his lecture struck people as being quite as odd as the circumstance of his lecturing at all. He was asked, " How on earth came you to choose a Latin title for your lecture ? " Others who took even a more serious view of the matter asked, " What does he know about Latin ? " adding with the authority of well-informed observers, " He may know a little about Saxon, but of Latin he knows nothing." Still, the lecturer, who had already begun to have more confidence in his own judgment than in that of his critics, thought there was wisdom in the phrase ; and evidently he did not care to have it altogether monopolised by the Roman Catholic missionaries. Hence, when he had consented to speak to the young men of London, and was asked what the subject would be, he at once replied, "De Propaganda Fide!"

The lectures had all been well attended; but no one present on this occasion could ever forget the extra excitement and the additional crowding. Long before the time of opening the doors the crowd was assembled, and the stairs leading to the great hall were blocked by the eager and expectant audience. When he came on to the platform, Mr. Spurgeon was perhaps even more cordially received than usual, for he had only recently recovered from what had been the most severe illness from which he had ever suffered. It was meet, also, to give some rounds of cheers, expressive of a little extra enthusiasm, when a young man of twenty-four was about to enter upon a new department of service. Never did a popular orator, in face of a vast audience, appear to be more self-possessed. Mr. Robert Bevan occupied the chair, and sitting beside him were such well-known personages as Dr. Campbell, Lord Ebury, the Hon. A. Kinnaird, Mr. George Hitchcock, and others.

Mr. Spurgeon remarked at the outset that he felt he should have to give a sermon, such being the force of habit in one who had contracted a strong habit of preaching; but the subject was so far a convenient one that if he wandered from it the people would be able to say that he did not understand his title. The first thing to be done was to explain what was meant by the Propagation of the Faith, a question which needed to be answered, first negatively and then positively:—

"By the Propagation of the Faith he did not mean the nominal Christianity of nations; to bring people merely nominally under the bond of the Covenant was nothing. It was in vain they were Baptists, and had Christian names given them—Chaos made way for John, or Lucius was displaced for Mary. While the Spirit of God was not in it, all was useless. The Romanists tried this, but all in vain. If it were possible to-morrow to gather all Mahomedans and heathens to bow down to the name of Christ; if they could dash down the Crescent and exalt the Cross; if all the gods of the heathen should be displaced by the idolatries of Rome, Christianity would not be advanced one inch. The Propagation of the Faith meant nothing of that sort. Nor did he mean the bringing of large numbers to make a profession of love to Christ, however pleasant that might be in the eyes of a pastor. There were some churches, he regretted to say, which, in the paroxysms of a revival, relaxed the discipline, and were not so cautious as to the character, motives, and habits of those who applied for admission, as they otherwise would have been. Now it was, indeed,

of small account that they should multiply their churches, unless they were genuine
Christians—if they had not the grace of God in their hearts, they were better out than
in. For the effect of such a course was perilous in the extreme; first, it was a
sedative to the mind of those who embraced the fallacy; it was a kind of armour with
which these persons surrounded themselves when addressed as sinners : 'Oh, we are members
of a Christian church.' Again, addition was not always increase. They might add much of
the wrong materials, then the Church was not increased, but adulterated; they would break
her down, not enlarge her; have defiled her, not increased her. The wider the gulf could
be kept between the Church and the world, the better. He did not mean by the Propagation of the Faith the mere conversion of people from one sect to another. When the
Church was increased, she must be increased from the world, and not from herself. Any.
one could see that. He had heard of an American who was so cute that he had made ten
per cent. on his money by putting it out of one pocket into the other. He was sure they
could not increase the Church by simply taking them out of one church into the other.
If a regiment of cavalry wanted recruits, that sergeant would be a fool, and would perpetrate a robbery on her Majesty, were he to recruit from the infantry. Perhaps the army
might be greatly improved by removing men from one section to another as a last resource,
but to look at that first was the very height of folly. First they must 'go out into the
highways and compel them to come in and fill the place.' They were to bring them to the
Bible, and after that set the other matters right. To bring up their sectarianism at the
present time would be absurd. If in the great movements for the cause of Christ they
should say, 'Whose shall these be—shall they belong to the Episcopalians, Presbyterians, or
Independents?' it would be useless to strive for the Propagation of the Faith. No, they
should rather say they shall belong to Christ first, and then let them, as shepherds,
take some little trouble to put them into the best pastures fully suited to them. The
Propagation of the Faith was a person. They might ask one another's religion, but he
would reply, the Gospel was a person—something solid on which they could rest. If the
twelve apostles had been asked what their faith was, they would have replied, not in a long
sermon, but by pointing to Christ, whose life was the Alpha and Omega of the Christian,
and save in which no summary of Christianity could be obtained."

Thus to spread abroad the faith was to diffuse a knowledge of
Christ; it was not an affair of cold logic, but of the heart. William
Huntington and John Wesley represented the extremes; but who
would dare to say that each did not effect great good? The lecturer
then went on to take a review of Christian work as it was at that
time, and to give some sort of an answer to the question, Was it
declining or progressing?—

"There were many favourable signs, but there were many others unfavourable. The most
favourable, perhaps, was the immense congregations assembling every Sabbath day to hear
the Word of God. If only seven years ago they had been told that St. Paul's Cathedral
would have been crowded every Sabbath evening, and Ludgate Hill blocked up, they would
have disbelieved it. A pleasing feature in this had been the unity of all denominations.
Nor was this all. He believed that all the Churches were more awake than ever they had
been. He often wanted to steal a march on his brethren, but was unable. He wanted to
do something new, something attractive; but before his idea was matured it was commenced
elsewhere. In every district it was the same, and nothing was so conducive to spiritual
progression; it was a neck-and-neck race who should do most good. Another good thing
was the increased unity of the Church. The objects the Evangelical Alliance had been

hammering at for so many years were achieved. The Dissenter thought the Churchman might have retained him if, in bygone times, the latter had been more gentle. Let them, however, now cease to talk of men being out of their pales; they should have no pale faces at all, but all be healthy and in unison. There was one thing he did not like in the special services, and that was the taking of things for texts not in Holy Scriptures. Let every man do as he chose; but he did think his brethren might find enough in the Bible alone for their use. It seemed to him a degradation, to say nothing else, of God's truth. All he knew was, that if some preachers had attempted this a few years ago, they would have been scouted as infidels. Then again there was the subject of prayer meetings. He knew there were still some large assemblies, nor did he think that the Spirit of God was not useful in them; but he was afraid to speak of their ordinary meetings, he knew they were very poor affairs. Again, preaching was faulty; the preacher lacked earnestness; he was not like Baxter, who spoke—

> 'As though he ne'er should speak again,
> As dying man to dying men.'

Again, in the Church itself there were faults; they were too worldly; there were among them men who would not keep open their shops on Sunday for fear of damnation, but who would yet hold shares in a railway whose dividends were made out of Sunday traffic— who would shrink from any false action in private, but who needed looking after when they and a few others got together."

The matter of worldly conformity was then touched upon, and it was thought that there was too much of it among Christian people. Mr. Spurgeon did not profess to be a Quaker in the matter of dress, to favour the " broad brim," and so on ; but nevertheless he found some satisfaction in looking back on the days when a Christian could be known, not only by the cut of his coat, but by his very brogue. He then made reference to the old Quakers, and to the then prevailing fashion of extended crinoline petticoats. " I would rather dress myself that way "—*i.e.*, like a Quaker— " than I would wear the things some men do ; and I would rather see my sisters in Christ habited as the Quakers, than that they should magnify, enlarge, and increase themselves as they now do." This produced a commotion of approval on the part of the men which seemed as though it would never end, and, as one remarked, it ought to have put an end to such a fashion. In a leading article on the meeting Dr. Campbell remarked, " The stroke was the most electric one ever witnessed in that hall. The ladies who were present —and the number was not inconsiderable—were placed in a plight most pitiable. The good-natured, yet deeply derisive, cheering was tremendous, and long, very long, continued. If that vast assembly

U

might be taken as a fair representation of the young men of England
—and we believe there can be no doubt of it—the ladies of the
nation stand reprehended, laughed at, and ridiculed by gentlemen
from John O'Groats to the Land's End." *

This matter of dress was regarded as an indication of there
being something wrong; but as the ladies appeared "to have had
enough of it," the lecturer went on to show that as the prophecies
were sure, the triumph of the faith was sure. They must all do
their part; individuals must work as such; and it mattered nothing
whether the preachers came from the colleges or from St. Giles's.
A somewhat gloomy view was taken of the work abroad. One
thing he never could bear or tolerate, and that was the argument
used whenever England went to war, "It was a providential opening
for the Gospel." For his own part, he could not understand how
the Devil could make way for Christ. What was war but the
incarnation of all that was wicked and fiendish? To

> "Cry havoc and let slip the dogs of war,"

and then say that this was to make straight a highway, knee-deep
in the gore of human beings, for the truth of the Lord, was a
monstrosity. God assuredly did evolve good out of evil, but he
confessed he could not see how war ever made a way for Christianity.
Let any other nation go to war if it chose, and if England then
sent missionaries, all well; she was not then accountable for the
devastation, not having caused it; but for an English cannon to
make way at Canton for an English missionary was a falsehood too
glaring for him to believe. He could not, he confessed, make it
out. If other nations would go to war, let them; but he blushed
for his countrymen when he saw crimes committed in China—for
what was the opium traffic but a crime, an enormous crime, out of
which a war arose?—regarded as means by which the Gospel was
to be forwarded. If he were a Chinaman he would assuredly ask
the missionaries what this Christianity was like—was it anything
of the opium sort? It was not this sort of propagation that foreign

* *The British Standard*, January 7, 1859.

countries required for the propagation of the faith; they must learn to feel and believe that England loved peace; that the English nation did not delight in blood, and that its only desire was—in return for the liberty with which God had blessed it—to maintain that liberty abroad; and that if the lion was sometimes roused it was not for blood, but because it believed it was bound to defend liberty. If the world believed that, England would be everywhere regarded as the defender of the liberties of the race; but whatever they did, let them put an end to this doctrine of "opening up" places to missions. He must, however, confess that the spirit was inherent in the English nation; it was of a pugnacious spirit. If he was passing along the street and saw two boys or two dogs fighting, he always felt disposed to stand and look on, and admire the stronger in both cases.

At the close of his address, Mr. Spurgeon was cheered with a good deal of enthusiasm, and it was generally thought that he had well maintained his prestige in the new character in which he had appeared. The discourse was characterised as being neither lecture nor sermon, and yet, for that occasion, something better than either.

Observers of Mr. Spurgeon's growth and progress in the Christian graces thought that he had made some advances since the illness which had overtaken him in the fall of 1858. In earlier days it had been remarked that he had shown the strength of Whitefield without that great preacher's tenderness or pathos. A change for the better had been observed in the Music Hall services, and also in the course of the "De Propaganda Fide" lecture. He seemed anxious to speak a good word to all classes while he condemned abuses and bad customs.

At or about this time Mr. Spurgeon was expecting to be able to make a tour through the United States, and the Americans were eagerly anticipating the expected visit. "Mr. Spurgeon is as much an object of interest in the United States as in his native land, and there is an intense desire to see him," remarked one journal. "Our readers must not be surprised should they shortly hear that an offer has been made him of £10,000 to preach four discourses in the splendid and spacious music hall of New York."* Later in the year *The Baptist Messenger*, which was then regarded as the organ of New Park Street Chapel, announced as a fact that the American trip would be undertaken, but the next month it was given out that the journey was abandoned "for the present year." Everybody thought that the visit was only postponed. " It is probable that he will by-and-by cross the Atlantic, but it will be on a wholly independent footing."†

When money was so urgently needed to pay the builder of the great Tabernacle, would it not have been easier to preach four times in New York for the magnificent honorarium the Americans offered, than toilsomely to travel about the British Isles making small collections? Mr. Spurgeon acted quite unselfishly in the matter. If he had secured any princely sum from the New World, he would not have used even a small portion of the amount for himself; all would have been given to the building fund ; and if the collections were small at home, he still had the satisfaction of preaching the Gospel to a far larger number of people.

If it was not advisable to cross the Atlantic, something might be got in Scotland; and, accordingly, in February, 1859, another visit was paid to the North. At this time there was considerable excitement in the country on the question of Reform, the Administration of the then Earl of Derby having a Bill in hand which

---

* *The British Standard*, January 7, 1859.

† *Ibid.*, March 4. I may here remark that the expected visit of the English preacher was being looked forward to in America with increased eagerness on account of the great revival which was then sweeping through the United States. The late John Angell James published a letter from an American friend, of which he said :—"It should be particularly noticed that this letter is the testimony, not of an enthusiast, or man of an impulsive mind or heated imagination, but of a cool, philosophic temperament. He writes from Boston, probably the most intellectual of the Transatlantic cities, the headquarters of Unitarianism ; and yet he tells us that a revival has taken place in America which has resulted in the hopeful conversion of half a million souls." Another writer remarked :— "Under these circumstances, the visit of the Rev. C. H. Spurgeon will be looked forward to with intense interest. He is to leave England early in April, and will preach at Rochester, and at Boston or Philadelphia, as well as at New York. It is true that Mr. Spurgeon had the offer of £10,000, as announced in the newspapers, but he preferred to go untrammelled." —*The Sunday at Home*, 1859, p. 128.

promised to be of more than usual interest as the production of a
Conservative Government. Accordingly, the discourse at the Surrey
Gardens on Sunday, February 13, was on *Reform;* but it was so
far from being a political sermon that its leading ideas had nothing
in common with the comprehensive scheme which Mr. Disraeli propounded in the House of Commons twelve days later. Mr. Spurgeon's
Reform was sufficiently indicated by his text (2 Chron. xxxi. 1), "Now
when all this was finished, all Israel that were present went out to
the cities of Judah, and brake the images in pieces, and cut down
the groves, and threw down the high places and the altars out of
all Judah and Benjamin, in Ephraim also and Manasseh, until they
had utterly destroyed them all." On the following Sunday the
familiar voice was not heard in the Music Hall; Mr. Spurgeon was
preaching in Scotland, where he secured nearly £500 for the building
fund of the Tabernacle.

The Scottish tour, with its preaching engagements, occupied about
all the week-days of a fortnight, the services being held chiefly in
Edinburgh and Glasgow. On his return, before commencing his
sermon, the preacher remarked that he had been addressing large
assemblies, and that the Spirit of God had been present to bless. Mr.
Spurgeon remarked further, "In visiting the North, the main object
I had in view was the assistance of the fund for the new building
which we propose erecting for the accommodation of the crowds who
flock to hear me Sabbath after Sabbath. It always was and always
will be my constant care to obtain the requisite sum, and I think
I may faithfully appeal to your sympathies to help forward the
project. The building would have been erected long ago if everyone who attends my ministry had acted as they ought to have done.
If each would give the smallest sum, it would not be long before a
building was raised where God's truth would be proclaimed for ages
to come."

It was no small matter for a preacher who had such a congregation as that at the Surrey Gardens to be away from his pulpit for
only one Sunday; but it was not expected to happen again soon,

and when it did occur the greatest possible care was taken to obtain a suitable supply. The crowd showed no signs of falling off; eminent personages were still present, while "carriages and vehicles of all sorts, as usual, thronged the surrounding thoroughfares."

Meanwhile the young preacher's popularity was tested in various ways, and it became increasingly evident that it was growing rather than declining. On Tuesday, March 1, at noon, he attracted a full house at Whitefield's Tabernacle, Moorfields, the service being on behalf of the London City Mission. In the evening he preached again in the same place for the same object, when the crowd was so overwhelming that "to prevent conflict and confusion at the doors the gates were early closed."

With such a vast enterprise in hand as the building of the great Tabernacle for his own congregation, however, Mr. Spurgeon at last found it advisable to alter his methods somewhat; and it was announced, therefore, that it was the young pastor's wish to appear in the principal chapels in London, first for the purpose of preaching the Gospel, and then of collecting funds on behalf of the vast undertaking.

The influence of Mr. Spurgeon was now being felt in various ways in all evangelical denominations; and welcome evidence was seen in the great "special services for the working classes" which were becoming fashionable. The outcry, which could even make itself heard in Parliament, that the Church itself was being "Spurgeonised," found little or no sympathy with the public. St. Paul's, Westminster Abbey, Exeter Hall, and St. James's Hall each attracted a full congregation, some leading man preaching in each instance. These services were spoken of as representing a most re-markable feature of English religious life, and as being an evidence of progress. The movement then extended to ordinary parish churches, and the wonder was not so much that full congregations assembled as that the working classes and the poorer kind of people generally were actually attracted. Thus, when the late Dr. Tait, as Bishop of London, preached in a West-end parish church, the vicar was able to report : "All St. Giles's turned out. The church as full as it could hold ; all the doorways and middle aisle blocked up with persons standing, and many had to go away. Every variety of the labouring class was here this evening." *

On June 26 a violent thunderstorm passed over the southern suburbs of London ; a tree was struck by lightning on Clapham Common, and a man who had sought shelter from the rain beneath the branches was killed. It occurred to Mr. Spurgeon that an effective way of impressing people with the solemnity of this occurrence would be to give a sermon on the spot and make a collection for the widow of the deceased, for whom much sympathy was felt. Accordingly, a notice was circulated to the effect that the pastor of New Park Street Chapel would address whoever liked to come beneath the fatal tree at three o'clock on Sunday, July 10. About 10,000 persons assembled, the preacher being accommodated with a wagon for a pulpit. After a striking prayer, Psalm C. was sung to the Old Hundredth tune, and the discourse was founded on the words, "Be ye also ready." The collection for the distressed widow, whose fourth child was only a few weeks old, amounted to £27 10s. 4d· A deep impression was evidently produced; and as the great concourse quietly dispersed, much sympathy was expressed with the object of the meeting, and all appeared to be thoroughly well pleased.†

* *The Sunday at Home*, 1859, p. 127.—"We certainly live (as our fathers and grand-fathers before us would have said) in extraordinary times. As regards the immense amount of preaching, we surely shall not err if we say there never were such days before. The Puseyites have opened Westminster Abbey for Sunday evening services; it is full to over-flowing. The aristocratic Dissenters have opened Exeter Hall for the same purpose; it is crowded to excess. Mr. Spurgeon, as everybody knows, has opened the Surrey Gardens Music Hall; and he keeps it full from top to toe. Besides this, we have in our part of the metropolis, preaching stations and lecture-halls almost in every street; forsooth, we say, we ought to be very good people nowadays. Every denomination seems to be on the stretch to do its utmost to gather up, and to get in the masses to hear something; the days are surely come when the prophecy is fulfilled—'Many shall run to and fro, and knowledge shall be increased.'"—*The Earthen Vessel*, xiv. 45.

† *The Christian Cabinet*, July 20, 1859.

CHAPTER XXXV.

THE METROPOLITAN TABERNACLE.

Interest in the Great Chapel—Laying the Foundation-stone—Speeches of the Pastor and
several Eminent Personages.

SOON after the work of collecting funds for the great Tabernacle
was commenced, prizes appear to have been offered for designs,
the building committee selecting the one which would be adopted.
After a large number had been examined, the design which gave most
satisfaction bore the motto, " Quod erat faciendum "—*Which was to be
done.* Mr. Pococke was the architect. A large number of designs
were sent in, for three of which, I believe, premiums were given.

When it was generally known that a large chapel was really to
be built for the young preacher, great popular interest in the
enterprise at once showed itself. The novelty of such an enterprise occasioned it to be written of and talked about in a way that
the present generation would hardly understand. It was "a mammoth undertaking," "a denominational wonder," and in a sense a
new thing under the sun, peculiar to the times.

While things were thus progressing in London as the best friends
of Mr. Spurgeon desired, things were also happening elsewhere such
as could not fail to gladden his heart. While the foundations of
the Metropolitan Tabernacle were being dug, a subscription had been
commenced at Southampton towards the fund for the enlarging of
Portland Chapel, of which Mr. James Archer Spurgeon was pastor.
The chapel was so excessively crowded that numbers were compelled
to leave the doors on Sunday evenings. At this time also took place
the conversion and baptism of Thomas Cooper, the ex-Chartist, who
had travelled up and down the country as a Free-thought lecturer.
The Radical politician and Mr. Spurgeon became good friends, and

from time to time Mr. Cooper gave lectures at the Pastors' College which tutors and students heartily appreciated.

The land on which the Metropolitan Tabernacle is erected was purchased, as has been said, from the Fishmongers' Company; and it had been the site of almshouses which the Company had put up in the seventeenth and eighteenth centuries. The main building was called St. Peter's Hospital, and this, as an asylum of the Fishmongers' Company, has been re-erected at Wandsworth. The forsaken ground was an uninviting spot until the new buildings were erected upon it.

The preliminary services in connection with the ceremony of laying the foundation-stone were commenced at New Park Street Chapel on Monday evening, August 15, when the prayers were offered and addresses given by Mr. Spurgeon and his father—the latter being at that time under fifty years of age—and others. There was another prayer meeting on Tuesday morning, the 16th. About three thousand persons attended the ceremony in the afternoon, and most of them were in their places by two o'clock. There was little or no display with flags and decorations. One inscription on white calico—the letters being formed by laurel leaves—was, " CHRIST IS THE CORNER-STONE ; " and one other ornamented with evergreen boughs read, " YOU ARE TRULY WELCOME." Mr. Spurgeon called on the audience to " raise a glorious song of praise to the God of heaven by singing to the Old Hundredth tune the hymn, ' Before Jehovah's awful throne.' "

The crowd appeared to show more than ordinary interest in the stone-laying ceremony. Sir S. Morton Peto, who occupied the place of honour, was cheered with some enthusiasm. Mr. B. Carr read a history of the church from the beginning, which he had himself prepared ; and although " the reading of this admirable document elicited frequent and hearty cheers," it was no doubt a relief when the reader came to the end, and so made way for Mr. Spurgeon to come forward with a bottle to be deposited beneath the stone. As something lighter was needed after the literary elder's solid historical statement, Mr. Spurgeon was equal to the occasion :—

"This bottle contains not the current coins of the realm; for we have none of them to spare. It contains no newspapers, for, however much we may appreciate the newspaper Press, we still think it inappropriate to place papers in such a place. It contains the Bible, the old-fashioned Baptist Confession of Faith, which was signed by Benjamin Keach, your former pastor; the declaration of the deacons which you have heard read, written on parchment; an edition of Dr. Rippon's Hymn Book, as published before he died; and lastly a programme of this day's proceedings. These will be for the perusal of the New Zealander who is to sit on the ruins of London Bridge, when this great nation has gone to decay—if ever it does so; and if such is the case, I have no doubt that they will eventually be stored up in some Australian or American Museum."

At that time Sir Morton Peto was a man of commanding influence among the Baptists, and was otherwise generally respected on account of the liberality with which he subscribed to philanthropic enterprises. To the worthy baronet it was like entering on a new era; and after showing that the new building was a necessity, he went on to say that he rejoiced to hear that the church, though strictly denominational, would be in no respect sectarian. While believing that there was no other mode of baptism than that prefigured in the Scriptures—being buried with Christ in baptism—his friend, Mr. Spurgeon, would at the same time proclaim that truth in such a spirit that all who might differ from him would only regret the difference, while they loved him not the less. He wished also to state to his Christian friends that this church would not only be their church, but would be a point from which Christian influence would radiate to the furthest ends of the world. His friend, in preaching the Gospel there, would not forget upon every fitting occasion to urge the claims of the heathen upon the attention of his church; and he rejoiced to know that while the hearts of the congregation would be sufficiently expansive to grasp the whole world, those who were perishing at our own doors would not be forgotten or neglected. There was a great work yet to be done, and many who were connected with other churches had gladly come to their aid and assured them that they would do all in their power to assist them in their undertaking. He could not but rejoice that this would be something of a cathedral to his denomination. It was quite right that they should have a Tabernacle in which not only the largest congregation could assemble, but which should, when schemes of Christian usefulness were to be promoted, be placed at the disposal of persons of any other denomination. This Metropolitan Tabernacle would therefore have claims upon other denominations. Those whom he addressed had a large and heavy burden to bear, and they were delighted to bear it, because it enabled them to evidence their love to Christ; still he could not but feel that Mr. Spurgeon and his deacons had a very strong claim for assistance upon all other Christian churches of the metropolis and of the kingdom at large; and he trusted that when Mr. Spurgeon ascended the pulpit for the first time, he would be able, while preaching a full, free, and finished salvation, to say that he did so in a chapel entirely free from debt.

Mr. Spurgeon complimented the baronet by saying that that was not the first time he had borrowed light from him, as he once received from him a reading-lamp which had often enabled him to read while on long railway journeys. All had reason to be satisfied with the receipts of the afternoon; for one anonymous friend at Bristol had sent a cheque for £3,000 to be laid upon the stone, in addition to which others gave £1,000 each. The speech of the occasion was, of course, that in course of which Mr. Spurgeon himself referred to the enterprise in hand:—

"I never answer slanders against myself, and very seldom answer any questions about them whatever, and I never mean to do so. When I have done wrong, it is always enough for me to have my own condemnation. I am quite satisfied with that, although I have plenty. If I am wrong, I will be accountable to my own Master, and to no other person living or breathing. This place, I said some time ago, when our brethren were half afraid —It is to be built, and God will fill it with His presence. There is no doubt about the money being raised. I have a solid conviction that the money must come. I give my hearty thanks to all that have helped me, and to all that have not helped me—they all mean to do so, and therefore I will thank them beforehand. There is one gentleman who is going to speak after Mr. Dowson, and the best speech will be made with his hands. He will give a donation of £3,000. He would not like me to mention his name, and therefore I shall not do so. And now, my dear friends, the place that is to be erected—I have a word to say about it. It is a matter of congratulation to me that in this city we should build a Grecian place of worship. It seems to me that there are two sacred languages in the world. There was the Hebrew of old; there is only one other sacred language—the Greek, and that is dear to every Christian's heart. We believe in the five great points commonly known as Calvinistic. We look upon them as being five great lights which radiate from the cross of Christ. I like to preach pure Gospel truth; but still, at the same time, I am no Antinomian, I belong not to that sect that is afraid to exhort the sinner to Christ; and while we are Baptists also—and we cannot swerve from that—we must have one Lord, one faith, and one baptism, and dear to our hearts is that word—the communion of saints. Whosoever loves the Lord Jesus Christ in spirit and in truth has a hearty welcome to communion with the Church of Christ. I see around us our Independent brethren, and I see also before me a Strict Communion brother, and he will address you. I have some of my dearest friends ministers of the Church of England, and I glory in the fact that, however firmly a man may hold the truth, he can give his hand to every man that loves Jesus Christ. And now with regard to our prospects. We are about to build this place, and I hope it will be paid for; and if our friends do but give well now, then when the chapel is built, those of our friends who want seats can buy them. There is not a chapel in London used up as ours is; they always hack it up; they say, We will hear all we can, and they never give me a chance of getting into the seats. Our brother told us last evening that churches should be like a man who milked the cow, and after she was milked she was so fond of it that she wanted to be milked twice a day. God sparing my life, I will not rest till the dark county of Surrey be filled with places of worship. It is only within the last six months we have started two churches, one in Wandsworth and the other in Greenwich, and we will do so to the one hundredth time, God being our helper."

After the stone-laying ceremony was over, and after the young pastor had himself thanked each contributor who came forward with a gift, between two and three thousand persons adjourned to tea in the adjoining Horse Repository. The great repast was served without hitch or confusion; and the otherwise not very inviting interior was decorated with flags and flowers, mottoes and illuminated lamps, until it presented quite a pleasing appearance. By the time that the Lord Mayor arrived to take the chair at the evening meeting, the popular enthusiasm was shown by the great crowd in the street which was eager to enter the already well-filled building. After the hearty cheers which greeted him had subsided, the Lord Mayor (the late Alderman Wire) referred to the advances made since olden times, and said he looked on Mr. Spurgeon as one who was called to accomplish a great work for God.

When the pastor looked round on his friends on that memorable day, he saw a strong muster; but while James Grant, of *The Morning Advertiser*, was present, Dr. Campbell was unfortunately absent, having made another engagement on the understanding that that meeting was postponed. Mr. Spurgeon thought that, as an editor, his friend had lived long enough not to believe things which he saw in the papers:—

"At any rate, my friend ought not to believe in those paragraphs unless he knows of his own knowledge that they are true. For my own part, I only wish I could compel the papers to make good their statements except when they are abusing me. Some of the papers have discovered that a magnificent fortune has been left to me, of which, however, I have myself no knowledge whatever. . . . I approve of ministers getting a good salary for preaching; and in this respect I would cordially say I am, for my own part, perfectly satisfied; but if anyone should leave ministers a large sum of money, they generally lose their voice or get an attack of bronchitis, or something of the sort, which puts an end to their preaching."

Mr. Spurgeon added, in regard to the Press, that he cared not how he was attacked, or his doctrines combated; he would come out all the stronger for opposition: it was when the newspapers praised him and friends surrounded him that tears came into his eyes, and he felt the more need of divine support.

To notice all the speeches that were made on the occasion would too greatly extend this chapter; but some were too important to be altogether passed by. Thus, the father of the young pastor, who was a comparatively young man himself, confessed that he was there to acknowledge a fault. He had thought that his son had done wrong in not going to college, and again in coming to London; but he now saw that God had opened the way. The speaker continued:— "This is one of the happiest days of my life. I feel beyond myself when I think of the kindness shown to my son when but a youth; and I ask all to go home and pray that God will preserve him from temptation. A meeting like this is enough to carry any man away, but the grace of God is all-sufficient. Several told me that my son would not do in London; he had not sufficient education; but he had, after all, the best education, for God had been his teacher. If anything could have crowned my happiness, it would have been to see my son's grandfather present. He is always speaking about him."

Mr. Spurgeon senior then told the anecdote about the way in which his wife had prayed for her son Charles, and said he attributed much to her prayers. Mr. James A. Spurgeon also spoke, and said he felt he was "taking up no sinking cause;" and if there were "sermons in stones," there was surely a good one in the stone they had laid that day.

One of the most forcible of the addresses given at the evening meeting was by the Rev. George Smith, who was then Secretary of the Congregational Union of England and Wales. A few sentences may be given; for they indicated how completely the tide had turned in Mr. Spurgeon's favour:—"I am here to testify on behalf of myself, my people, and my brethren generally, the very high regard we have for that gifted young man, not thirty years of age, whose name has become of world-wide reputation, and who everywhere has been honoured of God in turning multitudes from darkness to light—from the power of Satan unto God. I think we are all, whatever portion of the Church we belong to, deeply indebted to Mr. Spurgeon. For myself, I never had any doubt about him from the beginning. I never entertained a suspicion of him from the commencement. I never uttered one unkind word about him from the time when he commenced his ministry. I always thought Mr. Spurgeon was raised up of God to a great and good work; and we may well rejoice if men are raised up in a way rather different from what we had anticipated. . . . Every prediction about unsoundness, about erratic conduct, about failing in power, has utterly fallen to the ground."

Judge Payne was also present, and there were roars of laughter at his witty allusions, all being concluded according to time-honoured custom by the indispensable "tail-piece." Mr. Spurgeon held this friend in high esteem on account of his Christian character and self-denying labours as a chief ally of Lord Shaftesbury in the earlier days of the Ragged School movement; but he was not regarded as a model judge, because he showed a disposition to pass sentences which were at times believed to be too severe. One or two passages from his address at the evening meeting after the stone-laying ceremony may be given:—

"Among all the beautiful decorations there is one I do not see, but I have it before my mind's eye; I mean the three letters C. H. S. What do they mean? Why, first, Charles Haddon Spurgeon; but I do not mean that. C. H. S. means Clear-Headed Speaker who is Clever at Handling Subjects in a Cheerful-Hearted Style. He is a Captain of the Hosts of Surrey; he is a Cold-Hating Spirit; he has Chapel-Heating Skill; and is a Catholic Humbug-Smasher. He is a Care-Hushing Soother; he is a Child-Helping Strengthener; he is a Christ-Honoured Soldier, and a Christ-Honoured Servant. These are all the C. H. S.'s, and a very good lot of C. H. S.'s they are.

"I said he is a preacher that does not mumble; he is also a man that does not grumble. I have heard him say how pleased he is with the salary given him by the people of Park

Street. There was once a bass singer at a cathedral, and he sang in such a way that the dean did not like it, so he said to him, 'I recommend you to sing better; you are very careless.' 'Sir,' said the singer, 'I sing at the rate of £10 a year, and if you want me to sing better, you have only to increase my salary.' Our friend, Mr. Spurgeon, does not say that. He is perfectly satisfied with what he gets, although it is not half that he deserves. He is also a preacher that does not stumble. Did we ever see a man walk more firmly than he does before the world and the Church? He walks firmly, physically, morally, and religiously, and sets a good example to his flock. He is a good shepherd, or, if you like, a bell-wether sheep, whom you may follow. It is said that if one lives next door to a lame man, one very soon learns to walk lame also. Mr. Spurgeon is not a lame man at all, but walks well; he walks holily and happily, and those who follow his steps will do the same. Then he is a preacher that will not crumble. The man himself will die—many, many years let it be before that consummation is arrived at—but the reputation and character of a faithful preacher of God's free and glorious Gospel will never die. We may address the character and reputation of such a man in the language of the poet and say:—

> 'The stars shall fade away, the sun himself
> Grow dim in age, and nature sink in years.
> But thou shalt flourish in immortal youth,
> Unhurt amid the war of elements,
> The wreck of matter, and the crash of worlds.'"

Thus did this ever-memorable day come to a close. Mr. Spurgeon had just commenced the sixth year of his work in London, and he was beginning to reap the full reward of his labours. The great chapel which had entered into the day-dreams of certain enthusiasts soon after the young preacher had settled in London was becoming a fact; and the promise seemed to be that the work which would there be carried on in the future would be one to attract the attention of the entire Christian world. It was a supreme moment in the experience of a man, especially when that man was only twenty-five years of age. In this case there was no self-elation or ambition, however; the great preacher was even more humble and self-possessed than some of his friends and followers. He had a work to accomplish, and he was determined it should be done; but he was entirely unselfish. He was still true to what may be called the motto of his life—
"SEEKEST THOU GREAT THINGS FOR THYSELF? SEEK THEM NOT!"*

* For accounts of the proceedings on the occasion of the laying of the foundation-stone of the Metropolitan Tabernacle, see *The British Standard* for August 19, and *The Baptist Messenger* for October, 1859.

CHAPTER XXXVI.

LAST DAYS AT THE SURREY GARDENS.

Extreme Inconvenience of New Park Street Chapel—Prospect of leaving the Surrey Gardens—
Open-air Services—A Visit to Cheltenham—A Deliverance on Slavery—A Missionary
Meeting—Remembering Faces—Last Service in the Music Hall—Reappearance at Exeter
Hall—Death of John Angell James—Spurgeon's growing Influence.

WHILE an army of workmen were engaged in rearing the Metropolitan Tabernacle, the young pastor of New Park Street Chapel
and his congregation were feeling even more than they had previously
done the extreme inconvenience of not having a building of their own
large enough to accommodate the vast congregation. As regarded New
Park Street itself, it became more inexplicable how such a site could
have been chosen by shrewd Nonconformist leaders for their religious
home. "A more dingy, uninviting, and repelling region than where
the chapel is situated I have seldom explored," remarked one visitor.
"It is within a short distance after you have crossed Southwark
Bridge from Queen Street, in a gloomy, narrow street, surrounded
with small, dirty-looking houses. Within a minute's walk of the
chapel you see written up at the corner of a little street, 'Bear
Garden.'"* Of old this was a disreputable quarter, and though its
character may have improved, squalid streets and busy hives of
industry did not render the surroundings any more attractive. To
make matters worse, there was a prospect of the Surrey Gardens
Music Hall being used for Sunday evening concerts, in which case
the building would cease to be available for Mr. Spurgeon's morning
congregation. On one or two previous occasions the directors had
thought of attempting to replenish their exchequer by opening the
hall for such entertainments, and had been checked by the intimation that in such a case Mr. Spurgeon's Sunday morning congregation

* "Traits of Character," pp. 11, 109, 110.

would find accommodation elsewhere. At length, however, the managers appear to have supposed that the Sunday evening amusement would pay them better than the morning worship, and they resolved to carry out their scheme. It was a mistake which ended in disaster; for not only was a large rental, out of which a dividend had been paid to the shareholders, sacrificed, but a beautiful building, which some had said could not even be set on fire, was at length burned to the ground.

It would, of course, be impossible to notice even a tenth part of the services in various parts of the country which Mr. Spurgeon at this time was continually holding. Writing at the time in reference to the " immensely crowded congregations," a correspondent remarked, "He seems as if standing on Pisgah's top, 'viewing the land that is afar off,' though in sight; his soul mounts up as on ' eagle's wings ' to the very throne of God." It was thought to be no cause for wonder that such a man should have many ardent admirers on the one hand and detracting enemies on the other. " His heart-probing appeals to sinners, and his stern and unflinching rebukes of their sinfulness are sure to bring down upon him an avalanche of wrath from those who prefer the world to Christ, and are still wallowing in the mire." *

When the season and the weather permitted, Mr. Spurgeon at this time frequently preached in the open air when visiting country districts where the buildings available were small; and when a sermon in the afternoon was followed by another discourse in the evening, a part of the day's programme was a monster tea-meeting in a marquee on the greensward. An example of what pretty frequently occurred was seen at Carlton, Bedfordshire, early in October, 1859. In the afternoon the great preacher spoke from the words, " Come unto Me," to four thousand persons in a field. As the days were shortening, the service concluded at four o'clock, when the eager crowd hastened to the tea-tables which were set in the meeting-house, in the schoolroom, and in a large booth. Having finished

* "A Layman," in *The British Standard*, October 28, 1859.

V

this repast and enjoyed an hour's pleasant conversation, all again turned out into the field, when another sermon was preached by Mr. Spurgeon from Hosea ii. 14.*

A notable visit to Cheltenham was made towards the end of October, when Mr. Spurgeon preached at Cambray Chapel for his friend James Smith, who, besides being himself a famous preacher and voluminous writer, had been a predecessor in the pastorate at New Park Street. It was on this occasion that the young Baptist preacher met with the present Dr. H. Grattan Guinness, who was about to give a valedictory address prior to his departure for America, while Mr. Spurgeon's object was to make a collection in aid of the debt on the Baptist Chapel. *The Cheltenham Examiner* thought that the visit to the town of two such preachers at the same time was a striking occurrence; while "the electric shocks of their eloquence" had "already fired many a soul to a sense of its proper position." The vast crowd which assembled to hear Spurgeon in the afternoon gave ample evidence that the preacher's popularity was not on the wane. Mr. Smith assisted in the service; and Mr. Spurgeon's discourse was founded on Hosea ii. 14, "Therefore, behold, I will allure her, and bring her into the wilderness, and speak comfortably unto her." As this sermon was an admirable example of the preacher's early style, a passage which came in towards the close may be given:—

"'I will allure her.' Many souls are brought to Christ, not in the storm, but in the calm; some in the tempest and some softly floating in. Of such a description as the last is this, 'I will allure her.' I must explain this term 'allure.' I frequently observe from my house, coming down the road, especially on a Sunday morning, a number of men with small cages containing birds, which they use as 'lurers' to catch the wild birds in the fields. It is only the other day I noticed one of them had a little robin redbreast, which was singing to allure other birds from the liberty of which it had itself been deprived. I thought that was a lesson for me, and I remembered this text, 'I will allure.' The birds were not caught, they were enticed, and so got into the possession of the fowler. The fowler did not put a cat to catch the robin, but he used a robin because he wanted to catch robins. And so the Lord took me a sinner and set me there preaching, that one sinner might bring other sinners. I am, then, the lure bird; I am one of yourselves and have sinned much against God. 'But,' one would say, 'I am unworthy to be saved.' So think I. Another would cry, 'But if I went to Jesus He would reject me.' And so I thought, and much I now grieve to know that I should have slandered Christ by thinking

* *The Baptist Messenger*, November, 1859.

so. 'But,' says another, 'I would go if I thought He would have mercy on me.' So I said; but I did more, I put it in practice. I said I would go to the King of Mercy; I was resolved to try, for if I stayed away, I knew I must for ever die. And God did not reject the poorest of mankind. He would receive him, put away his sin and say, 'I have blotted out thine iniquities, thy sins are forgiven thee, go and sin no more.' Would to God that some of you would go and try for yourselves. Every Christian ought to act the part of the 'allure bird.' Some would bring others to the truth, but without this many must have a sad fate. Many people would say, 'To be a Christian is to be miserable;' but it is a mistake; you must seek by a cheerful and happy conversation, and a holy and consistent walk, to entrap others to come to Christ; you are left here to do a work for Him, therefore must endeavour to allure many for Christ. But the text says, 'I will allure.' That is God Himself. A mother had a little child which she desired to teach to walk. She knew it would not be made to walk, it could only be done by teaching, which in its turn must be effected by 'alluring.' The child is placed against a chair, fearing to trust its little feet; the mother holds out to it an apple or a sweetmeat; the child looks, and at last makes the first toddling step; the mother is reached, and there stands the child at rest, the marvellous feat performed of walking the first time in its life. Oh! what is not a mother's love? And what the love of God to His children? Are they conscious of their own weakness? He said, 'Come to Me and take the first step.' His mercy will be about them; another step and another will be taken, until they are brought to Him. Jesus said, 'Come to Me, come! come!' I beseech you, therefore, resist not His allurements; despise Him not that speaketh. One would say, perhaps, 'If He would but threaten me I should be saved; if He were full of terror I think I could come to Christ.' Nay, nay, come! He allures you; He stretches out His hands and says, 'By these nailed prints come to Me; by this thorn brow come; by My bloody sweat, and by My cross and passion, come. Shall it all be in vain?' I pray the Spirit of God may now go forth among you, that you may freely come to Christ. The more abject, ruined, and undone you are, the greater reason that you should go to Christ to have your guilt removed and your miseries cast away. Oh! come ye to Christ. 'Even as Moses lifted up the serpent in the wilderness, so shall the Son of man be lifted up, that whosoever looketh on Him may not perish, but have everlasting life.'" *

To those who are old enough to remember the strong man in his prime, when his matchless voice was not in any degree broken, such an example of his preaching as the above will awaken some delightful memories. It is an echo of the good old times when Spurgeon, in a physical sense, was at his best.

In regard to the preacher's anti-slavery sentiments there was never any doubt, although when the quarrel between North and South in the United States became a matter which could only be settled by the sword, the slave-holders would have been glad, had it been possible, to claim Spurgeon as a sympathiser, or even as a " moderate " compromiser. How far he was removed from this, however, was shown at a meeting at New Park Street Chapel on December 8, 1859, when, after the usual week-night lecture, John

* *The Christian Cabinet*, November 2, 1859.

Andrew Jackson, a fugitive slave from South Carolina, was allowed an opportunity of giving an account of himself. The story of this man's wrong awakened lively interest, while his sentiments drew forth outbursts of applause which were peculiarly English. He spoke for an hour, and did so from the pulpit; and when the ex-slave had finished, Mr. Spurgeon himself expressed satisfaction at what he had heard, and gave his opinion on American slavery in general. He alluded to the insurrection under John Brown, and said that if that leader were to fall a sacrifice to the cause he would die a martyr's death. The pastor continued :—

"Slavery is the foulest blot that ever stained a national escutcheon, and may have to be washed out with blood. America is in many respects a glorious country, but it may be necessary to teach her some wholesome lessons at the point of the bayonet—to carve freedom into her with the bowie-knife, or send it home to her heart with revolvers. Better far should it come to this issue, that North and South should be rent asunder, and the States of the union shivered into a thousand fragments, than that slavery should be suffered to continue. Some American divines seem to regard it, indeed, with wonderful complacency. They have so accustomed themselves to wrap it up in soft phrases that they lose sight of its real character. They call it a 'peculiar institution,' until they forget in what its peculiarity consists. It is, indeed, a peculiar institution, just as the Devil is a peculiar angel, and as hell is a peculiarly hot place. For my part, I hold such miserable tampering with sin in abhorrence, and can hold no communion of any sort with those who are guilty of it." *

Among the pleasant gatherings which came off during the fall of the year 1859 may be included a visit which Mr. Spurgeon paid to the City, being entertained by the friends of the Fox and Knot Ragged School. The occasion appears to have been valued by the pastor, because it gave him an opportunity of meeting friends whom he might not otherwise see from one end of the year to another. Mr. Cutler, one of the chief speakers, had for long been associated with the New Park Street Church, and remembered well the days of decline and of difficulty before Mr. Spurgeon came to London. He it was, moreover, who had enjoyed the privilege, in a scantily attended church meeting, of proposing that the young preacher of Waterbeach should be invited to the pastorate.

Meanwhile New Park Street Chapel was often used for other purposes than the ordinary services which the pastor himself conducted.

* *The Christian Cabinet*, December 14, 1859.

At one time the late W. G. Lewis, of Westbourne Grove Chapel, would give his popular lecture on the " Pilgrim's Progress," with the much appreciated lantern pictures; at another time you might walk in and find in progress a valedictory service on account of one or more missionaries going out to their destination. On Monday, October 17, Mr. Klockers, who was about to proceed as a missionary to China, was thus commended to the Lord in prayer. The late J. Howard Hinton, W. G. Lewis, and the missionary-elect himself, took part in the service, after which Mr. Spurgeon "gave the charge in a style peculiar to himself. He thought that the undertaking to convert four hundred millions was a human impossibility; if only a twentieth of such a number had been thought of, it would have been equally impossible; but, after all, if the Spirit of God was with the missionary, blessing him in his endeavours, who could tell what the results might be which would follow?"* This meeting was long remembered by those who were present.

At this time, and through his life, it was a characteristic of Mr. Spurgeon that he could remember people's names and faces in a most remarkable manner, although he was continually shaking hands with hundreds of new friends. An American friend, who was struck with this peculiarity, gives this amusing illustration: "In a throng of people an earnest man tried to grasp his hand, and at last succeeding, inquired in a very vehement manner whether the famous preacher did not recognise him. For once in his life the ' famous preacher' was at fault. He did not, however, hum and haw, and say, ' My dear fellow, the fact is I have forgotten your name, but your face is quite familiar to me;' but he owned right out that he had no recollection of him whatever. Whereupon the excited individual replied, very much to Mr. Spurgeon's amusement, ' Well, that is singular, seeing you rendered me the greatest service one man could render another—you buried my wife.' We must, of course, do the bereaved husband justice to suppose that he did not mean exactly what his words denoted; but nevertheless it was a good joke at the expense of the

* *The Baptist Messenger*, November, 1859.

usually exact and careful pastor, and one that, I have no doubt, he must frequently have repeated with considerable relish." *

The last service in the Surrey Gardens Hall took place on Sunday, December 11, when the preacher enlarged on the text of Acts xx. 26–27, " Wherefore I take you to record this day, that I am pure from the blood of all men. For I have not shunned to declare unto you all the counsel of God." Immediately on ascending the platform pulpit for the last time, Mr. Spurgeon said :—

"The service this morning will partake very much of the character of a farewell discourse and a farewell meeting. However sorrowful it may be to me to part with you, whose faces I have so long seen in the throng of my hearers, yet for Christ's sake, for the sake of consistency and truth, we are compelled to withdraw from this place, and on next Sabbath morning hope to worship God in Exeter Hall. On two occasions before, as our friends are aware, it was proposed to open this place in the evening, and I was then able to prevent it by the simple declaration that if so I should withdraw. That declaration suffices not at this time, and you can therefore perceive that I should be a craven to the truth, that I should be inconsistent with my own declarations, that, in fact, my name would cease to be Spurgeon if I yielded. I neither can nor will give way in anything in which I know I am right; and in defence of God's holy Sabbath the cry of this day is, 'Arise, let us go hence !'" †

The congregation at the Surrey Gardens was now practically dispersed; for when, on December 18, 1859, Mr. Spurgeon again stood on the platform of Exeter Hall, his hearers probably numbered only about a fourth part of what they had done for such a lengthened period in the great structure erected for M. Jullien's concerts. ‡ It

---

* Dr. Lorimer, " C. H. Spurgeon: A Monograph," pp. 101–102.

† *The British Standard,* December 16, 1859.

‡ As so many exaggerated notions regarding the capacity of Exeter Hall are entertained, the following trustworthy statement may be given :—

"The dimensions of the hall are, in length, 131 feet 4 inches; in breadth, 76 feet 6 inches (6 feet 6 inches wider than Westminster Hall); and in height, 45 feet. Eighteen windows admit the day; when the evening shades prevail, numerous gas-burners diffuse a strong but mellow light. The platform is five feet from the ground, and from front to back rises five steps of two inches each. In the body there is a level of fifty feet from the platform, after which, a rise of twenty-seven steps, each two inches high and two feet broad, thus enabling those at the greatest distance to see all that transpires with as much ease and comfort as the nearest. The numerical capacity of the hall, as recorded on a plan printed in 1849, is the following :—Upper back platform seats (seldom filled), 210 side platform seats, 180; central platform seats, 190; north and south galleries, 40 (total platform seats, 620); level area seats, 428 ; raised area seats, 1,182 (total area seats, 1,610); end gallery seats, 280 ; general total, 2,510. About 100 additional platform seats have been the gain of recent alterations. This estimate allows eighteen inches to each person, so that rarely, if ever, can more than 3,000 adults be assembled in the hall at one time."—*The Scottish Review,* July, 1857.

appears that a sum of £15 was paid for each service held in the hall. In June, 1861, the famous structure was destroyed by fire.

This sojourn at Exeter Hall continued throughout the whole of the year 1860, and until March 1, 1861, when a removal was made to the new Metropolitan Tabernacle. When the services were recommenced in December, 1859, a hard frost prevailed, so that "the weather and the parks" attracted the usual attention. Mr. Spurgeon preached on the "Inexhaustible Barrel," and on the following Sunday, being Christmas Day, a seasonable sermon was founded on the words, "Unto us a child is born."

Some little time before, Mr. Spurgeon had made a visit to Brighton, and numbers who had been interested or edified on that occasion were somewhat dismayed on reading an announcement that the great preacher had changed his views by giving up Calvinistic doctrines. In common with some other journals, *The Brighton Examiner* gave the news, but in the following number the matter was set right by a few lines from Mr. Spurgeon himself:—"The statement you have made with regard to my recantation of Calvinistic doctrine is a fabrication from beginning to end, and one which could only have been invented for malicious purposes. I am the same in doctrine as I have ever been, and I hope to remain faithful to the same grand truth until death."

During this year the young pastor lost by death his good old friend John Angell James, of Birmingham, for whom he appears all along to have entertained the very highest regard. Mr. Spurgeon was continually attracting new friends, however, so that the inevitable passing away of old ones may not have been so severely felt as might otherwise have been the case. One notable man, who about this time was tempted to read for himself *The New Park Street Pulpit*, was the late Dr. James Morgan, minister of Fisherwick Place Church, Belfast, who, as a competent critic, wrote as follows:—

"I have procured a copy of Mr. Spurgeon's Sermons for the library, in five volumes, and resolved to read one every morning after dressing. Rising at six o'clock, I am ready to begin the sermon at seven, and it takes me more than half an hour to read it. I have gone over about twenty, and find the exercise profitable. Although the sermons are hastily sent forth, they are still very valuable, plain, sound, and practical, and well fitted to be useful. There is a tone of faithfulness in them that makes them powerful." *

The work to which Mr. Spurgeon had put his hand was now making way all along the line. The pastor, as a preacher, was an acknowledged power in the metropolis; while his congregation was a recognised institution with provincial and Continental or American visitors. There were still certain newspapers which spoke of him unfairly; but the majority were of a different mind, especially since *The Times* had come over to his side. In *The British and Foreign Evangelical Review* for 1859 will also be found an article, the writer of which gives the preacher his due, showing how manifest were his earnestness and self-denial. It is probable that the latter even exceeded what could have been expected; for I believe that at this time he gave half, or even more, of his income to the work of the College. It was one of the most singular cases on record of an eminent man receiving a large income, and able to earn a much larger one, being content to live in the most frugal manner on far less than what hundreds of City clerks were receiving. This mode of living was really continued till the end; for although more was expended in later days, much more was also given away. The College was thus founded with the pastor's own money.

* "Recollections of my Life and Times," by James Morgan, D.D., pp. 320-321.

CHAPTER XXXVII.

MR. SPURGEON AND THE AMERICANS.

Interest in Spurgeon's Visit to Paris—The Question of Slavery—Altered Sermons published in America—The Pro-Slavery Journals and the English Preacher—The Open Air Mission.

AT the opening of the year 1860 great interest was felt on both sides of the Channel in the matter of Mr. Spurgeon's visit to Paris, which was to take place in February. The excursion was not to be by any means a mere holiday trip, for it was arranged for several services to be held in different buildings, and the preacher would not consent on this occasion to be absent from his own congregation on a Sunday. In anticipation of the young pastor's visit *Galignani's Messenger* said, " It is impossible for him to be absent from the immense congregation of 10,000 persons in London to whom he preaches on Sundays—the largest concourse of people that was ever known to assemble on every consecutive Sabbath for years to hear the Gospel faithfully preached." The writer in the Paris journal was struck by the way in which the popularity which had been at once achieved had been retained, and like many others, he wished to account for it :—

"He had no prestige in any line whatever to form an introduction. He flashed like a meteor upon the public eye at once, but unlike the meteor he still remains visible and attracts the same attention. . . . The adaptation of his conceptions and style to all classes is surprising; for while the nobles of the land, and some of the most cultivated intellects of the forum and the bar, are constantly amongst his hearers, the poor hear him with evident pleasure. He is blessed with good health and great energy, and is no idler in the vineyard. . . . But the most noticeable trait in his character is his apparent unconsciousness of his gifts and the influence which he wields. . . . During his short ministry upwards of 3,000 have become consistent Christians, hundreds of whom had previously abandoned themselves to vice, wickedness, and infidelity. . . . No wonder, therefore, that Royalty and the Government look favourably upon his efforts to benefit the population, and many of the most distinguished professions attend his ministry."*

The better part of the French people were also charmed to learn that so young a man had resisted brilliant offers to change his sphere

* Quoted from *Galignani's Messenger* in *The British Standard*, January 6, 1860.

of labour, the most tempting offers of all coming from America·
It was understood that the object of the visit to the French metropolis
was simply to preach the Gospel to the people—to such as understood English; for although Mr. Spurgeon could read French, I
am not aware that he ever attempted to give an address in that
language.

On January 7 of this year died Mr. Arthur Morley, the Nottingham philanthropist, for whose prize for an essay on Romanism Mr.
Spurgeon had unsuccessfully competed eight years before, when he
produced "Antichrist and Her Brood." Mr. Morley was only forty-
eight years of age; and he died suddenly on the railway while on
his way to Poplar to visit his sister, who was the wife of the Rev.
George Smith, a well-known Independent minister of that day.

American slavery had now become one of the burning questions
of the day; and from the fact that Spurgeon's Sermons were being
issued in the United States with certain passages omitted which the
publishers knew would be distasteful to their constituency, many
inferred that the English preacher had changed his views on that
question, or at least had greatly modified them. Mr. Henry Ward
Beecher called attention to this fact; and it appeared like a challenge
for the real truth to be made known. As one American anti-slavery
journal said, "neither Mr. Spurgeon nor his publishers can afford to
overlook the charge." Even the denominational organ in London
said, "The charge is one which cannot be treated with silence, and
Mr. Spurgeon is too manly and too much the friend of liberty to
allow it to remain unnoticed." * Later on the work of suppression
was shown to be the work of the publishers alone.†

Thus it happened that *The New York Independent* and some other
papers gave out that the great English preacher had changed his
views on the question of slavery; and an entire absence from the
published discourses of any unpalatable views on that question gave
some colour of truth to the rumours. Passages relating to open
communion were also taken out of the American edition of the

* *The Freeman*, January 4, 1860.   † *Ibid.*, March 7, 1860.

Sermons. Determined to arrive at the truth, Mr. F. W. Chesson, of the Emancipation Committee, wrote to ask Mr. Spurgeon if he had given his " consent to the publication of an expurgated edition of his sermons suited to the pro-slavery prejudices of Brother Jonathan." Mr. Spurgeon wrote in reply :—

"As the vile iniquity is not an English sin, I have not in my sermons been led to denounce it; and, so far as I am aware, there are no allusions to slavery in them, or, if any, they are so few that I cannot charge my memory with them. I do not see how the Americans can have expurgated the anti-slavery sentiments, for I do not think it was a subject which thrust itself in my way in the ordinary duties of my ministry. I have written a letter to an influential paper in America, and will see to it that my sentiments are really known. I believe slavery to be a crime of crimes, a soul-destroying sin, and an iniquity which cries aloud for vengeance. The charge against my publishers of altering my sermons I believe to be utterly untrue, and they are ready, as their best contradiction, to print a work on the subject if I can find time to write it, which I fear I cannot, but must be content with some red-hot letters." *

When he gave publicity to the above letter, Dr. Campbell advised that Mr. Spurgeon should publish something on the subject. It was not necessary that such a production should be voluminous. " A great book is not necessarily a great power. What is required is a thunderbolt—a concentration of truth and force such as Mr. Spurgeon well knows how to prepare."

The "thunderbolt," or, as the author himself regarded it, the "red-hot letter," duly appeared in *The Watchman and Reflector*, and had the slave-holders been actually attacked with heated shots the excitement could hardly have been greater. One passage from this letter may be quoted :—" I do from my inmost soul detest slavery anywhere and everywhere, and although I commune at the Lord's table with men of all creeds, yet with a slave-holder I have no fellowship of any sort or kind. Whenever one has called upon me, I have considered it my duty to express my detestation of his wickedness, and would as soon think of receiving a murderer into my church, or into any sort of friendship, as a man-stealer. Nevertheless, as I have preached in London and not in New York, I have very seldom made any allusion to American slavery in my sermons. This accounts for the rumour that I have left out the *anti-slavery*

* *The British Standard*, February 10, 1860.

from my American edition of Sermons. This is not true in any measure, for, as far as my memory serves me, I cannot remember that the subject was handled at all in any of my printed sermons beyond a passing allusion, and I have never altered a single sentence in a sermon which has been sent out to my American publishers beyond the mere correction which involved words and not sense. However, if any think me capable of such double-dealing, I doubt not that they judge of me by themselves, and from such persons esteem is not desirable. I do not, therefore, regret the loss of it. I have this much to say to all who respect me in America—I did not want to be blaming you constantly, while there are sins enough in my own country, but I shall not spare your nation in future. I shall remember that my voice echoes beyond the Atlantic, and the crying sin of a man-stealing people shall not go unrebuked. I did not know that I had been so fully adopted a citizen of your Republic; but finding that you allow me to be one of yourselves, I will speak out quite severely enough, and perhaps more sharply than will meet with approbation."

A Boston correspondent wrote:—"Our Baptist papers are over-flowing with indignation, and call on all publishers and booksellers to banish the books of your worthy young friend from their counters. . . . The poor slave-holders are at their wits' end, and know not what to do to save their doomed system. *The Montgomery Mail* says the Vigilance Committee at that place is engaged in burning dangerous books, and that two volumes of Spurgeon's Sermons have been contributed for their bonfires, and that they will be burnt. *The Mail* calls for more, and I have no doubt that Sheldon and Co., Mr. Spurgeon's publishers, would be glad to furnish them." *

For the time being the anti-slavery controversy raged around the name of Spurgeon. At first the English preacher's sermons were exceedingly popular in the Southern States; but when his sentiments on this question were discovered, there was a turn in the tide. Out-and-out anti-slavery sentiments such as Mr. Spurgeon uttered were

---

* *The Freeman,* March 28, 1860.

rare, even among those who professed to disapprove of slavery as an institution. Even *The Watchman*, which printed the young pastor's letter, did not do so without a half apology. Americans had more charity for those who were born the victims of the system; they had broader comprehension, and so on. This, however, was how a representative religious Southern paper referred to Spurgeon and his utterances :—

"If the editors of *The Watchman and Reflector* had any agency in procuring from Mr. S. such a letter, they are no better than he, and they all deserve the fate of Brown. We had just received a box of Mr. Spurgeon's Sermons to sell, but have *sent them back* to the publishers, Messrs. Sheldon and Co., New York, with all possible despatch. WILL NOT EVERY BOOKSTORE AND COLPORTEUR IN THE SOUTH DO THE SAME SO SOON AS THEY READ THIS LETTER? Can any Southern men ever purchase another volume of a man's sermons who denounces him as no better than a murderer, and who virtually counsels the torch of the incendiary and the knife of the assassin as appropriate arguments for the extermination of African slavery? We sympathise with his American publishers, Messrs. Sheldon and Co., for they have shown themselves to be highly conservative patriots and Christian gentlemen. We shall be happy to correct the false position which Mr. Spurgeon has assigned them at the close of his letter, so soon as they will authorise us. *Let the Press of the South universally pass Mr. Spurgeon round.*" *

Of course, it will not be inferred from such outbursts as this that the pastor of New Park Street Chapel was not as popular as ever with a large proportion of the American people. The fact was that the controversy which the friends of freedom had with the pro-slavery party of the Southern States became more fierce, and uncompromising in proportion as the inevitable final conflict, and which any shrewd observer was already able to foresee, drew nearer. The ignoble passions which were aroused and the brutal violence with which slave-holders resented the efforts of abolitionists can now hardly be understood unless we study the times in such a record as the Life of William Lloyd Garrison. † Nor were the fierce threats and angry

* Quoted in *The Freeman*, March 28, 1860, from *The South Western Baptist.*

† In proof that the language used is not too strong, take this incident :—" A Mr. Salisbury, deacon of a Baptist church in Oswego County, New York, went to Virginia four or five years ago, and purchased one of the worn-out plantations, which he has since been working by free labour and designed to make it his future home. He there united himself with a church of his own order and lived a peaceable Christian life, without calling in question the right of his neighbours to hold slaves, or in any way interfering with the institutions of Virginia. This, however, could not secure him from suspicion, and lately he has been waited on by a Vigilance Committee, and his house searched throughout for anti-slavery documents, but without success, till at length a few

words mere raving; the slave-holders and their leaders meant all that they said, and were at any moment ready to suit their actions to their utterances.

In common with many others, Mr. Spurgeon found this out; but although the sale of the Sermons in the United States yielded a handsome return, he did not hesitate to denounce slavery more heartily than ever when the opportunity came, and this deprived him of supplies which he had given to the Pastors' College.   Meanwhile a certain large-hearted American showed in a private letter how the English preacher was still revered by the better sort of people :—

"At the beginning I felt concerned for him, lest popularity might turn his head and lead him off, like Mr. Irving, into some vagary where his influence for good would be nullified. And ever since, as I have seen the height of the pedestal to which Providence has raised him, I have trembled lest something might topple him from that elevation, and hush his voice by the fall.   Knowing human nature, his continued popularity and usefulness have been a mystery which I could not solve without reference to my original conviction that he is one of God's chosen agents to do an important work and the belief that he is under the special care of the Master whom he serves.   He seems not to be ambitious of such fame; he evidently feels his responsibility; he caters for no man's taste; he preaches fully the most unpopular and unpalatable truths; he flatters no class; he spares no sin in high places or in low; he aims, not to wreathe his own brow with human honours, but to save as many of his hearers from perdition.   If some are watching for the decline of his influence, thousands pray for him that he may be kept from temptation, and that his bow may long abide in strength.   The preacher has not lived for a long period whose name was so widely known, or whose influence in six years affected favourably so many thousands. The whole evangelical ministry of the British Isles feels the throb of that warm earnest heart which beats in London, and there is an improvement in the preaching that is obvious to the stranger who has had the opportunity to compare the past and the present.   The example of pulpit power has a widespread effect.   The weekly sermon, accurately reported and quickly published, is read in all parts of the kingdom, thus multiplying many thousand-fold the stirring impulse.   Eternity alone will reveal the amount of good issuing, by the grace of God, from that one mind fired with the love of Calvary.   I heard Mr. Spurgeon both at the great Music Hall and at his chapel in New Park Street, and was in no respect disappointed.   He preached the truth of God as if he believed it, and was sure that others must believe it or perish for ever.   If some forms of expression would not have satisfied the exact theologian, and if some things would have been considered as violations of the canons of a severe taste, they were few, very few, and not worth mentioning, in comparison

copies of *The Albany Journal*, sent to him by some Northern friend, were found, and the good deacon, a grey-haired man of sixty, was brought before a justice of the peace, a brother, too, in his own church, and was remanded to prison.   He has since been released, and, at the advice of his friends, has come back to his native State.   He expects to make a heavy loss in the sale of his Virginia property; but there is no help for it in the present excitement."— Quoted from *The New York Examiner* in *The Freeman*, February 15, 1860.

with the clear, earnest, impressive exhibitions of saving truth. While I admired the originality, simplicity, and fervour of his utterances, I was impressed most of all by the prominence which he gave to Christ and Him crucified. When, therefore, my opinion is asked respecting the secret of his power, I am unable to express it more definitively than by referring to this characteristic of his preaching. His pleasing expression of face, his perfect self-possession, his melody of voice, his fluency of utterance, his easy manner, free from all over-action, his whole air of deep, unaffected sincerity, are doubtless auxiliaries of no small importance; but they will not account for the efficiency with which his labours are distinguished." *

The church of which he was the pastor is spoken of as being the largest in Europe, and 300 new members were added every year, the conversions being eminently sound on account of the humbling Gospel doctrines which he preached. Such a testimony at such a time under such conditions was no doubt very cheering; but one can hardly doubt that the slavery disputes had the effect of obliging Mr. Spurgeon to abandon his proposed visit to the New World. He would have no wish to make a tour through a country divided against itself; and the fanaticism which led to the murder of the greatest of the Presidents might even have rendered public appearances unsafe to so distinguished an abolitionist.

In a letter which appeared in an American newspaper at this time, Mr. Spurgeon gave a reminiscence of his own early days in connection with his late friend, John Angell James, who had died a few months previously:—" In an early part of my ministry, while but a lad, I was seized with an intense desire to hear Mr. James ; and, though my finances were somewhat meagre, I performed a pilgrimage to Birmingham, solely with that object in view. I heard him deliver a week-evening lecture in his large vestry on that precious text, 'Ye are complete in Him.' The savour of that very sweet discourse abides with me to this day, and I shall never read the passage without associating therewith the quiet but earnest utterances of the departed man of God." †

Mr. Spurgeon was always a strong advocate of open-air preaching, and in the course of his duties at the Pastors' College, he gave very

* Private letter by Dr. Stow, of Boston, quoted in *The Freeman*, January 25, 1860.

† Quoted in *The British Standard*, February 10, 1860.

carefully prepared lectures to the students on this practice. Those
who founded or nurtured the Open-Air Mission appear to have enjoyed
his friendship from an early period, and when the opportunity came
they advocated the cause on the same platform together. At the
end of January, 1860, the Southwark auxiliary of the Mission
assembled at "The Horns," Kennington, when addresses were given
by John Macgregor, the veteran "Rob Roy"—who has lately passed
away, but who in his day did more to promote this service in
London than any other man—Judge Payne, and others. The speech
of the evening was given by Mr. Spurgeon, and though extremely
brief, every sentence was telling :—

"I feel strongly with regard to this mission to the perishing thousands. If an angel
was to fly over London to determine where such a meeting as this should be held,
methinks he would stay here; for when churches and chapels were closed against the
great Whitefield, and he could find no building large enough to hold the crowds who
flocked to hear the Gospel from his lips, he preached in the open air on Kennington
Common. If anyone were to ask me to defend from Scripture the practice of ministering only in certain buildings called sacred, I could not do so; but open-air preaching
needs no defence—it stands of itself. It is necessary, because if we want to save souls,
we must go where the souls are. It is the going after souls that constitutes our divine
mission; and especially it is our duty 'to seek and to save that which was lost.' Open-
air preaching reaches many who otherwise never would hear the Gospel. People talk
sometimes about the dignity of the pulpit. That is very well. But I think the dignity
of the pulpit must be measured by the number of converts chained thereto. I have my
own ideas about colleges. A Canadian backwoodsman's letter came to me this morning,
and it stated that colleges were machines, and the college men machine-made men—not
at all fit for backwoods work. I don't hold with all this; but I do believe that the men
of our colleges are not fit for much of the rough work. But there are men who are
especially fitted for it—men who are born and bred among the people—who speak the
people's language, and whose hearts beat with the same impulses as the people among
whom they live. Such men are the Open-Air Mission supplies. God bless the Open-
Air Mission, because it give us such ministers. But there is a large amount of responsibility resting on Christians. The great clouds of divine grace have been hovering over
the United States; they have crossed the Atlantic to Ireland, and the droppings of the
rain have been felt in Wales. Shall they pass away without giving us a blessing, because we are not sufficiently earnest for the salvation of souls? Let it not be so. There
is a great harvest gathering for us. The masses are in an incandescent state. Ye
open-air preachers, strike and make the sparks fly, and weld the once cold iron. Stay
not behind your bulwarks, but go out into the field, and fight for the Lord our
God." *

The late Gawin Kirkham, of the Open-Air Mission, was present
at this meeting. Mr. Kirkham was preparing for this work a sketch
of Spurgeon as an Open-Air Preacher when death overtook him.

* *The British Standard*, February 10, 1860.

CHAPTER XXXVIII.

A VISIT TO PARIS.

A Visit to France — Preaches Five Times in Paris — Opinions of the French Pastors — M. Prévost-Paradol in the *Journal des Débats*—Deaths of Eminent Persons—A Day at Moorfields—Dr. Campbell as a Journalist.

MR. SPURGEON made a flying visit to Paris in the early part of February, 1860; and as he would not consent to be away from his congregation at Exeter Hall or New Park Street for even one Sunday, the trip represented a very hard week's work, although to outsiders it may have appeared like a pleasant excursion. The subject of the discourse at Exeter Hall on the first Sunday morning of the month was, "Mr. Evil-Questioning Tried and Executed," the evil question on which it was founded being, "Are not Abana and Pharpar, rivers of Damascus, better than all the waters of Israel?" (II. Kings v. 12). The sermon was an unusually long one, and taken as a whole it was one of the most remarkable examples of the preacher's early style. It was very much of an allegory; and as Mr. Evil-Questioning and his large circle of family connections—all being descendants of Mr. Human-Reason—were brought to the front and examined, the spellbound audience must have thought that John Bunyan the Second was speaking to them.

On the following morning, February 6, Mr. Spurgeon appears to have crossed the Channel. He had been invited to Paris by an Episcopal clergyman, who was of opinion that a series of services conducted by such a preacher would be fruitful in the best results. The expectation appears to have been in a large measure realised, the appearance of the young pastor being anticipated in the gay capital with the most lively interest. Five services were held, two at the Church of the Oratoire, and three at the chapel of the American Ambassador. The eagerness to be present was great, many persons of fashion, foreign visitors of rank, ministers of all Protestant denominations,

W

as well as a large number of Roman Catholic priests, being among the hearers. The preacher spoke with all of his accustomed force and earnestness, and the effect was such as had hardly been seen in Paris since the days of the Reformation. One gentleman of high position told the New Park Street deacon, Mr. James Low, that he had never in his life before felt so much interest in a religious service; the touching illustrations and searching appeals so affected him that he concealed himself behind a pillar in the church and there wept. The various pastors of Protestant congregations were of opinion that the visit would leave permanent good results.

Each evening during his stay in the city Mr. Spurgeon was invited to the house of some resident of social position and influence, and on each occasion a large number of friends were also invited, so that these *salon* gatherings were as remarkable in their way as the public services. Neither Scotland nor Ireland at first had shown such interest in the English preacher, while the French geniality was altogether charming. The visit to the college at Passy, where a number of students were being educated for missionary service, was a memorable event in connection with this visit. The young men were as much interested as Mr. Spurgeon himself, and appear to have expressed themselves as being very grateful for the visit. The address given to the students was translated by the President.

Various leading inhabitants of Paris were so struck with the effects of this visit that they hoped it might be repeated at an early date. A sum of nearly £70 was collected at the American chapel for the debt on the building; but the managers refused to keep the money, and insisted on its being given to the building fund of the Metropolitan Tabernacle; and in order that it should be sent without deductions, 400 francs were subscribed for the preacher's personal expenses. Two other good collections were also made for the poor of the city.

The comments of the Paris newspapers were as remarkable as they were satisfactory: for mere literary men as well as Roman Catholic writers were charmed with the exhibition of Gospel truth

by this young man of twenty-six.   Dr. Grandpierre, of the National
Protestant Church, told the late Dr. Steane, of Camberwell, how
greatly he was struck with the young English preacher's voice
and distinct enunciation at the Oratoire.   Although it was a
Protestant church, much of the teaching given forth in its pulpit
was of a very doubtful kind.   Dr. Grandpierre himself was an
Evangelical, and so also were some others who preached in turn with
him; but others who had access to the pulpit are said to have
been Arians, if not actually Socinians.   To hear Spurgeon in such
a place, therefore, was like the opening of a new Reformation.   The
French pastor just named was also impressed with the even flow of
Mr. Spurgeon's eloquence, the logical development of his thoughts,
and with his facile and always elegant language.   Another of Dr.
Steane's friends, Dr. Frédéric Monod, was chiefly delighted with the
young English preacher's catholicity.   Dr. Monod was at that time one
of the most devoted of French Protestant ministers, and he had left
the National, to join himself with the Free or Congregational, Church.
In Spurgeon this ardent reformer saw a man who took into the
pulpit no pet theories of his own; he had no system, he wanted to
gain no partisans for this or that denomination; his one and only
desire was to win converts to Christ.   " Mr. Spurgeon is a new proof
that God does nothing by halves.   If He calls one of His servants
to some special work, He gives him the special endowments necessary
for it.   So in this case; not only have intellectual and spiritual gifts
been bestowed, but physical faculties as well : a clear musical voice,
an indomitable constitution, and strength which ten sermons a week
from year's end to year's end can neither subdue nor exhaust.   I have
heard him converse, after having been engaged in the pulpit for
nearly three hours, with a voice as fresh and clear as before he entered
it." *   It was said that many remarkable conversions occurred as a
result of the services.

In England no one was more delighted at the result of this visit
than Dr. Campbell, who insisted that the voice of Paris was virtually

* Quoted in Dr. Steane's letter to *The Freeman*, March 14, 1860.

the verdict of Protestant France. "Gold is the same all the world over," exultingly exclaimed the friendly editor. "Latitude, longitude, clime and season, have no effect on its weight, sound, or lustre. So it is with a genius for Christian eloquence. Sect and nationality, manners and politics, affect it not. It controls them all. Mr. Spurgeon furnishes an illustration. No matter where he may appear . . . . all do homage to the truth, the nature, the attraction, and the power of his preaching." *

As coming from two of the leading Protestant teachers of France the utterances of Pastors Monod and Grandpierre attracted some attention. In the course of an article on Mr. Spurgeon, the former wrote :—

"In hearing him you forget man, you forget the preacher, and think only of the truths he utters. You are not under the false spell of a vain and high-sounding eloquence, but the heart is touched, the conscience is awakened, and that which thus subdues you is the power of the truth of God. You are not tempted to applaud and cry 'Bravo!' but you feel constrained to retire into yourself, to pray for yourself and for others, and to say from your heart, 'Amen! Lord! Amen!' The basis of the doctrines drawn by Mr. Spurgeon from the Bible is what we call Calvinism; he believes, and he preaches, that the Bible teaches the election of grace and the final perseverance of the saints. But how admirably practical is this Calvinism, how broad and grand it is! He would never straiten the limits of the infinite mercy of God in Christ Jesus. Without reserve, he calls all men to the foot of the cross, and tells them in his Master's words, 'Whosoever cometh shall in no wise be cast out.' His Calvinism is as far removed from Antinomianism as it is from self-righteousness, and would rather lead to holiness, without which no man can see the Lord." †

Pastor Monod then enters with some enthusiasm into his subject, and like all other inquirers had done, he asked what was the reason of such astounding success in one who was still so young, and whose church members had increased in six years from 150 to 1,500. He would not have it that imagination, voice, wealth of anecdote, etc., would account for such moral phenomena. It was rather the man's faith that accounted for the thing; the words spoken were mighty because they were founded on eternal truth :—

"His eloquence consists not in the mere clatter of words or in the pleasant arrangement of studied phrases; and if Joseph de Maistre had heard him, he would not have retired, saying, 'A Protestant minister is a man dressed in black, who says soft things.' No; Mr. Spurgeon is powerful because he possesses the faith which he teaches, and that

* *The British Standard*, March 9, 1860.

† *Archives du Christianisme*, February 20, 1860; translated for *The British Standard*, March 9, 1860.

faith possesses him; because he has tested in his own experience the reality and efficacy of those truths he preaches; and because, like John the Baptist, he is willing that Christ should increase and that he should decrease. He speaks because he believes and loves; and one feels that his eloquence has been learned on his knees before God and His Word, and has not been studied in any school of rhetoric. He preaches the truth, all the truth, in all the fulness in which he knows and loves it, because this truth, and this alone, is able to save the soul. Add to this a rare and perfect independence of character— he fears not men, he seeks not their favour; he shrinks not from their anger, but announces 'all the counsel of God' as he finds it revealed in His Word. He knows no other limits than those prescribed by the Gospel. He never asks, 'What will be said of me?' but rather, 'What is the truth, what is the will of God?' and then, when he sees clearly the road which God has marked out for him, he walks in it resolutely, and nothing can stop or hinder him. And is not this the only right way of doing good to men? We have heard of a bishop who, one day addressing the celebrated actor Garrick, said, 'How is that you, who represent only fiction, yet produce such lively impressions upon the people, while we, who preach of realities, too often leave our audiences cold and indifferent?' 'My Lord,' said Garrick, 'perhaps it is because we speak of fiction as if it were reality, while in the pulpit realities are treated as if they were but fiction!' Here then is the secret. When Mr. Spurgeon speaks of sin, of hell, of heaven, of Jesus Christ, of His cross and His blood, of pardon, of salvation, and of life eternal, one feels that these are all realities—aye, as real and earnest as the facts of everyday life. He cries to souls to flee from the wrath to come just as he would cry to a man asleep in a burning house to awake and save his life."

The expositions of the Scriptures are said to be as interesting as the sermons, the explanation of Psalm xxiii. at the American Chapel being referred to as especially striking. What struck the Parisians as being chiefly remarkable, however, was the unaffected simplicity and freedom from pride which were characteristic of the young genius. Pastor Monod then gives this interesting passage :—

"Just think for a moment what strong temptations to pride must beset this young preacher of twenty-six years! Not only week after week, but day after day, thousands of eager listeners crowd around his pulpit! From all parts of Great Britain and the United States he receives the most urgent solicitations to go and preach the Gospel. God blesses his words to the conversion of very many souls. His name is a 'household word,' his portrait is sold everywhere, his sermons, taken down in shorthand, are published every week, and then bound in volumes, which are rapidly translated into nearly all the European languages. Now, we ask, seeing a young man in this exalted and dangerous position, do we not expect to find in him—and should we not be even ready to pardon—a certain consciousness of his importance and superiority? But one is most delightfully surprised to find in him a brother full of simplicity and cordiality, possessed of a cheerful, amiable disposition, and without the slightest trace of affectation or pride. This was the impression of all who saw Mr. Spurgeon in private, but especially of those who on Wednesday and Thursday evenings met him at the house of M. Grandpierre, who kindly procured for the numerous friends who desired to be better acquainted with Mr. Spurgeon the opportunity of speaking a few words with him and pressing his hand. He seemed not to be aware that he was the one object of interest to all present, and had a stranger entered that crowded drawing-room, he would have had some difficulty in ascertaining who amongst that motley group formed the chief attraction."

Pastor Grandpierre also gave an article on the same subject in *L'Espérance,* of February 15, and from this a short passage may be quoted :—

"Spurgeon is truly a poet, and without having heard him one cannot even form an idea of the richness and power of his conceptions, and this, too, without even swerving from the simplicity which beseems the Christian pulpit, or the dignity which becomes a minister of Jesus Christ. . . . Both before and after his sermons, public and private prayer-meetings were held to invoke the blessing of God on his labours, and we are sure that souls were converted and believers edified, nourished, renewed in their inner life, and stirred up to fresh activity. Our dear and honoured brother received a most cordial welcome from Christians of all denominations in the capital, and he left us interested and grateful, happy in the reception which has been accorded to him, and promising soon to revisit us. On our part, we bless God that the Presbytery and Council of the Reformed Church of Paris considered it an honour to throw open to him the doors of its largest temple, which was filled at both services by an eager crowd. And of this grand assembly, the members of our Church happily formed no inconsiderable portion, thus proving once again that we have in our midst very many souls who know how to love and appreciate the earnest and faithful preaching of the 'Gospel of the grace of God.'"

But the good opinion of brethren in the faith such as the evangelical French *pasteurs* was to be expected, and the full effect of this visit to Paris of the distinguished English preacher was not fully seen or realised until the merely secular papers had made their comments. One of the most distinguished literary men in Paris at that time was M. Prévost-Paradol; and when such a writer, a Roman Catholic, sent forth a eulogy on the Calvinistic Spurgeon in one of the leading daily papers of France, it was looked upon as something very surprising. M. Prévost-Paradol wrote as follows :—

"Mr. Spurgeon has spoken; the indefatigable apostle has passed three days amongst us, and has preached five times without anyone being able to remark in his privileged nature the least trace of fatigue. And yet we do not think that any orator could throw more of humility into his speech or deliver himself with more ease to his audience. Without ever declaiming or becoming too much excited, Mr. Spurgeon is animated and interesting from one end of his discourse to the other. His subject is often a common one and its development is foreseen: that which one cannot understand before having heard Mr. Spurgeon is the persuasive, familiar, and yet commanding manner which draws on his auditor and conducts him, without fatigue, through that long chain of recitals, images, exhortations, and prayers of which Mr. Spurgeon, with so much art, composes the rich and solid tissues of his discourses. But why speak of art with reference to the most natural, and we would willingly say the most inspired, orator we have ever had the pleasure of hearing? Never has anyone spoken with less apparent preparation, or previous study been less felt, and yet what hearer of Mr. Spurgeon has remarked, we do not say the least indistinctness, but the least feebleness or the least hesitation, in the perpetual flow of his simple and forcible eloquence? One listens with security to that powerful and sympathetic voice which never falls too low, or is raised too high, and which, during whole hours, filled with its even flood the vaults of the church. The man who has received all these gifts, and who makes so generous a use of them, is not yet twenty-five years of age. It is impossible to look at this energetic and loyal character without reading in it the conviction, the courage, and the genuine happiness of doing good. This orator, who is perhaps more listened to than any other citizen of a free country, where freedom of speech exercises so noble an empire, is at the same time the most modest and simple of all men. It is true he has the happiness of addressing a people who do not think themselves obliged, in order to be liberal, to be unjust towards religion; but, after all, Mr. Spurgeon owes to himself alone the considerable and salutary influence he has acquired, yet no one would suspect him of being proud of it. Truly, and without affectation, he ascribes it all to God. It seems to us that all religious differences ought to lose themselves in rendering justice to such apostles. As for us, who have seen in this eloquent and benevolent young man one of the happiest examples of what can, in these modern times, promote Christianity and liberty, we have felt it a great honour and pleasure to shake hands with him." *

On the Sunday after his return from Paris Mr. Spurgeon preached at Exeter Hall on the Immeasurableness of Sin, the text being Psalm xix. 12, " Who can understand his errors? " The freshness and force with which he treated the subject would not have led anyone to suppose that he had just gone through such an arduous week's work on the other side of the Channel. There can now be no doubt that he was working too hard ; but so far were all from believing this at the time, that they supposed the iron constitution to be capable of meeting whatever demands youthful enthusiasm might make upon it.

On Wednesday, March 14, Mr. Spurgeon visited Dr. Campbell, who was, in the young preacher's estimation, a veritable Greatheart and the Luther of the nineteenth century. The conversation related to the sudden deaths of certain well-known personages which had recently occurred, all present little thinking that news of the death of the veteran editor's son, Mr. George C. Campbell, was even then on the wing. This promising youth, whose manners were frank and genial, had chosen the sea as his profession, but, after completing a few voyages, he perished by drowning during the heavy gales in the Atlantic in the early spring of 1860. The sermon preached at Exeter Hall on March 18 Mr. Spurgeon called " Memento Mori," the text being Deut. xxxii. 29, " O that they were wise, that they understood this, that they would consider their latter end ; " and references were made to Dr. Campbell as a champion of the faith, and to the brave young

* Translated and quoted in *The Freeman* (March 14, 1860), from the *Journal des Débats.*

officer who had been washed from the deck of the barque *Native*
during a storm in mid-ocean.*

The visit paid to Dr. Campbell was an annual one, and these
occasions were something more than mere exchanges of friendly
intercourse. The veteran editor himself once explained their
object:—"Every 365 days Mr. Spurgeon and his dear companion,
and the two little Princes Imperial, honour my family with their
presence for a whole day. We count on it; it is a high day with
us. By two sermons on that day I may say Mr. Spurgeon supports
almost entirely our City Mission at the Tabernacle." The reference
was, of course, to the Tabernacle in Moorfields which had been erected
for Whitefield, and of which Dr. Campbell was pastor, although
through loss of voice in the later years of his life he devoted his
energies to journalism rather than to preaching. Mr. Spurgeon's
opinion was that the religious Press of that day had two sides, and
that the doctor represented the better side. "He has the most
thundering pen in all the universe," the young pastor once emphatically
remarked. "If he will give me some portion of the kingdom of the
tongue, I shall willingly let him have that of the pen. His pen is
like Ithuriel's spear: it has detected many of the toads of false
doctrine now in existence, and I have no doubt it will detect and
turn up many more."

* A brief account of this accomplished young man, who was an author of promise as
well as a sailor, appeared in *The British Standard*, March 16, 1860.

CHAPTER XXXIX.

A PROTEST AGAINST FALSE TEACHING.

Progress of the Tabernacle—Sermon on behalf of Young Women—Brown's "Divine Life in
Man"—Protest of Spurgeon and Six Other Leading Ministers—Visit to Birmingham—
Visit to South Wales—Tour on the Continent.

THE Metropolitan Tabernacle being now in course of erection, great
interest was naturally felt in its progress, not only by the congregation it was intended to accommodate but by the public at large.
Hence, on Monday evening, April 2, a full meeting was held at New
Park Street Chapel to report progress and to adopt measures for
securing further subscriptions. Mr. Spurgeon himself presided, and
was able to congratulate his friends on the success which had already
been achieved. From what was further said, the audience inferred
that the new Tabernacle was to a great extent a copy of the Surrey
Gardens Music Hall. The panic in the latter building had taught
some useful lessons. As Mr. Spurgeon remarked, " A great improvement has been made in the mode of access to the galleries, there being
a staircase to each of them, so that no crush or inconvenience would
be felt in the ingress or egress. It takes about twenty minutes for
the people to get out of the Surrey Hall, but this building, though
crammed, would be cleared in some five minutes." The great building
was then described, and it was spoken of as a place which was being
built with large intentions. The subscriptions to date were nearly
£19,000, leaving over £12,000 to be subscribed before the sanctuary
would be free from debt.*

On Thursday, April 12, Mr. Spurgeon preached at Bloomsbury
Chapel on behalf of the Society for the Rescue of Young Women and
Children, the text being St. John viii. 10–11, " When Jesus had lifted
up Himself, and saw none but the woman, He said unto her, Woman,
where are those thine accusers ? " etc. After making some references

* *The Freeman*, April 12, 1860.

to the calamities which sin brought upon its victims, the preacher went on to speak of Christ's methods of dealing with particular sinners :—

"He did not condemn them but said, Go and sin no more. The reason He did this was because the condemnation against this sin had but a very feeble effect. Moses decreed stoning; but how ineffectual it was, seeing that a whole host of Pharisees indulged in it. The penalty had evidently failed to produce the desired effect. This one instance might be confirmed by all history. When any very stringent law was made against a crime, they had generally seen that that very crime increased. Forgery, horse-stealing, etc., were far more rampant when punished by execution than they were in their own day. Mere punishment, mere law and terror, had always failed in subduing the wickedness of the human heart. Certainly he did not deny that it had had a slight check on wickedness, but at the same time the thing had been a defeat and not a conquest. The conduct of the Lord was right towards the woman, because, unless they were prepared to say that Jesus Christ's motive was a mistaken one, they could not say He was mistaken in this act. But he (Mr. Spurgeon) did not see how Christ could have condemned the woman. There were two taken found committing adultery, and only one of the guilty persons brought before Him. If she had been before any judge, surely he would have said, 'Bring the other,' and when they saw the Christian Church acting as a mighty matron, looking down on the fallen daughters of Eve, did they not all say, 'Why does she not do so to the men?' because they were the ringleaders in sin, they first pulled their daughters from the stars and hurled them down to the depths of miry clay. Now that the law had proved a failure, let them try what the Gospel could do." *

It was about this time that the late James Baldwin Brown published a volume entitled "The Divine Life in Man," which showed the author to be a disciple of Maurice. To this work, John Howard Hinton wrote an answer, and when these "Strictures" were reviewed in the Baptist organ, appearances showed that the writer of the review agreed with Baldwin Brown rather than with his critics:—

"Mr. Brown's chief fault is inconsistency with himself, and it would have been better if Mr. Hinton had paid particular attention to this, and exposed his inconsistencies in detail, instead of conjuring up to himself a bugbear of heterodoxy beginning to be rampant in the churches which it shall be his 'mission' to destroy. We have no belief in this phantasmal hydra, and regret much that it so haunts the brain of some of our venerated and beloved brethren. We believe it to be a delusion of Satan's by which the great enemy has grievously succeeded in weakening the spirit of mutual confidence, and in destroying unity of action amongst the ministers of Congregational and Baptist churches." †

* *The British Standard,* April 16, 1860.
† *The Freeman,* April 4, 1860.

It almost appeared as though this reviewer wished to run with the hare and hunt with the hounds: he favoured or corrected each side in turn; for while Mr. Hinton's production was "most objectionable," the doctrines it advanced were "important to be upheld." Accordingly the next number of the paper contained what was not only a protest against Brown's erroneous teaching, but a condemnation of the bias of *The Freeman* itself, this being signed by Mr. Spurgeon and six other foremost men in the denomination.* The passages singled out by Mr. Hinton are spoken of as containing "pernicious error," and Mr. Hinton was held to have rendered "valuable service to Evangelical Christianity" by the publication of his "Strictures":—

"We are no more lovers of controversy than your reviewer, but if errors subversive of the Gospel are advocated by some of her ministers, it is the duty of others to withstand them. . . . Without conjuring up any 'phantasmal hydra' of heterodoxy, as your reviewer speaks, and imagining that it is beginning to be rampant in our churches, which we do not for a moment suppose or believe, we take the liberty of saying that we trust our ministers will continue to be students of Howe and Charnock and Hall and Fuller rather than draw their theology from Maurice, Professor Scott, and others of the same school whom Mr. Brown so strongly recommends."

The preacher thus publicly reprimanded wrote a short note to *The Freeman*, complaining that Mr. Spurgeon had joined six others in an endeavour to prejudice his ministry. The apologist for T. T. Lynch during "The Rivulet" controversy also preached in his own defence at Clayland Chapel, Kennington, on April 22. The matter, too, was mentioned in the pulpit at New Park Street Chapel on April 15. *The Nonconformist* devoted a leading article to the subject, and thought that a mistake had been made, and to this Dr. Angus wrote a vigorous reply. *The Freeman* also referred to the subject again at length; and it was in reply to this that Mr. Spurgeon wrote a letter which filled over two columns of *The British Standard* of May 25. After some introductory remarks as regarded the reasons which led to the sending forth of the Protest, Mr. Spurgeon asked:—

"How, think you, was this admirable document received? Why, sir, it was supplemented by an editorial postscript, the marrow of which consisted in a joke upon the juvenility of three of the brethren, who are yet old enough to know some who are their juniors in years,

* Edward Steane, Daniel Katterns, Charles Stanford, W. G. Lewis, Junr., William Brock, and Joseph Angus.

and a few who are far more their juniors in decency. A ghastly smile, like that which flickers upon the face of a man who is confused and confounded, but who longs to conceal his fears with the mask of levity, was the only answer we received. We were dealing with divine realities, and with verities which concerned the very basis of our holy religion; the reply was a play upon a harmless sentence, highly appropriate in the mouths of most of the seven, and not indecorous upon the lip of any one of them. This absurd trifling was esteemed to be so terrible a piece of artillery that it must needs be fired off again at Exeter Hall on the Missionary occasion, to the disgust of many of the audience, by a gentleman who was so alarmed at the stupendous engine with which he was entrusted that the echo of his own voice seemed to startle him, and one word from an indignant hearer extorted a trembling apology. Was he the reviewer who caused all the mischief? Did an uneasy conscience blanch that cheek, and cause that grim sarcasm which received a cheer or two because it was not understood? If it be so, it is time that the *incognito* of reviews should be rent away, when common decency cannot restrain a man from stepping forward to be his own champion, to defend in his public position a deed which he dares not avow to be his own."

This refers to the speech of one who was easily recognised. The controversy shifted somewhat from the book complained of to the conduct of a newspaper. At all events, it is the paper which Mr. Spurgeon is chiefly concerned with in his memorable letter to Dr. Campbell's journal. One more passage may be quoted:—

"*The Freeman* affirms that some of us had never read the book to which we referred. I am sure I had both read and marked it, but as to inwardly digesting it, I am not nearly enough allied to an ostrich to be able to accomplish that feat. Next, it unfairly takes it for granted that the letter of Dr. Angus was a joint affair, although it is his writing, and his alone. Admirable as it is, that letter is no more the composition of the whole seven than is this epistle, which the Editor will take care to observe is mine, and mine alone. A worse act than this imperiously demands inquiry. *The Freeman* must make good a statement to which I am now about to refer, or tacitly admit that its courage and truthfulness have vanished. *It dares to say that one of us had previously approved of Mr. Brown's book.* Name the man. Why stab the whole seven in the dark? In the name of common honesty, not to say religion, point out the individual. None of us would take the pains to deny an accusation so indefinitely worded. The charge is so serious that, to whomsoever it may be falsely applied, it will be his duty, for the protection of society, to visit the author of the libel with the fullest punishment the laws of his country can enforce, unless an ample apology be forthcoming. The imputation is tantamount to calling a man dishonest, if not a liar; and what remains to any of us when such charges are allowed to pass unchallenged?"

While the excitement occasioned by this Protest was at its height Mr. Spurgeon visited Birmingham. He arrived in the great Midland town on April 24 and remained until the next day. Without having to notify the fact of the services, 6,000 tickets were disposed of in a few hours; and the distributor of these is said to have had his bells broken down by the unceasing peals of applicants. Soon after this, Mr.

Spurgeon found rest to be necessary, and the commotion occasioned by the Protest against false doctrine died away.

It is evident that Mr. Spurgeon intended to write more on this subject, but he found more profitable employment, and does not appear to have given the matter further attention. On Wednesday, May 30, he visited South Wales, and preached in a field at Abercarn to 20,000 people. Lying in Mynyddyslwyn parish, this busy town has its tin-plate works as well as its great collieries; and the seat of Lord Llanover is the great house of the neighbourhood. " Among those present," says a local newspaper, " were the Lord-Lieutenant of Monmouth-shire, and Mrs. Leigh; Lord Tredegar, Lady Tredegar, and family; Lord Llanover, Lady Llanover, and family; and a large number of the leading gentry of the county." No more pleasing sight could have presented itself to the preacher than such a congregation made up in large measure of the working classes, and an incident occurred which showed him to be above all else a preacher to the people. The personages of the county were there in great force; but their four-horse carriages were on the outside of the crowd, and not in the best place for hearing. A cry arose for the people to move aside so that the vehicles and their distinguished occupants might approach nearer to the preacher. When he discovered what was being at-tempted, Mr. Spurgeon at once called out, " I did not come here to preach to horses but to men; four horses and a carriage would occupy the ground of fifty people, and therefore the horses and carriages must remain where they are." After the service the Lord-Lieutenant sent for Mr. Spurgeon and asked him to visit Pontypool; but it appeared that such a visit would be impossible, as preaching engage-ments had already been made for two years.

It was now nearly seven years since Spurgeon had first appeared in London; and the hitherto unrelieved strain of his heavy labours at last began to produce symptoms which could not be ignored. He complained of weariness, such as had not been experienced before. Since the days of Wesley, there was no record of a preacher having gone through such a term of service; for during the seven years an average of ten sermons a week had been preached, the congregation occasionally showing a total of 30,000 persons. The only way to prevent a complete breakdown was to seek relaxation for a time from such exhausting toil; and accordingly, arrangements were made for a tour on the Continent. On Monday evening, June 4, a crowded meeting was held at New Park Street Chapel, several well-known friends giving addresses while the assembly took farewell of the pastor and his wife, and wished them God-speed on their travels. Arrangements were made for various eminent ministers to conduct the services both at Exeter Hall and New Park Street during the pastor's absence.* It was also felt to be desirable that the erection of the Tabernacle should be proceeded with as rapidly as possible, so that a meeting might be held in the great building before the end of the summer. It was thought that such a meeting would not only be of general interest, but would stimulate the collection of the money still needed.

But even this necessary break in the round of toil was not a complete holiday, for sermons were given in some of the chief cities of the Continent. After June 3, Mr. Spurgeon did not preach in London again until July 29. As the first holiday in seven years, this was not too long; and it would have ceased to be a holiday at all if he had responded to all the demands which interested persons would have made upon him. For example, there were publishers who would gladly have issued a book of travels by the popular preacher; but he felt that taking notes for such a purpose would be too irksome, and that it would be as profitable to continue work at home as to become a slave abroad.

---

* One of the supplies was Mr. Henry Northrop, as we see from the following notice :— "On Sunday his (Mr. Spurgeon's) place was occupied by the young evangelist of America, Mr. Northrop. In the evening Exeter Hall was crowded in every part; but we noticed the absence of many of Mr. Spurgeon's usual hearers, their places being occupied by strangers, amongst whom were many Americans, one of them Mr. J. B. Gough, the temperance orator. Many of those present, who seemed to have read the 'Sketch of Mr. Northrop's Life,' just published by Mr. Stevenson, of Paternoster Row, were freely remarking on the juvenile appearance of the preacher, scarcely believing he could be more than twenty years old. In the evening New Park Street Chapel was as full as ever, and Mr. Northrop delivered a touching and impressive sermon to the young."—*The Christian Cabinet,* June 13, 1860.

CHAPTER XL.

ALTHOUGH Mr. Spurgeon did not consent to take notes for a
book such as would have delighted the heart of a publisher,
he supplied his friend Dr. Campbell with at least one ample letter
which is even now of historical interest, especially when read in connection with what has since happened in France and Germany. The
young pastor happened to be at Baden-Baden at the time of the
Conference of June, 1860, which was attended by the late Emperor
of the French, and eight other crowned heads. "One could hardly
walk in any direction without stumbling upon a Grand-Duke, or being
run over by the horses of an Emperor," we find it remarked. The
hotels were not only overcrowded; the demands of their regal visitors
were so urgent that more humble patrons, whose custom at ordinary
times was welcome, had to stand and admire at a distance.

The late Emperor of the French passed through Strasburg on Friday,
June 15, when the streets were abundantly decorated and crowded
with sightseers. One striking feature of the scene was the large number
of country people who came in to see the pageant. Garlands of oak-
leaves and tricolour flags decorated the quaint-looking old houses of
the more ancient streets, as well as the more elegant mansions of the
newer thoroughfares. Even the guards, of whom travellers had sometimes to complain, were in a good humour. Across the river, "the
town of Kehl was resplendent with the orange and red colours of the
Grand-Duke of Baden." It was supposed that there was enough of
the "French element" in the populace to account for the existence
of this "Imperial fever" on one side of the river as on the other.

What Mr. Spurgeon wrote of the French Emperor, who then had ten years of rule before him, will be read with interest:—

"If the people of Kehl received the Emperor heartily, they were the only Germans who would have done so, for everywhere throughout Belgium, Prussia, and the small German kingdoms, he is either dreaded or execrated. It is the universal belief that he will never be content until he has completed the 'natural boundary' scheme by subduing all the territory on the west of the Rhine to his imperial sway. If the English are no friends to Napoleon, the Germans go even further, and are more anti-Imperial than ourselves.

"On Saturday the Emperor might be seen early in the morning walking in the garden leaning upon his walking-stick, and looking more decrepit than his age might justify. It is a theme for great gratitude that he is not a young] man, and that, be his ambition what it may, he has no great time before him in which to work out his political adventures. On horseback or in his carriage, all men confess his noble bearing, and no signs of decay are manifest, but when he is walking, the spectator foresees that the greatest of men are mortal. During the greater part of the day the Emperor returned the visits of the Princes who had waited upon him in the morning. Possibly the laws of etiquette may in this case have been very agreeable to the great one, for it enabled him first to see all the Princes together, and then to give them a lesson privately and individually. Who can tell what devices were in the heart of the mighty? Who shall fathom the depth of the thoughts of kings? May the Lord rule and overrule, and out of every evil may His glory spring. The Princes and Dukes may have rejoiced at the coming of the Lord of France, but the people wondered what it all could mean, and forebodings of evil were neither rare nor frivolous. As for the little Kings, they came to this place like moths to a candle. Uninvited and unexpected, they must needs come forth to the presence of the potentate, if not to be lacqueys to his pride, at least to sun themselves in his superior glory. It is to be hoped that the dexterous player has not succeeded in throwing the apple of discord among these minor monarchs: divided they would soon be overcome, but united they might oppose a serious barrier to any aggrandisement he may anticipate. I like not to see either thieves in company or kings in conclave. Eagles come not together unless they scent the prey. All may be well, and the meeting may be a friendly visit and an exchange of courtesies, but uneasy thoughts will suggest themselves; for when the wolf inspects the sheepfolds and dines with the shepherds, the silliest of the sheep are troubled at nightfall.

"When the Emperor came forth from the hotel to his carriage, the populace of Baden gave him unmistakable evidence of their feelings towards him. Several gentlemen have assured me that the hissing was very far in excess of the few notes of acclamation. Even in the Conversation House, where the *élite* of the visitors were assembled, the hisses were very distinct, and must have been an unpleasant sound to one who breathes the air of flattery and eats the bread of adulation. When the Grand-Duke afterwards appeared, the people cheered him very heartily, as if to show for whom the sounds of disapproval had been intended.

"After all, as far as I can judge, it is not what he has done, but what he may do, which causes this ill-feeling towards him. Some men would have done less and have had more credit for it, but this man continues to mar all his good deeds by a crooked policy which leads most men to suspect his best actions and to impute to him designs which may be very far from his thoughts. Worse men than he have been better liked; and yet there is no injustice in this treatment of him, for his conduct courts suspicion and his dark reserve creates distrust." *

Sunday, June 17, appears to have been the day chosen by these magnates for their chief time of deliberation. When neither crisis

---

* C. H. Spurgeon's letter in *The British Standard*, June 22, 1860.

nor disaster was impending it seemed to be a scandal to the young London preacher that this should be the case. "Here were all the days in the week, all equally available, no haste compelling, no wars alarming, and yet none of their own six days will suit them: they must usurp God's peculiar day, as if they were lords of the Sabbath, or irresponsible to the laws of Heaven." In what degree were these potentates responsible for the gaieties of the Continental Sunday, which deprived the weekly rest day of its use and charm? Mr. Spurgeon continues:—

"The companies of country people who filled the roads were very interesting to observe; and as I looked from the windows of my quiet chamber upon the gaiety which the advent of these princes had caused upon a day consecrated to rest and worship, I could not fail to remember that men in high places have vast responsibilities, and God alone knows how much of the sins of the nations will be visited upon the heads of their governors. They are not only partakers of other men's sins, but creators of evil. Surely there are chains of darkness of unusual weight reserved for these ringleaders in rebellion."

Mr. Spurgeon witnessed the departure of Napoleon III. for Strasburg, and he penned this little word-picture of what was an interesting historical scene:—

"The Emperor left for Strasburg at 10 o'clock p.m., and his train started in the midst of a silence more profound than I had ever remarked before. Standing on the edge of the crowd, I was astonished to the utmost at a stillness like that of death—a quiet which was not broken until the cause of it had departed; then every man breathed freely, and as the Duke of Baden rode back to his castle, the people gave him loyal cheers, which contrasted with the gloomy silence with which the Gallic despot had been greeted. To my mind there was something truly dignified in this noiseless censure: to hiss might be but a display of weak impertinence, but to be sternly silent was the noble rebuke of resolute minds. I ought to have said that on Saturday there was a fine illumination at the Conversation House, which is the grand resort for the company who are staying in the neighbourhood, and the building in which is concentrated the gambling for which the town is famous. Beyond this one display I did not perceive a flag or light upon any house or hotel. This was very strange to me, for if in any English town there had been but one king, much less nine, there would have been some sort of display, unless, indeed, the unpopularity of one of the number had been great enough to compel the people to ignore the existence of the other eight."

These passages, as coming quite fresh to readers of this generation, will be read with keen interest. They are a fair sample of the book which such a writer would have produced had such work been the object of his tour. The truth was, however, that the storing up of illustrations for his discourses, and thus to utilise all other material that might be gathered on his travels,

x

was much more advantageous to Mr. Spurgeon than it would have been to give it in books or in newspaper letters. What the pastor says about the Emperor shows him to have been a keen observer of life. What were the notions of the once mighty potentate respecting the great English preacher? I once heard that, when Napoleon was a refugee at Chislehurst, in his last days, a friend who encountered him in his walks asked the fallen ruler a question concerning the pastor of the Metropolitan Tabernacle. " The Rev. C. H. Spurgeon, I thought your Majesty might have heard of him?" It transpired, however, that the ex-Emperor had been so engaged with other matters that he knew nothing about the most popular of English preachers.

Mr. Spurgeon gave an account of his adventures during this tour at a large gathering of friends, who, on his return to England, welcomed him home in the then half-finished Tabernacle; but it will be more convenient to conclude the account of the holiday before any reference is made to the business meeting.*

When he left London in that March-like month of June, the pastor was accompanied as far as Gravesend by a number of friends; and, after taking farewell of these, he proceeded to Antwerp with an Essex captain, who was well competent to exchange anecdotes with a genially communicative passenger. Concerning this veteran Mr. Spurgeon said :—

"We soon chimed in : I began to tell him some anecdotes and he began to tell me some. Some of his were original : I will tell you one, because it tends to illustrate the town in which we landed—Antwerp. Antwerp is so full of Virgin Maries that you cannot turn the corner of a street without meeting one—sometimes under a canopy of many colours and arrayed in all manner of pretended jewellery. Well, so many of these Virgin Maries are there that the sailors believe every image they see to be the Virgin. A sailor who landed went and bought some tobacco. When he came to the ship, one of them said, 'This is very good tobacco, Jack; where did you get it?' 'Oh,' he said, 'you will know the shop, for there is the Virgin Mary sitting over the door smoking a pipe.'"

Judging from appearances, it was inferred that more was thought of the Virgin Mary in the city than of Christ Himself. A grand procession from the fine old cathedral, the priests and their

---

* For accounts of this tour, as given by Mr. Spurgeon himself, see *The Times*, for August 22, 1860; *The British Standard*, for August 24, 1860; and *The Freeman*, for August 29, 1860.

attendants carrying lamps and candles in the daylight, made this even more apparent. They were said to be taking the sacrament to certain sick persons; and, as the ecclesiastics passed the houses, candles were lighted, although these were blown out as soon as the procession had passed. What was regarded as being especially scandalous was the fact that even Protestants were seen to light candles in honour of the host. "I should like to have seen Martin Luther with a candle before his door," remarked Mr. Spurgeon. "If there had been one, it would have been to set the priests' dresses on fire, or to have burned the Pope's Bull." Beneath the shadow of the cathedral, things too grossly indecent on the one hand, and crosses on the other, might have been purchased, thus showing that Romanism failed even to affect for the better the morals of the people, so that the English preacher had his Protestant sympathies strengthened :—"When I saw the gems that were in the shrines, the costly marbles, the rich and rare pictures; and when I saw their Calvaries, as they call them, with representations of Christ and His Apostles, and all those things, I felt my spirit stirred within me at the sight of a people so wholly given to idolatry. I believe Antwerp to be the most religious place on the face of the earth in a bad sense, that is, the most superstitious."

It was found that the Emperor Napoleon was as much disliked in Belgium as he was feared in Prussia, so that the storm-clouds of war, which were to burst with such disastrous effect ten years later, were already gathering. Mr. Spurgeon judged of the national feeling from what was said by a party of gentlemen with whom he had some conversation, and who maintained that, as Napoleon had already been permitted to annex Savoy, no hindrance would be offered by England to his taking Switzerland, or rectifying the borders of the Rhine, should he feel so inclined. The preacher appears to have said the best that could be said for his country. "Do you not think that if Napoleon were to touch any of your provinces on the Rhine, England would certainly speak out?" he asked. "No," replied one of the Prussians; "your nation never speaks out except it touches your commerce: you are a people that care for nothing or nobody except Manchester." This was thought to be not far from the mark. While shrinking from doing anything which might stir up the war spirit, Mr. Spurgeon maintained that Oliver Cromwell was the best peace-maker; for to say the right word at the right time, and to strike evil-doers, tended to peace-making more than did vacillation.

Brussels was visited, but that city was not found to be of any remarkable interest. What such a divine found reason to say of the preaching of certain priests in the Romish communion, however, must be given:—

"I heard a sermon in a Romish church. By the side of the pulpit was fixed up a crucifix, and the good man—for I believe he was a good man—was continually pointing to it and preaching Christ crucified. He did preach Christ crucified; he spoke of the love of Christ so that I, who am a very poor hand at the French language, could understand him. He did not say 'justification by faith,' but he did say 'efficacy of the blood,' which comes to very much the same thing. He did not tell us we were saved by grace and not by works, but he did say that all the works of men were less than nothing when brought into competition with the blood of Christ, and that blood was in itself enough. I was pleased to find my opinion verified that there are some even in that apostate Church who cleave unto the Lord—some sparks of heavenly fire which may perhaps guide poor souls to the rock Christ Jesus. I saw in that church a box for contributions to the Pope. He will never grow rich with what I gave him. I have seen money-boxes on the Continent for different saints—Santa Clara, San Francisco, San Dominique—another box for the Virgin, and another for the poor. But I could never make out how the money got to the Virgin and to the rest of them."

Something was said about several towns, and the long hours which the people worked, especially the women, who, in some parts, appeared to be strong and masculine, while they did more than the men. Many Irish were also met with here and there—men who volunteered to serve in the army of the Pope, and to whom no compliment could be paid. After passing through Frankfort and Heidelberg, a stay was made at Baden, and the gaming found to be going on there was characterised as the most dreadful sight this young pastor had ever beheld:—

"The Conversation House is a most gorgeous building. Wealth could not make it more splendid than it is. You are admitted without charge. The most beautiful music that can be found is there; and if there is a special concert, it is always free. The theatres are free, all the places of amusement are free, even the public library is free; nothing has to be paid for. You ask me how this is supported. To the left of the building there are two rooms for gaming. I went in. Here is a great table and a

GAMBLERS AT BADEN.

357

large crowd standing round it. Four men sit in the middle with a kind of rake pulling money this way and that way, and pushing it here and there. I hardly ever saw such a lot of money except at a banker's counter. You see a young man come in, he looks round him, but he does not seem like a gambler at all. He puts down half a napoleon. In a minute it is shovelled away and he has lost his money. He walks round again, puts down another: this time he is successful, and has got two. You see women sitting in this place all night long playing high stakes. Some people win, but everybody must lose sooner or later. The banks clear a tremendous sum every year by simply making the odds so great against those who play that they must lose; and thus all these splendid places, the theatres and so on, are kept up by the gains of sin. Besides this, a large sum of money is paid to the State, and the shareholders divide a large percentage upon their money. None but fools will go there to play, yet I had the sorrow of seeing many such. Some will spend so much there that they have scarcely enough to take them to England —some not enough. Such is the infatuation, that you feel you must put down something; and if you had not strong principles you would be carried away by the torrent. Some defend the system, but I hold it to be fraught with the deadliest evils of anything ever invented by Satan himself. I saw an old, respectable-looking man, not unlike my friend Dr. Campbell. He came there and put down £10, he won; put down £20, again fortune favoured him—£40—£80—in a few minutes he won £160; then he took it all up, put it in his pocket, and walked away as coolly as possible. That man will certainly lose, for he would come on the morrow, and play so deep that he would sell the house that covered his children's heads, and the very pillow from under his wife. The worst thing that can happen to a man commencing to play is to win."

Some earnest warnings against gambling were given; and the change from the gaming-tables at Baden to the Alps at Schaffhausen was a grateful one. The first sight of the "everlasting hills" made an impression which was lasting. "Is that solid—that snowy glitter that I see yonder? Is it the sunrise, is it cloud, or is it a mountain?" Passing on to Zürich, the fair was found to be interesting, while the costumes of the country were remarkable. The Reformation had also its agents still in the country :—

"At Zürich, I saw in the fair, what I also saw at Baden, that which gave me great pleasure. Opposite the house at Baden, where sin and wickedness reigned, there was an agent of the Bible Society selling Bibles and Testaments. I purchased a Testament, and felt quite cheered to see that little battery erected right before the fortifications of Satan; for I felt in my soul that it was mighty, through God, to the pulling down of his strongholds. In the midst of the fair at Zürich, where, like at John Bunyan's Vanity Fair, all manner of things were exposed for sale, stood a humble-looking man selling Bibles, Ryle's tracts, and somebody's sermons. I must confess I felt pleased to see my own sermons, for they have been translated into French, German, Dutch, and Welsh, so that you may scarcely go anywhere where you may not hit upon a copy."

After a Sabbath at Lucerne, the party ascended the Rigi, and then a visit was paid to the pastor of Geneva and historian of the Reformation, Dr. Merle d'Aubigné, and also to Pastor Bach. The doctor missed the great English preacher at the railway station; but, while in the city, he met with a friend who gladly recognised him, and who said, "Come to my house—the very house where Calvin lived." Mr. Spurgeon appears to have been entertained in the house of an eminent banker named Lombar, who is described as a "godly and gracious man." The company was in all respects suited to his taste, and his enjoyment correspondingly great. The Established and the Free Churches had had some differences, but their differences occasioned less friction than of old, and all welcomed most heartily their distinguished English visitor. Some of Mr. Spurgeon's further experiences in this city of Calvin and of the Reformation may be given in his own words :—

"I was really allowed to stand in the pulpit of John Calvin. I am not superstitious, but the first time I saw the medal of John Calvin I kissed it; and when the pastors saw my reverence for him, they presented me with a magnificent medal. I preached in the cathedral of St. Peter. I do not suppose half the people understood me, but it did not matter about understanding, for they were very glad to see, and to join in heart with the worship in which they could not join with the understanding. I did not feel very comfortable when I came out in full canonicals, but the request was put to me in such a beautiful way that I could have worn the Pope's tiara if they had asked me. They said, 'Our dear brother comes to us from another country. Now, when an ambassador comes from another country, he has a right to wear his own costume at court, but, as a mark of very great esteem, he sometimes condescends to the weakness of the country which he visits, and will wear Court dress.' 'Well,' I said, 'yes, that I will, certainly; but I shall feel like running in a sack.' It was John Calvin's cloak, and that reconciled me to it very much. I do love that man of God, suffering all his life long, and yet not only enduring persecution from without, but a complication of disorders from within, and yet serving his Master with all his heart. I want to ask your prayers for the Church at Geneva. That little Republic stands like an island surrounded by France. But I can assure you there are no greater anti-Gallicans in the whole world than the Genevese. I took rather a wicked delight in saying to them, 'Why, you are almost French people.' At last they hinted to me that they did not like me to say so, and I would not say it any more. They are afraid of being Frenchified; they cannot endure it. They know the sweets of liberty, and cannot bear that they should be absorbed with that huge monarchy. M. d'Aubigné charged me with this message, 'Stir up the Christians of England to make Geneva a matter of special prayer. We do not dread the arms of France, nor invasion, but something worse than that—namely, the introduction of French principles.'"

At that time arrangements were being made for the Evangelical Alliance to meet at Geneva in the following year, and Mr. Spurgeon was regretting that he would not be able to be present. The journey from Geneva to Chamouni was an exhilarating experience never to be forgotten :—"You feel that you are going up to heaven just as these mountains are." Then came the passage of the Simplon Pass, and the entertainment at the famous Hospice on the summit, in which were found four or five Augustine monks. The very name of the illustrious Christian Father made this a congenial retreat :—

"They asked us to go in; we entered, and were shown into a very nice room, where cake and wine were awaiting us, and, if one had chosen to order it, we could have had soup, or fish, or anything we liked, and nothing to pay. They told us that they always fed a hundred people every day gratuitously, and sometimes as many as twelve hundred. Of course, no one who could afford it would go away without giving anything to the poor-box. I was delighted to find that they were all Augustine monks, because, next to Calvin, I love Augustine. I feel that Augustine was the great mine out of which Calvin digged his mental wealth; and the Augustine monks in practising their holy charity seemed to say :— 'Our master was a teacher of grace, and we will practise it, and give without money and without price to all comers whatsoever they shall need.'"

While on his interesting tour Mr. Spurgeon passed through France, Belgium, the minor States of Germany, and Switzerland. Two sermons were preached at Geneva, and these discourses were published both in French and German. The medal of John Calvin was voted to the preacher by the congregational authorities as a memento of his visit. The principal places on the Rhône, Milan, Mantua, Verona, and Venice were visited, five days being given to the last-named city.

Mr. Spurgeon was very cordially welcomed back by his people on Sunday, July 29, when he preached at Exeter Hall. The text was Job xii. 9, 10; and the improved health and spirits of the pastor afforded great satisfaction to all friends. The Tabernacle builders had made considerable progress with their work, and a determined effort was now necessary in order to obtain the needful funds in time for the opening. Many difficulties had to be overcome. Some of these were of the usual commonplace kind; and then there was the drawback of an unfavourable season through excess of rain. Under such conditions, and when the building would cost over £31,000, it required some courage for a young pastor to declare that he would not conduct a Sabbath service in the chapel until the builder was fully paid.

CHAPTER XLI.

A THANKSGIVING MEETING.

Meeting in the unfinished Tabernacle—Letters to Mr. T. W. Medhurst—Strict Baptist Objectors—
Visits to the Provinces and to Scotland—Preaching in a Barn.

ON Tuesday, August 21, 1860, Mr. Apsley Pellatt presided at a great meeting in the only half-finished Tabernacle, "for the purpose of offering up devout thanksgiving for the success of the undertaking, and making an attempt to raise the remainder of the required funds so as to open the place free from debt." The chairman referred to the old times of John Bunyan and Rowland Hill, to the progress made in relation to religious liberty; and, as one of a different denomination from the pastor's, he wished him all possible success. Mr. Spurgeon made some characteristic allusions to certain of his friends who were present, especially to Dr. Campbell, and to Hugh Allen, who was then rector of St. George the Martyr, Southwark. Mr. Spurgeon himself was in good spirits, and concerning the building itself he said :—

"If my unbaptised brethren on the platform were to fall through the floor, they would find themselves in the baptistery. There is no water in it now, but whoever of you want, in obedience to your Master's command, to be immersed, I shall be glad to be your humble servant. I believe the acoustic arrangements of the building are excellent, though I do not think the science of acoustics is understood. I have heard people say that the building is not so large as they expected it would be, but that just shows that it is excellently proportioned. It is so big that it would hold two chapels like the tabernacle in Moorfields. I do not care a single farthing about the exterior: I will have no towers, for they are only for show. The building is magnificent without being gaudy, and it shows neither extravagance nor meanness."

The young pastor went on to describe other parts of the building, and expressed the hope that, following in the wake of his predecessors, he might be spared to minister for fifty years in the chapel. He added that he should feel like "a guilty sneaking sinner" if the chapel had a debt upon it when he preached his first sermon from its pulpit, for the Scripture said, "Owe no man anything." A hope was also expressed that the rector of St. George's would accept an invitation to preach in the building.

The rector made a short speech, and was followed by Dr. Campbell, who, as one of the London ministers who at first had some misgivings about Spurgeon, had at last came round to be his most enthusiastic advocate. The doctor said :—

"I sat in perfect astonishment as I listened to the record of the facts as set forth by the treasurer, and thought of the young man, Mr. Spurgeon, coming to London from the country, unnoticed and unknown. I thought of the historian who says of one who went down to Egypt, 'God was with him.' Now, Mr. Spurgeon came here, and God has been with him. The work is a mighty one. I came with Mr. Spurgeon and saw this gigantic edifice some three or four months ago, and was filled with amazement. I had never seen such a structure before, and rejoice that I live in the period when such a one has been brought into being."

After wishing that the pastor might be spared to labour in the chapel for fifty or sixty years, Dr. Campbell had to make a confession to the effect that he had once suspected that the young preacher from Waterbeach was an upstart. He had even declared that Spurgeon should never preach in the pulpit at Moorfields, but he was now proud to see him there on the occasion of his annual visit on account of the City Mission. Others, such as the Revs. Jonathan George and William Arthur, also gave addresses, and the people then inspected the building. In the evening Mr. Spurgeon gave an account of his Continental tour, and the subscriptions amounted to £1,050.*

On Thursday, September 6, a visit was paid to Holyhead, two sermons being preached in a large marquee erected for the occasion at great expense. About five thousand persons were present at each service, while on a great platform were a large number of ministers, as well as of the nobility and gentry of the neighbourhood. The admission was by ticket, ranging from 3s. 6d. to 6d., the proceeds being devoted to a new chapel at Newry, the foundation-stone of which was laid by Mr. Spurgeon after the evening service. This service was partly in Welsh, and a contemporary account † says that

* A very full report of this meeting appeared in *The British Standard* of August 24, 1860. An account was given in *The Freeman* of August 29, 1860; see also *The Times* of August 22, 1860.

† *The Freeman*, September 12, 1860.

a prayer offered by a minister from Denbigh "seemed to electrify all present." An historical sketch of the rise and progress of the Baptist denomination in Holyhead was read, and an address was delivered by Mr. Spurgeon, who also laid the stone.

In the autumn of this year Mr. Spurgeon lost, by death, his old friend Dr. Alexander Fletcher, whose funeral took place in Abney Park Cemetery on October 8. On Lord Mayor's day, 1860, another good friend also passed away in the person of Alderman Wire, who two years before had been installed Lord Mayor of London, and who had taken the chair at the evening meeting on the occasion of laying the stone of the Metropolitan Tabernacle.

Mr. Spurgeon always showed great regard for those who passed through the Pastors' College, and he seems to have harboured peculiar affection for those who had been the earliest of his students. He kept up a correspondence to the last with his "first student," Mr. T. W. Medhurst, a friend who has made several contributions to this biography. In sending the enclosed Mr. Medhurst remarks:—

"Here is a characteristic letter, showing his yearning desire for the spread of the Gospel, and the increase of the Lord's kingdom in the villages:—

"'Clapham, 1860.

"'MY DEAR MEDHURST,—Your kind letters always do me good. I have had nothing but joy in you, and such joy that it takes away many of my bitters. Your grateful recollections of the very little which I did for you come like a refreshing breeze on a sultry day.

"'Allow me to suggest the establishment of Baptist churches in villages around Coleraine, to be supplied by lay, *alias* local, preachers.

"'I am labouring to increase our stations, and have seen great success. We have Malden, Beddington, Cheam, Staines, New Court, Dockhead, Brentwood, and Grosvenor Street. In two of these there are now rising churches. My own opinion is that if there are only eight or nine in a village, they should be formed into a church, and set to work to increase and multiply.

"'There were, in 1653, Baptist churches in Waterford, Clonmel, Kilkenny, Cork, Limerick, Galway, Wexford, Carrickfergus, and Kerry. Where are these now? Could they not be recommenced, if only in small rooms or cottages? It is a solemn thing to lose one church: it is like blotting out a tribe from Israel. See to it, brother Medhurst. Try to be the Oncken of Ireland. God bless you and yours.—Yours very truly,

"'C. H. SPURGEON.'"

Mr. Medhurst further remarks:—

"Possibly, at one period of his life, Mr. Spurgeon may have

had the thought of forming a distinct body, not separate from the Baptist denomination, but a body of men within the denomination who should be 'set for the defence of the Gospel,' as he believed and taught the 'truth is in Jesus.' Here is an extract from a letter written to me on my removal to Glasgow from Coleraine, Ireland, which seems to hint in this direction:—

"'My dear Medhurst,—I hope ever to see all our Churches perfectly one in heart. The time approaches for the formation of a distinct body or confederation, and to have two large interests in Glasgow will be noble indeed if they agree in one.

"'We had such a meeting last night. The Lord is with the College. We only want faith, and that is growing. We will fill the nation with the Gospel, and then send our armies out the wide world over. Big words, but written in faith in a great God. God bless you and yours.—Yours ever lovingly,

"'C. H. Spurgeon.'

"The following note, on my leaving Glasgow for Portsmouth, is characteristic:—

"'Clapham, S.W., August 2, 1869.

"'My dear Friend,—I suppose you maun be flittin', but it's nae weel for Glasgie. God be wi' ye.

"'C. H. Spurgeon.'"

On Monday, December 5, another meeting was held in the schoolroom of Islington Chapel, Upper Street, at which Mr. Spurgeon presided, and at which the progress of the Tabernacle was reported. The pastor showed that he should not like the chapel to have a debt, because it would not do to have it said that they had had to borrow the money. "But do not imagine that because you subscribe now, you will not have to do so hereafter, because you will be most mightily mistaken," remarked the chairman. "Other things will occupy attention which, if we were in debt, we should not be able to perform. You are all aware that I have undertaken to prepare a few young men for the ministry; but I hope, when the chapel is paid for, to raise the present number to a hundred. I believe I have a call in this matter. I am not to bring out scholars, but rough thunder men that can preach and be understood. I have often felt that there is a lack of these men— men who suit the people and speak to them in their own language." At that time over £6,000 had to be subscribed. "I intend to be a beggar to-night," said Mr. Spurgeon; "a beggar as bold as brass.

It is a matter that will only occur once in my life, and I therefore feel like the man who said, when he was doomed to be hanged, 'It's only once, and I should like it done thoroughly well.'"*

The Strict Baptists still affected to look with misgiving on the pastor at New Park Street. One of the first of those who went forth from the Pastors' College to accept a pastorate was the late Benjamin Davies, of South Street Chapel, Greenwich, a man who was held in great esteem, and one who regarded Mr. Spurgeon with great affection. Davies had a friend at Leicester who belonged to the straitest section, of which James Wells was a leader, and this friend had been recommended to read the published sermon on "God's Sovereignty and Man's Responsibility," if he wished to have doubt removed respecting Spurgeon's orthodoxy.

The sermon was procured and carefully read, but it failed to yield satisfaction. The Christian brother wished there was more in it than there was, so that he could have spoken better of it. "He certainly has the form of the doctrine of sovereign grace in it, and as much of the power of it as any intelligent mind might attain and be altogether carnal." In other days the writer had known as much about this grace as the preacher, but was, at the same time, "as dead in sin as a stone is to natural or animal life." Hence it followed, "if Mr. Spurgeon has no better testimony to the power of sovereign grace in his own soul than he has given in that sermon, I believe it is quite possible that he may be like King Saul, have *another heart*, but not a *new one*." The hope was charitably expressed that Mr. Spurgeon would not "go over to Popery," while the method of his conversion seems to the writer to be unscriptural.† There still remained a section therefore who would not accept the Gospel as preached at New Park Street, or who would not admit that the preacher really understood the matter in his heart.

It was at this time that Mr. Spurgeon consented to become

* *The Freeman*, December 5, 1860.

† "Mr. Spurgeon's Views of Responsibility and Sovereignty," in *The Earthen Vessel*, xvi. 58–60.

joint-editor of *The Baptist Magazine*, the other editors being Messrs. Daniel Katterns and Samuel Manning, the one pastor at Hackney and the other at Frome. In days when no Baptist newspaper existed, the monthly denominational organ had been successfully conducted by Mr. William Groser, who was born in 1791 and died in 1856.* In the number for January, 1861, Mr. Spurgeon had a characteristic article on *Charity*, in which Gurnall's saying was quoted—"Love goes ever armed with zeal, and draws the dagger against all opposers of truth."

With the Metropolitan Tabernacle approaching completion and with no signs visible of their pastor's popularity declining, the congregation at New Park Street saw a great future before them. Though only twenty-five years of age, Spurgeon was now very commonly spoken of in newspapers as "the great preacher of the age." *The Bookseller* notified the fact that six millions of his sermons had been sold in six years; and, in addition to those read in English on both sides of the Atlantic, there were translations into French, Welsh, Dutch, German, and Swedish. "For a preacher to produce a sermon every week for publication is something wonderful," remarked *The Wesleyan Times:* "for those sermons to sell by thousands and even by tens of thousands is more wonderful still. When such remarkable facts come before us, we must note them."

Flying visits to the provinces were still made on week-days, and vast crowds were attracted. Towards the end of January, 1861, services were conducted at Sunderland, Stockton-on-Tees, and York. Leeds was visited on February 12, the service being in the Town Hall, when the tickets of admission ranged from a shilling to half-a-crown. A sum of £50 was given to the Tabernacle fund. On the following day, and under similar conditions, services were held in the United Methodist Free Church, when the Wesleyans were delighted with the preacher's account of his own conversion in the Methodist Chapel at Colchester.†

---

* *The Baptist Year-Book*, 1858.   † *The British Standard*, February 22, 1861.

Meanwhile enthusiastic meetings were held in London, from time to time, in order to raise the funds which were needed to clear the new Tabernacle from debt. One of these meetings came off on the day after Christmas Day, when Mr. W. G. Haynes lectured on Alpine Rambles, Mr. Spurgeon following with the subject of Southwark in the Olden Time. "The interval was occupied with music and various other amusements." * On New Year's Day, 1861, Mr. W. Roupell, M.P., took the chair, when nearly £1,000 was collected. The chairman spoke as an earnest philanthropist. In the following year, as all the world knows, there came a melancholy sequel to such apparently enthusiastic utterances. On Monday, February 4, a number of friends assembled in the Tabernacle itself, when £4,000 still needed to be raised, and when Mr. Spurgeon repeated what he had often said before, that he would not preach on a Sunday in the new building until all the money needed was either given or promised. If the funds were not forthcoming, the new and completed chapel would stand unused, while the congregation would still have to assemble at Exeter Hall and New Park Street, suffering all of the inconveniences with which experience had made them familiar. Early in March a circular was issued to notify that the building was nearly completed, and that only £3,000 was then needed to complete all payments. It was believed that this amount would be raised by a bazaar, and by the gifts of friends at the opening services.

In the early part of March, Mr. Spurgeon undertook a northern tour, preaching at Preston, Carlisle, and Newcastle, then proceeding to Scotland, services being held at Edinburgh, Glasgow, Perth, Dundee, Montrose, and Aberdeen. We find this tour described in one journal as "quite a triumphal march." At Edinburgh services were held at the Music Hall and the Assembly Hall. A number of Havelock's men were then at the Castle, and these were specially invited by the preacher to be present. "About one hundred attended, and allusions were made to their late commander and to their services in India."

* *The Baptist Messenger*, February, 1861.

Concerning the services in the Scottish commercial metropolis, *The Glasgow Examiner* said:—

"On some former visits we heard, among the captious people of very refined taste, of odd sayings and unwarrantable eccentricities, and very offensive sayings for ears polite; but, on this occasion, not a syllable of such criticism has been heard. The newspapers have been either silent or complimentary, and the people who listened to the discourses are entirely agreed about their gravity, soundness, and vast importance. The matter of the various discourses was such as to disappoint the envious, the fastidious, the critical; but those who went to find occasion against the manner or matter of the preacher could find nothing on which to lay hold."

The same journal gave a view of Spurgeon as a worker, and of his treatment by the Americans :—

"Some of his discourses have passed rapidly through many editions. Some volumes of his sermons sold in America to the extent of 250,000 copies; but, since his famous letter against slavery, matters have taken such a turn as to give a melancholy view of the power of slavery. He has been burned in effigy in every slave-holding State. His sermons have been publicly burned as unfit to be read in a State founded on the principle that all men are free and equal; and, what is most marvellous of all, the sale of his sermons has been completely stopped! Such is slavery in America at this hour, and it is not wonderful that a nation that tolerates such outrage on free opinion should be in trouble and about to explode. As much was got from the sale of his works in America (for though some will not believe it, he found honest publishers there) as went far to support his twenty-five students; but that source of revenue has been dried up, and these young men must be otherwise supported."

According to *The Morning Journal* of Glasgow, more than half the clergy of the city were present at the services at the City Hall and at the Queen's Rooms. "A Glasgow magistrate" gave a glowing account of the services in *The British Standard*, quoting the couplet in regard to the preacher's style—

"Though deep, yet clear; though gentle, yet not dull;
Strong without rage; without o'erflowing full."

At Aberdeen 5,000 tickets, ranging from a shilling to half-a-crown each, were sold long before the preacher entered the town.*

Mrs. Spurgeon accompanied her husband on this tour, and

* It was during this visit to Aberdeen that Mr. Spurgeon publicly referred to a well-known weekly paper:—

"One thing I always like to have—the hatred of *The Saturday Review* and the love of God. No movement can ever hope to be established as a movement until it has had both. When it has both, then it is all right. When you have the hatred of *The Saturday Review* you may be quite sure it is according to the mind of God." In reply to this the journal in question remarked: "The formula is neat and exhaustive—neatly and tersely put; only we have something to say about the terms." See the entire article, "Mr. Spurgeon Across the Tweed," in the number of the paper for March 23, 1861.

Sunday, March 10, was passed at the manse of John Anderson, the pastor of Helensburgh. Mr. Spurgeon preached twice in the Free Church; and in addition conducted another service in the manse garden, which is very beautifully situated on rising ground. There was a very large congregation, and the preacher addressed them from a table according to the example, which he ever admired, of Wesley and Whitefield. All the people in Helensburgh had not the discernment of their minister, Mr. Anderson, however; for one old Scotchwoman, who was accompanied by a younger friend, was far from satisfied. "I ne'er did hear sic a mountebank performance," she exclaimed at the conclusion of the service; and when the preacher came down and offered to shake hands, while passing, neither of them would countenance that civility. Nevertheless, after she became converted, the younger of the two hearers learned to admire the great preacher very greatly for his work's sake, and when he died she mourned for him as for a brother. On one or two occasions she communicated by letter with Mr. Spurgeon, and she treasures certain notes of acknowledgment which came in reply. If Mr. Anderson had lived, he would have been able to give some striking reminiscences of this and other visits. On one occasion the two took a drive to Loch Lomond, and while this was greatly enjoyed by the London pastor, he gave his more elderly Scotch friend ample evidence of the way in which he could choose a text, and then arrange the divisions and chief ideas which were suggested.

The preacher continued to meet with adventures, the details of which were more or less amusing. In May, 1861, a London correspondent told an anecdote relating to something which happened at Tring, in Hertfordshire, while Mr. Spurgeon was staying there. The people wished him to address them, but no building was available:—

"A Nonconformist minister was first applied to for the loan of his chapel, but returned an indignant refusal. An application to the vicar for the use of the parish church met with a similar response. An open-air meeting in the existing state of the weather was out of the question; and, there being no room in the village sufficiently large to accommodate a quarter of the expected audience, it began to be feared that the whole affair would drop through, more especially as Mr. Spurgeon had to leave for town by an early train on the following morning. In this dilemma a small farmer in the neighbourhood offered the use of a large barn, which was gladly accepted. An extemporaneous pulpit was hastily constructed, and long before the hour appointed every corner of the place was crowded with expectant listeners. On entering the pulpit Mr. Spurgeon informed his congregation that, although he had been only asked to give one sermon, it was his intention to deliver two. After a long and brilliant discourse in his own peculiarly forcible and impressive style, he paused for a few minutes, and then proceeded:—'And now for sermon number two—a plain practical sermon. Our friend who gave us the use of this building is a poor man. When I saw him this morning he wore a coat all in tatters; his shirt absolutely grinned at me through the holes. Let us show our appreciation of his kindness by buying him a new suit of clothes.' The suggestion was immediately adopted, and in the course of a few minutes some £10 or £12 were collected. On his return to London Mr. Spurgeon related the circumstance to some of his congregation, who testified their appreciation of the respect paid to their pastor by subscribing a further sum of £20 for the benefit of the Hertfordshire farmer." *

At the end of March, 1861, the Metropolitan Tabernacle was completed, so that the pastor and his people now entered on a new era of usefulness.

* *The Glasgow Examiner.*

Y

CHAPTER XLII.

OPENING OF THE METROPOLITAN TABERNACLE.

First Sermon in the New Chapel—A Bazaar—A Memorable Easter-day—Week-day Services—
Ireland and the Irish—Work at Southampton—Baptists and their Literature—Spurgeon
"Waxing Morbid"—Dr. Guthrie's Testimony—In Wales.

MR. SPURGEON preached for the first time in the Metropolitan Tabernacle on the afternoon of March 25, 1861, the text being Acts v. 42, "And daily in the temple, and in every house, they ceased not to teach and preach Jesus Christ." The opening service had taken the form of a prayer-meeting at seven o'clock a.m. on the Monday preceding, however, and on the next day there was a bazaar. This was visited by some two thousand persons, including many members of the aristocracy, the stalls being well furnished with goods needed in every-day life as well as things of a more fancy kind. It was remarked that "the centre of attraction seemed to be a large stall presided over by Mrs. Spurgeon, who had the most miscellaneous assortment of goods in the bazaar; for she not only sold baby-linen, pictures, and other fancy goods, but also dealt in daggers, one taken at Delhi, and another, if we correctly remember the fair lady's statement, at Sebastopol. Mrs. Spurgeon tried, *à la* Robins, to dispose of these articles, saying that they would be very useful to those fond of curiosities, but had not found a purchaser for them up to nine o'clock on Tuesday night." *

On Tuesday evening, March 26, a meeting of the subscribers to the building fund was held, when three thousand persons assembled, and one chronicler reports, "When the building was lighted up, the spectacle was one of the grandest and most imposing we ever witnessed." Sir H. Havelock presided, and while

* *The British Standard*, March 22, 1861.

he had to confess that a sum of £3,000 was still required to discharge all liabilities, he hoped their experience on that occasion would correspond with that of the Israelites who brought more than enough for the requirements of the house of the Lord. The pastor still resolved not to preach in the chapel on a Sunday until all the funds needed were subscribed; and yet his desire was to preach in the building on the next Sunday. Mr. Spurgeon said:—

"It was thought at first that it would be a foolhardy thing to attempt to raise £12,000 for the erection of the building; but, as they proceeded, they looked for £15,000, and afterwards for £30,000; and, as their own ideas swelled, the liberality of the Christian public increased, so that his faith did not stagger through the weight of the difficulty, but through the weight of God's mercies. Money had flown in upon them from America, Australia, and every part of the world. His wish was that whatever income was to be derived from the sittings might be devoted to the training, under his direction, of young men for the work of the ministry."

After several other addresses had been given, the announcement was made that the amount of money required was subscribed; on hearing which the people rose, and sang the Doxology, and at the pastor's request repeated the verse.

On Wednesday evening, March 27, Dr. Steane presided at a meeting of members of neighbouring churches in the new Tabernacle, when, after acknowledging himself to be everybody's debtor, Mr. Spurgeon added:—

"My dream and the promise are fulfilled—the promise God would help me to build a place the income of which would be devoted to the training of young men for the ministry, not with any view of interfering with or setting aside the colleges, but to bring out rough earnest men, who would lose their vigour if too highly polished. I hope you will all say something this evening, however short it may be. Some of you who have the gift might say a sovereign, and others, who have not such golden eloquence, half-a-crown, a shilling, or even a sixpence."

On Sunday, March 31, Exeter Hall was crowded in the morning, that being the last service prior to the final removal of the congregation to the Tabernacle. On the preceding Friday, being Good Friday, the pastor preached twice in the new building; and then on the evening of Easter Day he had the happiness of conducting the first Sunday service in the chapel, which was free from debt. The discourse was based on passages which had reference to the building of Solomon's Temple. The building was crowded, and the outer gates had to be closed to keep back the throng in the street. Dr. Campbell characterised the spectacle as "stupendous and unparalleled." Never before had he set eyes on such a congregation beneath one roof, and the sight was almost oppressive to the mind. In the graphic description which the veteran journalist gave at the time he seems to have thought the building to be in all respects successful. Perhaps the strangest arrangement of all to one over sixty years of age was the pulpit, or rather, what would appear to him as the absence of any pulpit. "What may be considered as the pulpit" was to him "a handsome gallery with a table and a desk," being furnished with a sofa. "At the back are six separate seats resembling those of first-class railway carriages, where the deacons sit in state like so many judges," he remarks; "while Mr. Spurgeon in front sustains the combined offices of Lord High Chancellor, Lord Chief Justice, and Attorney-General, doing the whole of the speaking with a vigour and a vivacity which enliven all around." The doctor then depicts the preacher as he saw him on that memorable night:—

"There stands the herald of salvation: he reads the word of the Lord, and every utterance falls distinct on the ear of the thousands around him. The multitudes lift up the voice of praise, which is as the sound of many waters. It ceases: the accents of prayer succeed—prayer, true prayer, the utterance of the heart, simple, direct, fervent, vehement, penetrating all and moving very many. . . . There stands the preacher as a man amongst men: he seems quite at home, but the idea of display, either in matter or manner, appears never to have entered his mind. . . . It was clear, however, that now the preacher has found at last a burden to try his strength. He might be likened to a powerful man under a ponderous load: he still walked firm and steady, but every muscle was tried to the uttermost, and his tread was heavy on the ground—any material increase would have brought him down."

As he sat behind the preacher on that Sabbath evening Dr. Campbell asked himself what would be the effects of the ministrations of such a man in such a building? The shrewd observer looked at the matter as an Independent, and the conclusion he seems to have arrived at was that his co-religionists would never be able to hold their own against such a competitor. Thus, in *The British Standard* of April 12, he said:—

"The building will inevitably form a powerful magnet, especially to young people, in all quarters of the city, who will hardly endure the old-fashioned churches and chapels of their fathers. The result will be to confer on it a leviathan monopoly. This monopoly will operate in two ways: it will bring multitudes from the world to the Cross—an event in which we shall most sincerely rejoice; it will also draw multitudes from the churches to the Water—an event in which we do not rejoice. This Metropolitan Tabernacle, we believe, will do more to make proselytes than all the other Baptist chapels in London united. It will lift the thing into respectability and even dignity. It will become an object of ambition with sentimental young women and poetic young men to be plunged into a marble basin so beautiful that it might adorn a palace, and so spacious that dolphins might play in it. Then Mr. Spurgeon knows well how to go about this matter: his noble catholicity has not sufficed wholly to eliminate his baptismal bigotry. His manly eloquence will most powerfully minister to the triumph of the polished marble. He showed last Sabbath evening that, while prepared to die for the Gospel, he is not less prepared to fight for the Water!"

After the first Sabbath evening service the Lord's Supper was celebrated; and, while the galleries remained nearly full, the ground floor was filled with communicants, the number of visitors being so large that their names could not be taken according to the usual custom. As an observer belonging to another denomination Dr. Campbell was struck with Mr. Spurgeon's method of administering the ordinance, a manner which may at first have been peculiar to himself, but which was generally followed by those who came forth from the Pastors' College. Thus, after reading the words of Scripture instituting the Supper, the pastor asked his deacons to assist in breaking the bread, which they did in the face of the congregation instead of having the bread cut up and placed on plates beforehand. Then as the Supper as instituted by Christ was taken in a reclining position, all sat while singing the hymn. Though this method was new to him, Dr. Campbell declared it to be "right in principle and happy in effect. The domestic aspect was complete."

The opening services of one kind and another kept on week after week. "Never was such an edifice so built," we find it remarked; "never was any edifice so opened." On Tuesday, April 9, there was a sermon by Hugh Stowell Brown, followed by a baptismal service. This was sketched by Dr. Campbell, who thought, however, that nothing sectarian should have marred the programme of such a glorious month:—

"The interest of the thing was overpowering. We doubt if it was a whit inferior to that of Taking the Veil in the Church of Rome. There was the young orator, the idol of the assembly, in the water with a countenance radiant as the light; and there on the pathway was Mrs. Spurgeon, a most prepossessing young lady with courtly dignity and inimitable modesty—the admiration of all who beheld her—kindly leading forward the trembling sisters in succession to her husband, who gently and gracefully took and immersed them, with varied remark and honeyed phrase—all kind—pertinent to the occasion and greatly fitted to strengthen, encourage, and cheer. Emerging from the water, there were two portly deacons in boxes at the side of the steps, with benignant smile, to seize their hands and bring them up, throwing cloaks over them; two other deacons received them at the top of the steps, and another two politely led them backward to the vestry. It was quite an ovation, an era in the history of the neo-phytes. It had really not been wonderful if all the ladies in the place had been candidates for such distinction. We have ourselves seen several who were there whose heads seemed completely turned."

Among the chief of the meetings which followed was that for the Exposition of the Doctrines of Grace on April 11; and that of the following evening, when Mr. Henry Vincent gave an oration on Nonconformity, the audience being worked up to a high pitch of excitement by the lecturer's rhetoric. The services throughout were regarded as a novelty and as a whole unparalleled. *The Freeman* thought the time given to the discussion of the doctrines of Calvinism the dullest evening, which from the nature of the subject before such a mixed audience may have been the case.

Throughout the progress of this great enterprise, the conduct of the young pastor had been so entirely removed from any self-seeking that he had been generally commended by the Press and by outsiders, although there still remained a minority of onlookers whom nothing could move into approval, and who could see no self-sacrifice in the man whose whole life had been a resolute turning aside from all temptations to mere personal aggrandisement. Thus, one Scottish journal, which was supposed to be in some sense a Christian paper, reminded "Sympathetic Aberdonians" that no more money-boxes were needed for the Tabernacle, as the place was opened and paid for; and as the building was "Mr. Spurgeon's own property, pew-rents and all," he would be able to ride in a carriage for the rest of his days. That being the case, it was hoped he would "finally dissociate the work of the Gospel from the pursuit of Mammon." Mean writers of this calibre could not understand Spurgeon : the truth about his devotion to the Cause, and extraordinary self-sacrifice, had to be told by others :—

"Mr. Spurgeon is still in the morning of life, yet how vast and varied his achievements! How extended and merited his renown! Only six years ago, a stripling in the
nineteenth year of his age, he entered this Metropolis a stranger; but, like another
Joseph, 'God was with him'—a fact which explains all that has followed. He has in
everything far outstripped the most favoured of his contemporaries. The annals of
English Christianity present nothing analogous. His piety, genius, eloquence, and labours
have reared for him a monument which will endure to the latest posterity. When all
that now live, and their children's children to the hundredth generation, shall have passed
away, the Metropolitan Tabernacle will remain the memorial of this wonderful and
Heaven-favoured youth, who was the instrument of its erection. As a well of salvation
of matchless magnitude, an aggregate of millions may be expected to have drunk at it
the water of life before the close of ages. In the salvation of that mighty host, he will
have been indirectly instrumental, and in the world of glory, peopled with the spirits of
the just, myriads will claim him as a sublunary benefactor." *

Now that the Metropolitan Tabernacle was an accomplished fact,
the building was found to be a far more convenient place than Exeter
Hall for May meetings. The first gathering of this kind that was
held in the new chapel appears to have been the annual assembly
of the Irish Society on April 22. The speeches were by those who
understood Ireland, and who were in hearty sympathy with the
work. A passage from Mr. Spurgeon's address on the characteristics
of an Irishman may be given:—

"I am sorry that we have not an Irishman with us, as they are always such
interesting speakers. I have heard the most wonderful speeches from brethren who, I am
sure, must have been Irishmen. When it was said that if I preached so much I should
kill myself, one of these brethren said he believed I should never die while I went on
preaching as I do. Another brother, on rising to address an audience, said, 'Before I
speak to you at all, I should like to say a few words.' I wish to say a few words
about the character of the Irishman. I cannot say too much in praise of the tenacity
of the Irish character when once it lays hold of what it believes to be true. If the
raw material for martyrs were needed again, you must get an Irishman—he is the man
to burn for what he believes to be true. I do not think it an ill sign that, with all
the harsh treatment and grasping character of his priest, he still adheres to what he
believes to be his father's Church. I like the man because he will not give up what he
believes. I will not commend bigotry, or stupid, senseless adherence to a dead creed,
but still there may be good in—I must not say a holy—but certainly an admirable
tenacity which, when modified and trained, might make the Irishman the truth's foremost defender. There is another thing about the Irishman which makes him well worth
looking after—his wonderful fire. We want a few Irish preachers—I will not say in
our own denomination, but in many Dissenting bodies; men who do not require stoves
in their chapels, but who are stoves themselves. We have had enough of those dry
brethren who understand magnetising people till they go to sleep. We need preachers
who cannot say anything better than has been said, but can say it in a more lively way.
If we had an Irishman or two in our committee, I think it would be a good thing.
He is the man to suggest new schemes of raising money. I have heard of an Irishman who
proposed to teach the people by Sabbath-schools held two days a week, and of another,

* *The British Standard*, April 12, 1861.

who, when the tithing-man came, proposed that it should be diminished from a tenth to a fifth. If we had such a man, he would be going about proposing that instead of 10s. a year subscription, it should be 5s. a quarter. An Irishman on the committee would be worth almost as much as the Secretary himself."

All this time the pastor of the Metropolitan Tabernacle felt great interest in the progress of his brother at Southampton. On May-day Mr. Spurgeon preached in Above Bar Chapel, which was lent for the occasion; and a tea and public meeting in Carlton Rooms followed. A piano, worth seventy guineas, was presented by the people to Mrs. J. A. Spurgeon; and on the following day Mr. Spurgeon, of London, presided at the meeting at which the church was formed, of which his brother James was to be minister—"A Particular Baptist Church, strict in fellowship, but holding open communion."

At the end of the spring, or at the beginning of June, a feeling of great weariness again came over the young preacher, so that engagements were cancelled, and Mr. James Spurgeon preached at the Tabernacle for one Sunday, thus allowing his brother to be away in the country for some days. Dr. Campbell received the following note for publication:—"Mr. Spurgeon begs to inform the public that he is knocked up with hard work, and is compelled to go into the country to rest. This will upset all arrangements, and he begs his friends to remit his promises, and the Christian public not to inundate him with invitations."

The strain and the excitement of the spring had been great, so that there was nothing surprising in the fact of the pastor being reminded that he possessed only human attributes. At one communion after the chapel was opened, a hundred persons were admitted to church membership, and one hundred and forty at another. Dr. Campbell remarked, "This is pretty well as times go, making, we believe, a total membership of nearly 1,900 members." An article was mentioned which had appeared in *The Record*, pointing out the kind of powerful popular preaching that was needed for the times, not mere learning or rhetorical eloquence, but faithful messengers of Christ speaking in the spirit of the Baptist—"Prepare ye the way of the Lord." Such preaching was to be heard at the Metropolitan

Tabernacle; and while Calvin himself would have put his seal on the doctrines taught, Whitefield would have certified to its eloquence. It is then said:—

"Charles Haddon Spurgeon is not one of a class, but an individual chosen for the accomplishment of a special work; and mentally, morally, and physically, he is every way admirably adapted to his mission. His seeming defects, in the eye of some, are special excellences. He is not to be judged by the petty rules that poor mortals have derived from the creeping experience of the past. Nothing were easier than to prove that he is often wild and erratic, and transgresses the canons of the schools. He is above the schools. He is a law to himself, and wholly unamenable to the tribunals of criticism. He simply exerts the powers, peculiar and wonderful, with which God has endowed him. He reads, he expounds, he prays, he preaches, as nobody else ever did, or, probably, will ever do. He is an original and a rebel in everything. But, his insurgency notwithstanding, he is the impersonation of the profoundest loyalty to a higher law. Comets are not less amenable to rule than suns. Through his disobedience he achieves his triumphs and rules the millions."

At the same time it was feared that the young pastor was going to extremes in the matter of baptism. As an editor of *The Baptist Magazine*, Mr. Spurgeon at this time contributed an article on Ministers' Libraries, in course of which he said, "We are not a literary people, and the few scholars among us are hardly denominational enough to add much to Baptist reputation." It was also thought that important advantages were being lost through failing to cultivate a denominational spirit.

To this exception was taken — "The great orator is waxing morbid, we might almost say rabid," it was remarked. The Baptists were not thought to show any shortcomings in the direction of zeal in advancing their own distinguishing tenet on the question of baptism: the tendency was believed to be rather in the opposite direction. There was a text which Spurgeon might venture to speak upon—"Christ sent me not to baptise, but to preach the Gospel"—words of the great Apostle in which the mere ordinance seemed to be thrown into the shade, and which thus seemed to breathe a spirit different from that which moved the pastor of the Metropolitan Tabernacle. "With the one the ordinance is secondary; with the other, primary. With Paul the water is merged in the truth; with Spurgeon, although the truth is not merged in the water, it seems almost, if not altogether, placed on a level with it." * It was thought that there might be danger in what seemed like excess of zeal for baptism. But the fears of Pædobaptists were never realised so far as Spurgeon was concerned.

Another observer, who was equally warm-hearted, harboured no such fears concerning his friend. In the course of a speech made about this time at Edinburgh, Dr. Thomas Guthrie said:—

"When in London two years ago, I went to hear that great man Mr. Spurgeon. I didn't care about how he affected duchesses and countesses who were among those that thronged to hear him, but what I wanted to know was how he affected the people down in Surrey. With the view of testing that, I fixed my eye upon two persons sitting opposite to me in the gallery. From their appearance I judged them to be a greengrocer and his wife. We heard a noble sermon—noble in its truth, its talent, and its telling effect. Some things among those that were said did, I do confess, grate on my ear; but, after all, they were as mere spots on the sun; and what I was interested in was to watch how the greengrocer and his wife were affected; and this is what I saw. Regularly at each recurring passage that jarred on me I observed that they were stirred and thrilled, for they looked in each other's eyes with a quickened intelligence, and by the light of the glance which they reciprocated I read their feeling. 'Well, isn't that fine!' There was, I believe, a ploughman once in Wales who was gifted of God with a rare faculty of speaking in a manner that at once told upon the rich and affected the poor; but God's ordinary method of endowment is to give different gifts to different men. He is pleased to use a variety of tools, some being rough and some smooth, some sharp while some are heavy. One man he uses to break up the fallow ground, one to plant the seed, and one to water what has been entrusted to the ground. One man is a Boanerges, and another a Barnabas—one a son of Thunder, and another a son of Consolation."

Soon after Midsummer, 1861, Mr. Spurgeon was again suffering from overstrain; and on July 4 his brother had to take one of the great preacher's engagements at Islington Chapel. A short time was passed on the shores of Lake Derwentwater, which helped to bring back the needed health and strength.

It was about this time that a visit was paid to Swansea, which excited the greatest interest in the town and neighbourhood. Although the preacher did not arrive at the railway station until nearly midnight, hundreds of persons were waiting in order to accord him a hearty Welsh welcome and, if possible, to shake hands with him. The scene was of a kind that must have been novel even in such a person's experience. "Good-bye, my friends," said the visitor, as he was driven away to Mr. E. M. Richard's house at Brooklands, "I hope to say a word of great import to you to-morrow."

* *The British Standard,* June 7, 1861.

On the morrow the rain came down most depressingly, but all were disposed to look at things on their brightest side, especially as Mr. Spurgeon himself offered to act in the most self-denying manner. The service was to have been in the open air, according to Welsh fashion on a great occasion; but, as that could not be, it was arranged that two services instead of one should be held in the morning. This involved double labour, which was cheerfully borne; and then, as the weather cleared, a great open-air service was held in the evening. Long before the time for commencing the approaches to the field were thronged with people. The service itself was described in a local paper at the time:—

"We could not help feeling that the spot was well chosen, commanding as it does a panoramic view of the town and its matchless bay, with the Mumbles Lighthouse—a beacon and a warning—resting in silent solitude in the distance. The hymns, too, and the beautiful manner in which they were sung, and the sound wafted by the summer breeze from side to side, were grand beyond conception. . . . Then, when he spoke, the plainness of his features, the bluntness of his manner, the brisk hearty sound, the clear spontaneous volume of his voice struck us as in strange contrast to the ordinary type of clerical first-raters. It was, however, when the tide of sympathetic speech rolled mass on mass, and heap over heap, and began to flow over the souls of the hearers, bathing and suffusing them with its influence, that the orator proved himself worthy of his fame. He took a solemn portion of Holy Writ for his text—'O earth, earth, earth, hear thou the voice of the Lord'—and as he went on, swaying the mighty multitude of his temporary congregation, forcing their thoughts to follow the bent of his mind, and working and winning them to his point of view, it became clearer and clearer that he had a master's power."

The Welsh are a people whom the most sanguine adventurer must not expect to captivate all at once. Even as regards such a feat, however, Mr. Spurgeon so far succeeded at an early date in his career that one admiring ancient dame ventured the opinion that the London preacher only needed to be blind of one eye to take rank with Christmas Evans himself.

Cardiff, Newport, and other towns were also visited. The afternoon service at Cardiff was interrupted by a somewhat violent thunderstorm; but that of the evening in the market-place drew together a congregation of ten thousand persons. From this time forward Mr. Spurgeon appears to have found peculiar pleasure in visiting the Principality. He is said to have declared that he never found so much pleasure in ministering to any people as the Welsh.*

* The Baptist Messenger, 1862, p. 226.

CHAPTER XLIII.

A GREAT MISSIONARY ADDRESS.

Centenary of Carey's Birth—Spurgeon's Speech—A Wesleyan Critic—A Summer of Accidents—
Spurgeon on the Ways of Providence.

ON Monday, August 19, 1861, the centenary of the birth of William Carey was celebrated at the Tabernacle. As many as 700 assembled at tea in the lecture-room, and at the public meeting at seven the chapel was well filled. Over the platform, in white letters on a crimson ground, appeared the motto—

"Expect great things from God.
Attempt great things for God."

Sir S. Morton Peto presided, and addresses were given by Messrs. J. P. Chown and Francis Tucker, the former of whom had some time before given an eloquent lecture on Carey in Exeter Hall on behalf of the Young Men's Christian Association. Mr. Spurgeon depicted Carey as an example to young men. In his day it was a new thing to talk of sending the Gospel to the heathen, and to many it was but a dream; but nevertheless the words, "Go ye and teach all nations," etc., were not Carey's, but Christ's. But to the people of his time Carey was a daring innovator. And was there not room for innovation now? We had master-minds in mechanics and manufactures, and should the Christian Church be without them? Should the Church ride on a heavy-wheeled chariot when the world was flying behind steam? Was the Church not to have some men of daring genius, who would think out new things, attempt new things, and carry them to a successful issue? Let them put down the inventor of Sabbath-schools among the greatest of innovators. Let them write down the man who brought out the ragged-schools as no mean genius; but let Carey, who taught the Church to carry the truth of life among the dead, be chief among the discoverers and

innovators who were worthy of honour. When a man once had a
good thought, he should not be afraid of it because nobody else had
thought of it. He should do it and dare it, defying custom if it
thwarted him, tearing it to pieces if it stood in the way of right.
All God's true servants were innovators. Those that turned the
world upside down were the very descendants of the Lord Jesus
Christ. Next to Carey's originality must be extolled his brave
determination. No one could now measure what he had to put up
with on first commencing the missions. He was sorely troubled in
his church by those who held Antinomian sentiments, and who perpetually declared that he did not preach the Gospel. Carey's theology,
however, was the produce of the noblest type of divinity that ever
blessed the world. He and his friend Ryland were students and
admirers of Jonathan Edwards, and if there ever was a man who
came nearest to the achievement of what was an impossibility—the
reconciliation to the minds of finite men of the two great truths of
human responsibility and divine sovereignty—it was Jonathan Edwards.
Brainerd and Carey were the living models of the Edwardian
theology, or rather of pure Christianity. Theirs was not a theology
which left out the backbone and strength of religion—not a theology,
on the other hand, all bones and skeleton, a lifeless thing without a
soul : their theology was full-orbed—Calvinism, high as you please,
but practical godliness so low that many called it legal. He did
not know whether the people in those days called Carey a Fullerite.
Perhaps they did; and to this day there were some inhabitants of
the innermost recesses of the cave of Adullam who thought it a
reproach to be called a Fullerite. He (Mr. Spurgeon) did not think
there was any reproach in the term, and although he was not prepared to endorse everything which Fuller said or wrote, he thought
it would take a long time to produce a greater theologian than he
was. A great many who scoffed at him might have been put by
his side without his knowing where they were. The old members
of Carey's church said that God's decree would be carried out without missionaries being sent to the heathen. Others said that God

had an elect people: no doubt, though they did not think there were any in India, or if there were, the Lord knew how to have His own. But Carey was not thus to be turned aside from his purpose, never doubting that if God had an elect people He would have every one of them, but equally certain that this was the reason why he should go and preach—because the Lord had much people there. There might be young men there who had been put back from preaching because some old ministers had said they did not believe in their call. If they had a right call, they would not be put back by any such thing. Some Sabbath-school teachers might have been discouraged by hearing some say they were not good, efficient teachers. Some persons wanted the Lord to send them to heaven on fine, sunshiny days, and then they would put on their best patent-leather boots and walk to glory; but the moment the Lord sent a storm, they had not got the clumped, hob-nailed boots to go trudging through the mud with. They wanted to conquer all their enemies, but they felt themselves so very valiant that they thought their backs were enough to frighten them, and so ran away. They could not put up with sneers or harsh words. But such faint hearts—such carpet knights—were not worthy of being God's soldiers and workmen. Let all young men be like Carey in determination, and when the world saw their spirit, they would honour them when their work was well done.

Carey's faith was then commended. It was a faith in God above all things; and it showed that nothing was impossible to such as believed in the Creator's power—the power that created atoms on the one hand and worlds on the other. He admired Carey all the more for being a Baptist: he had none of the false charity which might prompt some to conceal their belief for fear of offending others; but at the same time he was a man who loved all who loved the Lord Jesus Christ. The founder of the Indian Mission was then commended for his indomitable zeal, which prompted him to go through with whatever he undertook to do. If all the riches of India had been offered to him to forego his mission work, he would have laughed the offer to scorn. Was there a man of like spirit in that congregation? He would use the old term again—was there a man of like pluck? Was there a man who felt that God had called him to the ministry in foreign lands? Let him, in the name of "Him who liveth and was dead, and is alive for evermore," be a missionary, not heeding discouragement. Was the cold shoulder offered to such a one? Let him put both shoulders to the work and make them warm. Could he not see the way? Let him walk by faith and not by sight. If there was a man there who could put his teeth together, and his feet to the ground, and say, "I know that God has called me to this work, and I will do it"—do it he would, though all the committees should reject him, if he did but stand firm to his purpose. But, perhaps, some got stirred a little under an earnest sermon, or were induced by a speech like those they had heard that evening to say that they would go and do something, and yet, after a time, became cool again. It was better to make no resolves than to make them and not to carry them out. Let those who felt their spirits stirred within them go and teach in the ragged-schools, or stand up and preach in the streets of London. It was not more pleasant to preach beneath a banyan tree in India than under no tree at all in London. Sometimes after a missionary service, ten or a dozen young men would come to him next morning all anxious to be missionaries. In nine cases out of ten the resolution was probably a genuine one, and he had always told them, if they did not happen to have the exact qualifications for the missionary work, that they could be usefully engaged in winning souls here if not in other lands. He should never be happy, however, till many from that church had been sent to preach in other lands.*

Mr. Spurgeon lived to have his wish fulfilled, for numbers who are now labouring in various parts of the world have gone forth from the Pastors' College, many being members of the church at the Metropolitan Tabernacle.

In the summer of this year an able *brochure* appeared by Richard Wrench, a Wesleyan minister, entitled "The Popular Preacher;

* *The Freeman*, August 21, 1861.

or, Who and What is Spurgeon?" It was considered to be an excellent piece of literary work, and thoroughly impartial in its criticism. The pamphlet was written in an admirable spirit; and while the friends of the preacher might see good qualities recognised and defects pointed out, it was thought that Spurgeon himself might profit by the perusal of such a lecture.

The summer of this year was remarkable for its accidents, such as certain unthinking people are too ready to recognise as the direct judgments of God. On Sunday morning, August 25, a collision occurred in the Clayton Tunnel on the Brighton line, and twenty-three persons were killed on the spot, while over sixty were injured. On Monday, September 2, a collision occurred on the North London line, thirteen lives being lost. In addition to these there happened various calamities of a lesser kind. Because the victims of the mishap on the South Coast line were Sunday excursionists, some declared it was to be accepted as a manifestation of the divine wrath, and such extreme notions were even uttered in some instances by Christian ministers. Accordingly, on Sunday morning, September 8, the pastor of the Metropolitan Tabernacle enlarged on the words of Luke xiii. 1–5. It was worthy of remark, he thought, that in every age of the world many accidents of one kind or another had taken place, and just as calamitous as those which were being deplored; and those which were recorded as happening in the days of stage-coaches were just as many and as fatal as those which had followed since the invention of the steam-engine. He repudiated the notion that the collision in the Clayton Tunnel was a judgment from Heaven because of Sunday travelling: it was as likely to have occurred upon any other day as upon the Sabbath. In fact, the catastrophe at the Hampstead Junction had occurred on a Monday, and when the excursionists were going upon an errand of mercy.

FROM A PHOTOGRAPH BY THE LONDON STEREOSCOPIC CO LTD.

THE

LIFE AND WORK

OF

CHARLES HADDON SPURGEON

BY

G. HOLDEN PIKE

AUTHOR OF "THE WORLD'S WORKERS—CHARLES HADDON SPURGEON" ETC.

ILLUSTRATED WITH FIFTEEN FULL-PAGE PHOTOGRAVURE PLATES

VOL. III

CASSELL AND COMPANY LIMITED

LONDON PARIS & MELBOURNE

CONTENTS.

CHAPTER LXIII.

SPURGEON AND THE FRIENDS.

PHOTOGRAVURE PLATES.

THE LIFE AND WORK

OF

CHARLES HADDON SPURGEON.

CHAPTER XLIV.

"THE SCEPTICS AND THE SCORPIONS."

Adventures at Bristol—"Shrews"—"Eminent Lord Mayors"—Attacks of the Press—"Sceptics and Scorpions"—Reply of "Aristides."

BRISTOL was visited on Wednesday, September 11, for the purpose of opening City Road Chapel, of which Mr. Probert was then the pastor, and the riotous behaviour of the crowd appears to have had a disastrous effect on Mr. Spurgeon's nerves. The demand for tickets was very pressing. The opening sermon was announced to begin at half-past two, but crowds began to assemble an hour earlier, and "when the doors were opened, there was a tremendous rush," says a contemporary account. "In a few minutes every seat was occupied, and afterwards the passages were blocked up by a crowd that occasionally showed itself noisy and restless." When the first hymn was announced, the noise was almost too great for anything to be heard. All ended well, however: it was not until the evening service at the circus that anything more serious occurred. The building itself was crowded, even the passages were packed, but notwithstanding there were thousands outside, numbers of whom were sufficiently uncivilised to keep up a persistent knocking on the wooden sides of the house for admission, or it may have been to induce the preacher to speak to them out of doors. The service was commenced, but it was impossible to proceed. After intimating that he could not preach in the open air, Mr.

z

Spurgeon added:—" I am in the predicament of a man who has too many to hear him, and I wish that some other man would come forward to take one-half of them to himself. My nerves are thoroughly shattered by a late accident. I hope that some person will go to the police-station for assistance."

This was no easy thing to do; but someone volunteered to be let down by a rope outside. The ordeal proved almost too much for the nerves of the once strong man, who showed signs of fainting while he made the touching confession, " I wish I had the strength I had a few years ago; but I have preached ten times a week; I am thoroughly knocked up; I am getting old before I am young. After the sermon was commenced, further violent interruption occurred; but by some means, after a very short address, the preacher, whose popularity was more than his nerves could always bear, contrived to escape from his tormentors.*

It is no wonder that soon after this Spurgeon was overtaken by increased nervousness, which prevented his taking extra service for some time. He was to have preached for Dr. Evans at Scarborough, but the visit had to be indefinitely postponed.

But while preaching engagements in the provinces had to be accepted with more caution, the work at the Metropolitan Tabernacle itself was still carried on with vigour. In October a series of Friday lectures was instituted, and one of these, on the Gorilla, in consequence of the large attendance, was given in the Tabernacle itself. Usually, however, these lectures were given in the lecture room, and a small charge was made. This drew forth some hostile criticism, and was besides misrepresented.† An address on " Shrews, and How to Tame Them," which followed, seemed to have the

* For a full account of what occurred, see *The British Standard* for September 13, 1861, and *The Freeman* for September 18, 1861.

† " Misrepresentation " would appear to be too mild a word for the comments which were made on this lecture; some things which were said about it were not only disgraceful for respectable journalists to have written, they are too disgusting to be quoted. The following is mild and harmless compared with some others: " To say that Spurgeon is as good as a play is to say nothing. No play can equal him. The jest of the thing is that the popular preacher of the day, the man of the day, our neighbour's ass—the ass

effect of completing the discomfiture of the quidnuncs who were always glad of an opportunity of raising a laugh at Spurgeon's expense. In the course of this lecture he made some humorous remarks on the little animal called the shrew, and then dilated upon the human "shrew," male and female, beginning with Xantippe the wife of Socrates and coming down to Mrs. Wesley. Mr. Spurgeon, in solving the problem of "how shrews, whether male or female, are to be tamed," referred to Shakespeare's well-known play, from which he read several passages. In nine cases out of ten, he was of opinion, where a husband did not get on well with his wife, it was his own fault. There was a clergyman once who had had too much to drink when he was called upon to "sprinkle" a child. He fumbled at his book, but could not find the place, whereupon he stammered out, "What a very difficult child this is to baptise!" Mr. Spurgeon's advice to husbands with bad wives was, "Keep your temper, for love mingled with good temper will assuredly tame the most stubborn creatures." Christian women have often much sorrow of heart because they are yoked to ungodly husbands. The lecturer enumerated several instances of men having been converted through the instrumentality of the patience and forbearance exhibited by their wives.*

On November 8, the subject of the lecture was "Eminent Lord Mayors." Mr. Spurgeon was a good deal surprised that this series of lectures, instituted for the benefit of his own people, should have attracted such wide notice and such hostile criticism. Some timid souls suggested that the lectures should be discontinued, but as that

of the conventicle, whom the wise old Bishop has reminded his brethren of 'the Establishment' that it is a sin against the Tenth Commandment to covet—should be as great in the easy-chair of Rabelais as in the heights of his professional dignity. Spurgeon—it were an affront to his peculiar claims on attention to designate him as Mr. Spurgeon, and we no more think of giving him the conventional prefix than we do to Sam Hall, if such a gentleman exists, or to Mr. Robson—has been coming out again. His weekly facetiousness presents a formidable rivalry to the comic journals, and though perhaps it suggests that his other attractions are failing, it is something that a popular preacher has two strings to his bow, and that a broken-down Boanerges can make so good a Merry-Andrew." —*Saturday Review*, October 19, 1861. Much more of this kind of thing might be quoted, but it would now hardly be pleasing either to church people or dissenters.

* *The British Standard*, October 18, 1861.

would be showing the "white feather to the enemy," the pastor
declared he would do nothing of the kind. He believed that the
licentiousness of the Press had reached its height, and that if his
opponents had only rope enough allowed them, they would soon
hang themselves. In introducing the subject of Lord Mayors, he
expressed the belief that the Guildhall was a good standpoint from
which to study history impartially. As a rule the Corporation of
London had been on the side of liberty, and deserved respect : it
had done something for Protestantism. Having mentioned several
Lord Mayors, he came to the insurrection of Wat Tyler. He
declared it as his opinion that history had done but scant justice
to Wat Tyler, who had been a patriot in the early part of his
career, though he might have used his power arrogantly afterwards.
Walworth thought that Tyler was proceeding most unjustifiably in
his interview with Richard II., and therefore he slew him with a
dagger. Historians had taken different views of this act. By some
Walworth had been condemned, and by others censured, but we
probably had not the materials for forming a true judgment on
the matter. Liberty was not advanced by sanguinary deeds or by
mob violence : the boasted republicanism of America, out of which
despotism threatened to spring, gave a lesson which all ought to
ponder. He next came to Sir Richard Whittington, and having
given the chief particulars of his so-called history, he said that not
one word of it was true. He was sorry for it : he wished it were
true, and he had no doubt they and the people who came after
them would go on believing it. Whittington's father was a man
of substance, and he had come of a good family. Richard II. was
then reigning, and Whittington gave him one-tenth of his property
to carry on the war in which he was engaged. Richard was in
the habit of getting the London merchants to send him blank
cheques, which he filled up with any amount he thought fit.
Whittington invited the king to a magnificent banquet, and when
his Majesty remarked that the fire burned with a bright glow,
Whittington said he would soon make it burn brighter. He

then threw into the fire bonds to the amount of £60,000, which the king had given over to the citizens of London for the money he had obtained. Probably Whittington had bought the bonds at a cheap rate, as the citizens would know that the king was not very likely to pay his debts, and so the Lord Mayor in an easy way got the honour of paying them for him. Then came the career of Lord Mayor Barton, who lived in 1418; and that of Stephen Browne, who, in 1438, at a time when there was a famine in the country, sent to the Prussian ports for corn. In 1549, Sir Rowland Hill, the ancestor of Rowland Hill, was in office as Lord Mayor. He was a godly man, and in his case the promise of the Lord to be gracious to the descendants of His people had been strikingly fulfilled. He next came to Sir Edward Osborn, who had jumped out of a window and saved the life of a young lady who afterwards married him. Following him, in the reign of Elizabeth, was Sir John Spencer, from whom the Sovereign borrowed money, and who refused her the granaries which she desired. After him came Sir Richard Gresham, Sir John Gresham, and Sir Thomas Gresham. They knew the story of the grasshopper which was current about Gresham, but there was not a word of it true. The City had greatly aided in deposing Charles I. The dissolute times of the restoration of Charles II. were described, and an anecdote was told showing that the Lord Mayor of London at that time was addicted to the most debasing intemperance.*

About this time a little work of some interest appeared, the subject being "Baptism: or, a Contribution to Christian Union," the author being Daniel Fraser, M.A., of Lerwick, in the Shetland Isles. The author had found that the fame of the New Park Street pastor had reached even his distant parish: he admired the printed sermons, and thought that Spurgeon himself was a gift to the Church, and thus regarded his progress with pleasure. "In the midst, however, of the pleasant feelings, I had one serious draw-back, in respect of which I could not but feel that, at least, 'one

* A summary of this lecture is in *The British Standard* for November 15, 1861.

thing thou lackest,' and that as yet the treasure is found only in earthern vessels. You are a Baptist! or, expressing more precisely the drawback to which I allude, you administer baptism by immersion, and holding immersion to be baptism, you baptise only professing believers, or believing adults." The object, of course, was to convert the young preacher from the errors of his ways—an easy achievement, as was thought, if both sides would but rid themselves of prejudice. *

Some further notice may be taken of the criticism to which the weekly Friday evening lectures at the Tabernacle were subjected towards the end of the year 1861. This seems to be the more necessary because the young pastor was misrepresented by his enemies and misunderstood by his friends, who were misled by giving heed to the misstatements which were circulated. Dr. Campbell divided the young preacher's enemies into Sceptics and Scorpions; and both of these sections are said to have been in raptures with the sermon on the railway accidents. "Misapprehending or perverting his words, they hailed him as a powerful auxiliary in their blind combat with the idea that 'there is verily a God that judgeth in the earth,'" we find it remarked. "The idea produced uneasiness; and the man who, as they thought, helped them to get rid of it, was viewed as a benefactor and extolled as a sage." † It was thought by Spurgeon's friends that the censure of such people would have been preferred to their praise; for the question would arise whether he had not expressed himself incautiously. Whether that was so or not, the truce between the preacher and his friends was of very short duration; for the lecture on "Shrews," already noticed, afforded an opportunity for misrepresenting Spurgeon too tempting to be resisted. One of the daily papers, not distinguished for any liking for the Gospel as preached at the Metropolitan Tabernacle, professed all at once to be concerned for the cause of evangelical religion. As the shrewd onlooker, "Aristides," remarks, this oracle, "to serve its

---

* See *The Freeman*, November 6, 1861.
† "Aristides," in *The British Standard*, November 1, 1861.

purpose, commenced Pharisee, assumed the phylactery, and sounded the trumpet at the corners of the street, affecting profound reverence for holy places." The Sceptics having thus stated their case, the matter was taken up by others of the weekly Press, especially by one of the reviews of great literary ability, which all along showed a bigoted hatred of Spurgeon and his work which was interesting because it was phenomenal. At the same time, the articles of this journal were characteristic of superfine writers who, despite their high assumptions of birth and education, were utterly incompetent to speak on the merits or demerits of Christian work, or of those who did it, because they were altogether empty of the spirit pervading the New Testament. They knew how to do their work in their own way, however. "The Scorpions elaborated the spurious report of the lecture into a heinous offence against religion; and, soaking it in malice, they sent it forth among their misguided readers." Had this school of critics had the affair all to themselves, no great harm would have been done; it was when friends believed in the over-coloured reports of the lecture, and when, through being deceived, friendly newspapers expressed regret, etc., at what had occurred, that the need of correcting error appeared.

Dr. Campbell enlisted "Aristides" to discharge this duty, and he was the man for the hour. He mentioned the witness who confessed before the eighteenth-century magistrate that the Methodists had converted his wife, who hitherto had had the tongue of a shrew, but was then as quiet as a lamb. "Can there be a doubt that men are often driven to violent courses by the shrewship of their wives?" it was asked. "Does it not lead to strife, to separation, to abandonments, and even to bloodshed?" Hence anybody who could diminish the supply of shrews and scolds was a public benefactor; and the worst thing wished for "the scribes of the sceptic and scorpion school" was that each might get hold of a thorough, a matured, and an incorrigible shrew for a wife. That wish was hardly consistent with the principle of returning good for evil; but it was very natural.

That the public might not be in any doubt as regarded the

character of the Friday evening lectures, a visit was made to the
Tabernacle, and the scene was described:—

"At seven o'clock precisely, Mr. Spurgeon made his appearance on the spacious platform of the Lecture Hall—a building which is well lighted, well fitted up, every way
commodious, and capable of containing about 800 people. It was crowded in every part·
At the back of the platform hung a number of diagrams of lions and other animals,
the subject of the night's lecture. After prayer, Mr. Spurgeon opened with a pleasant
descant on the King of Beasts. He seems always to do best what he is doing last,
and he is eminently fitted for a public lecturer. It is difficult to conceive of anything
more instructive, innocent, and amusing. He continued to delight the assembly for an
hour and three-quarters! Although interspersed with wit and pleasantry, and apparently
extemporaneous, it was evidently got up with care and considerable labour. The diagrams were a highly useful appendage, enabling the eye to aid the intellect, and giving
occasional repose, both to the speaker and the audience. To show the earnest, business-
like way in which the matter is gone about, I may observe that Mr. Spurgeon keeps an
artist on the premises to prepare the diagrams, and, after they have been used there,
they are lent-out to societies and public bodies for lecturing purposes. The expense of
this arrangement is of course considerable, but it is met, and only just met, Mr.
Spurgeon told the assembly, by the twopence charged for admission. Such a lecture
must have been a great addition to the toils of Mr. Spurgeon for the week. Throughout
this hour and three-quarters, he frequently spoke with almost all the force and vehemence
which distinguish his ordinary preaching; and then, be it remembered that this was
after four hours' labour in the lecture-room and the exertions of the previous Thursday
night, while only forty-eight hours remained till the commencement of the overwhelming
services of the Lord's Day." *

Despite the howl of disapprobation raised by one section of the
Press, the Friday evening lectures thus continued, and the interest
of those for whom they were intended seemed to increase. As
Aristides said, Spurgeon seemed to do best whatever he undertook
last.

* "Aristides," in *The British Standard*, November 1, 1861.

CHAPTER XLV.

" COUNTERFEITS."

AS the Metropolitan Tabernacle was still a new institution, it continued to be a great centre of attraction. As a chapel, its mere size made it an object of the greatest novelty to all Christian visitors from the provinces and from foreign countries. If the congregation at the Surrey Gardens had presented a striking spectacle, this was still more wonderful, because the vast permanent building seemed to bear its silent but still overwhelming testimony to the lasting popularity of the preacher. Whoever properly understood the man and his surroundings fully realised that he was master of the situation; and that while no one could well be further removed from self-seeking, he perfectly understood how to turn all things to account in the service to which he was called. Thus, when the pastor was depicted in clever articles as being all that was objectionable without any redeeming traits, large numbers, who would not otherwise have been attracted, visited the Metropolitan Tabernacle to see the strange creature for themselves. So far that was satisfactory: only let the people come within earshot, and the preacher would give forth what was good for them whether they liked it or not. Large numbers who came went away benefited. The following account of the pastor and his daily life belongs to this time :—

"No one is so well able to judge of Mr. Spurgeon as those who are constantly associated with him in the work of the Lord, and who know something of that part of his life which is hidden from the public eye. As one of those so associated, I do most solemnly bear witness that it is impossible for any man to be more fully consecrated in body, soul, and spirit to the service of the Lord and His Church than he is. For that alone he lives and labours; not only is it the duty, but it is the joy of his life; and often has it been our lot to witness him labouring ardently, nay, joyously, under physical ailment the most severe, such as would have alarmed and prostrated an ordinary man. Very little of his time, comparatively, is spent at his own home. At the same hour in the morning that City merchants are seen wending their way to their counting-houses, he may be seen on his road to the Tabernacle, where he frequently remains fully occupied in the Master's work until ten o'clock at night. As to his income, save what is barely sufficient for his domestic expenditure, he gives all to the darling object of his heart, the College for young men, and other benevolent objects; and with respect to that College, if you did but know the glorious success some of the young men have had in the conversion of souls by the Lord's blessing, and who are now pastors of prospering labour, it would gladden your heart as it has done ours in no small degree; and, great as Mr. Spurgeon's work is as a preacher of the Gospel, you would say it is small compared to what the Lord is doing by him through the instrumentality of the College." *

The year 1861 was drawing to a close amidst apprehension and shades of gloom. What would come of the quarrel between North and South in America? What would happen in Lancashire if the cotton supply were suddenly stopped? While some may have been trying to answer such questions, the news of the Prince Consort's illness caused alarm to be felt throughout England, and then came the shock of the good Prince's death. The nation was in mourning; sympathy for the widowed Queen was universal. In thousands of pulpits reference was made to the subject, and Spurgeon spoke out in a way which did credit to his heart as well as his head. On Sunday morning, December 22, the Tabernacle was draped in black, and a large number of the congregation were in mourning. The text was Amos iii. 6, and referring to the royal death-bed, the preacher said:—

"Evil may be taken to mean calamity, and the saddest of calamities has just visited our city. You have lost a man who deserves nothing but good at your hands, and who, standing as he has always done in a most perilous position, has conducted himself so as to have become not only revered but beloved by all classes in the country. Our grief at the calamity is enhanced by the natural apprehension that must arise as to what may come next. We have lost one of the great ones of the land, and the dread sounds of approaching war can be heard rumbling from across the waters. It is at such a time that the very corner-stone of our royal house has been taken away, and our Sovereign is left a widow. What next? and next? We have great faith in our Constitution, but it is to God we must turn in faith to redeem us from the peril. Saddest and tenderest part of the calamity is that by it the Queen has lost her husband. Widows in the ordinary ranks of life have friends, relatives, and neighbours to condole and strengthen them in their affliction, but our Queen has lost in the Prince Consort her only friend and counsellor, and is in fact the saddest widow in the land, standing as she now does on her lofty pedestal in the very desolation of isolation. You feel that not for all her honours and advantages would anyone stand in the situation of our beloved Queen, thus

* Thomas Moor, in *The British Ensign*, November 7, 1861.

left lone and desolate in her deep sorrow. I regret that I have not the powers of a Robert Hall, or a Chalmers, to paint truly the sorrows of our Queen. My lips are unaccustomed to courtly phrases; I can only stammer and blunder out my impressions, but my heart weeps for that royal lady who in the seclusion of her chamber now mourns the loved husband, the wise counsellor, the steadfast friend and adviser, who has gone never to return. And in saying this I feel that I only echo the sentiment of my congregation, for I believe that in our whole history of royal personages there is not another case of a single death which has caused so much sorrow in the land." *

These were the preacher's honest sentiments, for his words always came from his heart, and he cordially recognised the good example set by the Queen in maintaining the purity of the Court. At a festive assembly of ministers and denominational representatives I have heard Mr. Spurgeon, as chairman, remark that the loyalty of the English people was founded on real appreciation of the monarch. On that sad Sunday in Christmas week, 1861, there was no prominent man in the country who more warmly sympathised with the Royal Family in their affliction than the pastor of the Metropolitan Tabernacle.

Thus the old year closed in gloom, and 1862 came in with wars and rumours of wars which seemed to impart to its opening days an ominous uncertainty. Neither public calamities nor personal ailments seemed to interfere with the great and ever widening work in progress at the Metropolitan Tabernacle, however. The pastor was still only twenty-six; but great as his popularity had been at the opening of 1861, his influence at its close appeared to be even more commanding. The printed sermons were attaining to a popularity which gave to the preacher an audience scattered over every part of the English-speaking world. On account of the discourses being given extempore, a fair crop of printers' errors occurred; but otherwise the doctrines given were so identical with what they had been at the start, that the pastor declared his motto to be *Semper idem.* The old theology was held to be incapable of improvement, despite the commotion which the publication of " Essays and Reviews " had occasioned. It was

* From the summary of Mr. Spurgeon's sermon in *The British Standard,* December 27, 1861.

therefore no small satisfaction to see the printed copies of the
sermons increasing in popularity. During the year 200,000
numbers were presented to all who were in any way connected
with the Universities of Oxford and Cambridge. A special edition
in German was also printed for the Leipsic Book Fair. The
translators did not even overlook the aborigines of New Zealand;
while the circulation of the discourses in English became still more
extensive by the United States newspapers, which reprinted them
entire.

Though not in the best of health, Mr. Spurgeon struck a
cheerful note on Sunday morning, January 5, when his subject was
"A Psalm for the New Year" (2 Peter iii. 18), "But grow in
grace," etc. The weekly sermon now began to be printed in larger
type, the size of each number being increased from eight to twelve
pages.

On Tuesday, January 7, Mr. Spurgeon again appeared before
the Young Men's Christian Association at Exeter Hall, the subject
of the lecture being "Counterfeits." Mr. Robert Bevan was again
in the chair, a number of notable persons being also on the
platform. The hall was so densely crowded, and the curiosity of
the audience so manifest, that Mr. Shipton's general order to "sit
down and sit close," was by no means untimely.

The interest of the occasion was probably heightened by certain
paragraphs and letters which had appeared, and which showed that
a distinguished University doctor had declined to fulfil an engagement to lecture before the Young Men's Christian Association
because his name was associated with that of Spurgeon. "If Dr.
Thomson has declined to row in a boat in which Mr. Spurgeon
takes an oar, we entirely approve of his, or any other gentleman's,
reluctance to be bracketed with a person of this sort," said *The
Saturday Review.* "It is an indication that a better type of
Palmerston bishop has at length been thought of. A bishop is
not in his place coquetting with Spurgeon, writing pretty letters
to him and to 'shining lights of the Nonconformist pulpit,' and

congratulating them on their labours and successes." The late Dr. Tait, who was then Bishop of London, was happily not of this order; and he had recently written a letter to Mr. Spurgeon which did credit both to his head and heart. No civility to Spurgeon could be tolerated by his more bigoted and uncompromising opponents. "Assuming that the letter is genuine," it was meanly remarked, "it is very likely that the bishop only meant to be civil to the Baptist preacher, and wrote a letter of ordinary conventionalism and platitude." Then it was added, "Most likely Mr. Spurgeon publishes it only to avert the waning popularity which the newspapers announce." The preacher's "waning popularity" received a curious kind of illustration when Exeter Hall was again densely crowded, and the young pastor rose amidst prolonged acclamation to give his lecture on "Counterfeits."

The lecture began by showing that it was almost generally allowed to be a good thing to be a follower of Christ. "To be, or not to be"—"To be, or to seem to be"—that was the struggle of the present age, as it had been the contest of all times.

"Nowadays there is a temptation for men to act as if to look like a Christian was as useful as to be one. The demon Counterfeit says, 'If charity be an admirable grace, let our name figure in every subscription list. If it be a great and a good thing to do something in the service of God, let us help others who are doing something and that proxy service will do as well. If to possess godliness be difficult, let us profess it, and we shall have all the advantage of it without the labour.' Again he will tell you that if you wish to win the confidence of your employer, and religion stands in the way, you must seem to be religious and you will succeed; but you must keep a guard upon your lips and tune your speech after the orthodox fashion. Then he argues, 'How much cheaper it is. Where sculptors have produced statues in marble, you fill up with figures in plaster. They will not cost a hundredth part as much, and will answer every purpose. Economy should be the order of the day. It is troublesome to repent; it is expensive to give up sins, to tear off lust's right arm, to be born again, and to pass from death to life. By the pretence of godliness you will win all and without any trouble or pain.' How many, tempted by this short cut, accept the counterfeit and neglect the reality? Then saith the Evil One, 'It looks quite as well and will last as long. Play your cards well, avoid all appearance of evil, and the keenest observer will fail to detect you.' Now you may play at this masquerade all through your youth and manhood, and even when you grow old you may scatter a halo of saintship around your hoary head, while your heart is as black as hell. Time was when men boldly declared what they believed was right; but, says the fiend, 'We know better now—this is not an age of bigots. We may swear to certain articles while we mean the contrary thing, and yet be thought good men.'"

So expansive indeed was the charity of the age that men who accepted one thing and preached another might even be recognised as ministers of Christ. Mr. Spurgeon himself had got into the habit of calling a spade a spade, and of expressing what he believed in plain Saxon language, so that he confessed to hardly knowing where he was, whether he was standing on his head or his feet, or whether he had any brains at all, when he heard what was evidently black heresy described as orthodox things to believe. It was the same when a man gave out what was opposite to the truth, and then declared that all came to the same thing as the truth. The lecture then proceeded :—

"Now Counterfeit is the man for such an age. He will never grow angry with an opponent because he has nothing to be angry about. He is a very nice man for all companies, a very delightful person for a drawing-room, because he will never raise any controversies. He is just the man for editors of periodicals and the conductors of newspapers. He is the very individual to whom the age points as one up to the times, and free from all the stereotyped notions of the barbaric past. Now it is fair to admit that there is something in this style of reasoning—that is to say, just enough to make it take. Alas! how many there are both in high and low places who profess that they never experienced, and wear colours which are not their own. How many tradesmen are there who hold themselves out as honest simply because it answers their purpose? They would not wish to be thought rogues, but they are rogues for all that. How many young men in warehouses are there who, if their master compelled them to lay aside scruples, would not do so? Thank God, we have thousands of employers and tradesmen who would not do the wrong thing, but still we read of daily disclosures of the contrary. No doubt some men make a good thing of their religion. By the mere profession of godliness their shops may be thronged and their business advanced. Goods will move off more rapidly when perfumed with godliness. In England at least the advantage is as much on the side of profession as non-profession. It is but honest to say so, and therefore men have inducements to counterfeit the possession of the quality I have mentioned. It is said that there were many hypocrites in Cromwell's time. I do not think many were to be found in Charles II.'s reign, as it did not pay. If a man then professed godliness, he lost his emoluments and soon got in the common gaol."

It was a matter for congratulation that times were so different from the days of persecution that services were even held in theatres, and churches were active. Nevertheless, the same showers which made the flowers rejoice, also brought out snails and slugs from their hiding-places. Persons in whom the habit of imitation was stronger than honour, at times professed to have undergone conversions which had never been experienced. The Church seemed to be under peculiar danger from pretended religion on account of the plentifulness of religious books and biographies. The Romish Church was then depicted as "Satan's Masterpiece of Counterfeits."

"The honest eye of Luther, kindled with the light of heaven, saw through the fabrication and told us the whole truth, and now the world rejected with loathing the counterfeit which it once so joyfully received. There might be some who would bring it back again, but surely they would fail. It could not be possible that the counterfeit of a counterfeit—Puseyism—could ever succeed. It was base enough when the harlot of Rome put on the garments of Christ's spouse; but to wear her rags was something execrable. To say the least, there was some attraction in the glittering pretence of the Roman Church; but paint and glitter, instead of gold and marble and precious stones, surely would not influence the enlightened minds of this century, so as to bring back an old counterfeit in place of the Gospel of Christ."

The young men were then urged not to pretend to be what they were not: it was a miserable thing to be thought a rich man and to be in reality a poor one.

"You are waited upon for subscriptions for every charity, and you must keep up establishments, but bills will at last come in for payment. That is just the position of a man who pretends to be a follower of Christ. He is like a drunken man whom I have seen attempting to walk on both sides of the street at the same time. Shops are sometimes filled with shams—parcels which contain nothing, empty bottles, drawers which do not pull out, and tea-canisters which never came from China. Going the other day into a cheesemonger's shop, I happened to tap a large cheese with my stick, when I found that it sounded hollow. I asked the proprietor what was the matter with it, and he could only reply that I had discovered a hypocrite in his window. Now, in churches we find people of hollow character like that, who look extremely like what they should be, but if you happen to tap them, you readily find of what they are composed."

The course of lectures given at Exeter Hall during the winter of 1861-2 was abundantly interesting; for the list included "Miracles," by Dr. Candlish; "The New Testament Narrative," by Dr. Miller; and "Lord Macaulay," by Morley Punshon. Mr. Spurgeon had previously been unwell; he did not preach on the last Sunday of the year; yet now, as one observer remarked, if there was not "the usual amount of electricity in him, yet it required a skilful eye to make the discovery." We find the scene generally described as "a grand spectacle," the discourse itself being "novel, startling, and useful, instinct with life and overflowing with eloquence." The magnitude of the audience showed the interest felt by the public in the lecturer and his theme.

As he had done before, Mr. Spurgeon disclaimed all pretensions to being a lecturer: he was only a preacher; but one, in refusing to admit this plea, said that he should like to have lecturing and preaching clearly defined. Dr. Campbell remarked that there need be no fear of giving the people too much Gospel; and it was because Spurgeon gave the people as much of the Gospel as he did, that his lectures deserved to be so highly valued.

"Let not the admirers of gifted men be offended if we say that we deem the discourse of last Tuesday of greater value than the whole of the previous lectures of the present course. It was a hundred times more adapted to promote the salvation of souls. We shall not be surprised if some scores—it may be hundreds—of the vast assembly should be roused to a sense of their true condition by the feeling and faithful appeals which were then addressed to them." *

At this time the work of the Pastors' College was being vigorously carried on, the expenditure being at the rate of about £1,600 a year. Over twenty students were being educated, and nineteen had already settled in pastorates. In addition to these, there were 150 young business men who were receiving instruction in the evening classes. Mr. Spurgeon still regarded this institution as being the chief work of his life, next to preaching the Gospel; and he still endeavoured to make all of his friends understand that the methods of the tutors differed from those of other colleges. The one qualification for admission was a gift for preaching, and possessing that, a man was acceptable, however poor his general education might be. This method of dealing with candidates was thought to be altogether consistent with common sense. "It is certain that many men who are toiling at Latin and Greek with very slender success, would be far more profitably engaged in learning English and getting general information," we find it remarked in a general statement of the time. "Such men only prove a drag upon their fellow-students in the classes, and get little good themselves. If a man can learn Greek and Hebrew, he finds the tutors ready enough to admit him into the classes; but in cases where no good could come of such an attempt, he is not dragged along in order to make him keep in rank, but is directed to a course of study suitable to his capabilities."†

* *The British Standard,* January 10, 1862.
† *The Baptist Messenger,* 1862, p. 16.

The annual meeting of the College was held on Wednesday, January 29, when the founder gave a full account of the origin and progress of the work. As the College Buildings were not then in existence, the rooms and lecture-hall of the Tabernacle had to be used for all purposes, even when, as would sometimes be the case, 1,200 or 2,000 persons would come to tea. On this occasion, the tutor-in-chief, George Rogers, was described as "a quiet, modest man, of rare endowments, who ought long since to have been at the head of an academic institution." What was more entertaining, however, were Spurgeon's references to the characteristics of the students themselves. Thus, soon after the start was made, and when at least one student had been turned into a success, another aspirant appeared on the scenes who was "quite as original." If his mind had been locked up in an iron safe, it could not have been more inaccessible to the tutor; for although it was plain to ordinary people that two and two made four, this well-meaning youth could hardly be made to rise to the apprehension of that fact. Professor Rogers was quite ingenious in the methods he used for stimulating this intellect into action, but all were in vain until the main facts of astronomy were set before him. The awakening touch was then given—"his mind seemed to burst the shell: he became a new man." In a word, he developed great preaching powers, and in what had been an empty chapel gathered a large congregation.

In January, 1862, the country was shocked by the news of the dreadful catastrophe at Hartley Colliery, in which over two hundred workpeople in the pit were killed. The sympathy awakened was very general: collections for widows and children left destitute were made at the Mansion House and elsewhere. At the Tabernacle week-night service on January 30, Mr. Spurgeon gave attention to the subject and made a collection for the survivors. The text was Job xiv. 14, "If a man die, shall he live again?" It was shown that people in general thought too little of death, and hence Providence thrust it before them. The warning had lately been heard in the palace; and now among common workpeople, who were as apt as

A A

others to neglect the future life, it was also being heard in tones of thunder. The question of the text was answered negatively and then affirmatively :—

"'If a man die, shall he live again?' No! he shall not live again here—he shall not live again for himself to make glad his household. If he lived a sinful life, this life shall never be repeated. If there were pleasures in sin, the dead would not come back to repeat them—to take in vain the name of that God who had daily loaded them with benefits—in whom they lived and moved and had their being. They would have no more opportunity for their base ingratitude to their Maker, whom they treated worse than the 'ox which knoweth his owner, and the ass his master's crib.' Nor would they ever live again to stifle the remorseful conscience. And it was quite as well for the wicked that they could not live again; for, whatever they might think to the contrary, if they lived again they would live as they had lived before—the filthy would be filthy still, and they would increase their condemnation. On the other hand, the righteous would not live again to repent of sin, to suffer for their righteousness. They would not bring back to strife and contest the victor when he wore the crown, the mariner who had gained the shore! And if a man would not live again for himself, neither would he live again for others. If there were any in that fatal pit who led others into vice, they would not live again to do so. The man who was living an idle and useless life, would not live again to set his bad example. There was no moral quarantine; but if they only had a clear perception of the leprosy of vice, they would shudder at those overt and covert influences by which some men were daily exercised for evil. There were some men who carried, as it were, a moral plague about them; but those would not live again to pour out moral poison and pollute the very air they breathed. As with the evil, so it was with the good. They would not live again to do their duty to their God and to their fellow-men. In the pit with those poor men at Hartley were some of the Primitive Methodist local preachers, men selected to preach to others because they could preach from the heart to the heart, though not perhaps grammatically. That was the true principle of New Testament Christianity—to select men for ministers, not for their scholarship, but because they had the Christian life within them. They would do more good amongst the working classes in London if they were not quite so squeamish on these points. If a man die, shall he live again? Yes! but not here. His soul would live again in a resurrection life. The poor mangled forms in the pit would live again. They would all live again, the consciences of the evil would live again and be their continual tormentors. Their victims too would live again; and those whom they had wronged would live again and reproach them. The good would also live again as flowers transplanted from one spot, where they could only bud, to another where they would bloom with everlasting freshness."*

In February of this year died James Sherman and Dr. Reed the philanthropist, two earnest men for whom Mr. Spurgeon felt a strong regard. The old-time leaders were fast passing away.

* *The British Standard*, January 31, 1862.

CHAPTER XLVI.

WORK AND PROGRESS IN 1862.

A Young Men's Mission Aid Society—Meeting at Bunyan's Tomb—A great Company of Emigrants—Bi-centenary of the English St. Bartholomew—Spurgeon refuses to take part in the Celebration—A Service at Cheddar Cliffs—A Memorable Open-air Service—Barnums in the Pulpit—Death of James Smith.

ALTHOUGH he very much disliked writing prefaces or introductions to books by other people, Mr. Spurgeon would occasionally undertake such a task, or he would even volunteer to do the service in an exceptional case when he thought some good purpose might be served. Thus at this time we find him supplying a prefatory notice to Mr. John Stock's "Handbook of Revealed Theology," a closely printed volume of over 350 pages.

When the roll of Church membership at the Metropolitan Tabernacle became the largest in the world, nothing pleased the pastor better than to see a number of friends exercise a spirit of self-denial by going elsewhere to start or strengthen another interest. One of the places which thus received attention was the chapel in New Court, Old Bailey. It was determined to resuscitate the cause by reopening the Sunday-school and engaging one of the members of the College to conduct the services. This succeeded so well that towards the end of February, 1862, the congregation was in a position to remove to what had been the Welsh Independent Chapel in Aldersgate Street by purchasing the lease. Mr. William Olney lent his aid and did much to make the enterprise a success. The student who undertook the pastorate was Mr. Alfred Searle, whose rare devotion, success, extreme youth, and early death conspired to make him a subject of more than common interest. He died of consumption, while staying at

Hastings, September 20, 1863, being then in his twenty-first year. At the time of his death he had only just accepted a call to the pastorate of Vernon Chapel.*

On Monday, May 5, the Young Men's Missionary Association in aid of the Baptist Missionary Society had its meeting at the Tabernacle, Mr. J. E. Marshman being in the chair. It was arranged that there should be no resolutions, but that each speaker should choose a subject and enlarge upon it. Mr. Spurgeon decided to speak upon the Society. It was shown that the day was past when anyone harboured suspicion in regard to the righteousness of the cause; and some references were then made to Calvinism past and present:—

"We know that the Calvinism of a former time—although I trust we still maintain it in all its great fundamental principles—but the Calvinism of that former time was not able to reconcile to itself the text where Christ is represented as weeping over Jerusalem. The commentators of that day laboured hard to prove that Christ did not weep, or that He did not weep over the fact that men would perish. They could not reconcile it with the Sovereignty of God and the doctrine of election. Now I trust our Churches know that God's purpose is fully consistent with free action on man's part, and that while it is God's to choose and God's to effect, it is ours to attend, and to be employed as instruments in God's hand. We are no longer afraid to say, as Peter did, 'Repent, and be converted, every one of you,' though we can still feel with the Apostle Paul, that it is not of him that willeth, nor of him that runneth, but of God that showeth mercy. We can say fearlessly, in the name of Jesus Christ, 'He that believeth and is baptised shall be saved.' Yet there are still a few survivors of that ancient tribe who will have men do nothing because God works in all; but they are happily very few, and I do not suppose there are any in this assembly. There are also difficulties raised by enthusiastic people who think that God will surely, all of a sudden, make one day as a thousand years, and cause all the nations to be born at once. Perhaps their hope is true. I think it more than likely that such an event will transpire—that at the coming of the Lord from heaven with a great shout, the nations shall behold the Messiah, and in the Glory of His second advent shall perceive that it was He of whom Moses and the law and the prophets did speak."

In the retrospect it seemed a marvellous thing that such a man as Dr. Stennett should have looked coldly on missionary enterprise. If they looked on sick persons and knew of medicine which would cure them, would they not tell of it? If well clothed, they pitied the shivering beggar on a cold day; and thus Christian instinct prompted them to make known the precious secret that God was ready to receive and forgive the sinner:—

* *The Baptist Messenger*, April, 1862; *The Baptist Year-Book and Almanack* for 1864, p. 24.

"When the love of Christ gets into the soul, it can never be hidden. Persecution could not check its hallowed fire from spreading. The angel of Prudence once said to a spark which fell into a field of stubble, 'Spread not, for if thou dost, the next particle of stubble will be kindled, and another and another, and who can tell where-unto this may lead?' And lo! ere the angel had finished speaking, the spark had kindled the next atom of stubble, and the next, and the next, till it burst into a blaze, and the angel was fain to spread his wings and fly away. Though the man zealous for God were to be confined in a prison, I would work there for Christ; if not in the cell, yet I would find some means of being heard beyond it. Let a servant of God be put in cramping irons, and be told that he must not do that which the Spirit of God within him compelled him to do. As well tell the river it must not flow to the sea, or the sun that it must not shine, or the stars that they must no longer cheer the darkness of midnight. They must—it is not *may* with them—they must. 'Woe is me,' said the Apostle, 'if I preach not the Gospel.' We feel it like fire burning within us, and we feel constrained by a holy force more powerful than even that of gravitation, which makes the earth revolve within its orbit. We feel that the omnipotence of love and of grace compels us, so far as we have opportunity, to make known the great plan of salvation for the souls of men."

When they comprehended Christ's sufferings and character, it was hard to understand how there should ever have been any indiffer-ence to His cause. Young men seemed to have a special mission in the world; but while it was an instinct of youth to be radical and destructive, Mr. Spurgeon himself confessed to being conserva-tive. Who were the best qualified for missionary work?—

"It is for the young men to venture. During the winter, when the ponds at Clapham get frozen over, I have seen stones thrown on to the ice to see if it were strong enough to bear. If the stone does not go through, a small boy will be sent on, and if he makes the transit in safety, full-grown men will venture. I think that in the mission work, young men should feel that they are to make the venture where others cannot. The young man, perhaps, has not got a wife yet; he has thought of it, but still, not seriously, and he has laid it aside; he knows that it is good for a man to wear the yoke in his youth, but still he does not intend to wear that particular yoke at present. When he puts on his hat he has covered his house, and when he goes abroad he can take his worldly goods and chattels with him, for he is at present, 'self-contained.' This is the young man to go out as a missionary. Perhaps the committee may say, 'Well, but you would be better if you had a wife; is there no young person of your acquaintance?' 'Oh, yes,' says the young man, 'that could be managed; there's a young sister living so-and-so: it *could* be managed.' These are the sort of folks to venture if there is any hard work to be done. If there is any difficult place, or any suffering to endure, they are just the people. These are the men who, when God has touched their hearts, will be ready to lead the forlorn hope, to run into the ditch, to put up the ladder and make the irons rattle on the coping of the wall. It is God's will that some should abide by the stuff, while some should go forth to the battle; and who so fitted to do so as the young?"

There was some rough work to be done, and it would not be done by people in kid gloves. There were grand opportunities, the

Baptist communion being the finest under heaven; but a man must be qualified for the service required:—

"Many come to me who think they are called to be preachers, and from the very cut of their mouths I can tell they were never meant to be, that they would never make fluent speakers. There are always two sides to a revelation. A person wrote to me, saying it was revealed that he was to preach for me one morning in the Surrey Music Hall. Far be it from me to be disobedient to any sort of heavenly vision. I wrote back to say it was a lop-sided revelation, but when it was revealed to me that I was to let him preach, I would let him know; at present I had not had such a revelation. You may perhaps see clearly enough that they are the men for the mission work, and that they ought to go out to some land where the cannibals will eat them up in a proper manner; but if the committee does not think them the proper persons, it is much better that they should be cut up at home. But if they believe they are called, and the Missionary Society will not send them, let them go without. There are plenty of missionaries unconnected with any society. It is possible for them to find friends who would take a pleasure in maintaining them; if not, might they not, in answer to prayer, be so prospered in life as to be able to maintain themselves in the mission work?" *

On the day after he had given this advice to young men who might be desirous of entering the mission field, Mr. Spurgeon paid a visit to his brother at Southampton, whose congregation assembled in the Carlton Rooms. A service was held in the afternoon, 900 persons sat down to tea, and an enthusiastic public meeting came off in the evening in aid of the fund for the chapel which was subsequently erected.

In the spring of this year Bunyan's tomb in Bunhill Fields was restored, and with the Earl of Shaftesbury and some others, Mr. Spurgeon attended the inauguration on May 21. It was a wet afternoon, so that after a very short ceremony in the grounds the large company sought shelter in the City Road Chapel. Following his friend Lord Shaftesbury, Mr. Spurgeon spoke at some length on Bunyan as a preacher, an author, and a sufferer. The tinker's style was commended, that style being "not the spread-eagle style of long and lofty sentences, but plain and homely speech which all love and by which all are attracted." In regard to Bunyan's works, Mr. Spurgeon did not hesitate to value "The Holy War" more than "The Pilgrim's Progress," the one being a sketch of the Christian life, the other the filling up; the

* *The Freeman*, May 8, 1862.

one being adapted for babes in spiritual experience, the other being meat for full-grown men.* "As the works of Dr. John Owen have been well described as the Thesaurus of theological wisdom, so are those of Bunyan the Thesaurus of allegory." After some references had been made to the sufferings of Bunyan from imprisonment and extreme poverty, the people were advised to raise monuments to the allegorist in their hearts, becoming his spiritual descendants by accepting and cherishing the truths which he taught and thus keeping his memory green.

During the spring of this year Dr. Merle d'Aubigné, of Geneva, visited London as the guest of the Kinnaird family in Pall Mall. On Sunday morning, May 18, the historian of the Reformation visited the Tabernacle, when the pastor gave what he called an Exhortation founded on II. Samuel xi. 1, which was followed by a Salutation from his visitor. The latter spoke English with some difficulty; but showing great earnestness, he made the people understand him, while he quoted the Apostle's words, " The whole Church saluteth you," and made reference to the tercentenary of the death of John Calvin, which in 1864 it was hoped they might celebrate in the famous Swiss city by erecting a fitting memorial of the Reformation. On the Tuesday following the Hon. A. Kinnaird gave a conversazione in the furtherance of this enterprise. It was proposed that the memorial should take the form of "A Hall of the Reformation," in which the Gospel would

---

* Notwithstanding the extraordinary opinions on Bunyan which nowadays pass as literary criticism, Mr. Spurgeon was not alone in the high value he set on "The Holy War." Lord Macaulay's opinion, that next to "The Pilgrim's Progress" that work is the best allegory ever written, is well known. The accomplished editor of "Bunyan's Complete Works," George Offor, studied "The Holy War" with ever increasing delight for over forty years. James Montgomery was hardly less ardent in his admiration. To such, certain later utterances would have been regarded as little less than utterly puerile. Thus in the Clarendon Press edition of this great work we are told : "The spiritual career of the human race, the fall of mankind, and the subsequent salvation of the just, cannot be treated of under the form of an allegory." A London morning paper in reviewing the Clarendon Press edition also remarks : "It can hardly be said that 'The Holy War' in these busy book-laden days will repay perusal, either from the point of literary invention or spiritual edification." One might almost as well accept the enlightened dictum of "The Penny Cyclopædia," which pronounces "The Pilgrim's Progress" itself to be "mean, jejune, and wearisome."

be preached, the building being also available for the "great ends to which Calvin devoted his life." It was also proposed to circulate the Reformer's works more widely. Mr. Spurgeon, who was present, cordially advocated the scheme, which was warmly taken up by friends in various parts of Christendom. It was hoped that £10,000 would be raised in Great Britain alone.

On May 27 a more than usually novel kind of meeting was held at the Tabernacle, to take farewell of a thousand emigrants who were about to proceed to what was called the Nonconformist Settlement in New Zealand. A tract of territory comprising about sixty thousand acres was secured, and two-thirds of the land was supposed to be suitable for settlement. The distance from Auckland ranged from thirty-five to sixty miles, and a sum of £2,500 had been set apart for the construction of roads. All the arrangements which had been made appeared to give satisfaction to those in England.

Mr. Edward Ball, M.P., occupied the chair, and Mr. C. J. Middleditch, who spoke on the general subject of Christian Colonisation, emphasised the fact, that the gathering was of a very unusual character. "The spectacle of a thousand Christian people going forth at once amid the sympathies and benedictions of such an assembly as this has probably never been beheld." Dr. E. Tomkins gave a kind of charge to the pastor elected to accompany the emigrants —Mr. S. Edgar, B.A. Several other addresses were given. Mr. Spurgeon said:—

"In the history of the Church, the first sower was the devil, and in his efforts he scattered the seed everywhere. Satan is unwittingly the servant of God—fool as he is; though not intending it he accomplishes the purposes of Heaven. His object at one time was persecution; now he is endeavouring to hug the Church. But He who has delivered the Church out of the jaws of the lion, will also deliver it out of the paw of the bear. By Satan even emigration has been prostituted to the worst of purposes; now we are going to defeat him. You are going forth not so much to found a colony, as a Christian Church. Many who hear me will remain to sing at home; but the emigrants are going to sever the ties of home. They are going to the Antipodes, and instead of lips being together, the nearest part of their bodies to England will be their feet. They will have to forget some of the highest associations under heaven—

'Wherever we wander, there's no place like home.'

Your condition after a while will not be quite so respectable as it has been. We talk about being sturdy Nonconformists, but even a sturdy Nonconformist getting hungry is not in a very respectable condition. The proof of the pudding is in the eating of it, but the trouble is in the making. After a while some of you will be feeling for the softest bit of wood on board ship, or enjoying the cold comfort of a bed in a hut with the wind blowing through it. You have had experience of England but not of New Zealand. In making the change you will perhaps feel the force of the arrow all the more, because it is a new one and has never been shot before. In going to the place on the banks of the river, the name of which I do not remember, I expect you will be strictly loyal, and as a reminder I will ask you to sing 'God save the Queen.' * In addition to loyalty I hope you will always keep up what I will call the Englishness of your hearts. Let that word 'home' be held sacred, whether the home be a log hut or a palace. I expect you will keep your arms strong—strong to wield your axes and reap your harvests. You will also require strong doctrine—sixteen ounces to the pound —of election and perseverance. Religion is a blessed thing in all ranks, but best proved among the poor. But you tell us you expect something of us. I rejoin, blessed are they who expect nothing, for they shall not be disappointed. But in the prayers of dear friends you will not be forgotten. Prayers will be heard in England for you, prayers will be heard in New Zealand for us. I trust you will go out good soldiers of the Cross—strong in the omnipotence of the Master." †

During the year 1862, great attention was given to the subject of the secession of the two thousand ministers from the Church of England two centuries before—men who gave up their parishes because conscience would not allow of their subscribing to all that was contained in the Book of Common Prayer. On Sunday, August 24, that being St. Bartholomew's Day and the 200th anniversary of the secession, discourses were very generally devoted to the subject in the pulpits of England and Wales, the opinions of leading preachers being given in the newspapers. Mr. Spurgeon did not follow the example of his brother ministers, however; for his subject on that morning was "The Loaded Waggon" (Amos ii. 13). He objected to the celebration as a one-sided one, and thought that Churchmen as well as Nonconformists ought to have united in such a commemoration, agreeing to confess their faults in common, and to bury past grievances. That would have tended to sweep away anything that remained which might be opposed to religious liberty. There might be some things yet remaining to be complained of; but he believed they would have been granted by Churchmen if they had been asked for in the right way.‡

* The National Anthem was then sung.

† For a full account of this meeting, and of the striking demonstration at the Docks on the Thursday following, see *The Freeman* for June 4, 1862.

‡ These sentiments were vigorously applauded at the Bunyan Meeting in the City Road Chapel already referred to. See *The Freeman* for May 28, 1862.

On Wednesday, September 10, a more than usually interesting service, attended by 10,000 persons, took place at Cheddar Cliffs. The congregation showed the keenest curiosity to see and hear the preacher, and a large proportion had come together from a radius of twenty miles. Indeed, the scene altogether was of the most striking description, the preacher standing on a platform erected for him with his back towards the rocks. The hymns, "Before Jehovah's Awful Throne," and "Rock of Ages, cleft for me," were sung with grand effect; and then came a sermon on "I am the way," such as Spurgeon alone could have given. A contemporary account compares the service with one of the gatherings of the old Covenanters among the hills of Scotland; and such was the power of the young pastor's voice at that time that an outdoor assembly of twice the number could easily have heard every syllable. This passage occurred in the sermon :—

"Ye rocks that have listened now and heard the words I speak; ye rocks that have felt as much as some have felt; ye rocks that have trembled as much as some have trembled; ye rocks, give witness before God against this people if they believe not in Christ, when your head shall bow down at the last great day, still bear witness that Christ was lifted up in Cheddar, and His name exalted. Shall they bear witness against you every time you pass them; shall they say, 'You had an invitation, but you rejected it ?' " *

Meanwhile, work at home was being carried on with vigour. Nothing afforded the young pastor greater satisfaction at this time than to see one handsome chapel after another rise up as a result of the preaching of men who had been trained in the College. Wandsworth now gave rise to one of these interesting stations. About three years after his first preaching in London, Mr. Spurgeon

* *The Baptist Messenger*, 1862, p. 275.—A somewhat puerile article on this service at Cheddar appeared in a local paper; and, being quoted by a high-class weekly paper opposed to Mr. Spurgeon, was of course heartily approved, *e.g.* : "This sort of criticism is certainly exceedingly creditable to the good sense of the local Press. It is thoroughly friendly, but nothing more damaging to Mr. Spurgeon can be thought of. His doctrine, his style are all upset. We may say what the local writer would not say, but what his remarks clearly imply—that the exhibition of Spurgeon at Cheddar must have been exactly as edifying, and no more, as the exhibition of Blondin at Glastonbury." By innuendo, as we have seen, doubt was cast on the genuineness of a letter received by the preacher from Bishop Tait; and in a similar way it is inferred that the people returning home from the Cheddar service had had too much to drink.

gave a sermon in the Assembly Rooms, the regular ministry in which was afterwards carried on by one of the students, Mr. J. W. Genders. He commenced with a Church of eight members, which he soon increased to over 150, the main part being baptised by himself. The result was that Mr. Spurgeon laid the memorial-stone of a new chapel to accommodate 700 persons on October 6, 1862. The estimated cost of the chapel was £2,100.

During that same week the annual meeting of the College was held, when the pastor referred to his students in affectionate terms. There were then thirty-nine students in course of training, besides over one hundred young men who attended the evening classes, the cost altogether being then £2,000 a year.

The Friday evening lectures were still in favour; and on September 19, the subject was "George Fox." The founder of the Society of Friends was described as a man whose faults had been excused by his disciples, while opponents had falsely given him a scandalous character. Macaulay's estimate was to be taken for what it was worth; and even Carlyle, unexcelled as a shrewd thinker, had still "done serious injury to religious faith in the present century." Concerning Fox himself, it was remarked:—

"He lived in a time when men were in earnest, and some went beyond enthusiasm into fanaticism. Prophets were in every street, and prophetesses were as plentiful as blackberries on bushes; but George Fox was one of the soberest men in that strange time. Some of his professed followers committed actions that disgusted him, and against which he protested; but he could not prevent all who were his followers from doing something that was outrageous. They should not therefore confound George Fox with his associates; they should not lay other men's sins at his door; they should let him stand in his own shoes. George Fox was probably the best judge of what was his duty, and two hundred years ago knew better what God required of him than they could know in the present day. If he had as much grace as George Fox, with George Fox's temperament, he might have done the same thing. The marvel was, not that the man was extravagant, but that he was not much more so. Even in early life George Fox had shown the most tender spirit. Plays and games had no charms for him, and, shocked at the conduct of some old men, he once expressed a hope that when he grew old, God would prevent him from doing as they did. His parents had not the means of giving him much education, but he had the power to pick up a great number of things. When he said 'yea,' it was ended so; and when he said 'nay,' it was impossible to change him, because he meant 'nay.' When certain men would swear, and professing Christians would declare upon their honour or their word, George Fox would say 'verily,' and there was an end of it. George Fox could always deal with other men's hearts and see them thoroughly, because he had been prepared by temptation for his high and noble mission. One of the first things he perceived was that human learning was not necessary for religious teaching; and was there anything extraordinary in that? No! because no man could pretend to make a minister, for that was God's work. He next said that human profession did not make the Christian, and that was the fact; but for protesting that, George Fox was put in prison." *

Many of the opinions held by Fox were accepted by the speaker, but the doctrine of sinless perfection could not be endorsed, because no such example had ever been met with. The acts of the old Quaker were also generally approved; although it was a silly thing to enter Lichfield without shoes and stockings, to cry out against the city. Macaulay had charged him with indecency, besides calling him a madman; but there was no indecency in an act "which merely caused the cooling of his feet and the losing of his shoes."

During this year, the distress in Lancashire, consequent on the stoppage of the cotton supply, was very widespread, and amounted to a national calamity. Large sums were collected in different parts of the country and distributed among the sufferers from enforced idleness. Into this work Mr. Spurgeon entered with great heartiness. He sent money on several occasions; and on November 9, when collections for the distress were made at the Tabernacle, the sum realised was £713 6s. 9d.

Like Whitefield, with whom he was so often compared in these early days, Mr. Spurgeon delighted in the open air. Some of the most memorable of his discourses were given in fields or on a hillside; and a complete account of what he did from first to last in this department would certainly be a record of extraordinary interest. As this work proceeds, I may be able to give reminiscences supplied by friends of some of the happy occasions referred to. Meanwhile, I will give here a description of a field service in 1862, which my friend Mr. William Cuff, of the Shoreditch Tabernacle, has kindly supplied:—

"The first time I heard Mr. Spurgeon preach in the open air

* *The British Standard*, September 26, 1862.

was in the year 1862. The place was at Naunton, eighteen miles from Cheltenham. I was but a lad, just then converted to God. Of course I had heard of the mighty man, and went to hear him full of wonder and expectation. The service was held in a lovely meadow, through which meanders the famous Naunton Brook. It was a faultless day, and crowds gathered from all parts round about All classes came. Work in the fields was suspended, and smock frocks were plentiful in the audience. Horses were tethered every-where, and the roads seemed blocked with all kinds of vehicles, from a four-wheel waggon to a brougham. I am not sure, but I think the pulpit was a waggon. A crowd of thousands had gathered long before the time to commence the service. We waited eagerly, and some prayed fervently for saving power to be upon preacher and people. One old man standing next to me scarcely ceased praying all the time we waited. When Mr. Spurgeon stood up to commence, he said a fervent ' Amen ' and ' Lord help him.' It thrilled me.

"Then came the preacher and the service. I shall never forget the ring and tone of that musical though powerful voice as the words fell on our ears—'*Let us pray.*' A profound and holy hush fell on the crowd. It was as still as death. The prayer was simple, short, mighty. Every word was heard. Every tone was felt. It lifted the mass nearer God, and transmuted the meadow into a very house of the Lord. Sinners must have trembled, while saints rejoiced in the presence and power of the Lord. But the prayer was calm and measured. So was the pleader. Mr. Spurgeon did not look or seem the least excited. He stood then as ever he did, *like a master of assemblies.* The reading and exposition were very powerful, yet most simple and unaffected. Another prayer, not long ; but a tender, intensely earnest plea that souls might then and there be saved. Then came the text and the sermon. It is as impossible as it is needless to describe the sermon or its effects on the crowd. The text was in Acts xiv. 9–10. The sermon is printed in Vol. x., p. 145, of the printed sermons.

"One curious incident happened at the close of this service. A poor old man came up to Mr. Spurgeon and shook hands with him in a manner that shook him all over. He said—' I have heard of thee by the hearing of the ear; but now mine eye seeth thee.' ' Go on, sir, and finish the text,' said Mr. Spurgeon. There was a pause, and some confusion, and then Mr. Spurgeon added—' Wherefore I abhor myself and repent in dust and ashes.' There was a sharp but kind rebuke administered for misquoting, and wrongly applying Scripture. That service took place thirty years ago, but the whole thing is as vividly before me as it could be if it had been yesterday. The result will be known when the secrets of all hearts shall be revealed."

By this time Spurgeon had in the main lived down opposition, but here and there was found one who still looked on him with suspicion or actual dislike. At an ordination service at Bristol a well-known doctor of divinity, who gave the charge to his own son, was heard giving the preference to dumb dogs to such as were always barking; and the young pastor was urged to be on his guard against " the Barnums of the pulpit who draw large gatherings, collect large amounts, and preach many sermons."

Taken altogether, the year 1862 was one of progress and encouragement. The improvement in the weekly issue of the Sermons ensured a greatly increased circulation. From all parts of the world news was continually being received of the good effected through the reading of the discourses in many tongues.

In the closing days of 1862 occurred the death of Mr. Spurgeon's predecessor at New Park Street, James Smith, of Cheltenham, an uneducated man in a literary sense, but one possessed of genius and of rare devotion in his calling. As pastor of Cambray Chapel, he preached to a large and appreciative congregation; and such was the respect accorded him by the townspeople generally, that while Mr. Smith lay in his last illness, and within a few days of his death, the rector of Cheltenham, I believe, presided at a meeting at which a sum of £400 was subscribed for the Baptist pastor's necessities.

CHAPTER XLVII.

PROGRESS OF THE COLLEGE.

Losses by Death—Spurgeon ceases to edit *The Baptist Magazine*—Spurgeon and Punshon—
The Tabernacle depicted—Societies—Work of the College Students—Temperance—
Baptisms at the Tabernacle—Exaggerated Reports of Spurgeon's Income.

MANY friends of Spurgeon, both in the Establishment and in the ranks of Nonconformity, passed away during the year 1862. Beresford, Primate of Ireland; Sumner, Archbishop of Canterbury; and Horne, the well-known author of "The Introduction to the Scriptures," were among the Churchmen; the losses of Dissent included George Clayton, James Sherman, Drs. Reed and Leifchild, and lastly Sheridan Knowles, who commended Spurgeon when he first came to London on account of his correct elocution and dramatic power.

During the year London had been enlivened by the second Great Industrial Exhibition; but the untimely death of the Prince Consort, who had laboured hard to make that international show a success, cast a gloom over the country, which was deepened by disasters in mines and on the railways. As we have seen, Mr. Spurgeon was ever ready to turn to account the events of the day by drawing useful lessons from them.

Other matters also, in which the pastor of the Metropolitan Tabernacle was more interested, because they more affected him in his work, were taking place. At the opening of the year 1863, a controversy between the assailants of the authority of Scripture and the defenders of plenary inspiration was at its height. "Whatever may prove to be the distinguishing characteristics of the year 1863, one feature it is already seen to possess in common with that which has just elapsed—that arising from the struggle between the assailants and the defenders of the veracity of God's Word," remarks a religious chronicler of the time. "The controversy would seem to

be just commenced, and we appear to stand in a position not dis-
similar from that occupied by the men who, thirty years ago, were
called to contend for the faith against Tractarianism. Then it was
superstition, now it is scepticism, which threatens to sap the Church's
foundations. In the ultimate discomfiture of the one we read a
prophecy of the certain defeat of the other." *

These disputes touched Spurgeon in his most tender place, for
he seemed to realise that his life mission was not only to preach
the Gospel, but also to stand for the defence of the Truth. His
attitude in this respect was always uncompromising, although
his hearty denunciations of Arminianism in the pulpit did not
prevent his fraternising with the General Baptists in their work
and everyday life. At the same time the smooth progress of
the pastorate and of service in the world was occasionally hindered
by hitches and obstacles which were more ominous than reassuring.
Thus, with the opening of 1863, Mr. Spurgeon ceased to have
any connection with *The Baptist Magazine*, which he had jointly
edited for two years. It was in relation to this change that a letter
was sent to Mr. Medhurst, now of Cardiff, to whom reference
has been made as the "first student." After showing that it was
impossible to carry on the joint-editorship so as to please all, Mr.
Spurgeon added :—

"We hope to start another and cheaper magazine in which we may teach the truth
and discover error, without being called to account by a denomination far too heterogeneous
ever to be represented at all, and, I fear, too unsound to endure plain speech. If I may
leaven the denomination with scores of men like yourself, I shall rejoice indeed, but earnest
preachers of the whole truth are too few.

"Pray that the Lord may guide me in some tremendous struggles which now await
me."

Referring to this communication, Mr. Medhurst remarks in a
private note :—

"The magazine of which the above letter speaks as to be started was *The Sword and
the Trowel*, commenced in 1865, in which truth has been taught and error exposed with
unwavering fidelity from the commencement even down to the present time.

"From the beginning of Mr. Spurgeon's marvellous ministry, he was eagerly stretching
out his hands towards the 'regions beyond,' longing for the time when the results of
his ministry should be far-reaching."

* *The Sunday at Home*, 1863, p. 79.

It cannot be said with certainty to whom the allusions are made; but we should go wide of the mark if we were to interpret too literally expressions which were written down in letters, or which were spoken in private conversation, at the date in question. The fact seems to be that the misgivings with which Spurgeon had been regarded in the earliest years in London had not altogether died away. It is certain that many good Christian people who read *The Baptist Magazine* would have taken exception to his sound Calvinistic teaching. The young preacher had a favourite expression—a full Gospel, "sixteen ounces to the pound;" but some did not care for what he regarded as full weight.

About the middle of January the welcome news reached England of the arrival in New Zealand of the Albert Land emigrants previously referred to, and in whose welfare Mr. Spurgeon was deeply interested. Speaking of the land allotted to them, a daily paper said much of it was of excellent quality, while the remainder was average. "There is ample room for cattle-runs with the present population. We regret that for a few days the special settlers suffered considerable privations. Nothing had been done by the pioneer agents to provide shelter for the immigrants on their arrival, although this could easily have been arranged." * Some inconvenience and extra expense were occasioned by somebody's negligence; but some of the more opulent settlers were sufficiently pleased with the country to purchase much more land than was originally allotted to them.

About this time, Dr. Campbell published a series of articles, entitled "Eloquence. The Young Men's Christian Association," the pieces having reference to the lectures given at Exeter Hall, and to those who gave them. In one of these studies particular attention was devoted to Morley Punshon, comparison being also drawn between that distinguished orator and Spurgeon; and these utterances seem to be the more interesting because the two men were always sincere friends. They differed on theological points; but they were content to differ. Mr. Spurgeon would himself occasionally attend a

* *The Southern Cross* (New Zealand).

B B

lecture at Exeter Hall; and I have reason to think that he has there been profoundly impressed by the power of Punshon's oratory. I have heard that Spurgeon once said after an address by his Wesleyan friend, "If I could speak like that, I would turn the world upside down." At the same time no one knew better than the Baptist preacher that Punshon was too rhetorical. As is the case with writing, speaking may be too highly finished to produce the best effect, especially when all that has been prepared has been learned by heart. Hence, notwithstanding the admiration which Spurgeon justly accorded to his friend, he never really coveted his art. "What did you think of Punshon's oration?" "Well, I felt like the country-boy who, on being requested to ask a blessing at a feast, said: 'Lord, we thank Thee that we do not get such a good dinner every day, else we should be ill and want the doctor.'" It had to be admitted that in the best sense highly ornate preaching is not successful. It does not seem to have been so even in the case of Robert Hall; and it was still less so in the case of some who came after him—men who, as talented elocutionists, were much run after by the crowd.

In his study of the famous Wesleyan preacher, Dr. Campbell showed that his speaking was "novel, startling, grand," but it was not sufficiently natural; and in this respect he differed from Spurgeon, who had "surpassed all his contemporaries by his fidelity to nature." The great preacher performed "nearly the whole of his mighty marches in the pace of a Titan:—His is Cicero's first style on the very largest scale possible. It consists of gigantic conversation. He could trot, and that to purpose, and so could he gallop, but he rarely does either, unless the latter sometimes, when waxing indignant with the Neologists, Rationalists, or the American slaveholders, and then he thunders and lightens like Jupiter."

As had been the case with Jay, of Bath, Samuel Martin, of Westminster, achieved "his wonders" like Paganini, who charmed all Europe with one string. It was worth while giving attention to such exemplars:—

"Why should not Mr. Punshon take a leaf out of the books of Martin and Spurgeon? It would mightily add to the pleasure of his audience and to his general usefulness. It would to that extent increase even his present immense popularity. As the matter now stands, he has, to men of taste and culture, too much the air of merely a brilliant rhetorician, an English Isocrates, a leviathan declaimer. The trot, the gallop, are doubtless a great thing, but they must not constitute the whole, else it will savour of a performance, a display, an exhibition, a notion everywhere fatal to dignity, grandeur, and power. It is not thus that the great business of life is carried on in courts of law and halls of legislation: not thus spake Chatham, Pitt, and Burke, Erskine, Plunket, and Flood." *

Whether or not Spurgeon had at this time reached the height of his popularity, it was a fact, as we find one insisting, that his name was the most popular in Christendom. At the same time, there were large numbers even in the metropolis to whom the Metropolitan Tabernacle as a term conveyed only a vague idea. The place was indeed one of the most wonderful centres to be found in the world; but only by being visited and looked into could such a hive be properly understood. One friend in particular seems to have become more and more astonished and delighted at what was being achieved as he advanced in years; and the aim of his writing and speaking was to lead persons to visit the great chapel for themselves. "You arrive," wrote he, "at a few minutes to six o'clock on a Sabbath evening. The streets around are crowded with respectable people. At length the gates open, and in a trice the whole of the vast area within is gorged; the noble flight of steps and the spacious portico are literally loaded with an expectant throng. At length the doors are opened, the bulk of the seat-holders having been already accommodated, and in the visitors pour as a torrent, which very speedily covers every foot of space. Try now, good stranger, if you would form a proper estimate of the wondrous sight."

In the distant region of the upper gallery there was a large congregation; there was one even larger in the middle gallery, and one more numerous still in the area. Indeed, we find this spectacle described as really consisting of half a dozen chapels, each being larger than the average, but all having the advantage of being under the ministry of one master mind and one unrivalled voice.

* *The British Standard*, February 6, 1863.

What was more, the tendency was to increase rather than fall off, notwithstanding that "scathing envy and green-eyed jealousy" had confidently predicted that this would not be the case. At the opening of 1862 the quidnuncs who were well versed in the signs of the times gave out that Spurgeon's power to attract might survive the summer, because people coming into town to the Exhibition would hear the hero of the hour, but when all the visitors had returned to their homes, the whole thing would naturally collapse. The fact was, however, that the eagerness of people to attend the services was greater than ever. The additions to the membership averaged about nine a week, and the Church of nearly 2,500 members was already the largest in Christendom. It was held, too, with some reason by Mr. Spurgeon's friends that the congregation, large as it was, had the privilege of being even better looked after than many smaller assemblies. The town was divided into districts, each having a discreet and vigilant elder to look after it, who had to give in a report at special meetings. These we find described as presbyters, the pastor being the bishop. "He repudiates the idea of isolated independency, holding by something which may be designated Baptist Presbyterianism."

The preacher with his surroundings on a Sunday morning at this time we have depicted thus:—

"You see the clock; Mr. Spurgeon will be here in a moment. Mark him as he softly glides down those steps, and drops upon the sofa. Note his lustrous and beaming eye. The countenance is not so much sallow as bloodless. His whole face, you will see, is radiant with benevolence; he seems the happiest man in the assembly. You see those gentlemen that sit in those enclosed seats. That is the sanhedrim; those are the deacons. Do they not present a really aldermanic appearance? What a fine-looking body of men! How hale and hearty they are! They certainly adorn their position, and speak well for their profession. Their presence is a standing proclamation of the fact, that godliness has promise of the life that now is, as well as that which is to come. They seem to say with Moses to Hobab, 'Come with us, and we will do you good, for the Lord hath spoken good concerning us.' The introductory prayer, you will think, is a somewhat strange affair. Men from a distance, more especially from the systematic and orderly kingdom beyond the Tweed, are often startled at its seeming irreverence. They doubt if the good man be praying at all; or they think he is still but a learner. Well, he certainly *talks* to God as if he *meant it*."

It was pointed out that at this time Spurgeon really gave at every service what might be called a lecture as well as a sermon;

and it was thought that the comments on the read portions of Scripture which constituted this lecture were quite as valuable material for the printer as the ordinary discourses. It needed no unusual sagacity to make the suggestion that these readings should be published; for had they been issued in a way similar to that adopted by Dr. Cumming, the volumes would no doubt have been extremely popular. The fact is, however, that there was never an excessive amount of enterprise in connection with the publication of Spurgeon's works.

The annual meeting of the College took place on January 30, and was a more than usually good gathering. "Here we are in the midst of a most interesting company of tutors, Church officers, leading men, students, and friends," we find one of the guests remarking. "The assemblage takes place at five o'clock, and the tea is of course excellent. Mrs. Spurgeon, with her modest vivacity and modest attention to all, is the soul of the hour, and the young bishop is moving airily about, loving all, the beloved of all, pleasing all, and amusing not a few." After tea there was a crowded meeting, and the history of the institution for the year showed the College to be a thing by itself—something unlike anything else in the British Islands. If such a school of the prophets did not prove the founder to be actually revolutionary, its existence at least showed him to be thoroughly original. He did not wish to be singular or eccentric; but desiring above all things to be useful, his genius enabled him to find out new paths. He cared nothing for conventional ideas nor for prevailing customs unless they happened to fall in with his plans and aspirations. "He acts in everything as if he had been the first actor, and as if this were the first age of Christian society, with neither ancestry nor precedent," we find one remarking. "What is good? What is better? What is best? This point settled, to work he goes, and he rests not till the object has been accomplished."

But while this eminent leader possessed sterling characteristics which enabled him to move as a chief among his fellows, it was not to be taken for granted that he was always necessarily right in speech or action. Obstacles to the success of the College had been overcome in a wonderful way; the objections of early opponents had been triumphantly answered by the progress made; the prophecies concerning failure or undesirable results had never been fulfilled. At the same time, while the devoted young pastor was extolling the liberality of the people which under God had enabled him to achieve what he had done, he was simply carried away with his own enthusiasm when he publicly declared, "The days of societies are over and gone." Exception was very generally taken to such an assertion in the newspapers. It was maintained, with some show of reason, that in a Christian sense the day of societies had only begun; that they would be as lasting as the nations, with which they had much in common; and that they were necessary for the accomplishment of Christian work which could not be carried out by individuals. It was shown that some of the best things which had blessed the world had been carried out by associations.

Connected with the College at that time were three Jews, one of whom with his own hands had distributed 3,000 copies of the Scriptures at the Great Exhibition of 1862. They had some Primitive Methodists among their number; and it was then thought to be a singular thing that about half of the students in course of training should send up a memorial in favour of teetotalism. Mr. Spurgeon was not then an advocate of total abstinence, believing that intemperance, like other sins, would have to be cured by the Gospel. Still, he characterised the memorial as a good one, though its very mention provoked a round of laughter. At all events, it showed a becoming disposition towards economy in men who received only fifteen shillings a week.

When the President rose to make a further statement, he was able to say, "My once despised lath-and-plaster institution is actually, in point of numbers, already at the head of the colleges of the Baptist body." There were over fifty students, and on this fact one authority remarked:—

"The circumstance is alike remarkable and cheering. But this is only one view of the subject ; it regards only the College proper. There is much, very much good, however, besides being done in the way of intellectual culture and fitting men for usefulness. The evening classes comprise thrice the number of the College students, and these classes are supplied with instruction adapted to their circumstances of an exceedingly interesting and important character. In addition to the College course and the diversified exercises of the evening classes there is every Friday night a popular lecture, very often by Mr. Spurgeon himself, and otherwise by the most eminent men, lay and ministerial, that he can find. This is one of the most attractive features of the system. He stated on Friday night that Mr. Paxton Hood had been engaged for the next series of lectures, embracing pulpit eloquence and a variety of subjects, all enlightening and attractive." *

It was thought that the institution was exercising a power which was wanting in other colleges, and that Spurgeon was not only the presiding genius, but "the animating soul of the system." Hence persons who by no means underrated an educated ministry predicted that vast good would come to the Church from the evangelistic enterprise of a band of men who were taught that the ingathering of converts into the Church was to be the ambition of life. The training, as a whole, seemed to be well fitted to develop enthusiasm, as well as to draw out latent talent. "Everything is done to nourish the spirit of devotion," wrote one friend. "The tutors and the students form a species of Protestant fraternity of the ancient type, with all its good, and without any of its evil ; a spirit the most paternal seems to obtain among them ; nothing can form a greater contrast than the cold proprieties of the old Dissenting Colleges and of the National Universities." According to Principal Rogers, the law of love was dominant ; then profitable social intercourse was encouraged, while they communed together once a month at the Lord's table. The institution may have shown some shortcomings ; it might not be the place for such young men as had enjoyed exceptional advantages, and had set themselves to attain to a high standard of scholarship, but it was nevertheless such a training-school as the age required. While expressing his admiration, Dr. Campbell ventured to give forth a prophecy destined never to be fulfilled :—

"In addition to the tongue power which it so strenuously

* *The British Standard*, February 6, 1863.

cultivates, it initiates the young men into all the chief branches of human knowledge, and, although there is obviously little time for general reading, yet mind is awakened, directed, and put in the way of improving itself indefinitely. Rightly speaking, education only begins in colleges. It was well remarked, both by Hume and Gibbon, that no man was ever great who did not put himself through a second course of training after leaving the university. It is well known that Swift obtained his degree in Dublin by special favour, having no literary claim to it; but afterwards he laboured fourteen hours a day for seven years, and hence that brilliancy of wit, and that vigour of intellect, and that multifarious-ness of knowledge which lifted him so high above his compeers. If we do not greatly miscalculate, mankind will hear more of this matter. Should Mr. Spurgeon, who, we believe, is only yet in his twenty-sixth year, have before him forty or fifty years of life and health, which is quite possible, and the present measure of Divine approbation, his work will be its own witness. He will very probably, however he may deprecate the idea or struggle against it, become the founder of a denomination bearing his own name, which will occupy a place of no ordinary usefulness and honour both at home and abroad."

Among those who were baptised at the Tabernacle during February, 1863, appear to have been the present Sir Arthur Black-wood, of the Post Office, Captain Hawes, and Mr. Ord. According to *The Record* their immersion took place in "Mr. Spurgeon's baptistery adjoining the Tabernacle," but, as most persons are aware, the baptistery is beneath the lower platform, directly beneath the chair which Mr. Spurgeon used while conducting a prayer-meeting.

The Friday evening lectures were still kept up, the pastor him-self giving one occasionally. In the main, other lecturers had now to be engaged, however, and amongst them we find the author of "My Wanderings in the East" delighting the audience on February 13 with an account of Palestine. The Tabernacle itself was on this

occasion nearly filled, and Mr. Spurgeon spoke in high terms of
Mr. Gadsby both as a lecturer and writer.

It was not customary for Nonconformist chapels to be open on
Good Friday, but on that day in this year, Mr. J. A. Spurgeon
appears to have preached twice at the Metropolitan Tabernacle on
behalf of his new chapel at Southampton.

Exaggerated notions of the amounts which Spurgeon received
from America on account of his works gained currency from time
to time. We find it reported that Sheldon and Co., the Transatlantic
agents, had sold 300,000 of the Sermons, and that they were accustomed to remit the preacher £1,000 at one time. Mr. Spurgeon in
contradicting the report said that he would like to see such a remit-
tance, or even one of a thousand pence.

CHAPTER XLVIII.

"NUMBER FIVE HUNDRED."

Distress in Lancashire — No. 500 of the Published Sermons — A Week-night Festival — Spurgeon's Address — Speeches of Friends — *The Watchman and Reflector* — Spurgeon attacked by J. B. Gough—Visit to Whitefield's Tabernacle—Spurgeon and the Wesleyans.

THE distress in Lancashire continued to attract attention, and individually Mr. Spurgeon seems to have done all that lay in his power to relieve the sufferings of those who were chiefly affected. The pastor of Pole Street Chapel, Preston, acknowledged the gift of £50 with a crate of clothing from the pastor of the Metropolitan Tabernacle. A little later, a sum of £150 was sent to the Lancashire Baptist Relief Fund.

Sunday, March 15, 1863, was an interesting day on account of No. 500 of the published Sermons being delivered at the Tabernacle in the morning. The text was 1 Sam. vii. 12, "Then Samuel took a stone, and set it between Mizpeh and Shen, and called the name of it Eben-ezer, saying, Hitherto hath the Lord helped us." On the following Wednesday the publishers invited a number of friends to a supper to celebrate the event. Mr. J. Spicer, who had rendered great service in procuring the site for the Tabernacle, was to have presided, but though present, he desired that the place of honour should be taken by Mr. Rogers, the Principal of the College. Mr. Spurgeon explained that it was quite a social party and not a public meeting; and they were assembled in the lecture-room because their entertainers had not a drawing-room large enough for their accommodation. The general object of the meeting was to obtain additional subscriptions for extending the work of the College. Mr. Spurgeon said he trusted he might ask them to join with him in very sincere and fervent gratitude to God for the help which He had given him, so that he was able to say "Ebenezer—hitherto the Lord hath helped me." They could sympathise with him in some degree, he was sure, in the pleasure, in the surprise, that he felt in that God had been thus gracious to him. It would be utterly impossible for them fully to enter into the depth of the debt which he owed to the Lord his God. He remembered what he was, and therefore he marvelled that there should have been found Christians to listen to him all these years. He remembered when he was, some twelve or thirteen years ago, teaching small boys in a country place—an occupation by no means congenial to his tastes. Goldsmith had said that a man had better be hanged than have such work to do, and he was quite of that opinion. He should hesitate, perhaps, for a time, but in the end, no doubt, prefer the alternative of hanging. He was not, at the time alluded to, big enough to be a master; and not small enough to be a boy. He had had no college education. This he said not by way of boasting—far from it. He would have learned more if he had had the opportunity; but, that not being the case, he did what all ought to do—he made the very best use he could of such opportunities as he had. He should never forget the first time when he went out to preach. His friend Mr. Trestrail recollected his addresses in the Sunday-school, but before then, while yet in a jacket, he had addressed the boys, and there were always found large numbers of persons to listen to him. The schoolroom was crowded. It was in a queer little cottage that he delivered his first sermon, with a ceiling so low that a hole had to be cut in it to enable tall preachers to stand upright. That hole, however, was not necessary in his case. He was very glad when his sermon came to an end, and as he sat down an old woman asked him how old he was. He said he would talk to her after the benediction had been pronounced; and so he did, and told her that he was under forty. She held that he must be considerably under twenty. As to his five hundred sermons, the later ones were rough enough, no doubt, but they were exceedingly superfine as compared with the earlier discourses of the series. The fact was that he had used a homely oyster-knife where a razor would have been but of little use. Nothing could be of more real service to a young preacher than the style of criticism to which he had been subjected—men who not only expressed their opinions very frankly, but sometimes in a bitter, nasty way—and many a joke had been cracked at his expense. Young preachers never liked such critics, but after all they were their best friends.

Reference was made with good effect to the out-of-the-way places to which the sermons found their way, such as Central Africa, the Bahamas, New Zealand, etc.; and to a preacher who had, since coming to London, preached nine times a week, it was an encouraging thing to be able to maintain sufficient freshness to command an increasing circulation. There were, no doubt, persons who harboured the opinion that preaching was such an easy thing that a man had only to elevate his arms and the words would run out of the mouth; but a great mental strain was necessary in the case of one who preached so frequently.

Some interesting facts relating to the circulation of the weekly issue were given at this meeting. The publication had gone on for eight years—an average of a million numbers a year had been sold; and one friend who attended the meeting had himself circulated a quarter of a million of the discourses. As the object of the gathering was to help the funds of the College, Mr. Spurgeon gave some facts relative to the work of the students as supplementary to what he said about the sermons. The German translation, he said, was sold off at the last Leipsic fair; in Holland a Dutch version had had a large sale; and on a visit to that country he found that many knew his name though they could not pronounce it. In fact, he did not know himself what they called him. In Sweden and in Norway editions had been published; and in France the discourses appeared in three different shapes. A friend had also arranged for an Italian edition. Since he had been pastor of that church he had baptised 3,000 persons, most of whom he might call his spiritual children, they having been brought to a knowledge of the Truth either by hearing or by reading those sermons. As to the College, they had now fifty-four students preparing for the ministry; and so greatly had the cause prospered, that if they had four hundred instead of fifty-four, they could place them out at once in suitable spheres of labour. These students, in fact, did not wait for what were called promising openings, but preferred rather to go into unlikely places, where their efforts might be blessed. Referring to the liberality with which the College was supported, he stated the case of a lady subscriber, who, on coming into the possession of considerable property, offered to support at her own cost a minister in her locality, and allow him to preach in her own drawing-room till he found a congregation, when she would build him a chapel. During the first six weeks of this year £600 had been subscribed towards the College, and he had no doubt that if they had faith enough to double the number of students, the funds would be forthcoming. They received a great many one-pound notes from Scotland—some of them, he thought, must come from Presbyterians, because there were not nearly so many Baptists in Scotland as they had received one-pound notes. Some young men who had attended their other classes at Scottish universities came to his college to complete their theological course, and some came even from the colleges in America, so that he felt greatly encouraged in his work.

Mr. Spicer characterised the whole thing as unparalleled. There was no other minister, either in London or the provinces, who would have liked to be published to such an extent as Mr. Spurgeon had been. A Churchman who had not seen the Tabernacle had been encountered, and the advice given to him was, "If you wish to have your mind enlarged, go: you little know what is done there."

Many other speeches were made, the most interesting being those by James Grant, of *The Morning Advertiser*, and Dr. Campbell, who, as champions of the cause which Spurgeon represented, were regarded at the Tabernacle as two of his chief friends. The former said that public speaking was not his vocation; and had he known that he would be called upon for a speech, the probability was that he would have remained in his editorial quarters in Fleet Street. When the tongue of the popular journalist became unloosed, however, he said some good things :—

"It may not be known to anyone here that I was the first person connected with the newspaper press who made reference to Mr. Spurgeon. Since that time I have had very great pleasure in frequently referring to his public ministrations as well as to his public works, and no one rejoices more cordially than I do in all the success which has attended him. Mr. Spurgeon has referred to various quarters from whence he had received most gratifying evidence of the good his works have been productive of ; and only the week before last I received a communication from a person in London, educated for the Church of England, in which he spoke of the very signal service he had received from a sermon of Mr. Spurgeon's. I know from various quarters that the printed sermons have got into places where very few of us would ever imagine, where the persons have been educated in all the fashionable pursuits of the world, where the Gospel was altogether unknown; and from my own knowledge I know that in many instances persons who have read those sermons have been led to abandon their evil ways. Some time ago the daughter of an Archbishop being recognised by a friend in the Tabernacle, and feeling that she had no right inside a Dissenting place of worship, put her hand to her lips as much as to say, ' Don't say I was here.' "

When the turn came round for Dr. Campbell to speak, that veteran was loudly cheered as the hero of the evening ; and this was not only on account of his private and public worth, it was the manner in which those assembled expressed their satisfaction at his success in what the chairman called " bearding the lion in his den," in connection with an action for libel against a leading weekly paper. For reasons best known to the proprietor, this journal manifested a strange kind of dislike to Spurgeon, while Grant and Campbell were hardly more favoured. Campbell took the bull by the horns, however, and in a suit for libel won £50 damages, an application for a new trial being unsuccessful. It was on account of this victory that the audience cheered the name of Campbell, and repeated their plaudits when the old journalist rose from his seat. In the course of his speech he showed that his neighbour of the *Advertiser* " did not exactly do justice to himself. The truth is," it was added, " he was the first of our public writers to sound the tocsin, to blow the trumpet, and to announce that there was a young prophet among us." The doctor confessed to having been one of the last of the London ministers to become reconciled to Spurgeon's methods. He then showed in what sense the young pastor was an innovator :—

"There was no preaching in . . . great public edifices till Mr. Spurgeon went to Exeter Hall; but now people, both Churchmen and Dissenters, are eager to imitate him. Deans and chapters and bishops and clergy are all imitating him; and as if the great cathedral were not enough, they actually go to Exeter Hall; nay, they rush to the very theatres. All this, whether for good or for evil, undoubtedly originated with Charles Haddon Spurgeon. Is that nothing? Why, it is a mighty thing. This unpretending, humble, but gifted youth, who came from the country, this lad with the little basket and the 'barley loaves,' to use a phrase supplied us by the Holy Book, has set all, from the Bishop of London downwards, in motion. All Mr. Spurgeon's movements have been new; the form and character of this stupendous structure are new; his style of talking is new; his style of praying is new; his style of preaching is new; everything is new—and there is something else that is new—the idea of preaching and printing a weekly sermon. That never entered the head of anybody; but then, next to that in novelty and wonder, is the assembly this evening to celebrate the five-hundredth sermon. Why, Steele with his *Tatlers*, Addison with his *Spectators*, and Johnson with his *Ramblers* and *Idlers*, were all little men compared with this stripling. The sale of their papers was limited to London, while Charles H. Spurgeon has supporters throughout these Isles and all over the world. For a time he was in mighty favour with the States of the South; but they discovered at last that he was not to their liking, that he was too much the friend of the slave, and then cursed him as much as they had blessed him before. They have a mighty gift of cursing. They burnt his sermons from the time that they discovered his principles, and there was an end of the sale among the Southerners, as you have heard. They will come to their senses by-and-by."

This little festival, at which Mr. Spurgeon's publishers were the hosts dispensing hospitality to a choice circle of supporters and admirers, was talked about and written about in a way which at least testified to the preacher's unique popularity. One weekly journal which never showed anything save hostility to Spurgeon thus referred to the celebration:—

"It appears that Mr. Spurgeon is gradually declining the comic business of which he has proved himself so great a master. The publication of his five-hundredth printed sermon was celebrated on Tuesday evening by a sort of festival at the Tabernacle. Many hundreds of people were collected by the attraction of tea and speeches at a shilling a head, or speeches simple without any charge. It would not be just to say that those who did not pay for tea got milk-and-water, for no enemy would venture to call Mr. Spurgeon's speaking weak, and several of Mr. Spurgeon's young men performed creditably, considering their inexperience. The objects of the meeting were: first, the consumption of tea and cake; secondly, to hear Mr. Spurgeon recount his own rise and progress as a preacher; thirdly, to promote the collection of a fund for the support of the College which he has established for training ministers; fourthly, to give some of the pupils of that College an opportunity of exercising their powers of public speaking; and lastly, to combine with these more serious exercises a little of that jocosity which seems requisite to maintain the popularity of the Tabernacle. The history of Mr. Spurgeon's ministration was traced by one of his admirers through the volumes of his five hundred sermons. It would be superfluous to criticise Mr. Spurgeon's conduct in presiding at a meeting while this elaborate compliment to his abilities and success was being read; because it is evident that if he were a man of sensitive delicacy he would not have a Tabernacle to preach in. Mr. Spurgeon's followers are a good sort of people in their way, but it would not be likely to occur to them that there was any impropriety in puffing spiritual commodities. But if Mr. Spurgeon's sermons were to be examined by an impartial critic, it would not be difficult to derive from them a conclusion more flattering to the preacher than to his congregation. The truth is, that Mr. Spurgeon used methods to acquire popularity which he began to lay aside when he saw that his position was secure. He has gained by extravagance a power and influence which he means to use discreetly, and, having become prosperous, he thinks it time to cease being amusing. . . . As an example of practical sagacity, let us just observe him trotting out his best pupils before the meeting. He wants to make these young men preachers like himself, and, knowing that public speaking can only be learned by practice, he seizes the opportunity of putting them up to speak to a sympathising audience on a congenial theme. In this respect the Church might possibly learn a useful lesson from the Tabernacle." *

It was remarked at this meeting that the idea of printing and publishing a sermon weekly was a new idea which never entered the head of anyone before; but as was pointed out, the late Joseph Irons, of Camberwell, issued through Mr. Collingridge, of *The City Press* office, a discourse weekly from June 4, 1848, till the preacher's death.

Some interest was shown by Mr. Spurgeon in the Surrey Mission, a society which had for its object the spread of the Gospel in the county. On April 16 we find the pastor preaching on behalf of this cause at Union Chapel, Brixton. There earnest evangelists were already employed, and the committee, being greatly encouraged by their past efforts, were hoping to engage others for service in distant parts of the county.

When he accepted the joint-editorship of *The Baptist Magazine*, Mr. Spurgeon discontinued his letters to the Transatlantic journal *The Watchman and Reflector*, but during the year 1863 that correspondence was resumed. A letter which appeared in April contained some personal allusions which show what methods were adopted in answering the slanders of enemies :—

"I have a good friend whose common sense is of the richest kind, and I have frequently heard him observe that it is a great mercy that bad men are allowed to use ill-language. 'For then,' says he, 'I know what they are and how to deal with them.' If lions could bleat like lambs, they would be far more dangerous. The rattle of a rattlesnake is a useful appendage, for it sounds a warning to the unwary. Every man, then, after his own order. It should be very shallow wisdom to make all men speak by one rule, or to induce them to adopt a language which is not in harmony with their hearts.

"Pardon me, friendly readers, if I here digress a little. You will excuse me if ever you have been the subject of the same provocation. Continually am I assailed with accusations from every quarter, bringing to my charge words I never uttered and deeds I have never dreamed of. From the first day till now I have never answered a slander. I have seen

* *The Saturday Review*, March 28, 1863.

my best motives impugned, my holiest aspirations ridiculed, and my most disinterested actions calumniated, and hitherto I have held my peace. The silence which at first was one of moral courage, now assumes a tinge of contempt. 'I am crucified unto the world, and the world is crucified unto me.'

"Its loudest censures are almost as powerless as thunders in a dead man's ear, and its praises have even less effect upon me. There is no love lost between me and a world which despised Christ. Let it speak ill of me, for I have good cause to say far worse of it than it of me."

Then comes a passage concerning John B. Gough, which will remind us that at this time Spurgeon was not a teetotaller, and that the popular Temperance advocate did not speak of him in the kindly strain that was characteristic of after days:—

"I have turned aside from copying from the dear companions of my study, to write out of my own heart, because, singularly enough, a paper has reached me since I have written the last extract, containing a most cowardly and undeserved attack upon me by Mr. Gough, the temperance orator. I will not be tempted even by so urgent a case to turn aside from my fixed rule. I had always honoured Mr. Gough as a great and good man, far removed from any suspicion of falsehood, and equally clear of the folly of attacking God's ministers in order to defend his opinions. I imagined that he knew too well the cruelty of slander to spread a libel against another. I had supposed, also, that he was a gentleman, and better still, a Christian, who esteemed the cause of religion even more highly than that of teetotalism. We live to learn, and there is some learning which costs us bitter grief and the deepest sorrow. When my tongue knows how to speak evil of my fellow-labourer's character, let it rot from my mouth. If I have a cause near to my heart which cannot be defended without slander, perish the cause, even though my heart break from the disappointment.

"Friends, let us leave this personal matter, for I am half inclined to put this letter into the fire even now, and would do so but that the lesson may be useful to us. Let us believe nothing against God's people unless the testimony be ample and decisive, for there are ever those about us to whom it is sport to do mischief. We have been harshly judged; let us not commit the same sin, but ever rest assured that there is real grace upon the earth, and far more of it than some would have us believe."

This was the kind of rebuke which Gough would be able to lay to heart, and although many years were to elapse before the preacher would accept the principles of the teetotal champion, the day ultimately came when Gough and Spurgeon were good friends, and when costly presents were exchanged. The lecturer once sent the pastor a magnificent gold-headed walking-stick, to which a Clapham burglar unhappily took a fancy; and I was at the Tabernacle when a beautifully bound set of Spurgeon's Sermons was presented to "the most extraordinary of English orators," as Gough was called by his more gushing admirers.

On April 15 Mr. Spurgeon, accompanied by his wife and sons,

C C

paid his annual visit to Dr. Campbell, and preached twice on behalf of the Whitefield Tabernacle Auxiliary of the London City Mission. The party at dinner was a brilliant one, and the day was long remembered by the veteran editor as one of the happiest of his life. George Smith, then the well-known pastor at Poplar, was present, and as a good conversationalist did much to enliven the occasion. Even more attractive in regard to the reminiscences he was able to give of other days, was Thomas Jackson, who in his time had served the Wesleyan body as President of the Conference, as Principal of Richmond College, and as editor of many denominational works. This "father" among his own people held Mr. Spurgeon in great respect, and though he was an Arminian in the company of Calvinists, he got on very well. The crowd was so great in the evening at the chapel that the outer gates had to be closed to keep the people back. The aged Wesleyan leader made one of the congregation, and it so happened that the sermon was a decidedly Calvinistic one, powerful throughout, and peculiarly searching in certain passages. When the friends met after the service, the old Methodist remarked in kindly tones to the young pastor—"If I had heard you sixty years ago, I should have preached better." One friend was of opinion that Spurgeon felt this compliment, for the Wesleyan patriarch was so well pleased with the appeals to the unconverted which he had heard that he meant all he said. As host, Dr. Campbell himself was perhaps the best pleased of the party. He looked at a matter like this from a thoroughly Catholic standpoint. "The God of love and mercy blessed, and blessed equally, both Whitefield and Wesley, and it ill behoves their followers to reproach or unchurch each other. It is a proof that both have 'the root of the matter' in them, that both 'hold the head,' and that both embrace the Lord Jesus Christ as Prophet, Priest, and King."

CHAPTER XLIX.

A VISIT TO HOLLAND.

A Night at Sea—Landing at Rotterdam—At the Hague—Interview with the Queen—Preaching Services — At Amsterdam — Utrecht — *The Manchester Examiner* — Spurgeon at Exeter Hall—Pure Literature—Paxton Hood's Lectures at the Pastors' College.

ON Tuesday, April 21, Mr. Spurgeon left England for a tour in Holland, " not with a view to rusticate, after a year of Herculean labours, among the locks, docks, and smiling gardens of that moist and rheumatic region," as one journal remarked, " but to preach twice or thrice a day throughout the great towns and cities, and to address the students in the university." This visit to the land of his ancestors afforded some satisfaction to the pastor's friends; for the Low Countries were understood to have come down in a religious sense until the people were enveloped in the darkness of Egypt. " Out of its 1,500 parish pulpits, in little more than 100 is the Gospel trumpet sounded," we find it stated. Hence, it was thought to be " a matter of great moment that the truth should be proclaimed, as Mr. Spurgeon is wont to proclaim it, throughout the length and breadth of the country."

Thirty years ago the communication between England and Holland was far from being so perfect as is the case at present, and those who sailed from the Thames for the Continent fre-quently suffered from the discomforts of the voyage. Mr. Spurgeon and his friends set sail at midday on Tuesday, the 21st; and after " a very rough and boisterous voyage, though an unusually rapid one," they arrived at Rotterdam in a sickly condition at six a.m. on the following day. In that old town they were cordially wel-comed by friends who were looking out for them, of this number being Mr. Davis, the English pastor, and some of his church officers. After breakfast they went to the church in which a service

was to be held when some other towns had been visited; and after
a short prayer-meeting a start was made for The Hague, which was
reached early in the afternoon. In that historical place the distinguished London preacher was met by Baron van Wasnaer, who
entertained him at his mansion during the visit. This official, who
held a high place at the Court, was a genuinely pious man, and his
wife was in full sympathy with him; and to have his acquaintance
was a great advantage. On their arrival at the house, the
visitors found themselves in one of the most stately residences of
the city: the rooms were magnificent, and in one of the saloons,
on that same evening, Mr. Spurgeon gave an address to 120 persons
from the words, "We have seen the Lord." It was said that religion was fashionable in Holland at that day, and that as it was a
reproach rather than otherwise not to make a profession, hypocrisy
was common. In a plain but forcible manner the necessity of
personal and genuine godliness was set forth; and one who was
present said he believed that the Word was with power to many
hearts. After the service the people lingered about the saloon, now
offering words of welcome to the young English pastor, and then
offering congratulations on what he had been able to do. Spurgeon
was already quite popular among the Dutch; for through a translation his sermons, as we have seen, were already read in all directions.

On Thursday, April 23, there was service in the King's Church
at two o'clock; and the Queen would have been present but for the
illness of her son. The Princesses were in their places, however,
as well as others from the Court, and as these appear to have
understood English, they all, as one present remarked, "for once
in their lives heard the Gospel fully and faithfully preached." One
who was present describes the service :—

"Mr. Spurgeon was mightily helped. His text was from 1 Peter v. 12, 'This is the true
grace of God wherein ye stand.' It was like a great swivel gun, made to turn every way,
and aim at all deceivableness of unrighteousness. He spared no powder, no shot, but went
on demolishing all their refuges of lies till they were left desolate and unsheltered before
God. Then he preached Christ, showed them their only refuge, pleaded with them for their
souls' salvation as if it were for his own life, and finished by urging them to self-
examination by picturing the awful result of deception in so momentous a matter. There

were many tears from many eyes. May the Lord grant that there may have been many a broken heart." *

In the evening, Baron van Wasnaer had another assembly at his mansion; and before a brilliant assembly of many of the chief personages of Holland, Mr. Spurgeon spoke for an hour and a half on the opening words of Psalm xxiii. Of this address the correspondent already quoted, says:—

"It was very sweet: he spoke as he sometimes does, calmly, gently, with a persuasiveness which melts the heart. Said one lady to me, 'This is like dew after a thunderstorm; that was a terrible sermon this morning.' He gave us pictures of Eastern life among the shepherds and their sheep, showed us the fond ones who kept close to the shepherd and fed from his hand, and said that if we were sheep, we had the privileges of guidance, provision, and protection; and our duties were obedience, trust, and love."

The Dutch audience were thoroughly charmed with their English visitor; and the gratitude of the pious among them was very manifest. While blessings on the preacher were generally invoked, there came from every direction requests that he would come again to The Hague.

On Friday morning, April 24, Mr. Spurgeon's attendance at the royal palace was commanded, and he had an interview with the Queen of over an hour's duration. At noon the party left for Leyden, celebrated for its university, which was founded in honour of the manner in which the citizens held out while besieged by the Spaniards in 1574, when 6,000 persons died of famine and pestilence. Spurgeon here held a service in the spacious Church of St. Peter, and the professors and students were present in great force; the discourse was founded on the words of Christ, "I am the way." When he left the church at two o'clock, the great English preacher appeared to be more than satisfied with his adventure, for the smiles which lit up his face told of joy in the heart. "The Lord gave me great power in preaching," he said to his friends, who were equally gratified. The preacher thoroughly realised the characteristics of those who made up so large a proportion of the congregation. He said, "I preached very boldly, ridiculing their new philosophy,

* *The British Standard*, May 1, 1863.

and exposing their errors, but very simply setting before them the Cross, and warning them against knowing anything among men save Jesus Christ and Him crucified."

Amsterdam, famous for its wonderful harbour and magnificent royal palace, was reached on Friday night. On Saturday morning a sermon was given to a densely crowded congregation at the Mennonite Church, and in the evening another service was held at the Dutch Reformed Church. On Sunday there were two more services, in the morning at the Scotch Presbyterian Church of Mr. M'Braith, and in the evening at the Dutch Church of Pastor Schwartz. A correspondent who accompanied Mr. Spurgeon said :—

"These four sermons in Amsterdam have caused quite a commotion there. Rich and poor, old and young, Dutch and English, are there alike enthusiastic in their joy. Such a reception as Mr. Spurgeon has met with in Holland is, I should think, rarely enjoyed. Everywhere his presence has been hailed with rapture, and the people seem to feel that the Lord has indeed sent him among them to do a great and special work. Many a fervent blessing has he received from the poor. They read his translated sermons, and get good from them, and then, though they cannot understand his language, they come just to gladden their hearts by a look at the man whose printed words have comforted, refreshed, or edified them. One peasant-woman, at the door of the Dom-Kirk at Utrecht, caught his hand, and with intense emotion said (in Dutch, of course)—'Oh, Mr. Spurgeon, God bless you! If you had only lived for my soul's sake, you would not have lived in vain. God bless you!' So from the Queen upon the throne to the humble peasant, God has given him favour in the sight of all the people."

The party left Amsterdam on Monday, April 27, and reached Utrecht in the afternoon, the University, the Cathedral, and the pleasant gardens of the environs having an attraction on the one hand, while the manufactures had an interest of their own on the other. Spurgeon had come with his message of peace to a town which was remarkable for its foundry for cannon-balls. An hour after his arrival the preacher was in the pulpit of the Cathedral, and here also professors and students from the University attended in force to hear what he had to say. The audience was immense, and representative of the people of all classes.

In Utrecht, Mr. Spurgeon was the guest of Baron van Boetyclace, who in the evening gave a reception, at which between one and two hundred persons were present, all of whom were supposed to understand English. All of these had come for an address, and they were privileged to listen to one of two hours' duration on the words, "I have given thee all them which sail with thee." At the close the expressions of approval were many, and they came from every direction. "I am more and more astonished at the spirit of hearing which seems poured out on the people of Holland," remarked one friend who was present. "They seem to thirst, to pant after the living water; their souls long for the pure simple Gospel, but their preachers give them instead Rationalism, and well-nigh starve them to death."

The next stage was to Rotterdam, of which Erasmus was a native, and which next to Amsterdam is the greatest centre of commerce in Holland. The round of visits arranged for was now completed: the preacher had arrived at the port where he had landed a week before. Several services were arranged to be held in this city, as well as some gatherings in private houses, ministers and others being invited to attend.

This was in all respects a striking journey, and no one was more surprised than Mr. Spurgeon himself at the size of the congregations and the enthusiasm of the people. Although the May meetings were in progress when the preacher returned, the tour excited considerable interest in England. In the course of a leading article a provincial daily paper said:—

"Mr. Spurgeon has recently made a short tour in Holland. Merely as a tourist in search of the picturesque he would probably not have selected a country without mountains, trees, or springs, but he went there in the exercise of his calling as an eloquent preacher of the Gospel, and had reason to be abundantly satisfied with his reception. The event is singular in its way, but withal unimportant, and we should not raise it above the dignity of small type were it not that the incidents of this preaching tour are rather startling to English prejudices. Everybody knows that Mr. Spurgeon belongs to almost 'the straitest sect of our religion.' He himself, of course, would trace his ecclesiastical lineage to the days of the Apostles, but his pretentions lack the visible seal of sacerdotal rank and Act of Parliament orthodoxy. In short, he belongs to a class of tolerated personages usually known as 'Dissenting ministers.' Measured by success he is the first preacher of the day, and those who include character and motive in their estimate of a Christian minister will find all possible suspicion as regards Mr. Spurgeon dispelled when they learn his incessant labours, his unwearied zeal, and his pecuniary disinterestedness. Yet, who can doubt that if it was announced to-morrow that he had been permitted to preach within the walls of any consecrated edifice in England, the most tremendous consequences would follow? The preacher's voice would do for our venerable Establishment what the celebrated rams' horns did for Jericho. Its hoary walls would fall down flat, crushing to death a host of beadles and bell-ringers, and disclosing to view a helpless host of mitred bishops and portly deans, rending their lawn robes, and howling over the day of conquest and profanation. We cannot for a moment suppose that Archdeacon Denison would survive such a catastrophe; but if he did, it would only be to end his days in pious solitude or to grasp his pilgrim staff and march off to Rome. We need not add that a fatal blow would be struck at the religious sensibilities of the nation, and that ten thousand pulpits would re-echo to terror-stricken audiences the voice of weeping lamentation and woe."

After giving a brief account of the tour itself, the writer goes on to take a more optimistic view of religion in Holland than the English preacher himself held, and a contrast is drawn between the Low Countries and England in regard to Protestantism:—

"Mr. Spurgeon gives, as well as might have been expected, a rather cheerless view of Dutch orthodoxy. 'Holland,' he says, 'is fifty years ahead of England in infidelity.' We are sorry to hear this statement, and we are tempted to fancy that his oratorical labours left him insufficient leisure for forming an accurate opinion, since it must be admitted that if the Dutch are fifty years ahead of us in infidelity, they are a couple of centuries ahead of us in Christian charity. It is not given to any man to be at once a fervid preacher and a calm and accurate critic of the tendencies of other minds. Certainly the immense crowds which followed him in the principal towns of Holland proved anything but a state of religious apathy, and if the tree is to be known by its fruits, Mr. Spurgeon must admit that the Dutch stand the test uncommonly well. But we do not care to dwell upon this point. Our purpose in referring to the subject at all is to hold up before the eyes of the Protestant public in England the singular contrast which Dutch Protestantism presents to ours. We sometimes fancy that we enjoy a monopoly of 'civil and religious liberty.' We never tire of felicitating ourselves upon the triumphs of freedom, as if nowhere else in Europe was the same unfettered scope permitted to the manifestation of religious conviction. We pass no judgment upon this complacency. Perhaps we are better Christians than the Dutch, and our way is more excellent than theirs, but it is also worth while to ask whether or no this is really the case, and at all events the contrast is instructive. Amid the fierce sectarianism of this country, religious people absolutely make fools of themselves if they chance to light upon some little humble flower of Christian charity. If the Archbishop of Canterbury shook hands with a Dissenting minister, the great event would forthwith have the run of all the papers, and provoke the fiercest denunciations in some section of the Press; and if a Dean just popped into a Methodist prayer-meeting, there are thousands who would set him down as worse than Colenso. The excellent Bishop of Melbourne once visited the dying bed of a distinguished Independent minister, and offered prayer with his family. It was a glorious prodigy of Christian sentiment; a sure sign of the millennium. A Dissenting minister in London preached a sermon on the marriage of the Prince of Wales, and having been induced to print it, he sent copies to Her Majesty and the Prince, who graciously accepted them. A denominational journal thought it worth while to chronicle this pleasing fact, and to moralise upon it as showing the immense advance we have made in late years in something, it is hard to say what, unless it be a sense of common politeness at the British Court. Yes, it is added, this sermon actually bore on its title page proof of its 'Nonconformist origin,' and yet it was not flung back in the face of the sender, as happened to an eminent Nonconformist divine under similar circumstances twenty years ago! It must, no doubt, be very grateful to a minister to have a copy of his sermon accepted by the Queen. He is justified in telling it to his wife, or explaining to his children the honour conferred upon him, or even perhaps in making a note of it in the family Bible, just to let his descendants know that they had a distinguished ancestor; but to inform the world that the loyal offering was not disdainfully rejected, and to parade it as a proof of wonderful liberality, makes us painfully aware how deeply the iron of State Churchism has pierced the soul of English manliness and self-respect. The process is quite natural. Preference leads to patronage and servility; assumption on one side provokes flunkeyism in the weaker natures on the other. We don't envy for Dissenting ministers the honour of being invited to Court, and it is not a matter of transcendent importance that they should be allowed the run of the Cathedrals. But it is a matter of some moment that Englishmen should become wiser, less prejudiced, more appreciative of mutual differences, more proficient in the graces of Christian charity. It is a matter of some moment that some of the many walls of partition which fence class from class, and make us strangers and aliens to one another in our own land, should be broken down, and the great elements of Christian character, wherever found, be recognised as superior to clashing doctrines. All this pertains to the growth of the nation in solid virtue and the development of the Church in honesty, manliness, vigour, and breadth." *

The effect of this tour was so exhilarating that the pastor felt stronger and more refreshed when he returned than when he set out. Some references were made to the subject at the Metropolitan Tabernacle on Sunday morning, May 3.

At the annual meeting of the Religious Tract Society at Exeter Hall on the following Friday, Mr. Spurgeon was among the speakers. Some allusions were made to Christian union, as it had been understood, and as it was understood and practised at that time. The duty of putting good doctrine into all publications intended to diffuse the Gospel was then insisted upon by Mr. Spurgeon. The day, he said, had happily gone by already when it was thought necessary to talk much about Christian union, because it had been realised. It used to be thought something like the "Happy Family" on Waterloo Bridge to see ministers of different denominations met together on the same platform. They had now learned to see this to be their duty, and to feel that when they had done all in this matter they were unprofitable servants, that they ought to have loved each other long ago, and even now far better than they did. There was still "one holy Catholic and Apostolic Church"— and that Church was not loose in its creed. It had a creed as firm as if it were of cast-iron, and could no more be removed than the granite foundations of the globe; God the Father, God the Son, and God the Holy Ghost, seen most plainly by us around the

---

* *The Manchester Examiner and Times.*

cross where the bleeding Saviour offers himself a sacrifice for sin. These truths constituted the warp and the woof of the Christian's creed; they felt that they could not disbelieve them, could not be Christians if they did not hold them fast, especially those truths about Jesus, of whom they could always say, "We cannot be right in the rest unless we think rightly of Him." But there were some rising up who objected to doctrinal preaching. It was not necessary, they said, in these days: practice, and perhaps a little experience, but no doctrine. But really, if you take away the doctrine, you have taken away the backbone of the manhood of Christianity—its sinew, muscle, strength, and glory. These men reminded him of Philip when he wished to enslave the men of Athens, and would have them give up their orators. Demosthenes replied, "So said the wolves; they desired to have peace with the shepherds, but the dogs must be first given up—those pugnacious dogs that provoked quarrels. The wolves would lie down peaceably with the lambs, and delight themselves with the sheep, if only those bad-tempered dogs were hanged." So perfect peace was promised among the sects if doctrines were given up; but, depend upon it, these were after all the preservation of the Church, which without them would soon cease to be. These men said they loved the house; they would not touch the furniture in it, not they; they loved the doors thereof, and the floor thereof, and especially the table thereof, and the cupboard thereof. They would by no means touch those things—they only wished to remove certain stones that projected a little above the floor; they would be quite content to get rid of the foundations, to have them torn up and sold for old bricks. His reply was, "We don't see it, gentlemen; we cannot agree to the terms." The men and their communications were known, and the school in which they had studied; and they were not ignorant of his devices who is the master and head of the school. "Burn the charts; what's the use of the charts? What we want is a powerful engine, a good copper-bottomed ship, an experienced captain, and strong, able-bodied mariners. Charts!

Ridiculous nonsense—antiquated things; we want no charts; destroy every one of them. Our fathers used to navigate the sea by them; but we are wiser than they were. We have pilots who know every sand and sunken rock, who can smell them beneath the water—or by some means find them out. Men know what's o'clock nowadays; we don't want chronometers." So they put out to sea without the charts; and looking across the waters, they might expect to witness the shipwreck of those who thought themselves so wise, and fear sometimes lest they should hear their last gasp as they sank and perished. Supposing themselves to be wise, they became fools.

The cry of those who were opposed to sound teaching was "Liberty;" but that did not mean liberty of conscience in the proper sense; it was the liberty to insist that black was white—a kind of freedom which was once illustrated by a diverting occurrence which took place in Ratcliff Highway. A man had a menagerie of wild beasts; and the elephant, fumbling about with his trunk one night, got hold of the peg which fastened his den. So he got out, and, being a member of the Liberation Society, he proceeded to let out the lions, and the wolves, and the jackals. There was soon a terrible noise in the back yard; and the master, waking up, rushed in among the animals with his whip, and soon had them back in their respective quarters. But for his promptness there might have been great mischief done to the people of London. The teachers of false doctrine were playing the part of the elephant, and the lies which they were letting loose upon society must be hunted back to their dens. There must be no liberty to pull up the buoys and to destroy the lighthouses of the Christian Church. It was an entire mistake to suppose that the people did not want doctrine; for the unlettered folks were just those who would receive it best and love it most. An illustration of this had lately happened to himself. Staying at the house of a lady in Holland, he was requested to speak to the three female servants, who had been interested in the reading of his sermons. He asked them in the course of the conversation which sermons they had liked best. One mentioned a discourse on the doctrine of election, the second one justification, and the third one on imputed righteousness —all devotional sermons. Depend upon it, if rich people did not want doctrine, the poor did. And observe, the Reformation had never succeeded in any country where its principles had only taken root in the minds of the higher classes. There were several nobles among the martyrs during the Reformation in Spain, but it was short-lived, because the people were not with it. When the sun shone only upon the mountain-tops the day had not fully dawned; but when the lowest valleys were flooded with its light, then the day had fully risen.

It was pointed out that if the Gospel was to be generally diffused throughout England, it would be necessary to begin low down; but if the people were to be instructed by reading, the reading needed to be made interesting. There were tracts so dry that they resembled chips in porridge, and their stupefying effect insured the reader a sound sleep. Mr. Spurgeon always held that the most effective way of opposing error was to proclaim the truth. Thus, he said on the present occasion, "You may shoot at the man of straw in the cherry tree if you will; but assuredly the best controversy in the world is the preaching of truth." He was also of opinion that Sunday reading was often duller than need be the case; and by way of proving this, he pointed out that the readings for Sundays in Kitto's "Daily Bible Illustrations" were less interesting than those for weekdays. "I see no reason why the highest truth should always be done up dry," he added. "A stroke of humour even in a sermon is not always out of place; but, like a flash of lightning on a dark night, it adds to the general impressiveness and the effect upon the mind."

From this it will be seen how well the pastor of the Metropolitan Tabernacle understood the fact that no man could really gain and hold the attention of the multitude unless he succeeded in making his addresses interesting. This was always Spurgeon's aim as a preacher and a platform speaker, and how well he succeeded can be testified by those who listened to him. He also tried hard to get his students to imitate him in this respect, insisting that devotion and hard work would commonly carry a man through; and that genius, even if possessed, would never become a substitute for labour.

Some little time before the breaking up of the College for the summer vacation this year, Mr. Paxton Hood concluded a series of lectures which he had been requested to give to the students. Mr. Spurgeon and the other tutors attended most of these lectures, and expressed themselves as being greatly pleased. The session ended on Friday, July 31, with a meeting at the Tabernacle. "This is my one life's work, to which I believe God called me, and therefore I must do it," said the president on that occasion. "To preach the Gospel myself, and to train others to do it, is my life's object and aim." Only a short time before, one who was converted through reading one of Spurgeon's sermons had come all the way from Ceylon to be admitted into the College, and was not disappointed. Fourteen students also found settlements during the year.

At this time, Mr. Spurgeon often preached in the open air, and seemed to delight in the practice. A London friend supplied the late Gawin Kirkham with the following reminiscences :—

"In the year 1863 I was living at St. Ives, Hunts. Hearing that Spurgeon, the young preacher, whose fame was everywhere, was to speak in the open air, my sister desired me to be ready for the driver who was to take me at the appointed time for 7 o'clock service in the summer evening.

"I sat somewhat behind, but where I could plainly see the dark figure and earnest countenance, and the clear voice was well heard all round.

"The portions read were from Numbers xxi. and St. John iii.; the text, Numbers xxi. 8, 9. I hear him now, as he said, 'How those mothers would lift their children up and bid them look, and turn their faces toward the serpent. We cannot *make* our children look to Christ, but we can lift them up and turn their faces hitherward.' The service ended, but it was not forgotten. For many years afterwards I had charge of a mothers' meeting, and the one sentence quoted, if no other, was often repeated.

"I never saw Mr. Spurgeon again until the Sunday morning of October 19, 1879, when being within walking distance of the Tabernacle—or, at least, distance which I did walk—I went with a friend to hear him. After a time I had a seat in front of the platform, and not very far from it. The preacher entered, facing a mass of living souls—a mighty throng, above and below, every corner full, his students around him, near a small table a chair, on the back of which he laid his hand. Oh! what a different Spurgeon in physique those years had made him, in evident pain all the time he stood: the service proceeded. The hymn—

> 'So did the Hebrew prophet raise,
>   The brazen serpent high,'

seemed to savour of a past day, but when the portions were read, and the text was given out as Numbers xxi. 9, I felt the coincidence to be remarkable. Waiting for the well-remembered sentence to mothers, I was not disappointed, and was able to recognise the whole sermon as the same. At the end of the service, a lady next me hastened to express to me her admiration; when I told her I had heard the same sermon twice, I fear she considered it a poor 'tribute,' for she remarked, 'He does not often preach the same sermon twice.' I replied I thought it was a good feature that he preached the same sermon in the little Huntingdonshire village that he did fifteen years afterwards to the great London congregation in the Tabernacle.

"At the close of the service Mr. Spurgeon told us that that sermon would be the 1,500th in the published series."

CHAPTER L.

Preaching Tours—Waterbeach Chapel burned down—Spurgeon's Visit—Birmingham—The New Zealand Settlers—Spurgeon in "The Ingoldsby Letters"—Weekly Communion—Mr. J. A. Spurgeon removes to London—Scotland revisited—Death of Friends.

AFTER his return from the Continent, during the spring and summer of 1863, Mr. Spurgeon was frequently found away from home, opening new chapels or preaching on special occasions. On Tuesday the 5th of May he again visited the pretty Cambridge-shire village of Melbourne. At such a time the congregation came in from the surrounding country, there was a great tea-meeting, but not as a rule anything very considerable in the way of a collection. The money was not the first thing which entered into the preacher's calculations, however; he accepted no honorarium for his services, and the ingathering of converts into the Church by the preaching of the Gospel was the only reward he sought.

On Monday the 1st of June the pastor had the happiness of attending the opening meetings of Wandsworth Chapel, Mr. J. W. Genders, who had been trained in the College, being the pastor. He made an earnest speech on the duty of giving, remarking that the collections of Christian people were as sweet music in the ears of the Lord. Judge Payne was also present, the subject of the indispensable "tailpiece" being the seasonable one of "The glorious first of June." On the day following Mr. Spurgeon preached twice on behalf of the cause, and in addition he and his people sent £100 to the building fund. On the following day he was found at the stone-laying of Walworth Road Chapel, Mr. Howieson, his neighbour, being the pastor. Mr. Spurgeon strongly commended this enterprise, remarking that though he did not believe in salvation by works, he knew that God still poured out His blessing on works which were rightly done.*

* *The Baptist Messenger*, 1863, pp. 192–193.

On Monday the 27th of July, Waterbeach presented a holiday-like appearance, the occasion being the laying of the memorial-stones of a new chapel which now occupies the site of the older structure wherein Mr. Spurgeon commenced his pastoral labours. At that date the sanctuary was hardly sixty years old, having been opened in the spring of 1803, and comely as it may look in a picture, it was hardly adapted to modern requirements. After it had stood for nearly sixty years, on April 25, 1862, the building was totally destroyed by fire, and had it not been for the unique associations of the previous decade, the loss need not have been very greatly deplored, a more commodious meeting-house being desirable. As it was, the villagers looked with dismay on the havoc wrought by the fire, and as a member of the congregation afterwards remarked to the writer, they revered the very smoke as it ascended, so closely connected seemed the great London preacher and that odd-looking little chapel.

When they thus lost their chapel, the people did the best they could under the circumstances: they made a barn their Sunday meeting-place, and meanwhile the builder of the Metropolitan Tabernacle in London supplied plans for a new chapel at a cost of £750, which were generally approved. There was some ambition to erect a chapel worthy of the village and its great memories.

On the summer day already mentioned, Mr. Spurgeon went down to Waterbeach, and in the presence of between one and two thousand people laid the first memorial-stone of the new building, to the fund of which he presented a sum of £120. The silver trowel, which was brought away as a memento of the occasion, was presented by a deacon of the Tabernacle. Deacon King, an old friend of the preacher, offered prayer, Mr. Ewing, then the pastor at Waterbeach, gave an address, and a second stone was laid by Mr. James Toller, a local gentleman. Then followed a great tea-meeting, and in the evening there was the irresistible attraction of a sermon by Spurgeon in the capacious barn to two thousand delighted hearers.*

* *The Baptist Messenger*, 1863, p. 246.

From a photograph by R.H.Lord, Cambridge.

REV. T. G. TARN.

From a photograph by Martin & Sallnow, Strand, w.c.

REV. WILLIAM WILLIAMS.

From a photograph by the London Stereoscopic C°. 1st Regent.St.w.

REV. ARCHIBALD BROWN.

From a photograph by Fredk. Thurston, Luton.

REV. WILLIAM CUFF.

From a photograph by Debenham & C°. Southsea.

REV. T. W. MEDHURST. (FIRST STUDENT)

DISTINGUISHED MINISTERS TRAINED IN THE PASTORS COLLEGE.

The preacher's incessant labours at this time prompted Dr. Campbell to remark, "Mr. Spurgeon would seem to be superior to all the frailties of humanity. In point of labour every day is almost a Sabbath, while his Sabbath efforts are such as might well exhaust and lay up for a day or two the strongest man." The pastor of the Tabernacle was compared to Whitefield, for as the great evangelist of the eighteenth century had had to travel far and wide on account of the orphans he undertook to feed, so did his modern successor have to itinerate in the interests of his College. Immense as was the liberality of his own people, he had to seek additional supplies in the distance. Thus we find Spurgeon preaching twice at Birmingham to 6,000 people, the collection of £132 averaging 4¾d. each person.* Two sermons were also given to 3,400 people at Dudley, where the collection of £112 averaged 8½d. At Wolverhampton 3,000 gave £91 at two services, the average being 7¼d. Smaller places were also visited in turn, and to such an observer and lover of nature as Spurgeon some of these were of far greater interest than the large manufacturing towns. Take by way of example the visit made at this time to Lymington and the New Forest district:—

"This celebrated preacher paid his long anticipated visit to Lymington on Wednesday last. The event having been duly set before the public in the shape of handbills, posters, notices from the pulpit, etc., one of the largest crowds ever seen in this town gathered from all parts of the neighbourhood to welcome Mr. Spurgeon to Lymington. A monster booth had been erected, capable of holding from two to three thousand persons. It was, however, not large enough to hold the congregation, many of whom had to listen outside the booth to the preacher. The weather was showery, but the people were so determined to hear this remarkable man that the rain was scarcely heeded. Mr. Spurgeon preached in the afternoon and evening, the booth being crammed each time. The appearance of the huge congregations as they defiled out of the tent was very remarkable and striking. We fancy no other man living could create such an excitement in this usually steady-going town. We trust Mr. Spurgeon will pay Lymington another visit, and can assure him he will meet with a cordial and earnest welcome from the public. We are not bold enough to criticise his preaching. His style is peculiarly his own, and is not to be judged

* On the whole, the reception of the preacher at Birmingham was extremely cordial; but he was still occasionally greeted with coarse abuse, e.g. :—" Our *Birmingham Gazette* has indeed been honouring Mr. Spurgeon with bitter ridicule and sneers, and has set him down as nothing better than a mimic and stage buffoon, treating him as the comedian Foote did Whitefield in the playhouse and by the Press; holding him up to public scorn as Dr. Squintum."—Peter Sibill, in *The British Standard*, June 19, 1863.

D D

by ordinary rules. He is a gifted, earnest, eloquent man—cut out for hard work and plenty of it—and will leave a name behind him when his work is done that will excite the envy of many and the admiration of all. We wish him God-speed."*

The news which came to hand from time to time respecting the large body of New Zealand settlers on whose behalf the great farewell meeting was held in the Metropolitan Tabernacle must have been somewhat disappointing. "We regret to find that a very serious misunderstanding has occurred between Mr. Brame and his co-trustees," remarked the denominational organ. "The lands in question were sold under the authority of Mr. Brame, who is charged with having secured a Crown grant of them in his own name, while he was understood by the settlers to be acting only as their agent. He, in return, makes large money claims upon the settlement."† This would be a sore disappointment to Mr. Spurgeon, who had shown such interest in the welfare of the emigrants. The deserters from the settlement increased rather than diminished, and the number who remained had gone down to about two hundred. The outlook, nevertheless, was in some respects promising. The Sabbath services were well attended; the sale of intoxicants was prohibited, but there was a lack of good schools. The courage of some had failed on account of the heavy expenses of transit.

About this time, some interest was excited in the portraiture of Spurgeon, as given to the world by a High Churchman in the second volume of "The Ingoldsby Letters." It was manifestly a sin in such a writer, as he ingenuously confessed, to leave his parish church for the sake of repairing to the Metropolitan Tabernacle. The indiscretion, being once committed, however, was repeated, and the visitor was so deeply moved by what he saw and heard that he could not well refrain from giving his impressions to the public.

The service commenced at 10.45, and lasted two hours, and half of the time was occupied by the sermon. In regard to this, it is observed, that "it is not so much the absolute length as the

---

* *Hampshire Independent.*   † *The Freeman,* May 1, 1863.

unvarying routine, the repetitions, and icy formality of our Church system which renders the usual morning service tedious even to religious persons, and notoriously repulsive to others." The preacher appeared exactly to time, "dressed in a plain frock-coat without any robes or bands;" but it excited no small astonishment when the first hymn was sung to the tune of "God save the Queen." Having no book and no knowledge of the words of the hymn, both mind and tongue were disposed to get into the groove of—

> "Confound their politics;
> Frustrate their knavish tricks," etc.

So that it was submitted "to the Coryphæus of that vast assembly whether it might not be in better taste to confine his selection of tunes to such as are commonly applied to words of seriousness." The writer continues:—

"The hymn concluded, Mr. Spurgeon walked to the table, and taking his stand between it and the sofa, opened a large and handsome clasped Bible (the gift, I was told, of the congregation), 'and when he had found a place,' which was on this occasion the latter part of the sixth chapter of Ephesians, he proceeded to read it with a slow and articulate voice, dwelling upon the more impressive passages, which he illustrated by a short extempore comment as he went along. Never did I hear the 'first' or 'second' lesson in our churches delivered with like effect. Often, too often, have I mourned to hear them mangled in the reading, or hurried through as if a secondary portion of the service for the day, and never (as is well known) accompanied by the smallest attempt at exposition, however 'hard to be understood,' or however fertile or profitable instruction for the humbler class of worshippers. Not a word must pass the lips of the orthodox minister—the unfeigned-assent-and-consent-subscriber to our Liturgy—during the time of reading the prayers and appointed lessons of the day, but what is set down for him in the book, and has been so set down for the last two hundred years, and (according to the Bishop of Oxford) will be set down for the next two hundred. If the officiating minister break this rule—if he attempt, for example, on the 26th of next month, upon reading the second lesson for the evening service, to interrupt the course of Scripture by explaining how the feet of a Christian may be shod with the preparation of the Gospel of peace, or his head covered with the helmet of salvation—he renders himself liable to an action for brawling in church, and may be sequestered from his living for as long a period as if he had been guilty of immorality, or had contravened any of the Thirty-nine Articles of religion.

"This same chapter, or rather a portion of it, explained as he went along by Mr. Spurgeon, was a sermon in itself; and was listened to with profound attention, and I will venture to say, corresponding edification, by all that multitude, who thus drank in the words of the Apostle, made plain and intelligible to the humblest comprehension, at the same time impressed upon all with a fervour and simplicity of illustration worthy both of the matter and object of the writer."

Attention was drawn by the writer to the singing of the second hymn and to the second prayer, which was more special in its character than the first, cases of individuals being mentioned, thus bringing home to each present the value of personal prayer, the Established Church service, with the exception of the Litany, being defective in that respect. Other things are also mentioned; then follows something concerning the preacher himself and the causes of his unique popularity :—

"Meanwhile, I would ask my readers to review calmly what I have written, and to bear in mind that I can have no possible motive in exalting the Conventicle at the expense of the Church; while I would fain have the latter, where it can, take a lesson from the former; as on the other hand, as far as rests with myself, I would see the former amalgamated with the latter by such a relaxation of the terms of subscription as I am persuaded might with safety be undertaken.

"That something is wrong somewhere, when thousands are thus seen to rush Sunday after Sunday (for several years' continuance) to listen to an unauthorised teacher, and to partake of what, without offence, I must designate as a schismatical form of worship, is but too manifest; while the contrast is made more painful by the languid manner in which the ministrations of the Establishment are but too frequently attended, and the vacancies seen along our benches, notwithstanding all the appliances used to induce a cheerful and ready attendance.

"All the learning and piety in the world will not supply the want of a good delivery, and the tact to suit your discourse to the character of your audience. Herein lies the first secret of Mr. Spurgeon's success. He has taken the measure of his congregation's taste and capacity, and adapts himself to it. Like the cunning doctor in Lucretius, he anoints the lips of his cup with honey, and so cheats his patients into swallowing the salutiferous draught. Religion was made agreeable to his hearers, but it is still religion. He makes it apparent both in his preaching and practice that her ways are ways of pleasantness and all her paths are peace.

"The second great cause of Mr. Spurgeon's continued popularity is that he is mighty in the Scriptures. This is his deep well, and he is not sparing of its resources. He draws and draws again as he has occasion, and he does it without forcing. He has carefully studied John Bunyan, and copies him here with considerable skill. Thirdly, he is evidently a man of prayer, and feels therein a hidden source of strength which will not fail him at his need. The same gift which empowers him to pour forth his two extempore prayers in the early part of the service, accompanies him throughout his sermon, and chastens and subdues even the more attractive portions of the discourse. In his lightest illustrations he does not forget the object and the occasion, and thus escapes splitting on a rock that has foundered many a preacher of oratorical powers equal or even superior to his own."

So far, the gifts and attainments of the preacher, in this writer's opinion, were sufficiently striking to account for his success; but of course the portraiture would not have been complete without reference to his "full, clear, and melodious voice," which struck most of his hearers in those early days as one of the preacher's most unique endowments. In connection with his manner in the pulpit, however, there were other things which attracted this shrewd observer's attention :—

"He has, moreover, an accurate and quick ear and an expressive eye, developing in a remarkable degree the organ of language, aided by those of ideality, comparison, gaiety, wonder, veneration, and constructiveness. His manner is agreeable, and he is blest with a large fund of animal spirits and considerable strength. Such are Mr. Spurgeon's natural and acquired qualifications as a preacher, to which he has not disdained to add the great advantages of careful study and long cultivation. He understands, too, the art of concealing his art. He holds himself entirely under control. And if for a moment he appears to give way to the excitement of the topic and allows free rein to his tongue, he still has it under subjection, and returns to a quieter mood without effort and without constraint. His transitions are natural, and pleasantly relieve the outline of his bolder strokes. He is no windy orator, and knows when to pause, when to turn. He does not run either himself or his subject out of breath. His diction, though rapid, is sufficiently choice; his figures well selected and full of meaning. His energy is prodigious, and his earnestness bears all the appearance of sincerity and truth."

Spurgeon had thus recommendations which would have made any preacher popular; but there was something else which had to be reckoned among his peculiar advantages, and which so largely accounted for his standing in the front as the "phœnix of Nonconformity." This lay, the writer unhesitatingly declared, in the *freedom* of the preacher's position :—

"Mr. Spurgeon neither prays nor preaches in chains. He is unconscious of the sword of his bishop hanging by a hair over his head. He is not, I believe, of the Independent persuasion, but he is independent (notwithstanding) of everything except the favour of his flock, who are worthy of him and he of them. They are mutually fond of one another; exacting and expecting no more than is the due between minister and people. The latter not extreme to criticise; the former not fearful to give offence.

"It is this mutual good understanding which, as it first contributed largely to secure his congregation, now serves to cement it. Meanwhile it should not be forgotten that Mr. Spurgeon possesses the additional stimulus of a remarkably propitious soil for the full development of his genius. His tabernacle stands in a densely peopled district of the middle orders, where the voluntary system will always work to the best advantage; a system which, be its effects what they may (and we are far from advocating it for general adoption), has at least the merit of drawing out and bringing into the foreground all the talent and capabilities of its teachers. Under it a preacher finds his level as surely and almost as quickly as do air and water. No envy depresses him. No nepotism or favouritism keeps him perpetually in the background. Conservatism or Radicalism form no part of his religious profession. He has neither to crawl into favour with his diocesan, nor to set his barometer daily to the level indicated by the public horizon.

"Can the same be said of the 20,000 ministers under the Establishment; and is it, then, surprising that we meet with few or no Spurgeons in the Church? I have heard it remarked by a London physician of extensive practice, that there is no profession in which there is such a *waste of power* as in the Established Church."

What was the remedy for this state of things? The answer of this writer was, "Let us Spurgeonise the Church." The skill which enabled a preacher to give the Gospel to the people in the most acceptable manner could hardly be supposed to be the possession

of only one man : Churchmen as well as Baptists could adopt
popular methods. In bygone days Simeon, of Cambridge, had
attracted a full congregation : why should he not have imitators
of his example ? There were a few already ; but what would be
said if there were to be a Simeon or a Spurgeon in every church ?
" Let them say what they please, so long as they cannot say,
with some show of truth, that while the ministers of the Establishment are idly busy purging away common sense amidst whole acres
and furlongs of empty benches, their would-be congregation is being
gesticulated away by the fervid eloquence of a Spurgeon, or the
ungrammatical nonsense of Mr. Stubbs." *

The sentiments of this talented author may possibly have found
as much sympathy among Nonconformists as in the Establishment
itself. The two volumes contained 128 letters which had previously
appeared, and three letters were devoted to Mr. Spurgeon. " Men
of such a spirit are the bonds of all that is good in the Establishment, and the magnets of all that is good beyond it," said one
reviewer. " A thousand men, such as the author of ' The Ingoldsby
Letters,' in twenty years would put a new face on the Church of
England, and would operate in a manner the most salutary on the
spirit of Dissent."

A work published in 1863 drew attention to the question of
the Lord's Supper, advocating the practice of a weekly celebration,
references, by the way, being made to Mr. Spurgeon. As is well
known, the Church at the Metropolitan Tabernacle maintained the
rule of open communion, while the membership was strictly confined
to Baptists. This rule was pretty common in the denomination to
which Mr. Spurgeon belonged, while the General or Arminian Baptists
on the one hand, and the Strict Baptists on the other, were usually
of close communion principles. The book just referred to was not
concerned with such controversies, however ; the object of the author
was to prevail on all the Churches to practise weekly communion.

* "The Ingoldsby Letters, in Reply to the Bishops in Convocation and in the House
of Lords on the Revision of the Book of Common Prayer." Vol. II. London, 1863.

Some references were made to New Park Street Chapel and to the Metropolitan Tabernacle as follows :—

"I may here remark that Mr. Spurgeon had fortnightly communion when in Park Street Chapel, and found nothing inconvenient, much less impracticable, in it, although he had latterly in that place a congregation numbering more than 2,000 persons, and a Church consisting of about 1,000 members. And if Mr. Spurgeon administered for years the Sacrament of the Lord's Supper to his large Church in Park Street Chapel once every second week without any inconvenience whatever, the inevitable conclusion to which we must come is, that there can be no admissible excuse on that ground for not commemorating the death of Christ on the first day of every week. Indeed, I have great pleasure in being able to say that I have ground for believing that ere long Mr. Spurgeon will see it to be his duty to institute the weekly celebration of the Lord's Supper in his Metropolitan Tabernacle, with its congregation of between 5,000 and 6,000 persons, and members of the Church numbering not much short of 2,500. I fondly trust that my expectations in this matter will be speedily realised, because the fact of weekly communion being established by him would have a powerful influence on other ministers of the Gospel and Churches throughout the land; while the circumstance of weekly partaking of the Supper in the largest place of worship—having also the greatest number of Church members in the world—would prove an unanswerable argument in opposition to those who urge, as their reason for neglecting weekly communion, the inconvenience, if not the impracticability, of dispensing the Sacrament of the Supper weekly in large congregations and Churches." *

The removal of his brother from Southampton to London during the summer of 1863 would naturally be a matter affording great satisfaction to Mr. Spurgeon. Sir Morton Peto had erected a handsome chapel in Cornwall Road, Notting Hill, and of this Mr. James Spurgeon accepted the pastorate. The chapel was opened on Wednesday, the 1st of July, and the pastor commenced work immediately afterwards. Among the speeches on that occasion was one by Henry Ward Beecher,† who had been present at the

---

* "The Dying Command of Christ; or, the Duty of Believers to Celebrate Weekly the Sacrament of the Lord's Supper." By the author of "God is Love." London, 1863.

† Mr. Beecher's speech is in *The Freeman* of July 8. The great American preacher appears to have been on very friendly terms with Mr. Spurgeon at the time when the former was thus depicted :—

"There is not a rag of the parsonic about him, though I heard him twice declare that he was a 'clergyman;' apart from which declaration I should have pronounced him a thriving farmer on some of the sunny slopes of the Hudson, extremely partial to fine horses, and not averse to a good generation of shorthorns. I could not smell so much as a text in his velvet-collared coat, and my private opinion is that not even one of Watts's hymns would have had the courage to get into the wide-awake with which he covered his noble head. He may be a 'clergyman,' but I have grave doubts whether any bishop on earth would own him. Judging from his face I should say he looks like a man whose opinion is always made up, and like a man, too, who always comes out of the front door when he wishes to give his opinion an airing."—Joseph Parker, D.D., "To the Coming Man," in *The British Standard*, November 6, 1863.

Metropolitan Tabernacle on the preceding Sunday morning to hear
Mr. Spurgeon's sermon on "The Rainbow."

Another visit to Scotland appears to have been undertaken during
the summer; and Sunday, the 9th of August, was passed at
Helensburgh at the manse of the Free Church minister, John
Anderson. It was not quite a day of rest to Mr. Spurgeon, however; for after preaching in the church in the morning he preached
again in the evening in the open air near the railway station. The
text of the first sermon was St. John xx. 25, "We have seen the
Lord;" that of the evening was from the same Gospel—vii. 37:
"If any man thirst, let him come unto me, and drink."

As regarded entertainment, Helensburgh was probably at this
time the place which Mr. Spurgeon loved best to visit in Scotland;
but now he had the additional satisfaction of seeing his son in the
faith and "First Student" settled as pastor over the Frederick Street
congregation in Glasgow. Mr. Medhurst had accepted that charge only
a few months previously, and was doing a work which gladdened the
heart of his Chief. Great advances had been made by the Baptist
denomination in the city; for we find it stated on good authority
that a century before "there was not an individual to be found in
Glasgow who avowed his conviction of adult baptism." We find
it added, that "when a native of a neighbouring parish had his
attention drawn to the inquiry, there was none with whom he could
communicate." The individual referred to, Archibald McLean, became
a Baptist at the age of thirty in 1763. That being then a hundred
years ago, we find that there was some desire to have a centenary
celebration. "Dr. Gill has passed away," it was remarked. "Mr.
Spurgeon treads in his steps, Mr. Medhurst follows in the rear, and
the Baptist friends in the capital of the West gather round him to
sustain and support him." *

From first to last it was a most unusual thing for Mr. Spurgeon
to leave his own pulpit on a Sunday in order to preach elsewhere;
but this happened on Sunday morning, October 18, when he gave

---

* See "Glasgow One Hundred Years Ago," in *The Earthen Vessel*, xix. 24–25.

a discourse to his brother's congregation at Cornwall Road Chapel, founded on Deut. i. 38, "Encourage him." The people received some excellent advice in regard to their conduct towards their minister, some things being said which were very necessary to put in practice, but which the pastor himself could not have spoken with so much effect.

The progress made during the year 1863 appears to have been in all respects satisfactory. The Church at the Metropolitan Tabernacle was rapidly growing in numbers, while the College, which was now seven years old, had a staff of competent tutors and sixty-six students, besides nearly two hundred young fellows in its evening classes. The money for all this enterprise was never wanting; no debt was ever incurred; and the pastor himself always declared that all the necessary supplies came in answer to prayer. George Müller, at Bristol, and Spurgeon, in London, were thus alike in their faith and methods. The students prepared for service readily found openings; forty had already settled, and the applications were more numerous than the men to respond to them. The men who were sent forth were found to be peculiarly successful in breaking up new ground, or in making new spheres for themselves. Thoughts of erecting a college building were now first entertained. What was being effected by certain of the more successful of the former students was already justly regarded as striking evidence of the success of the College; and in the number of his paper which appeared on Christmas Day Dr. Campbell said:—

"As one example, take Mr. Gange, of Portsmouth. He has laboured there a year. His hearers at first were fifty; in a few weeks nine hundred. To protect those who hold seats, he has been obliged to adopt the ticket system of his metropolitan patron. Not a single sitting is unlet. Many persons go away unable to get in. He has received into Church-fellowship considerably more than a hundred persons, his own converts. Besides an inquirers' class and male and female Bible classes, he has also a preachers' class—that is to say, no fewer than thirty-five men, probably young men, meet him every Saturday night, when he trains them in the art of extempore speech as preachers, which holy art they exercise on Sunday afternoons in the open air."

The chapel which was soon afterwards erected was the largest Nonconformist place of worship in the county of Hampshire. There for some years Mr. Medhurst, the "First Student," also laboured, Mr. Gange having succeeded to the pulpit of Robert Hall, at Broadmead, Bristol, where he still remains.

The last day of the year falling on a Thursday, the usual week-night sermon at the Tabernacle was succeeded by a watch-night service. The weather was very wet, so that the attendance was not so large as usual. Those who waited were regaled with refreshments in the rooms below; and at eleven o'clock, when the pastor again appeared on the platform, there was a very large congregation. The address was founded on Heb. iii. 7, "The Holy Ghost saith to-day." It was, he said, a short text, and he meant to preach from it a short sermon. They were words full of meaning and import to every-one present. They set forth, in the first place, their opportunity. That opportunity was the day of mercy. That day might not be past to them; but they must remember it was "to-day." To-morrow it might be gone, and once passed it was lost for ever. It was very variable in its duration. To some it was seventy years, to others not so many weeks, and to some there might not be seventy minutes. Let them, then, seize it while it was to-day. Then the words implied his importunity. The thought of eternity made him earnest in his entreaties with them to flee to the Saviour, and he concluded by calling upon them to spend the few remaining moments of the year in silent and fervent prayer to that Saviour, that He would hear their cry for mercy and enable them by the Spirit to lay hold upon Him as the only medium through which it could be extended towards them.

According to custom, the people spent a few moments in silent prayer while 1863 passed away and the new year came in.

Among those who died during 1863 were Dr. Reed, the philan-thropist, Dr. Raffles, Sir Culling Eardley, and Archbishop Whately. Perhaps the loss which would most affect Mr. Spurgeon, however, was that of Dr. Gaussen, the Geneva professor, whose work on the Plenary Inspiration of Scripture the London preacher afterwards re-published as one of the books on this subject which he most valued.

CHAPTER LI.

THE WORK AT THE METROPOLITAN TABERNACLE.

Statistics of Church Work—The College—The Annual Supper—Intellectual and Moral Growth of the Preacher—Success of his Students—Death of Mr. Spurgeon of Stambourne—Walworth Road Chapel—At Exeter Hall—Winslow.

AT the opening of the year 1864 we find the Metropolitan Tabernacle spoken of as "that great ecclesiastical wonder," the spiritual influence for good of which was still extending. While he looked upon it with astonishment, Dr. Campbell likened the place to a great healthy tree which was continually extending in every direction. The chapel was no longer a novelty, but it seemed to be ever growing, and were it double the size there would be a congregation to fill it. "The aggregate, with the households it represents, would form a considerable township, requiring, for decent accommodation, well-nigh 3,000 residences," it was remarked. At the rate of increase of Church members which had been going on, it was calculated that the regular communicants would soon exclude the ordinary congregation of outsiders who were attracted. It was supposed that that might occasion some perplexity; but in point of fact Mr. Spurgeon did something to keep the numbers down by encouraging the secession of a body at one time who settled elsewhere to found or revive another interest.

During the year 1863 the number baptised was 311, while 116 were received by letters from other Churches, making a total of members received 427. There were 22 deaths, 50 were dismissed to other Churches, 4 were excluded, and 23 names were removed from the roll for non-attendance, the total number of members being 2,517. The small number of deaths in proportion to the congregation was regarded as something like a phenomenon :—

"How is this to be explained? Only in one way: the mass of the people consist of persons in the prime of life or in its early morning. Nor is this all; the male sex, who in London are the better lives, preponderates to an extent we have never witnessed elsewhere in any regular assembly. But while the vast majority are males, the bulk of them are also younger men, which, we believe, goes some way to account for the absence of the usual mortality, as well as for the moral force which distinguishes the place in everything. It also serves, to some extent, to explain the extraordinary liberality in the way of pecuniary contribution. The power of a mass of men and a mass of women, although their numbers were equal, is not for a moment to be compared, because of the difference of their respective earnings and incomes. But here a question occurs. Whence this mighty gathering of young people? The reply is, we think, obvious : the preacher began a lad, and is still but a young man, with an extraordinary power of fascination over his own class. Youth naturally cleaves to youth. There is also in the place, its associations and employments, an endless attraction, an inexhaustible excitement, which carries all before it. There is about the whole concern a social grandeur, a moral romance, that dazzles, delights, and captivates the rising generation."

Other characteristics of the congregation were also sufficiently remarkable to such as took intelligent account of them. The general liberality of the people for all purposes was far above the average, and thus beyond what might have been expected. The assembly was a middle-class one, the very rich being as conspicuous by their absence as the very poor. The amount raised in 1863 for all purposes was £7,645 15s. 10d., or something like an average of thirty shillings a sitting.

Because every member who joined the Church was expected to do something in the way of Christian service, the aggregate accomplished was very great. The pastor himself was not only an earnest worker, his enthusiasm appeared to be contagious. Many compared him with Whitefield, who frequently actually commenced preaching at six o'clock; and Cornelius Winter, who lived with the great eighteenth century evangelist, was wont to say, "There was no rest for man or beast after four o'clock in the morning." One of Wesley's comrades also said of him, "While calm and even cool himself, he set fire to everything around him." Spurgeon was regarded as an inheritor of the characteristics of these great leaders. He seemed to understand the art of prompting people to give and of stimulating them to work. It was thought that the wide world contained nothing worthy of being compared with the Metropolitan Tabernacle's system of instrumentality. The golden motto of Methodism was clearly applicable to Spurgeon—" At it, all at it, and always at it." It was evident that the pastor was " alike ready to run a race with John Calvin in doctrine and with John Wesley in practice."

The College had, at this time, outlived most of its early difficulties; and those who had at first put down the idea of founding a college without large funds and titled professors as " fanatical and preposterous," found out that their misgivings had been unfounded. The work widened and became more important as it progressed; and it was thought to be not a small wonder in the history of Providence when over £100 a month was put into the Tabernacle collecting-boxes to make good the failure of supplies from the United States.

On Wednesday evening, February 10, of this year, Sir Morton Peto presided at what would appear to have been one of the first of the annual suppers on behalf of the College, which have been continued until the present time. In the first instance the feast was wholly given by one friend; but afterwards the cost was subscribed by Mr. Spurgeon himself and one or two others. On this occasion, in 1864, two hundred persons attended and gave £2,000 —a striking success when compared with the £500 which had been raised when the publication of the 500th sermon was celebrated. The facts of the year's work, as given in *The Morning Advertiser* of the time, were regarded as being remarkable. There were seventy students in course of training; and some who had gone out had gathered congregations for themselves, and had managed to get their own chapels erected. One young Jewish convert had undertaken a preaching tour in Poland at the expense of the College; and other things which had been done showed that the managers were hampered by no strait-laced rules. They did whatever promised best to further the gathering-in of the people into the Church. They maintained that they were succeeding in a way which had never been surpassed. As a Pædobaptist, Dr. Campbell was not likely to be over-biassed in favour of the Baptist president's methods; but when he contrasted his own experience with what he saw at Newington, he yielded the palm to Spurgeon :—

" We have ourselves gone through the full University curriculum, half in one and half in another of the national institutions, and we feel bound to say that the system then, however admirable in other respects, was most defective as it related to the preparation of preachers. It did not admit for a moment of comparison with the method pursued at Spurgeon's College. The last thing that seemed to be thought of was the preacher and the pastor. The exercises in the Divinity Halls, which followed the courses of language, literature, and philosophy in those days, were of small account. When a man had finished his seven or eight years, whether for platform or pulpit labour, or pastoral work generally, whatever might be his talents, or even genius and scholarly attainments, he would have been eclipsed by a large portion of Spurgeon's young men, even at the close of the first year. Allowing for the immense improvements which have been made on all sides since that day, there is still, we feel assured, need of great advancement. Spurgeon has the true idea of the wants of the Church and of the times, and he has fully provided for them. He is not the foe of learning by any means, but he is more the friend of souls. What he deprecates is, not education, but *non-adaptation to the work contemplated*, and every man of sense and reflection will join him. He does not view the great national establishments as *over*-educating, but as *mis*-educating the labourer for his field of service. With respect to numbers, the absence of all academic training had, on the whole, been better than a training which only tended to incapacitate a man for preaching. Real ability, sound conversion, fervent zeal, a thorough knowledge of the Word of God, and constant practice in speaking will, in the end, go a great way to make a man a good and an able minister of the New Testament. Such was that prince of commentators, Thomas Scott; such was that prince of epistolary writers, John Newton; such was that prince of polemical authors and genuine theologians, Andrew Fuller; such, too, were Abraham Booth, Adam Clarke, and Richard Watson—men constituting the mighties of the age they lived in."

We also find it remarked at this time that the College which Spurgeon had founded, and which he managed with a success that surprised his friends while it dumfoundered his enemies, was a standing protest against read sermons. The students learned their leader's ways until it was not to be wondered at if they were suspected of unduly imitating him. At all events, they learned to preach without a manuscript, and it was considered that this was so far a gain that it was one of the things which contributed to the preacher's wonderful success. It was impossible to conceive of Spurgeon with a MS.; and it was declared that the use of paper would have reduced his hearers from thousands to hundreds.

The ninth volume of the Sermons appeared at this time, and enabled those who were interested in him to take notice of the intellectual and spiritual growth of the preacher, and also to mark the progress of his work. It was already clearly seen that these discourses would be the preacher's greatest and most enduring monument. " Where is the man in England or Europe who preaches a discourse every Sabbath morning throughout the year, which will bear publication every week, and sell in all lands by the million?" it was asked; and then it was added, "He pours out sermons as Shakespeare did plays, apparently as unconscious as the poet was of doing anything at all extraordinary." By some of his more ardent admirers the preacher was thought to be almost past criticism; and so greatly had he improved that the volume for 1863 appeared to be better than any which had preceded it. "It is replete," said this friendly critic, "with truth and love, force and fervour. From the archbishop down to Thomas Blyth, the worthy bargeman, who speaks a word to the weary on Sunday evening, there is not a preacher in the land who may not read and ponder the volume with benefit. Spurgeon was born with a key to the heart of humanity in his hand; and the volume before us shows the marvellous skill with which he turns it. It is interspersed with numerous passages which for power and pathos are equalled by very· little, and surpassed by nothing, in the sermonology of the world." *

A remarkable circumstance in connection with the Pastors' College is, that many of the men who have achieved the most striking success were students in the early days now under notice. Among these is Frank H. White, who settled at Chelsea, and whose work has for some years been associated with Talbot Tabernacle, Notting Hill. At the outset of his course, Mr. White was pastor at Paradise Chapel, Chelsea, and he was one of the men in whose labours the president of the College showed the greatest interest. It was proposed to erect a new chapel to accommodate a thousand persons at a cost of £3,500; and when a meeting was convened to further that object, Mr. Spurgeon wrote :—

"My dear friend, Mr. Frank White, has worked hard in that inaccessible place so blunderingly called Paradise Walk; his ministry has been blessed to the conversion of many; but he now sees what I have long seen, the imperative necessity of leaving Paradise and *walking* elsewhere—an emigration which, I trust, will be for the good of thousands. The Church at Paradise Walk is very small, and quite unable to erect a structure such as the denomination requires; but with the help of Christian friends the task will be accomplished. I shall give Mr. White my most earnest aid, and trust that all lovers of Jesus will do the same. The edifice will be of such a character that I may safely guarantee that no money will be wasted either in expensive ugliness or trifling ornament."

* *The British Standard*, March 4, 1864.

Mr. White cheered the heart of his Chief by advancing to far greater things than might have been looked for in those days. In due time he became the recognised Remembrancer of the College, and as such, at each successive annual Conference, he gave an account of the collections which had been made by the Churches during the year on behalf of the institution.

Mention may here be made of Mr. James Cubitt, pastor of the church at Thrapston, Northamptonshire, who assisted as tutor in the College for over two years, commencing with the summer of 1861. Health failing, he retired for a time from active service; but disease had made such inroads into his constitution that he passed away at the age of fifty-five.*

On Friday, the 12th of February, 1864, the venerable James Spurgeon, of Stambourne, passed away at the age of eighty-seven years. After the afternoon service at the chapel on Sunday, February 21, the remains of the late pastor were buried in the adjoining grave-yard, thirty children and grandchildren of the deceased standing around the grave. Mr. Spurgeon does not appear to have been of the number; but at the Metropolitan Tabernacle he preached from St. Matt. x. 22, "Enduring to the end," and paid a glowing tribute to his grandfather's memory.

Born on Michaelmas Day, 1776, James Spurgeon, of Stambourne, was almost a nonagenarian at the time of his death. The Spurgeons appear to have been a long-lived race, and from this, and also from the fact that former pastors of the Tabernacle church had held their office till old age, it was inferred that C. H. Spurgeon's pastorate would also be a long one. Like Gill and Rippon successively, the young pastor of Waterbeach had been first asked to preach at the age of nineteen, and having commenced like the veterans of the past, it was fondly hoped that he would finish like them. "It is not decreed that we can know of certainty," we find it remarked, "but it seems both possible and probable."

---

* For some account of the work at Chelsea, to which Mr. Spurgeon's letter refers, see *The Baptist Messenger* for January, 1864, which also gives an account of Mr. Cubitt.

Some account of James Spurgeon, of Stambourne, has already been given; but it may be added here that his father, Clement Spurgeon, was a cane-reed maker of Halstead, who gave his sons the best education possible under the circumstances—James remaining at school until he was sixteen. At the date of his death in 1864, *The Wesleyan Times* gave some particulars which may be quoted, as showing the condition and surroundings of the Spurgeon family a century ago:—

"Some difficulty presented itself at that time as to the best way of disposing of the youth, his father not being anxious to put him out as an apprentice; but a friend of the family recommended him to a gentleman at Finchingfield to learn the combined business of grocer and linendraper. Here, as far as worldly circumstances went, he was favourably situated, meeting with great kindness and consideration from the family in which he was placed. But the young man was not happy, there existed within him a feeling of void, a consciousness of something wrong, which required prompt and decided attention. Religion had no place in their dwelling, and even the form of family worship was not observed. In a state of mind far from happy, he heard of the illness of his father, after he had been three years in the general store at Finchingfield; and in 1795 he left the place, glad that even so sad a dispensation as the failing health of his father had interposed to bring about the change he desired. He had given his heart to God in very early life whilst attending the ministry of the Rev. Mr. Ball at Halstead.

"Remaining at home till Christmas of the same year, he had anxiously prayed that whatever opening for him might next be made, he should be placed in a religious family; and his prayer was answered. Mr. Rudkin, of Coggeshall, Essex, engaged his services in his business, and there he found himself surrounded with all the blessings of a God-fearing family. These, however, were considerably restrained by the low religious condition of the Independent church which the family attended at Coggeshall. The old minister had run his course of useful labour, and young Spurgeon heard the old man on only one Sabbath, the pulpit being afterwards supplied with students from Hoxton. One of the students thus sent was Mr. Fielding, whose piety and amiability soon won over to him the affections of the young shopman, so that a very close acquaintance was formed between these young men. An invitation to the pastorate was given and accepted. His mind being already prepared by Divine grace for the sacred union, Mr. Spurgeon shortly afterwards joined the Church. So entire was the change which grace had wrought in his mind, he diligently set himself to do good to others; and one way in which he carried out his holy purposes was by establishing a prayer-meeting in the vestry of the chapel on Sabbath morning and evening, which was well attended; and in carrying it on the founder had the satisfaction of seeing much good done. At first he was content with reading the Scriptures and prayer; but after receiving encouragement from his minister, and prompted by the kindness of his employer, Mr. Rudkin, he advanced a step further, and occasionally gave a short address of encouragement or warning as an exhortation. For nearly eight years—namely, from Christmas, 1795, to the year 1803, Mr. Spurgeon continued to conduct this excellent and profitable means of grace; and he had the joy of seeing much good result from his labours.

"Prompted by his pastor, Mr. Fielding, and encouraged by his good friend, Mr. Rudkin, with whose family he resided, he consented to go to Hoxton College to prepare for the ministry; there he spent two years, having knowledge of several instances of conversion during his labours as a supply at various places near London. In 1805 he received a call

E E

to the pastorate over the Independent church at Clare, in Suffolk. There he commenced his stated ministry at Christmas, 1805, and was ordained on the 23rd of the September following; the ministers who took part in his ordination being Mr. Fielding, of Coggeshall; Mr. Ray, of Sudbury; Mr. Stevenson, of Castle Hedingham; Mr. Hickman, of Larringham; and Mr. Beddow, of Stambourne. The desire to be a minister of the Gospel entered his mind in very early life, and it was strengthened when his conversion took place. He had a very pious mother, who tried to instil into the minds of her children the fear of sin and a love of God, and her efforts were not in vain as far as her son James was concerned."

After serving during five years at Clare, James Spurgeon settled at Stambourne in 1810. He had many converts; and in his latter years, before the death of his wife, he spent about six weeks of every year in visiting friends who had been benefited by his ministry, although even then he found time to write letters of Christian counsel. It was his opinion that all ministers should have some knowledge of a secular business; for the attaining of such a knowledge was a profitable discipline, while it extended their knowledge of human nature. The multitude who gathered at the graveside on the occasion of the funeral sufficiently testified to the venerable pastor's popularity.

The large chapel in the Walworth Road, of which Mr. Howieson was pastor, and which is a near neighbour of the Metropolitan Tabernacle, was opened on April 20. Mr. Spurgeon attended the opening service and gave a vigorous speech, congratulating the pastor, and hoping that the chapel might become the scene of a genuine revival.

Spurgeon had now become such an attraction at any great gathering that his services were eagerly secured for any May meeting whenever he could be prevailed on to appear. On April 28, 1864, he attended at Exeter Hall to advocate the cause of the Baptist Missionary Society; and we find it remarked that he then spoke " with a warmth, a vigour, and an eloquence surpassing even himself." He was thus thought to be as capable on the platform as he was in the pulpit, and if the work of the platform had been too much eschewed, it seemed that the error might profitably be corrected.

At the great missionary meeting referred to, something happened which helped to enliven the scene, and so to add interest to the speeches. As Dr. Campbell tells us, Mr. Spurgeon " seemed to think

that one of his cherished notions touching church action and obligation was hinted at, and questioned, if not repudiated, by Dr. Angus,
and he broke out into an argumentative oration in favour of his
own principle, which carried the assembly with him as a whirlwind."

Mr. Spurgeon began by remarking that he harboured profoundest
respect for Liberal politicians who were for reform; and he had
also some respect for the Conservatives who sat under the nearly
rotten branches of their favourite shelter and sang, "O woodman,
spare that tree," etc. There was something so beautiful in all this
that he could not find it in his heart to speak against the old
Conservative tree. There was, however, something beautiful about
the youthful flash and fire, which, in order to put things right,
turned them upside down. A middle course was nevertheless to be
preferred, although true lovers of their country were probably to
be found in both extreme roads. The Missionary Society might
have friends among those who would have nothing altered; but
they were equally friends who would follow more closely what was
believed to be a more Scriptural method. There had been some
misapprehension, for one and all had prayed for a blessing on the
society. It was not a question as to whether there should be a
society or not, but rather whether the churches should not be more
fully recognised, and individual action be brought more fully into
play. "When the gage of battle is thrown down I am not the
man to refuse to take it up," said Mr. Spurgeon; and then after
this reference to Dr. Angus, and to the solemnity of the work in
progress, he added:—

"Did it not seem strange, according to human reason and the law of cause and effect—
did it not seem absurd and ridiculous that a few people in England should meet together
to talk about the conversion of India? I excuse Sydney Smith for his belief that it was
indeed the freak of a raving madman, though I cannot excuse the ribald language in which
he expressed the thought. But it does seem, on any principle but a supernatural one,
to have been the maddest enterprise in which men ever engaged. We must understand,
then, where we are. We take our stand on the supernatural. We are to depend for our
success on Him who has bidden us go and teach all nations, baptising them in the name of
the Father, and of the Son, and of the Holy Ghost. It becomes us, then, to be exceedingly
careful how we lose this principle or do anything whatever that might rob us of its
strength, for we must lean entirely on that arm. If neither committee, funds, nor subscribers
can do anything without Him, we must mind we do not grieve Him; but we must go

to work on such principles as may ensure us success, because He has promised it. We are willing, dear friends, to hear arguments on the other side at all times, provided they are not those equivocal arguments which say 'the thing is right in principle, but in practice it is right but not important.' To us to be right is to be important, and to be true is to be necessary. Let it only be shown that a thing is wrong and unscriptural, and in an assembly of Baptists we never ask the question whether we shall keep it any longer. If it be wrong, to the winds with it. When I joined this denomination I was enchanted with that which seemed to be written on the banner. We will have nothing but what we find in Scripture. We will not even have infant baptism, because we think it merely a tradition, and we will order our church government on Scriptural principles. It seems to us that to say a thing is right and Scriptural, but does not signify, would be to cut the rock from under our feet and stand upon the sands for ever; and to this, by the grace of God, we cannot possibly submit. Now, it has seemed to us that an association of good men working out God's purposes was a noble idea, but indeed the outgrowth of the idea of a Church, and we have therefore never said a word against it, but have, on the other hand, fondly cherished the hope that we might see such an association. We have not believed in an association composed of ten-and-sixpences; and we have always said piety is an essential, and the profession of that piety before men. We have always thought that any connection with the world, merely on account of ten-and-sixpences, or even thousands of pounds, was almost as great an evil as uniting the Church with the State, which contains so many worldly elements. And therefore we have not spoken about words and phraseologies, but about what is to us a very solemn principle. We are prepared, as Christian men, to maintain in its fullest strength this society, but we are not prepared to work with any society which either ignores the Churches or does not distinctly make itself a Christian society by having no members but those who profess to be Christians. We don't believe we could expect to have God's blessing unless we purge out the old leaven. We think that just as in the human body, if there is a piece of bone that is dead, there will be an ulcer and a swelling till the bone is cut out; so the admission, even in phraseology, of anything like a dead world, and the unrenewed nature of man, into the working society of Christ, would only be to breed an ulcer in it, which would mar the whole body in its beauty and strength."

Leaving that question, the pastor went on to say that he wished to see a more widely spread interest in the work of the Missionary Society, and dissatisfaction with what was then being done. He wanted the Churches to do more and to see more done in India to advance the kingdom of Christ. His heart rejoiced at what had been done; but when he thought of millions being still unconverted, the dread thought came that the world still lay in the power of the wicked one, and that the prince of darkness swayed his sceptre over mankind. If they desired greater things, however, greater things would come :—

"To a great extent our prayers and expectations are prophetic. They show what God is going to do, and if we are content with what we have—grateful I know we must be— if we do not pant after wider and larger things, we shall not have them. But when the groan has gone up, 'O God, we cannot endure this any longer; Lord, Thou who didst work so mighty a work at Pentecost, is Thine arm shortened that it cannot save; were not whole continents covered with the truth in a short space of time, and may we not expect the like wonders now?—then we may expect to see something more done by God for the salvation of men. Now, it struck some of us that to get the whole country into something like dissatisfaction with the results hitherto obtained would be one of the best ways towards making every man feel more than he does his own individual responsibility, and to make every church feel more than it does its own individual responsibility. If you could see my heart, you would see nothing in it but the purest love to this society, even when I say everything about its faults. It is because I love the society that I want to see a more thorough revival of the sense of individual responsibility. To whom did Christ give His commission? Not to a society, but to individuals. We gain immensely for God and His cause when we make every believer begin to cry over souls and to say, 'Lord, what wilt Thou have me do?' If our committee get on fire with enthusiasm, we will get water and pump on them, and do our share to save them from combustion, spontaneous or otherwise. Yea, if they should do anything absurd, and be arraigned for attempting impossibilities and getting into debt, some of us will come and plead guilty side by side with them, for we shall be too glad to find them offending—delighted to catch them falling into something like extravagance for God. Oh, for a circular all round to pray for a sevenfold blessing, setting forth the faith of the society in her God, and then for immediate action, depending upon God!"*

On Tuesday, May 3, an interesting visit was paid to Winslow in Buckinghamshire, where a Southwark predecessor, Benjamin Keach, laboured in the Puritan days. A large tent was erected, and in this Mr. Spurgeon preached in the morning from Rom. i. 16, and in the evening from St. Mark vii. 32. A cold collation was provided in the assembly room of the Bell Inn, after which the ceremony of laying the foundation-stone of a new chapel was gone through by Mr. Henry Kensall, of Rochdale. Mr. Spurgeon gave £20 to the building fund, and promised to contribute the last £20 required. There were 400 persons at the tea-meeting which followed, and the evening service, conducted by the popular London pastor, attracted an overflowing congregation. Another stone-laying ceremony, of great interest to those who took part in it, came off soon afterwards in connection with Mr. F. H. White's chapel at Chelsea.

On June 20 a visit was paid to Golden Lane, the occasion being the opening of the Evangelists' Tabernacle, which a City merchant had erected at his own expense. Mr. Spurgeon preached, and was evidently greatly interested in the surroundings. "The neighbourhood in which I am preaching was two hundred years ago inhabited by the fashionable and wealthy," he remarked, "but now they have migrated

* *The British Standard*, April 29, 1864.

to the West End of London, whilst poverty and crime crowd together in the adjacent courts and alleys, and souls are dying unnoticed and uncared-for by Christians who live in more respectable localities."

One of the preachers in this building was the present Mr. W. J. Orsman, L.C.C., who laboured perseveringly on until the headquarters of the costers became one of the most successful mission-stations in connection with the Metropolitan Tabernacle. As a youth, Mr. Orsman served in the Crimean commissariat department during the war, and on his return to England he accepted an appointment in the General Post Office. His philanthropic work was carried on after business hours, and Mr. Spurgeon always regarded him as one of the most valiant of his sons in the faith. As will be seen presently, Mr. Spurgeon more than once visited Mr. Orsman's head-quarters to preach to the costers and others who are chiefly benefited. Since the clearing away of the rookeries of Golden Lane, the work has been transferred to Costers' Hall, Hoxton, which was also visited by Mr. Spurgeon.

In 1864 the late Dr. Campbell entered upon his seventieth year, and Mr. Spurgeon subscribed £50 to the testimonial fund which was raised on behalf of the veteran journalist. No one realised more than the young pastor the sacrifices which his older friend had made. It was said that in Dr. Campbell "the Evangelical churches of all lands have an enlightened exponent and defender of Christian truth;" and he was regarded as an advocate for philanthropy, a helper of Sunday-school teachers, and a bold leader in the enterprise of ensuring a cheap Press for the people.

CHAPTER LII.

SPURGEON AND THE BIBLE SOCIETY.

The Strict Baptists—The Bible Society—Great Speech at Exeter Hall—The Calvin Tercentenary—
Estimates of the Reformer—Evangelical Alliance Soirée.

DURING this year (1864) the Strict Baptists still regarded Spurgeon as the hero of the Metropolitan Tabernacle, as well as a figure in the religious world of singular interest, although there does not appear to have been any controversy in regard to practice and doctrine. To them the popular preacher was, of course, much more than he could otherwise have been to persons who viewed him from the standpoint of the Surrey Tabernacle, because he came so near to their recognised standard, and yet not near enough to be altogether approved. Thus it happened in due course that the same people who maintained that "Fullerism" wanted the marrow of the Gospel, saw little or nothing more in Spurgeonism than the practical side of Christianity. At the same time, Spurgeon's old friend, Charles Waters Banks, as the chief literary veteran of the Strict Baptists, still continued to harbour sincere affection for one whom he had been among the first to welcome to London. In taking a retrospective and prospective view of things about this time, Mr. Banks wrote :—

"It is now eight or nine years since we bent our knees beside Mr. Spurgeon's little bed on a certain occasion when he was very ill; and in the arms of our faith, and in the simple affection we feel for all young men who are enlisted under the banner of Christ, we were helped to plead with the Lord for his speedy recovery. It was such a season of holy fellowship and of earnest wrestling with God as we have known but seldom during our five-and-thirty years' pilgrimage in the truth; and so fully did we receive that young brother into our heart, that neither his rapid rising, nor our circumstantial descending, has ever caused us to forget. He has gone up into the skies of popularity; we have gone down into the valley of adversity; he has stretched himself so extensively as to take in almost everybody; and *almost* everybody, in some shape or other, has taken him in : the circles of his ministry are so immense that you can never say of him he is the same yesterday, and to-day, and for ever. He travels round the whole of the evangelical globe, and touches, more or less, at every point; while we, having sunk almost into obscurity, can, perhaps, understand but little of what passes in these days for religion, for revivals, for conversions, and for Christian churches. . . . We have always believed him to be a tender-hearted child of God; and although he hurls dire contempt down upon us poor little Zionites, Zoarites, and Bethlemites, sometimes, still, having had some boys of our own, we know they will be naughty now and then; but love covers their folly and aims to correct their fault. Whatever C. H. Spurgeon may do, or not do, on this imperfect stage of time, we hope, through grace, to meet him in that kingdom where pleasure in perfection is, and all are like their Lord. We have thought—we hope it is not a wicked thought, but we have thought—what a changed scene it will be if, in that bright celestial world, on some future period, and sitting on one of the heavenly hills, we should happen to see a company of the Southwark divines, good old George Francis, in all the youth and beauty of a Saviour's healing life; 'dear Master Thomas Gunner,' with a heart as soft and a mind as refined as the loving John and the holy Jesus Himself; Hugh Allen, as tame as Noah's dove; James Wells, in the shining robes of his loving Master's righteousness; and Charles H. Spurgeon close beside John Foreman and J. A. Jones (for we believe the ancient Jireh patriarch will go home some day), and then and there, as our favourite poet says, we, yes, even we, hope to see—

> 'The glorious tenants of that place
> Stand bending round the throne.' " *

Apart from the fact that Mr. Spurgeon was the chief speaker the great meeting of the Bible Society at Exeter Hall this year would seem to have been of more than ordinary interest. The report of the year's work was encouraging, the income being larger than in any former year; ambassadors from Madagascar were upon the platform, and the speakers included Lord Shaftesbury, who was in the chair, the then aged Bishop of Winchester, Lord Charles Russell, William Arthur, and Dr. Edmond.

Mr. Spurgeon was no doubt at his best. He thought the history of Scripture was to be divided into certain epochs—the Reformation being the period when the Bible was liberated. With its feet, as it were, in the stocks, the Word had borne its testimony through the dark Middle Ages, "When suddenly there was a great earthquake, and the bonds of all thought, of all science, of all truth, were loosed, and then, like Paul and Silas, the Bible came forth to its glorious liberty." The period of bondage was over, and that of the multiplication of Scripture had come. When the Bible first came, it might, by reason of the fewness of its copies, be compared to the one glorious angel who heralded the advent of Christ; but in its multiplication it more resembled the host who sang "Glory to God in the highest." The multiplication needed to go on so long as mankind multiplied;

* *The Earthen Vessel*, xx. 108.

ERASMUS AND THE BIBLE.

but the Word needed to be brought home on a larger scale to the masses of the people. That was better than controverting objections, which did not appear to be the particular work required of Christians. Really to know what were the fruits of the Gospel, the Gospel needed to be applied. The speaker then proceeded :—

"There is a tale that when Scanderbeg's sword was hung against the wall, one who had heard of the trenchant deeds of valour done by the barbarous conqueror, said, as he looked on the sword, 'I can see nothing in it.' 'No,' said the man who showed it; 'but if you could have seen the sinews of the brawny arm that was wont to wield it, you would have admired the sword and the arm too.' Now, the Word of God is nothing but a dead letter till the Spirit of God, with omnipotent arm, grasps it, and then it cuts to the dividing asunder of soul and spirit, and is a discerner of the thoughts and intents of the heart. And we want to cry out to-day, 'Lord, if Thine adversaries doubt whether this be Thy sword, lay Thou hold upon its hilt, and cut them to their very quick, and make them know that there is a God in Israel still, and that there is still God's word.' Merely to circulate the Bible will not prove its virtues. There is no virtue in the Bible any more than there is harm in a three-volume novel, if I do not read the one or the other. If they lie there on the shelf unread, the one will do me no good and the other no harm. Erasmus laughs at the idea of the man who attaches a benefit to the mere possession of the Bible. He likens him to one whom he calls Cyclops, who wears in his belt on this side a goodly bottle of sack, and on the other side a richly ornamented copy of the Word of God, and says in his swaggering style, 'In truth I am as good a saint as any.' Erasmus tries to disprove this, in his witty way, and says, 'Prithee serve thy sack bottle as thy Bible. There are many virtues in that bottle of sack; it warms you when you are cold; it gets your valour up when you are half afraid. But do not take it; never take the cork out of it, and then see what its virtues are.' Of course our friend objects. He admires the bottle of sack, but he likes it better when the cork is out, and, most of all, when it is against his lips, and the stream is flowing merrily. 'Aye,' says Erasmus; 'but what do you say to this Book?' He says, 'It is tedious.' But begin to read and study it. 'Ah,' he replies, 'it is all dry matter that does not concern me.' 'Verily, then,' adds the other, 'I see thou art indeed a true disciple of the sack, but a false disciple of the Book.' There is much truth in that wit. If people carry their Bibles as Erasmus wished this man to carry his sack, they will get no good out of them. We may scatter Bibles by millions, and reduce the price to twopence or nothing, but we have done nothing but add to men's responsibility, unless we pray earnestly that God will lead men to study it, and by His Spirit bless it to their conversion, their edification, their sanctification in righteousness. I take it that while this is necessary to show the true quality of the Bible, it is also necessary to show the true answer to objectors."

The speaker went on to speak the true sentiments of his heart when he declared, in face of the cheering thousands in Exeter Hall, that he was of that kind of metal that he thanked God when the adversaries of truth were loudest in their objections; for he feared a sleeping devil more than a roaring one. "Let the devil roar; he shall but wake us up from our slumbers, and make us the more earnestly to contend for truth." How had it happened that in the generation before there had been no objections to Scripture from persons in high places? Because they were not necessary to Satan's ends? What was the Bible then to many of us who were slumbering and even sound asleep—what was it but a harp that was getting out of tune because it was not played, a sword that was growing rusty because it was not used? "And Satan said within himself, 'As long as they do not handle their edged tools I will not care to blunt them.' I am glad to think that the Church is being urged to activity, and I am reminded of the cynic who, sooner than be still, would roll his tub about. Sooner than the Church should be still, I would have her roll her articles and doctrines about. Keep the Church still, permit its voice not to be heard crying in the wilderness, 'Make straight the way of the Lord,' and you are hindering its course and depriving it of all power to bless the world." Hence the need of bringing home the Bible to the people, in order that they might be better acquainted with its doctrinal truths and historical narratives. When spoken to angrily by his envious brethren, David, by giving no answer, set the best example; and then he proceeded to kill the giant, which was a triumphant refutation of all cavils. The best answer to objections, therefore, was to verify the truth of the text, "The entrance of thy words giveth light." Let the Bible go forth into the courts and alleys of London, as well as into the dark places of the Pagan world. That was the best logic; and the Bible Society should promote Bible reading and Bible understanding as well as merely promoting the circulation. To show the importance of this, a contrast was drawn between the youth of Scotland and the young persons who came from other parts of the empire—the men from the North who entered the Pastors' College being, as a rule, much better acquainted with the Scriptures than Southerners. That was no doubt one of the good results of catechising. Mr. Spurgeon then entertained his audience with the story of the apple in the bottle:—

"One of my earliest difficulties was—not the source of the Nile, I had not got the length of that; but a certain matter which was far more wonderful. On a shelf in my grandfather's parlour was a little vial, containing an apple just the size of the largest part of the bottle. Now, I had no business to touch anything on the mantelshelf; that was forbidden. But whenever I could get alone, I took a chair and got the vial down, and tried to find out how the apple could possibly have got down that small neck. I thought the vial must have had a false bottom, and I really wonder how it was that in my various essays I did not, in my zeal and scientific diligence, manage to break the bottle, and so get a sound thrashing. But it happened, quite accidentally, that this great mystery of nature—one of the problems that I thought scarcely the wisest men of the East could solve—became unravelled. One day, as I walked in the garden, it came to me that my grandmother had put a little apple inside the bottle while it was growing, and that it grew there to its present size. And thus,

'Nature, well known, no prodigy remained.'

I could not but think of that while standing here. We cannot get men under Biblical influence very readily after they are grown up; but if we can put them inside the bottle when they are little ones I am sure we shall be following the analogy of nature. And we have quite a Scriptural precedent for it, for we find that Timothy knew the Scriptures from his youth up. I am afraid that some Sunday-school teaching is not what it should be with regard to distinct Bible teaching; and I should like all of us who have to teach others to look very much after this, labouring for the good of the young people. And then, again, I think that the exposition of Scripture should become more and more a distinct feature in our congregations. It may possibly be that, in some cases, the service will not allow a practice into which some of us have fallen, of always expounding the Lessons as we read them; but there might be extra services, of which that should be the main feature. There might be little Bible-reading parties, intended to break up difficult parts, and presided over by some brother who had the ability to study the chapter, and that would be exceedingly profitable. In Wycliff's days it was the classes that used to do so much good—classes that met and studied Scripture, and then dispersed, scattering abroad the knowledge they had gathered in that manner. It was these classes that brought on the Reformation; and I say it is thus that we must maintain the Reformation. We must get an intelligent knowledge of what God tells us in His Word, by studying therein, and then spreading abroad that same intelligent knowledge amongst others by expounding it."

A greater deference or respect for the Word was necessary; and texts which refused to open to them otherwise became plain to them in prayer. It was then forcibly shown that in Scripture alone would they ever find a basis of true Christian unity :—

"When we shall all become reverent subjects of God, and obedient to God's will, as we find it in Scripture, we shall all come close to one another. All attempts to create unity apart from truth must fall to the ground, and let them. Unity of action for God's glory we can have, even despite our minor differences, and I trust we ever shall have it; but to attempt to form a Church on any other basis than that of definite fixed principles, must be an attempt to build a house upon the sand, and it must come down. First purity, and then unity; first truth, and then oneness. I would not sell a principle of God's Word for all the brotherly love under heaven, because I hold that brotherly love which will not let me keep my conscience clear is not such brotherly love as Christ inculcated in the Holy Scriptures. Firmness to truth there must be—aye, and to every particle of it—to everything that you have received of the Lord. Let us seek no union by throwing aside those truths which God has clearly revealed to us. The Bible is to be the great pacificator of all sects—the great hammer of all schismatics. The Bible is to be the end of all disunion. The Bible, when we shall be brought to read it with reverent eye, and receive it with meek and humble heart, bringing us to itself, shall, in the Spirit of God, bring us to one another. I would rather have a little discussion now and then as to the principles which divide us, and then, if we have dissented on any point without due grounds, let our dissent be ended. Oh! if we could get the Bible spirit, and say, Whatever I do not find here I will throw overboard, we should have a blessed unity established. And it is because this unity is coming on that Satan is very wroth. We shall live, some of us, to see the day when we shall be distinguished the whole world over for our unity. I think I see looming in the future the rising of the sun that shall scatter all the mists of our bigotry. Some of us shall live to behold that happy day. Already this very meeting presents to us the blessed presage of it, but the consummation can never come except we hold the Bible, spread the Bible, and press the Bible home upon the heart and conscience of everyone with whom we meet. May I beg of you—most of whom I have never seen before—this very day to try and teach something scriptural to somebody. Every day a line, and then what a poem will your life's psalm be! Every day a soul, and, oh, what soul-winners you will be! Every day a seed, and then what a harvest shall you have! Every day a star, and then what a galaxy of glory shall glitter there! Every day a gem, and then what a crown of honour shall you have to put upon the head of your Christ! Every day a note, and then what a song shall that be which shall roll from you poor mortal, but God-inspired, God-helped men, up to the throne of the great One who sits above us all!" *

Mr. Spurgeon this year attended one other May meeting: he was one of the speakers at the early breakfast of the Young Men's Christian Association on the 6th of the month. The chair was occupied by Mr. Joseph Gurney Hoare, and the interest of the occasion drew together an overflowing congregation.

Mr. Spurgeon joined with great heartiness in celebrating the tercentenary of the death of John Calvin. The celebration itself took place on Friday, May 27, both at Geneva and in London; and the sermon at the Metropolitan Tabernacle on May 29 was in commemoration of the event. The discourse—"Laus Deo"—was pre-eminently one of praise to God, the text being Rom. xi. 36, "For of him, and to him, are all things: to whom be glory for ever. Amen." The distinguishing doctrines of the Reformation were well brought out; and the contrast between Luther and Calvin was that while one was the pioneer and iconoclast, clearing the way, or even knocking down what seemed to obstruct the progress of the Gospel, Calvin was the teacher, himself enlightened by the Spirit of God, who followed after. To such a preacher as the pastor of the Metropolitan Tabernacle, the Reformer of Geneva was second only to the apostle Paul himself as an interpreter of the oracles of God.

* *The Bible Society Reporter*, June, 1864.

Was Spurgeon's estimate of the Genevan Reformer's acquirements, genius, and devotion set too high? Some would have declared this to be the case; but it closely coincided with the estimate of other competent and conscientious judges. In the sixteenth century Knox wrote: "In my heart I could have wished—yea, and I cannot cease to wish—that it might please God to guide and conduct yourself to this place [Geneva], where I neither fear nor am ashamed to say it is the most perfect school of Christ that ever was in the earth since the days of the apostles. In other places I confess Christ to be truly preached; but manners and religion so sincerely reformed I have not yet seen in any other place besides." Then the historian d'Aubigné says: "After the mighty Luther, the bold Zwingli, the indefatigable Farel, such a man as the meditating Calvin was a necessity. The first three *fought*, the last *built up;* though at heart they all did both. Luther, Zwingli, and Farel held the sword; Calvin, humble and poor, yet held the sceptre. If the former were the generals of the Reformation, Calvin was its legislator and its king."

The pastors of Geneva desired to observe the tercentenary of the Reformer's death in a becoming manner; but many difficulties seemed to hinder their plans. It was proposed to erect a building to be called the Hall of the Reformation, and Dr. Barde, a pastor of the National Church, was deputed to visit this country and invite Christian people to co-operate. On Friday, May 27, that being the 300th anniversary of Calvin's death, the Evangelical Alliance had a soirée at Exeter Hall, attended by leading men of all denominations of the Church; and a meeting also took place at Edinburgh. At Geneva the interesting ceremony of dedicating the site for the memorial building came off, the scene being one of enthusiasm. "Here the members of all Churches will meet, with those who belong to no Church at all, and the net of the Gospel will be cast," said Pastor Demole. "That net, though it has often been exposed to the world's stormy waters, is unbroken still; it is powerful, and in it we shall gather those who will be brought to salvation. In doing this we shall lay a just claim to Calvin's inheritance."

The question might be asked, Why was Spurgeon, at the great Evangelical Alliance reunion at Exeter Hall, in honour of Calvin's memory, so conspicuous by his absence? No one present at the meeting could have replied to such a question; but to us, as we look back through the vista of nearly thirty years, the matter is plain enough. The great preacher was meditating on a subject which gave him some trouble; and when given to the world by the printing press, the sermon preached at the Metropolitan Tabernacle on Sunday, June 5, would create a sensation which was almost unparalleled. What this was will be seen in the next chapter.

Meanwhile, there appear to have been some honest souls in the world who thought that Spurgeon might have a counterpart, and some would, no doubt, have found pleasure in introducing such a rival of the popular preacher to the world. Of one who was expected to do great things we find it said in a newspaper leading article :—

"Our attention has been called to a young man from the country on a visit to town, who, if we do not much mistake, will yet be better known among us. We doubt not he is destined for distinguished usefulness in the vineyard of the Lord. He is richly endowed with every attribute required to great instrumental efficiency. The first condition of success to the popular preacher is voice; this constitutes a full third of his qualification, and in this respect the stranger we speak of has few, if any, superiors, either among Churchmen or Dissenters. So far as our experience has gone, it surpasses that of every speaker now in our midst, except Mr. Spurgeon's, and we incline to think that it will by-and-bye prove at least equal even to his. It is specifically a voice of the same class; so much so, that again and again, while there is not the slightest imitation, it suggested to us the magnificent accents and intonations and electric force of the great Metropolitan Tabernacle orator. It has, in a measure, all its excellencies, and defects there are none. There is the same clearness, fulness, energy, flexibility, and lashing power. The compass at times seems even somewhat greater; that is, it rises a note or two higher, adding to the sharpness and pungency of questions, and the scale of climaxes. It is also in a very high degree manageable, and hence, with Mr. Spurgeon's skill and experience, which years will impart, it will prove not less adapted to dialogue and bursts of the dramatic, a thing of wondrous potency, fraught with special pleasure in the ministrations of Mr. Spurgeon."

CHAPTER LIII.

SPURGEON AND THE CLERGY.

Baptismal Regeneration Controversy—Attack on the Evangelical Clergy—The Hon. Baptist Noel's Letter—Mr. Bardsley's Reply—The Gorham Case—Mozley's View—Dr. Campbell's View—Other Disputants.

WHAT is known as the Baptismal Regeneration Controversy belongs to the year 1864; and as that dispute occasioned the publication of a large number of pamphlets on both sides, this chapter may properly be devoted to it. The matter is even now not wholly forgotten; for Mr. Spurgeon's discourses on the subject have commanded an extensive sale, which has, in some measure, continued to the present day.

I have heard that the idea of exposing the unscripturalness of the doctrine of baptismal regeneration originated in Mr. Spurgeon's mind at Bury St. Edmunds, where he saw some things in a church which displeased him. Be that as it may, he resolved to preach on the subject, although at the time he seriously believed that the publication of such views would have a disastrous effect on the sale of the weekly sermon. When he had attacked slavery as "the sum of all villainies," the preacher had been burnt in effigy in the Southern States of the American Republic, and the fire had been stimulated with volumes of his sermons, which appear to have been withdrawn from circulation because no bookseller would have dared to sell them. It was thought that this experience, or something similar to it, was about to be repeated in England. Mr. Spurgeon told his publishers that he was about to ruin the weekly publication of the sermons; but he did not on that account flinch for a moment in carrying out his resolve of preaching the sermon on "Baptismal Regeneration," which he full well knew would be distasteful to a very large section of the Christian public.

This discourse was given at the Tabernacle on Sunday morning, June 5, the text being St. Mark xvi. 15–16, " Go ye into all the world," etc. The preacher felt that the burden of the Lord was upon him; and that although his opposition to what he believed to be serious error might result in the loss of friends and the stirring up of enemies, he was obliged to go forward. Belief in baptismal regeneration seemed to be spreading, so that there was need of an antidote. It was shown that baptism without faith could not save; and if the Church of England taught that it did, even the morality of evangelical teachers might be questioned, when they remained in such a communion for the sake of retaining their livings. Thus, as it was worked out, the sermon was virtually a formidable attack on the evangelical clergy for holding an invidious position. The High Church party, if they believed in baptismal regeneration, were of course held to be more consistent than the others, and were on that account to be commended. In speaking as he did, it will be noticed that the preacher boldly assumed that the Prayer Book really taught the doctrine he denounced; and if so, it naturally followed that men who taught one thing and subscribed to another occupied a position which was more than anomalous. Hence, the controversy was not one on the question as to whether baptismal regeneration in itself was right or wrong; the question was, Does the Prayer Book teach it as a Scriptural doctrine? If this could be proved to be the fact, Spurgeon was master of the field; but if, on the contrary, the Church of England favoured no such teaching, her evangelical pastors had been misrepresented and maligned in a way which they might well be excused for resenting with some warmth or even indignation. The manner in which such men regarded the determined onslaught which Spurgeon had made upon their honour was well shown by an article in *The Gospel Guide*, a weekly newspaper of that time :—

"A nice little country boy comes to London; he loves the Lord; he preaches (at least some of) His Gospel; his voice is of an amazing, yet well-balanced, power; his face, and all his features, are full of affection and zeal; he preaches, he prays, he weeps; he wrestles with God and with man, and prevails. Thousands flock to hear him; thousands profess to be converted by him; all the world is talking about him; he is the wonder of the age. No chapel, no church, no hall, no tabernacle, is large enough to hold the people who crowd to hear him; he resolves to erect a Metropolitan Tabernacle of his own. He outsteps David, for when David essayed to build a house for God, and Nathan encouraged him, and all the people were ready to help him, the Lord stepped in to stop him. It was not Heaven's will that David should build the temple, therefore he did not build it; but when C. H. Spurgeon said, 'I will build a tabernacle for God,' he did it. And clergymen and laymen—yea, men of all sorts and sizes, shapes and characters—stepped forward and poured their thousands into his lap. The Tabernacle was builded, and, as far as sight and sense was concerned, its opening was grand and significant. And from the day of its opening until now it is believed by many that the glory of the Lord has filled the house; and that the once little country lad is, in a few years, become the pastor of an immense people, the preacher to an overwhelming congregation. His College lads are building chapels in all directions, and Spurgeon's name and influence is immense, beyond all calculation.

"Is it any marvel that such a man should, at length, be found turning round upon the brethren with whom he has fraternised, laboured, and prayed; and in an unguarded moment publicly censuring, condemning, and almost anathematising them? Wonder or not, he has done it; and all the unthinking masses of the community applaud this grand onslaught made upon the clergy. The doctrine of baptismal regeneration is decidedly a Popish error; but the Church of England does not hold it, nor do her good ministers preach it; and this is proved by nearly all the published replies made to Mr. Spurgeon's sermon."

Undoubtedly one of the most effective of the replies to this famous sermon was "The Evangelical Clergy Defended," by the Hon. Baptist W. Noel, who had given up a distinguished position in the Established Church to take the more humble standing of a Baptist minister. Mr. Noel accused Spurgeon of violating the fourth of the General Resolutions of the Evangelical Alliance, of which he was then a member—the resolution in which everyone promised "to avoid all rash and groundless insinuations, personal imputations, or irritating allusions." Mr. Noel then addressed these words to his brother in the faith at the Metropolitan Tabernacle :—

"When you spoke of evangelical ministers of the Church of England as unworthy of the friendship of honest men, did you remember that your words were blasting, as far as they were received, the memory of some of the most excellent men who have ever lived? Thomas Scott was eminently honest, conscientious, devout, and useful; Henry Martin, with talents of the highest order, relinquished all the objects of ordinary ambition that he might preach Christ among the heathen; Charles Simeon bore bravely, for many years, the scorn of the ungodly at Cambridge; John Newton was full of love to God and man; few men have been so heavenly minded as Fletcher of Madeley; and John Venn, when dying, was so filled with joy at the thought of being speedily with Jesus, that for three days he could not die. All these, when on earth, belonged to that class which you denounce as unworthy of your friendship. Had you criticised the services, and said nothing of the men, you would have done more for the cause of truth. I shall not attempt to explain or to justify their views ; but I may mention one obvious fact. According to the Articles which contain the recognised doctrines of the Establishment, persons are justified by faith

F F

through the call of God; those who are thus justified by faith become the sons of God by adoption; and those who are adopted attain to everlasting felicity, so that it follows, according to their doctrine, that ungodly persons, who live and die in sin, never were adopted or regenerated. To these Articles the evangelical ministers in the Establishment adhere, endeavouring to explain the Liturgy in harmony with them; while their opponents, by teaching baptismal regeneration, contradict them. Let me ask, therefore, why you accuse of 'gross and pestilential immorality' those who maintain the Articles which they have subscribed, while you compliment the honesty of those who subscribe and contradict them? When, further, you charge those brethren with dishonesty, without hearing their defence, you violate your own rule; for in one page you say, 'I shall not judge the peculiar views of other men,' and in the next page you do judge them."

Those who are old enough to remember this dispute will not need to be told that the rebuke of a man like the pastor of John Street Chapel, Bedford Row, produced immense effect on the public mind. Mr. Noel was more than respected, he was regarded by Nonconformists pretty generally as a hero in their camp, who, as the scion of an honourable house, had made such great sacrifices for conscience sake that there could be no doubt about his earnestness and sincerity. By leaving the Established Church to join the Baptists he had to some extent sacrificed a social position of commanding influence, such as even a devoted Christian man might highly value. Indeed, we can hardly doubt that he also turned his back on a prospective bishopric; for when the Earl of Shaftesbury became Lord Palmerston's "bishop-maker," Baptist Noel would probably have advanced to the episcopal bench had he been eligible.

When, therefore, such a man spoke on this unhappy controversy between Spurgeon and the clergy, he stood forth as an ex-clergyman of the very class which was so bitterly assailed. At the same time, he spoke for himself as well as for others; and the calm Christian dignity of his letter added force to words which to large numbers were already irresistible as regarded their conclusive testimony.

Though equally respectable, Mr. Bardsley, the secretary of the London Diocesan Home Mission, was of another class; but he forcibly stated the case of himself and his brother clergymen in opposition to Mr. Spurgeon's representations:—

"I ask for the reader's attention to the reasons why he should not believe the fearful charges to be true which Mr. Spurgeon brings against a large body of the Church of England. He accuses them, as we have seen, not only of shuffling and equivocation, but of perjury and lying. He argues thus: The Church of England teaches baptismal regeneration, the evangelical clergy do not believe in this doctrine, and yet for the sake of keeping their livings they swear that they do believe it. I meet this statement with a simple denial: the evangelical clergy do not, in the sense described by Mr. Spurgeon, *believe that the Church of England teaches baptismal regeneration,* and therefore do 'not swear before God that they do when they do not;' and in this lies the whole fallacy of Mr. Spurgeon's statements. Is he ignorant of this fact, that the 'evangelical clergy' do *not believe* that the Church of England teaches the doctrine which, in the 'gentlest' manner, he describes as 'one of the most atrocious of all the lies which have dragged millions down to hell'? They do not believe that the Church teaches it, and this of itself disposes of the charge which he brings against them of being dishonest, by 'swearing before God that they do when they do not.' Mr. Spurgeon believes the Bible teaches that God has decreed from all eternity to save a definite number of Adam's posterity which can neither be increased nor diminished. The whole body of the Methodists, with but few exceptions, reject this doctrine; they not only do not believe it, but teach the very opposite; both accept the Bible as an infallible revelation from God, yet both would repel *with indignation the foul charge* that either party was guilty of perjury and dishonesty. The simple matter of fact is this. Mr. Spurgeon and those who hold his views on election believe that the Bible teaches that doctrine; the Methodists do not believe that the doctrine, as held by Mr. Spurgeon, has any place in the Bible. There are between thirty and forty bodies of Dissenters who accept the Bible as their rule of faith; on some question or other they all hold different opinions. Now, if *they* are allowed, without being charged with dishonesty, to differ as to the teaching of the Bible on these questions, why are *clergymen* to be branded with infamy because they differ among themselves as to the meaning of some portions of the Book of Common Prayer? People who live in glass houses should never throw stones." *

This is plain speaking from the standpoint of an uncompromising evangelical within the Episcopal pale. Of course, all the objectors were not of this class. Thus one incumbent, whose Arminianism must have closely resembled that of Laud himself, remarked in a letter to Mr. Spurgeon: "The fact is, infant baptism does not, and never can be made to, square with the sour doctrine of election which you are so strongly pledged to uphold." He then defends regeneration :—

"All that I can gather from your sermon is, that in your opinion regeneration means the *salvation of the soul.* I am bold to aver that from no part of our Service Book can you legitimately draw such a conclusion. True, the catechumen is taught to express his thankfulness to his Heavenly Father for having, through baptism, called him to '*a* state of salvation;' but, and in order to show that this is a distinct thing from salvation itself, he is immediately instructed to pray unto God to give him His grace, that he '*may* continue in the same all the days of his life.' It is a *state* or condition of salvation which can only lead to a successful issue by the use of the means of grace, and by the fulfilment of the obligations which the covenant, entered into at baptism, of necessity involves." †

* "What is it All About?" etc. By Joseph Bardsley, M.A. London: 1864. This tract was widely circulated.

† "A Letter to C. H. Spurgeon, touching Baptismal Regeneration." By J. C. Napleton, B.A.

Concerning this question, however, What does the Church of England really teach in regard to baptismal regeneration? the authorities have seemed to give forth contradictory statements. Of this the historical Gorham case was in itself a notable example. When Dr. Phillpotts, the High Church bishop of Exeter, refused to institute Mr. Gorham into the living of Brampford-Speke, because spiritual regeneration in baptism was rejected as being contrary to the teaching of the Church, the bishop maintained that he was upholding what the Church demanded should be taught as Christian doctrine. When the case was tried in the Court of Arches, Mr. Gorham lost his case ; but on the occasion of its being heard by the Judicial Committee of the Privy Council, the decision of the Court below was reversed, so that the appellant had to be allowed to take his living after all. The bishop instituted proceedings in three courts of law successively ; and, by losing the case in each instance, learned a lesson of a very wholesome kind. This shows in what sense Phillpotts himself understood the language of the Prayer Book. We find that when he preached, this was apparently a favourite theme ; and he would go to the Homilies and the Prayer Book for proofs to show that the Church taught the doctrine of spiritual regeneration in baptism. No wonder that the evangelical clergy were greatly chagrined when Mr. Spurgeon maintained that such teachers as this were alone consistent when they subscribed to all that was contained in the Prayer Book.

One of the most remarkable contributions to this controversy appeared in *The Record ;* and singularly enough, this was merely the reprint of an article which had appeared two years previously. In the course of a brief preface, the editor recommended the article —a critique upon Mozley's " Review of the Baptismal Controversy "— to the notice of Mr. Spurgeon himself, and offered this explanation :—

"Mr. Mozley is a well-known scholar of the Ultra-Church school. He was one of those who signed the protest against the Gorham judgment, and conscientiously believed that the literal interpretation of the baptismal service ought to exclude evangelicals from the Church ; but when he came to examine the subject calmly he saw reason to change his opinions, and, with a candour which entitles him to the highest respect, he has declared that he was mistaken, and that the words of the baptismal service were not intended to 'IMPOSE THE DOCTRINE THAT *all infants* ARE REGENERATED IN BAPTISM.'"

According to *The Record*, the great value of the Gorham judgment consisted in its defeating the attempt to put a Popish interpretation on the Protestant Formularies. "It was also important as silencing, by the interpretation of the highest judicial authority, the unworthy taunt of insincerity which has often been thrown upon evangelical clergymen, who receive the baptismal service and the catechism in the sense understood by the fathers of our Reformation; because those words may *appear* to assert something different." It cannot be denied that the words may have had a somewhat different meaning in other days, that being the case with many other old English words.

Thus, the offence which the evangelical clergy held Mr. Spurgeon to have committed was the acceptance of the words of the Prayer Book in their modern sense, when the testimony of history showed that such meaning was directly opposite to what the compilers intended. Mr. Mozley carefully examined the English baptismal service and the catechism, as well as the Articles, giving some attention to the methods of interpreting "the baptismal language both of Calvinism and Lutheranism," and then he said:—

"The statement, therefore, that the Calvinistic hypothesis is inconsistent with the language of the Prayer Book, is an ill-considered statement, reflecting only a rough, offhand impression, which proper reflection would correct. It has obtained currency because it has appealed to this offhand impression; but an act of thought at once reveals its groundlessness. . . . The Prayer Book was submitted to the criticism of Calvinists after it was compiled; it was afterwards protected by Calvinists when it was attacked; it has been used quite naturally by thousands of pious and devout Calvinists of every generation, from the Reformation to the present day. The great battle of the sixteenth century in defence of the Prayer Book was conducted by two Calvinists—for Whitgift was the author of the Lambeth articles, and Hooker held the doctrine of the 'indefectibility of grace.'

"We have, then, in the facts appealed to in this chapter, the comment of an actual course of things upon the statement in the baptismal service; the truth being that this statement was inserted in the Prayer Book by men in intimate relation with divines of the Calvinistic school who distinctly held that only the elect were regenerate; that it was acquiesced in by the most rigid Calvinists of that period without a word of complaint; that the hypothetical interpretation of this statement was the dominant interpretation for a century after the Reformation; that the Laudian school, in its full power and highest ascendency, never thought of interfering with it; and that, lastly, an interpretation which was thus coeval with the very service itself was never legally called in question till the other day.

"The whole evidence, viewed collectively, appears to me conclusive in favour of the judgment of the Court of Appeal—viz., that our formularies do not impose the doctrine that all infants are regenerate in baptism."*

When the controversy reached its height, and every day during the summer some fresh contribution seemed to appear, some surprise was felt because the preacher's veteran champion, Dr. Campbell, remained silent. For weeks or months his paper had little or nothing to say on the subject beyond a passing reference; and when at length, on September 2, he commenced a series of seventeen articles, which were afterwards reprinted in a volume, the doctor did not write as a mere apologist of Mr. Spurgeon, the controversy was entered into on an independent footing. Both Churchmen and Nonconformists now urged him to publish his views. In the preface to his volume, Dr. Campbell attempted to define his position as a friend of Mr. Spurgeon, being careful to show that their relation to each other was not quite what it had been some years before, when the young preacher's friends had been far less numerous than his enemies. Apart from that, Spurgeon was no longer a sapling who needed holding up, but an oak of the forest and more than a match for all who assailed him. Dr. Campbell had, moreover, already

* Quoted in *The Record* (August 31, 1864) from Mozley's "Review of the Baptismal Controversy." How different the conclusion was at which Dr. Campbell arrived will be seen in this extract from his article of December 30, 1864:—

"In connection with this great subject, it may be well, as lawyers say, to traverse the case, and to widen the area of inquiry. To obtain a satisfactory verdict, it is necessary to go beyond the Established Church. Let us, then, in fancy, appeal to the entire body of the Nonconformists of England, whether ultra or moderate, Independents, Baptists, Presbyterians, and Methodists of every class and species. Let the baptismal service be transcribed and sent to every man among them, and let each be requested, as in the presence of the searcher of hearts, to state his views of the true import of the service as it stands, without note or comment. What think you would be the result of such an appeal? My knowledge of these several bodies is large and intimate enough to enable me to answer the question. Had I ten thousand lives I would stake them all upon the issue. To a man, I affirm, they would explicitly and emphatically declare that the 'regeneration' of the baptismal service meant the salvation of the soul, as set forth in the Holy Scriptures—a new creation, a passing from death to life, neither less nor more, and maintain that every theory which excluded that was false. By them the various explanations which have been given by gentlemen of your body would, one and all, be viewed and treated as forced, as unnatural, as doing violence to truth, and outraging the common-sense of mankind."

written on the subject, and still professed to have much at heart
"the correction and purification of the Liturgy of the Established
Church." This led to his determination to go over the ground
again. As, however, the matter in dispute was not whether baptismal
regeneration was unscriptural—nearly all acknowledged that it was—
but whether the evangelical clergy accepted the doctrine in their subscription to the Prayer Book, Dr. Campbell did not undertake to
decide between the combatants. In the preface to the volume containing his articles, he thus referred to the controversy in general :—

"In my view, then, the statements of Mr. Spurgeon as to the general doctrine, in
point of accuracy, are unimpeachable; truth has obviously, from first to last, been the
sole object of his inquiry. His argument is, in my view, clear, cogent, and unanswerable.
His complaints and remonstrances are, I think, well founded, and such as deserve the
candid and serious consideration of those to whom they are addressed. His appeals and
protests are, nevertheless, occasionally marked by an acritude of spirit, fitted to startle,
scandalise, and exasperate.

"His style, too, more especially in the first discourse, is vehement and trenchant in a
manner which has rarely been exceeded. His conceptions on the enormity of the evil
in question are most vivid, and his convictions are in consequence exceedingly strong.
The power of the discourse, however, arises less from its logical than from its rhetorical
qualities. The error has been exposed and exploded in a manner the most convincing a
thousand times; but never, I believe, was it exhibited to the public eye with colouring so
vivid, and never was it pressed home on the clerical conscience with a force so thrilling,
resistless, and terrible! But even Mr. Spurgeon's clinching logic, apart from his devastating eloquence, would have left things very much as it found them. In that case, Messrs.
Passmore and Alabaster, the publishers, would not have had to report the unparalleled
issue of 350,000 copies of these discourses. Mr. Spurgeon's opponents have been so
dazzled, I might almost say, concerning some of them, so infuriated by the daring drapery,
as to lose sight of the subject-matter. They have merged the essentials in the circum-
stantials. There has, I think, been a mutual oversight. Neither party has duly estimated
the position of the other. Mr. Spurgeon, in my view, has not made the allowance which
equity and charity required, and which is made in the following articles, for the clergy ;
and the clergy have not made the allowance, the large allowance, for which we equally
contend, on behalf of Mr. Spurgeon, whose training has been thoroughly scriptural, and
in all points anti-Romanist. They have not, moreover, duly estimated the condition of
a gentleman still far short of manhood's prime—a gentleman endowed with great powers
and strong passions—holding forth in the midst of five thousand hearts beating in unison
with his own, and with ten thousand admiring eyes converged on him. The case of such
a man is extraordinary, unparalleled, and when placed in the balances of critical judgment
and severe propriety, charity apart, it is, I contend, but just and fair to make a very
large allowance for strong language—language stronger than I could have used; but, with
his talents, temperament, views, and convictions, and placed in his circumstances, I might
have spoken as he spake, without at all feeling that I had violated the strict rules of
verity, justice, and Christian propriety."

Dr. Campbell had spoken at last; and although his views of
the matter as a whole may not quite have satisfied his younger and

more vehement friend, it is hard to see how the veteran journalist
could have said more or less than he did in relation to both sides.
He looked at the question in a calm judicial spirit; and while
strongly condemning the doctrine itself, he did not see any reason
for breaking off his friendship with evangelical friends in the Church
of England. On account of the extreme bitterness which it stirred
up, the dispute was to be regretted; some thought Spurgeon
might have exposed the unscripturalness of a Romish figment
without alienating friends in the Establishment who did not believe
in it any more than he did himself. Some of those friends
reminded Mr. Spurgeon that they had helped him to rear the
Tabernacle; and they thought that he had broken faith with them,
or, at least, that continued friendship was rendered impossible. In
the end, however, old friendships seem to have been renewed, and
to have remained strong until death. On the other hand, there were
evangelicals whose harsh language far surpassed anything Spurgeon
himself had said, and, as was pointed out, violated the rules of the
Evangelical Alliance. Take this example by Dr. Goode, Dean of
Ripon, a voluminous writer on the subject in hand:—

"As to that young minister who is now raving against the evangelical clergy on this
point, it is to be regretted that so much notice has been taken of his railings. He is to
be pitied, because his entire want of acquaintance with theological literature leaves him
utterly unfit for the determination of such a question, which is a question, not of mere
doctrine, but of what may be called historical theology; and his charges are just a parallel
to those which the Romanists would bring against himself as well as others for the
interpretation of the words, 'This is My body.' But were he a wiser man than he is, he
would know better what his qualifications are for passing judgment on such a point, and
be willing to learn from such facts, among others, as the Gorham judgment and the
cases of Mr. Maskell and Mr. Mozley, what ground there is for his charges against the
evangelical clergy. Let him hold and enforce his own view of doctrine as he pleases;
but when he undertakes to determine what is the exclusive meaning of the Book of
Common Prayer, and brings a charge of dishonesty against those who take a different view
of that meaning from what he does, he only shows the presumptuous self-confidence with
which he is prepared to pronounce judgment upon matters of which he is profoundly
ignorant. To hold a controversy with him upon the subject would be to as little purpose
as to attempt to hold a logically constructed argument with a child unacquainted with
logical terms." *

At the best, Dr. Campbell did not find this controversy to be
congenial to his taste; but though he did not acquit Mr. Spurgeon

* Quoted in Dr. Campbell's Preface.

of using heated language, he vigorously properly resented such utterances as this of Dr. Goode.

Several deliverances on this dispute appeared in *The Freeman*, and among the letters were two by "A London Curate," which were written with some force. In the following passage the position of the evangelical clergy as they understood the matter themselves is very succinctly stated :—

"The real drift of Mr. Spurgeon's charge seems to me to be this, in rather quieter language—that the Church of England, by her doctrine of baptismal regeneration, teaches men to undervalue the necessity of a renewed and converted heart—the vital importance, that is, of spiritual life. This he might argue, giving even their real meaning to the phrases which I have quoted before. I shall at once endeavour to meet him by the example of the spiritual lives of the best Churchmen, by a claim for as much spiritual life amongst our 20,000 clergymen as there is amongst 20,000 ministers of any other form of religion, by an assertion that amongst the godly Church of England poor there is as much spiritual humility, as little confidence in mere privileges, as little trust in the flesh as will be found amongst any other godly men. I know that this would be only assertion, but Mr. Spurgeon's statements on these points are only assertions. If our mutual assertions are said to prove nothing, we must go back to the discussion of the standards of Church of England teaching —viz., her Liturgy and Articles ; and there I am firmly convinced, as I have said before, that giving the Prayer Book that which cannot in justice be denied it—viz., the benefit of interpretation in the sense in which it was written, and not forcing upon it a sense invented after it was written—we shall find nothing about baptism saving the soul without spiritual life, any more than we shall find literally stated the benefit of 'the praying windmills of Thibet,' to which Mr. Spurgeon alludes." *

As an authority of that day remarked, Mr. Spurgeon's censors or critics were indeed legion. Clergymen of the Establishment of various grades, as well as Baptist ministers, and even City missionaries, assailed the preacher as one who was speaking beside the mark, or who did not very clearly understand the matter in hand. Occasionally even members of the Evangelical Alliance appeared to add to the confusion by publishing what were supposed to be their utterances in the interests of charity. While a large proportion of the combatants were opposed to Spurgeon, there was not a little disagreement among themselves. One who stood before the world as a clergyman of the Establishment sent forth· "The Spurgeon Antidote." Another showed to his own satisfaction, if not to that of his readers, that what he called "the Popish error of baptismal regeneration" was not a doctrine of the Church of England. In opposition to this, another

* "A London Curate," in *The Freeman*, July 13, 1864.

clergyman showed to a demonstration that it was in reality the teaching of the Church. One curate thought he was able to prove that Spurgeon himself taught such a doctrine; while another curate attempted in his way to impose the closure on the controversy by his *brochure*, "The Rev. C. H. Spurgeon Settled." There was much besides, hard hitting by angry opponents being diversified by unexpected rebukes from friends. If any industrious reader should succeed in wading through a complete set of the publications of this controversy, he will never be tempted to repeat the experiment should he survive the first entertainment. "Seriously, one is quite bewildered," remarked one editor, as he surveyed his table, amply furnished as it was. "To read with patient attention so much crude theology is really beyond our power." The majority of the pieces printed were not by any means contributions to our standard literature. "We have looked through each pamphlet or tract sent to us with the honest desire to find something worth noticing," said *The Freeman;* but in the main there was little or nothing of interest. What really appeared was that recognised Churchmen were "chiefly angry with the matter of the attack," while others objected to the manner. *The Freeman* agreed with Mr. Spurgeon without so many qualifications as some others, such as Dr. Campbell, for example; but this, of course, arose from the subject being viewed from a Baptist standpoint.

Here we may take leave of a controversy which stirred up much angry feeling on both sides, and which probably did not do so much for the furtherance of truth as the combatants hoped. But even those who regarded the evangelical clergy with most affection felt that the revision of the Prayer Book was more than ever necessary. Hence, Spurgeon did not speak in vain.

CHAPTER LIV.

WORK AND PROGRESS IN 1864.

Temperance — Helensburgh — Work at the Tabernacle — A Remarkable Service — *The Christian World* and its Editor—The Divine Decrees—Glasgow.

FOR years after his coming to London Mr. Spurgeon was so little of a teetotal advocate in the conventional sense that, as has been already shown, he said something which J. B. Gough resented in language too warm to be pleasant. There seems to have been a tendency towards total abstinence in the College, however, which the President had no desire to check; and in the summer of 1864 a temperance society in connection with that institution was formed. The late Dr. Hannay attended as a deputation from the National Temperance League; and the chair was occupied by Mr. J. R. Selway, who was then scientific lecturer in the College, and who accepted the post of president of the society. To-day a large proportion of the pastors educated in the College are ardent teetotallers.

During the days now under review, many friendly messages passed between Clapham and Helensburgh, where John Anderson, the Free Church pastor, still preached, in a sense, after the manner of Baxter—"As a dying man to dying men." In the early summer Mr. Anderson made one of his flying visits to London; and having hastened back to Scotland without calling at Nightingale Lane, the following letter was sent to him on Midsummer Day:—

"Helensburgh House,

"My Dear Mr. Anderson,   "June 24, 1864.

"You deprived us of a great pleasure by flying home without alighting at our nest; but we felt very much comfort in the thought that your wings had grown strong, and that you were hoping to sing the old sweet song. I am very much your debtor for the kind token of remembrance you have sent me; I shall read it with great pleasure.

"The good work grows in my hands; the battle thickens; the victory is all the nearer. My sermon on baptismal regeneration has stirred up the rattlesnakes' den; but as their venomous fangs cannot reach me they may rattle as long as they please. Of course, I lose the friendship of the evangelicals; but I can bear that sooner than an ill conscience.

"The College prospers abundantly. The men are much in request, and usually succeed in the highest degree—especially in soul-winning. Passmore is out sniffing the salt sea, and we are beginning to look, like Elijah's servant, in the same direction. We cannot, however, venture into the 'land o' cakes,' for an habitation is already secured in the little village of Walton-on-the-Naze. My kindest regards I hereby present you; praying that your health may be confirmed, your ministry blest, and your heart encouraged. Mrs. Spurgeon and the boys send also their love.—Yours ever truly,

"C. H. SPURGEON." *

Although he made no pretensions to being a teetotaller, we find Mr. Spurgeon about this time giving a lecture on Poland on behalf of the funds of the Band of Hope Union. The pastor's deliverance on the subject of the oppressed Poles so delighted Dr. Campbell that he called the lecturer "that mighty man-of-all-work." What had been spoken in the British Senate on this subject was declared to be "but fribble and babble" in comparison. The young patriot's old friend added: "We wish Mr. Spurgeon could have found his way into the House of Commons for the occasion, and have poured himself out in the hearing of the gallery, that his grand, glorious, and philanthropic aspirations might have gone forth to the ends of the world on the wings of the British Press." This may be grandiloquent, but it is characteristic.

Dr. Marsh, for whom Mr. Spurgeon harboured a high opinion, died in August at the age of ninety years. The doctor may be

* Communicated by Miss Stewart, Sea-Bank House, Helensburgh.

regarded as the last member of the original Clapham Set; for he had been associated with Simeon of Cambridge, Henry Thornton, and William Wilberforce.

The progress of the work at the Metropolitan Tabernacle during the year 1864 was in all respects encouraging and satisfactory. Mr. Spurgeon had now been ten years in London; and the way in which the small and scattered congregation at New Park Street had been revived was generally regarded as the most striking thing which had ever occurred in the annals of Nonconformity. The old chapel, capable of seating 1,200 persons, had been crowded from the outset of the pastor's career; and the great Tabernacle, into which 7,000 could be packed, had been filled on Sundays from the day of its opening. The church which removed from New Park Street in March, 1861, numbered nearly 1,200 members. At the close of 1864 this total had increased to nearly 2,900. Altogether, Mr. Spurgeon had received close upon 3,600 into membership; and out of this number 47 had become ministers of the Gospel, 7 were working as City missionaries, while 3 were Biblewomen. The aim was to make this great organisation a good example of a working church. In the general oversight of his large flock, the pastor was assisted by ten deacons and over twenty elders. The deacons, who were elected for life, had to "serve tables," or look after the temporal affairs of the church; the elders were chosen annually, and it was their business to see candidates for membership, etc. It was necessary thus early, also, to have an assistant in the pastorate, whose duty it was to attend to cases of discipline and to visit the people in their own homes. Mr. J. T. Dunn succeeded Mr. Ness in this office. Great care was taken in the matter of selecting candidates, or the roll of membership would have been a much greater one. No candidates save those who had made a favourable impression on one of the elders were seen by the pastor, and he was thus saved from work which others were as capable of doing as himself.

In the course of his duties in connection with the Church and the College, the pastor came in contact with many remarkable characters. One good man, who is said to be still living, was a convert before he was even able to read. His wife was accustomed to read the Scriptures to him; and with the texts in his memory he would go out into back streets, or wherever he could draw together a congregation, and then proclaim the Gospel with a power which was altogether singular under the circumstances. In due course others were themselves converted; but there were persons who did not quite approve of a man undertaking to preach who was so illiterate. Complaints of the assumed irregularity were even made to Mr. Spurgeon, and it seemed necessary that the pastor should see the offender. " Well, brother, so you are out preaching," said Mr. Spurgeon. "I do not know much about preaching, sir," replied the other; " but bless the Lord, I must tell of His love to me, and try to bring others to love Him." " But I am told that you do not know grammar." " Grammar! What's that, sir?" asked the young Christian, with an expression of perplexity on his features which at least showed his honesty. The conversation went on a little longer, and after further explanations had been given, Mr. Spurgeon turned to his deacons and said: " This good brother means to preach, and there is only one way to stop him that I know of, and that is to take his head off." My informant remarks that no deacon, " not even in those days," was equal to such an undertaking as that; and, being in full sympathy with them, the pastor added, " If you do not feel disposed to take his head off, the next best thing will be to put something in it." The result of the interview was that the illiterate evangelist was taken in hand; he was first of all sent to a night-school, and afterwards he was received into the College. He has now been preaching, with good results, for over thirty years.

About the same time that this happened, Mr. Spurgeon was continually meeting with adventures in the provinces, of which it is to be regretted that a more particular account was not preserved by those who accompanied him. Thus, when a visit was paid to Ogbourne St. George, near Marlborough, the service would have been held in the open air; but wintry weather came on, and other arrangements had to be made. There was a wealthy farmer in the place who had a tent erected to accommodate a thousand people, and to provide seats for them he ordered a stack of prime meadow hay to be cut into trusses as level as forms, and the perfume of which filled the tent. When this was done a heavy fall of snow came on, which covered the ground for over fourteen inches. The distance from the village to the tent was a quarter of a mile; and in order to give the people a dry path, the farmer who had put up the tent had a rick of straw cut up, and with this the road was plentifully covered, so that no one had to complain of damp. "I know I have many Primitive Methodists here," said Mr. Spurgeon; who then added, "I was converted in a Primitive Methodist chapel; but I soon got over to the other side of the hedge." It was a memorable occasion; and one who heard Mr. Spurgeon many times afterwards says that he never heard the great preacher with more pleasure or profit than when the sermon was given in that village tent at Ogbourne St. George.

Among the friends who stood by Mr. Spurgeon and advocated his cause in the days now under review, must be reckoned the late Mr. James Clarke, editor and proprietor of *The Christian World*. For some years the pastor of the Metropolitan Tabernacle strongly recommended Mr. Clarke's paper; and when he felt that he could no longer give such a recommendation on account of its broad theological tendencies, Mr. Spurgeon still received his old friend's annual contribution to the College funds.

Like Mr. Spurgeon, James Clarke was an Essex man, though his early days were spent at Ipswich. When he came to London as a young man to make his way, he for a time acted as shorthand amanuensis to Dr. Campbell. The young man, who had been reared in an evangelical school as strict as that in which Mr. Spurgeon himself had been brought up, was not only in hearty sympathy with all Christian work, he was himself an active worker, who would preach, as opportunity offered, in lodging-house kitchens or in the open air. At that time Spurgeon was no doubt regarded by the young journalist as one of the best models of a Christian worker the times had produced ; but while the pastor still adhered to his grandfather's teaching, Mr. Clarke embraced broader, and what he regarded as more liberal, views. At the same time, the busy journalist looked on the varied work in progress with a friendly eye ; and not only gave money to it, but in his paper, in a way, advocated Spurgeon's cause. In addition to accounts from time to time of meetings and of work, helpful notices of Mr. Spurgeon's works also appeared in *The Christian World*. The attitude of each toward the other was that of a man who agreed to differ with his fellow and to remain friendly. Without any compromise of principle on either side, I wrote for Mr. Clarke's paper at the time I was serving Mr. Spurgeon on *The Sword and the Trowel*. Each was well aware that I served the other, and I was handsomely treated by both.

A man who preached a sermon every week could not expect never to utter a sentiment from which none even of his best friends dissented. On May 8 a sermon was preached at the Tabernacle on "Divine Decrees ; " and one passage, which seemed to declare that every act and thought of man was pre-ordained by the Creator, was taken exception to as savouring of fatalism. One writer, who called attention to this discourse, says its doctrine was pointed out to him by a friend. "It had filled him with consternation, and he was carrying the sermon about in his pocket in order to keep it from falling into the hands of his young people." The writer proceeds :—

"Now, the first thing that occurs to one to ask on reading such a passage is, How does Mr. Spurgeon *know* this ? Has he access to some source of information not open to other intelligent men ? He cannot find it, nor anything like it, in the Bible. If he can, he can tell us where, and so place the matter beyond dispute. The truth is, the Bible is very reticent on this subject of the Divine decrees ; while I believe there is not one of its writers who would not have shrunk with horror from identifying the contents of that 'hidden roll' with the black and troubled history of this bad and miserable world. But has Mr. Spurgeon seen the 'roll' himself ? Or has someone else seen it and told him all that it contains ? In either case it is no longer a 'hidden roll,' and it must be competent to Mr. Spurgeon, if he chooses to use the power he has acquired, to make the whole world acquainted with its contents. That would, indeed, be a new revelation, and such as would throw utterly into the shade the Book which God has given us to be our guide.

"But if Mr. Spurgeon does *not know* this, his assertion is very bold, and I, for one, think it is a very daring one. If 'God had written down with His wise finger every thought which man should think, every word which he should utter, and every deed which he should do,' then He had so written down all that Mr. Spurgeon was thinking, saying, and doing at that moment. Mr. Spurgeon's sermon, therefore, is nothing more than a copy taken from that 'hidden roll' and first preached to his people, and then handed to Messrs. Passmore and Alabaster for the purpose of a wider circulation. And not only so, but all the worst thoughts which men have indulged, all the vilest words they have uttered, and all the wickedest acts they have performed, are traceable to the same paternity. Let the world once come to believe that, and there is an end of conscience and duty together." *

In such a case as this, the preacher probably did not intend to teach all that "Delta" inferred, and it was a case in which a public man might well have offered some further explanation. In itself, as quoted, the passage looks very much like what a fatalist might have said; but Mr. Spurgeon was no fatalist, and the discourse must be read as a whole before any fair judgment can be given.

While the year 1864 was drawing to a close, all the works carried on at the Metropolitan Tabernacle showed no signs of flagging. Some thought that increased energy was apparent. The preacher had no doubt alienated a certain number of friends by the action he had taken in regard to the question of baptismal regeneration, but his popularity was not in any way diminished. The question which had been asked before again arose—Would Spurgeon found a sect after the manner of Wesley or the Countess of Huntingdon? Some supposed that this would be the natural development of his system. As one said, "He is being rapidly surrounded by a system which will probably go on to develop itself till nothing further remains to effect this end. He is less of an Independent, be it known, than of a Presbyterian; and the probabilities are that his community will be worked up into a close, compact structure, which will render a hundred churches more efficient for good than several hundreds united by no tie." This is no doubt a correct representation of the case. If Mr. Spurgeon

* "Delta," in *The Freeman*, June 1, 1864.

G G

had not been a Baptist, he would probably have joined one of the Presbyterian communions.

One of the stations which had been among the first to be visited by Spurgeon when he was the boy-preacher of the Fens, had been Milton, in Cambridgeshire; and on the 9th of November, 1864, the memorial-stone of a new chapel was laid. For half a century the place had been visited by the Baptist local preachers, the services being carried on in an ancient barn fitted up as a chapel. At length a friend presented a site for a new sanctuary, and the stone-laying festival was a high day at Milton. New Testaments were given to all young persons who chose to apply for them; a tea-meeting was held at the White Horse Inn, and the stimulating addresses were followed by a good collection.

On November 14 Mr. Spurgeon preached in a chapel situated close to Vauxhall Gardens, Mr. Hearson, one of the College students, having done some good aggressive Christian work in that district. The building was not a new one; it had been erected some years before by the Independents, and after being vacated by them it was used as an Episcopal chapel. Mr. Hearson had already collected a congregation, and the chapel being available, he and his people removed into it.

On November 25 another visit was paid to Glasgow, when Mr. Spurgeon preached at Elgin Place Chapel and also at the City Hall, on account of the somewhat heavy debt on North Frederick Street Chapel, where Mr. T. W. Medhurst, the first student, was stationed. Great congregations were attracted, and a sum of £100 was collected.

On December 15 the autumn session of the Pastors' College was brought to a close, and on Friday, the 16th, there was a tea for friends, after which a meeting took place in the Tabernacle. The popularity of the work at this date may be inferred from the fact that close upon two thousand persons came to tea, and about double that number attended the after-meeting.

CHAPTER LV.

"THE SWORD AND THE TROWEL.."

AT this time Dr. Cumming ranked as "*The Times* Bee-Master;" and in a work on bee-keeping he made some remarks on Spurgeon and the baptismal controversy which were not at all approved at the Metropolitan Tabernacle. "I wish that somebody would send Mr. Spurgeon a super of good honey. Three months' diet on this celestial food would induce him to give up those shockingly bitter and unchristian tirades he has been lately making against the clergy of the Church of England." In answer to this prescription issued for his benefit, Mr. Spurgeon recommended that his brother of Crown Court should give less honey and more salt in his public ministrations. If he saw the reasonableness of this, and liked to follow the advice, Dr. Cumming was promised that a brick of the best salt should be sent to him carriage paid.

The first wedding that took place in the new Tabernacle was solemnised at the opening of 1865, Mr. G. D. Evans, who had been educated in the College, being married to Miss Sarah Hockett. Some two or three thousand persons assembled to witness the ceremony, and in the name of the Church the pastor presented the happy pair with a family Bible. It is to be regretted that Mr. Spurgeon's wedding addresses and prayers were not all taken down.

For several years it was Spurgeon's custom to preach on the first Sabbath morning of each year from a text of Scripture selected by "an esteemed brother," who was a clergyman of the Established Church. On New Year's morning, 1865, the subject was "True

Unity Promoted," the text being Ephesians iv. 3, " Endeavouring
to keep the unity of the Spirit in the bond of peace."

The annual week of prayer, at the beginning of the year, was
also observed as usual, the weekly prayer-meeting at the Metropolitan Tabernacle being crowded and pervaded by much fervour.
This gathering was, according to arrangement, the central one for
London, and really commenced at three o'clock in the afternoon.
On successive evenings similar meetings were held in other chapels
in various parts of London, these being visited by Mr. Spurgeon,
who appears to have given an address at each place.   Edward
Leach, Mr. Spurgeon's literary assistant, thus referred to these
gatherings, which appear to have been remarkable for their fervour :—

"'A little cloud . . . like a man's hand.' A few ministers who had set their congregations the bad example of not knowing much of one another, formed themselves into
a little society.   Once a month they met for conference and prayer at the Metropolitan
Tabernacle, under the presidentship of C. H. Spurgeon.   Expectancy should always follow
prayer. A blessing was expected. First it came as a little cloud.   An earnest spirit
of revival then manifested itself in the central church. The flame spread. The new
year approached. It was decided to open it with a special week of prayer. The first
day 6,000 souls filled the Tabernacle, earnest addresses were delivered, sobbed-out petitions
presented to the Throne of Grace, and the Holy Ghost descended, making saints feel
intensely their miserable insignificance, and sinners their wretched condition, as unsaved
and undone. . . . On the Tuesday following the second great meeting, Sabbath-school
teachers met at Upton Chapel, where the Rev. G. D. Evans labours so acceptably, and
invoked the Divine blessing on this means of extending the Saviour's kingdom.   On
Wednesday evening meetings were held simultaneously at the houses of at least fifty-
five members of the Tabernacle church, where earnest souls sought unitedly for the blessing
of revival upon the Christian churches. . . . The Baptist denomination, unfortunately,
has much to answer for. Its lukewarmness for years past is most incredible. Its slothful-
ness, its lack of care for sinners on the one hand, and its wilful perversion of doctrine and
blindness in preaching free-grace invitations on the other, have, we fear, caused it to be
a byword in the land. And yet out of these dry bones God is creating, and will more
abundantly create, new, young, and invigorated life. The Baptist churches of England
will soon have to bear a mighty witness for God. Some of them, headed by Mr. Spurgeon,
have made a valiant stand for truth against the Popish dogmas of baptismal regeneration
and priestly absolution. Other antichrists have to be dethroned, and these most of all,
for though they have had a severe bruising, the mortal stab has yet to be given." *

At the beginning of this year, a testimonial, amounting to £3,000,
and supplementary to a donation of £500 previously subscribed, was
presented to Dr. Campbell.   As already intimated, Mr. Spurgeon
subscribed liberally to this fund ; and we find that he referred to
the veteran journalist and his friends in genial terms.

* *The Baptist Messenger,* 1865, pp. 67–68.

One of the chief things to be noted in connection with the year 1865 is the issue of Mr. Spurgeon's magazine, *The Sword and the Trowel*, which commenced in January, and has been continued until the present time. It would appear that during some years previously there was an inclination to found such a monthly periodical; but one objection was, that it would have a tendency to injure the sale of *The Baptist Magazine*, the recognised monthly organ of the denomination, which had already been in existence for over half a century. When he became joint-editor of that venerable publication, Mr. Spurgeon's attention was diverted from the enterprise which had suggested itself to his mind; but now that an experiment, which had ended in failure, had been made, he was more at liberty to follow his own inclination. The constituency at the Metropolitan Tabernacle was at that time almost large enough in itself to be represented by an organ of its own; but when to this was added the large number of friends throughout the country who ranked as friends of Mr. Spurgeon, the prospect of success was encouraging. The circulation attained ranged from ten to fifteen thousand, and till the editor's death this was well maintained.

Of course, the success of such a venture could have been more striking had " success," as conventionally understood, been the one aim of the projector. Mr. Spurgeon had his own notions, however, concerning what such a magazine should be, and the path marked out would not be departed from for the sake of any temporary advantage. The magazine would not be undenominational, for example, and that alone would be likely to bar its progress in many quarters. As regarded the staff, the editor depended mainly upon himself, well knowing that his own name would attract buyers in the book-market quite as readily as the most brilliant list of contributors. Thus, in the very first number, he commenced the exposition of the Psalms, which, as " The Treasury of David," in seven volumes, is no doubt his greatest literary achievement. He was helped by several competent friends who surrounded him, some who had passed through the College being of the number, while Mr.

Rogers, the Principal of that institution, assisted in the editorship. One of the early contributors was Edward Leach, who became sub-editor until the end of 1871, when he resigned his position and accepted the editorship of *The Freeman.*

On March 6, what appears to have been the first conference of the Pastors' College was held, and this has been continued annually until the present time. It was felt that some bond of union was needed to hold together those who had been educated in the College, and consequently an Association was formed. It was proposed and agreed upon that the members of this brotherhood should believe in the doctrines of grace, in believers' baptism, and that they should be earnest in their endeavours to extend the kingdom of Christ. There appear to have been nearly 140 members present. On Wednesday, March 8, a tea and a supper were given by a friend, who continued the practice for some years; and the President appears to have been quite in his element as he described the character of the work in progress. The surroundings were of a kind to make him cheerful; for among those present were not only some of the best men who had gone forth from the College, the work promised to extend in all directions in a way which at first could not have been anticipated. Mr. Spurgeon went over the old story of how he had commenced with one student; and how the supplies from America, on which he had depended, suddenly fell off in consequence of his anti-slavery views. The President added:—

"The funds of the College got very low, and when they were at the lowest, some lady unknown sent a cheque for £200, and afterwards another for £100 was sent. The number of students is now ninety-three, and means has never yet been wanting for their support. The weekly offerings of the church began at £3, and now they are £50 or £60 per week. Money, in fact, is sent from all parts of the world. The number of students settled over churches during the past year is about thirty. A fund has been established, which now amounts to £5,000, to assist in the enlargement and rebuilding of chapels, on the principle of advances without interest, repayable by instalments extending over a series of years. The expenditure of the College is now about £3,500 a year. About sixty-two of the students of the College are now settled as pastors of churches in various parts of the country." *

* *The Freeman,* March 15, 1865.

Ministers, such as Mr. Gange of Landport, and Mr. Medhurst of Glasgow, gave accounts of their work, which were regarded as the best possible testimony to the success of the College. The health of the Queen was drunk with loyal enthusiasm, and then followed a toast in honour of the friend who provided the supper. There were 300 guests at the tables, the pastor's father being of the number.

On Tuesday, March 14, the Tabernacle was densely crowded, the attraction being "Sermons in Candles," illustrated by emblems and dissolving views. Mr. Charles Gilpin occupied the chair, the lecture being given on behalf of the Band of Hope Union. Mr. W. R. Selway, the scientific lecturer to the College, appears, as we have said, to have been an ardent total abstainer, and both among the students of the College and among the congregation generally, he did what he could to advance teetotal principles. On that evening he had the satisfaction of inaugurating a Band of Hope in connection with the Metropolitan Tabernacle, and the first members to be received were the twin sons of the pastor, who were then eight years and a-half old. The two boys stood forward, and, amid the loud applause of the congregation, Mr. Selway placed around the neck of each a Band of Hope medal. "Master Charles, in a clear voice, which was distinctly heard by nearly, if not quite, all present, thanked the audience for the kind way in which they had welcomed him into the Band of Hope, and said he hoped he should always be a teetotaller. Master Thomas said: 'My dear friends, I thank you for your kindness, and hope I shall grow up to be an honourable man, and to keep my promise.'"* The chairman confessed to being deeply moved by this incident. In reply to a vote of thanks, Mr. Spurgeon said: "I am not a teetotaller myself, and it is not likely that I ever shall be. I believe, however, that if children are brought up to abstain from alcoholic liquors they will never need them; and therefore I think it right that they should have no instruction in the use of them from their parents. I will

* *The Freeman*, March 22, 1865.

go quite as far as that with the Band of Hope, and knowing that the society does a great deal of good, I am glad to help it as much as I possibly can." *

On the following evening Mr. Spurgeon was again at the Tabernacle, and presided at a meeting of evangelists, who, working in connection with the church and congregation, carried on a most genuine and far-reaching work. The present Mr. W. J. Orsman, of the London County Council, as the honorary secretary, gave an account of what was being done. Quite apart from students trained in the College, there were some fifty young men who, in various ways, voluntarily devoted their leisure hours to evangelistic service, preaching in cottages, halls, or in the open air, as opportunity offered. There were also about eighty others of both sexes who, on each Sabbath, took Spurgeon's sermons bound up as loan tracts, and left them at the houses of the poor and the working people who liked to receive them. A branch of the British and Foreign Bible Society had also been established, by which means over 1,100 copies of the Scriptures had been circulated in the course of two months. Among those who gave addresses on that occasion were Judge Payne and Gawin Kirkham, both being valued friends of the pastor. Mr. Spurgeon was always cheered by those who laboured in this disinterested manner, the work of Mr. Orsman being especially valued.

---

* There were those present who looked on this pretty ceremonial with different eyes, *e.g.* :—

"But the crowning absurdity of the whole business was wisely reserved for the end. After Mr. Spurgeon had done with his candles and the rest of his apparatus, a veteran teetotaller got up, and, after some remarks on the glories of water, summoned two little boys with knickerbockers and red stockings to the front of the stage. The more flippant of the spectators might have anticipated a light gymnastic performance, either as a testimony to the unimpaired strength of the aged abstainer, or as emblematic of something in the Bible. However, the teetotaller announced that they bore a name which would be honoured in history; so the audience, who had been in a manner guessing riddles all night about the candles, conjectured, and rightly, that they beheld the sons of their 'pastor.' Then solemnly each was admitted a member of the Band of Hope Union, and ceremoniously invested with the medal of the order. The enthusiasm of the multitude knew no bounds. They cheered and waved hats and handkerchiefs, and the little boys made two tiny speeches, and then the several hundreds of people cheered and waved hats and handkerchiefs again till they were all hoarse and dizzy. This is the kind of thing for which the multitude are to be got at!"—*The Saturday Review*, March 18, 1865.

On April 24 Mr. Spurgeon attended a meeting of the United Methodist Free Church at Exeter Hall, when a notice of a coming lecture on " Mind Your P's and Q's" afforded him an opportunity of indulging in some humorous remarks :—

"I am very glad to be here, but am sorry I have to speak, having already spoken twice during the evening and hurried from one meeting to another. But then one is always at home with Methodists—because they are full of warmth ; and more at home still with those Methodists who are quite free ; and again, with those Methodists who are not, like Mahomet's coffin, hanging half-way between heaven and earth, with regard to the State Church, and not knowing where they are. I am glad to be among you because I know you are sound in that matter, and that when that question comes to be fought out we shall find you, having been true to principle in other things, true in this ; and you will not, when the time comes for the fresh Reformation, act on the plea of Erasmus, 'Are there not good people in it, and must it not be spared?' whereas from pinnacle to foot-stone it must be pulled down."

Reference was then made to the great work in which the Primitive Methodists were engaged. Mr. Spurgeon enlarged on the miracle of the loaves and fishes, showing that the lesson taught to believers in this age was that substance, talents, and all things available, must be consecrated to the work :—

"The United Methodist Free Churches must take stock. How many loaves and fishes have they? Bring them, though they may some of them be barley loaves—little fishes, though some of them may chance to be ;—bring them to the Master's hand, and He will bless and break, and there will be enough for all the millions ; yes, enough and to spare. The resolution recognises the claims of the ignorant, benighted, and spiritually destitute millions both at home and abroad. That is enough ; if a Free Methodist recognises a claim, he says, 'I intend to pay you.' If you cannot pay just now all the claim, if you keep on recognising it at every collection and every opportunity, the debt will hold good at law, and it will still be right to recognise it. The churches at home have been blessed by having kept before them, by means of missions, the duty which they owe to Christ. I like missions most of all for this peculiar reason of my own—they secure an issue for the higher spiritual life of their churches. There are brethren whose prayers seem as if they shake the gates of hell and open the doors of heaven—brethren who have communed with Christ till you know they have been with Him. If we have not missionary work, these people will be thorns in our sides. As the walls of Jericho are invested, so are we going round the walls of heathendom. Let us not expect so much for the present, but wait for the future, remembering that the measure of what we should do must be the claims which we recognise, rather than the results which we may expect. This is God's work, and our work under God, and we must undertake it as for death and life, with time before us fleeing, and eternity behind us hastening on. We must all take our places by prayer, by gifts, by efforts—by all means we must all be at it ; but we will never bring down the walls of this Jericho except by prayer and faith. The text says something about hastening on the coming of the kingdom. I cannot quite get into that part, but I will just illuminate you a little as to my own view of the second coming of the lord if you will bear with me. This I do by graphically comparing our position to that of Prince Immanuel's troops when they fought outside the walls of Mansoul with Diabolus and his crew, ere the shrill sound of the trumpet heralded the approach of the Lord Himself. I assure you, in conclusion, that I am thrice happy to be here ; let us still go on and conquer both at home and abroad, having as our motto still that of John Wesley, 'The best of all is, God is with us.'"

In consequence of his leaving England early in the month of May, Mr. Spurgeon did not do much in the way of speaking at the religious anniversaries. Indeed, he was showing signs of great weariness, and may have hurried away to escape the ordeal; for notwithstanding the seeming ease with which he got through such work, it was always a heavy trial of strength to him. Before taking some weeks of needed rest, however, he preached a fine discourse on behalf of the Baptist Irish Society.

A quarter of a century ago, a certain school of theologians, who also became prophets, were looking forward with great interest to the year 1866, predicting, with some confidence, that it would be "a year of wonders." On one occasion the subject of Mr. Spurgeon's sermon was Joshua and his army encompassing the walls of Jericho. The modern Jericho was believed to be Romanism; her walls were destined to come down, and when that happened, the glory of the kingdom of Christ would shine out more resplendent than ever. A friend, who had a brother labouring in Ireland, was attracted to the Tabernacle to hear this discourse, and he wrote down the impressions which were made upon his mind :—

"The divisions of Mr. Spurgeon's sermon were *Work, Wait,* and *Win.* It was well calculated to stimulate zealous souls to action ; and there is no immediate necessity for finding fault with Christian people for overmuch working ; there has been so little done by Protestants and so much done by Papists, and all the dark and death-like forces, that really we seem to need some stimulants to set us going. There was one point in Mr. Spurgeon's sermon I distinctly noticed. Referring to the 'signs of the times,' he said, there always had been 'signs of the times,' which remark was quite true ; but the sweeping sentence was this : Mr. Spurgeon did not believe in the near approach of any remarkable crisis, for many reasons ; one was, because all the prophets said we were fast approaching the end ; 'but,' said he, 'all the prophets are liars ;' of course, he meant those prophets who made a profit out of their prophesying. As I do not know who these prophets are, I will not say much. Dr. Cumming has, doubtless, made large sums by his literary productions ; but, having carefully read some of his works, I am not prepared to pronounce all his predictions false. The fact is, Dr. Cumming in England and Mr. Baxter in America are two great collectors of the testimonies and predictions of all the students of prophecy for many centuries ; and it is remarkable that multitudes of grave, gracious, and intelligent writers have all *thought* that ere 1875 has come solemn changes would be seen, and that

1866 did stand in their eye as a great culminating period. I am afraid of that spirit—
' *Where is the promise of His coming ?* ' etc. etc. And to pronounce 'all the prophets as
liars' came to me exceedingly harsh ; yea, more than that, it was calculated, I feared, to
influence thousands of minds, and lead them in a wrong direction." *

Mr. Spurgeon continued to manifest great interest in the prosperity
of the Baptist interest at Winslow; and at the beginning of May
he again visited and preached two sermons in the little town in
which his distinguished predecessor in the pastorate, Benjamin
Keach, had laboured in the seventeenth century. About forty of
the leading people dined together, and the balance-sheet of the
building fund showed that the chapel—the memorial-stone of which
Mr. Spurgeon had laid about a year previously—had cost £638.
He not only encouraged the enterprise by his presence, he successively
gave several handsome donations to the building fund.

Some few weeks after this a visit was paid to a village in Berk-
shire, which is still vividly remembered by Mr. Goldston, of Hastings,
who was present, and who supplies a description of the scene. Mr.
Goldston was then living at Caversham, near Reading, but he afterwards removed to London and became a member and an elder of the
Metropolitan Tabernacle. I much regret that other friends have not
preserved similar records of many other days which were equally
memorable. Mr. Goldston writes :—

"A few miles from Caversham is a village called Pepphard. Here,
in the summer of 1865, the usual annual gathering was held, when
the country churches for miles round met to make a holy-day of
their annual holiday. A religious service is held in the open air,
and a collection is made for the village minister. On this occasion
Mr. Spurgeon had promised to preach.

"For months previously the people had talked of his coming;
yet there was a doubt, as gout had already prevented his fulfilling
some engagements. However, although suffering in the right foot
and in great pain, the beloved servant of God was able to take the
journey.

* *The Earthen Vessel,* xxi. 146.

"To describe the scene on our way from Reading to Pepphard, with the increasing multitude of pedestrians, and the hundreds of vehicles from Henley, Reading, Wokingham, Bracknell, and other places, would be to say, 'it was like going to Henley Regatta.' The opportunity was limited, as there was to be but *one sermon*, and that in the afternoon; consequently, the privilege was a rare one for the country people, and they were determined to be there in time. But haste was impossible, for it was difficult for one conveyance to pass another in those narrow country lanes.

"Assembled in a spacious meadow, surrounded by all that is beautiful of nature's bounty, in farms, fields, flocks of sheep and herds of cattle, it was a fitting time to have the mind 'drawn up to Nature's God.' On this occasion, also, a waggon was used as a platform, and the opening prayer brought sweet calm with holy expectation.

"The preacher took for his text the words, 'Thy name is as ointment poured forth,' Sol. Song i. 3. It was one of his happiest seasons. One said to another, referring to the preacher, 'He gets deeper down than most of us, sir.' 'Yes; he do put the spade in deep, don't he?' was the reply.

"This sermon occupied nearly an hour in its delivery, and the people (although standing all the time) gave no evidence of weariness or of inclination to leave; and it was said that the preacher's voice could be heard at a distance of more than a mile. Twenty-five years and more have passed since that day; but there are still living in the villages of Pepphard and Caversham, also in the town of Reading, those who saw more of Christ that day than they had ever seen before."

At this period visits of this kind were continually being made to country congregations, and the results, in the way of stimulating local revivals of religion, are no doubt visible even in the present day. That the preacher was wearing out faster than he supposed must now be recognised; but his temperament was such that, so long as health and strength held out, he could hardly rest save by changing his work.

CHAPTER LVI.

IN SWITZERLAND AND ITALY.

Rest Needed—Among the Swiss Mountains—Venice—Italy—The Continental Sunday—The Island Church—Sacra Monte—The St. Bernard Hospice—Dr. Pritchard and Constance Kent—*The Freeman*.

AS the spring of the year 1865 advanced, it became again evident that there would have to be another lengthened break in Mr. Spurgeon's round of toil. Although he was only thirty years old, he had already done what might have passed for the work of a lifetime: he had gathered an immense congregation, he had founded a college, while the ten volumes of his published sermons might have ranked as a respectable body of divinity. Now the preacher had to confess, however, that preaching the Word had been somewhat of a weariness or a drag—symptoms of an ailment which rest alone could cure. Accordingly, on Sunday, May 7, he told the congregation that he found it necessary to leave England for a season for change of scene, and to seek refreshment both for mind and body. Before the end of the week the report was circulated that the pastor of the Metropolitan Tabernacle had gone to the Holy Land; but in point of fact Mr. and Mrs. Spurgeon had started off together for a tour on the Continent. The object he had in view this time was rest above all things, so that the journey differed from other European rounds which had been undertaken, because it was not made laborious by formal visits and preaching on extraordinary occasions.

The tourists passed through France into Switzerland, and made their first stop at Basle, the capital of the canton of the same name, and the richest city in Switzerland. The next stage was to Lugano, with its beautiful lake of deep transparent water and matchless amphitheatre of hills. Though a small place in comparison with

Basle, the surroundings of Lugano would be more interesting; for to spend any time amid such scenery was to Spurgeon a more profitable exercise than reading books, because the thousand and one things he looked upon gave him illustrations for future use. Como, the birthplace of Pliny the Younger, was next reached, the journey thus increasing in interest at every stage. The old town, with its double walls, strong towers, and narrow crowded lanes, which passed for streets, was a contrast indeed to the surpassing beauty of the natural surroundings, or to the attractions of the shores of the justly celebrated lake. Amid the olive gardens and vineyards, the orchards and richly productive fields of the country around the base of the mountains, Mr. Spurgeon found a country after his own heart. It was possible to rest, and at the same time to gather materials for future service. As the preacher looked out upon the striking scenes which Nature presented, he called it the Work-Volume of the Creator, as distinguished from the Word-Volume which it had been the work of his life to expound.

The party next went on to Venice, which was then under the Austrian yoke; but apart from that, and apart from the degraded superstition of its Romanism, it was a city in which Mr. Spurgeon saw hardly anything but beauty. The characteristics of the city rendered a sojourn in it as novel as it was delightful to one of the distinguished visitor's temperament. "We did not need to walk," he said, "for in a gondola one might travel all day long in that wonderful city." The fact was, that a person wishing to walk could leave an hotel by one door, and step out into the solid street; by going out at another door, a canal with its gondolas offered a more delightful method of transit. In the city itself, however, the eye was entertained more than the ear. To a sturdy Calvinist, who had just come straight from Switzerland, with its stimulating memories of the Reformation, Venice was a beautiful place, but a spiritual desert. "It would be a great mercy if one could dispense with ears whilst there," said Mr. Spurgeon; "for there is an infinite number of churches, and the bells are ringing twenty-five hours out of the

twenty-four. I give that as a guess as to the number of hours," he
added; "they began to ring as soon as they left off. By night
and by day there was nothing but a perpetual ringing of bells. Out
at sea in a gondola the sound was lovely, but near it was a horrid
ding-dong." All this discord, which the people associated with the
worship of God, carried home its lesson to the ready mind of such
an observer as Mr. Spurgeon, however. "I think it is very like
some churches and some people," he remarked, "who are very beautiful in the distance, making you think how much you would like
to belong to such communions; but on getting into their midst
and understanding what is going on, all that was so harmonious is
nothing but ding-dong."

But, notwithstanding all such drawbacks as these, the offspring
of the priestcraft of Romanism, the famous city of the Adriatic
was a place in which it seemed impossible to go an inch without
learning something. To Mr. Spurgeon it was not only full of
interest, it was the most enchanting of all the places he had visited;
for a profitable holiday he seemed to think the city preferable to
all others, so that anyone who even walked thither would find himself well repaid. Among the places visited was a famous charnel-
house, in which were to be seen no less than two thousand skulls, as
well as coffins containing the remains of former citizens, and which
were variously decorated. That scene so impressed itself on the
preacher's memory that, on his return to England, he spoke and
wrote about it. In a week-night address at the Tabernacle an
account was given of this charnel-house: "What a picture it is of
many professors who are well decorated with the flowers of morality,
and well garnished with a knowledge of the Gospel doctrine, but
who, seeming to be living, are yet dead." The preacher prayed
that such might never be the effects of his own preaching, simply
making people outwardly fair to look upon; on the contrary, he
prayed that all who came within his influence might really have
the heavenly life.

It does not appear that very much was seen of the Italian

villages, otherwise we might have heard something about the de-
plorable condition of the peasants, but some particular attention was
given to the life of the towns. In one town where the party happened to be staying there was a funeral procession, and Mr. Spurgeon was tempted to follow in order to see how it would end.
Each of the mourners carried a lighted candle, but, as it was broad
daylight, the English preacher thought a candle was unnecessary
so far as he was concerned. The procession went on until a certain
church was reached, the coffin being then put down to be sprinkled
with holy water. No sooner was this ceremony over than a number
of those who had followed took off their funeral robe and stole
away out of the church. When first seen there had been about a
hundred following, but when at length the graveyard was reached,
the whole of the mourners had disappeared, Mr. Spurgeon and his
friends being the only followers. As usual, the adventure taught a
useful lesson, which he brought with him to England for the benefit
of others. "I thought this was wonderfully like some ministers,"
he said. "When they first begin their ministry, what numbers of
people follow them, and how they admire and respect those pastors!
But gradually they slip away, and turn the corner. May it never
be so with us."

The traveller also saw enough of the Continental Sunday to make
him prize more than ever his English privileges. On one of the
Sabbaths he was away he much desired to have a quiet day, and it
was arranged that the time should be passed in a town on the
shore of a beautiful lake. One might have fished from the bedroom window of the hotel, and there was an abundance of the finny
tribe to catch. Here a complete view of the Italian Sunday, as it
was observed on a high occasion, was obtained. The day happened
to be King Victor Emmanuel's birthday, and thus, early in the
morning the popular festivities commenced by an incessant firing
of guns of various sizes. After this din had been kept up for some
time, those who were piously inclined went off to church, while
others prepared themselves for further enjoyment. In the afternoon

From a photograph by permission of Mr Tom Brine.

From a photograph by Mr S.S. George, Barnsbury St N.

From a photograph by Mr M.G. Wilde, Blackpool.

From a photograph by the London Stereoscopic Co Ltd.

THE LATE REV. JAMES SPURGEON OF STAMBOURNE.

Mrs C.H. SPURGEON.   THE LATE Mrs JOHN SPURGEON.

REV. JOHN SPURGEON.   REV. J.A. SPURGEON. L.L.D.

there were divers diversions such as would be associated with a low fair in England. There were bonfires, climbing greasy poles, and such-like diversions to suit a low taste. Italy thus proved herself to be far lower down in the scale of civilisation than England. "I thought what a mercy it is that in England we have our quiet Sabbaths," said Mr. Spurgeon after he returned. "Although in London there are Sunday trading and other objectionable things, I thank God that we have not gone so far as the Italians," he added. "Wherever the Sabbath is used as a day of pleasure, there it is also a day of drudgery. Wherever they have fêtes on the Sabbath, in those same places we see carpenters and bricklayers at work; trade goes on just the same throughout the seven days of the week; and the workman gets no more than the wages of six days' labour. Sabbath consecration ensures Sabbath rest; and when once the Sabbath is desecrated, it ceases to be a Sabbath altogether." With such views, Mr. Spurgeon was naturally opposed to the Sunday opening of museums and picture galleries.

But there was always something fresh or novel to see in that sunny land. When Sabbath was passed, Monday happened to be a fête-day, and there was sure to be something in prospect far more interesting than the most brilliant of London pageants. On the other side of the lake was a mountain, which would repay those who undertook the passage across the water in order to visit it; and while in a boat accomplishing that voyage, the English preacher was privileged to look upon a spectacle which in itself struck him as being one of the most charming sights that had ever met his eye. There was a beautiful little island in the middle of the lake, and on that was a church, to which, on certain occasions, people from the surrounding towns and villages went to worship. These small companies, of course, put off from land in boats of various sizes, but they formed, as it were, but one procession. At the bows of the craft which led the way a crucifix was visible, and behind that there was a picture of the Virgin Mary. The scene was pre-eminently picturesque, and the chanting of the whole of those who were in

H H

the boats which followed produced an effect which was peculiarly striking. "It struck me that this was no new picture," remarked Mr. Spurgeon when speaking of this scene. "I thought of the whole Church of God coming across the sea of life to the land of the hereafter, with the Cross at the prow, gently rowing along and singing the praise of God."

One fête-day may follow closely on the heels of another in Italy; but the picturesque and suggestive of to-day may be succeeded by something far more objectionable on the morrow. This was Mr. Spurgeon's experience: he saw what he called "an exhibition of idolatry." This was, after all, neither more nor less than an ordinary procession of priests, before whom was carried an image of the Virgin, at sight of which persons in the streets fell on their knees to worship. That was a very ordinary sight; but it was also a most saddening and depressing one. "Roman Catholics sometimes tell us that they are not idolaters, and that they do not worship these things; they had better take out the eyes of observers at once," said Mr. Spurgeon when speaking of this procession. "I saw," he added, "the people bowing down before what seemed to me nothing but a doll which only a little child would cry for, and which I could not worship even if I felt some reverence for the Virgin Mary."

The ascent of Sacra Monte, "the Holy Mountain of the New Jerusalem," was described as "a very stiff pull," but the waxwork show to be seen there was of a kind never to be forgotten. As Mr. Spurgeon said:—

"The first thing we saw was the 'Birth of the Saviour;' in a square building were seen the Virgin Mary and the newborn babe, with the shepherds and angels in figures large as life. We also saw Jesus Christ represented in the Garden of Gethsemane, just like life, and exquisitely done. There were great drops of blood on the ground, the three disciples asleep, and the others in the distance. A little further on we came to the Crucifixion—a dreadful sight. There was also a tomb, in which lay the representation of Jesus Christ's body. The Resurrection was exhibited, too, and the Ascension. The whole was very remarkable, and if it were not that the people came to worship these objects, I can scarcely blame them. Though we deplore the idolatry that leads multitudes of pilgrims there, we cannot but feel that we have a very lifelike picture of the scene of our Saviour's life and death."

Some further experiences in the Alps Mr. Spurgeon also described, as follows :—

"On one mountain we came to an inn, surrounded by the most lovely scenery; and although it had been recently built, yet, on going to the bedroom window, close under me was the most splendid dunghill I ever saw. This is the general custom, but it struck me it was human nature all over. When God makes an object beautiful and lovely, we must bring something close under our nostrils which must be offensive; we must have something to fret about. I have become quite an adept in riding; I should not think anything of riding up to the top of the galleries before me. I did not carry my wife on my back, but I will not say that some other person did not do so. In ascending we were accompanied by a man whose duty it was to dig us out of the snow, for there was a great deal to get through in some places. But going down-hill was ten thousand times worse than getting up. I started over the slippery shingle, when my feet went under me, and down I came, and in order to hold on I stuck my fingers right into the earth. I thought I would crawl back again to the top, but, supposing the other side of the mountain would be as bad, I did not do so. I saw a mule drift more than a quarter of a mile. My heart was in my mouth, and I expected to follow the mule. I wished I was at home in the Tabernacle. Cowardly people ought not to go on such journeys. In some places it was necessary to tie the mules together, so dangerous was the road. I thought it was a good picture : whenever the road got bad, it was good for Christian people to unite together, so that when one slipped the others should help him up."

In travelling among the Alps, it was found that the snow variously affected people's eyes. As a rule, those who lived high up the mountain were superior to such as were located in the valleys; they were superior in intellect as well as in physical strength. The party reached the St. Bernard Hospice, which was found to be at the time of this visit deeply embedded in snow up to the second floor. That hospital, capable of entertaining six hundred guests, was certainly one of the most extraordinary houses of entertainment in the world, rich and poor being alike welcome, and no donation being expected from the latter. It was a wonderful place, which had its weird sights while it afforded hospitable shelter. Nothing was wanting to make even Protestant visitors happy, for there were pianos on which the accompaniment to their hymns might be played. But any who slept there would think of the corpses in the Morgue, for there were there the remains of some who had perished centuries before, preserved from corruption by the atmosphere.

Mr. Spurgeon was refreshed and even wonderfully benefited by this tour. In addressing his people on his return, he spoke in the

characteristic manner of a man who was in love with his work,
and who was encouraged by his people's bearing towards him :—

"I have heard that it is worth while for a man and his wife to fall out for the
pleasure of coming round again; but I had my suspicions as to the correctness of that
remark. Still, I really think it is worth while to go away for the pleasure of coming back
again. I thank you ten thousand times for the kind expressions I have received from one
and all. I feel that my absence has been of very great service to myself; and how far
serviceable it may be to you, you must form your own judgment. You have looked in my
face pretty well. I am not complaining, but am rather thankful, and I think you will
have observed a material difference. I cannot help thinking that I am ten years younger
in feeling; but I hope not ten years sillier—there is no need for that. I feel ten years
more elastic in body, and I hope ten years fuller of life, spirit, life and soul for the preaching of the Word."

The fact was, that, prior to setting out on this eight weeks'
holiday, the ominous symptoms which are produced by overwork
had begun to show themselves. Preaching had become a task and
a drag rather than a pleasure; the work seemed to have lost some
of its freshness, although to observers in the pews there did not
appear to be any falling off of power, nor of good effects following. As regarded the "supplies," all had not been satisfied, while
the funds for the support of the institutions had fallen off. This
was in some respects a disappointment, although the money began
again to flow in immediately on the pastor's return. As regarded
those who had occupied the pulpit in his absence, he said : "I
had been hoping that I should receive some such intimation as
that given by an old lady to Dr. Leifchild. She said, 'There,
now, you are a good man ; you are not like some preachers, who,
when they go away, get dull sticks to fill their pulpits ; whenever
you go away, you always get a better preacher than yourself.'" On
the whole, all things had gone on well, however ; and one who
had preached most acceptably was a young man from the College,
that fact yielding peculiar satisfaction all round.

The time occupied by the Continental tour represented the
vacation of the College, so that during that same eight weeks Principal Rogers had visited several of the College men who were
stationed in pastorates. As Mr. Spurgeon himself explained : "Mr.
Rogers has been travelling episcopally through the diocese of England,

ordaining the young men, or something of that kind, visiting five or six places where their students had settled, stirring up the Church, and holding confirmations—confirming the young men in the faith."

At this time Mr. Rogers was about sixty-six years of age, and he was so popular among his former students that he was often engaged to preach on special occasions. While going from place to place during the summer of 1865, he was greatly encouraged at the signs of progress which he witnessed. The College was now recognised as the chief work of the Church, and it already numbered about a thousand subscribers.

The cases of Dr. Pritchard, the notorious poisoner, and Constance Kent were now attracting notice. The former had poisoned his wife and mother-in-law. Constance Kent, who was twenty years old, had confessed that she murdered her brother, aged four, on June 29, 1860. Dr. Pritchard was hanged, but Miss Kent was sentenced to penal servitude for life. After serving twenty years, she was liberated on ticket-of-leave on July 18, 1885. In the course of his sermon at the Metropolitan Tabernacle on July 23, Mr. Spurgeon said :—

"It was deserving of note in regard to Pritchard that he pleaded Not Guilty before the judge, and that he then endeavoured to throw the whole blame of the offence with which he was charged on the unfortunate woman, Mary M'Leod, whom he had led astray from the paths of virtue. It seemed that the convict would have been glad if he himself could have escaped by making her suffer in his stead. This conduct reminded one of Adam throwing the blame on Eve, and of Eve throwing it upon the serpent. Then, Dr. Pritchard made no confession whatever until after the case against him had been proved. In fact, he pleaded innocency, and only pleaded guilty when he must have been stark mad to do otherwise—namely, after his conviction and sentence of death was passed upon him. He then confessed after a sort and after a fashion, something like as sinners usually confessed—when the confession was wrung and squeezed out of them. In Dr. Pritchard's case it was very partial at first; villain as he was, he would only confess to one part of his crime : that he poisoned his wife, not his mother-in-law. This, too, was what sinners usually did, confessing part, but not all their offences. When he made his last confession, supposing the last to be true and complete (and of this we could not be quite sure), there were no words of extenuation in it, but a sort of madness, and the influence of strong drink, were made to bear the blame. All this was done not through ignorance, but in the teeth of an excellent education, and in the teeth, also, of a knowledge that he was doing evil. Had it been done by a person of a low order of intellect, who might throw the blame on the nation for his want of culture, there might possibly be some excuse; but he was a man who, he supposed, had listened to thousands of sermons, read the Bible, knew well the difference between right and wrong, and yet who had sinned grievously, and made no confession until he made a lying one, and then made a second confession with as much coolness as when he was denying the whole of his crime with a lie in his right hand."

Reference was then made to Constance Kent, whose crime was creating immense sensation throughout the country:—

"In the other case—that of Constance Kent—no doubt an atrocious sin and a very great crime had been committed. She appeared in court under her own confession. Her life was not in danger when she made that confession. She surrendered voluntarily to justice, and when asked whether she pleaded Guilty or Not Guilty, she unhesitatingly replied Guilty. Several persons had asked her to plead Not Guilty in the hope that through some flaw in the evidence she might be acquitted upon her trial, but she said Guilty, and though an offer was made to her to retract that plea, she exhibited no signs of wavering, and again said Guilty. This was the sinner's true and only plea. Then, she was anxious to free all others from blame. If her counsel spoke, it was to assure the judge that, upon her honour, she alone was guilty, and that no father, sister, brother, or friend was implicated in the crime. Her language was that of the Psalmist, 'Against thee only have I sinned, and done this evil in thy sight.' She needed no witness to come and convict her. No one saw the deed committed; it was done in secret. Collateral evidence there might have been to prove her guilt, and she might have been sentenced to death if she retracted her plea. But she confessed all. I think it must have been a solemn moment when the judge said to her, 'You are charged with having feloniously and maliciously killed and murdered your brother.' Yes, she was Guilty. This was her reply. She did not object to those words. 'Guilty of malice?' 'Yes.' 'Of malice aforethought?' 'Yes.' 'Of murder?' 'Yes.' Not a word of extenuation; she took it as the judge put it. She had not, nor had her counsel for her, a single word to say by way of apology. Her counsel might have said she was very young, being young that she was easily led away by evil passions, and that the murder was committed long ago, when she was younger still. But no. It was her own confession, and nothing of the kind was said. The judge might think all this if he pleased. There was nothing said by her or for her upon the subject. The confession came so thoroughly and truly that not a word was put in to render that calm stream of confession muddy or impure. When asked whether she could give any reason why sentence of death should not be passed upon her, nothing why the solemn and dreadful sentence that she should be hanged by the neck until she was dead should not be carried into effect, she was silent. It was no wonder the judge wept; he could not help it. She did not speak the confession in the spirit of bravado, saying, 'Yes, I did it, and I will do it again.' She seemed to know what guilt was. She felt that she could not make any atonement to society for the offence she committed except by confessing, and accordingly she confessed as one who felt within the guilt she felt without. Sin, in the sight of God, could not be taken away by mere confession, but law, in the case of man, might remove the penalty in consequence of it. Dr. Pritchard had asked for the prayers of the public on his behalf, and those prayers would not be withheld, although one could not help feeling a loathing for his denial of his guilt. But in the case of Constance Kent, if it were put to a show of hands in England to-morrow whether mercy should be extended to her, I feel confident that the verdict would be, 'Let the penitent sinner live. A great and dreadful crime she committed, which must blight and blast her life; but she has confessed, and let her be spared—spared, not on the ground of justice, but this is a case in which, if the sovereignty of mercy is to be exercised at all, it should be now exercised.'"*

* *The Freeman,* July 26, 1865.

It was about this time that, through lack of adequate support, the denominational weekly newspaper, *The Freeman*, was taken in hand by a limited liability company. From the first Mr. Spurgeon had been somewhat disappointed with the paper, because he considered its theology to be too broad. In one of his letters to the American *Watchman and Reflector* some time before, he had remarked, "I must beg that neither you nor your readers will regard any newspaper as the organ of the English baptists. We have no organ which represents the Calvinistic Baptist Churches of England." The change of management which was soon afterwards effected resulted in a change of tone, which Mr. Spurgeon heartily approved. Under some responsible advisers, Mr. Edward Leach now became acting editor; but the high price of fourpence a copy naturally hindered the paper from becoming popular in the widest sense. It might possibly have been an advantage if the plan, adopted some years later, of issuing the paper at a penny had been adopted then; but that was opposed by friends who thought that the Baptist denomination in England was too small to allow of a representative penny paper being able to hold its own.

CHAPTER LVII.

THE LONDON BAPTIST ASSOCIATION.

Archibald G. Brown and his Work—Work of the College—Baptist Leaders—Baptist Union—
Persecution in Saxony—The New London Association—Dr. Parker—New Chapels.

AMONG those who were trained in the Pastors' College were several who were destined to turn out first-class men, and whose service has proved itself to be of the most far-reaching kind. Foremost among the successful is Archibald G. Brown, "my curate," as the President would call him, and whose work at the East-End of London Mr. Spurgeon reckoned to be only second to his own. Mr. Brown, senior, was for years a deacon at the Metropolitan Tabernacle; the family ranked high among commercial circles in the City, while the family connections included Dr. Geikie, author of "The Life and Words of Christ," and Sir Archibald Geikie, the geologist. Young Archibald was intended for a mercantile life; but after being converted under the preaching of the present Sir Arthur Blackwood, he found his way into the Pastors' College to become one of the most popular of the preachers ever sent forth from that institution. A month after he was received into the College Mr. Brown was sent to preach at Bromley, his first congregation consisting of twenty persons, who assembled at the White Hart Assembly Room. The memorial-stone of the present chapel was laid by Mr. Spurgeon on July 4, 1864, when the outlook from small beginnings had become most promising. Early in 1867, Mr. Brown removed to his larger sphere in the East-End of the metropolis, where, in due course, Mr. Spurgeon had the happiness of opening the East London Tabernacle, in which a full congregation has ever since assembled. Mr. Spurgeon and Mr. Brown were ardent friends to the last; they were agreed on most points; they heartily co-operated in Christian work; and when the

Chief died, the sorrowing survivor assured me that life and service could never more be to him what they had been.

The aggressive work of the Pastors' College at this time was well illustrated also by the erection of the chapel at Drummond Road, Bermondsey, the memorial-stone of which was laid by Mr. Spurgeon on August 4, 1865. Planned to accommodate 600 persons, the sanctuary cost £1,500, two-thirds of which was subscribed by Mr. Spurgeon and his people. A preaching station with a Sunday-school already existed; but as Bermondsey had added over 2,000 souls to its population during the three previous years, this additional place of worship was felt to be a necessity. " My object in having the chapel built in this neighbourhood is a purely disinterested one," said Mr. Spurgeon. " I and my congregation would be as happy in our own Tabernacle, so far as we personally are concerned, if this chapel had never been contemplated ; but when I look around and consider the spiritual destitution, I feel constrained to strive to supply the need by every means in my power. It has been said that working men would not listen to the Gospel, but I believe that is a libel on them, and I hope to see this chapel full of them, for I am sure they are attached to the Bible, and value their souls as much as any other class." Later in the day, after tea at the Metropolitan Tabernacle, the pastor congratulated the people on the commencement of this work, he thanked them for their co-operation, and added, that he hoped to have their assistance in supplying the needs of other destitute localities in a similar manner.

At this time the Baptist denomination in Great Britain and Ireland had about 2,400 churches and 250,000 members, but the general condition as regarded working and leadership was put down as pre-eminently unsatisfactory. There seemed to be no lack of able men, but there were none apparently who cared to take the part of leaders. This led to a want of united action, while at the same time the Missionary Society was curtailing its operations in India through want of funds. " There are voices in our midst which would ring through the land, but which are silent except to their own congregations," said *The Freeman.* "There are men whom we should all gladly follow, but they carry no standard, and utter no call. Almost the only exception to this statement is Mr. Spurgeon." The question then arose, Could not Spurgeon do something in the way of taking the lead, and thus benefit the denomination at large? *The Freeman* seemed to think it was hardly his own fault that he did not do so:—

"By his wondrous popularity and wondrous power—aided, as we believe, by much of the Divine Grace—Mr. Spurgeon has obtained a following not only in London, but throughout the land. His voice is heard by thousands every Sunday; his written words are read by hundreds of thousands every week. But, through the peculiarity of his position, Mr. Spurgeon has hitherto stood much alone. He is the head of a denomination *within* a denomination. He takes little part in the concerns of the Baptist body *as such.* We believe this is not Mr. Spurgeon's own desire. If we are not mistaken, he has expressed, again and again, the desire to unite more heartily with his brethren. Why should he not do so? Is there anything that keeps him apart from the Baptist body in spite of himself? Truly, he has much to do already; but there is no man who could do more to rouse the body as a whole to action, no man who would be welcomed more cordially by the denomination generally as a counsellor and a brother beloved. If *The Freeman* could do anything to bring Mr. Spurgeon and the Baptist body generally in cordial and loving union and co-operation, the day on which such union was effected would be to its conductors one of the proudest of their lives."

The autumnal meetings of the Baptist Union, which in 1865 were held at Bradford, appear to have served a good purpose by leading both pastors and people to see that there ought to be more unity for concerted action. Just at that time much sympathy was felt for Baptists on the Continent, who were suffering from persecution; and at the Bradford meetings the question was discussed of how assistance could best be rendered. It was stated that "Since the year 1861, when the church was formed in Saxony, their brethren had been exposed to a series of bitter and unrelenting persecutions and hostility from the Lutheran clergy, so that their assemblies had been again and again dispersed, their pastor had been arrested, treated like a felon, and spoiled of his personal property, and he had to meet brethren in the Lord for the purpose of consultation in the dead of the night, and in the depths of the forests of Saxony." In the discussion various opinions were expressed, and with some there seemed to be a disposition to leave all action to the

Evangelical Alliance. Mr. Spurgeon strongly advocated a petition direct from the Union to the King of Saxony, that being, in his opinion, far preferable to any remonstrance to Lutheran pastors. "If snubbed by the King of Saxony, at least they would be snubbed by a king, and that was better than being snubbed by a parcel of Lutherans." It was in connection with these gatherings that Mr. Spurgeon preached at St. George's Hall, Bradford, on Thursday evening, October 12. The discourse was founded on Psalm cii. 16, "When the Lord shall build up Zion, he shall appear in his glory." We find that on this occasion the hall was not only "most densely crowded," but that "the crush for admittance was tremendous."

What may be called the reorganisation of the London Baptist Association belongs to the fall of 1865, and Mr. Spurgeon took a leading share in the business, which yielded a more than usual amount of satisfaction to a large number of people. "There are but few amongst us who will not remember the old Association of Baptist Churches in the Metropolis," said the denominational organ; "an association which for many years did some good, until at last, through sheer inanition, it died out; killed, because at length it ceased to find anything to do. During the years which have intervened since then, the process of isolation has been working steadily and disastrously amongst us, until at length the Baptists in London have seemed to become utterly powerless for any concerted action, and, what is worse still, for any mutual sympathy." An endeavour was made to put an end to this state of things by forming what was virtually a new association, and a circular, inviting the co-operation of all who could lend their aid, was sent forth by Mr. Spurgeon and some other ministers. It was arranged that three meetings should be held at the Metropolitan Tabernacle. The first meeting was for ministers only, who would discuss the articles of association; the second gathering would include both pastors and deacons, who would together further discuss the resolutions of the first meeting. This was to be followed by a great meeting for prayer "in the spirit of the union formed."

Eighty pastors attended the preliminary meeting, and Mr. Spurgeon presided at the devotional service which preceded the business. An excellent spirit of true catholicity prevailed. As *The Freeman* said : "The brethren assembled represented well-nigh every shade of opinion amongst us, although, if any party predominated, we should say it was that of our strict communion brethren. Still, it was most apparent that the ruling wish of all present was to give as little place as possible to differences of opinion, and rather to find out the common basis on which they could practically agree."

It was felt that practically the past had been characterised by disunion, and the time seemed to have arrived for something better. Mr. Lewis, pastor of Westbourne Grove Chapel, sketched out the programme of the new Association, the first thing had in view being the cultivation of brotherly love. By way of advancing the cause of Christ in and about London, one chapel in each year was to be erected. The members, ministers, and delegates were to assemble quarterly, the first gathering in each year being regarded as the annual meeting. A church of less than 250 members was to send one delegate ; if there were over that number two delegates were sent, and larger churches were allowed one representative for every 250 members. The President was to be elected annually, and the expenses were to be collected in small subscriptions. *The Freeman* thought that all things were about as promising as they could be. "We are thankful, too, that the basis of this new Association is so broad," it was added. "It does not rest on the technicalities of a creed, but simply on the wide basis of evangelical sentiment." No one worked more heartily in the new movement than Mr. Spurgeon, whose addresses at the meetings were always characterised by the fervour of a man who was thoroughly in earnest.

The visit which Mr. Spurgeon paid to Newcastle on November 7, was to the church and congregation which then assembled in the Town Hall under the pastorate of Mr. Wildon Carr, who in after years was closely identified with the work at the Metropolitan

Tabernacle. A chapel for Mr. Carr's congregation was in course of erection, that being the second chapel he had been instrumental in erecting in Newcastle in the course of four years. The people first met at an old chapel in New Court; a handsome new sanctuary was then provided on Rye Hill, and on retiring from this pastorate, Mr. Carr was followed by a large number of the congregation, who met in the Town Hall until another new meeting-place was provided in Marlborough Crescent. Mr. Spurgeon not only preached on behalf of the cause, he gave £400 to the building fund.*

On two successive Friday evenings in November Dr. Joseph Parker, who then held a pastorate at Manchester, gave two lectures at the Metropolitan Tabernacle, Mr. Spurgeon occupying the chair on each occasion. The first was on "Nonconformity in Relation to the Book of Common Prayer;" and this was followed by "Reasons for a Nonconformist Aggressive Policy." These lectures created some sensation in Manchester, and similar interest appears to have been excited in different parts of this country, and also in Scotland. On the evening of the second lecture the Tabernacle was crowded, and Lord Ebury was one of the audience.

Some reference has already been made to prophecies uttered about this time by self-constituted seers concerning wonders which were to happen in earth and heaven during the year 1866. Some credulous persons appear to have given out that the end of the world would actually occur in the year named, for certain tracts, in which such opinions were given, were said to have been written by the pastor of the Tabernacle. Someone sent these productions to Mr. Spurgeon, and asked if he had written them. At a meeting in the chapel answer was given to this question:—

"You will hear of me in Bedlam when you ever hear such rubbish as that from me. The Lord may come in 1866, and I shall be glad to see Him; but I do not believe He will, and the reason why I do not believe He will is, because all these twopenny-halfpenny false prophets say He will. If they said that He would not come, I should begin to think He would; but, inasmuch as they are all crying out as one man that He will come in 1866 or 1867, I am inclined to think He will not arrive at any such time. It seems to me that there are a great many prophecies which must be fulfilled before the coming

* See *The Freeman*, November 22, 1865.

of Christ, which will not be fulfilled within the next twelve months; and I prefer to stand in the position of a man who knows neither the day nor the hour in which the Son of man cometh, looking always for His appearing, but never interfering with those dates and figures which seem to me to be only proper amusement for young ladies who have nothing else to do, and who take to that instead of reading novels, and for certain divines who have exhausted their stock of knowledge about sound doctrine, and therefore try to gain a little ephemeral popularity by shuffling texts of Scripture, as the Norwood gipsies shuffled cards in days gone by."

On November 28 Mr. Spurgeon laid the memorial-stone of a chapel at Redhill, and gave £100 to the building fund, an additional £100 being promised when the work was somewhat more advanced. A few days later we find that immense congregations were addressed at Woolwich, the collection being divided between the Pastors' College and a local Dorcas Society.

The annual tea in connection with the College was held at the Tabernacle on the evening of December 20, an excellent repast being provided by the ladies of the congregation. The accounts of work done, and of the funds which still came in for the support of the work, were still encouraging. Thirty students had been sent forth into pastorates during the year, and when such men as Messrs. Cuff and Spurrier stood up to speak enthusiasm was, of course, re-enkindled. Mr. Spurgeon entertained the audience with an account of William Knibb and his work, and Dr. Underhill followed with an address on the condition of Jamaica. This was thought to be one of the most encouraging anniversaries which had ever been held in connection with the College.

During three days in Christmas week, 1865, a great bazaar was held at the Metropolitan Tabernacle, the proceeds being devoted to the building of new chapels in and around London. The bazaar opened on December 26, on which day 1,700 persons visited the rooms. The receipts of the two first days amounted to between eight and nine hundred pounds. In one account we read that, " Mrs. Spurgeon's stall, as might have been expected, was a source of great attraction, and that lady drove what may be called ' a roaring trade,' and the amount placed against her name as cash received is consequently much higher than that of the other amateur shopkeepers." The students of the College also had a stall all to themselves, but notwithstanding their natural and acquired advantages, they were outrivalled by some others. The visitors to the stalls all had a letter by Mr. Spurgeon placed in their hands, in which he showed the solicitude with which he viewed the spiritual destitution of London, *e.g.* :—

"Impressed with the necessities of our ever-growing city, I have used my utmost exertions to increase the number of our Baptist churches, and, as a result, solid and flourishing churches have been founded in Wandsworth, Stepney, Bromley, Redhill, and Ealing, while the small place in Paradise Place, Chelsea, has become a noble house of prayer; and in Bermondsey a chapel is nearly completed for the use of a congregation now in connection with the church in the Metropolitan Tabernacle, and worshipping in a small room. From the success already achieved, I am encouraged to attempt yet greater things, and to seek the erection, during the year 1866, of several new buildings. My faithful friends, to whose generous co-operation, under the blessing of God, all is due, intend to hold a bazaar. As the object is one which concerns all our Baptist brethren, and, indeed, all Christians, we make a very earnest appeal for aid, and confidently look for it. We have no personal end to serve; we have no motive but the glory of God. London needs the Gospel; its thousands perish for lack of knowledge; the teachers of error are leaving no stone unturned; Puseyism is compassing sea and land—why should we sit still? Other churches are doing their best but the Baptists are hardly lifting a hand. Better days are dawning. Let us now arise and build. On the south side of the water we have the nucleus of three churches all needing buildings, and promising success if these can be erected. On the northern side, Buckhurst Hill, Kingsland, Clapton, Barking, and Bow, and several other districts, crave our aid. Why should not all be assisted? They shall be, if the Lord's people will aid us." *

In these earlier years of work at the Tabernacle ministry, a young preacher occasionally came to the front of whom one and another would say that he was destined to become a second Spurgeon. Thus, in the days of his early popularity as a preacher, the present Dr. Grattan Guinness was spoken of as "a bright particular star," and he was also described as "bidding fair to rival the renowned Mr. Spurgeon as another modern Whitefield." The comparison with Mr. Spurgeon was not a happy one ; for the characteristics of the Irish preacher showed that he had little in common with the Essex lad, who had risen to eminence by his naturalness of manner and devotion to the cause in general. Then, when the late Brownlow North turned aside from the world of sport and of fashion, in which he had lived until middle age, to preach the Gospel with an attractive

* *The Morning Advertiser*, December 29, 1865.

power which called forth general admiration, he was called the Northern Spurgeon. There was never any real similarity between such preachers and the pastor of Southwark, fond as people were of drawing comparisons. No one was more pleased than Spurgeon himself when another arose to preach the Word with power; but none knew better than he did himself that, as a preacher, he virtually stood alone through having no successful rivals.

The year 1865 ended more cheerily than some others; for though Lincoln had fallen a martyr to the cause, freedom was advancing both in the Old and the New World. In April, Richard Cobden and John Cassell had also both passed away, their deaths leaving a blank which could not be filled. Mr. Spurgeon always regarded with admiration the work of the great publisher, whose influence lives after him.

CHAPTER LVIII.

MRS. BARTLETT'S BIBLE-CLASS.

The Origin of a Great Class—Presentation to the Editor of *The Christian World*—Mr. E. H. Bartlett's Reminiscences—Spurgeon and the City Missionaries.

ONE of the largest Bible-classes ever collected was gathered at the Metropolitan Tabernacle; and the conductor, Lavinia Strickland Bartlett, was ranked by the pastor among his chief helpers. This lady was a widow, whose husband had died of cholera; and having commenced Christian work when quite a young girl, she went forward until her success in teaching a class of young women—first at New Park Street, and afterwards at the Metropolitan Tabernacle—drew forth many an expression of surprise and admiration.

On a certain Sunday afternoon in the year 1859 Mrs. Bartlett consented to take a senior class which had only three in attendance; but after persevering for a month, notwithstanding that she suffered from an affection of the heart, Mrs. Bartlett had the happiness of seeing the numbers increase to fourteen; and when the Tabernacle was opened in March, 1861, the total had increased to fifty. Her first meeting in the new chapel was in the upper gallery, before it was finished; but eventually, after one room and then another had proved too small to accommodate those who came, the lecture-hall was occupied, the class gradually increasing until over 700 would frequently be present. By the end of 1865 something like 600 persons had joined the church who came from this class.

Those who were thus willing to accept Mrs. Bartlett as their teacher were not all young women; the majority might be young, but many were as elderly as the leader, or even older. By her daily example as regards dress and other matters, this devoted woman sought to teach her following more effectively than by mere precept. The cases

I I

of reformation of character which took place were some of them very striking, and the converts came from various ranks in life.

In course of time the claims of this class required that the undivided attention of its leader should be devoted to it; for not only were there week-night meetings on Tuesdays and Fridays, but inquirers were allowed to see Mrs. Bartlett personally at her own residence at any time; and it was on this account that Mr. Spurgeon was wont to speak of the place as " the house of mercy." Collections were also made among the members on behalf of the Pastors' College, and from time to time considerable sums were collected in this way. On one occasion, in company with Mr. Spurgeon and other friends, the late Mr. James Clarke was present, and he wrote out a graphic little sketch of what he saw and heard :—

"Many have probably heard of 'Mrs. Bartlett's class' in connection with the Tabernacle, but certainly nobody who has not actually witnessed its magnitude will possess any true idea of what it really is. That it is a large class of young women conducted by Mrs. Bartlett would be the natural inference, but who would imagine the class to consist of SEVEN HUNDRED members, meeting frequently for loving conference with its devoted President? Every half-year, it seems, Mrs. Bartlett is in the habit of inviting Mr. Spurgeon and a number of friends to meet her class, to hear something of the progress made, and to receive a report of the amount subscribed by the class towards the support of the Pastors' College. It was our privilege to be present, for the first time, at such a meeting on Wednesday evening. The visitors were scarcely less numerous than the members of the class, and made up the company to at least fourteen hundred persons. Mr. Spurgeon, having taken the chair, delivered an animated opening address, and mentioned the remarkable fact that no less than fifty of the young women attending Mrs. Bartlett's instructions had joined the Church, upon a public profession of their faith in Christ, during the past year. What reason had they all to be thankful for so abundant a blessing resting upon the earnest and self-sacrificing labours of their devoted sister! And this was, happily, not at all an exceptional state of things, for conversions had ever attended Mrs. Bartlett's loving ministrations. Since the formation of the class, now some years ago, the goodly number of five hundred of its members had avowed themselves on the Lord's side. Several hours having been devoted to speeches on set themes, of practical religion, by gentlemen leaving the College, upon invitation to pastoral work in the provinces and in Australia, Mrs. Bartlett herself spoke at some length, and with intense feeling, to the female portion of the audience, exhorting them to listen to the voice of wisdom, and to walk in the ways of holiness all their days, looking forward to hallowed joys here and to a blessed immortality hereafter. Mr. Bartlett stated, on behalf of his mother, that the sum contributed by the class during the past six months towards the funds of the Pastors' College was ONE HUNDRED and THREE POUNDS, which he handed over to Mr. Spurgeon amidst the general applause of the audience. Mr. Spurgeon warmly acknowledged the gift, and expressed his thorough conviction that the cause of Christ could not be more surely advanced than by bringing out and preparing young men for the ministry of the Gospel; for let an earnest minister be p'aced in any position, and there would immediately spring up all those other means and appliances adapted for the instruction and elevation of the people. The sending forth of evangelists from that College had already led, again and again, to the necessity of erecting new places of worship. This fresh work was indeed growing upon their hands, and demanding fresh efforts to accomplish it." *

It was on this occasion that the President of the College specially honoured Mr. James Clarke, as editor of *The Christian World*, by presenting to him, by way of a testimonial, the ten volumes of *The Metropolitan Tabernacle Pulpit*, handsomely bound. Mr. Clarke had collected from the readers of the paper a sum of £160 for the Institution; and Mr. Spurgeon felt sure that many readers would be angry that so much money had been given to such an arch heretic as himself. Amid the cheers of the people, the volumes were presented as an acknowledg-ment from the congregation of the practical interest Mr. Clarke had shown in the progress of the College. The editor accepted the books with sincere pleasure, and said he was always glad of an opportunity of co-operating with Mr. Spurgeon in his many laborious and valuable efforts. " Any earnest man may well feel proud of lending a helping hand to Mr. Spurgeon in his college and chapel-building efforts, whether agreeing with him in all his opinions and ways of doing things or not," added the journalist. " There is this peculiarity between myself and Mr. Spurgeon which makes me feel in some sort as standing on the same platform with the renowned pastor of the Metropolitan Tabernacle : Mr. Spurgeon preaches habitually to by far the largest congregation in England; and I have myself the pleasure of conducting a weekly journal possessing a circulation greater than all the other religious papers of the metropolis combined, of whatever price. I am quite sure that many of my readers are warm friends of Mr. Spurgeon, and believe that at any time when they are informed that his College funds are low, or that special donations are needed for other purposes connected with the evangelistic work of the Taber-nacle, they will be prepared to give liberally according to their means."

From this it will be seen that in the year 1865 there was not only a strong bond of sympathy uniting the Southwark pastor and the Fleet Street editor, but that Mr. Clarke had full confidence in the College as

* *The Christian World*, September 8, 1865.

an evangelistic institution. He favoured none of the prejudices or objections against it which arose in certain quarters; and, as already shown, he continued to be one of its liberal supporters, when his theology had become much broader than that of Mr. Spurgeon. Some maintained that there were colleges enough; that the setting up of a new one would only create jealousy; and that, consequently, if the pastor of the Tabernacle desired to educate men for the ministry it would be far better to send them to colleges already existing. It was no doubt an innovation; the promoters felt it to be so, but they insisted that it was a special effort to meet a pressing want of the age.

What was greatly objected to was the notion that an effort was being made merely to Spurgeonise the Christian church. It was represented in America that Spurgeon was more and more extending his influence, and that a body of preachers imbued with his own spirit, and copying with "ludicrous fidelity" their Chief's manner and mode of speech, were going forth in all directions. " More and more is Spurgeon separating himself from the general organisation of the religious world, and even of the Baptist denomination, and concentrating his work upon his immense church, his college, and the churches throughout the kingdom that have taken his pupils for pastors," said one New York journal. " If this goes on for another twenty years," it was added, " Spurgeonism will be a vast organic and wondrously vitalised body; and, should circumstances warrant, this body may, as many intelligent Baptist ministers think probable, assume the name of its founder." It was thus assumed that the pastor of the Tabernacle would copy the example of Wesley in founding a sect; but, in point of fact, his action at the date in question was showing directly opposite tendencies. He protested against such misrepresentations. The word " Spurgeonism " was utterly distasteful to him, and in connection with the subject he was wont to say, " Let my name perish, but let Christ's name last for ever!" The heartiness with which he had entered into the business of forming the London Baptist Association showed that he was in full sympathy with existing agencies, and had no desire to form a fresh community.

Having given details respecting the remarkable work of Mrs. Bartlett, it may be added here that a son of that devoted woman was among the converts of Mr. Spurgeon's ministry in London, and being still a member of the church at the Metropolitan Tabernacle, he continued to the last to be associated with his pastor in Christian service. Mr. E. H. Bartlett has written and published a biography of his mother, to which Mr. Spurgeon wrote an introduction in 1877; and he sends to me the following account of work in which he has been engaged during the long period of thirty-seven years :—

" I was brought to the Lord through the instrumentality of C. H. Spurgeon, in 1855, at Exeter Hall, during the enlargement of New Park Street Chapel, was baptised on the first Sabbath of February, 1856, and have retained my membership to the present day. Soon afterwards I was elected to the Secretaryship of the Sunday Schools, Great Guildford Street, Southwark, and remained until the church and congregation removed from New Park Street to the Metropolitan Tabernacle. The Mission Hall was given up, and many of the teachers took possession of the schoolroom at New Park Street. Soon afterwards I was called to the superintendence of the school, and continued so till the chapel and schools were sold. From there the teachers and some of the scholars went to a schoolroom in Short Street, Brandon Street, Walworth, as a temporary place during the building of the schoolrooms in Station Road, Walworth, which are attached to the Metropolitan Tabernacle Almshouses. In 1875 I took up my late mother's work, which I still carry on. A special Sunday evening service for the young (which is still carried on by Mr. George Cook) was established. Besides this, there was established a Loan Tract Society (which is still in a flourishing condition); and to this was added a Maternal Society for poor women on the districts. For some years a Police Mission was maintained by the youths of the Special Service, who visited every week the police-stations of the South of London with the late pastor's sermons and other religious periodicals. A Coffee-house Mission was also carried on by the young women, who visited the coffee-houses monthly and left a copy of *The Sword and the Trowel* for the use of

customers. Many were greatly blessed by this means, and led to come
under the sound of the Gospel at the Tabernacle. When the Stockwell Orphanage was opened for the reception of children there was
commenced a Special Sabbath Morning Service, which is still carried on."

All of these operations are traced back as an outcome, direct or
indirect, of Mr. Spurgeon's early ministry. The details are given here
as coming from one who is old enough to remember the Essex lad
as he was at the outset of his London career, and who remained
associated with him in Christian work till the last.

From first to last of their acquaintance with Mr. Spurgeon his
troops of friends have been struck with his keen interest in all
kinds of Christian work, especially among lowly people in London
and great, populous towns. His interest in what is called " Ragged
London " was stimulated in the days of his youth by reading some of
Dickens's vivid descriptions, and that interest became strengthened in
later years. Thus, the large number of articles published in *The Sword
and the Trowel*, on Low London, will testify to the editor's deep
interest in the work of the City missionaries, and of all who are
endeavouring to raise the humble classes from squalor and degradation.
His sympathy with the agents of the City Mission in their arduous
service was all the greater, probably, because he realised to the
full that he himself lacked those qualifications which alone will enable
a man to do such work successfully in face of difficulties and obstacles
which might well discourage even a Greatheart.

More than once Mr. Spurgeon addressed the assembled band of
City missionaries ; and on one of these occasions, after cordially
thanking the men for their service in the name of the Church at large,
he added, " Little can we tell what London would have been without
you. If there has been a great moral change pass over it—and I am
sure there has—it is owing, doubtless, to the ministry, but equally as
much to your untiring labours from house to house. I can scarcely
dare to draw a picture of what London would have been if it had
not been for the City Mission. I am quite sure that, had it not
been for this instrumentality, our ministry would have been utterly

powerless, in the darker parts at least of those thickly populated lanes and alleys, where the voice of the ministry cannot be heard."

In speaking to the men on earnestness in their work, he could find no better exemplar of an industrious evangelist than Richard Baxter, who himself visited every house in Kidderminster. " There was not a child in the parish whom he had not catechised; there was not a backslider whom he had not warned; there was not a reprobate whom he had not addressed with solemn awe." Thus the whole parish knew that Baxter was not only a preacher, but a pastor in the fullest sense. What was possible in Kidderminster in the seventeenth century, however, was altogether impracticable in London in the nineteenth. " I say honestly, from my inmost soul, I do not conceive myself to be guilty of any dereliction of duty in the fact that I do take only one part of Baxter's work," said Mr. Spurgeon. " It is utterly impossible that I should take the other." If he preached as an evangelist up and down the country, and in such a service taxed his powers to the utmost, that was enough; the pastoral work in London had necessarily to be done by City missionaries, and Richard Baxter was held up to them as a pattern—a man who was on fire in his zeal for God, and who would have been nothing had it not been for his earnestness. That earnestness Mr. Spurgeon recommended to the men as the only proper excuse for invading an Englishman's house; but while thus giving good advice he was willing to accept it himself. " I say that my yearly income is robbery to the Church unless I serve it with my whole soul. And so is yours: if you do not put your whole soul into your work you have eaten bread for nought, you have taken money for services which you have not rendered. The Church does not support you and me that we may be images to look at, but that we may be servants to labour."

Like all great men of his class, Spurgeon was a shrewd reader of human nature; so that even while speaking to a large body of men, such as the City missionaries, he not only realised that they were fellow-workers with himself, but that they were confronted with the same kind of difficulties all round. They had to strive against habit; for even good habits might possibly become antagonistic to zeal, and the preacher was able to illustrate this from his own experience:—" I frequently catch myself, when reading the Scriptures for my own private devotion, looking at the verses to see what sort of texts they will make; and I must confess that, while in private prayer, pleading my own case before God, I find a very strong influence, which would carry me off at a tangent, to pray as a *minister* rather than as a *man.*" This danger was not peculiar to a class: it was common to all Christian workers. Much as this great man hated what he called "ministerialism," he confessed that he sometimes found its spirit entering into him:—" Unless we look very carefully to ourselves, we get like a machine wound up, and we are something like the toys which sometimes our children have, which only need a certain quantity of sand at the top and they run on until they run down." At times Spurgeon seemed to speak as though there were no honours associated with Christian work but such as those which all workers in common were entitled to share. At all events, the City missionaries occupied a place of honour in the vanguard of the Church militant; and therefore there was reason for enthusiasm in discharging their duties. There was also some excuse for one speaking in glowing terms while advising or exhorting them; and once, when addressing the entire body at the mission-house, he as nearly imitated the style of Robert Hall as ever he did in his younger days, *e.g.*:—

"I charge you, by the names of those saints of God who have suffered in Christ's holy cause, by all the men and women who in devotedness have given up their whole substance and their whole time to Christ, be ye worthy of this glorious cause. Runners, open your eyes, and look at the glorious assembly that surrounds you. See ye not the cloud of witnesses? Play the man, if ever ye were men—play the man before such spectators. When such spirits look on, who will not run? 'Lay aside every weight, and run with patience the race that is set before you, looking unto Jesus, the author and finisher of your faith.' If at the old Olympic and Isthmian games men thought they must strain every nerve and muscle, because Greece looked on, what shall we say to you, when the world looks on, and the Church looks on, and Hell looks on, and Heaven looks on? By all these, the spectators of your warfare, fight—fight lawfully, and win the crown, through the grace of your Lord Jesus Christ."

CHAPTER LIX.

WORK AT THE TABERNACLE.

Baptist Colleges—London Association—College Conference—Students and Books—The Baptist
Union—Evangelists.

ACCORDING to the custom which he had observed for many years, Mr. Spurgeon preached on the first Sunday morning of 1866 from a text selected for him by a clergyman of the Established Church who lived in the suburbs. The subject was " Unity in Christ," the text itself being the words of John xvii. 20, 21, " Neither pray I for these alone," etc. The discourse was able and helpful, and struck an excellent note at the threshold of a year which had been anticipated by self-constituted prophets as certain to be a year of supernatural wonders. There were those, as we have seen, who professed to expect that the Lord himself would come in 1866.

As the organ of the evangelical Presbyterians, *The British and Foreign Evangelical Review* at this time gave a survey of Mr. Spurgeon's work, viewing him " as a man, as a preacher, as a divine, and as a Baptist." The Presbyterians and the Particular Baptists being then in hearty sympathy as regarded their theological beliefs, Spurgeon's teaching was generally commended; but when the writer came to view the great preacher as a Baptist his attributes were not so pleasing. In regard to the Baptismal Regeneration Controversy, the Review sided with the evangelical clergy, and declared against Mr. Spurgeon in no half-hearted manner. " We are compelled to endorse the excellent letter by Mr. Baptist Noel, and to say that the charge thus brought by Mr. Spurgeon against the evangelical clergy of the Church of England is as indefensible as it is injurious and uncharitable. In one point of view," it was added, " we might even characterise it as partaking of ingratitude; for nothing admits of being more clearly demonstrated than that to this unhappy dogma of baptismal regeneration, as held by many in the English Establishment, the communion to which Mr. Spurgeon belongs owes much of its success in England." That is to say, people were driven from a church, which they believed taught a semi-Romish doctrine, to seek a home among a body whose methods and teaching emphatically protested against it.*

The great success which had been achieved by the Pastors' College at the time now under review can only be fully realised by comparing the receipts with those of other similar institutions. Thus the denominational paper gave the following in a leading article :—

"Baptists are not unmindful of the necessity of a collegiate training for their ministers, nor is the amount contributed to college funds indicative of any lack of interest in the work. Bristol rejoices in an income of £1,663 11s. 3d.; Rawdon reports its receipts at £1,412 2s. 6d.; Regent's Park possesses an income of £2,047; Chilwell receives yearly about £740; while the Pastors' College, at the Metropolitan Tabernacle, has an annual income almost equal to the combined receipts of Bristol, Rawdon, and Regent's Park, expending, and therefore, so long as under the management of Mr. Spurgeon, receiving £5,000. In the Principality, the college at Pontypool reports its income at £951 15s. 7d.; Haverfordwest at £853 19s. 4½d.; North Wales at £460 5s. 9d.; making the total for Wales upwards of £2,226. Scotland, several of whose ministers have been educated at one or other of the national universities or in England, has but one college, whose income last year was £250. The Baptists of Great Britain have nine colleges, which are educating 264 young men, with a yearly income of £13,379. It is significant and suggestive that one college receives nearly a third of these students, and more than a third of these receipts. Evidently Mr. Spurgeon and his friends are more earnest and liberal in the work of providing collegiate training for the ministry than are the major part of our pastors and ministers." †

To those who had merely been familiar with the work of the older colleges, it was a matter to excite amazement when ninety-three students could be received into one institution, the income of which not only sufficed to support them and their tutors, but actually left over something for chapel-building besides. Nor could it be said that those who went out from the College were not successful, for the settlements of students which were constantly being chronicled showed otherwise. Thus, early in 1866, Peniel Tabernacle, Chalk Farm, a large and beautiful chapel, was erected through the efforts of Mr. Swann; and accounts of the successes of former students came about the same time from Dunfermline, Aldeburgh, and Bedford.

* See *The British and Foreign Evangelical Review* for January, 1866.
† *The Freeman*, January 24, 1866.

The annual meeting of the church at the Tabernacle was always a great occasion with the members, so that it was only an average gathering when 1,500 sat down to tea on the evening of January 24. The current expenses of 1865, including some repairs and alterations, etc., amounted to £3,333. In addition, a sum of over £700 was dispensed to the poor of the congregation alone, while a number of smaller sums had been voted to missions both at home and abroad. The treasurer who made the statement was then the venerable " Father " Olney, who in the early days of the Tabernacle was a very familiar figure among the deacons on the preacher's platform. During the year 1865 no less than 438 persons were baptised, and the total membership now stood at 3,258. A series of revival meetings were held during the month of February, and a powerful impression appears to have been made, especially among the younger portion of the congregation.

The first meeting of the newly-formed London Baptist Association was held on February 7, at Bloomsbury Chapel. The Association at this time represented sixty-four churches. Mr. Spurgeon, who showed the greatest possible interest in the new brotherhood, gave a stirring address. The outlook at this time was thought to be of the most promising kind.

The second conference of the College opened on Monday, March 12. On the following morning the members assembled at Upton Chapel, Lambeth Road, when the President gave the annual address from the chair. In the evening, about four hundred friends, who were subscribers to the Institution, assembled at the Tabernacle, being specially invited to tea and supper. The account for the year, as related by Mr. Spurgeon, was thought to be a marvellous story. About £4,400 had been expended in the twelve months, of which close upon £1,600 had been subscribed by the contributors to the weekly offering at the Tabernacle. Referring to the income in general, he said that it had all come in spontaneously, and it was not intended ever to seek to have a roll of subscribers on whom dependence would be placed.

" Believing it to be God's work, they looked prayerfully and with confidence to Him to send the means necessary for its maintenance and prosecution, assured that when these failed the time would have come for giving it up. The funds had at times been very low, but never wholly exhausted. The amounts received had been spent in the most economical manner possible: chiefly upon the students' board, and in the purchase of books for their use. Mr. Spurgeon reminded the meeting that there were charges in connection with this College not incurred by any other. It sometimes happened, for example, that students had to be clothed as well as fed and educated; while, beyond the limits of the College proper, large evening classes were conducted, into which any Christian young man in business might enter and receive a good education free of all cost, except, perhaps, in the matter of elementary books. From these classes many of the College students had been obtained. Proceeding to specify the settlements of students during the year, Mr. Spurgeon mentioned the names of no less than a score of young men who had gone forth, either to gather new congregations or to revive old and almost defunct Churches, and who had met with success that in several cases seemed perfectly marvellous, and in nearly all exceedingly gratifying. It was pointed out, moreover, that the most rigid discipline is exercised in respect of the students, and that men who discover unfitness for the ministry, in respect either of their talents or characters, are dismissed. Mr. Spurgeon deeply regretted to say that some who had turned out badly were sent to him with the strongest recommendations, and that others whose aspirations for the ministry were discouraged and repressed by their pastors and the Churches to which they belonged, had proved themselves to be divinely called to the work. He begged that ministers and gentlemen would never recommend to him any young man about whose character and qualifications they had the least doubt, or unless they knew him thoroughly. To do otherwise was to commit a grievous wrong, and that in many ways. Testimonials ought to be sacred things, and not signed, as they often were, on mere hearsay evidence. Regarding the Chapel-Building Fund started two years ago, to which £5,000 was to be paid in during five years, to be lent out without interest, £2,500 had been received, and the whole of it lent; and this was not more than half the sum that could be so employed with excellent effect, if it could be obtained." *

The students were encouraged to purchase books by having them supplied at a cheap rate; while settled pastors who needed assistance in chapel-building were assisted in their enterprise by having money lent to them free of interest. An endeavour was also made to teach the men the value of life insurance; and as editor and proprietor of *The Sword and the Trowel*, Mr. Spurgeon offered to give the profits of the magazine to a fund for reducing the premiums. It was a very animated meeting, although the absence, through illness, of Sir S. M. Peto, who was to have presided, was a disappointment. " In the course of the supper a gentleman offered to give £100 to the funds of the College, on condition that £1,000 were subscribed during the evening. Lists were sent round, and by half-past ten o'clock it was announced that £750 had been contributed, without reckoning the conditional

* *The Christian World*, March 16, 1866.

£100. Numerous further sums were speedily promised, and no less than £907 were obtained before the proceedings closed at eleven o'clock."*

Mrs. Bartlett's service had now gone on for seven years; the work was increasingly valued by the pastor, and we find it characterised as "one of the most remarkable classes of modern growth." In Mr. Spurgeon's eye the class was in itself a large congregation, which needed the undivided attention of its teacher. The members were accustomed to contribute to the funds of the College, and on April 13 they met together and presented the President with £100. We find it remarked, in connection with this meeting, that "the service, which is conducted by this remarkable lady with only casual assistance, consists of singing, a prayer, and an address, sometimes founded on a passage from Scripture, and as often from an incident which has occurred during the week, and which has been impressed on the mind of the teacher. The addresses are simple in character, and are delivered with considerable eloquent earnestness." As the members of the class had furnished a stall at the bazaar, the £100 now presented did not represent the whole of their gift; so that, while speaking of the spirit of self-consecration manifested by the class, Mr. Spurgeon expressed surprise at the largeness of the amount. Their work was one of love and devotedness, and he blessed God for all that had been accomplished through Mrs. Bartlett. A short printed account of the work of the College was distributed among the company, in which it was stated that the results of the College work had not been paraded before the subscribers, much less before the world; their desire was to avoid boasting and vain-glory, and simply to give the facts in order that God might be glorified, and that the subscribers to the work might be encouraged. "Our plan in London," said Mr. Spurgeon, "has been to do little where we could not do much; to open many rooms, and to start many small communities, in the hope that some of them would live to become self-supporting churches. . . . Our building fund is of the greatest possible

* *The Baptist Messenger*, April, 1866.

assistance to our good work. We have been much cheered by our success in London, and hope to sow yet more largely in that fruitful field." The College had already supplied nineteen pastors to the London district alone; and in that area eight new churches had been formed which had had chapels built or secured. Ten other churches had been started which needed chapels, while preaching was carried on at seven stations at which it was expected churches would be formed. In addition, several old or decaying churches had been revived. Altogether there were at this time about eighty men from the College who were preaching the Gospel in Great Britain and Ireland, and nearly all of whom were ordained pastors.

The Spring Session of the Baptist Union opened at Upton Chapel, Lambeth Road, Mr. Aldis, of Reading, being Moderator. It was noticed that the attendance at such gatherings was much smaller in London than was ever the case in a provincial town. There were only ten spectators in the gallery, whereas at centres such as Bradford or Birmingham, the spectators crowded the space allotted to them. The Chairman's address was on "The True Nature of Dissent." A party of students from the Pastors' College acted as waiters, to whom a vote of thanks was given. To this Mr. Spurgeon himself replied, when the opportunity was also taken of saying something in reply to what a minister present had said concerning students for the ministry. "It is always a great pleasure to differ from Mr. Landels, as well as to agree with him," said Mr. Spurgeon, amid much laughter. "The 'muffs' are the very men who will preach," he added, "and if you do not educate them they will be worse than ever. I find what a friend has remarked—that you get about one good preacher out of every eight students; and I believe that nothing can change that proportion."

At the afternoon meeting in the Metropolitan Tabernacle there was a discussion on the education of ministers' children, a scheme having been propounded which would provide a school, the supporters to have votes after the manner of some other charities. This voting system was strongly condemned by many present. Mr.

Spurgeon advised that no scheme should be entered upon which could not be carried out; let them remember the advice of Mrs. Glass in regard to the cooking of a hare—first catch it. After referring to the fact that he had himself at one time been the un- happy victim of such a school, Mr. Spurgeon went on to say that he abominated the voting system because it involved a great and useless expenditure of money. "For example," he added, "I have recently received as many as fifty letters at once for the few votes I have in connection with the Orphan School at Haverstock Hill. Of course, I do not answer them, and thus four shillings and twopence is spent upon me alone quite fruitlessly."

In the year 1865 the Baptist Home Mission and the Baptist Irish Society, which for half a century had been separate institutions, were united. On the occasion of the first anniversary (April 26, 1866), at Bloomsbury Chapel, Mr. Spurgeon attended and gave his views on "Home Evangelisation the Work of the Churches." That was in any case a congenial theme, for to such a speaker the extension and maintenance of Gospel work was so far the work of the Churches that societies were to be looked upon as nothing more than a make- shift, until the time should come when the Church would properly understand her proper work. Mr. Spurgeon went on to say:—

"Jesus Christ recognises but one pillar of the truth—namely, the Church of the living God; and the Church is not only the house which He has built, but He also supplies builders for the house. I hope that the societies will flourish, and that God will bless them, but I hope they will grow until they are not wanted, which will be a consummation devoutly to be wished. The day will come when even as a denomination we shall cease to be, because when everybody sees right on the subject of believers' baptism, there will be no need of any distinction. No doubt the way in which societies originate is this: the Churches settle down into the idea, first and chiefly, that the main end of a Church is not to glorify God, but to enjoy itself for ever; they think that 'celestial fruits on earthly ground' will grow without faith and hope; some of them count it to be the end of a Church to maintain a minister, though they do but little of that. The keeping up of the old form of doctrine, the maintenance of the five or of the fifty points, and the contending, not earnestly, but savagely, for the faith, is the first, last, middle, of everything in Church existence. It was a grand thing when Fuller felt that if the Church would not do its work, the work must be undertaken apart from Church organisation, and it is a noble thing that if the Churches will not do their home mission-work there should be a society to take it under its care; but I take it that they will all ultimately come to this— that the Churches, as Churches, will do all the work by the employment of their own mis- sionaries. I believe that this is the tendency of the age, as well as a right and proper principle to act upon. To teach people that it is their duty to work, and that, therefore, the societies are not to do it, would be dangerous, because it would be pulling down without building up, and would be radicalism without any pinch of the salt of conservatism, which is necessary in all good things, lest they should run to seed, and become bad in the very process of growth. It is only natural that one of the first wishes of a Christian should be to spread abroad in the world those precious truths which only by the grace of God have been made vital to him, and in this respect he is a true revealer of secrets. Even if he were charged by the highest authority to keep silent he would scarcely be able to do it, and I question whether it is not an instinct of the new-born nature to tell the good news to others. Thus, one of the first works of the Church would be that of home evangelisation. Much is said about not allowing small Churches to be formed where they would not be self-supporting, but the attempt to suppress such modes of action would be more injurious than their permission; and if we attempt always to gather up our strength, and to centralise it too much, we might perform an act of spiritual suicide in our attempt to make ourselves strong and healthy. The more we leave everything to the guidance of God's Spirit, we will have to rejoice more in the wonder-working of the Great Head of the Church. We cannot expect to spread much if we go on at the same rate as we have been going. It is not nice to find fault with ourselves, but we do not do all that we should do. We want to grow faster."

It was shown that there were many towns in the country in which there was no Baptist Church, and thus persons of Baptist principles joined other communions. If such were to come out, there would be no difficulty in the matter of forming new interests; but in the meantime, it would be well if persons who were able to do it undertook evangelistic work in a place and then removed to another place. What was wanted, however, was action on the part of the Churches :—

"If the Churches did more in the work of home evangelisation it would be a cure for many ills. Fuller said that his Church was in a very sad state, and that there was a deal of quarrelling till someone proposed that they should send a missionary to the heathen, and then they had no time to quarrel. If the Churches have objects before them to work for, there is not much likelihood that the mighty energy which the Baptists possess will spend itself in internal conflicts, but in the service of God. This work will also be a means of spiritual edification. There is no making a thorough soldier unless he sees some real service, and there is no hope of making advanced Christians without setting them to some earnest Christian work. The growth which comes only from meditation will be the growth of the conservatory, but if we work hard as well as pray, we shall grow so that the wintry frost will not be able to bite our root, nor touch our leaf."

Mr. Spurgeon went on to say that he trusted the mission would be carried on in faith, especially in Ireland, where Christianity might seem to be in even a worse state than in England. Was not Ireland really the rampart "which, if taken, might lead to the taking of the whole length of the wall?" He urged them to prayer, to call

down the divine aid, and then advised the employment of a number
of earnest evangelists. It was maintained that there were many who,
though unable to preach in a refined style, yet understood how to
get the ear of the people. "If I were a wealthy man," added Mr.
Spurgeon, "it would seem to me to be one of the grandest things I
could do to find a man who was really fitted for the work of an
evangelist, and to give him a yearly salary—£100, or whatever I
could afford—to go round from place to place preaching the Gospel;
and if judicious persons could be selected for this, they would do
great service to the cause of Christ." By way of illustrating what
might be done by earnestness and perseverance, something was
mentioned which had happened at the interesting little Buckinghamshire town of Winslow, which had been so intimately associated with
the work of Benjamin Keach. A young man at Winslow had
gathered a congregation in two years, and had actually sent to the
Pastors' College for a pastor to settle in the sphere he had made.
Just at that time Colportage had been revived in England as a new
enterprise in connection with the Metropolitan Tabernacle, and this
was recommended, although the notion then hazarded that the colporteur might become a self-supporting agent was afterwards found to
be a mistaken one. The practice of Sunday-school teachers meeting
their classes on week-nights was also recommended, while it was
thought, too, that catechetical classes might serve a useful purpose.
Though they were not in love with class-meetings as held among the
Wesleyans, they still seemed to need something of a similar kind.

The idea of employing evangelists as suggested was thought to
be a good one, and the Hon. Baptist Noel, who was present, suggested that the experiment should be made.

CHAPTER LX.

THE REVIVAL OF COLPORTAGE.

Need of the Work—Character of the Men—The Work in Scotland—Mr. W. Corden Jones's
Reminiscences—Lord Shaftesbury—Luther's Inkpot.

IN connection with the work at the Metropolitan Tabernacle, the
year 1866 was remarkable for being the period in which the
service of the colporteur as an itinerant bookseller was revived in
England. When he fully realised the importance of such an effort,
Mr. Spurgeon wondered that it had not been revived before; and
when a number of men were actually placed in their districts, he
was surprised that greater interest was not shown in the work by
the Christian public. The colporteur was so far from being a new
character on the scenes that he was merely a copy of the agent
who in the days of the Reformation carried about, with other wares,
the evangelical publications which, by enlightening their readers,
helped on the great movement. Colportage was then, in some
measure, a service of danger; but now, to Mr. Spurgeon and his
friends, it promised to supply a missing link in the work of rural
evangelisation. A few persons saw what great possibilities were
within reach, and were correspondingly enthusiastic in their advocacy
of the enterprise; but the association at first made only slow progress.
Colporteur and *colportage* were words which had a strange sound in
English ears, and they were not readily understood. It was also
soon found to be a mistake to suppose that such work could be
self-supporting. On the average, every colporteur employed represents
an outlay of £40 a year, which has to be made up by subscriptions.

The men whom Mr. Spurgeon sought to bring together for this
service were usually of the better working-class standard, although
I have known a man with a college degree to be in the ranks.
Besides being of good Christian character, each man needed to be

sufficiently strong in a physical sense to bear the strain of carrying a heavy pack from village to village. Then, in addition to his book-selling, the colporteur was expected to be an all-round friend of the common people to the extent of his ability. As a rule, each man gave full satisfaction to his employers in this respect. The books were sold, the cottagers were visited, the sick received atten-tion, and at many Sunday and week-night services the colporteur was the minister. The work was entirely undenominational, in strict accordance with the interpretation Mr. Spurgeon put upon that term. It is true that there is a so-called undenominationalism which will hardly allow the agents employed to call their souls their own; at all events, they are denied that liberty of free speech which is, or ought to be, every Englishman's birthright. With Mr. Spurgeon it was quite otherwise. Men of all evangelical denominations were welcomed into the Colportage Society, and each man was expected to be outspoken and to do the best he could for his own body. The Wesleyan worked as such, and so also did the Baptist, the Churchman, or the Congregationalist. What more effective method could have been devised for promoting brotherly love?

Colportage had really been commenced in Scotland about ten years previously, and in 1866 the Northern society had about 150 colporteurs at work. The experiment in Scotland was at once a great success, and by way of showing what could be effected in one rural district the Committee said :—

" About seven years ago a colporteur was started in an agricultural district in the South of Scotland, with instructions to visit only the villages, hamlets, and separate dwellings, and to leave unvisited a populous town within it. When he began his labours he found that the people read little except newspapers and frivolous or pernicious publications, and that they had so little interest in literature, or desire for it, that it was often with difficulty they were persuaded even to look at the publications which he carried with him. But it was not long till a favourable change took place. Cheap and attractive periodicals found their way gradually into many families, the number of subscribers increased from year to year, till they have reached the vast amount given below : a result which bears the highest testimony to the power and value of the aggressive principle adopted by this and other agents of the society."

The sale of magazines and numbers soon averaged 1,600 monthly in this parish alone ; and it was therefore added :—

"Who can adequately estimate the amount of wholesome influence which these publications must be exercising from month to month over the minds and hearts of this people?
And there is every reason to believe that, with few exceptions, the subscribers would have
been without them still had they not been carried into their dwellings.

"This, however, is only a small portion of the literature sold by the colporteur. A
growing interest in religious books has been awakened throughout the district, and of these
the annual sale is now very large, including between three and four hundred Bibles and
Testaments.

"And let it be remembered that the society's agents are no mere book-hawkers, but
pious men, who know and love the truth, who commend it by their lips as well as by the
publications sold by them, and who feel it to be their privilege, and make it their endeavour,
to introduce the Gospel message into all the families in their districts.   They distribute
tracts, read and pray with the sick, aged, and dying, hold prayer-meetings, and are most
valuable auxiliaries to ministers, missionaries, and all who are seeking to extend the Redeemer's
kingdom."

Even in Ireland the work proved so successful that in one year
the colporteurs sold 64,136 Bibles and books and 367,752 periodicals.
It was, no doubt, through noticing these results achieved in the
more remote parts of the United Kingdom that Mr. Spurgeon was
prompted to take action, and to found an association in connection
with the Metropolitan Tabernacle.

Mr. W. Corden Jones, who in his early days was associated
with Spurgeon's old friend, Richard Knill, of Chester, supplies the
following particulars about this agency:—

"I send you a few particulars concerning my personal connection
with the Colportage Association and the late beloved President.

"After several years of evangelistic service I was admitted to the
Pastors' College as a student, and formed one of the comparatively
small band who, in its earlier years, first linked hands in the formation of the Pastors' College Association.   Well do I remember him
saying on that occasion, as we looked upon his manly, vigorous form :
'Some of you will remain until you see the hairs on this head turn
grey, and will perhaps say, as you see me toddling along, "There
goes old Spurgeon."'   Would that his honoured figure had been
spared to toddle among us for many a year to come !

"Mr. Spurgeon baptised me in the Metropolitan Tabernacle.
Never shall I forget, while standing on the steps of the baptistery,
his solemn exhortation to be a faithful preacher of the Gospel of
Christ.

"During one of those inconvenient intervals in the pastorate to which so many ministers are liable, I was invited by the Committee of the Metropolitan Tabernacle Colportage Association to the secretariat. Of course, before accepting the office I first saw Mr. Spurgeon. He received me very kindly, and said, 'Jones, I should prefer to see you continue fully engaged in the work of the ministry; but try the colportage, and if you do not like it I will find you a church.' Accordingly I entered upon the work January 1, 1873, and have thus for over twenty years continued in it, preaching on Sundays as opportunity offered.

"When I entered the Association it was in its infancy, only ten colporteurs being employed, and these supported with great difficulty. Although a novice in the technicalities of colportage, I had received the advantages of a thorough business training. I also fully realised the great need for the work, knowing full well the immense quantity of trashy, impure, and infidel literature circulated with baneful effect throughout the land. To counteract this by taking to the people good, sound, moral and Gospel books and periodicals, presented for sale by Christian men, I saw to be a grand home missionary enterprise. Accordingly, I devoted myself to the work in hand, and sought to make it known as widely as possible.

"For a time Mr. Spurgeon seemed to feel the society a burden to him, and would say, 'It is one child too many for me; I wish someone would take it off my hands.' However, I was not discouraged; the number of colporteurs increased from year to year until now nearly one hundred are employed. This greatly cheered the President, and when a well-known gentleman offered to take the Association off his hands, Mr. Spurgeon said, 'No, you go your way and we will continue ours; there is room enough for both.' And so it has proved.

"The Association has been eminently successful in spreading the Word of God and good literature, visiting the afflicted and aged, and conducting Gospel services in the open air, cottage meetings, etc. During the year 1891 the value of the sales reached £11,255 0s. 6d., and from the beginning £153,784 3s. 6d., many millions of publications being thus scattered broadcast as good seed. The President rarely interposed in any details of the work, but if any special need arose as to funds (which was not infrequent), he would say to me, 'You go on with the work, I'll find the money.' This he did nobly to the end, besides contributing generously from his own purse. On the occasion of his jubilee, when a large sum was presented to him, earnest representations were made to induce him to appropriate the whole to his own use. In replying, he told the friends that he wished to divide it among his various institutions, and said, ' I wish to give £200 to the Colportage Association,' which he did.

" Mr. Spurgeon was much pleased with the extent and value of the work, and said repeatedly from the platform of the Tabernacle that it was second to none of his institutions in value and utility.

" Alas ! in the zenith of its prosperity he was taken to his rest and reward ; but the work and the workers remain. Surely, apart from the immense amount of good accomplished and the intrinsic merit of the work being done throughout the country, no stronger appeal than the memory of the beloved founder can be made to friends to contribute the necessary funds to maintain and extend the Colportage Association. At least £1,000 a year is required, besides the sums contributed by districts, to retain the present staff of colporteurs. The total expenditure annually is about £7,000."

On the whole, the Colportage Association has probably succeeded in a greater degree than the founders could have anticipated at the outset ; for there are now about ninety men in as many districts in England and Wales. Bibles and wholesome books and periodicals, of the value of about £11,000 a year, are distributed, and people are gradually awaking to perceive the value of the work. As the late Lord Shaftesbury said ten years ago, " The records of the system in many parts of the Continent, in various districts of England and Ireland, but especially in Scotland, prove that we have long passed the period of trial and experiment, and that we have entered on a career of certain and great success."

The aim of the Colportage Association was not only to enlighten the people by giving them what was elevating : a great deal needed to be done in the way of counteraction. As the great philanthropist just referred to added : " The infidel and immoral agencies of all kinds would, but for movements like these, have the field all to themselves ; and few, except those who have been forced into an investigation of what is said, done, and written by the circulators of impure and seductive literature, can form an estimate of the number and variety of their efforts, and of the zeal and subtlety in which they are conceived and executed."

Probably Lord Shaftesbury knew more about the havoc caused by impure literature than Mr. Spurgeon, but no leader could have more highly valued a band of humble agents, who were proud to own him as their Chief, than the pastor of the Metropolitan Tabernacle valued his colporteurs. Again and again, on the occasion of the annual meeting in May, have I sat near the pastor to take notice of the eager interest with which he followed the unadorned stories of service told by the men fresh from their country spheres. They spoke in an uneducated way, but their anecdotes of adventures, which could never have happened to men not in earnest, were always greatly relished, not only by Mr. Spurgeon himself, but by the entire audience. It was on one of these occasions that the services of the late Dr. Samuel Manning, of the Religious Tract Society, were enlisted, when the doctor referred to the mark on the wall in one of the rooms of the Wartburg, said to have been made by Luther when he threw his inkpot at the head of the devil. " There is nothing so likely to make the devil flee as a good, well-administered pot of printers' ink," said Dr. Manning. " Depend upon it, it is more powerful to exorcise the devil than all the holy water that ever has been sprinkled by priests from the beginning of the great apostasy to the present time. This is precisely what this Colportage Society is doing all day long, and every day all the year round—throwing pots of printers' ink, which has been put upon paper, at the person of the arch-enemy."

CHAPTER LXI.

CHURCH AND STATE.

The Liberation Society—Spurgeon on the State Church—Misrepresentations—Visit to Scotland—. The Sabbath Question—Spurgeon at the Free Church General Assembly—Address on Home Evangelisation.

ON Wednesday evening, May 2, the Liberation Society held its annual meeting at Hanover Square Rooms, and Mr. Spurgeon was among the speakers. Those chiefly interested in such a meeting seemed to be in good spirits, for the principles of religious freedom appeared to be making progress. Although church-rates were not yet finally abolished, and would hold on until July, 1868, the principle of abolition had been once more reaffirmed by the House of Commons after an appeal to the constituencies. Thus it was thought that the cause represented by the Liberation Society should be advocated with increased earnestness, and it was a resolution worded to that effect which Mr. Spurgeon moved. On rising he was greeted with loud cheers, and he was apparently in one of his happiest moods while discoursing on the characteristics of a political Dissenter :—

"There is an old proverb that if you give a dog a bad name they will hang him; but this does not hold true as to men unless they are of the doggish stamp. All sorts of bad names have been given to those in connection with the work of this society, and they are called by the terrible name of 'political Dissenters.' It used to be bad enough to be a Dissenter, but now certain of them are picked out as being troublesome, radical, noisy boys, who must be at once put down because they are 'political Dissenters;' and there are even some of their own brethren who are mightily afraid of the title, and creep like snails into their shells when it is applied to them. A political Dissenter, according to some people, must be something very horrible; but I have been looking round the meeting, and I see that it is composed of some of our most earnest deacons and evangelical ministers, and I am persuaded that they are as spiritually minded a body of men, and as active in the spread of the Gospel, as any that could be brought together. I intend spending a few moments in expostulating with those of my brethren who think that it is wicked thus to agitate, and especially to teach, anything political. Some of these are superfine, hot-pressed, spiritual-minded people. I myself was met by a man of this sort when I was returning from going to vote at the last election, who told me that he wondered how I could interfere in politics, because I was not a citizen of this world, but was a stranger and an alien. I replied that this was true of my spiritual nature, but not of the carnal nature. The man went on arguing the matter, but such people are perfectly absurd and inconsistent; for if they were attacked in the streets they would cry for the police, which they have no right to do according to their own dogma. If their property was in danger they would employ a solicitor to take the case into court, but the judge might very justly tell them, as they are not citizens, they have no rights. I hold it to be a dishonest thing to join a community and enjoy its privileges without discharging its duties; and insomuch as in this country we do, happily, enjoy very great privileges as citizens, we are bound, as honest men, to discharge the duties which devolve upon us as citizens. I hold that in this, as in some other respects, we are very much like sailors on board a ship, where each one is bound to do his duty. What is the State but a goodly ship?—and we are borne across the billows of life in it, and surely, whenever a crisis comes, we ought to take our fair share of the work."

The speaker then had a word with those who maintained that engaging in the business of the world would act as a damper to their spiritual-mindedness. If, however, they were so spiritually minded that they could not take any part in abolishing what was oppressive and erroneous, they ought to be consistent throughout, and not to claim any assistance from the State in the way of protection. Mr. Spurgeon proceeded:—

"Another class of people are those terrible conservative brethren who have sung to us as their lullaby those famous words, 'As it was in the beginning, is now, and ever shall be, Amen.' These people are all for peace, and would do anything for a quiet life. They are very amiable, but their amiability is only gilded weakness. It is said of some that they are 'as easy as an old shoe,' and if they are so, they are worth no more than old shoes. But this wish to lead a quiet life savours of a very base kind of selfishness. If they had a principle which they would uphold, and about which they would not be silent, they might make up their minds that between here and heaven there is stormy weather for them, and that they will have to sail among many rocks, and have to feel their keel grating upon the quicksands. How is it possible to do anything for light without coming into collision with darkness, or to do anything for truth without being antagonistic to error? Though some may think it to be a very pleasant grace to be very quiet, there are other virtues in a Christian soldier besides a retiring disposition. I very much question whether a court-martial would think it a good excuse if a man were so extremely modest as to consider himself unworthy of the attention of the gunners on the opposite side. We are sometimes told that Jesus Christ would never have interfered in this question. I am not so sure about that; but I never could believe in the Jesus Christ of some people, for the Christ in whom they believe is simply full of affectionateness and gentleness, whereas I believe that there never was a more splendid specimen of manhood, even in its sternness, than the Saviour; and the very lips which declared that He would not break a bruised reed uttered the most terrible anathemas upon the Pharisees, who formed the State Church in that day. These people themselves seem to lack manly vigour, but this should not be; and I would that they were rather like Job's war-horse, smelling the battle from afar."

Mr. Spurgeon went on to show that many Dissenters did not

heartily join in the work of the Liberation Society for want of thought. The government was in the hands of the people, however, and if the principles of the Constitution were not carried out, the people were responsible. Unless they protested, they were all really responsible for church-rates, for Maynooth, for Dissenters being excluded from the universities, and for State Church persecution. It was then asked :—

"Is there anyone here who would like to be accountable for the action of the Established Church in relation to the burial of unbaptised infants? A singular instance of this has just occurred. A poor woman in the country had three children at a birth, and, as they were likely to die, the curate was sent for to baptise them. The curate was busy, and did not go, and during the night two of the children died. Next morning the curate baptised the child left alive, which soon after died, and the mother asked if all three might be buried in one coffin. The curate consented, but the evangelical rector heard of it, and would not allow the service to be read over the two who had died during the night! The three children were put into one coffin, and when they got to the church the two were taken out and left on the belfry stairs while the service was read over the other; some dirt was thrown in, which was afterwards removed, and the two other children placed in the coffin. Could there be an atrocity so fearful? Yet these men were only acting in accordance with the regulations of the Church of England, and every one of you present will have a share of the responsibility of such an enormity if you do not fearlessly enter your protest against it. I take it to be the duty of a Christian man either to join this society, or in some other form to advocate its principles, not only on the considerations which I have already ventured to offer, as to escaping from responsibility of sin, but from the very highest principles of our religion. I look upon the society as a most potent and impressive declaration against persecution. They stand up boldly and declare their hearts and consciences are God's, and God's alone, and that none on earth shall interfere with them or control them. I look upon the society, too, as lifting up a very bold testimony in the face of all men for the spirituality of religion. The day has gone by for controlling religion by the rack and the stake, but the same spirit still remains, and men are foolish enough to imagine that they would legislate for spiritual things by Acts of Parliament, whereas the spirit of true religion is too divine, too mysterious to come under the domination of man."

Such were the principles by which, according to Mr. Spurgeon, Nonconformists would have to sink or swim. Amid hearty cheers, he finished up by urging all to increased diligence in the common cause, expressing the belief that in the end victory would be with truth and right.

This speech attracted much attention, and in some quarters was misquoted; for the popular preacher was made to say that he wished the Church of England was worse than she was, in order that she might the more speedily come to an end. On being questioned by a correspondent in regard to this matter, however, Mr. Spurgeon wrote in reply:—" I entirely repudiate the language imputed to me; but it probably suggested itself from a misunderstanding. In view of the Tractarianism which the so-called Church of England fosters, and the general mischief which the State Church works, I am sorry that so many good men continue to give it the sanction of their presence; and I wish they were all gone from her, that the evils might become too glaring to be borne with any longer. I have no hostility towards Evangelical Churchmen, but the reverse; and it is for their real benefit that I wish to see that unhallowed union of Puseyism and Evangelism, which goes by the name of the Church of England, entirely abolished. A Free Episcopal Church might then win for itself the esteem of all believers."

Late in the spring of 1866 Mr. Spurgeon again visited Scotland, and being in Edinburgh during the sitting of the Free Church Assembly, he attended some of the meetings. He probably listened with interest to Dr. Candlish's great speech on the Union question;* and he also heard the arguments for and against the Glasgow morning newspaper compositor who had appealed to the Assembly against a sentence of excommunication for Sunday labour pronounced by the local Presbytery. A large part of the people of Edinburgh is always greatly interested in these annual reunions of the Free Church; but to judge of the interest he excited by the eagerness there was to hear him, Spurgeon eclipsed the General Assembly, while at that Assembly itself he was, to the majority, the principal figure. When it was known that the great London preacher would occupy the pulpit of his old friend, Dr. Candlish, at Free St. George's, on the afternoon of Sunday, May 27, the demand for tickets was enormous, and a vast crowd assembled, which could not be held in check; for many who had no tickets climbed over the iron railings, and so entered the

* " There had been some indications of a desire to embrace the Established Church in the negotiations for Union, and this appeared in the Assembly, in more than one of the speeches, along with an insinuation that some of the fathers were abandoning their old principles. This thoroughly aroused Dr. Candlish, who repudiated the charge with a vehemence and power characteristic of his best days."—*Life of Dr. Candlish,* p. 544.

building. In the evening, when Mr. Spurgeon preached in Dr. Thomson's United Presbyterian Church, the scene was, if possible, even more animated; for one door, which barred the encroaching crowd, was broken down.

As regarded the Sunday labour case, in which Mr. Spurgeon manifested great interest, *The Freeman* thought that "the appellant, who argued his own case very ably, had clearly the best of it." The undaunted compositor maintained that Free Church ministers who read the newspapers on Mondays were really the employers of the printers, and as such were answerable for the Sunday evening work. Moreover, those who employed servants for purposes even less necessary than newspapers, could not throw a stone at a compositor. The man even dared to affirm that there were Free Church ministers who on Sunday prepared their sermons for *The Daily Review* —a Sabbatarian paper, the action of which did not agree with its avowed principles. More than this, he was able triumphantly to flourish in the face of the august assembly *The Daily Review* of that morning, which contained a full report of Mr. Spurgeon's address in Dr. Candlish's own church of the day before—an achievement of Sunday labour on the part of reporters and compositors. In common with those who had excommunicated him, the compositor acknowledged the necessity of keeping the Fourth Commandment. *The Freeman* thought that "if he had insisted that in keeping, according to Jewish hours, from Saturday evening to Sunday evening, he was nearer the exact observance than they, we do not see what their answer would be; for Paul at Troas appears to have begun the Sunday at evening and sailed the next morning." The compositor was thought to be a right-minded man, and it was held by many that Dr. Candlish and the General Assembly would have acted more wisely if they had been guided by the Apostle Paul's ecclesiastical law—"Let every man be fully persuaded in his own mind."

If Mr. Spurgeon did not take this view of the case it was because he sat in the Assembly Hall during the trial and was in possession of all the particulars. After he had listened to both sides he had a presentiment that the matter would be misrepresented. The Assembly did not seek out the case, and would have been glad not to be troubled with it. Further, it was not a case of working merely a few hours on Sunday evening; the man worked a great part of the Sunday, and at type-setting which could easily have been done on Saturday, which day he preferred for his weekly holiday, however. If any error had been made, Mr. Spurgeon thought it to have been on the side of leniency.

The entire General Assembly anticipated with extraordinary interest the address on Home Missions which, according to arrangement, Mr. Spurgeon was to give on the evening of Tuesday, May 29. The bare mention of this had drawn forth a hearty cheer, and several speeches were shortened in order to give the great preacher ample time in which to work out his subject. He began by conveying the Christian salutation of his own people to the Free Church of Scotland, and then continued :—

"The significant circumstance is that I am here as a Baptist. You have seen the shepherd gather the sheep from the hills—gather them into one flock, just when the storm was coming on. Here, I think, the Shepherd of Israel is gathering us together, for doubtless a storm is lowering. We may hear His voice calling, 'Come ye closer together, and confess yourselves to be one flock, for the time of tempest is near.' The Captain seems to say, 'Close your ranks, my soldiers: let every man draw nearer to his brother man;' and if some of you do not belong to the same regiment, still let all strive as brethren to get closer together, and nearer yet to the common standard. I can remember, some years ago, when I was in Scotland, in coming hither we came to a certain water which divided the two countries. We passed it so rapidly that it scarce made any difference at all. I hope that our different views upon baptism may be no more formidable a barrier to communion. I have gone from Scotland to England in former years, and when we passed the boundary my luggage was a little rudely shaken before I entered England. My countrymen were afraid of my taking with me a more fiery spirit than I should be allowed to carry. I have never had my bags shaken in coming this way; you were not afraid of my bringing among you the water in which I take delight. I can go back, and hope, without being overhauled for it, to take with me some of your strong spirit. I need not explain that I do not mean whiskey, but some of your stern, strong spirit of orthodoxy and firmness which I think infinitely better."

In the course of an ample address, Mr. Spurgeon showed what was the object of home mission work. All classes were to be sought; no place was to be left unoccupied. The so-called hopeless class were singularly hopeful; and reclaimed sinners, in the hand of God, made the best agents for the reclamation of others. It was then shown that, to be successful, great movements have to begin with the common people :—

> "I believe I am historically right in saying that wherever the Reformation was carried on only, or mainly, by the nobility, it did not succeed. You hear much of Anne of Bohemia, but you do not hear of the peasant people of that country largely taking part in the work of the Reformation; and where is the Gospel in Bohemia now? The Spanish nobles also took the most active part in the work in Spain, and though there were noble martyrs among them, the lower class did not take part in the work; and where is it now? But in the Reformation in Scotland, under John Knox, it was not only the lords of the congregation, but some of the peasants were the first to draw their blood to sign the covenant, and the work then begun stands now. You have in the midst of you still John Knox's house, and the house, though not now in an aristocratic neighbourhood, would not be on that account, I daresay, objectionable to honest old John. He would be as glad to preach the Gospel to the dwellers there as to those in your new town. The spiritual interests of those on that side of the town would be as dear to him as the spiritual interests of those in the highest circles in the land."

The Assembly was warned of the insidious encroachments of Romanism, to resist which the churches south of the Tweed needed to be up in arms, but it was not apprehended that there was much danger of the Pope gaining any ascendancy in Scotland. "When I walked through the ruins of your abbeys, I fancied the nests had been so effectually pulled down that the birds could not come back again," said Mr. Spurgeon; "and if they be built again, if you do not pull them down in a literal sense, you will down with them in a sense far from metaphorical, even though it be spiritual." There was still danger, however, in latitudinarian laxity. The most effective of home missionaries were the pastors of churches; the working of the whole agency depended very much upon the pulpit. The Edinburgh Castle noonday time-gun then supplied a telling illustration :—

> "I was sitting over there yesterday, when this house seemed to shake with a terrible sound. I soon perceived what it was when all the brethren pulled out their watches to see if they corresponded to the hour-gun. Now, I thought to myself, this is how I should like to preach; I would like to startle all my hearers into seeing whether they are right in the matters which concern their souls. But how can I do that? The electric wire brings down the force by which the gun is fired. The sun gives the time of day, and soon you get it flashing along the wire. Union to the everlasting Sun of Righteousness will enable us to deliver ourselves with a force more startling, and our hearers will soon learn not only where we are, but where they are themselves. How necessary is it that we should be right, for how many hundreds set, not their watches, but their lives, by what we have told them on Sunday. And, in addition to being right, how necessary is it that we should speak with force, so that those who do not want to hear may be made to hear."

A word was said on the most effective way of putting things in the pulpit. On the preceding day reference had been made in the Assembly to hot dinners on Sundays, but while such might be "very terrible things," they were by no means so mischievous as "cold divinity on Sundays."

"Always let us have the doctrines of grace served up thoroughly hot and warm. There are sleepy people in our congregations. That is sometimes their own fault, for they go to sleep before we begin to preach. There is an old story of a minister who recommended an old lady to use snuff in church, and she suggested to him that it would be better to put the snuff into the sermon. I would recommend a little snuff in the sermons—a lively and warm way of presenting the truth before the hearer's mind. Sermons should be as much as possible simple in style. You would not have a man say that 'Deity is my pastor, I shall not be afflicted with deprivation;' but, 'The Lord is my Shepherd, I shall not want.' You don't like the Psalms put into any shape so well as your good old rugged metre. Though there may be prettier ways of putting the Gospel, the plain, old rugged way will take the ear, and be the readiest way to the heart."

Earnestness and hard work were insisted upon. And then came the importance of the prayer-meeting. " Go into a cotton-mill; see all its departments in operation; walk along the rooms; wander out by that door, and in the outside you may see an ugly shed, with a black-looking machine, making black smoke that is spoiling the blue sky. In that engine-house is the motive power." References were made to the Sunday-school, to female agency—the wonderful work of Mrs. Bartlett being mentioned—and to the work of adults in the church. In connection with the latter were given some personal reminiscences :—

" Somebody asked me how I got my congregation. I never got it at all. I did not think it my business to do so, but only to preach the Gospel. Why, my congregation got my congregation. I had eighty, or scarcely a hundred, when I preached first. The next time I had two hundred : everyone who had heard me was saying to his neighbour, 'You must go and hear this young man.' Next meeting we had four hundred, and in six weeks eight hundred. That was the way in which my people got my congregation. Now my people are admitted by tickets. That does very well; a member can give his ticket to another person and say, 'I will stand in the aisle,' or 'I will get in with the crowd.' Some persons, you know, will not go if they can get in easily, but they will go if you tell them that they cannot get in without a ticket. That is the way in which congregations ought to bring a congregation about a minister. A minister preaches all the better if he has a large congregation. It was once said by a gentleman that the forming of a congregation was like the beating up of game, the minister being the sportsman. 'But,' he said, 'there are some of our ministers that can't shoot.' But I really think I could shoot a partridge if I fired into the middle of a covey, and I might not do so if there were only one or two."

It was insisted that the Church needed to be aggressive. " O, that word Church ! " he wished that there was another word for it, for in England it simply meant " a heap of bricks and a spire ; " but that could hardly have been the kind of church which fell on Paul's neck. It was in connection with giving to the cause that Mr. Spurgeon then told a story in his most effective manner :—

" A certain merchant had been waited upon during the day by someone for a subscription for a society. He replied, as some merchants do, ' I cannot, for I have so many calls.' At night, when he got home, and his wife and family had retired to rest, he drew a chair in front of the fire and sat down, and as he sat looking into the fire he thought thus :—I refused that good man a subscription to-day. I have refused subscriptions before, and told the people I had so many calls. There was a time when I gave more than I do now. The reason was because I built this new house. The other house was very good ; still, my wife thought it was not quite the thing. We went to the new house, had to get new furniture, and then got into a new circle. The girls want more for dress, and the boys want more. My expenses have risen, and I am afraid I am entrenching upon what I have been giving to the cause of God. He is then supposed to fall asleep—whether he did so or not I am not here to say—but as he sat by the fire in came a stranger, a singularly mild and majestic-looking man. He came up to the merchant, and said to him, presenting a paper, ' I am come asking a subscription for foreign missions.' He asked it very tenderly, and the merchant, with a good deal of hesitancy, said, ' Really, you must excuse me ; I cannot, I have so many calls.' The stranger looked very sad. There was no anger in his face, but there seemed great grief. He took out another paper, and said, ' You do not give anything to foreign missions ; will you give something towards home evangelisation ? There are many heathens at home.' The merchant again said, ' I can't afford it ; besides, I think there is more said about home heathenism than is necessary.' ' Well,' said the stranger, who seemed to look more sad than ever, ' there is the Bible Society ; will you give something to it ? ' He was a little vexed, and said, ' I really do not like to be pressed in this way ; I can't give.' The stranger looked sadder than ever ; but in a moment seemed to change, and there stood before the merchant one like unto the Son of man. And he said to him : ' Five years ago your little child lay sick, near unto death. You went upstairs into your chamber ; your heart was bowed down with bitterness, and you prayed that that dear one might live, your soul being bound up in the life of that child. Who raised your darling to life and spared her to your house ? ' The merchant covered his face with his hands. ' Ten years ago,' said the same soft, tender voice, ' you lay upon what seemed to be your dying bed. Your affairs were then in a bad state, and if you died you left your children penniless. You turned your face to the wall, and prayed that you might be spared until, at least, you might leave your children something. Who heard your bitter cry, and raised you up ? ' The merchant was more confused than ever. ' Fifteen years ago, in a certain chamber, you knelt, a broken-hearted sinner, with a weight of sin on your conscience and soul. Filled with bitterness, you cried for mercy. Who came to you and said, " I have blotted out your sins like a cloud, and like a thick cloud your iniquities," and opened His heart to wash you from your iniquities ? ' There was no reply, except a sob. ' If thou wilt never ask anything of me again I will never ask anything of thee. Thou shalt not be troubled with my many calls if I am not troubled with thine.' The merchant fell on his face before the stranger—' My God, my Lord, forgive me, and take all that I have.' And lo ! it was a dream—but not a dream, for his life was changed thereby."

CHAPTER LXII.

WORK AND PROGRESS IN 1866.

Foreign Missionaries — State of London — The Cholera — Final Closing of New Park Street Chapel — A Street Adventure — Baptist Union at Liverpool — Spurgeon at New College — Sermon on Ritualism.

MR. SPURGEON appears to have learned some things in Scotland which he was able to turn to good use; and at a meeting of the Metropolitan Tabernacle Chapel Building and College Reserve Fund, on Wednesday, June 13, 1866, he gave the people some account of the visit to the North. He seems to have been struck with the systematic way in which the Free Church organised its various enterprises, and with the mode in which printed reports were presented to the presbyteries. There did not appear to be any prospect of the Baptists ever working in union in a similar manner, however, although some of the methods of the Scotch might with profit be adopted by the congregation. It was recommended that committees should be formed — one to promote the circulation of pure literature, one to see after the Sunday-school and to arrange for the establishment of a day-school, and one for benevolent purposes. There should also be one for foreign missions, and another to look after political privileges and present petitions to Parliament, as necessity might arise.

The continued interest which the people at the Metropolitan Tabernacle manifested in the work of foreign missionaries was shown by a meeting which was held on Monday, July 30, when farewell was taken of certain missionaries who were about to proceed to India. Mr. Spurgeon said that they wanted to see the heroic age of missions come back; they wanted some examples of self-sacrifice such as should stir up the hearts of the people :—

"Some have spoken of the astonishing labours of such men as Francis Xavier, and of the Jesuits of China, whose zeal was truly apostolic. I think that if something rare were done—something so rash as to astonish people, as in the case of poor rash Carey—that a

K K

greater blessing might accompany our missionary work.   There is a feeling growing up in many churches—I only say what others have stated—that there is less preaching by missionaries than in former times.   Translations, writing tracts, and teaching knowledge are, I consider, subordinate things to preaching the Gospel.   The pulpit is, I consider, the great Thermopylæ of Christendom, and, as I am accustomed to say to the students of the College, 'If you cannot preach, you can do nothing.'   I venture to say that because missionaries are apt to forget it."

The year 1866 is still remembered as a time of panic and of cholera.   The insanitary condition of the more crowded quarters of London encouraged the spread of the plague when it once appeared, and what that condition was may be inferred from what the pastor of Commercial Road Chapel said of his surroundings:—

"In this often ignored and overlooked district of the teeming multitudinous world of London there are thick jungles of immorality and heathenism uncleared and almost unvisited, where are always more deadly foes than fever or cholera, plague or pestilence, which kill the body and leave no more that they can do.   I myself know well a locality where 10,000 or more inhabitants are huddled together in filthy narrow streets, and where for years, amid the lowest forms of vice and the greatest profanity and Sabbath desecration, only a solitary and heroic missionary has been found toiling and labouring for the good of the people." *

On Sunday, August 12, special attention was drawn to the cholera visitation in a sermon founded on Amos iii. 3–6.   The preacher did not think that every such affliction was a judgment sent by God on the nation; and he did not believe in judgments coming on particular persons except in extraordinary cases.   Individuals were rewarded or punished in the next state; but as there would then be no nations, nations, as such, were punished in the present world.   The national sin of drunkenness was enlarged upon :—

"Alas! alas! this drunken city may well expect that God should visit it.   The debauchery of the streets is a pestilence which is enough to cause God's health-giving providence to refuse to walk with us.   I think that the constant neglect of the worship of God is a sin of which London is peculiarly and pre-eminently guilty.   In some of our country towns and villages the accommodation in places of worship is even larger than the population, and I know places in England where there is scarcely a soul to be found at home at the hour of public worship—certainly not more than absolutely necessary to nurse the sick, care for the infants, and protect the doors—for the whole population turn out to attend the place of worship.   But in London the habitual forsakers of public worship are probably in a large majority.   It must be so, because we know that, even if they wished to go, the provision of seat room is most lamentably short of what they would require, and yet, short as it is, there is not half so much want of churches and chapels in London as there is of inclination to go to either the one or the other.   The masses of

* Thomas Goadby, in *The Freeman*, August 24, 1866.

our people regard not God, care not for the Lord Jesus, and have no thought about eternal things. This is a Christian city, we sometimes say, but where shall be found more thorough heathens than we may find here? In Canton, Calcutta, or even Timbuctoo, the people have at least a form of worship and a reverence for some idea of a God, but here tens of thousands make no pretence of religious worship. I protest unto you all that whereas you think Christianity to be well known in our streets and lanes, you only think so because you have not penetrated into their depths, for thick darkness covers the people. There are discoveries yet to be made in this city that may make the hearts of Christendom melt for shame that we should have permitted such God-dishonouring ignorance, that in the very blaze of the sun, as we think our country to be, there should be black spots where Christian light has never penetrated. One design of the cholera seems to be to wake up the indifferent population—to make them remember that there is a God, to render them susceptible to the influences of the Gospel, to drive them to the house of prayer, to influence their minds to receive the Word, and, moreover, to startle Christians into energy and earnestness, that they may work while it is called to-day. Already I have been told by Christian brethren labouring in the east of London that there is a greater willingness to listen to Gospel truth, and that if there be a religious service it is more acceptable to the people now than it was, for which I thank God as an indication that affliction is answering its purpose. There is, perhaps, no part of London more destitute of the means of grace, and of the desire to use the means, than that particular district where the plague has fallen; and if the Lord shall but make those teeming thousands anxious to hear the Gospel of Jesus, and teach them to trust in Him, then the design will be answered."*

Towards the end of the summer of this year, the congregation which had been accustomed to meet in New Park Street Chapel finally took leave of the building, which they had learned to love on account of its hallowed associations, and despite its uncanny surroundings. During the preceding eighteen months Mr. George Kew had conducted the services, and on leaving the place he was presented with a handsome family Bible. As the old sanctuary now, as it were, disappears from the scenes, we may ourselves take account of what is called Dr. Rippon's Prophetic Prayer, which that veteran offered up towards the close of his long pastorate. The doctor is said to have asked the Lord that it would please Him "to anoint and to commission a young minister, who peradventure is not yet born, to be witness for the Gospel, and a leader of God's flock, and whose successful career shall throw the great annals of the past into the shade." The congregation which had overflowed in the time of Mr. Spurgeon's pastorate had again dwindled to a very small company. The sale of the property gave the funds needed for the establishment of a day-school, while the almshouses were rebuilt on a more eligible site.

* *The Freeman,* August 17, 1866.

It was also at this time that the public heard for the first time of the proposal to found an Orphanage in connection with the Metropolitan Tabernacle, the report now gaining currency that a lady had promised Mr. Spurgeon £20,000 with which to found an Orphanage.

Among other things that were given to the world in 1866 was a report concerning a "Miss Spurgeon," who was supposed to exist, and which at least served to prove that fiction is sometimes stranger than truth. Thus *The New York Home Journal* said:—"Miss Spurgeon, the daughter of the popular preacher, accompanied Queen Emma to this country. Miss Spurgeon is on her way to the Sandwich Islands, in the hope of being able to instruct the natives in the doctrines of Christianity. She is twenty-four years of age, has a fine intellectual face, and very prepossessing manners." At this time the reputed father of this imaginary young lady was himself only thirty-two years old.

The great preacher would occasionally meet with adventures in the streets which would be more or less diverting, according to circumstances. I never knew of his ever travelling by omnibus, and in his later years he was not accustomed to walk about the streets; he would employ either his own brougham or a cab. In the earlier years of his service he walked about, however, and this is a relation of one of his adventures as told by himself:—"I remember, in the streets of London, a man took off his hat and bowed to me—'The Rev. Mr. Spurgeon; a great humbug.' I took off my hat, too, and said, 'I am obliged to you, sir, that I am great at anything.' We passed on, parting very amicably. I have not had the pleasure of meeting him since, but I felt highly flattered that day." Commenting on this interchange of civilities, a weekly journal, which always looked at Spurgeon through the green spectacles of the narrowest Anglican prejudice, said, "The story is a good one, and does credit to the discrimination of both parties. The gentleman who politely characterised Mr. Spurgeon in this way certainly did not hate him; and the kind way in which Mr. Spurgeon accepted the compliment showed his character and his appreciation of notoriety. Any notice was better than no notice at all; any pre-eminence, even as a pretender, was grateful; and notoriety, even that of censure, is acceptable." *

A paragraph which appeared in the newspapers at the end of August, 1866, had the effect of making the young pastor appear extremely peculiar in the eyes of a large number of people :—" Mr. Spurgeon has just notified, on smart pink paper, to a member of his flock, that he discourages as much as possible the practice of returning thanks after childbirth by any of his congregation, since, in most cases, it is an absurd superstitious practice."

The Baptist Union autumnal meetings took place at Liverpool during the second week of October, Mr. J. Aldis, of Reading, being in the chair. The proceedings in general were probably of more than average interest. The denomination appeared to be making progress, for it was stated that one-fourth of the Baptist chapels of England had been erected during the preceding twenty years. Congratulations were given and received in regard to the generosity of the churches during the cotton famine; might they now band together to ward off a still worse famine—that of " The Bread of Life? "

A paper was read by Mr. James Benham, then treasurer of the Baptist Building Fund, on " The Deacon's Office in Relation to Church Finance." A discussion followed. Then the scene suddenly changes :—

" Whispers are numerous, and speedily a loud burst of applause is heard. It greets a brother whom all love to see and delight to honour, and there he stands—the Rev. C. H. Spurgeon. He speaks of elders as well as deacons in the Tabernacle church, and from grateful experience recommends sister churches to have them too. Many business men are not needed in a church, but elders are. Let them be employed; the result will justify the step. A pastor's support is no gratuity. ' The labourer is worthy,' not of ' what Providence sends,' or ' what can be raised,' but ' worthy of his hire,' and the Master enjoined this because He knew that certain influences in churches rendered the injunction necessary. We ought to rise to that munificence which only entire consecration to Christ can secure. An inefficient deacon is to be remonstrated with, and if he go away offended we lose only a bad man; if he remain and improve, we keep a good one." †

It was on this occasion that Mr. Spurgeon made the confession that he had once received the offer of a partnership in a mercantile

* *The Saturday Review*, March 23, 1861.
† *The Freeman*, October 19, 1866.

firm with £3,000, on which he might have made himself comfortable and retired, had he been so disposed.

On Wednesday, the 17th, he attended the Welsh meeting at Myrtle Street Chapel, preferring that to the conversazione held at the Philharmonic Hall at the same time. Several of the addresses at Myrtle Street Chapel were in Welsh, a dialect which the London preacher never attempted to learn, though he always affected to believe that it must have been the language of Paradise. He had a liking for the Welsh people, however, and was gratified by finding that the volume of his sermons then recently translated was meeting with a ready sale. In addressing the Welsh friends on this occasion, something was said about what is called Welsh fire in preaching, and then followed some remarks which must have gone home to the hearts of many of those present:—

"I always desire to mingle with the preaching of the Word as much of fire as is characteristic of Welshmen and is consistent with its being fire from off God's altar. Englishmen have been very apt to lie back on the laurels of William Knibb and men of that class among them, and some of my Welsh friends are always talking about their Christmas Evans. That is all well enough, but every minister ought to seek to emulate the heroes of the past. It is a good thing to think of the men who went before us, in order that our courage may be strengthened and our pulse quickened; but to rest there would be the saddest thing that could occur to the Church. Our honour before God must depend on the exertions of to-day—nay, our very existence much longer might depend on our making advances on the foe. Ministers must make up their mind that they will preach better. If they preach the best they know they must learn more, and if they have attained unto some degree of success, they must forget what they have attained unto and press on for something yet beyond; for if the kingdom of Christ is to be spread, very much depends upon the ministers being quickened in all respects in the work of the ministry. The Welsh churches furnish a considerable proportion of members to the English churches through the constant progress of immigration. May I ask you, with the deepest affection and respect, to see as much as ever you can to the discipline of the Church? We do not complain of our churches as they might exist, but we have to complain that sometimes Welshmen in London are very different from Welshmen among the hills; that, although they may be very useful members of their own churches, they do succumb very terribly to the temptations of London. Whether or not this indicates that there must be some of them unconverted, or whether they are simply backsliders, I leave to my brethren to judge. But we must be very scrupulous about our membership."

Lotteries, or "gambling for the glory of God," as Mr. Spurgeon described it, appears to have been comparatively common at that time; and, while he strongly condemned the practice, he mentioned having had two tickets sent to him, which were then sent to the

Home Secretary. Some references were made to the spread of Romish practices in the Established Church; and it was then shown how the mere patronage of royal and great personages was not enough to advance a great reformation:—

"How well the Reformation went on under Martin Luther until kings came in to help it! The king's hand is said to cure the scrofula or king's evil; I believe it gives it. As soon as ever the kings touched the Reformation, the Reformation ceased. It never went further; it could not, it was impossible. There was another Reformation in the days of Oliver Cromwell, but that Reformation was very much achieved by carnal weapons. I deplore the fact that men who loved God so well ever took sword and pistol in hand at all. The next Reformation must be by the clear, sheer force of the Holy Ghost's power, earnest prayer, and the faithful preaching of the Word of God. Though I think we must use all political means as citizens, yet as Christians this is our chief means, and we may rest assured that the old battering-ram of the Gospel, which shakes the walls of heathenism, though it is hoary with age, and makes them come tottering down in one colossal ruin, will shake the walls of Antichrist, and make them come down too. It is a part of patriotism to denounce that which will lead us back to Popery. It is a part of our Christianity, not only to preach truth, but denounce error. I urge you, by your love of souls, to spread abroad the Gospel; by your love of Christ to spread that Gospel lovingly; by your hatred of everything which touches the crown jewels of Christ, which sets up any king but Jesus in the Church, which brings out any law but the Bible, and which would teach us to trust in anything but the precious blood, to rely on anything but the finished work of the Saviour; by your hatred of these to be instant in season and out of season; to let your testimony be bold, clear, strong, united, consistent, honest, and true."*

After the pastor's return from Liverpool his earnestness in the work to which he had set his hand seemed to become more manifest than ever. His sermon to the Union, preached to an immense audience, in the Philharmonic Hall, had been founded on Ephesians v. 14, "Wherefore he saith, Awake thou that sleepest, and arise from the dead, and Christ shall give thee light." The discourse seems to have been like a call to renewed diligence and consecration. When he again settled down in London Mr. Spurgeon read Dr. Manning's pastoral letter, asking for daily prayers for the Pope, and that suggested the institution of daily prayer-meetings at the Tabernacle to ask for a special blessing upon the Church at large in its varied operations. The morning meetings were at seven o'clock,

* In this and some few other cases in which the speeches are amply reported, it has seemed preferable, in order to bring out their full force, to let the preacher speak in the first person. Spurgeon's speeches are reported in various ways, at times verbatim; but often in an eccentric mixed style that needs some extra care in transcribing.

and those of the evening at seven, or half an hour later. The fifth of November was also set apart by the London Baptist Association as a day of fasting and prayer, that being thought to be more profitable than bonfires and fireworks.

Having done so much in the department of ministerial education, Mr. Spurgeon was naturally regarded with much interest by the tutors and students of other colleges. At this time Dr. Halley was principal of New College, and for years that veteran writer, preacher, and teacher had asked the pastor of the Metropolitan Tabernacle to pay him and his students a visit. Not until the evening of Friday, October 26, however, was Mr. Spurgeon able to accept the invitation. Dr. Halley presided at tea, and a meeting was afterwards held in the library, a battalion of young men from Regent's Park College being also present. Mr. Spurgeon, having offered prayer, was cordially welcomed, and he then proceeded to give an address on " The Power of the Pulpit " :—

" By the pulpit I do not, of course, mean the large, wooden box in which many men are shut up; though, in passing, I may say a word or two about this as a hindrance to the efficiency of preaching. It has been said that pulpits are scriptural, and that Ezra had a pulpit. But a reference to the passage shows that the pulpit held fourteen people. The Saviour did not preach from a pulpit; Raffaelle, in his cartoon of 'Paul at Athens,' has not represented the Apostle as addressing the people from a pulpit. It is one of the greatest proofs of the inspiration of the Bible that it has survived the introduction of pulpits. When a man is in earnest his whole body speaks, and he ought not to be concealed from his congregation. The main business of a minister is his pulpit. The visitation of the sick, private visitation among his people, organisation of useful and benevolent institutions, platform speaking, occasional contributions to magazines and reviews—these are all good and important; but the work of the pulpit is more important than any of them. The pulpit is the Thermopylæ of Christendom. It has not done everything; it is not intended to do everything; but it has done a great deal. Look at its history. It over-rode philosophy and bigotry, which is almost as strong as philosophy. Against these Paul had nothing but preaching as an instrument. It overthrew idolatry and the colossal system of the Church of Rome. Much was done for the Reformation by the writings of Erasmus, by caricatures, by translations, but the lever by which was lifted the monstrous stone covering the sepulchre of spiritual life was the preaching of Luther. The pulpit did much to overthrow Stuart tyranny; Cromwell's Ironsides could not have done without a sermon. Great were the effects of the preaching of Whitefield and Wesley last century; and nowadays, with all its defects, men cannot do without the pulpit. Preachers are worth all that their congregations give them, and worth a great deal more. If any young man present is conscious of having received more than he ought for his occasional ministrations, let him stand forward and say so. If there is such a one he is a *rara avis*, or rather a goose. In all ages preaching has been the great instrument of conversion. Then as to edifying: it is true that some men have the gift of dispersion largely developed, and their power of thinning a congregation is wonderful; but, after all, the pulpit is a great instructing power."

It was then shown that, even in the matter of purely secular education, a good deal was done by preaching; and the pulpit did much also in the way of encouraging and directing beneficent action, as was proved by the collections for good objects which were made by congregations. Thus, in some measure, the pulpit affected the entire well-being of the country. Wherein, then, consisted the power of the pulpit?—

"The preacher must be a man. He must have force of character, and personal life above suspicion. There is much, also, in his manner: how powerful are the tears which sometimes testify to the power of the subject over the preacher! and more powerful still are those dry tears which tell of inward agony. But the main force of the pulpit is in the matter; a preacher must not talk book. Men first thought of communicating by talking to one another. Speaking came before writing. As to the choice of matter, I can speak from a point of experience. For twelve years most of my sermons have been reported and printed, and yet in my search for something new, I pace up and down my study, embarrassed with the abundance of topics, and not knowing which to choose. If John B. Gough were to take Exeter Hall, and twice a week speak on teetotalism, or Mr. Bright do a similar thing with reference to politics, I will undertake to say that at the end of twelve months they would have to turn to something else. Their subject would have lost its interest. It is not so with the preacher. He goes back into the council chambers of Jehovah and far into eternity; up to the Triune God and down to the degradation of the soul in sin. Then as to the doctrine: correctness is of more importance than most men think. A man may go over a great many big stones, but one little one in his shoe will trouble him. So we may know a thousand heresies, but if we get one into our creed, it will bother us. Doctrine is the food of thought and the mainstay of practice."

The chief element of pulpit power, of course, consisted in the promised presence of the Holy Spirit. Mr. Spurgeon then passed on to show how the pulpit might be overturned, or have its power for good destroyed:—

"It may be done by putting empty-headed men in the pulpit, men who have nothing to say, and say it; or frothy, feathery men, men who introduce a joke in the pulpit for joking's sake, and who, not being particularly conscious of any other mission in the world, make themselves generally agreeable and think that sufficient. Iron men, too, are dangerous in the pulpit—men who in preaching the wrath of God do it without a tear, men who will discuss and wrangle, clear-headed, but cold and hard, like a snowy night with the moon shining. Then there are idle men. Idle students are bad enough; but idle ministers—what shall I say of them? There are also what I call men of putty—men who are influenced by everybody, and have no opinions except those of the last person they met. There are starched brethren—men wrapped in dignity, who come from the pulpit, and walk down the aisle, their minds absorbed by heavenly contemplation. Finally, there are weathercock brethren—men whose religious opinions veer with the prevailing doctrinal current in their neighbourhood—men who in their time have boxed the spiritual compass, and said that every point is the North Pole. Of course, I speak of these as curiosities; probably no one present has ever met with them."

Some of the qualifications for pulpit efficiency were then mentioned—unflinching faithfulness to themselves and to others, a
growing spirituality, hard work and holy boldness, all being supplemented by much prayer and love of souls. Then came the
conclusion of the address, which had lasted for two hours :—

> "Above all, it is imperative to see to our weapons and their efficient handling. We
> have to fight against Ritualism and against Rome. We must preach the truth of Christ.
> It was not to listen to moral essays and rules of ordinary conduct that, in the old perse-
> cuting days, brave men and women assembled at dead of night under the walls of
> Antwerp. It was not to inculcate simply domestic and social duties that Cameron and
> Renwick preached on the hill-sides of Scotland while the Claverhouses with their dragoons
> were hunting them from place to place. Let us be worthy of our sires, and do better
> even than they did in the cause of truth and God."

Many men who are now settled in the ministry, but who were
present on this memorable occasion, have probably carried with them
into the world the words of the great preacher—his wise counsels
drawn from actual experience, and his earnest exhortations to faithfulness which were the outcome of his glowing enthusiasm for the
Gospel cause. It was on such great occasions that Spurgeon
was carried away, as it were, by his subject; and it was not until
he reached home that he realised how much the effort had taken
out of him.

On Sunday morning, October 28, a very different theme engaged the preacher's attention at the Metropolitan Tabernacle; for
he then spoke on Ritualism and its work in the Established Church.
The text was Isaiah lix. 19, "When the enemy shall come in like
a flood, the Spirit of the Lord shall lift up a standard against him."
It was remarked that no language could well exaggerate the sad
condition of things in the Church of England, and Mr. Spurgeon
then went on to say :—

> "It was not now from without, but from within, that the greatest danger manifested
> itself. High Church! What was it? Bastard Popery. Broad Church! What was that?
> Dishonest infidelity—not honest enough to come out at once and say it did not believe in
> Scripture, but dishonest enough to take pay for that which it did not believe. Both those
> parties were making a great noise, so much so that some Evangelical friends were being
> somewhat cast down, and asking what was to be done. He saw no help likely to arise from
> any quarter except this one—that the Holy Spirit would now interpose and show His
> strength; and there were signs that the Holy Spirit was coming. He did not want the
> bishops to interfere with the Ritualists, because what service had the bishops ever rendered

to the Church, or what benefit would they ever render to it? Neither did he want Parliament to interfere with them. He wanted the Holy Ghost to lift up the standard against them. He thought he could perceive that there was a general spirit of prayer coming over the Churches that were faithful to Christ. He had appointed the 5th of November * as a day for fasting and prayer at the Tabernacle, and the friends at Birmingham, without any dictation on his part, had appointed the same day for a like purpose. The brethren, then, were creeping together and preparing for the conflict which was impending, and he was happy to say that among them minor points were being given up. They must stand together shoulder to shoulder in this day of trial. He was happy to say, too, that there was coming back to the Protestant churches a greater love of the old truths than there was before, that some of the ministers were getting sick of their philosophical speculations and geological views, and were giving more of Matthew, Mark, Luke and John to their flocks. They were beginning to see that wherever the old standard was borne to the breeze it would bring victory. Let them press to that standard everywhere, and let every man do his duty now in the Church, and be found faithfully at his post. And let them never despair, let them not even fear for the result, but let them be of good courage, for God was with them; and, if only they acted very courageously and very earnestly, they might rely upon it that the Spirit of the Lord would lift up the standard." †

At the time when these words were spoken there appears to have been some extra commotion in the ecclesiastical world in regard to the practices of the Ritualists. The Church Congress had just been held at York, and while *The Pall Mall Gazette,* in commenting on " A Catalogue of the Ritualistic Show " in the northern city, remarked that it might be " accepted as a pocket edition of the *Directorium Anglicanum,*" *The Times* thought it was time that " some decided measures should be taken to repress such pernicious extravagances." In a letter to the leading journal, the then well-known writer, " S. G. O.," warmly reprimanded the bishops who had taken part in the meetings at York for not protesting against " the Tussaud exhibition of ecclesiastical millinery."

Monday, November 5, appears to have been a day set apart for special prayer. At the meeting at the Tabernacle in the evening prayer was asked on behalf of Mr. Gillet, who had been met with in Oxfordshire; and having now passed through the College curriculum, had accepted the offer of an Indian gentleman who was desirous of assisting a young man with a view to missionary service.

* Readers of Nonconformist history will be aware that this was a great anniversary with patriotic Dissenters in the early part of the last century. The famous Thomas Bradbury, of Fetter Lane, always piously observed this day in commemoration of the landing of William III.

† *The British Standard,* November 2, 1866.

CHAPTER LXIII.

SPURGEON AND THE FRIENDS.

A Week-night Address—George Fox and his Work—The Friends' Testimony—A Stirring Appeal
—Visit to Paris—Golden Lane Mission.

THERE can be no doubt that Mr. Spurgeon had much in common
with the Quakers; for he never forgot his ancestor Job, who,
as an early member of the Society, suffered for conscience sake in
Chelmsford gaol during one of the severe winters of the seventeenth
century. The young pastor was therefore interested in the Society
of Friends; and he felt some regret that the members were not maintaining the prestige of their ancestors in the Puritan age, by doing
all that they might do for the world in the department of Christian
work. Some reference to this was made in a private letter, and
the writer expressed a desire of "addressing the members of the
Society of Friends on the necessity of maintaining, in these perilous
times, those spiritual principles which were brought out so clearly
by George Fox." An opportunity of carrying out this wish occurred
on Tuesday, November 6, when Mr. Spurgeon arranged to speak
at the Institute in Bishopsgate Street. There was a very crowded
meeting, and Mr. Charles Gilpin, M.P., occupied the chair. Among
those present were Lord Houghton, Mr. W. E. Forster, M.P., and
a number of the leading members of the Quaker denomination.
There was "silent prayer" after the manner of a Quaker meeting,
and then the chairman said he hoped that Mr. Spurgeon had
found that, whatever else they might have been, George Fox and
his followers were God-fearing men, who hated covetousness. Thus,
if it was found that the living generation had fallen from the
standard of the fathers, what was said should be accepted as coming
from a friend, while all should be turned to profit.

Though it may have appeared otherwise to certain observers, Mr. Spurgeon no doubt felt quite at home with his remarkable audience. He confessed that the desire to speak to them had pressed heavily upon his mind; but his idea had been not to deliver an ordinary lecture, but to speak for a few minutes. "I look upon the Society of Friends as a picked body, who are the representatives of spiritual religion," he said; "who have suffered long for it, whose history in times past is highly honourable to them, who still love the spirituality of godliness, and who are not to be bewitched by the formalism of the age. But I think," it was added, "their testimony just now is hardly made enough of; though clear as a bell, it ought to be loud as a clarion; and I have thought that if it so pleased God you would permit me to say a few earnest words to you, so that some amongst you, especially some young men, might be stirred up to lift up their voice like a trumpet, to cry aloud and spare not, and to tell this age of its sins and iniquities."

Instead of being allowed to speak in this manner, as he had proposed to himself, Mr. Spurgeon had received another programme: he had been requested to speak to a company of Quakers on the Life and Work of George Fox. That struck the preacher as being a most extraordinary proposition, for as Quakers they ought to know much more about their founder than a lecturer could tell them. If that was not the case it ought to be, for the life of George Fox was well worthy of being studied. "His journal is a rich mine of ingots of gold, which one may go on finding from month to month."

Some of the chief events in the life of the seventeenth-century veteran were then mentioned, and then those present, as "brethren and sisters in Christ," were asked if they did not think that the age required their services in a peculiar manner. The age, indeed, needed the testimony of all Christians, but it seemed most urgently to need that of the Friends. "If you wish to be at all like George Fox, was there ever a period since his day in which the existence of the Quaker was more necessary than now?" asked the pastor. "I think not," he added; and then went on to show that the

Quakers occupied special vantage-ground in fighting with Ritualism, and with the covert popery which seemed to be coming back to England :—

"The advocates of Ritualism cannot turn to the Quakers and say, 'Physician, heal thyself,' unless, as some wicked people say, they got to be as Ritualistic without a form as others were with one. But, as far as I can judge, you are clear of this sin, and therefore are the very persons constantly and vehemently to speak against it. Is there not need that you should do this? Is it not a most dreadful sign of the times that the public taste seems running that way? The taste in dress and in decoration is florid, and this to some extent accounts for the taste for florid religion; but over and above that, the principles of priestcraft are being intruded. One has not to complain so much of gaudy dresses, and crucifixes, and incense, as of the doctrine that a man is to confess his sin to one of his fellows, who by some mystic operation has received power to forgive sins. Is it not shocking that in what is called the enlightened nineteenth century men should be found to believe this; and that it is being spread at so great a rate by men who evidently have great power and skill, and who are good servants of Satan and serve him well? Should not all Christians bear their testimony against this? 'Yes,' you say; and so you do quietly in your meetings."

That was so far well, but something more was needed; and the Quakers exercised unusual influence, although they were only a small community. It could not be denied that they had indelibly impressed themselves on the political history of their country, some bearing names which would ever be held in honour. Certain Quakers were becoming famous in antiquarian and literary matters, but it was hoped that such things would never be their chief glory. "I hope you will never drivel into politicians, or scholars, or antiquarians," said Mr. Spurgeon with an emphasis his audience were well able to understand; and then he showed that that would be the case if they ever came down from being Christians for the sake of lower things. Possessing the great influence they did, as well as great wealth, and a number of meeting-houses, was all to be unused? It was true, indeed, that all had been utilised in a thousand excellent ways; for Quakers had been foremost as philanthropists, and freed slaves would always remember them in their prayers. "But I claim for Christ, for truth, and for the Spirit of God, this power which has been given you," said Spurgeon. "There are many honoured men among you who can preach the Word and testify to the truth, but should there not be many more such?" he went on to ask. "Would there not be many more if the Spirit of God visited you; and would not the time then come which was prophesied by Joel, when your sons and your daughters shall prophesy, when your old men shall see visions, and your young men shall dream dreams? Ought you not hopefully to desire this?" The audience was then asked to lend their aid to those who were fighting against Ritualism and idolatry. The Society of Friends was a small body, but its very smallness might even become an advantage. There were times when God would not use a multitude; He said, "The people be too many for me;" but if the Quakers were as the men who lapped, they might yet become instrumental in defeating the host of Midian. If there were some things to be given up, let them go, so long as they kept true to vital points. This earnest address was concluded very nearly as follows:—

"If George Fox was here he might not endorse all that I have said, but I believe that he would, as I do, exhort you now, if ever, to testify for the Spirit's work; to testify for the spirituality of godliness, to witness against idolatry, to cry aloud and spare not, to lift up a standard against the incoming of the foe, which is coming in like a flood. If Popery comes back, will you bear the blame of it? But you must do so if you do not now speak out; and you, indeed, will be highly culpable if you do not now join with others who know what spiritual religion means. I do think that it would be a great calamity if the Society of Friends ceased to exist—at any rate, till the great principles of which I have been speaking are proclaimed by the whole Church. The principle of the spirituality of worship needs to be testified continually, to be iterated and reiterated, and to be dinned into people's ears over and over and over again; and even then it will be useless unless the Holy Spirit impresses it on your hearts. I do beg you to hear this testimony. I do not know in what way you can do it, it is not for me to prescribe for you; but I do pray that God will bless you, and multiply you, and make you a great power upon the face of the earth. I and others will then rejoice with you; wherein we think you err we shall sorrow; but wherein we know you are right we shall rejoice. I can say sincerely that if God should multiply you greatly I know that there are thousands of the Lord's people who would be thankful for it, knowing that that increase would indicate an increase in England of spiritual religion." *

Although Mr. Spurgeon was supposed on this occasion to give the lecture on George Fox which had already been given in various places, the address was largely made up of a stirring appeal to the Friends to bear a stronger testimony for religion in the world. There were 1,200 persons present, a large proportion of whom occupied spheres of commanding influence. The opportunity to give

* Accounts of this remarkable reunion, by different hands, may be seen in *The Christian World* and *The Freeman* for November 9, 1866. I have been indebted chiefly to the former.

this address had been earnestly desired by Mr. Spurgeon; and now the time had come. It may have been apparent to some that the preacher was not quite the man he had been ten years before. While moving and delighting that distinguished audience, he was all the time suffering great pain. He felt a strong desire to offer prayer, but the chairman appears to have thought that *silent* devotion alone was consistent with the principles of the Society. Concerning this, Jonathan Grubb wrote as follows to *The Friend* :—

"It was my privilege to attend C. H. Spurgeon's lecture on George Fox at Devonshire House on the 6th inst. It is almost superfluous for me to say how cordially I united with his powerful, truthful, and loving appeal to our society. Indeed, his address altogether seemed to be an embodiment of what has been my own concern for years past, and which I have endeavoured, with far less ability, to impress upon my fellow-professors in religion.

"I cannot but view the whole thing as a message of mercy from the Almighty, and I am sure it will add greatly to our responsibility, as well as to our condemnation, if much fruit does not follow this renewed evidence of divine regard.

"I could really say in my heart, while listening to the earnest, simple pleading of this dear servant of Christ, 'It is the truth, the very truth, and nothing but the truth,' so entirely did my feelings and my judgment go with it all.

"One thing caused me sorrow, however. I do not think our views and our practice on the subjects of prayer and of worship were correctly represented on this deeply interesting occasion.

"No doubt there was a jealousy in some minds lest these views should in any way be compromised, and I apprehend that these honest, though groundless, fears were the cause of their being, to a certain extent, misrepresented.

"Our worthy chairman told us, at the beginning and at the end, that it was to be a *silent* approach to the throne of grace. Now, if I know anything of Quaker principles, we have no more right to *enforce* silence than to *enforce* a vocal offering. Either way, I believe the work of the Spirit upon or in the heart should be left unfettered.

"I am sure the spirit of prayer was over the meeting at the beginning, and still more evident was the spirit of thanksgiving at the end; and I believe there was a call from the Lord for vocal utterance, which was prevented by human interference.

"Surely we might have safely trusted our dear brother, the lecturer, to follow his own convictions of duty in this matter; and I know that if he had not felt called upon to address the Almighty there were other lips that would have been opened had liberty been granted; and I think such an end to such a meeting would have been altogether in accordance with Gospel order and with our own belief on the subject of divine worship.

"In conclusion, I venture to express a hope that should we be favoured with another visit from one who is clearly prepared to appreciate and to approve our leading views of Gospel truth, he may be left at liberty to do his Master's work in his own way, a condition to which he is fairly entitled, and which we claim for ourselves when similarly circumstanced."